Living Dreams

1 Van
3 Years
2 Parents
6 Kids

Through 15 Countries...
and Becoming a Functional Family.

`À Chiropratique ;
Sans Frontières
Voici notre Mission
Chiropratique !`

No Regrets

Ed

Published by Ed and Gaye Chicoine
P.O. Box 250,
Wakefield, Quebec.
J0X 3G0

www.livingdreamsbook.com

Maps created by Tanya Chicoine

Printed & Designed by Marquardt Printing Ltd.
240 - 250 City Centre Avenue
Ottawa, Ontario, Canada K1R 6K7

Cover Design & Page Layout by Wendy Clements

ISBN: 978-0-9731128-2-5

For Tanya, Ben, Dayna, Karina, Jake and Whitney
My children and greatest teachers

———◀○▶———

For Ed too
Because we do get the opportunity
to live out a few of our dreams

In Memory of my Dad and Mom

Stan Michlowski 1928-2001
Joan Wilkinson Michlowski 1934-2007

Table of Contents

Preface

One evening during the autumn of 2004, I got a phone call out of the blue from a woman whose first words were, "You don't know me, and I'm not quite sure how to begin what I'd like to talk to you about."

As it turned out, she had read one of my books (always a good opener), and had a manuscript of her own, a travel story. What she wanted, she eventually made clear, was some advice on editing and preparing her story for publication. Did I offer such advice? Would I like to see some of it?

Suffice it to say that there are travel stories and there are Travel Stories. And when my persuasive correspondent explained to me that hers was about a three-year journey through South America with her husband and six school-aged children — a journey that included time on primitive parts of the Amazon; in the wilds of the Andes; on the remotest coastlines of Chile and Argentina — I was tempted to have a look.

And did... and never looked back.

The manuscript Gaye Chicoine sent me a few weeks later was printed on a six-inch stack of bond paper and ran to a quarter of a million words... and was one of the most personal and engaging travel journals I had read in many years. Not only did it explore the planet, its people, its possibilities for redemption, it questioned everything in its path: cultural mores, community and family standards, conventional education.

And so Gaye and I went to work, shaping this fascinating document into a book. The months flew by. We exchanged emails and margin notes and phone calls, some lasting two hours or more and addressing not just the mechanics of writing and storytelling but (increasingly) ourselves, our families, our shared views of life.

One of the significant offshoots of my four-year editorial collaboration with Gaye is that I feel I have gained a friend — one who, in all the months, I have never met face-to-face. What's more, I have met a family the likes of which I do not expect to meet again. It goes without saying that Gaye and Ed and their children are an extraordinary group. I have been half way around the world with them, been exposed to their passions, personalities and private moments — and at times their inner fire and frustrations. I have followed Gaye's personal journey to the far corners of the psyche and spirit.

The result of all this is the book you hold in your hands: an adventure, a family saga, in some ways a revolution.

From the beginning the project has been a pleasure for me. And as I lend a hand now in passing the book along to you the reader, I want to thank Gaye for the satisfaction I derived from working with her and for her trust in my judgment and encouragement. As a reader, you will eventually want to thank her yourself.

Meanwhile, this wonderful book begins a journey of its own. I suspect that its travels throughout the world, like that of the journey that set it in motion, will be extensive and rewarding.

In all things planetary and spiritual, I wish it well.

Charles Wilkins,
April, 2008

Introduction

Our story was never intended to be a book. I just recorded our travel events to remember the experience in greater detail, and it continued to grow. Before reaching our initial destination of Chile, several people en route told both Ed and me that we should be writing a book. Eventually, for some reason, it felt like the powers that be didn't give me a choice in the matter. It took lying in bed severely ill for several days before I came to terms with the fact that the story was to be a book, at which point my health returned.

From then on every time I decided I was not going to turn my journals into book form, something happened to put me back to work, and try as I might to get someone else to do it for me, the task at hand always landed back in my lap. To some extent I am dyslexic and I didn't want to labour over a manuscript that I believed someone else could re-write in a fraction of the time. I have to watch my fingers type the letters on the keyboard, otherwise I cross them in my mind and end up with gibberish. My grammar skills at one time were atrocious but I did manage to work through most of that. So with plenty of encouragement from family, friends and many people who were simply interested—and patient coaching from Charles Wilkins, the last person onto whom I tried to dump the editing job—the book has materialized. I learned I could write a book. When I was sitting through a live talk, by Mark Victor Hansen in 1990, he told his audience that one out of every ten of us in that room would write and publish a book. I quickly claimed, "Well, it's not going to be me." God's plan isn't always my plan.

So this is the story of our young family travelling through two continents over three and a half years, and yet it is much more than that. It is about the expansion of chiropractic in South American countries, the education of our children (of all of us, really) using non-traditional methods, and becoming a more functional family. It is also a story of dreams, different kinds of dreams, listening and not listening to them, and learning from them.

It would be difficult to claim there wasn't some kind of spiritual force that directed events, protected us and gave us learning experiences when we had lost sight of the purpose of our journey. I incorporated that aspect of our travels and experiences; it was just too difficult to create the story and keep it true to events without that perspective.

On the morning of January 3, 1999, I decided I would put the story down without my dream journal entries. However, the decision was short-lived—on the afternoon of that same day, I was given the message that dreams should be part of the story. I had listened to the music tape, *The First Flute,* which had just arrived in a Christmas box from my parents. I read the legend then the background information by the musician, Ron Allen.

"Perhaps we all share a sacred bond through our dreams. Some people dream great things and act on them while others only dream at night and seek no meaning in their visions. Significant dreams should be shared—because they have meaning and can be understood."

When I read the phrase, "Significant dreams should be shared", my heart leapt into my throat; I felt like I was being told to rethink not including my dreams. They may not be significant to anyone other than me, but they have significant meaning relative to the story. Every one of us has the ability to live our intentions, ambitions, visions and dreams, or take heed of warnings when they are given through them, if we truly listen, believe in them, have intent with integrity, and act on them.

So with many dreams accomplished, many more promising, and several years after our return to Canada, here is our story. It is time to share the laughter, joy, tears, living, learning and one big dream come true.

Gaye Chicoine

Breaking Away

Those restless feelings that unwarily creep into the consciousness of almost every person sometime during mid-life forced Ed and me to take a good look at who we had become, where we were going and what we really wanted to do with the rest of our lives. Living in the same house and sleeping in the same bed together, we were going through the motions of life, yet it felt as if we were living separate lives. At one time we had goals, dreams and aspirations but they felt distant and unattainable while Ed was working in a profession and I was spending every hour of every day caring for our six young children.

We knew each other in high school, but it wasn't until years later when both of us were living in Toronto, Ontario that we started to spend time together. While getting to know one another, we discovered we had many of the same ambitions, dreams and life principles. We both wanted to see the world and had a desire to have a family. I wanted to be able to stay home with my children while they were young; Ed felt this was important as well. We had many of the same alternative ideas about health, and at the time we started seeing each other, both of us were exploring a vegetarian diet. It wasn't long before we found ourselves living in one apartment instead of two to save money for an extended trip to Japan, Asia and Australia when Ed completed Chiropractic College. Travel plans and saving were not exactly an easy task with him in school full-time, but it was something we both wanted to do, and together we made it happen.

So on August 13, 1983, after Ed's graduation, we were married. Five days later Ed left for Japan on a three-month contract to teach English to Japanese businessmen. I joined him in November, and we did our circle Pacific tour. We did what we had to do to get what we wanted together and it set a pattern in our lives.

One night during our trek through the Annapurna Range of the Himalayan Mountains in Nepal, we were sitting on a mountaintop with an extremely clear and different view of an abundance of stars, talking about differences between the countries, the people, children of Nepal and how so many of them spend their days begging. I wondered about children in North America. If they were able to see how children lived in other countries, would their attitudes be different? We then started to discuss the possibility of someday travelling with our own children and showing them what the world, other than Canada, was really like. Ed commented, "It is too bad our society is structured the way it is. Most people work hard to support their families but the work only takes them away from their growing children. By the time a couple is more financially independent and has more free time, their children are usually grown, have lives of their own and don't want to spend time with parents." Ed felt he wanted to spend as much time as he could with our children while they were young. It was that night we decided we would travel as a family on an extended journey when our children were a 'good age'. I was pregnant two weeks later.

After our return from Asia and Australia, Ed started practicing Chiropractic in Ottawa. Before long he had set up clinics in Wakefield, Gracefield, and Shawville, Quebec. We moved to the village of Wakefield and the babies just kept coming.

Ed has continued to further his education through professional courses and other seminars. I usually joined him and we both learned about the founding philosophy of Chiropractic, the "love principle", the power of intent when helping others improve their health, and that having faith, confidence and belief in your life purpose is right and good for humanity. There was so much to learn from so many successful people who had valuable insights and information. We listened to speakers such as Wayne Dyer, Bernie Siegel, Ed Foreman, Jack Canfield, Denis Waitley and Mark Victor Hansen, as well as Chiropractors such as Jim Parker, Jim Sigafoose, Charlie Ward, Kirby Landis, Larry Markson, Reggie Gold, John Demartini and a host of others. I often attended pregnant or brought along a nursing baby during those first years, and we always came home with renewed enthusiasm and a more positive mental attitude. In his work, Ed applied many of the spiritual principles we were discovering together along with the Chiropractic care, and the clinics grew to what he could physically handle on his own. People were getting well and staying well with some results that seemed unbelievable to even us. Ed's chosen profession became a passion. Our lives became peaceful, happy, content and busy.

Then came school for the children. Tanya attended pre-kindergarten and kindergarten half-days for the first two years. The following year was grade one and Ben started pre-kindergarten. It soon became apparent that an entire week could go by when Tanya and her Dad, living in the same house, wouldn't see each other. Ed was in the clinic when she arrived home, and she was in bed when he finished for the day. It was a difficult year for us as a family. Ben was plainly too young to be in school, as was the case with Tanya in grade one. When she came home from a full day of school, my happy-go-lucky little six-year-old girl would sit in the rocking chair staring out the window like a child withdrawn from life because of some kind of abuse. She was dazed, exhausted, had no spirit left, and had pages of homework to complete. On stretches of days that school was out, the content little person started to re-emerge.

Through one of the parenting groups I attended that winter I met a mother who was teaching her children at home. It sounded like a solution to my concerns, but I wasn't prepared for the dedication and responsibility my children's education would require from me. That soon changed. As a parent helper on a class trip to the Museum of Civilization in Hull, Quebec I decided that home-based education was the only solution. The trigger was my observation of the moral behavior of that group of six- to seven-year-old children, while one of the teachers just shook her head and looked the other way. We would get through the rest of the year while I prepared myself, but my kids would not be back in school the following September. Children at a young age need constant guidance. If they aren't given moral guidelines in a loving way by the people who are supposed to be there to provide it, how do we expect them to grow into adults who know how to conduct themselves as positive, confident and capable people with logical sense? I decided that if I had to spend time with a six-year-old child doing homework after school hours—the most out-of-control time of day for young children—I might as well have that child doing one-on-one instruction at nine o'clock in the morning when her mind is fresh and open. So needless to say, although we met some stiff opposition from the school and our families, home-based education became a part of our lifestyle.

I have often wondered if choosing to live differently from the norm of society has been beneficial, but I do see positive results in the children. During the winter of our fifth year of home-schooling, all six of the kids and I were shopping for a duvet cover. The salesperson was helping us out when a man came into the shop to pick up an item. He patiently waited his turn and observed the crew. When we were finished he said, "That's the best-behaved group of kids I have ever seen. I have two grandchildren who can't sit still five minutes." I don't know why I said it but it rolled out of my mouth, "Well, sir, it may have something to do with lifestyle. No meat, milk, sugar, TV, or school, and then there is the positive experience of gentle home birth, no immunization, regular Chiropractic adjustments, and they have just spent the last two hours doing gymnastics with the home-school group. They don't have energy left to misbehave." I don't remember much more of what was said that afternoon but the incident provided much food for thought and I went away feeling as if what we were doing makes a noticeable difference in the children.

During the last two years before we left on our adventure, although we were happy with our alternative lifestyle, Ed and I started to feel restless and wanted to do more, or something different. We found and purchased sixty-three acres of land on the Ottawa River with the idea of eventually building a home for our retirement. As winter wore on, we started to think that it would be fun to do that sooner rather than twenty years later. Both of us were losing our enthusiasm for day-to-day living. I felt pressured by the demands of community and started to resent every phone call or person who dropped in unexpectedly. Lack of uninterrupted time with my children was becoming a major concern.

Then there was our house. It had four livable floors, including the clinic—big and comfortable. It was everything anyone could ever need. But during the last years before departing, I started to feel like a slave to house and things. The house was full of belongings, chaotic, cluttered and out of control; a trap from which I needed to escape. It was more than I could handle and was affecting my mental-emotional health. I knew I needed to do something about it; I just had to figure out what. In small snatches of meditation time I managed to accomplish, I found myself asking for a solution to what I knew needed to be done.

An epic dream in February 1996, told me what was to come: I was on a tour of my own house, first guided by an invalid man in a wheelchair and then by a healthy young man. Each room I was shown had an aspect of my life symbolized before me. On the stairs to the second floor, a polar bear moved his head twice in the same direction—he was telling me I was supposed to be going that way. It felt as if the direction was north. At the door my shoes were tied together in knots, and I couldn't get them untied so I went barefoot outside. I was then sitting on a beach in the dark overlooking a body of water and watching vivid northern lights. I felt as if they, too, were trying to tell me something. I swam in the water but it was difficult to keep my head above the surface to breathe—something kept pushing me under although I still managed to get enough air. I then sat at my piano and started to play *Bless This House*. There was a mirror lying on top of the piano, making every note I played sound distorted. When I picked it up and looked into the reflection, my house and belongings around me melted away and I was left facing down a road.

The events that led us to South America over the next few months occurred as if they were pre-ordained and out of my personal control. In March, Ed had a visit from a previous patient, Pascal. His health had so positively improved with chiropractic care that he became a chiropractor himself. He was about to graduate and was looking for work opportunities.

When Ed came up from the clinic that day, the first thing he said was, "I offered to sell the house and clinic to Pascal today."

I looked at him in disbelief and exclaimed, "What on earth made you do that?"

"I don't know," he replied, "it just seemed to be right. We've been thinking of other things, maybe it's time for a change. We have the land. Maybe we should build our house now or travel with the kids like we wanted to."

It was the beginning of a long conversation about the possible opportunities that lay before us: our family spending a winter in Mexico and building a house on our land in the spring. It was fun to dream and plan.

Weeks went by. Reality set in again. Pascal was looking at work opportunities in Ottawa but wanted to show the house and clinic to his wife, Christiane. He wanted to buy us out if he could convince her to move away from the city. The house looked the nicest it had in a long time and they went through it carefully.

"What's wrong with this place?" she asked. "Why do you want to sell it?"

"It isn't on the market," I answered. "If you and Pascal will buy it and continue to provide service to the community, it is for sale. We are 39 and 41, restless, have dreams we want to live, and staying here won't make them happen."

More weeks went by, and in mid-June Ed received another call from Pascal. They came to see the house again, and after some discussion they told us they couldn't purchase both the clinic and house together. Pascal offered to purchase the clinic in the fall and the house when the mortgage was up in March 1998, pending financial arrangements.

July passed, and we made new plans. Without having the cash from the sale of our house to build another, Ed suggested we look into working somewhere for a couple of years. He regretted not working in Japan while we travelled through Asia and didn't want to feel that regret again. He contacted the World Federation of Chiropractic and asked for addresses of countries that would have work opportunities.

I wasn't so sure. I was looking forward to being away for the winter and building a house in the spring. But, Ed was right—if we tied ourselves down again immediately we would be in the same situation before long. I agreed to go someplace exotic. When the list came from the World Federation of Chiropractic, Ed sent twenty-five letters and résumés around the globe, some by mail and some by fax. He received positive responses from Honduras, Australia, and Indonesia. We decided against Australia when we realized it would take fifteen thousand dollars or more to fly our entire family there. That ruled out Indonesia as well. Ed talked to the contact person from Honduras who had replied to his letter and was told that all we had to do was arrive and there would be plenty of work.

The night Ed sent a fax inquiring about Chile, an answer came back within two hours: "Yes, I am interested. Call me in the morning. Let's talk. Steve."

As it turned out Steve had started working on setting up Chiropractic clinics in Chile, communicating with insurance companies about coverage and adjusting people on his visits to the country. He couldn't live there because of his family situation and was looking for someone to work in the clinics he had established. He wanted someone with experience and preferably not single. Ed fit his expectations.

Ed also spoke with a chiropractor in Peru. Like Chile, it had potential work opportunities. It looked as if we were headed for South America. Once again, we realized that flying to Chile or Peru was going to be costly, and after a short discussion about how we would get there, Ed nonchalantly stated, "We can drive it. We have a good van."

"You're crazy," I replied. "It would take forever. Why don't we just go through Alaska while we're at it?"

And the subject was closed—for a day. I took my dreamcatcher earrings off the next evening. They were Ed's Mother's Day gift to me just after the rumblings of change started to shake our home life. As I held them in my hands, I realized that this was the window of opportunity to make our dream of travelling as a family come true. It was now or never.

Driving to Chile with six young children was an absurd idea but it stirred some thought. Peru is a country that has intrigued me since learning about the Incas in public school. I soon began to see that travelling over land would be a great way for the kids to learn history, geography, climate, cultures, another language and all kinds of new things in a way they would never forget. I knew it could be fun—but also risky through those countries. Ed was confident—negative things just never cross his mind. He has always been an optimist. I soon felt opportunity outweigh risk and agreed.

By late July, the possibility of Pascal securing successful financing was looking slim. Disappointment set in before I convinced myself to let go of the idea of driving to Chile. I was at peace with the fact we were staying right where we were. Then everything changed again. It was mid-August and Ed received the final word: the chiropractic clinic was sold and we were going to change our lives.

The news came as a surprise to the community. People seemed to think we were either crazy or the total opposite. Some were envious, told us so, and thought the experience the children would have would be unequaled by anything else we could ever give them.

Steve wanted to meet us and discuss arrangements for Ed to work in his clinics. We agreed to meet in New York City in early October before Steve was to catch a flight to Santiago, Chile. We talked with him, about his family, our family, our desire to travel, chiropractic philosophy and the major topic, Chile. We told him of our plans to drive to Miami, put the van on a ship to La Guaria, Venezuela, then drive through Venezuela, Colombia, Ecuador and Peru to Chile. We figured we could be there by April. That was good for him; it was going to take that long to finalize the business arrangements. We parted with plans to keep in touch.

Two weeks later, Wayne Dyer was speaking at a chiropractic seminar in Toronto. Our going would be an opportunity to visit with Ed's brother, Dan, and his family and another chance to hear the inspirational speaker we so often enjoyed listening to.

Wayne Dyer spoke about his latest book, *A Promise is a Promise*, the story of a mother whose daughter had been in a diabetic coma for the past 27 years. She lived through trials and tribulations taking care of her daughter with little or no financial support, surviving pretty much on faith and miracles alone. When he described Kay and Edwarda's visit from the blessed mother, I almost sobbed as I remembered my own experience of being given strength to go on with my life by the same motherly symbol. While listening to him relay the story, I felt as if there was more than we were aware of to the journey we were about to take. Mr. Dyer closed the afternoon by playing a recording of *Amazing Grace* sung by Cecilia. We came away with a meditation CD, a Cecilia CD, his latest set of tapes, and two copies of the inspiring story, *A Promise is a Promise*, one for a friend and one for me.

Ed suggested I have my books signed. Children were the subject of discussion as Wayne Dyer was dedicating and signing his books. He asked, "How many children do you have, Gaye?"

"Six—four girls, two boys," I replied.

"Do you think you'll have any more?"

"No, six is good"

"Well, when you have six, a couple more wouldn't make any difference. We thought that and now we have eight."

There were many people waiting for signatures. I would love to have chatted, but am known for my long stories. "I'm sure. Thank you for signing the books."

I walked away feeling that someday he'd hear our story and will know the positive influence he has been in our lives.

I played the Cecilia CD constantly after that weekend. Her music touched my soul and I couldn't hear it often enough. One afternoon, days later, without the music playing, I was humming one of the tunes I didn't know the words to and suddenly felt compelled to know them. I found the song right after "Amazing Grace" and followed the words by Stuart Wilde, to "Silver Wings".

The past it taught me well
And even though I fell
It's plain to see
the lessons were for me
So let it be
It's come to set me free

If God's plan for me
Is to reach higher
I accept the call
That's my desire
For within my heart
The everlasting dwells.

T'was fate that showed me how
To profit in the now
The game of life
Is stepping past the strife
So let us be
It's come to set us free

Let me voice my plea
And let me touch my destiny
Fly me fly me on Silver Wings
To the place where Angels sing

I didn't make it through the song without shedding tears and again I felt there really was something for me to learn and give. Travel through South America was something we had to do.

By early November, Steve had returned from Santiago and everything he had been working on in Chile had fallen apart. There was no job for Ed to go to but it never crossed our minds to not go. Chile was our destination and our plans never changed.

The major task of emptying the house became a lesson in itself. I know when I dream of a house it is always a symbol of me as a person. The body is a house for the soul and a house is a place for the physical body to dwell, a representation of the self. I started with all the things stuffed into the attic cubbyholes. They had to be dealt with, and as I was doing so I wondered how many dark areas of myself I still needed to clean out. A beginning. Everything that had become useless to us could no longer be stored and was moved out. Books went to the second-hand bookstore, and a few things ended up in the house contents sale, but most sat at the edge of the road waiting for garbage day. The morning the garbage truck came, I was going through the closet of the girls' room. I stopped to watch from the upstairs window. The workers piled a load into the truck, squashed it in, piled more stuff in, squashed it again, piled more stuff in and continued on down the street. My past just rolled away in the garbage truck. What a metaphor! There was a lot of garbage there. The rest of the house was sorted into what we wanted to keep, what went into the house contents sale, and what waited for the next garbage truck. I started to feel lighter and freer with every item we let go.

We kept the basic house needs for our return—kitchen supplies, towels and bedding, some furniture and the books that have helped build our character over the years. The children wanted to keep their 'special things,' some of which meant security; we couldn't take that away from them. Each of them packed a "treasures box" to put away.

During the days of shopping for storage space for what we were keeping, Dad phoned. "We've cleaned out the attic of the garage for the kids' stuff. Just because you guys are getting rid of everything doesn't mean they have to. We'll bring the truck and take what they want to keep."

That was the beginning of a long conversation. My father just couldn't understand what we were doing. As it turned out he was willing to take our books and other basics as well. We arranged with Ed's sister, Lisa, and her husband, Pierre, to take what furniture we were keeping to their new cottage for the period of time we would be gone. It was a convenient arrangement for both them and us.

The week before we did the final clean-out of our belongings, I asked our home-school recorder group to gather and play one last time before we left. Everyone came. The children's attention span was longer than usual, and when they went off to do other things together, the adults continued. We ended up with eight extra bodies sleeping in our house that night. The children were having a tough time saying goodbye to friends and squeezed out as much time as possible together.

Dad arrived Friday evening in mid-December to help pack and take home what was being stored in his garage. On Sunday morning the truck was loaded. We then accepted an invitation to brunch at the restaurant of Lucie, Gilles and their family; another home-schooled family and close friends. A large table was set for both of our families and we were served a fabulous breakfast amongst great company. During brunch, their five-year-old daughter, Marilee, ran up to me, dropped a small gift into my lap and ran off without saying a word.

"I don't know what it is," Lucie said. "She did it herself this morning. She wanted to give you a present."

I opened it to find two precious little things, a stone and a small angel pin. I am sure she didn't plan it, but I felt as if she had just given me a divine message from another realm. A stone, a piece of the earth we were setting off to learn about, and an angel to remind us we were being taken care of while doing it. I was speechless, and when words did come I told Marilee I would keep her gift with me always on our journey.

Weeks earlier the woman at the Venezuelan embassy who had helped prepare the paperwork for the van told Ed we were crazy to drive to Chile and tried to convince us to change our plans or at least start someplace other than Venezuela. Ed explained that we had to go to her country to obtain the *libreta* for the van, a document only issued in Caracas. She sighed and replied, "Well you had better be taking your angels with you. I count on them whenever I am in Venezuela."

After that, little angels started to come into our life.

Dad and the four younger children were off to Grandma and Grandpa's house after breakfast and as they were leaving, Marie Francoise, Jan, Reine and Joelle, another home-schooled family, arrived with lasagna and helping hands. Marie quickly surveyed the house and said, "You're doing very well." The third floor had the things that Pascal had previously moved in and the furniture that Lisa and Pierre were moving to the cottage in the spring. The bedroom floor held only the furniture that Pascal and Christiane had purchased from us. I cleaned the second floor while Ed put together the heaps of paperwork that still needed to be dealt with. Marie and Jan packed our van for us and helped clean the main floor. Pascal and Christiane were moving things in that afternoon as we were still moving things out. We breathed a sigh of relief when we finished. Ed's Mom and Dad were expecting us for dinner, but it just didn't happen.

We walked nostalgically through the house that evening, saying good-bye, then crossed the threshold of the door, closed it behind us and locked our keys in. It didn't belong to us any more. As the saying goes, when one door closes, another opens, but in this case, it was the road.

Jan asked, "So how does it feel to be homeless?"

We laughed. "For me, easier than I expected," I replied. "I thought I would cry when the time came, but it's not there."

Ed, Tanya and Ben all agreed that it was too early to know. Everybody gave big hugs and thanks. We would have been packing until midnight if not for the help. Marie, Jan, Reine and Joelle got into their van and we got into ours. I would miss that family. They had given me much-needed support for home-schooling over the years. Marie is a professor of Religious Studies at the University of Ottawa, and was a home-schooled child herself. Jan is a stay-at-home dad and 'taxi driver' to provide for their busy life and activities. They have three girls and arranged their lifestyle according to their belief system, advocating home-base education. They were a confirmation to me that being different is all right.

We spent Christmas holiday with Dad and Mom. The gift-giving tradition was reduced to small gifts that would be useful for the days ahead. It was a happy and exciting time, but also a time of some sadness, knowing that we were leaving and that it could be years before we would see each other again. Departure was teary for grandparents and kids but there were no tears from Ed and me; the anticipation of being free and the excitement of the adventure ahead overpowered the grief. I knew we would be back some day—we just didn't know when.

We visited with Ed's family until our last day in Canada, and found his mom distraught about us leaving. I felt I needed to help her feel more comfortable with the inevitable. She is a faithful woman but her faith was being tested. The children chose and purchased an angel to give to her as a reminder that we were taking our angels with us. Various friends and family had given us a total of eight (coincidence?) small angel figures as gifts to take along and, every one of them was stuffed into corners of the van. Ed's mom said she would be praying for us every day.

We met Pascal and Christiane at the lawyer's office at 8 a.m., January 2nd, 1997. The papers for the sale of the clinic and house were in order and signed. Ed received the cheque for the clinic. We shed winter boots, coats and snowsuits. Diane, a sister of Ed's, put what we would use on our return in a closet in their home and took the smallest of the outdoor clothes to the snowsuit fund. There was one last stop to deposit the cheque, and we were at the American border by 11:30 a.m. Driving south and watching the road come toward us with no obligations to anyone but ourselves was the ultimate freedom. I guess it could be seen as, "We're free, let's put as much space between us and what kept us tied down as fast as possible." We were at our rented villa in Florida, and on the beach, by 2:30 p.m. the following day.

I watched everyone play in the water that afternoon and wished I didn't feel apprehension about going in myself. Twenty years ago I would have been with them. But it was too wavy, I'd be too cold when I got out—excuses or age? I just enjoyed the surroundings from where I was. Did it really matter if I swam or not?

Caressing the sand, my hand unearthed a broken, water-worn shell that looked like a calla lily unfolding; what was left of it felt soft and smooth. While rolling it in my fingers, it spiraled in and out, giving me the idea that it was breathing. There is a time to learn and there is a time to give back what we have learned. When a living organism looses the ability to take in and put back out, it dies, then, transforms into food for other organisms within the environment—a continuation of life. An understanding settled into my soul. Nature doesn't have anything mixed up—it is all so perfect on its own—even broken. The need to understand more about everything overwhelmed my senses and I found myself asking God to help me understand more. I am so naive in so many ways.

Ed joined me on the sand after his swim and asked, "Do you find yourself thinking, 'Oh no, what have we done?'"

I had to be honest. "I feel sick every time I think about it."

"Me too," he replied. "Do you want to go back?"

Surprised at his question, I answered, "No, we can't go back now."

"I know, I was just asking. We sure got ourselves out of our comfort zone, didn't we?"

We both took a deep breath; we were soon to be in a whole different world.

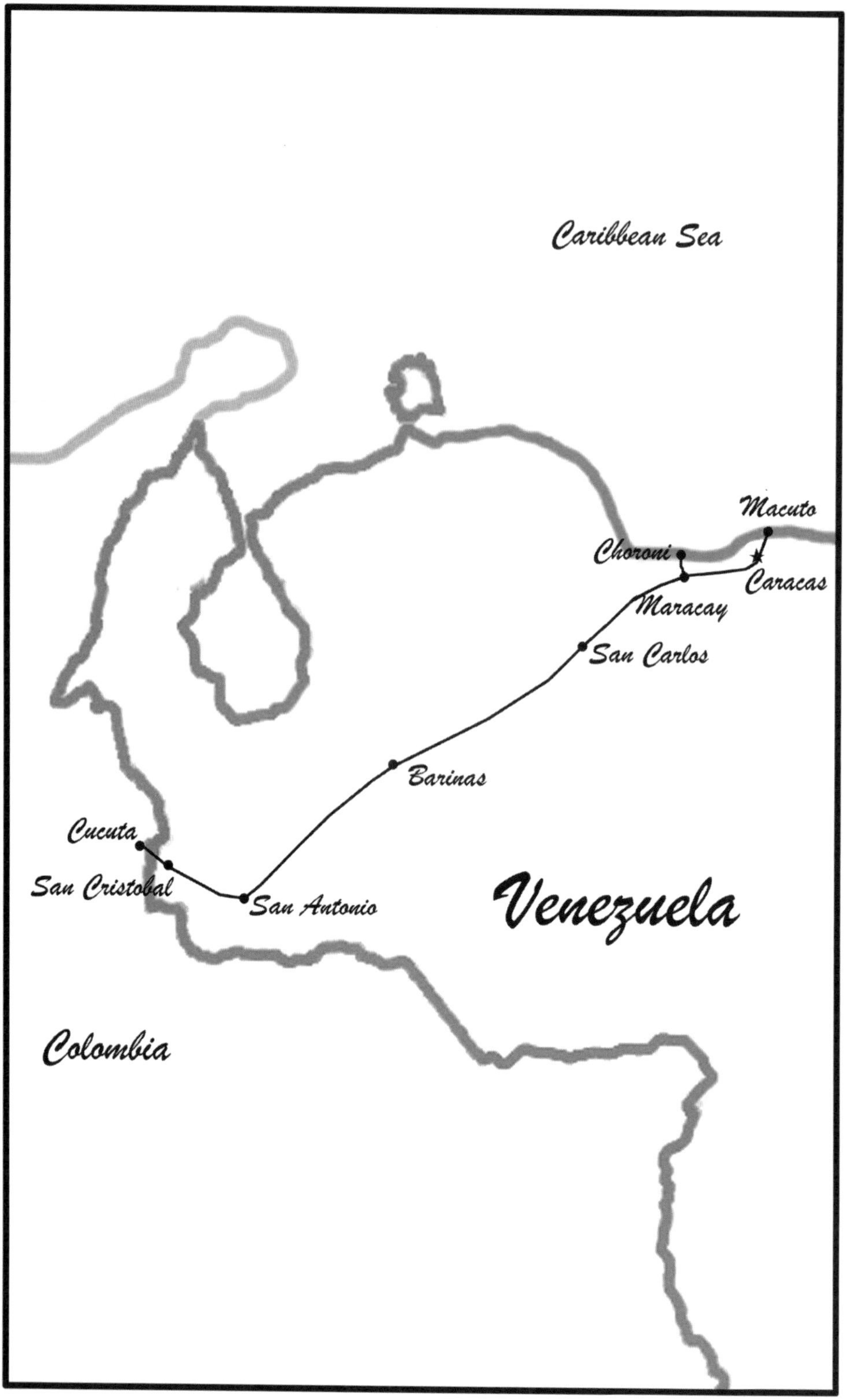

Caribbean Sea

Macuto

Choroni

Caracas

Maracay

San Carlos

Barinas

Cucuta

San Cristobal

San Antonio

Venezuela

Colombia

VENEZUELA

January 20, 1997: Pension Guanchez, Macuto, Venezuela

Our first week and introduction to South America has been one of excitement, confusion, being overwhelmed, and at times feeling like royalty. We have begun our South American education with a few lessons learned.

Ed was prepared for a long process at customs since we were arriving on one-way tickets, but the officer accepted his explanation along with the papers for the van and we passed through in less than two minutes. We were then faced with reality: the heat engulfed us as we left the building, and Ed and I felt total confusion. People, porters and taxi drivers bombarded us. One porter, speaking English, managed to grab Ed's attention and said he'd find a taxi big enough for us all. He and other porters guided Ed, the kids and me through the commotion and crowd of people to a waiting van. We laughed at the irony—it was a Ford Econoline.

"Hey, this is just like ours," Karina said.

"Just a little older," Ed said, then started speaking with the driver.

"You have a van like this?" he asked.

"Yes, it is arriving this week."

"It's coming here?"

"Yes, we are driving to Chile in it."

"What year is it?" He was the first person that didn't say anything about our intentions.

"92."

"Hey, that's not very old. I'll buy it from you. Do you want to sell it?"

"No, we brought it here to use."

"Well, when you don't need it anymore, come and see me. I'll buy it from you."

That was encouraging. The conversation continued as we drove from the airport onto the main streets of Macuto. There were no opportunities to move into the flow of traffic on the street, so our driver simply made his own opportunity, cutting into the stream. Others cut in front and honked their horns. Some cars moved to within six inches of our van many times during the fifteen-minute ride. I don't know how the vehicles didn't collide with each other. Ed looked at me and asked again, "Do you get the feeling of 'Oh no, what have we done?'"

My heart was beating so fast with the thought of us driving on those streets that I replied, "My feeling exactly—Ed, I can't drive in this."

Before we knew it the taxi driver announced, "Pension Guanchez, here we are."

It was majestic looking. On both floors wide verandahs wrapped around three sides of the inner building, and were furnished with couches and chairs for sitting in the shade. The pillars supporting the verandahs and roof gave it the look of a southern plantation mansion. The entrance to the first floor had railings on either side of the steps. The wooden banister was wider than the span of my hand and had a well-used look to it.

We were barely out of the van when three men and an older woman poured out of the doors chattering excitedly to us in Spanish. They appeared happy to see us and we were greeted like long-lost friends.

"We are the Chicoines," Ed announced. "We made reservations from Canada—a big room, six beds and bathroom".

One man, Edgar, spoke English. "Yes, yes come in. We were expecting you."

The smiling woman was doting on the children. We didn't know what she was saying but she kept talking. When I picked up a bag to carry to the room I was scolded. It was clear that I was not to carry my own bag. We were led down the hall. The interior of the pension had a homey feel and I absorbed the surroundings. The floor was inlaid with small white, brown, tan and grey mosaic tiles in patterns that formed squares and octagons. It drew the eye, balancing the effect of the seemingly excessive space above our heads. The ceiling must have been between fifteen and twenty feet high. We climbed the twenty-two wooden stairs and followed the hall. Ours was a comfortable room. There was no air-conditioning but it had a fifteen-foot ceiling with two big fans that we used continuously. There was a bathroom with shower up two steps on a higher level, a window with shutters, no glass, on the street side (very noisy), and two sets of double doors, one to the hall and the other to the balcony, each with small doors above to let the air circulate.

The small *mercado* (market) around the corner from the pension had an old "general store" feeling. The shelves were stuffed with all kinds of hardware, clothing, food, and drugstore supplies. The shampoo and conditioner we had stocked up on in order to have our favorite brand was sitting right there on the shelf. We bought bread, jam, honey, cookies, juice, beer, and limes and snacked to our stomachs' content during our first night on the South American continent.

The people at the pension liked us. Although we had asked for six plates of the breakfast they were serving, we were given eight bananas, eight glasses of orange juice, twelve fried eggs, bread, and two platters of two kinds of cheese, ham and coffee. We were given two kinds of excellent coffee to choose from: *café con leche*, (a pot of hot milk and a pot of very strong hot coffee to be poured to your preference) and *café negro* (a strong, black coffee served in a smaller cup with several packets of sugar on the side). The children ate almost nothing but white bread and cheese with ham. While watching the kids eat their breakfast that morning; I realized it was going to be difficult to maintain the diet we had grown accustomed to at home. We have been a "no meat, milk and sugar" family for several years.

A no-meat diet started for both Ed and me when we were living in our own apartments. My body functioned more efficiently without meat and I felt better when I didn't eat it. And, with modern-day production practices, I am wary of what is fed to cattle.

While becoming more diet-conscious, our decision to consume only natural sugars fell into place as well. My emotional ups and downs, especially the downs, became less severe. Imagine what happens to children who eat large amounts of refined sugars several times a day. For one thing, every time we consume refined sugars, our immune system functions at less than its full potential for up to five hours. Our alternative is maple syrup and honey, natural sweeteners in small amounts that are assimilated into the body at a slower rate.

We eliminated dairy products from our diet shortly after the birth of Ben, our second child. Tanya was born eight weeks premature when I contracted toxemia. The birth process and hospital stay was not a positive experience for me. During my pregnancy with Ben I looked for alternatives to the medical system. My search brought me to an experienced midwife, and home-birth became the goal if the pregnancy progressed normally. Once again at about twenty-seven weeks my body started to become toxic. At the midwife's suggestion I eliminated all dairy products and within days the toxemia ended. Ben was born at home, three days before his due date, a healthy eight pounds, ten ounces. That same day I started to enjoy my milk again, but with each passing day, Ben's breathing became increasingly difficult. He wheezed, sounding almost asthmatic. At ten days old I took him to a medical doctor who prescribed antibiotics to assist his lung function. At the midwife's next visit she suggested I try eliminating dairy again. I experimented and discovered that when I consumed dairy products and nursed Ben, his lungs filled with mucous and his breathing became laboured. I resigned myself to the fact that if dairy products had that kind of an effect on him, even indirectly through me, they mustn't be as healthy for us as we are led to believe. It wasn't easy giving up dairy but when we did, it had a positive effect on our health. None of the kids after Tanya had ear infections for example, and my irritable digestive system started to work more effectively. Now, on our first meal out, it didn't look good; we were in for a big change.

Before we left Canada, Señor Gustavo Contreras, here in Venezuela, had helped Ed prepare the van paperwork for entry into his country and South America. When he was informed that we had arrived, he came to Pension Guanchez to continue to be of assistance until we had the van back in our hands. Senor Contreras took Ed's passport, driver's license, car ownership, letter of intent, the freight papers and 10,000 bolivars toward his fee. Ed was back with us only minutes later, looking concerned, Ed thought he would be going to the customs office with him. "I just gave him all my documents. I don't know whether that was the right thing to do or not."

"I don't know about that either, but he is a customs agent, he was recommended in the travel book, and he can't do it without the proper papers. We will have to have faith in some people around us or we shouldn't be here."

"Yes, that's true, but I asked him several times how much this is going to cost me and he just said, 'Don't worry, I'll give you a special price, you are my friend.' Good words, but I don't like the sound of them. It's going to be Friday or even Monday before we get the van."

With the rest of the day to ourselves we walked to the waterfront, then along the park and past restaurants and shops to get to a swimming beach. There was garbage everywhere, along the waterfront and on the streets: paper food wrappers, plastics food wrappings, broken glass bottles, plastics of all sorts, cans from both beer and food, and in two places along the curb rotting heaps of garbage. Whitney said, "I just don't understand people putting garbage on the ground." She verbalized what the rest of us were thinking. There was just too much not to notice.

The beach was littered as well, but the kids had a nice afternoon playing in the water. We relaxed in the heat, played in the sand, and had ice cream from one of the vendors with coolers walking by. Ed and I had a beer from one of those coolers, too. When everyone was hungry again, we made our way back to the hotel, had a freshwater shower, and went to the restaurant across the street for barbecued chicken and yucca. We ordered three half-chickens and enough yucca for the eight of us. Ed paid the bill. While walking out he looked at it again, and realized it was more than it should have been. We were charged for three whole chickens.

When he went back to ask about the discrepancy, he was told by both the cashier and waiter that we had ordered three whole chickens. The smug look on their faces said that we had just been taken advantage of and it was easy to see they were lying. With Ed's limited knowledge of Spanish he couldn't argue and that was our first lesson learned. We definitely only had three half chickens—otherwise, there would have been no need for the tiff that we had over who got the three legs.

Gustavo returned that evening and informed us that the van had arrived late that afternoon—everything was in order. Ed would have his papers back in the morning and we would have the van on Friday.

The kids were in bed early and Ed went out on the balcony to talk with other tourists. Ian and Emma, from Britain, had come to spend four months in Venezuela to surf. However, the winter months are not surfing weather and Ian's surfboard has not been out of its cover. They were at Choroni, a small fishing village west of Caracas, and said it was a great beach but there was not enough surf there either. They were looking into flights to Mexico.

Ed went to the shipyard customs early Thursday morning to pick up his papers and was told to return Friday morning to claim the van.

Edgar had been tremendously helpful as a translator when it came to the legal paperwork. He called the *Touring Y Automovil Club de Venezuela* to inquire about purchasing the *Libreta de Pasos Por Aduana* and made arrangements with a friend to take Ed to the office in Caracas.

A woman named Dayana Palana wrote up the application form and said it would take three working days to complete. Ed was encouraged when he returned, mostly because he felt as if he was getting somewhere understanding Spanish. She spoke slowly and he understood every word.

The kids and I spent Thursday at the hotel playing cards, games, reading, and doing some math. They weren't enthusiastic about going to the beach again; the litter didn't make it inviting to return. That evening on the balcony, we got a euchre game going. Ian and Emma arrived back from a long walk and rested their feet while watching and talking with us. Ian couldn't believe these guys were playing euchre. He said it was a game played only by the fishermen on the wharfs at home, making it sound as if there were some kind of stigma attached to it. I said, "It's a fun game; it makes them think and work together with a partner, being competitive and cooperative at the same time. Those concepts are life preparation, and a simple game can instill them without the kids even realizing what is happening."

Ian looked at me as if he thought I was crazy. But then again, most people don't see things as such in the way we have learned to see them, so I guess I shouldn't really have expected him to understand.

Ian and Emma were looking into alternatives to Venezuela. They talked about Ecuador, but flights were expensive. Ed invited them to come as far as Quito with us, if they thought they could tolerate us, but I believe the kids will scare them off.

I wished Ed good luck and safe driving as he left to pick up the van. He took a deep breath and said, "Thanks. I'm not really looking forward to the initiation."

He and Gustavo went together to claim the vehicle. Gustavo had everything complete; there was both a military and a customs check of the papers. Everything was in order and it only took ten minutes. Ed paid Gustavo $200 (Canadian) for his services. There were so many papers involved and, not having knowledge of Spanish, if Ed had tried to do it himself it probably would have taken a week or more to complete.

While they were waiting at customs, Ed stirred up some curiosity talking about chiropractic and offered to treat Gustavo for the shoulder pain he described. Gustavo said he would take our family out on Sunday to visit Caracas, Junquito and Colonia Tovar in the mountains, so we had our first excursion arranged.

Gustavo warned that, having only one license plate might give us problems and suggested we make a photocopy to put on the front of the van. The headlights were another irregularity he thought was odd and couldn't understand why they were on all the time. Ed explained they were automatic daytime running lights, but to him it was a waste to be on during the day. Gustavo coached Ed on his initial South American driving experience and then received the promised chiropractic treatment on their return to Pension Guanchez.

The kids and I walked to the beach that morning. We didn't know how long Ed was going to take and I wasn't going to spend another day cooped up in the room. As we walked along the street toward the beach a young man sitting at a table watching us yelled in heavy accented English, "Hey you!" When I looked, he said, "Love." I smiled and continued walking, flattered, although what he meant exactly I am not sure.

The kids had just gotten into water play when Ed arrived. He had Ian and Emma with him and they knew of a cleaner beach east of Macuto. The kids were a happy group with that prospect and dried off quickly to hop in to the van.

The side mirrors made the van too wide to fit inside a standard crate so it had been open to everyone during shipment. Our garbage can, the big box of Kleenex, the safety triangles and three of the six travel pillows were missing. Whoever it was liked the soft velour pillows I made out of scrap fabric and foam chips and left the good ones.

The 40-kilometer drive to Las Caracas took us along the coast on a road squashed between the rocky shoreline on the left and the mountains on the right. Since it was a work day we had the beach almost to ourselves. The feel of the white coral sand, the smell of the sea, the soothing sound of gentle waves and a visual backdrop of cliffs and mountains covered in green tropical vegetation made our afternoon nothing less than extremely pleasant. Ian lent his boogie board to Ben who was in the water all afternoon and by the time we left had it figured out.

A person walking the beach with a basketful of warm, fresh *empanadas* (pastry filled with meat or cheese, deep fried or baked) showed up just as hunger set in. Ed purchased two for each of us, filled with chicken and cheese. They were tasty and cheap—we may be eating many more of these.

Ed spent Friday evening after the kids were asleep talking on the front porch with Pablick and his friends. Pablick runs the pension and is the son of the woman who owns it, but he informed Ed that it was still his mother who made most of the decisions. One of Pablick's friends, Oswaldo, spoke English so for Ed it was an evening of learning Spanish through translation and conversation. Otto and David didn't know a word of English and they were asking Ed the questions. The conversation eventually turned to chiropractic and everyone expressed interest in being adjusted after Ed explained that health is a gift of life; that a healthy body enhances every other aspect of our lives in this physical world; that when our natural life force—nerve impulses, are able to flow through our nervous system without being blocked by interferences, every muscle and organ in our body is able to function at its full life potential; that chiropractic care helps clear obstructions and maintains the nervous system, which results in a healthy body.

These are all facts of life for us as a family, and it became Ed's profession because it was what gave him optimal health. I was plagued with debilitating headaches that would last for days until I began chiropractic care. The headaches were greatly reduced and I eliminated the horrendous number of painkillers I was putting into my body. Our children have had the advantage of chiropractic from the moment they were born and are an extremely healthy group of young people with few health complaints.

On Saturday we planned to go back to Playa Las Caracas but Ed held a clinic and gave adjustments to anyone who was willing to receive them. People he hadn't spoken with started to turn up as well, including a friend of Oswaldo and the friend's mother, including Pablick's sister, Tamara, a medical doctor. She liked the concept of chiropractic when it was explained to her. We managed to get to the beach by mid-afternoon and another few good hours.

While playing cards on the balcony Saturday evening, we heard screams and car tires squealing that made our hearts jump. A man had been struck down by a car and lay on the pavement. We watched in a state of shock. The man didn't move. The traffic on the busy street had suddenly stopped in both directions, yet an ambulance arrived within minutes. The medics felt for a pulse and obviously found none. The man was totally wrapped in a blanket then quickly loaded into the vehicle. The ambulance left and there was barely a sign of an accident within fifteen minutes. It was unnerving to see a person's life ended so abruptly and the body swept away like that. There was a message for us to use extra caution; pedestrians have no priority on these streets.

The roads are not a safe place to be. So far, our impression is that beer is the common drink most of the time, rarely water. We saw a man, bottle of beer in hand, drive off in a car with a policeman standing right beside him and watching. There don't seem to be laws against drinking and driving, or if there are, it obviously doesn't make a difference.

On Sunday when Gustavo arrived to take us on our tour, Ed was giving treatments again. Gustavo had another treatment, as did several new people. Again we were late leaving.

While driving through Caracas toward El Junquito and Colonia Tovar, we stopped part way up the mountain to take photos of an overall view of the city and to visit a small shop to have fresh-made juices and *empanadas*. We continued to climb at a steep angle for an hour. Just before El Junquito at 2,006 meters, the motor started to miss and knock, and then eventually it stopped. The temperature gauge was reading normal, so we assumed that the altitude change was causing the problem. Gustavo went for water and filled the radiator. The van continued for only a short time before it started to miss again. It did manage to get us to the town of Junquito, only to choke itself out while we were parking. A great start. Since arriving in Venezuela I have been feeling less confident about travelling in our own van to Chile and already it was acting up.

Gustavo took us to a restaurant and the first thing Whitney wanted was to go to the bathroom. There was no toilet paper, we returned to the table to steal some serviettes. When we got back we found everyone having hot chocolate or beer. The air was cold. We needed sweaters but hadn't brought any, because we left Macuto at 11 a.m. in 32°C temperatures. Everyone was hungry and two huge oval plates of meat and cheese were set in front of us. Tanya, disappointed, turned up her nose and said, "I'm not eating that, I'll eat some cheese but I'm not eating that." Karina looked at the plates, then at me, and said, "Oh no" and sunk back into her chair thinking she was not going to get to eat. The platter had three types of meat: barbecued beef cubes, kielbasa-type sausage, and blood sausage. I discretely tried to explain to the kids that they should show appreciation to someone who is taking the time to show us around and that they should at least try the foods that are native to the country they are in. I convinced them to taste the one kind that was similar to their grandfather's kielbasa that they like so much. It disappeared along with most of the beef cubes. Dayna and Ben tried the blood sausage but without a positive reaction, so there was no way the others were going to put it near their mouths.

As we worked at the food before us, five men dressed in identical black suits climbed the stairs on the other side of the room. They stirred up some curiosity at our table. Each had gold braid along the side seams of his pants and black knee-high boots so highly polished you could see a reflection in them. They wore bright yellow ruffled shirts under waist-length, brass-buttoned and gold-braid-trimmed jackets. On their heads were the biggest, classic black sombreros I had ever seen. Ed and Gustavo continued talking. Whitney became impatient when some lively music started to play upstairs. She wanted to see and listen up close. I carried her up the stairs while Dayna, Karina, and Jake followed. At the top we found that every chair had been taken so we stood, watched and listened. The band played fiddles, drums, trumpets and a ukulele. One of the trumpet players took notice of the foreigners bouncing to the lively music. He used hand gestures to ask me if the four children were mine. I hand-gestured him back to indicate "yes" and that there were two more downstairs. He slapped his forehead, threw his head back, then put his hand on his upper arm and made a fist with the other. I'm starting to wonder about men in this country seeing me with my children. It was the second time I felt flirted with and both times Ed was not present. We didn't last long. There was a cold breeze blowing through the window that sent us for shelter in our skimpy clothing.

After the van had had a rest it continued the climb to Colonia Tovar at 2,426 meters without a chug or sputter. Colonia Tovar was founded and settled by German immigrants in 1843. It retains its old-style European architecture and has become a tourist attraction since the road was paved. The town is nestled into a flat area atop one of the peaks and is populated along the edge of one side. Overlooking the valley and peaks, farms spread out where they can, and cling to the slopes where they can't. Gustavo explained that corn, tomatoes, beans, and lettuces—vegetables and grains that like a cooler climate—are grown in the higher altitude. In the lower valleys where the temperature is hot all year, yucca, bananas, pineapples and coconuts are grown. He said almost anything would grow in the area. Colonia Tovar supplies the Caracas market with strawberries, rhubarb, garlic, flowers and leafy vegetables.

We found sesame seed honey bars in one of the shops. I asked for six and gave the vendor 1,200 bolivars for them but he only put five in the bag. When he handed it to me I opened it up, dumped the contents onto the counter and asked for another. He gave it to me without a word. I don't understand what they think they are gaining by being so dishonest.

Our descent to the coast was on a smaller road that wound and clung to the edge of the mountains toward Macuto. Jake's food for the day didn't stay down—he vomited three times, and then it was Karina's turn, twice. I hope they get used to it; we have a lot of mountains ahead.

We organized ourselves for travel and Ed spent the evening adjusting everyone again. He was asked to stay here in Macuto. Pablick said he would give Ed a space to set up a clinic and Tamara said she would refer everyone for chiropractic care. Ed felt encouraged by her openness to the concept of chiropractic. It was the first place where he has demonstrated Chiropractic and already he has had an offer of help to start a clinic.

January 24, 1997: Choroni and Puerto Colombia

By the time Tuesday morning arrived we were ready to move. Pension Guanchez is a home for the Guanchez family and the food was fabulous but it was a noisy place beside the main highway. One night I awakened out of a dream as the sound outside changed from automobiles to a hard rain falling. It was so good to hear a natural sound. My body relaxed to the rhythm of rain washing the streets. It was a peaceful sound yet from trying to figure out the dream, I didn't get back to sleep until long after it had stopped. In the dream I was in an auto repair shop, but it was the windshield that needed to be repaired. It was smashed on the driver's side of the van and I couldn't see out. I kept dialing the phone number of the shop that repairs windshields—562-6211—but the two last digits, the ones, didn't seem to be connecting and wouldn't show up on the number display. I kept pushing on the one to get it to enter but it just wouldn't. A man in the shop asked me what was wrong. I explained that the phone number wasn't working. He looked at it and said for the repairs I needed, that was definitely the number I needed to call.

The numbers stuck in my head: sixes, twos and ones. Six kids, two adults and the 2 ones were not connecting. Something in my life needs to be repaired now; most likely the way I perceive things, maybe Ed and I are the two ones and need to learn to connect to each other again. Maybe all of us as individuals in our family need to connect to each other. It is a puzzle, telling me something I don't understand as yet. It was a few days ago and the dream still comes back into my conscious thoughts.

David, Edgar, Ed and Pablick

I took some photos of Ed and the men he became friends with at Pension Guanchez and we were off, making stops for gas, money exchange, mail and the *libreta.*

The next challenge was to find our way out of Caracas. We managed to get to the freeway then headed down the ramp going east instead of west. Ed stopped the van.

"Gaye," he said, "get out and stop the cars from coming down the ramp so I can back out of here."

I jumped out and stopped the cars. He quickly backed up and we continued across the bridge to the westbound ramp. Anything seems to go here—the cars just waited for us to back up and get out of the way.

The freeway took us through hot, dry grassland with a wall of Andes on our right for two hours. We managed to find our way to Choroni through Maracay and along the main street, Pizza Hut, Yogen Früz, McDonald's and Burger King were lined up beside one other, making it look very much like a North American city. We stopped at Yogen Früz for a washroom break and a cup of yogurt. The bathroom situation was typically South American, though—there wasn't any toilet paper.

It was a short distance to the Caribbean Sea, but with the mountain range between the beach and us, it was still a three- to four-hour drive. The road climbed continuously through dense rainforest—a small road reduced to barely one lane with drastic drops in many places. You were expected to honk your horn at every corner to give warning to oncoming cars. There were hairpin turns, and in many places one vehicle would have to back up to let the other go by. The vegetation was lush with bamboo clumps in almost every corner of the road. It grew extremely tall, so that in many places it was bent over and broken. The road opened up onto the saddle of the mountain where there was an extreme drop on either side of us. From the crest we could see the Caribbean to our right and the grassland plain from which we had just climbed, on our left. Yogurt was the wrong snack to have while driving—Jake and Karina shared the front seat and took turns vomiting out the window. Do we have this to look forward to all the way to Chile?

Choroni is a quaint fishing village that has become a popular tourist destination because of the beautiful beach within walking distance of the main village. We found a small apartment with parking and enough space for the eight of us to sleep comfortably. Whitney, for some reason, decided to become independent and was angry at being expected to sleep with her Dad and Mom like she always has. She thought a bed of her own would be better now—of all times, when more beds mean more money.

We had dinner in a restaurant where the waiter was infatuated with Whitney. Pablo introduced himself, chatted to her and wanted to shake her hand. But the chatterbox clammed up, shy of the stranger: her lips were sealed. When she asked to use the bathroom, he led us to the back, showed us where it was, and talked to her in particular. She didn't say a word, scrutinizing him carefully.

He had a little girl three years old who was also born in August, but that didn't impress Whitney.

Tanya was not well or happy during our first day in Choroni. She is twelve-and-a-half, had started menstruating for the second time in her life, and didn't want to go to the beach. Ed took the others to the beach while we stayed in the apartment. She rested, I read a book, and then found myself wondering if we had done the right thing. I watched her sleep. It doesn't seem to matter how old they are, they still manage to take on that angelic look while sleeping. She just needed to let her body adjust to the changes. I found myself feeling sorry for her in a way. Babies growing up, a young woman dealing with all sorts of inner feelings, and no one her own age to talk to. I remembered my own experience of menstruating. I talked to my girlfriends at school about it more than with people who actually had some understanding. Which was the norm then, it seemed. I remembered the negative attitudes toward female bodily functions when I was in my teens. No one was ever very pleased with having a period unless they feared being pregnant. I remember dreading menstruation and it being called "the curse", mostly by the women in my family. My own attitude has changed dramatically since then. It has taken me twenty-five years to learn to accept this biological cycle that really is an asset. Our body is a remarkable thing. When a young woman starts to menstruate, her body is capable of producing a new little human being. It is the ultimate creation and nothing less than a miracle. I cannot figure out why our society perceives the process and everything connected to it as such a problem or taboo. When we cut ourselves the cut bleeds, carrying bacteria out of the wound before the wound heals itself. Bleeding is a way of cleansing the body, and that is how I perceive menstruation. A sexually active woman needs to menstruate to cleanse her body. For me, it is a beneficial monthly cleanse and I feel so good afterwards. Women need to learn to be friends with themselves. Watching Tanya sleep made me think about what kind of attitude I would like to see my girls have. It doesn't have to take them until they are forty years old to like themselves and their bodies, and to understand how their bodies function efficiently. It has been a long learning process for me. Maybe they can get a headstart with the right kind of knowledge and attitude and be more fully functioning women from the beginning. I find myself feeling comfortable and trusting the process.

The second day in Choroni we decided to hike to another beach east of the village. The kids couldn't swim or play in the water at Playa Grande; the surf was too dangerously strong. It took an hour to walk up the mountain and back down to the beach. Still, the surf was too strong to swim, but we did get wet on the edge. The waves filled our bathing suits with sand and since the small cove was our own, it wasn't long before everyone (except Tanya) was naked and playing in the waves. We snacked on what we had brought and lay in the shade. The kids climbed and played on the rocks of the shoreline. When it was time to return we encouraged Jake to lead so he would walk. He was so proud to be the leader that he forgot about being tired and didn't have to be carried. We went back to the same restaurant for supper and had a meal of fresh fish. Whitney cautiously said *hola* to Pablo, but that was the extent of her verbalization during our meal.

On our third day we walked to Playa Grande. The garbage bins along the sandy road were swarming with vultures—fascinating to watch. A treed area separated the beach from the road. There were restaurants and booths filled with food, souvenirs, beach wear and toys to sell to visitors. One man stood with a long snake coiled around him. You could have your photo taken with him, for a fee of course. The beach was a beauty—white coral sand backed with coconut palms and contrasting with the blue-green of the sea—but it was so disheartening to see the amount of garbage lying everywhere. Although there were garbage bins, it was difficult to find a spot that wasn't littered. While Jake played and dug in the sand he unearthed a tampon and was twirling it around by the string before I realized what it was and took it away from him. The surf being strong again, we barely got wet on the shore. What an undertow!

January 26, 1997: San Carlos, Venezuela

We plan to leave in the morning, the beaches get crowded on weekends. We left without breakfast, thinking we might avoid some messes, but Jake still managed to vomit the water he drank. It was a fast drive to Valencia on the four-lane freeway: the speed limit was posted at 80 kilometers per hour, but everyone drove 110-120. Valencia was another big city, and although it was our destination for the day, it was busy and confusing, so we moved on. San Carlos appeared to be the total opposite of Valencia—not such a rat race. We checked into Hotel Central, the best in town, and it wouldn't hurt any Canadian's wallet. It wasn't long before the kids discovered the HBO movie channel. Ed purchased snacks for supper and cereal and milk for breakfast. With lots of space to feel comfortable and lots of laundry to do we decided to stay an extra day to wash our clothes. After the laundry was complete we went to find a restaurant for a mid-day meal but there wasn't a thing open. This town takes the Sabbath Day seriously, and was absolutely deserted today compared to the bustling place it was last night. Every metal roll-up door was down; even the hotel restaurant was closed.

We found a phone booth and gave Dad and Mom a call to let them know where we were. We cut our conversation short. Ben had found a corner-type store that was open, but it looked like the shop owner was starting to close up. We arrived just in time to buy some boxes of yogurt drink, day-old bread, and the cold empanadas that were left. We returned to our rooms for the afternoon and made sandwiches with the tomatoes we had left from the day before.

The kids had worked out a system by which each had a half hour to play games on the computer but there was always a reason for someone to go longer and fights started. It was hard for me to stay out of it when I saw fairness and honesty lacking. We let them watch movies all day to take their minds off their stomachs, but television does not bring out the best of character in them.

The heat is intense at 35°C or more. At least we have a comfortable temperature inside. We have eaten everything.

January 27, 1997: Barinas, Venezuela

It is amazing how going a little hungry for a day made plain old cereal and milk a fabulous meal this morning.

It was a four-hour drive to Barinas across land that was flat, hot and dry with only a few sparse trees along the roadside. Where there were trees, people stood under them with things to sell.

Ed had a challenging day of driving. The gas pedal started to stick and the van idled high; it didn't want to slow down and was difficult to control when a slower speed was required. At one point we were almost forced off the edge of a bridge—one that didn't have a guardrail—by a truck taking up more than its share of the road. I thought we were going over the edge. When I glanced out the window on my side there wasn't any road underneath us. I looked straight down into the river below.

Driving into Barinas we spotted a Ford dealership on the main strip and a children's play park across the street. After finding a place to spend the night we backtracked to the dealership to have the van checked. The kids and I went to play on the swings, slides, and teeter-totters, but the three- to four-inch cones of sand on the ground held our interest much longer than the play structures. The sand cones were anthills with holes in the center about the size of a dime, the ants themselves being about a centimeter long. Not knowing whether they would bite or sting, we were careful not to disturb them and watched their activity from a distance. The kids thought the hills looked like little volcanoes.

A problem with the fuel injection caused the high idling and it was adjusted after the computer diagnosis. It took almost two hours before they had it running properly again but it cost only $16.00 (Canadian). That was a pleasant surprise.

We are in two rooms tonight to have enough sleeping space. At first the rooms were side by side but when Dayna was washing her hands at the sink, it fell off the wall. She caught it and screamed, "Help!" She couldn't move while holding it up and felt somewhat frightened that she had done something terribly wrong. Ed pushed it back onto the wall and carefully let go. It stayed. The man from the office came to the room and just lifted the sink off the wall, set it on the floor, and told us to take the next room. We moved. The boys are in the small room and the girls are in the big room; occasionally it's fun to be by ourselves.

January 30, 1997: Merida, Venezuela

Barinas was unbearably hot in the early morning, so we dressed in light clothing, but it was a mistake. Our route climbed in altitude from the moment we left town. The magnificent ride took three hours to Apartederos in the mountains and it kept getting colder until we were freezing.

Apartederos, at an altitude of 3,473 meters, is a long, spread-out town adjacent to the road. It was the first time I had experienced the effects of thin air. I was dizzy, couldn't get enough oxygen into my lungs, and my fingers would barely move, a weird sensation.

We dug out some warm clothes when we stopped for lunch at the Pargue Turistico. Ed read the *South American Handbook (SAH)* while waiting for our soup and learned there was a road to the CIDA Astronomical Institute—the highest place in Venezuela accessible by road. We took it and the views from the top were well worth the climb—what a clear sky. The road back to the main highway was barely one lane. Ed eased the van down the steep hairpins. At one point he had to back up to get around a corner. I don't know what we would have done if we had met another car. The road to Merida followed the Chama River continuously downhill, providing more incredible mountain views. We found Posada Leiz Carabello easily and since we planned to stay a few days, we brought all our belongings into the room and parked the van for the duration of our visit.

The city of Merida has a good feel to it. It stretches along an alluvial plain that is cut in half by the Chama River. The steep mountains prevent it from growing wider, so it is a long, narrow city. Level ground is non-existent—one either walks uphill or downhill. The city has many colonial buildings, several parks, and doesn't feel dangerous. The pace is more relaxed than that of Valencia, Maracay, Caracas and Macuto. From Merida, one can arrange trips into the jungle, camping, paragliding, and horseback riding; go trekking to Pico Espejo or on other circuits; and take jeep trips into the park. There are many travel agencies that can help out. Some provide proper clothing for hikes and almost all have someone who speaks English. A person could spend months doing all that is available here.

Merida boasts the world's longest (12.5 kilometers) and highest (4,756 meters) cable car. Built in four sections, it climbs from Merida to Pico Espejo. The kids wanted to do the cable car ride and when they want to do something it is so much easier to gain cooperation. We dressed warmly preparing for the cold at the top. Being some of the first to arrive at the starting point, we waited close to an hour before there were twenty-five people to go up the mountain. The first section of cable went over the Chama River Canyon, giving a good overview of the city. It took 15 minutes to get to the second station at 2,500 meters. Jake, fascinated with the gigantic gears that moved the cables, kept asking, "How do they make us go up?" Neither Ed nor I could give him an answer to satisfy the curiosity to his questions. He really wanted to know and displayed some frustration with his parents.

The second section took us up another 1,000 meters in altitude. From our perspective one tree stood out in contrast to the regular deep green, its foliage a greenish-white. Suddenly we were carried above the tree line. At 3,500 meters I could feel the effects of the altitude again. Jake and Whitney complained about anything and everything. Whitney wanted to be carried, she wouldn't walk; I believe the altitude was affecting her as well. The third section took us up to 4,045 meters. The area reminded me of the mountains of Nepal where Ed and I had trekked northwest of Pokara. The kids complained that they were hungry. The biscuits we had brought along were long gone and all we had eaten was a bowl of cereal in the room before leaving; everyone was grumpy. Ed got impatient with the kids while waiting to do the fourth section. There was a cafe but for some reason he thought they should wait to eat until we were back in Merida. They were miserable so I went for a walk; he could deal with them if he wouldn't give them what would be an effective remedy to their misery.

On the trail I encountered two mule trains coming to the cable car with supplies, just like what we had encountered on the trails of Nepal; the people had a similar appearance to the Tibetans as well. Take away the *teliferico* and it could have been the Himalayas as easily as the Andes. Ben and Dayna soon caught up to me. We found the two turquoise-blue Los Anteojos lagoons and had an excellent view of Pico Bolivar, the Timoncitos glaciers and the peaks of Humboldt and Bompland. Pico Bolivar, at 5,007 meters, is the highest in Venezuela and stays snow-capped year round. The flowers and plants were unusual. One in particular, the fraileyon or flannel flower, was intriguing. Its leaves were the shape of lanceolated plantain: thick, fuzzy and soft like cotton flannel. Its flower was as big around as, and resembling a three-inch cotton ball. It grows only at high altitudes in the tropical Andes.

Jake and Whitney were still miserable when we returned. I purchased a bowl of chicken soup for each of the kids and they devoured it. Everyone's mood changed for the better. Ed was angry with me and we had a tiff over not making them wait, but food would have been two hours away. I argued that Jake, Whitney and Karina are little kids; we couldn't make them wait hours. I tried to get him to understand that if we accommodate basic needs first, our trip will go more smoothly; the kids aren't able to go all day without food (like when we travelled alone) and stay in good humour. The altitude wasn't making it any easier on anyone. We waited more than an hour for the fourth section to start up, and when Ed inquired he was told that it wasn't working and wouldn't be for several months. We were not told that when the tickets were purchased at the bottom.

By the time we had lunch at the Mercado Principal it was 2:00. Afterwards we explored the market building full of handcrafts, shoes, baskets, clothing, foods, and souvenirs on three floors of shops and stalls. The long uphill walk back to the *posada* had the kids tired out and complaining again after our day of walking. Ed put them and me in a taxi and walked back on his own, frustrated with us.

When Ed listed off a few sites to visit, the Beethoven Park with its clock that plays an hourly Beethoven melody sparked an interest for the kids since they are familiar with Beethoven's music. To get to it, we walked uphill for 45 minutes, vaguely following the map through an affluent residential area, some of whose homes had exterior marble floors that shone in the sunlight. Every property had a high metal fence around its yard and bars over the windows of the houses, and all were adorned with flower gardens and lush vegetation. When we found the square with the bust of Beethoven, the clock indicated 9:50. It was not the right time, and after a few minutes we realized it wasn't working and that we wouldn't hear any tunes. There was some disappointment from the kids, but they enjoyed playing in the park until hunger set in again. Ed bargained with Whitney, "If you walk all the way to the ice cream store we saw on the way here we'll stop and get ice cream for everyone." It was a deal, difficult for her to honour, but with some encouragement from the others, she made it and we all enjoyed tasty cones.

The weeks before lent are festival time in Merida and a time when children from different schools (we could tell by the uniforms) collect in the Plaza across the street from our *posada*. They marched around the square to music played by a military band. We watched the parades today then walked to the archaeology museum. Jake was fascinated with the stones and crystals, but the main part of the museum was closed for renovations. The cathedral with its impressive stained glass windows was our next stop but there was a sign that indicated NO ENTRY without hats or if wearing short pants; we didn't have hats and all of us were in shorts. So we had two days of trying to do things and each time our ambitions were frustrated. Tonight while we were packing, about a hundred horses and people decked out in costumes trotted past our window and down the street. A large marching band accompanied them; there must be a good party somewhere.

Before bedtime, the kids watched the movie *Ghost*. Jake asked if the story was true. Good guys, bad guys, God, devil, ghosts, all made an impression on him and he had several questions I didn't know how to answer again. From watching the movie, he seemed to think that if you are a bad person the devil takes you away. I told him I didn't know if that was true or not, but felt that doing bad things just makes more bad things happen and doing good things makes good things happen; it is important to do the best we can all the time. He was satisfied with that and processed the concept with deep thought. These children of mine cause me to reach beyond myself more often then anyone else I have ever learned from.

I feel like staying in Merida. The atmosphere is enchanting, but Ed is anxious to move on.

January 31, 1997: San Antonio, Venezuela, on the border of Colombia

It rained almost all night; the streets of Merida were streams of water this morning. Ed parked the van outside the door of the cafe where we had breakfast. The two male waiters appeared to be intrigued with the kids and concerned for their well-being. (The one making the juice was sure to show me he used bottled water for theirs.) They conversed with them extensively, Ben in particular; who is learning Spanish quickly. They asked if we were on a holiday and were surprised of our intentions to drive to Chile. They told the kids how lucky they were and couldn't stress enough to Ed and me to be careful in Colombia; there are so many kidnappings. We piled into the van, both of them right behind us making sure the doors were properly closed and waving goodbye. People are different toward us with the kids around. The kids may limit us from doing the kind of travel Ed and I did on our own, but they open doors that wouldn't be there without them.

We drove through Merida, Tovar, Las Grita, San Cristobal, then San Antonio. It was a long day for the kids—seven and a half hours through the mountains, mostly in rain making for extremely poor visibility. January and February is rainy season in the Andes. Our road wound around on mountain slopes. In two places half of it had washed away down the mountainside and it was scary to use the section that was still there. We did get a few glimpses of agriculture in the fertile fields and valleys when the fog lifted, but not much.

We are at the Terepaima guesthouse, a decent place run by amiable people. At dinner tonight the kids were talking about how white rice doesn't have the same satisfying taste as whole-grain rice. It was the first time they've said something about the change of diet in South America, at the same time indicating something positive about the healthier food they were accustomed to eating at home in Canada.

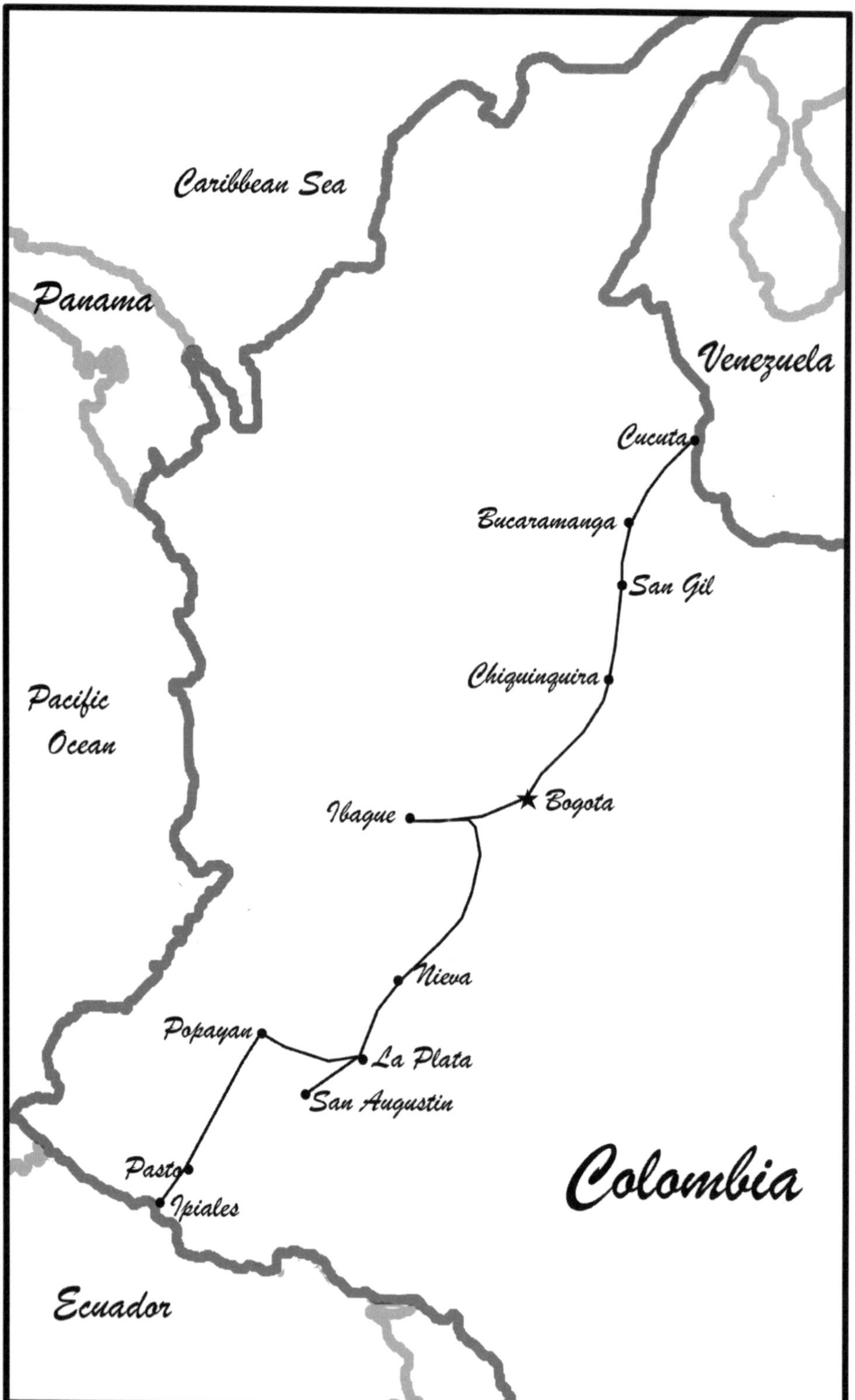

Caribbean Sea

Panama

Venezuela

Cucuta

Bucaramanga

San Gil

Pacific
Ocean

Chiquinquira

Ibague

Bogota

Nieva

Popayan

La Plata

San Augustin

Pasto

Ipiales

Colombia

Ecuador

COLOMBIA

Cucuta, Colombia

We crossed the Simon Bolivar International Bridge over the Rio Tachira and travelled toward Cucuta for five minutes before realizing we had missed something. Ed said, "We'd better go back."

The immigration building was set off the highway slightly—hard to miss, but we did. Colombians and Venezuelans move freely across the border. While the rest of us waited in the van, Ed had obtained all the necessary Colombian stamps and visas for everyone—within fifteen minutes. We then had a delay of two hours waiting for the agent who did the paperwork for foreign vehicles. Once he arrived the *libreta* took five minutes to complete, no questions asked.

I urged the kids to use the bathroom in the immigration building while Ed filled the van with gas. There wasn't any toilet paper in the women's washroom, of course (you'd think I would know that by now) so I went back to get a roll out of the van. (We did buy some at least.) Jake was being a wild man and decided he didn't want anyone to see him use the urinal and slammed the door shut. On my return, the door to the men's washroom was closed. There was no doorknob but there was a latch. Ben and Jake were locked inside with no way to open the door. Jake panicked and cried while Ben tried everything he could think of to get the door open. I tried unsuccessfully as well. Then Ben started to feel claustrophobic and panicky. Tanya ran to the van and returned with Ed who was armed with a screwdriver and needle-nose pliers. He managed to get hold of the latch and pull it open. It wasn't as traumatic as it could have been but it subdued the boys for a while.

Vehicle insurance is mandatory in Colombia and it took another hour and a half to find the insurance office that was recommended at the border, only to discover that it was closed on Saturday. When we realized we would be staying until Monday, we visited every hotel listed in the book, within our budget, all of them in the market area. Cucuta just didn't feel like a place where we should compromise because of cost and by the time we checked into Hotel LaPaz it was four o'clock in the afternoon. We had been in the van nine hours, but the distance we covered was all of 16 kilometers.

The room wasn't great but the hotel did have a pool and enclosed parking. The bathroom had a shower but no toilet seat. Dayna doesn't like to use a toilet without a seat and is having some adjusting to do, as a toilet seat is a rare luxury these days.

At the outdoor restaurant about a block away from the hotel, we had a dinner of chicken and rice and to drink, beer and Sprite. Shortly after returning to our room, the waiter from the restaurant was at our door. He had forgotten to charge for the second beer we had ordered and wanted more money. We must have been conspicuous and were obviously closely watched, if he knew where to find us.

Ed and I decided to find some food for Sunday in case we were to run into another situation like last week. Only Whitney came with us. The kids wanted to watch television, so we let them stay giving specific instructions that they were to open the door to absolutely no one but us—no exceptions.

At the nearest outdoor shop/stall we bought cereal, bananas and milk for breakfast. Whitney was perched on my hip and the shopkeeper talked with her. She replied with the Spanish words she knew, making him laugh. He then asked where we were from. When Ed replied "Canada" he stuck his index finger into Ed's stomach saying *peligroso*—danger. If our hotel was close by, he advised us to go back. Ed asked if the market would be open on Sunday. He said it would be, and it was safer during the day but still not a good place for *gringos*. We went straight back to the hotel without incident. If we hadn't had Whitney with us I'm sure there would have been less concern for our wellbeing from that man.

The long hot day got to Ben, he was extra moody and wanted to sleep in the double bed. It was supposed to be for Ed, Whitney and me. We refused his request; he had a good bed but still got angry and cried. The issue wasn't really the beds. He's just tired of being cooped up in the van and misses his friends. He really wanted to ski this winter and it is a big adjustment to the difference in culture. He did eventually sleep—in the big bed.

We spent another Sunday morning doing laundry in the bathroom and hanging it in the room. When the cleaning woman came in, she took the wet clothes to the roof to dry and brought them all back neatly folded a few hours later.

Ed put on long pants and shoes (people don't wear shorts, even in this heat!). He didn't take his waist pouch, instead putting his money in his pocket, and went to the market to purchase food for the day. He could pass for a Colombian with his dark hair and darker complexion.

We were at the pool when he returned with some familiar foods and a Colombian specialty—a boiled egg surrounded in curry-flavored rice and mashed potato, wrapped in pastry, and deep-fried. It was tasty and filling, as well as inexpensive and hit the spot. Ed enjoyed his disguise. He was Colombian as long as he didn't have to speak. When he told the woman at a food stall he was Canadian, she fed him several samples of the cooked food she had available. That's where he bought the eggs.

The kids were out of the pool only long enough for their turn to play games on the computer and eat. Jake's hands and feet were shriveled when we took a break from the sun. It was a good place to take a time out while waiting the weekend out.

When we knew we were in the area of the insurance office on Monday but still couldn't find it, Ed parked the van in the shade of a building on a quiet street. The kids and I waited for what seemed hours, and when the kids started to complain about the heat and having to wait, I felt like complaining too. It seemed Ed was taking much longer than he should have, and scary thoughts started to run through my head. What if something happened to him? What if he didn't come back? What would I do? I know so few words in Spanish—how would I manage? Just as all these negative thoughts were running through my head, a policeman appeared at the side of the van and started to talk to me. I looked blankly at him and thought, "my fear made this happen". I didn't even know how to tell him I didn't understand. The side doors were open to let the air circulate, and he looked in at the kids while continuously talking. Ben thought he said we were in a "no parking" zone, but there was no indication of that on the street. When I shrugged, he backed off, stood on the sidewalk and looked off into the distance wondering what to do. Ed finally returned. The policeman asked to see the papers. We were parked in a no parking zone, but it didn't seem to matter—he was more interested in where we were from, what we were doing and where we were going. Ed had just purchased the insurance so everything was legal for Colombia. He let us go.

Our driving expectation for the day was to get to Bucaramanga. Mountains, mountains and more mountains—the vistas even captured the kids' attention for most of the day and they did great in the van. Jake and Karina laid claim to the front seat so they could stick their heads out the window when necessary. It was the first time Whitney succumbed to the twisting mountain roads and she vomited all over herself. Ed stopped at a mountain stream immediately. For such a hot climate the water was so cold I couldn't put my feet in it. It was a cold bath for Whitney and she let us know it.

Bucaramanga was busy and confusing. It had the look and feel of Asia. The neon signs and clothes hanging out of the windows on poles reminded Ed and me of Hong Kong. Somehow we found the turn to continue south, so Ed kept going and we found ourselves climbing another mountain at sunset. The light was warm and the low sun cast deep shadows, creating heightened contrast and colour in the views. Ed drove slowly to enjoy it. He is usually a more aggressive driver but vehicles were passing us for a change.

February 5, 1997: San Gil and Chiquinquira, Colombia

It was dark when we arrived in San Gil and we found an economical hotel with enclosed parking. Again, we had been in the van a long time. We walked to the Plaza de Armas after dinner to stretch our legs. The kids needed to burn off some energy before they could settle into a night's sleep.

Tunja was our destination for Tuesday, and we drove at a leisurely pace, since it was only 175 kilometers away. During our breakfast of eggs and bread across the street from our hotel, two men having coffee watched our family zoo. Whitney was angry and created a fuss. Ed had cut up her eggs and she wouldn't eat them. She wanted an unbroken egg to dip her bread in. I traded with her to get her calmed down. One man spoke enough English to understand what was going on and laughed at the antics in an understanding way. We talked with them and found out both were stonemasons supervising the building of the new *Palacio de Justicio* for the province. One of the men explained that the stone for the main structure, which is a light pinkish-orange colour, was quarried from the mountains a half-hour from San Gil. The grey stone used as a contrast on the floors was from the south. The *South American Handbook (SAH)* refers to the "spectacular rock colors" around San Gil, and we did witness that the previous day. Out of interest, I asked questions about the stone and we soon found ourselves walking down the street for a tour. We entered an overwhelming stone structure through a small door in the tall board wall and were impressed immediately by the colonial style building with carved stone pillars and arches. Although it is a modern building, it is being built with the same everlasting skill and methods of the Incas. The stones have been carved, not cut, and fit together perfectly. We were given a tour of the entire building: three floors of courtrooms, judges' quarters, offices, and a library, all built from stone. I don't know why they took the time out for us but the tour did give us a better appreciation of the area. They are proud of their work, and have good reason to be. What a structure!

We were on the move by mid-day, but were immediately confronted by a road closure for construction just outside of town that would keep us waiting until five o'clock that afternoon. Ed asked if it was possible to go around and was shown an alternate route on our map. After an hour of driving we found ourselves in a small village where the people wore traditional clothing—women in full cotton dresses with long, black hair in tidy braids, which appeared to be of great importance to them, decorating their backs. Every woman, young or old, had incredible braids. The sidewalk market was bustling with people selling their wares, including stacks of cages with baby chicks—anything and everything. We had snacks and refreshments at a *panderia* (bakeshop) and Ed asked directions to Confines. They wanted to send us back to San Gil to take the highway. There was only one other road to Confines—over the mountain—and the locals reaction to us taking it was not encouraging. Nonetheless, we took it.

We climbed and climbed. The road was not really even gravel, just dusty dirt. I was thankful it wasn't raining. The road hugged the mountain, affording us wonderful views of the fertile valley farms. We were enjoying it, despite its narrowness and bumps, when the van started to sputter and choke, and then stopped. Ed cleaned out the air filter and added gas cleaner to the tank but this didn't appear to be the source of the problem.

During our wait, the kids did some exploring. I was useless to Ed and joined them. I noticed what looked like a sensitive plant. It folded up immediately when touched; the tiny compound leaves closed in to meet each other. The kids had never seen a plant move so quickly and were fascinated. Our long wait felt short, with the time taken up learning about the plants they found.

The van did eventually start but it sputtered and quit again as we made it to the crest of the mountain. Ed coasted down the other side in neutral with the engine off. Without power to the steering and brakes, it was a tough, dangerous drive. The kids were quiet and concerned. When I was nervously thinking about all the mountains ahead of us and the fact that the van was not performing well at altitudes over 2,000 meters, I realized I had missed out on my morning giving thanks ritual. I asked Ben to pass the crystal to me. It was a gift from a friend before we left, offering protection for our journey. I held it, shut my eyes and thought about all the things I am so thankful for, and simply said, "thank you". Maybe it was the altitude and we were low enough for the van to start, but during the time I was giving thanks, Ed started the engine and it worked without a choke or sputter for the rest of the day.

We lost ourselves on the one-way streets of Barbosa then saw a sign to Bogotá and assumed it was our road to Tunja. It was a truck route and a main road to Bogotá but not Tunja. We continued anyway, instead of going back. At one point on the highway there was a section of pavement about 10 centimeters lower than its surroundings. It was a big dip, as if that piece of land supporting the highway had slid down the mountain and then stopped. In some places the road was washed out without warning. It kept us alert.

There are mini-buses everywhere in Colombia, many of which are vans exactly like ours. People attempt to flag us down, mistaking us for a bus, and then shake their fists in anger as we drive by. Being a newer model, the van has headlights that are automatically on at all times. People here don't like to see the lights on during the day and they constantly point at them, flashing with their fingers, expecting Ed to turn them off. They keep doing it even though he shakes his head to indicate to them that he knows. It is becoming annoying.

We are in Chiquinquira tonight, another town similar to San Gil, but at an even higher altitude than when we experienced engine troubles earlier. It leaves me wondering what the problem was this afternoon—maybe a reminder to give thanks every day. Ed found this comfortable hotel and room with seven beds. It is the first time each of the kids has had a real bed since we left our own home on December fifteenth.

Ed phoned Gay Bernal and told her that we will be in Bogotá at about 3:00 p.m. tomorrow, if all goes well. She was glad to hear we were safe and gave Ed directions to the apartment she has arranged for us. She and Pacho will be awaiting our arrival.

Ed took Spanish lessons during the fall from Angela, a home-schooling mother and family friend. When he began his lessons, Angela's mother, Gay, was visiting from Colombia, so he had plenty of opportunities to practice Spanish. She invited us to visit with her and Pacho in Bogotá when passing through, and here we are.

February 5 to 12, 1997: Bogotá, Colombia

Ed had our route figured out on the city map and wanted me in the front seat to help with directions. Ben was angry, insisting it was his turn. It would always be his turn if you left it to him. He gets more front-seat time, more computer time, and a bed to himself more often than anyone else, yet he still thinks everything is unfair to him. From my point of view he is being unreasonable but he obviously doesn't see it that way. He stayed angry until we arrived at the apartment.

The directions were perfect, and we made it through the mega-city without error. Gay and Pacho were waiting for us. They introduced us to their friends, Blanca and Liez, who live in and take care of the building. We were given an apartment on the fourth floor. It is a large space with five bedrooms, three bathrooms, a fully equipped kitchen, a dining room with a beautiful wooden dining room set, and a window that overlooks the city to the north. It also has a living room with cable TV. Half the channels are in English and the kids are ecstatic.

We unpacked the van and parked it inside the garage. Carrying everything up all those steps was a job. The altitude of Bogotá is 2,800 meters, making the air thinner and always cool, despite the fact that the city is within five degrees of the equator. I had a slight headache and difficulty getting enough oxygen into my body. It took a long time to catch my breath after hauling our belongings into the apartment.

Gay took us in her Jeep to the supermarket. She explained that her vehicle is old and not so nice to look at, but it works. People are less likely to steal old-looking vehicles. The Jeep was secured with two chains and padlocks, one from the steering wheel to the door handle and another from the steering wheel to the underside of the seat, making it impossible to turn the wheel.

We bought vegetables which we have been missing in the restaurants. Gay explained that most establishments don't take the time to do what is required by regulation to make them safe for eating, so they just don't serve them. She showed us several different fruits we had not tasted before and we tried them out. Passion fruit was a big hit with everyone. Gay didn't think we should eat the lettuce. Up to now, any time we have eaten anything of the sort we have washed it with grapefruit seed extract and so far it has worked.

For our first day, Gay, who had previous commitments, made arrangements for Blanca to be our tour guide in Bogotá.

The kids wanted French toast for breakfast and since we had a kitchen we took advantage of the opportunity. It set a good mood for the morning. I put a lentil soup together for our return.

Blanca was ready to go at 10:00 a.m. She recommended we leave the van in the garage, explaining that it was too dangerous to leave it parked on the streets in Bogotá. We toured by city bus. Our first stop was a funicular ride up to Monserrate for an aerial view. This city of 6.5 million covers an area of 1,587 square kilometers on an interior plateau of the Andes Mountains. It stretches much farther to the north and south than what we were able to see. The buildings are tight together and most are covered in red tile roofs, creating an interesting visual rhythm on the cityscape. From the funicular we walked to the Museo de Oro (Museum of Gold) and took a break at a children's play park along the way. The museum has an unbelievable display of pre-Inca gold artifacts that were not found by the conquistadors. More than 30,000 pieces of pre-Colombian gold work are on display—sculpted figures, jewelry, masks, all painstakingly intricate work. We were told that every technique used by goldsmiths today was implemented in the artifacts. A five-minute visit inside the Salon Dorado (an inner vault with a concentration of thousands of pieces) was all that was allowed. All six of the children were as spellbound as Ed and I.

On the crowded bus ride home, Whitney was tired and not at her best. A man gave her and me a seat and when we were a little more comfortable she asked, "Mom, how do you say 'I'm hungry' in Spanish?"

"I don't know, you will have to ask your Dad," I replied.

He was several seats away from us, so she yelled, "Dad, how do you say 'I'm hungry' in Spanish?"

He replied, "Tengo hambre."

"Tengo hambre, then," she said, and continually repeated it. Everyone on the bus knew she was hungry.

That evening Gay called and wanted us to pick them up with the van at 9:30 the following morning. They had arranged a special day for us.

We went to a country house, the farm of a friend. We saw our first llamas up close and it was the first time that I have noticed eucalyptus trees in South America. Gay put together a wonderful meal of rice, lentils, papaya juice, several carefully prepared salads and a plate of tomatoes that had been hand peeled. There were more fresh vegetables in that meal than we had had for a week and it was a treat. After our mid-day meal we went to a perfectly circular lake in the mountains. At one time it must have been a volcano. A guard at the entrance gate explained that it was a sacred place and imperative that we be quiet while visiting. There was a trail for walking around the lake, but swimming was strictly prohibited. It was a tranquil, peaceful place; the vegetation was so green and the sky so blue. The kids were outside and in the open. To them it meant freedom to run and let loose, but it was not what was expected and we had to remind them several times to stay quiet. As we started down the path circling the lake, Ben let out one of his Tarzan-like yodels. Between Whitney wanting to be carried because of the altitude, Ben's behaviour, and it being late in the day, we decided it was better to leave the lake undisturbed. We turned around and went back to the van. Ben was somewhat disappointed, but for some reason he couldn't behave appropriately in the situation; he didn't get a second chance and complained. It would have been a lovely hike.

Pacho told Ed that Ecuador was not safe. People were trying to take over the presidency, and the border was closed for an indefinite period of time. What's more, on Tuesday there was a national strike scheduled in Colombia. The labour movement and government employees were having a disagreement and he felt that it could be a dangerous day to be on the roads. Pacho painted a picture of extreme danger; Ed didn't know what to think. It seemed as if Pacho wanted us to stay. We were discouraged, but with all the do's and don'ts that have been presented to us, Bogotá doesn't feel like the safest place either.

On Saturday, Blanca asked Ed if he would see a friend who had back pain and digestive problems. Señora Roja, in her sixties, came for an adjustment out of curiosity more than anything else, and Ed gave her a treatment after explaining how Chiropractic works. She liked him instantly and they talked at great length. Ed wanted more information about what was happening in Ecuador and she invited him to her house to call the South American Club in Quito as the phone in the apartment was limited to local calls only. When he came back from Señora Rojas' her entire family was with him: her husband, who is a medical doctor, her two daughters and their husbands, one of whom is a spinal surgeon, and all her grandchildren. Ed adjusted them all. The surgeon spoke English, so he and Ed discussed Chiropractic in depth. He then offered to help Ed start a clinic, saying there was a lot of money in Colombia and that with his skills Ed could easily get rich in Bogotá.

All this positive feedback about Chiropractic has filled Ed with enthusiasm. The big question is, do we really want to stay in Bogotá? There is a quality-of-life issue here. It is an interesting place to visit but if it is as dangerous as everyone has been telling us then it is not a place where we want our children to be for an indefinite period of time.

Blanca called a friend in Ecuador to inquire about what was happening; the friend hadn't heard of any problems. Ed tried the South American Club again after his earlier unsuccessful attempt, and the woman who answered said there weren't any problems.

Ed adjusted everyone that Blanca and Pacho sent for treatment, as well as Señora Rojas' entire family again on Sunday morning. It is the explanation of

Chiropractic and how it works that takes the time. Once there is an understanding of how an adjustment works, it is hard to refuse.

Señora Rojas and her daughter Marytza invited our family for lunch at a private Tennis and Golf Club. We followed them and Marytza's daughter to Marytza's. Ed said there wasn't any sense in taking two vehicles to the club and that they should come in our van. So the three of them came with us. Marytza was infatuated with Karina because of her blonde hair. She wanted Karina to sit beside her and gave her candies and chocolate. Karina was pretty smug about the special treatment, while Jake and Dayna complained that it was unfair.

We walked into the club wearing jeans, t-shirts and sweatshirts, and it was the first time in years that I have felt self-conscious about it. People in Bogotá dress well. Pacho always visits us in a three-piece suit, while Gay always looks so nice in skirts and jackets. We are comfort-clothing people, have a limited supply of even that at the moment, and were not dressed to the standard of the people in that restaurant.

Señor Rojas, Marytzas' husband, Jorge, and his parents joined us as well. The children were seated at a separate table. Señora Rojas ordered salmon and trout for us but the kids wanted chicken and fries. It was extremely busy and we waited more than an hour before the food arrived, by which time the kids were extremely hungry. We may not have been dressed very well, but the kids acted like royalty with their honed etiquette skills. During the entire meal, which took close to three hours, their behaviour and patience were more than what could be expected. They outdid themselves.

Señora Rojas kept ordering food: cream of asparagus soup, salad, tea, coffee and desserts. We had to have the house specialty, two thick slices of cheese with caramel sauce in between, heated until the cheese melted. I ate some, but with difficulty. I now understand why Señora Rojas has digestive problems. How do we get people to understand that a good part of health comes from what we put into our bodies, which need foods that nourish without causing stress? Nobody likes to work without getting paid, and yet we ask our bodies to do so, plying them with so many foods that are a liability as opposed to an asset. It is all a matter of choosing what we put into our mouths.

Jorges' mother was shocked at what we are doing. She just couldn't understand why we sold our house and belongings to live like "gypsies". She kept looking at us as if there was something really wrong. After dinner, in the ladies room, she cornered me and asked if I was happy. I had the impression she thought that Ed was dragging me along as an unwilling participant. Yes, I am happy with what we are doing. I like travelling. Other things can be an issue, but I do like travelling. I didn't know how to tell her more. She shook her head in disbelief.

Ben's heavy dinner did not sit well and his digestion was aggravated by his playing on the swings as well as the winding road. Ed had to stop the van so he could vomit while we were on our way to the dairy that Señora Rojas, Marytza and her daughter wanted to show us. The shop, as it turned out was full of cheeses, flavored yogurts and an extensive variety of desserts with whipped cream. Señora Rojas bought us more desserts, but we were still so full that even the kids didn't want to eat them. She had them boxed up to take with us.

It was dark when we dropped Marytza and her daughter at home and headed toward the apartment under Señora Rojas' directions. She was lost, so we drove back and forth, ending up in the south end of the city, which is not recommended. We turned around and tried again and again. The kids were patient and well behaved for as long as they possibly could be, then started to jump around. Jake stepped on one of the three plastic bottles of yogurt we had purchased for breakfast and the top popped off. Yogurt squirted across the floor, and some was even smeared on the ceiling. They used a whole box of Kleenex to clean it up.

Ed patiently took directions from Señora Rojas while the minor fiasco was going on in the back. This woman has lived her entire life in Bogotá and yet she didn't know how to get from her daughter's house to her own. She has three maids and a chauffeur. Her driver takes her wherever she wants to go. I wonder if she ever does anything for herself and where her self-satisfaction in life comes from. I can't imagine being that dependent on others. We did eventually get home, an hour and a half later; it should have taken fifteen minutes.

We were supposed to leave Monday but people just kept coming for adjustments. Tuesday was a repeat of Monday. While Ed worked, the rest of us settled into some reading and writing, but the kids got antsy being cooped up in the apartment. They can't take being confined for long with so little to do. Ed adjusted a man who did his Ph.D. in agronomics in the United States. He stayed for a visit, and had some dinner with us. He was well informed about what was happening in Ecuador. The problem is a truckers' strike at the border, which is in the process of negotiation, and he said it should be settled by the time we get there. Uneven tariffs imposed on trucks transporting goods between Colombia and Ecuador are the issue, and Ecuadorian truckers have the border blocked in protest.

Pacho and Gay were not happy about us leaving. He in particular wanted us to stay indefinitely, but it wouldn't be fair to the kids to keep them confined like that. It took most of the morning to get out of the city. The exhaust fumes in the stop-and-go traffic were stifling and caused sore throats by the time we got to open country roads.

Saturday, February 15: Ibague and San Augustin, Colombia

The road brought us out of the mountains and onto the plains of the Rio Magdalena. What a contrast in climate in such a short distance. It is consistently between sixteen and twenty degrees Celsius in Bogotá, and thirty degrees year-round only an hour's drive away. The flat, central plateau made for easy driving through extensive farm country. Across the Rio Magdalena, the vegetation eventually turned to jungle—with banana and palm trees that, in parts had taken over the landscape. As we started to rise into mountains again, the road followed a tributary of the Magdalena through a river gorge, twisting and turning alongside the rushing water

Whitney & Statue – San Augustin, Colombia

while hugging the edge. At one point the road cut into the cliff, the rock overhead creating a half-tunnel above us. There was a sheer drop into white water right beside us.

Transport trucks were lined up and stopped on the side of the road for 12 kilometers outside the city of Ibague. Ed asked a taxi driver next to us at a stoplight for directions to the road to Armenia. He said to follow him. Eventually he turned off and pointed in the direction in which we were to keep going. Within a minute, there were more trucks lined up, blocking the highway. A landslide, in the process of being cleared, had stopped traffic for several kilometers on both sides of the city. We were told that the road should be cleared by morning. We found a decent hotel for our evening in Ibague, and a market where we could purchase food. With our extra time we enjoyed a walking tour that took us to the plaza. There is always an impressive cathedral to visit.

Whitney and I played a "matching pairs" card game while the others played euchre. The idea is to obtain more matching pairs than your opponent, and the rules are whatever works for who is playing, which usually turns out in her favour. The numbers 6 and 9 are still somewhat confusing for her, and sometimes she has to count the pictures on the cards. We counted our piles; I had 22. She counted 1-2-3-4-5-... 27, 28, 29, and 20-10. She didn't miss a number right up to 20-10. She screamed, "I win, I win".

"Yes, you do, Whitney, but the number of cards you have is called 30."

"No, 20-10."

"No, 30. 20 plus 1 is 21, 20 plus 2 is 22, 20 plus 3 is 23 all the way up to 20 plus 10. 20 plus 10 is called 30."

"It's still 20-10" she insisted. There was no sense in arguing; at some point she'll figure it out.

We learned, after the van was packed, that the landslide was worse than anticipated. The road was still blocked and there was no prediction as to when it would be open. There were two choices: stay and wait, or go back the way we came and continue south through the interior plain of the Rio Magdalena and cross over the mountain range at Garzon to Papayan. The road we'd be following wasn't marked as a main road, but we were told that it was passable. Since we were packed, that was our choice. It was a hot day of driving with the Rio Magdalena on our right and mountains to our left. Fortunately, the road was in excellent condition and we made good time. A group of soldiers flagged us down in Natagaima. One asked the direction we were going, and Ed told him Papayan. He looked into the van, surveyed the passengers, and asked if we could give him a ride to Neiva. Again, it was Ben's day in the front seat and he didn't give it up without some angry words when Ed told him to move back. The soldier, a pleasant young man, said hello to everyone. He and Ed chatted as if they were long-lost buddies for the forty-five minutes the young man was in the van with us.

I read about San Augustin to Ed from the *SAH*. It was not much farther from the turn-off to Papayan. Ed asked the soldier about it. He said, "It usually takes about four hours to drive from here but with this van, no more than three, and if you like archeology it would be worth visiting." We let him out in Neiva and continued to San Augustin.

As we drove into the town of San Augustin, so many people surrounded the van that we were prevented from moving. It is a tourist town—tourists mean money. We didn't even get our feet on the ground before we were being solicited to buy things and go on tours. Ed asked if there was an office where tour and hotel arrangements could be made, and it eliminated all but one of our suitors. The kids and I waited in the van until Ed came back from Gustavo's office all smiles. He had arranged a good place to stay, a tour set up in the archeology park, and possibly a horse-back ride to visit some sites the following afternoon.

Our *posada* was a neat place. From the street they never look half what they are inside. The solid white cement walls had a couple of tiny windows with jail-like metal bars over them. Two heavy wooden doors opened onto a brick floor and hallway. The interior is a rectangle of two floors of rooms that face into the open courtyard garden. The latter was inviting with its tables, chairs and palm umbrellas, a lounging area, and a large circular cage for tropical birds that intrigued the kids.

Rossi, our guide (he has seventeen children), directed us first to the Bosque de las Estatuas. The stone-carved statues date back to 3000 B.C., Rossi worked with archeologists for eight years to excavate them. There is not much known about the people who made them but there are many theories. One that Rossi believes suggests the carvers and their culture came from Asia or Africa, in that the motifs of gorillas and elephants, animals that don't exist in South America, are carved into the rock in several places. The kids enjoyed running in the space and figuring out what animals or human activities the statues represented. Each one of them was different: male, female, serpents, squirrels, monkeys, birds, warriors, people playing instruments, people chewing coca, farmers, and the fertility goddess. At a small river, the rocks were carved out so that water could be redirected into pools for specific purposes. Theories suggest that amongst those pools, there was an area for purification, a place to give birth, another area for healing, and a place for both human and animal sacrifice. I was reminded that sometimes gaining knowledge just creates more questions and the realization of how little we really know.

Rossi is knowledgeable about plants. As we walked he pointed out a small plant, plentiful along the walkway, effective for female problems; a vine with burgundy, heart-shaped leaves, fuzzy on the back, called snake plant, which is good for reducing inflammation of snake bites when used as a tea or poultice; a tree whose leaves help heal lung infections; a small white flower for digestive problems. He showed us a plant for almost every common ailment. There was something wherever we walked.

Activities always take longer with a group of kids, and a three-hour tour turned into four, but Rossi was extremely patient with us. There was no time for lunch. We drove from the park and Ed dropped us off at Rossi's house, where the horses were waiting. Ed parked the van at the *posada*, and ran back bringing with him bananas and cookies for us to eat along the way.

The kids were excited about getting onto horses, and Jake was angry that he couldn't have one to himself. He and Karina rode together, Whitney rode with me, and the others had a horse to themselves. Ben's horse wanted to be in front at all times, and Ben thought that was great: he, too, likes to be the leader. We rode for three hours, during which we visited El Purutal, La Palotal,

La Chaquina, and El Talaban to see more stone statues, some of which date as far back as 3,300 B.C. A few of them were painted yellow and red, colours that had lasted for thousands of years. There was a moment when I was almost in tears. Heading back to the village, I was at the end of the line of horses walking down the mountain. On a higher part of the hill there was an incredible view of the Andes in Colombia and my family on horses. My heart almost stopped in overwhelming thanks to whomever, or whatever, for the opportunity to be doing what we are doing. Somehow it is difficult to believe we are where we are. I felt so thankful and happy at that moment that I probably would have cried if the horses hadn't jolted me back to reality by running for home.

We were saddle-sore by the time we put our feet on the ground. Jake, who had been anxious to get off his horse close to an hour earlier, had the comment of the day: "We rode all that way just to see those rocks!" It was a good day, and Rossi said he had never had so much fun with a group before.

Gustavo came to say goodbye. We were planning to go back to Garzon, but he didn't think we should have to. He said the shorter route was a gravel road and that we should be able to travel it because the van rides high off the ground.

As it turned out it had rained in the mountains, and the road was severely worn. There wasn't much gravel left, and there were many deep mud holes. After an hour of driving on an iffy road we got to a spot where a tandem truck was coming through. The driver stopped and said the road was very bad, with many places worse than the one he had just traversed. He was certain we wouldn't get to the main highway without big trouble. We turned around.

It took two hours of our day, and we were back to the beginning but on smooth highway, where after a while we were stopped by two soldiers who looked somewhat intimidating. They took positions on each side of the van. One spoke so fast that Ed didn't understand a word—he seemed to want something. Ed took out our papers, but he wouldn't even look at them. I was in the back with the little ones. He stuck his head into the van and counted, *uno, dos, tres, quatro, cinqo, seis*—we understood that much. He rolled his eyes, rapidly jabbered on, laughed, and indicated with hand gestures for us to continue. After seeing the kids, whatever it was he wanted didn't matter. He had a hard time believing his eyes. They probably weren't soldiers of the Colombian army.

In Garzon, Ed asked several people about the road to Papayan. We were told it would take six hours; it was rough, but passable. One person said there were guerillas and recommended going across the mountains via Ibague, Armenia and Cali. Ed then asked a policeman who said it was a fairly good road and if we drove in the daylight we would be fine. Ed spoke with a group of soldiers at the military post when we arrived in La Plata. Every one of them agreed that the road was drivable and that it would take three to four hours to get over the mountains. We were told there were both guerillas and soldiers between La Plata and the Purace Park, but we wouldn't be able to tell them apart, as they dress the same. All agreed that it would not be a problem for us to pass through in daylight. One of the soldiers stressed to Ed to be sure to tell whoever stopped us that we were Canadians—not: *if* they stopped us but *when*. There was no doubt it would happen. It was the first time we had more than one person agree on any kind of advice or directions, so we moved onward.

And sure enough it wasn't long before we were stopped by a group of heavily armed soldiers. They asked us to get out of the van while they checked inside; three of them checked our passports studiously. One soldier asked Ed the usual questions about our destination. When they were satisfied we just wanted to pass through, they let us continue on our way. A short while later we saw many army packs lying on the side of the road. Several army personnel, or perhaps guerillas, were standing around a jeep in the middle of the road; it had a smashed windshield. Ed carefully continued around as if it was no concern of ours and they didn't give us a second glance either.

The mountains and countryside were breathtaking. The altitude of the road is between 2,000 and 3,000 meters. The most spectacular 25 kilometers followed a lower pass along a gorge, with a river flowing hundreds of meters below, and mountains towering above us. Eventually, the road became a trail for barely one vehicle; it was hard driving for Ed. Fortunately, when the road was demanding, the kids slept. There was not a soul to be seen for more than an hour, and an eerie calmness enveloped the remote uninhabited mountains. We experienced sunshine and rain, and learned that the weather can change in a matter of moments at high altitude.

A strong smell of sulphur from the hot springs indicated that we were coming up to Purace Park. The soldiers in La Plata had told Ed that when we got to the park, we would be out of the guerilla zone and that the road would improve. We made it without incident. We had climbed over 3,000 meters, and the van had worked perfectly. We may have our angels to thank for more than just a working van.

In the town of Purace, there was only one *posada* and one place that served food. But after ten hours in the van, we decided to stay. Our room has whitewashed mud walls with four straw-tic mattress double beds. The toilets are outhouses, and two sinks hang on the outside walls. Our basic needs are met.

We slept well. The van sat outside on the street for the first time in South America and was untouched when we piled into it this morning, perhaps because military personnel occupy the streets at all times in Purace.

February 17, 1997: Through Higuirones and on to Pasto

Breakfast in Papayan consisted of delicious hot chocolate served the traditional Colombian way: in a bowl with bread for dipping. After our previous long day, Ed told the kids that we would be staying the night in Pasto, a four-hour drive away. The tarmac of the Pan–America Highway had felt so good for all of two hours. The highway was visible on the next mountain, and Dayna was the first to figure it out. "Hey look, that's our road over there and it just stops." We were

in good spirits and enjoyed the sunshine and mountains, until we spotted trucks parked along the side of the road again. A landslide had buried a tunnel entrance. People were saying it would be at least three days before it was cleared. It happened shortly before our approach and the clean-up job hadn't started yet. We

One of the landslides that diverted our route.

went back to the last town we passed through and Ed asked about an alternative route. There was one, but we were warned that it would take four to five hours on a gravel road to go the equivalent of about 30 kilometers on the Pan-America Highway. Our choice was between days of waiting or hours of driving and Ed chose the latter. We bought food to make some lunch and a rack of bananas to tide us over for the afternoon. The gravel road was good going for all of a half hour, then clouds started to roll in, turning blacker by the minute until it started to pour rain. There were three vehicles ahead of us taking the same route with many more following. High in altitude, the road was narrow and muddy. It rained so hard we could barely see ten meters ahead. Just as I allowed myself to think, "Well, it can't get any worse," we reached a small hill where a cargo truck had slipped off the edge and in the ditch, unable to move, but still blocking more than half the road. A mini-van attempted to get around the truck and ended up in the ditch on the opposite side. We sat and waited out the rain as another line of vehicles collected on another blocked road.

The rain slowed and a crowd of people emerged from their vehicles. One man showed up with a rope and everyone pitched in to pull the mini-van *up* the hill; no one got behind it. Small all-wheel-drive vehicles were able to pass, but one slipped off the edge and was pulled up the hill as well. Ed tried three times to get up the mud-slicked hill. He didn't get stuck but with the limited space, the van managed to climb only part way up. The man with the rope was gone by this time and the truck driver from directly behind us told Ed that the man had made not-so-nice comments about the Americans, said he wasn't going to help any gringo, and left with his rope. The vehicles going in the downhill direction were cleared through.

A bus driver asked his passengers to disembark. He then towed the truck backwards down the hill several meters. It stayed in the ditch but opened up some space to make the road passable. More four-wheel drive vehicles made it through but we were not given the opportunity to try again. The bus attempted the hill but was still unable to squeeze by and slid off the opposite side. An oncoming bus attempted to pull the stuck bus up, but to no avail, and once again the road was blocked in both directions.

It was dark. There wasn't any hope until morning. The truck driver, whom we were beginning to get to know through his interaction with the kids, suggested to Ed that we drive back to Higuirones. He said it would be safer in the village, and he knew there was a restaurant where we could get some dinner. Everyone was hungry. We had eaten every last thing in the cooler and all the bananas. Ed drove backwards a long distance before there was enough space to turn around. The line of traffic waiting to pass was almost four kilometers long.

The restaurant was closed but a young man on the street saw that we were potential customers and knocked on the owners' door. A friendly older man answered. His wife came to the door as well, looked at our crew, and agreed to cook us a meal. It took close to two hours, and word that foreigners were in the village travelled fast. As we waited, children crowded the doorway, peering in at us. The alarm to the van kept going off as the kids pulled on the door handles looking for a way to get inside. The night air grew very cold while we waited for dinner. I went to the van to get blankets to wrap the kids in, but it was a challenge to get to the blankets as I was crowded with village kids wanting to get into the vehicle. I let them look and then went back into the restaurant. It was barely a minute later before the alarm had gone off again. Ed went out to check the van and turn the alarm off and he came back extremely annoyed with me. Somehow I didn't lock the one side door and there must have been twenty kids inside. They were just curious.

While waiting for dinner and chatting at the table, I said to Ed, "I know you are going to think this sounds crazy but... I didn't hold the crystal, give thanks and visualize this morning and the only other day I missed was the day we coasted half way down the mountain at San Gil."

He replied, "Well, you'd better not miss anymore, right?"

We were served delicious beef broth macaroni soup, then tough, boiled beef, white rice, fried potatoes and sliced tomatoes. We ate everything, including the meat. Beggars can't be choosers; it would have been extremely rude to not eat what was prepared.

Five other people arrived after us, and they were fed as well. Ed asked the man if there was a *posada* or something of the sort where we could spend the night, but there wasn't. He then asked if it would be all right to sleep in the van parked in front of his restaurant for the night. The man said that it would be fine and went back to serving the others that had arrived. As we finished our meal the man conversed with his wife then offered us three beds in their home above the restaurant. Ben and Tanya were content to have good space in the van and the rest of us shared the three single beds.

We were awakened to tunes of Michael Jackson blasting in the square. Despite having slept with our clothes on we had little red marks all over our legs. It was a bright, beautiful morning and you wouldn't know it was the same place as the previous day. We were served hard, sugary, donut-like pastries to dunk into *tinto* to be softened before eating. *Tinto* is weak, sweet coffee that even children drink for breakfast in Colombia. The kids had some coffee with milk, but had a hard time with the "rocks", as they called them, and ate only what was needed to ward off hunger. Ed left us at the restaurant while he went to inquire about the road, and the kids were outside playing in the sunshine long before he returned. There was light-coloured, stringy whisps of material hanging on lines beside almost every building in the square and where there wasn't enough space it was laid out on the ground to dry. We had noticed it hanging on lines along the road during our detour and had wondered what it was then too. Ed asked the restaurant owner about it and he opened a garage door to display bundles piled to the roof. The strings are the insides of the cultivated cactus plant in the area. The bottom leaves are cut off and the outer layer of the leaf is removed to reveal a mass of fine string inside. The cactus grows similar in shape to an aloe vera plant, but the leaves are denser, the cactus itself is taller than a person and at least two meters in diameter. The leaves are harvested from the bottom as they mature. Jake asked if the plants were big pineapples, which is what they looked like after several of the bottom leaves had been trimmed off. The strings are hung to dry, bundled, then shipped to the city to be made into burlap bags and rope.

Ed paid for breakfast and asked if he could pay for the beds but they wouldn't accept money for them—we were their guests. All of us thanked our hosts sincerely for their hospitality and told them they made our overnight stay much more enjoyable. They said they enjoyed having us with them, as they have three grown-up sons who have all moved to Cali. They were extremely generous to us and I regret not having learned their names. After the fact, I find it odd that we didn't do introductions. The world is full of good people.

Ed didn't get any definite answers about the road, but traffic had been coming and going again, so that was a good sign. He handed me the crystal and said, "Gaye, do your thing."

The hill where we had been stopped appeared smaller than the previous day. The buses were gone but the truck had been pulled farther back again and was now deeper in the ditch and leaning to the side. The road was still a mud slick, but was clear of any other vehicles. Ed stepped on the gas to gain momentum up the slick and we almost made it. He backed down before we slid backwards. We sat quietly analyzing our challenge. Ed said, "I want you guys to get out, maybe with less weight I can make it."

Ben protested when the command included him but Ed didn't give in—he meant Ben too. He took a faster run at it and didn't hold anything back; the van slid to the side a little during the ascent, but made it to the top the second time. We did nothing but enjoy the mountain views the rest of the day and arrived in Pasto early afternoon.

The Koala Inn was described in our book as having "laundry facilities and hot water showers". Ed checked us in and we started to clean ourselves up while he and Ben took the van to be cleaned.

I asked the owner about using the washer. He spoke English and we conversed easily. He said, "You bring it to me, you are on holiday, I'll do it for you."

I replied. "Remember, we are the ones that walked in with six kids. I can do it; there are a lot of clothes."

"That's okay. Bring it to me. After what you have been through you need a rest."

He did the laundry himself and everything was returned neatly folded in piles of the same colour.

As it turned out however the cost for the service was outrageous and Ed was disgusted with me for not asking the price beforehand. I failed to do that, but I had been expecting to do it myself and had included absolutely everything that needed to be washed; we needed clean clothes. Ed stayed in the room for the evening. He was upset with me, upset with Ben for being miserable at the slightest thing, and didn't like being around other tourists. It has been a tough few days. Everyone is allowed to get moody occasionally. The rest of us watched English HBO movies in the common room. Our night of sleep felt so luxurious in clean beds, clean clothes, and clean bodies.

ECUADOR

February 19, 1997: Tulcan, Ecuador

The border and the bridge across the Rio Carchi were clearly visible from the hill above the Colombian immigration building. The approach was jammed tight with transport trucks allowing barely enough space to walk. The truckers strike was still on, and as we parked, seven people around the van wanted to help us get across the border on back roads. Ed accepted the assistance of one young man. As I mentioned, the grievance was an uneven trade agreement. Colombian truckers carry goods all the way to Quito, but Ecuadorian truckers are only allowed to go as far as Pasto.

Ed and his "assistant" brought the passports and *libreta* to the office and received the exit papers for Colombia. All passports were processed and again no one checked to see to whom they belonged. Ed and the young man then walked across the bridge through the trucks to Ecuador Immigration. Tourist cards for Ecuador were issued without a problem, but because of the strike vehicles were not allowed into the country. The border patrol officer wouldn't process the van papers. The young man who assisted Ed with the unorthodox entrance procedures then asked the officer what the fee was for filling out the van papers (more or less asking if he would take a bribe to do the van paperwork) and the *libreta* was immediately processed as well. Money does talk. With the paperwork in order the young man then joined us in the van and directed us over back roads and across the river to the alternate border control. This time the Ecuadorian immigration officer checked the identification papers of everyone in the vehicle and then let us pass. We were in Ecuador.

Tulcan was a forty-five-minute drive from Colombian immigration, on back roads. I was beginning to wonder if we were ever going to get to drive on anything but back roads.

Something was blocking Visa transactions at the banks and we were stuck without Ecuadorian currency—*sucres*. One banker told Ed that he should be able to give him cash the following morning. We had some American dollars, and Ed changed enough for dinner and a room.

We found a comfortable hotel but parking was a tight squeeze—the mirrors almost scraped the sides of the twenty-foot alley leading to the enclosed parking. Slowly, Ed made it through, touching the walls only a couple of times.

We had our evening meal at a small restaurant run by a young family: potatoes, rice, a marinated carrot salad, fried eggs and fresh mora berry juice. Everything was so delicious. One son of the owners, about eight years of age, was sitting at another table with his schoolbooks spread out before him. I am sure we distracted him, as he didn't do much work while we were at the restaurant. What a cute little guy, with an innocent round face, dark hair in a long grown-out brush cut so thick it stood straight out all over his head. Every time I made eye contact with him he gave me the biggest grin—his whole body smiled. I couldn't help but grin myself.

Ed was still unable to get cash in the morning but was told he could exchange money in Ibarra, 100 kilometers away. Once again we encountered trucks—strikers—blocking the road. It was an effective demonstration: vehicles were simply not going anywhere. Several people were hanging around, and Ed talked to a teenager on a bike. He learned there was a way to get around the obstruction. The lad pointed to a road on the mountain above and said he would show the way. We loaded his bicycle into the van, and he hopped in. We headed back toward Tulcan, off the highway, up the mountain and over a muddy road that became a mud track, but he delivered us to the other side unscathed. Ed gave him some *sucres* and he was a happy guy returning on his bicycle.

Once again we enjoyed the sun and scenery and noticed many people walking toward Tulcan. At one point after rounding a bend, we encountered logs lying across the road, blocking it in both directions. As we came to a stop, a group of young men ran up to the van. Each of them had farm tools in their hands: hoes, shovels, pitchforks and machetes. It didn't look good. Ed talked to them for a few minutes and when they found out we were Canadian, they asked for money. Ed emptied his pockets of change, totaling close to $4 (CDN). They split it amongst themselves and were more pleasant with us, but still wouldn't allow us to pass. We were told there were similar roadblocks all along the route to Ibarra. During the entire time Ed was talking to these guys there was one young man, maybe in his late teens, baton-twirling his machete in front of the van. The impressive part was his flinging it into the air, catching it by the handgrip, and never missing a toss. We wouldn't have found a better knife-juggling act in a circus.

A military truck full of soldiers came from the Tulcan direction. It barely needed to stop before the guys that were holding us up had the road cleared for it to pass. An older man, a civilian who was walking, pushed his way through the group of irregulars around our van. With an air of authority, he scolded them and they all backed away. He had on a good quality but well-worn, charcoal-grey wool suit with a knitted vest underneath his jacket. To Ed, he waved his index finger back and forth saying, "No, no, no. Don't go down that road. There is a car from Colombia down there with slashed tires. Go back to Tulcan." He had a salt-and-pepper mustache curled up at the ends and revealed a full head of white hair underneath his dressy felt hat as he gave us a more polite greeting. He carried a cane, a paper bag, and a carpetbag over his shoulder.

He may have been telling the truth, or perhaps just wanted a ride to Tulcan, as he said he had been walking since sun-up. We invited him into the van, and he sat in the front passenger seat. We then invited others to join us: a young woman and her daughter, as well as another man, all walking to Tulcan. The older man knew the countryside, took charge and directed us back the way we came.

Not being able to do transactions at the banks in Tulcan, our only choice was back across the border in Colombia to acquire some cash. The kids and I waited in the van while Ed walked across the border between the monstrous trucks that blocked the bridge and took a taxi to an Ipiales bank machine, all without entrance papers. The truckers were suspicious of Ed's speedy return from Colombia and started to question him before he got to the van. The tension of the not-so-friendly faces changed when they learned we were Canadians attempting to tour their country. One man said he would take us to Ibarra on back roads for 150 American dollars. But Ed decided to wait this one out.

Apart from the tight parking arrangements, we had been comfortable the previous night, so went back to the same hotel. I was in front of the van directing and watching Ed carefully maneuver the passage to the parking lot when he popped his head out and said, "déjà vu". There was a crunch and smash. In diverting his attention for just half a second, he had hit the passenger side mirror on the wall. It was partially ripped off and the force pushed it into the door. The mirror support smashed the front passenger window inside the dented the door. We have been weathering the setbacks fairly well up until now, but the broken window made us all feel like crying. After asking at repair shops, we were informed that the only place the window could be replaced was in Quito. We spent the afternoon taking the door apart, cleaning out the broken window glass, pushing the dent in the door back out, and putting it back together again.

While we were in the coffee shop of the hotel that evening, the entire town started to party. The Minister of Transport had been negotiating with the truckers all day and they had come to an agreement. Trucks were parading through the streets with their horns bellowing. The strike lasted twenty days. We were lucky that it had held us back only one. All the setbacks that had kept us in Colombia longer than anticipated were a blessing in disguise. Everything happens for a reason. Big Fiesta.

February 26, 1997: Quito, Ecuador

The Pan-American Highway to Ibarra had remnants of fires and roadblocks, but it felt like a deserted highway, there wasn't a soul to be seen. The relief map indicates that the highway is at an altitude of 2,000 to 3,000 meters between Tulcan and Quito. Despite our being at the equator, there was a cold wind blowing through the missing window. We arrived in Quito sooner than anticipated. Crossing into the southern hemisphere was supposed to be a celebration but it happened without our noticing.

We didn't have a decent city map of Quito but still managed to find the South American Explorers Club to pick up our correspondence from home. Ed inquired about a place to stay. A boarding and guesthouse, run by a woman called Graciela, was recommended.

Graciela is an older woman with three grown children: a daughter living in Britain, a son in the United States and another in Quito. The two who live abroad have children. She would love to be able to spend any amount of time with her grandchildren but doesn't have much opportunity to do so. It pleased her to have some children in her house and she gave us special treatment. We have the north section of the house to ourselves, with two bathrooms and three sleeping areas. She made sure we had enough space and blankets and then invited us to use the kitchen to make our own meals. There is a washing machine to use as well, but it is temperamental. Patita, her employee, will help us if necessary. The van was too wide to fit through the gate of her home so she made arrangements with a neighbour to park it there.

It is a rambling house on a quiet street above the gorge of the Madhangara River, with a view of an over-bearing mountain on the other side. At night the lights of many homes dot the slope. The front garden is small yet filled with many flourishing plants, mostly calla lilies. There is a set of spiral outside stairs to access the bedrooms over the common living area. A long, narrow kitchen stretches across the back of the house. It is not modern, but efficient. At the opposite end of the house from the dining area, a set of stairs climbs to Graciela's living quarters. Underneath her living quarters are the rooms we are occupying. Our front room opens up to the garden and the back room opens into the kitchen. Ecuadorian weavings hanging throughout the dwelling give the rooms a cozy feel. I like being up in the morning to enjoy the peacefulness of the east-facing living room which is warmed by the unobstructed sunshine.

Patita took us to a supermarket and reassured us that the van would be fine in the parking lot of the grocery store, even with the wide-open, broken window. We accepted what she said as truth, and returned after purchasing food and a birthday cake to find the van untouched. Karina was pleased with having a vegetable sauce with noodles (her favourite food) and birthday cake. I forgot to buy candles but Graciela was quick to furnish them along with a small gift—Karina didn't even get one from us!

During our stay at Graciela's, four other people were renting rooms for an extended period of time. Robyn is a woman in her twenties from Australia and is beginning a six-month tour of South and Central America. She is in Quito for four weeks studying Spanish. Carolyn is an American teaching English for a year. Nate, an engineer, is an American studying Spanish and looking for work. Richard is British and teaching English as well; he wants to stay in South America indefinitely. Everyone except Richard joined us for birthday cake and we had a little party for Karina.

The neighbour, at whose place Ed parked the van, told him of a shop where the window could be repaired. They didn't have one in stock and called several suppliers but there wasn't one to be found in the city. It didn't discourage them, they could still replace the window—it would just take a day to manufacture it. Ed was to bring the van back on Monday morning. On the drive back to Graciela's, we discovered a chiropractic office and wrote the phone number down so Ed could call and possibly visit.

Patita is the only person other than Graciela that is a permanent resident in the house. She does the cooking and cleaning for the temporary residents. Officially she is an employee, but it is clear that she is a dear friend of Graciela and takes care of her. The kids and I spent Friday afternoon at the house, mostly visiting with Graciela. She has the only television in the house, in her private area, and invited the kids to join her—to Patitas' surprise. I did the laundry.

Ed spent the afternoon having the brakes repaired and visited Edward Jarvis, the Chiropractor. He had practiced in California for 12 years prior to moving to Quito. He didn't like what was happening to the chiropractic profession in the United States and moved to a country where he was able to practice traditional chiropractic. He was impressed with what we are doing as a family and encouraged Ed to practice somewhere in South America. He recommended Colombia because of the economy. He, too, said there was plenty of easy money to be made there. He does a weekly radio show to educate people about chiropractic and said it always brought in new patients. He suggested to Ed that wherever he set up practice he should do a radio show or at least interviews. Ed arrived back at Graciela's encouraged with the positive prospects.

We visited Quito on foot and via trolley on Saturday. The kids chose to visit the cathedral that stands atop the hill overlooking the city. It caught our attention from a distance when we first drove into Quito. Quito is at an altitude of 2,850 meters; it took a lot of effort to walk uphill. The altitude made it difficult for us to get enough oxygen and Whitney wanted to be carried. The old city streets are cobbled and narrow, and it's rare to find one on level ground.

The Basilica is magnificent and is still being restored after the earthquake of 1987. It is decorated with gargoyles, each of them unique sculptures. It isn't usually open on Saturdays, but there was a christening, so we slipped in to take a look before the doors closed after the service. Tall pillars drew the eyes to the domed ceiling, while the stained glass windows competed for visual attention as the sunlight set them ablaze with colour.

Two days before visiting Quito I dreamt of needing to eat pumpkin seeds, finding a heap, and devouring them. They were delicious. (Pumpkin seeds are a natural vermifuge that eliminates some types of parasites from the body.) On the street of the cathedral was a woman with a heap of roasted pumpkin seeds displayed on a cloth, for sale. I didn't pass them by—we bought plenty. Whether we needed a parasite cleanse or not, we had a filling, delicious snack of roasted pumpkin seeds.

When it started to rain we waited out the downpour in a restaurant in the market and had a chicken soup lunch with bread and tea. We were a little shocked that the whole meal for the eight of us cost a total of four Canadian dollars.

Plaza Independencia was our next stop. The Colonial buildings with their repeated pattern of arches stood out in my mind. Unaware that the grass was for looking at and not walking on, we were kicked off of it while attempting to take pictures of the kids beside the impressive flower beds. The policeman had in fact been blowing his whistle furiously for a good length of time before we figured out it was because of us.

The original peoples of Ecuador are always dressed in traditional clothing. The women are in full, brightly coloured, woolen skirts that have a wide hand-embroidered band in colourful patterns around the bottom. All native people wear a hat, the style dependent on what area they are from. The majority of hats on both men and women in Quito are "Charlie Chaplin" style. They are made of varying colours of felt, with a band of ribbon, and a small curled-up brim. They sit high on the head and appear to be too small—a North American point of view.

During our walk back we stopped at Carolina Park, a large open expanse of grass (on which we were allowed to walk) with a play area for children and paddleboats on small man-made canals. Ben asked if he could use a paddleboat but the cost of one was unreasonably high considering the limits of paddling around in a circle. The kids wore themselves out playing on the swings, teeter-totter, climbing structures and rides. An ice-cream vendor came around and Ben asked for ice cream as well. When Ed found out that each ice cream bar was going to cost $3 (CDN), he refused. Ben was unable to see reason when $4 just fed the eight of us lunch. He was livid and screamed, "Why did I even bother coming on this trip?" He barely talked to anyone the rest of the day.

Graciela's son came to the house for a visit and gave Ed directions to the Mitad del Mundo – Middle of the World or Equatorial Monument, 23 kilometers north

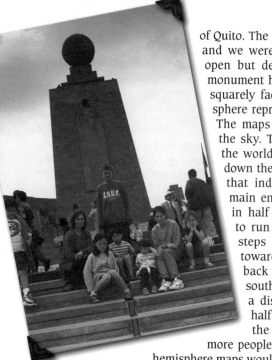

of Quito. The park was extremely busy on Sunday and we weren't sure we should leave the van open but decided we would trust again. The monument houses a museum. The building sits squarely facing each of the four directions. A sphere representing the world is perched atop. The maps of South and North America face the sky. The equatorial line of the sphere of the world aligns with the bright yellow line down the east and west sides of the building that indicates earth's actual equator. The main entrance, in the east wall, is divided in half by the yellow line that continues to run along the walkway and down the steps toward the parking lot. Walking toward the monument, the kids hopped back and forth across the line, north, south, top half, bottom half. We got into a discussion about why there is a top half and bottom half and Tanya cut into the conversation to say, "Probably if more people of the world lived in the Southern hemisphere maps would be the other way around. How can there be an up or down on a ball?"

We started at the top of the monument for a view of the countryside and then toured the museum. It has sections devoted to the different groups of original peoples of Ecuador. We noticed the extreme differences between mountain people and coastal people. Clothing, jewelry, dishes, tools, musical instruments and houses. What a social studies lesson for the kids! We now feel as if we know Ecuador a little more. It was well worth the visit.

Music coming from the square with its surrounding border of shops drew us in to listen. Pan flutes, guitar, *quenas* (an Andean flute) and drums. Even the lively tunes were soothing to the soul. The van was untouched again.

On our drive back to Graciela's, we stopped for vegetables at an open farmers' market. It didn't take long before almost everyone in the market was staring at us. It seemed as if they were as intrigued with us as we were with them. I am starting to learn enough Spanish to ask for some vegetables and clumsily spoke with several people to purchase food. Ed talked at great length to the man we bought potatoes from while I did most of the food collecting. The man asked many questions about what we are doing—and about the kids. He gave us twice as many potatoes as we asked for, and almost everyone in the market waved goodbye as we pulled away.

We enjoyed our meal of mashed potatoes, broccoli, tomatoes, cucumbers and *platanos*—plantain that Graciela showed me how to cook. While we were finishing up our dinner, Nate, Richard, Robyn, and Caroline came in for theirs. They sat down at their places and were served white sticky rice, noodles with cheese, fries and a piece of deep fried chicken. Nate ate most of his but pushed around the rice. Ed offered them some of our vegetables but they politely refused, probably not wanting to offend Patita, but Nate did help himself to some tomatoes. We discussed the food in Ecuador. Most people eat the same starchy foods every day without much variety. Vegetables are available; we don't understand why people don't eat more of them.

Graciela lit a fire in the living room fireplace for the evening, as it gets cool at night and houses in Ecuador are not built to keep heat in. We spent the evening with Robyn, Nate and Richard. Nate and I talked about how the kids are handling the whole experience. At one point, he interrupted me. "Ah ha! Now I know you are Canadian. You said 'eh'!"

"Does that surprise you?" I asked.

"No, not really," he replied, "but I thought I would be able to pick out Canadians like a Texan from the way they talk."

I wondered how many American people have the same ideas. We all have preconceived notions of what other cultures are like until we learn differently. It is so important to go into new territory with an open mind.

At some point the Quest question cards came out of the school box. Robyn played with the kids, and they found her weakness—mathematics—and she exaggerated it. They were rolling in laughter before the game stopped and the kids found something else to do in their room. Robyn had just returned from a weekend trip to Lago Quilotoa, a circular lake in the cone of a dormant volcano, and told us about how much she enjoyed the excursion. Richard had been there as well. Between the two of them they gave us an extensive explanation of what to expect. Richard was in a talkative mood and it didn't take long before he started to ask questions about us. As our discussion continued he spoke about Britain and his own family with anger in his voice; the happier expression on his face changed. His mother had died just two months earlier, he didn't go to the funeral, and has had no desire to return home. He has been in Ecuador almost a year. There appeared to be some deep family animosity connected to his anger. I listened to noise from the kids that sounded like a fight. Richard said, "I don't envy you guys travelling with so many kids. Why do you even bother? It can't be any fun." I could still hear the kids, (I try to stay out of their fights as much as possible) it sounded like it needed a referee and I excused myself.

When Ed came to the room he said, "Richard seems to hate the kids."

"You got that feeling, too?" I replied, "He doesn't envy us but I don't envy him either, alone and trying to find whatever it is he's missing in his life here in Ecuador."

"Whatever it is," Ed said, "we, as a family, sure hit a sore spot with him."

Richard showed Ed the route to Lago Quilotoa and gave suggestions for the beach. Ed had it figured out: Latacunga, Quilotoa, Quevedo, Porto Viejo, San Clemente and Crucita—a beach and some warmth for a few days.

Early Monday morning Ed took the van to the shop to have the window repaired, and he returned with two windows missing. On Tuesday morning both were replaced. They used the driver side window to make a mold, reversed it, and fabricated a passenger side window. It cost the equivalent of 39 Canadian dollars and the work was professionally done. It is good to have the windows back.

Graciela didn't like to see us packing up. She enjoyed our company as much as we enjoyed staying with her. Everyone gave her a big hug and when it was my turn she hung on longer than what felt sufficient for a goodbye hug. There were tears in her eyes as we got into the van. She loved having the kids around. She showed me several photos of her own grandchildren. I get the impression she is a lonely woman despite her busy house.

February 26, 1997: Latacunga and Lago Quilotoa

We had our route planned through the city but as usual something happened again and we got somewhat lost. After driving in what we thought should be the general direction, Ed stopped to ask how to get to the Pan-Americana Sur. The man looked at Ed as if there was something wrong—we were on it. After all that planning and figuring out directions, sometimes instincts work just as well.

The highway to Latacunga travels along on the plateau within sight of snow-capped peaks on either side. North American winter is rainy season in the *altiplano* of the Andes. We passed Volcan Cotopaxi but didn't really see it, as the dense cloud cover kept the mountain peaks of Cotopaxi National Park hidden.

We were in Latacunga by 3 p.m. and found Hotel Central, a family-run business. The owner's son, about fifteen, helped bring our bags to the room and then bid us follow him to the rooftop for a good view of the mountains. He said the mornings were best before the clouds moved in.

Tuesday happened to be market day and we didn't have to go far to find items of interest. We had passed up visiting Otovalo, known for the good quality woolen textiles, because of the broken window on the van, but most of the articles in the Latacunga market were from there. Tanya, Ben and Whitney chose similar warm, thick sweaters, machine-made but warm, perfect for the climate we are experiencing. Woven llama wool sweaters are plentiful here. When I reached up to feel the thickness of one, it was immediately pulled down for me to look at. The woman offered a price and when I didn't say anything she brought out more and the price came down. Ed bargained, buying the group of them together, and it became an even better price. We continued looking. Every person in every booth had something in his or her hands to sell to us. As we looked with interest at a poncho for Dayna, the vendor, an older man, said two of the sweaters we bought were synthetic and showed us the difference between those and what he was selling. He was disgusted with this artificial fibre, saying it's no good. Artificial fibre clothing isn't the same quality—it doesn't keep you as warm—and it is eating into the market for the real stuff. Dayna purchased her poncho of pure wool from him and he showed us how to tell the difference. Looking across the article with light from behind, artificial yarns have shiny fibres that reflect light—llama wool doesn't do that and is much softer.

We had to go back to the hotel for some warm clothing for dinner, and Jake tripped on the sidewalk in front, cutting his knee badly. He cried, attracting plenty of attention. The woman from the family that owns our place came running out through the doors, afraid that something drastic had happened. The sight of blood panicked Jake and he kept his hand over the cut, shoving us away. Eventually he settled down enough to have it taken care of. The woman from the hotel repeated several times to be sure to clean it well. She had her antiseptic out but Ed assured her we had everything necessary to take care of the cut in our room. It was a good gash but after the wound was cleaned and bandaged, Jake was himself again and still wouldn't wear long pants.

The food stalls within the market were arranged in two long rows, each run by a woman. All had huge pots of steaming soup over gas burners and *empanadas* or the makings for other kinds of meals. Finding something close to a vegetarian meal was an impossible task, as was finding a stall with space enough for the eight of us to sit. We were fortunate to walk by a table where a group of people was leaving and the dinner available was a chicken potato stew. Ed, Jake, Ben and Dayna sat on the bench at the table facing the women who was providing our meal. Tanya, Karina, Whitney and I sat at a picnic table that was shared with the next stall. It was a delicious stew in the cold, each serving included a piece of chicken, potatoes, onion, *zapallo*—squash pieces and broth. The woman at our stall and the woman behind me in the next stall talked to each other as we ate. I don't know what they were saying but I do know they were talking about the kids.

Jake managed to hit the edge of his plate, spilling stew over his sweatshirt, shorts and legs. He was having a tough day and now crying again. We cleaned him up at the sinks but he was cold. Tanya, feeling sorry for him, gave him her sweatshirt. A stray dog quickly cleaned up the spilled dinner on the ground, and when we sat back down to finish our meal, the table had been wiped clean and another full dish was at Jake's place without having asked for it.

We did have a few quiet moments of eating before Whitney started to pout. She wasn't eating and wouldn't move. I asked her what was wrong, but she just shook her head and pouted more. I tried to feed her but she refused and cried. She blurted out loudly, "I want to go back to the hotel, I want to go back to the hotel now!" We were attracting attention again. When I attempted to feed her again she glanced up to the right without moving her head. A man was standing about six feet away and staring at us. I don't know how long he had been there but certainly long enough for Whitney to get a scary impression. I have never seen a more desperate looking human being. He had wide bare feet, flat and black with dirt and was literally wearing rags. Both his shirt and pants, or what was left of them, hung in strips that barely covered his body. He held a walking stick in his soiled hands. He was bent over and his face had a partially greyed scraggly beard. His cheekbones were black with dirt and the whites of his eyes were hauntingly white. His shoulder-length hair hung in matted ropes. I did a double take, and understood Whitney's dismay. After I picked her up she sat on my knee still paralyzed with fear. The man stood there staring at us. I tried to get her to eat but she was just too upset. The two women wondered what was wrong as well, but quickly figured it out. Both of them, at the same time, moved out of their places toward him, waved their arms and told him to leave. He moved on and Whitney felt comfortable enough to continue eating. Our simple dinner turned out to be an ordeal, but it killed the hunger pangs.

We were wakened in the morning, the sun filling our room, telling us to get up to the roof. The valley was bathed in sunlight but every mountain around us was covered with a cap of cloud. Cotopaxi looked as if it had a hat on. The shape was visible, but not the actual mountain.

Ed asked a man standing at the side of the road the direction to Lago Quilotoa. He had a look of surprise on his face and then said; "If you take me with you I'll show you the way. I live just past there and am waiting for a bus home."

We invited Joselito along and he introduced himself with pride. He is a farmer living on a small farm a three-hour walk from Lago Quilotoa. He has twelve children ranging in age from seven months to twenty-three years. They are a poor family, with only cows and sheep. He asked about our family, where we were from and what brought us to Ecuador. When Ed told him we were driving to Chile possibly to work, he asked about where we were staying. He was curious and asked how much we paid for the night in the hotel. It was the equivalent of roughly 25 Canadian dollars. He couldn't believe it would be that much and thought we were very rich. He called himself poor but said there are many people who are much poorer than him in Ecuador. He had good clothes on and he was not starving. It is all a matter of perspective, isn't it? There will always be richer and poorer persons than oneself.

Joselito knew about the countryside we were travelling. He explained that the eucalyptus trees being harvested are sent to Guayaquil to be used for building furniture. He showed us the area where homes were destroyed and many people died as a result of an earthquake that hit last year. As the road climbed to a higher altitude the vegetation changed from lush and abundant to sparse and barren, while llamas became more prominent on the landscape. The farms were fenced with rows of cultivated cactus plants tangled together. Joselito showed us the *laguna,* and even he was in awe of its beauty. A blue-green lake in the crater of the volcano, it is almost a perfect circle at an altitude of 4,000 meters. Joselito offered to pay for the ride, but Ed refused. There wasn't public transportation to his home, so he continued on foot.

We met a couple from New Jersey at the lake. They had also driven from Quito but in a rented car. We talked of the craziness of driving, the people, the culture, and our experiences. The man had retired recently and the woman was a semi-retired journalist who occasionally still writes articles for magazines. After some discussion about our travels, she commented that we should be writing a book and was certain it would sell, adding that nobody in their right mind would attempt such a thing and people like to read about that kind of stuff. I didn't feel as if that was the purpose of our journey.

March 3, 1997: The Ecuador Coast

The moment we reached the west side of the Andes, the terrain again turned green and lush with vegetation. Rainy season made the road a mud slick—challenging driving in several places. One area was being cleared where a landslide covered the road; there was a trail through the mud but no real road. The bull dozer clearing the mess moved to the side to let us pass. Ed surveyed the situation and decided to go for it; there were large enough vehicles to help if we got into trouble. The van skidded from side to side but we made it to the clear gravel road. Ed said, "I'm sure glad that was downhill—we would never have made it up."

On the flat Pacific plain the air changed to stiflingly hot, and soon we were in banana country. Rancho Hosteria in La Mana looked appealing to the kids. It had two swimming pools, one large and deep with a tall water slide, the other round and shallow for younger children. We had a pleasant afternoon of swimming while enjoying rumba music over the sound system. The kids always make up games. At the pool the game was "who could come up with the most unique way of coming down the slide." When Jake realized it was easy to swim to the edge of the pool after coming down the slide, there was no turning back, and he spent his afternoon in gleeful play with the older kids.

Dayna enjoyed the rhythmic beat of the Latin American music, and just couldn't resist a good dance at the top of the slide. When I noticed her bum wiggling back and forth in time to the music, I told Ed to look. When Ben noticed, it was no secret any longer and everyone burst into laughter. Sassing us back, she gave her bottom a good wiggle and slid down the slide. Ed said, "Don't be embarrassed, Mom can't do that." She just giggled.

They got into swimming races as well. Tanya was the champion, even beating her Dad, but Dayna can consistently swim a longer distance underwater than everyone else.

I took a shower to wash my hair and when Ed was about to get in and join me, he turned me around to look up. A dark, hairy spider the size of my fist sat there perched in the corner. I caught my breath at the sight of it, finished rinsing my hair and backed out of the shower. Without thinking, Ed grabbed the hairbrush and smacked the spider. Yellow insides squirted across the wall; half the spider was on the brush, while the other half remained glued to the spot where it was flattened. It was relief to know the spider wouldn't be bothering anyone, but neither one of us liked the idea of having killed it. It may not have bothered anyone at all. The kids were surprised at the size of it and asked if it was poisonous. We didn't know. When Ben saw the spider he asked, "What did you kill him for?" Which only added to our guilt. The younger kids were full of questions but Tanya said she'd never use that hairbrush again. We do get conditioned away from that sense of wonder, don't we? That spider taught me something. Sometimes my senses are keen and aware of my surroundings, but at other times I can be totally oblivious. It would be a good idea to use a little more awareness at all times.

Driving through the village of San Clemente was a challenge. It appeared that mud holes are never repaired on the streets; some were extremely deep and filled with water from the recent rains. One such hole didn't look as bad as we thought, but it gave the van a good jolt. The pigs enjoyed the mud holes, as they roamed freely throughout the village. I'm not sure why they were loose, but possibly because when free to do so they are pretty good scroungers and can find their own food in places where it is scarce. In time, of course, they become food themselves.

We found a *hosteria* (a hotel-like hostel) set back from the shore. It was a tall building for the area, and each of the four floors had wide balconies used as living space and slung with hammocks. It looked perfect and the top floor rooms were available.

The beach sand was dark—almost black. The water was calm, shallow and as warm as a bathtub. It was a place where young children are able to play safely in the ocean water and many young families were on the beach. There were small crab-like animals, no bigger than a square centimeter, in the sand at the water's edge. Each wave swept the top layer of sand away, uncovering them, and each time they furiously dug back under the sand. It was impossible not to walk on the little creatures. We watched the ceaseless repetition, and played in the warm shallow water for the afternoon.

The evening air was warm, and we lounged in the hammocks and played euchre. Whitney and I cuddled up in a hammock and rocked to sleep, only to be wakened by the hammock string breaking and tossing us out onto the floor. It was the beginning of a restless night. The rooms were hot and stuffy, so we spent as long as we could outside until the abundance of bugs drove us in. The windows were just shutters, and we had to close them to keep the mosquitoes out, which reduced the air circulation. The kids did manage to settle and get some sleep. When we turned out the lights and our surroundings became quiet, Ed and I heard scratching noises on the roof. It didn't take long before we both figured out that there were bats clinging to the wall and roof outside our room, so we turned the light back on hopefully to discourage them from coming in. None did, but there was enough noise to keep us alert and awake. The bats were probably the reason the top floor was available. There were so many mosquitoes I kept getting up to make sure the kids stayed covered with a sheet to prevent bites. Tanya and Ben found it so stuffy in the room they wrapped up in their sheet in a hammock outside, took their chances with the bats, and had the best sleep of us all. Jake was played out from his afternoon on the beach, never moved and slept through everything. The girls complained about the mosquitoes buzzing in their ears. The only way they could get any peace was with their heads under the sheets, which was uncomfortable but necessary for protection. By the time the sun came up, we hadn't had much rest, but it didn't take long to pack.

We drove south along the coast of Ecuador, travelled inland through Porto Viejo and Jipigapa, over the coastal range of hills, and to the ocean edge again at Pito de Cayo. At some point that I didn't really notice, the coastal area turned into desert, and we began to see cacti growing on the hills.

We found ourselves at the Alandaluz Ecological Tourist Center, a place where tourists can spend time on the beach in a more earth friendly atmosphere, where, for example vegetables are organically grown and served in the restaurants, and composting toilets and biodegradable soaps are used. The cabins, with their palm-leaf roofs, are built of bamboo, as is all the furniture. Travellers on a budget would find this place a little pricey, but we treated ourselves for a night, rented a cabin with four single beds and doubled up in them. At Alanduluz and at a couple of other nearby places catering to the tourist trade, we saw, for the first time, South American beaches that were kept clean and free of garbage; it felt to be a refreshing change from what we were seeing elsewhere.

As we drove out the lane from the restaurant where we had dinner, a group of people was walking toward us. As we passed them, one man shouted out in English, "Are you guys really all the way from Quebec?"

Ed stuck his head out the window shouting, "Yep, all the way."

He yelled back, "You should be writing a book!" It was the second person to say that within a few days. We didn't even talk to him and he urged us to write a book.

We had another not-so-great night as Jake got tied up in the mosquito net several times. Despite the drawbacks, the nets certainly made a difference, reducing the amount of buzzing in the ears.

Whitney and I walked the beach in the morning and watched the sand crabs collect their breakfast. The others joined us soon afterwards and the mood was pretty somber. Everything was getting to us. A few days' rest on a beach would be welcome, but finding accommodation that isn't mosquito-infested, comfortable, and within our budget, is nearly impossible.

As we continued south, there were some interesting fishing villages on beaches that appeared beautiful from a distance. But once we arrived we discovered them to be dirty and littered with garbage. It is so discouraging. We found a place south of Manglaralto where the beach was cleaner and rented two rooms. The owners made us a dinner consisting of a small piece of deep-fried fish, a heap of white rice, banana chips, and a tablespoon of shredded cabbage.

We spent Saturday on the beach. There is nothing like the elements for improving the mood and healing my soul. The water was cooler than the beach at San Clemente and the surf was good for playing in. We found sand dollars exposed by the waves and watched them bury themselves using the tiny hairs over their shells to dig themselves under the sand. All four girls went for long walk up the beach and brought back twenty-two dead sand dollars.

Our "shrimp dinner" and meal for the day was a heap of white rice with a few dried peas and a few tiny shrimp mixed into it. I couldn't eat it; I was just too constipated on the diet of white rice. Relief didn't even come in the form of sleep. Again, outside where it was cooler, there were swarms of biting bugs, and inside, the room was so hot it was hard to breathe.

Some sleep did eventually come but in the morning I discovered my legs covered in bites from bed bugs again. I went to the beach while the others were still asleep, hoping to change my perspective. People live in these conditions all the time. I thought I was more flexible than I am, but I am not coping with what comes our way as well as I anticipated I would. What really keeps me going is exploring the mountains, countryside and coastline, but when even my explorations are marred with garbage and the ill effects of humanity, it is depressing. The kids joined me while Ed went to see if he could find something to eat. He brought back a small bunch of bananas and three pineapples. We enjoyed them. He said, "It was slim pickings." For a country that produces so many bananas one would think that we could at least find an abundance of those.

We headed toward the mountains. The kids found refuge from the insects in the van. Given the lack of sleep over the previous few days, every one of them slept for almost three hours during the drive. We missed the road we intended to take to avoid Guayaquil, so continued along the coast. Around every corner and over every hill there were incredible vistas of beaches and countryside, but the abundance of garbage is an unavoidable fact of life.

We navigated through Guayaquil surprisingly easily, only to be stopped at a police check 10 kilometers east of the city. The officer was not pleased to find Ed shirtless—it is against the law. He issued Ed a ticket for not wearing a shirt and told him to go back to Guayaquil to pay the fine. Ed pleaded with him, being a foreigner, unaware of the law and not knowing where to pay the fine, then asked if he could give the officer the money to pay it. He added that he now knew the law and would always wear a shirt. The policeman agreed. Ed gave him the 10,000-*sucre* (about $6.00 Canadian) fine and he allowed us to continue.

Driving east toward the mountains took us through banana country—field after field of bananas covered with clear plastic sleeves. The towns where we thought we might stay were in worse condition than those along the coast. Children roamed around without any clothing whatsoever, and only a few people wore any kind of footwear. Families live in rusty tin structures on stilts squashed between the highway and huge expanses of banana fields. This is where the bananas come from that we pay 39 cents a pound for at home. These people are certainly not making any profit providing bananas to the world. Apples that grow in our own country cost a dollar or more per pound in Canadian stores, which makes me realize that something is really wrong here. The pricing alone is a good indication of why Canadians eat more bananas than any other fruit. The problem is that our preference comes at the expense of people in countries living in conditions the average Canadian couldn't even imagine.

March 9, 1997: The southern mountains of Ecuador. Cañar, Cuenca and Vilcabamba

We opted to drive two more hours to get into the mountains. Cañar is a colonial town where indigenous people make up the majority of the population. It is much cleaner and more prosperous than what we experienced on the coast.

Donkeys are a common sight in the Andes since they are reliable work animals on mountain terrain. While we were moving through a settlement along the roadside before getting to Cañar, Dayna was puzzled and asked, "Dad, why does that donkey have two tails?" It was a peculiar question and Ed, curious to know why she thought it had two tails, slowed the van right down to find out what she was talking about. Once we got a look at the donkey it did appear that he had two tails. Well—it took a moment for Ed and me to stop laughing before we could give an explanation. The kids were shocked, dumbfounded and surprised to learn that the second tail was the donkey's penis with a full erection. (It was dragging on the ground.) I won't put down all the foolish comments that were made but it did become a biology lesson, along with some sex education and the subject of discussion for quite a while afterwards.

The man who runs Hostel Monica looks so much like Dad it is spooky. He was friendly, recommended a restaurant around the corner from the hostel, and said there were Inca ruins just a short drive away that are worth visiting. The kids couldn't get over how much he looked like their grandfather, and Jake asked with a longing tone in his voice, "When are we going to see Gram and Grandpa again?"

I answered, "I'm not sure when it will be, but they said they would visit us when we stayed in one place for a while. So they will come."

Cañar is located in one of the most fertile farming areas of Ecuador. Altitude creates several climatic regions within a small area and healthy soil gives a high yield of a variety of foods. Everyone ate every drop of the tomato vegetable soup we had that evening, and the potatoes and customary chicken; they were a real treat. We actually had some fresh orange juice in the morning, with eggs, bread and a

Ingapirca, Canar, Ecuador

tomato-cilantro-hot pepper salsa. After not having anything but soft drinks while travelling the coast, the kids appreciated the juice.

Ingapirca, at 3,190 meters, is known as Ecuador's most important Inca ruin. The Cañari people constructed its architectural predecessor on the site and by the 1500s they were totally integrated into Inca society. The Incas tore down all but the Cañari's sacred burial site and reconstructed what is left here today. The central structure, the Sun Temple, is the most intriguing, with its trapezoid cavities and doorways. It is a solar observatory constructed of fine Inca masonry and stands as an ellipse—the length exactly three times the diameter of the semi-circular ends. Ingapirca hosts the festival of Inti Raymi each year during the third week of June, celebrating the "Resurrection of the Sun" (the solstice), the recent harvest, and the beginning of a new farming year. As we moved from the upper platform the kids played hide-and-seek in the surrounding maze of walls which at one time made up residential and storage areas. Play and exploration became one, giving Ed and me an opportunity to take in the surroundings.

A late afternoon visit to the park so that the kids could wear themselves out gave me a chance to people-watch. The women here certainly know how to multi-task! Groups of them walked by socializing as they spun wool into yarn, each with a spindle that continuously whorled and collected thread. They carry a bag of carded wool under one arm, from which small amounts are gently eased out while the spindle in the opposite hand whorls and collects the spun wool. Others sit and knit or walk and crochet. All were dressed in brightly coloured, full wool skirts, scalloped and embroidered around the bottom in bright colours and patterns, each had a colourful and often multi-coloured woven shawl over her shoulders. The men wear black wool trousers and knitted wool sweaters. Both the men and women in the Cañar area wear straw hats that just cover the crowns of their heads and have a narrow turned-up brim trimmed with black cotton. Most people keep their head covered when outside. It is a strong tropical sun, directly overhead; hats are protection, not a fashion statement. In Cañar I noticed how hot the top of my own head got, deceptive in that the temperature of the air was cool.

Cuenca was a welcome reprieve and offered a few of the comforts that we enjoy in Canada. We lucked out and found Hotel Paradez, which felt like luxury and was within our budget. French provincial decor and high-quality wool area rugs created a rich feel and the atmosphere improved everyone's attitude.

Markets are always a highlight. Wool is a way of life—it is what every Ecuadorian wears and uses to keep warm. We ended up purchasing a blanket of llama wool.

Karina loved the full skirts the women wear and asked for one as a birthday gift. Since we hadn't really given her a birthday gift, it was a reasonable request. She chose a magenta skirt with a four-inch embroidered band of flowers around the bottom, and completed the outfit with a blouse and shawl to match. She was pleased and spent the rest of the day looking Ecuadorian—in spite of her blonde hair.

During our exploration of Cuenca we purchased a bag of croissants. Jake carried what remained in the bag after our snack and gave the last few to a man sitting on the sidewalk begging for money. Either he was impatient carrying them or was in a generous thoughtful mood. I hope it was the latter.

That evening we discussed how things were going. Food is a big problem: it lacks variety and nutrition, and too much of what we are eating is deep-fried. Hotels we stay at within our budget are not good unless we hit it lucky. All of us are learning what kind of conditions people here live in, and it is affecting us. There is a variety of food but it is unavailable to so many people.

The kids are taking most of the journey in stride, except for Ben. He seems to be having a hard time. I don't know whether it is hormones or that his space is too cramped, but he does not have any flexibility whatsoever. A simple touch from someone sends him into tears. Everything has to be even, but when it comes to the computer, "even" means he gets twice as much time as everyone else. He appears to be using it as an escape from the reality he is living.

The route to the border town of Machala was blocked with a sign indicating *derumbe*—landslide. The road would be closed for at least three days. Heading back to Quenca we caught sight of a sign for *cabanas* and decided to check it out.

The complex of buildings was Swiss Alps style surrounding an activity space. There were swings, a playhouse for kids, a volleyball court and table tennis, amongst flowerbeds and vegetable gardens. We were shown an apartment with a kitchen, fireplace and seven beds; it didn't take long to decide to stay for a few days when we learned we could cook our own food.

Peter Reidel and partner Suzanne are the owners. He is from Germany and her home is Ecuador. They met in Germany while she was teaching Spanish. They have been together for five years in Ecuador, where they purchased eight hectares of land, and have built the house and hotel complex themselves. A lot of love, attention and hard work have been put into the well-kept buildings and gardens.

Suzanne gave us a walking tour of the grounds. She is proud of their flower and organic vegetable gardens and explained that when they started to build them, they used the tried-and-true method of the Incas. All are terraced and produce enough food for Suzanne and Peter's personal use as well as the demands of the restaurant. Suzanne showed us the irrigation system they built, again using the Inca method, utilizing a mountain run-off stream. Gravity does all the work. Suzanne provided us with lettuce, Swiss chard, carrots, kale, onions, radishes and two-dozen eggs, all produced right here and six loaves of homemade whole grain bread that she baked herself.

We barely saw any of the children the rest of the day. Jake, Whitney and Karina played in the playhouse all afternoon and the rest of them just enjoyed the space. They picked and ate wild mora berries that turned their mouths deep purple-black.

Peter arrived late in the afternoon and we talked with him for a long while. He speaks English, German and Spanish. Twenty years ago he lived in Ottawa for a couple of years and helped manage a restaurant. Hotel and restaurant management has always been his business. He doesn't like the corruption and dishonesty in Ecuador but has resigned himself to it, although at times it drives him crazy. He says people in Ecuador pay only twelve percent tax but the people who are capable of paying find ways to get out of it. He shook his head and asked rhetorically, "How do you run a country based on that kind of value system?"

Both Ed and I had the impression he had been on the receiving end of some injustice. He is also frustrated at not being able to depend on people to do as they say. Would-be guests make reservations and don't show up, or order a meal ahead of time and when they actually get to the restaurant decide they want something different from what they originally requested. Employees feel no obligation to show up for work, and when they do they give contradictory excuses about why they were absent. However, Peter loves the mountains and the home he has made.

I asked about the eucalyptus trees, because they aren't native to South America, yet they are the only type of tree growing on the slopes of the area. Peter says they were introduced to Ecuador about sixty years ago and adapted well to the arid mountains. They have been both a curse and a blessing: they keep the bugs away but because of that there aren't any birds around either. They grow fast and prevent erosion on the slopes, but the native vegetation doesn't grow alongside or underneath them. They are used mainly for logging and the first planting is cut within ten years. Cutting stimulates the stump to send out shoots that produce four to six more trees. They are harvested up to five times, then must be replanted as with each cutting, the trunk of the next tree is smaller and not as usable for furniture and lumber. Eucalyptus is a strong wood; after a year of curing it becomes so hard a nail can barely be driven into it.

Peter asked if we had our firewood and said we would need it for the evening. We didn't have any, so he brought us a wheelbarrow full and asked if we knew how to make a fire. Ed chuckled, "Did you forget we are Canadians?"

Peter replied, "Just asking. People on vacation from Guayaquil come here and freeze because they don't know how to make a fire. They just never need one, so I make sure everyone who stays with us knows."

While he stacked the wood in the corner he recommended a hike up Mount Cabogama if we were looking for something to do the next day.

Tanya didn't feel like doing the hike and said she would stay with the little ones; it was a treat for me, and Ed, Ben, Dayna and I did the 1,000-meter-altitude hike. It wasn't long before the others were well ahead of me and I fell into a trance-like walk as several voices nattered around inside my head. One was making me feel guilty for leaving Tanya with the kids; I should have stayed and done some laundry. After much berating of myself a voice that didn't sound like mine said, "You need to do some fun things. The journey has to be enjoyable, and if you can't make it that, there isn't any sense in what you are doing." Often there are confusing voices that are difficult to sort out and trust, but that was a loud and clear message. I found myself singing Harry Chapin's song, "Greyhound"— *"It's got to be the going not just the getting there that's good"*. The journey—how do I make it better for all of us? Something is going on. Everyone is somewhat unhappy. It's not just me. Sometimes I think the kids just reflect what is going on inside me. I have inner turmoil, and I don't know what the cause of it is. I know it is not the travelling—the travelling is only making me face what is really going on. In a healing process, whether it is physical or emotional, the root cause has to be found before true healing will take place, and things usually get worse before they get better.

The vegetation out on the trail at a higher altitude was different from the eucalyptus forest. There were low, woody bushes, scrubby stuff with small flowers, a blueberry-like plant and all different from what is familiar to me. Best of all, I could take time to observe the little things. Two hummingbirds with eighteen-inch tails flew swiftly around while collecting nectar amongst the bushes where I photographed the flowers. Several times I ducked my head out of their way (I felt as if I were annoying them just being there) and didn't even have a chance to aim the camera at them before they were gone.

Ed, Ben and Dayna took a rest stop at a place with a good view and waited for me to catch up. By the time I did they were ready and raring to continue to the top. I decided to stay put, enjoyed the view, and took some time for photographs without being rushed. I have spent many years having babies, providing for their needs and not exercising; I am terribly out of shape. The three of them couldn't figure out why I would give up the climb so close to the top and berated me for quitting 200 meters below the peak. To them, getting to the top was important, and they did it. Sometimes, other things are more important than conquering. I needed the energy and stamina to complete the hike and make it through the rest of the day with the people who would be demanding my attention on my return. I don't like to put limitations on myself but one must be realistic as well. I can't do it all. Tanya and the little ones did fine for the day.

Mountain vegetation, Cuenca, Ecuador

Ben wanted to sleep in a hammock strung up in the living area and for some reason thought I wouldn't let him. He was angry with me again. Moms and Dads are so easy to blame for our troubles.

The fire gave a cozy feeling to the room and we enjoyed an evening of reading like we so often did at home during the winter. Ben slept happily in the hammock.

Ed read about Vilcabamba, another place he would like to visit. Suzanne exclaimed that Machala was so *horrible* and suggested we go through Macara. Vilcabamba wasn't far off that route. The plan changed to moving on instead of waiting out the landslide.

It is said that people in Vilcabamba live to be over a hundred years old more often than people in most regions of the world and that their longevity is attributed to the water. True or not, the town is located in a fertile and healthy valley where a water bottling company makes a profit off the rumours. Finding a hostel that had enough space for us took some searching, and the kids reached their tolerance level and started fighting long before we found accommodation, a three-room space without cooking facilities. I couldn't stand the scrapping and my spirits kept sinking deeper. Ben and Tanya screamed at each other over who was going to make chocolate milk for everyone. Jake, Whitney and Karina fought, screamed, and yelled at... I don't know what, and Dayna just sat and withdrew into herself. Ed couldn't understand why everyone was so angry and what the problem was. I reached my limit being a referee. I yelled, cried, separated them, and sat everyone down. Ben screamed at me to leave him alone and shut himself in a room until after we had made and eaten our cold dinner.

Everyone else watched the one English channel on television while I lay on the bed in a room by myself thinking about what is going on. I don't seem to help the kids cope at all; I am not in any great emotional state myself.

It rained most of the night; twice I was awakened by thunder and lightning; it was stimulating dreams. One was about having to see my Aunt Jean and her husband Mike which made me feel desperate in that I kept trying to get there but just couldn't make it. Another dream, about my Aunt Ruth's husband Patrick, he was standing in front of the cupboards in a corner of the kitchen of their house, looking nine months pregnant and about to give birth; something was very wrong with him. In another, Aunt Doris was crying uncontrollably. Another was of a family reunion at Babas' house—everyone there. Gedo (my grandfather) walked up the lane and dropped his load of tapestry carpets onto the front steps of the house in which all of the family had at one time lived. In the dream, he had been absent for many years, then just walked back into our lives. In yet another, the windshield of the car I was driving was broken on the driver's side, making it difficult to see out. And in another, the river beside where I grew up was flowing backwards. Brick walls were causing it to do that, and one was in the center of my favourite old swimming hole, ruining it. I was distraught. In the part of the river where the water was flowing the right direction, there were stepping stones to walk on. All I could do was observe them, I couldn't get to the stones to walk.

I wakened feeling as if I had been put through a wringer washer, and tried to sift through the information in the dreams. At first I thought there must be trouble at home but eventually realized that the only trouble is emotional baggage I carry from my family and upbringing. Everyone I dreamt about was a close family member. My vision-perception was obstructed in the earlier dreams and then in the last came some insight. Water in my dreams is always a representation of my emotions, and what I took from the dream is that I need to remove the walls so that the water can flow in the right direction again. There are steps to take that will help turn it around.

After the wild night, we got a sunny day for visiting Vilcabamba, where the people wear black more than any other colour, which I don't understand.

The altitude is only 1,500 meters and the temperature is warm, but this town is the first place we've come to in which the men wear short pants, albeit with black knee socks. Maybe there is some truth to the healthful valley. The people look healthy, both the men and women of all ages have such, thick, long hair and all wear it in well-groomed braids down the middle of their backs. I have noticed in the larger cities that there are a variety of hats but in smaller villages, people wear the same type and in Vilcabamba, black felt is the style.

When our destination for the day turned out not to have a suitable place to stay we opted to continue to the border. It meant two more hours of driving, but the kids agreed to carry on when Ed promised we would stay at the hotel with a pool listed in the book. The road became a challenge: it was mountainous and we encountered the results of several small landslides that weren't cleaned up, yet there were always tire tracks through the debris. At one in particular Ed laughed, saying, "We have to take a picture of this. No one at home will believe we drove on a road like it."

Within 50 kilometers of the border we were stopped at three police checks, each of which consumed time and after the regular questions were answered, ended up being more a social stop than anything else. At the third stop the policeman half-heartedly checked inside the van, I suspect as more of an excuse to ask us to get out at which point he called the others out of the office to meet us. We had a lengthy social visit, including the kids, and before we were back on the road each of the three policemen shook hands with each one of us and sent us off with the blessing of, "God be with you."

Macara is at an altitude of 600 meters. It is hot and not a pretty place. The hotel we promised the kids was abandoned, boarded up, fenced in, and the pool was empty. The grungy place we stayed at was awful, but the people were friendly. We brought only what we needed into the rooms and joined the owners on the verandah in the cooler night air. The older woman, mother of the owner, liked to talk. She didn't let anyone get a word in, asking a question and not even waiting for an answer. It was just as well. I didn't understand much of what she was saying. Ed managed to talk with her some, or at least listen to her. His patience amazes me. A Christian Reform Church was having a service across the street. It was mostly music and I let myself get lost in the uplifting happiness until the mosquitoes drove us inside.

Ben complained about the beds again, demanding his preferences and making it difficult for everyone else. Dayna sat on a chair outside the rooms waiting for a settlement; she doesn't care where she sleeps, she just sleeps. While Ed and Ben were sorting out the bed situation, I tried to figure out what to do to turn attitudes around. The "bathroom" was barely a toilet, without a seat, of course, and the water source was a fifty-gallon tin barrel. Water was scooped out with a bucket and used for whatever the need. The electric light bulb flickered off and on. I filled our biggest pot with water, added some drops of grapefruit seed extract and washed each of the kids, then Ed and myself with soap and facecloth. We went through several changes of water and it helped us feel a little refreshed. We passed on brushing our teeth, mostly because it was probably healthier to do so. Once Ben was satisfied with a place for himself, everyone else settled in. Jake and Whitney had slept while driving in the van and weren't tired. As a result Jake tossed and turned, while Whitney was up and down like a yo-yo. As I waited for her to settle down, I lay there surveying the grungy place. At least half of the people of this country live in such conditions all the time, and probably many in worse. All we do is complain. We have many lessons to learn.

The next morning, we looked for a restaurant for breakfast but the only thing served was meat and rice, so we declined. I bought a package of cookies and a carton of fake juice to help tide us over. After the fact, I realized that meat and rice would have been a healthier choice than processed packaged food. We get ourselves into such habitual ruts at times. Just because meat and rice was different from what we are used to, it seemed like the wrong kind of food for breakfast.

As usual, while exiting at the border, we sat in the hot van while Ed did the paper work. Again, nobody checked to see if papers matched people. When all was complete Ed drove across the bridge of the Macara River and we entered the country I have dreamt of visiting for many years: Peru.

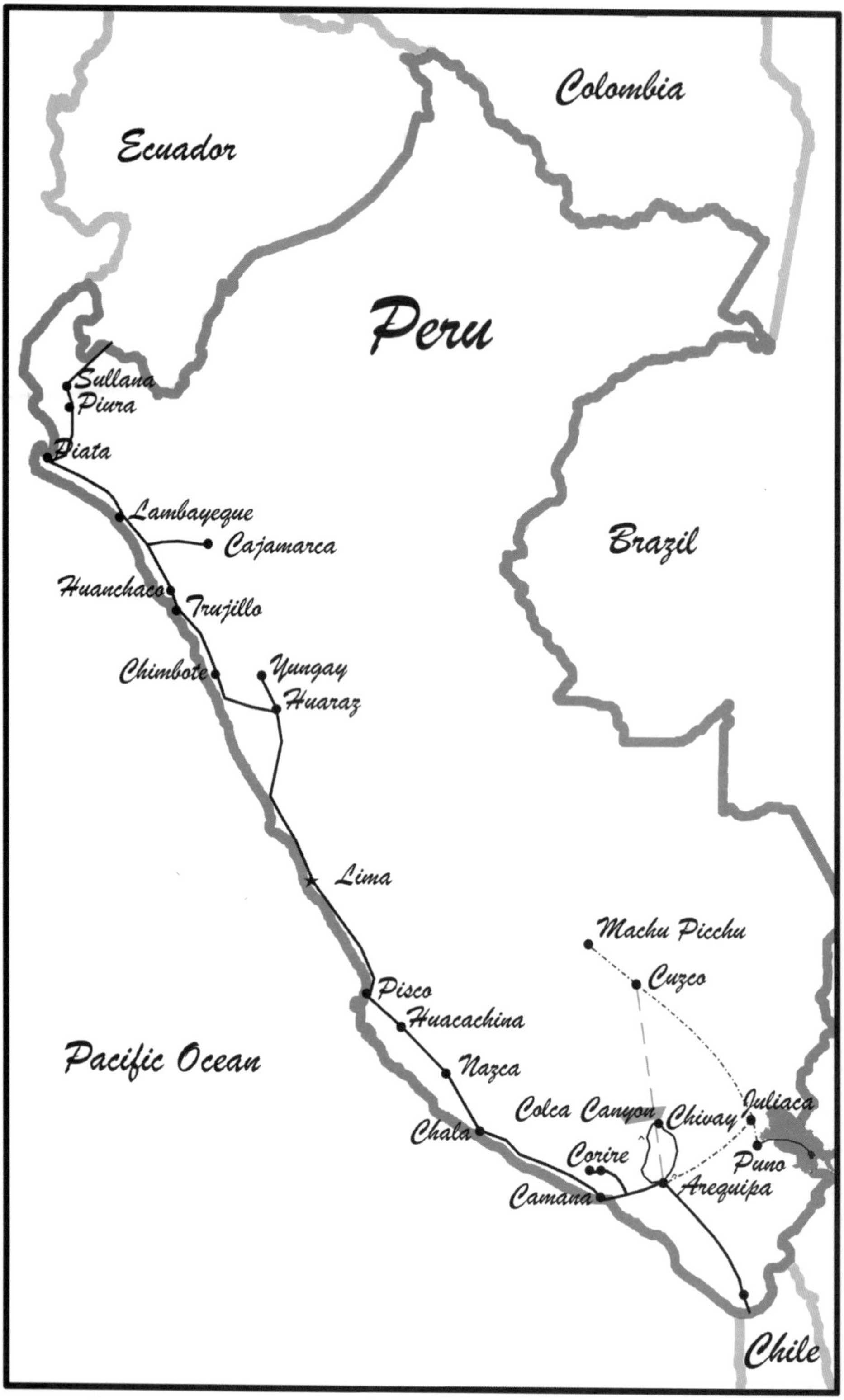
Colombia
Ecuador
Peru
Sullana
Piura
Piata
Lambayeque
Cajamarca
Huanchaco
Trujillo
Chimbote
Yungay
Huaraz
Brazil
Lima
Machu Picchu
Cuzco
Pisco
Huacachina
Pacific Ocean
Nazca
Colca Canyon
Chivay
Juliaca
Chala
Corire
Puno
Camana
Arequipa
Chile

March 10, 1997: The Northern Coast of Peru

The Peruvian immigration officials were more thorough, and the border control officer requested that all of us be present to fill out papers. When we were finished, he handed each of us our own passport back. At that moment, Jake and Karina were having an argument that ended up with Karina crying. As the officer handed Karina her passport, he said, sympathetically, "Don't cry, you are in Peru." I took it as a message for us all—we are supposed to enjoy our journey.

Sullana is a flat, dusty place where people appear to be in a hurry. The city streets are overrun with fast-moving tuk-tuks, the same little three-wheeled vehicles that we saw years ago on the streets of Bangkok, Thailand. We stayed only long enough to obtain some Peruvian *soles*.

Colan, on the coast, is a 40 kilometer drive through sandy desert. Both sides of the highway en route were used as garbage dumps that reeked in the heat. Either the garbage had been buried under sand and the wind had blown it off, or it was just dumped, and the drifting sand had partially covered it.

We found a restaurant on the beach, sat in the shade, and enjoyed the cooler breeze drifting in off the ocean. The menu was so unusual that we didn't know what to order. The waiter suggested *ceviche,* the seafood specialty of Peru. *Ceviche* is octopus, squid, or other kinds of raw fish marinated for 24 hours in lemon juice and salt. When it arrived the kids were not impressed. It was mid-afternoon and we had had little to eat that day. Ed and I thought it was fabulous. Tanya, Ben and Dayna ate most of what they were served but the raw fish was just a little too weird for the younger ones. So Ed ordered some deep-fried battered rolls of shrimp and fish, and even Karina, who would never eat seafood or fish before, enjoyed filling her stomach.

The sand on the beach at Colon was too hot to walk on with bare feet, but that was just as well—it was full of glass and garbage. Besides, the ocean had a disagreeable odour that wasn't an ocean smell. After the kids said they wouldn't be swimming, we drove on to the fishing village of Paita where people were bathing in ocean water that I wouldn't have set foot in, given the choice—it was black. We didn't find a suitable place to stay the night so continued inland to Piura. It was discouraging to the kids; who had wanted a couple of beach days.

Hotels with several beds in a room are harder to find in Peru. During our lengthy search, Jake and Whitney were oblivious to our predicament and had a good time giggling and playing in the back seat. It doesn't seem to matter where they are as long as their basic needs are met. At Hotel La Sol we found a room with five beds, a television and a small pool; we took it. As our afternoon of searching had worn on, a feeling of nausea had overtaken my body. Just as Ed parked the van in the hotel parking lot, my stomach had all it could take and expelled the contents of the meal I enjoyed so much. I crashed on a bed while Ed and the kids spent the rest of the day without me.

I was still not feeling the greatest by morning, and Ben was being difficult just for the sake of being difficult. He wanted to stay at a beach and was angry because we had chosen a hotel with a pool. However, when it was time to look for a place on a beach again he pouted because he wanted to stay at the hotel. Exasperated, Ed decided to stay another day for the kids to enjoy the pool and me recuperate. It seems he, too, is in emotional upheaval. He just wants to keep moving, but the reality of the situation is that he is dragging seven other people along who slow him down. I am sure he is somewhat frustrated but won't admit it. I got a good glimpse of this at dinner this evening when Whitney kicked up a fuss about her soup and he lost all patience, got up and left, gritting his teeth.

We attempted to find another place on a beach at Santa Rosa and San José but we are in Chiclayo tonight planning to head to Cajamarca tomorrow. We have given up on the idea of a beach. We had lunch in San José, and again all that was available was seafood similar to what we had the day I vomited. I am now sure I had an allergic reaction to one particular fish in the *ceviche*. I could eat everything else today, but as soon as I put this one kind in my mouth, I gagged, so I didn't eat it and have been fine this afternoon. We drove over more desert on roads in much the same condition as the highway from Sullana to Colan. The garbage is burned and bulldozed under the sand, but it doesn't stay buried. Today for the first time we really saw a mirage; it looked like blue water out over the desert but we never got to it.

Our highlight for the day was stopping in Lambayegue to visit the Bruning Museum, which gave us a good understanding of the archeological excavation that is taking place in the vicinity. It was an informative museum about the Lambayegue, Chavin, Moche, Viscus and Chimu cultures that inhabited the area before the Inca Empire became dominant. The exhibits included an extensive collection of finely woven ancient textiles, centuries old pottery in perfect condition, and some gold pieces. We were in awe of the mummified body of the ancient Lord Sipan, as he has come to be known. The children found the displays as captivating as Ed and I did.

March 16, 1997: Cajamarca, Peru

Although the ocean was at least 20 kilometers away as we drove south over the desert, ocean waves seemed to be rolling in on the sand just a short distance from the highway. It was an intriguing illusion. The road heading east to Cajamarca in the mountains followed the path of the Jequetepeque River and valley. At first the land was barren—rocks rose out of the sand. But soon the landscape gave way to rice paddies creating a strip of green out of the dry earth on either side of the river. Through irrigation and redirection of the water flow, rice that needs so much water to thrive grows on the desert.

The drive to Cajamarca tested everyone's patience. We started our day eating greasy, fried eggs on dry, sweet, white bread. We stopped at the cafés at the Cajamarca turnoff and got some fruit, but the only drink available was Sprite. (I know why my digestive system isn't working properly.) Dayna spilled a cupful of Sprite over herself, which took some time to clean up without water. Ben was upset three times: with me for not giving him the Sprite first, and then over having to give up one of two pillows he was sitting on so Jake could rest his head. An hour later he was angry again when neither Ed nor I acknowledged his request to stop so he could relieve himself, which was obviously a mistake. At the time, we were moving through a town figuring out which road to take, and it was not a good place to stop. He yelled out his request and second time and Ed stopped the van in the middle of town, acting as unreasonable as Ben, who didn't get out, of course, but cried uncontrollably. When Ed stopped on the side of the road at a more suitable place, Ben wouldn't get out of the van, angry with his Dad. Ed left instead of giving him time to calm down. I was at my wit's end and cried too. When we were able to talk with a little more sanity, Ben said he didn't know why he was here. I asked him if he wanted me to put him on a plane to Grandma's, but he said no. He is having a hard time being happy but is not ready to give up. We would have had to do some serious evaluation about what we were doing if he had said that he wanted to leave. Neither he nor I are coping very well with what we are facing. Nor is our family communicating with one another effectively. That's the biggest problem.

The mountainous road got to Jake again. Ed stopped the van for him to get some air and Ben to relieve himself. No sooner were we back on the road when the van started to act up while climbing to a higher altitude. It choked and stalled; again we coasted downhill, with the motor turned off, this time into Cajamarca.

Hostal Plaza on the Plaza de Armas is a great location, but our toilet's flush mechanism is broken, so we have to flush manually dipping our hand into the water reservoir. As usual, there is no toilet seat, and the hotel doesn't supply toilet paper. Otherwise the room is good.

I read about things to do in Cajamarca: visiting the ruins, thermal baths, cathedrals and the monument. Ed said it costs $1.25 each to go to the baths and was concerned about spending money. I didn't say anything, but felt much of what Ben was expressing that same afternoon. I know we are on a budget but why am I here if we can't see and do things in Cajamarca, or anywhere else for that matter? I would like to have stopped along the road to take some photos, but there was a truck behind us and Ed didn't want it in front of us. I would have liked to go to the Sipan excavation site, as Ben requested, but we have too far to go in our broader, travels and we can't take the time. But like Ben I'm not ready to quit either. After I vented my negative feelings on paper, I was able to talk to Ed without so much hostility attached, and we managed to have a good visit in Cajamarca without blowing our budget.

I read aloud to the children, from the *Lonely Planet* guide to Peru, about the Inca and Spanish history of the city. When the kids learned that the Spanish Conquistadors executed Atahualpa, the king of the Inca Empire, right in the Plaza we were overlooking, they were interested in learning more. We discussed the history, reviewed the story, and figured out some places to visit where events had taken place.

The thermal baths were invigorating and we enjoyed a good soak. The girls liked being alone for a while, as did the boys, and it improved the mood of the entire family. The natural hot spring water provided another simple geography lesson. We walked around the springs and sulphur ponds discussing how an underground river becomes hot, the evidence of it boiling and bubbling up out of the ground right in front of us.

As we arrived at the *ventenillas*, young people bombarded us with offers to be our guide or watch the van. The *ventenillas* are holes carved out of the rock cliffs and were used as graves. At one time, each *ventenilla* was sealed with a tight-fitting rock slab door. Skeletons found inside were rolled up in the fetal position. From a distance the series of holes in the mountain look like windows in a rock house, hence the name *ventenillas*—the Spanish word for windows.

During our walking tour of the city we ascended the steps to the Santa Apollonia Hill. The steps create a vertical line that is a prominent feature on the cityscape and visible from the balcony of our room. The wide steep uphill path accommodates stone statues at several intervals. Peddlers of pottery and a multitude of other things lined the path's edge with their wares. The view of the city from the top suggested an ocean of red tile roofs. We visited the carved stone "Throne of the Inca" where Atahualpa reviewed his troops. There are several carved stones on the hill, some are from the Inca era, others dated much earlier. Anywhere there is an Inca sacred site, there is often a Christian shrine or cathedral erected on top of or in close vicinity. We visited the Christian shrine as well and enjoyed the splendor of the flower gardens. We waited out a downpour under a stone archway at the top and started our descent after it stopped.

Whitney complained of being tired and wouldn't walk. She controlled our group until Ed consented to give her a piggyback. Content on her Dad's back, she promptly proclaimed, "I want to be called 'Boss' and I want everyone to listen to me." It cracked us up and she displayed a look of utter dismay when she realized we didn't take her seriously. This little person already wants more control of her own life.

While walking the streets and passing the many food vendors, we came across a stall in which a woman was deep frying pastries. The aroma enticed the kids and they had to have a look at what she was cooking. There in the pan were traditional French Canadian-like doughnuts, almost a foot long. The woman told Ed that they were sweet bread dough filled with *manjar*—similar to a jelly filled doughnut. She demonstrated how she made them, rolling out a long, narrow rectangle of dough, dropping a generous amount of *manjar* the length of the dough, rolling the dough around the *manjar* and pinching it together to seal it up. She then dropped these long slim rolls into the fat, and they expanded as they cooked. *Manjar* is a caramel flavoured condensed milk sweetened with sugar. It is used as a spread, like jam, on toast and in many desserts, from what we have learned. We had purchased a jar to try it but it had not been very popular with our gang. In fact, when Ed was about to purchase a sampling of the "doughnuts" it was Ben who said, "Don't bother, Dad, they have *manjar* in them, and they look like a donkey's penis. I don't want to eat that." Whatever enthusiasm the rest of the kids had for the treat at that point was quickly diminished. Between them having *manjar* in them and being referred to a "donkey's penis", we passed.

Our hostel was in a strategic location for catching the Easter festivities. In the courtyard of the cathedral, during the evenings, a brass band played and sang songs, drawing us out into the Plaza which was bustling with activity. Beyond the festivities, young people used it as a meeting place under the watchful eyes of adults. They walked in circles, changed direction, and walked the other way almost all evening, every evening we were there.

We walked through the market to purchase some food and found a stall that had freshly squeezed orange juice—what a treat! We had to buy a straw basket to carry our food in that plastic bags are not supplied and I forgot to bring a cloth one. Our troop is always a spectacle. Curious eyes followed us as we did our shopping and several people asked where we were from. We visited two more cathedrals, and saw Atahualpa's ransom chambers, as well as the rooms he filled with silver and gold for the Spanish, in a vain attempt to save his own life.

It rained so much last night the streets became rivers, all of which water will eventually reach the desert and sustain the rice paddies.

Before leaving Cajamarca today we went to refresh ourselves at the thermal baths again. Ben had some sort of nausea and diarrhea but felt better after vomiting. I gave him some grapefruit seed extract and made sure he drank lots of clean water.

As we descended out of Cajamarca, we saw a sign indicating the altitude as 3,240 meters. The drive was continuously downhill, following the cultivated valley blocked out in different shades of green. The moment we reached the flat expanse of desert, the colours that met the eye changed dramatically and instantaneously from green vegetation and blue sky to yellow desert and blue sky.

Tonight we are in Huanchaco, a fishing village just north of Trujillo. Fishing here is still done from *caballitos,* boats made from *totora* reeds, almost the length of canoes and shaped like a giant elves' shoe. The men sit balancing atop and paddle out onto the ocean to fish. The beach sand looks like ground black pepper and here, too, there is a tide of litter. We are in Sol Y Mar, a hotel with a pool, and the kids are enjoying it. Ben has started to feel more himself this evening but hasn't eaten all day.

March 20, 1997: Huanchaco, Peru

We managed to take a wrong turn on our way to visit the famous local sun and moon temples, but the mistake gave us an extensive tour of farming on the desert. We found ourselves driving on small, one-lane tracks through well-defined blocked-out plots, each growing different kinds of vegetables. What is so remarkable is the number of irrigation canals that run through the area. I find it amazing that the desert can become so productive when given some attention.

It was late morning by the time we reached the *Huaca de la Luna*— Temple of the Moon—and archaeologists were hard at work while we visited. The impressive part was the muralled walls being excavated. We were told that the structure was built in six stages, there was work and viewing on the fifth. The hole in the ground plummets, revealing each level covered in painted, patterned murals. Shards of a pot had just been brought up from the bottom. One archaeologist showed them to us and said that it looked as if the entire pot was there. They will put the pieces back together to restore it to the vessel it once was. He also showed

us several adobe bricks used in both the sun and moon temples and explained that each brick used in the construction of the ancient buildings has a specific symbol on it. Eighteen bricks were laid on the ground before us, each with its own markings. Almost a hundred different symbols have been catalogued. It is believed to be the "signature" of the group that made it. The theory is that bricks for temples may have been a means of tax, and the symbols were a way to keep track of contributions.

Huaca del Sol—The Temple of Sun—is the largest pre-Columbian structure in Peru, estimated to contain about 140 million adobe bricks. It is a solid structure with different levels on the exterior, which at one time were connected by sets of steep stairs. Because there are no chambers within, it is believed to have been a huge ceremonial site. Both structures are from the Moche period, about 1500 years ago.

Ed suffered from diarrhea and vomiting for a day while the rest of us enjoyed the pool and wrote letters home. I managed enough Spanish to do some food shopping on my own. Ed not being well and me learning to function in a language other than English—both are rare.

Chan Chan, Trujillo, Peru

There are so many historic sites to visit we needed to pick and choose. ChanChan, the largest pre-Columbian city in South America, is also the largest mud city in the world, covering 28 square kilometers. On our visit there a guide took us through to explain the city and the Chimu people who built it. He showed us the pole markers within the high walls, which give rise to the theory that the pre-Inca people surveyed and planned their cities in great detail. The inhabitants thrived as fishermen. It is believed they watched the sea birds to know where to fish, and they probably used nets to bring in their harvests from the sea. The molded figures and designs on the walls depict birds, fish and repetitive patterns resembling fishnets. Our guide explained that there are nine sections to the city, each built by a succeeding ruler and each containing a royal burial ground of its own. One compound, partially restored, took several hours to visit and was time well spent.

The heat was intense. Our guide wiped the sweat off his forehead and face with a handkerchief several times. He said the heat was not normal, which may indicate another El Niño year; it was hot like this before the damaging flood in 1983.

As I took photographs, I noticed that the light from the sun was different from what I had ever noticed before any where. It looked unusual to me through the camera lens as it played on the sculpted relief of the ruins. I knew it was different but didn't figure out why. When Ben was playing, raising his arms up and down and turning in circles, I asked him what he was doing. He said, "Looking for my shadow. Look, I don't make one unless I put my arms out." It became a game, as each of the kids discovered and played with his or her lack of a shadow. I then understood the daylight I had never seen before—more learning through playing, for both the kids and me.

Our guide took us to another site, *Huaco Arco Iris*—The Rainbow Temple—which was included in our entrance ticket to ChanChan. The Rainbow Temple was where the Chimu people prayed for rain in the mountains. The temple is a solid trapezoidal structure constructed of adobe bricks. Exterior panels in relief molding are decorated with rainbows, calling symbolically for rain. One panel had been fully restored and the others displayed evidence of the original existing colours. Before the 1983 El Niño the structure was in much better condition; the rain did a lot of damage. Our guide explained how the canals irrigate the desert. The pre-Inca and Inca people constructed most of the irrigation canals in use today, and the Inca people farmed three times as much desert as what is currently in use. The canals are still there, but many are buried under the drifting sand. It almost makes me think that our modern day civilization has moved backwards.

Palm Sunday, March 20 1997: Huaraz, Peru

Huaraz is the tourist center of the Cordillera Blanca and the base for trekking into the mountains. The Cordillera boasts twenty-three snow-crested peaks in close range. This is the only place in the tropics that incorporates such a large concentration of glaciers above 5,000 meters, including the highest mountain of Peru—Huscaran—at 6,768 meters.

We wanted to visit the Cordillera Blanca, but driving the main highway meant adding an extra 200 kilometers to our trip. Ed noticed a shortcut on a secondary road and stopped in Casma to ask two policemen if they thought it was passable. One didn't think it was such a good idea, but the other said the van could make it and told Ed just to go slowly and be careful. Ed then spoke with a truck driver who gave him the same advice; it is a hard road to drive but passable and could be done. Two people saying the same thing was enough for Ed. (So much for sticking to main highways!) It is just 70 kilometers to Huaraz as the crow flies, 110 kilometers on the gravel road shortcut, 260 kilometers to go around on the main highway. Looking back at it now, it would have been faster to go around.

We started toward the mountains facing a sheer cliff. Dayna shouted out, "Hey, look at the truck up there."

The truck eased its way around a corner out of sight, at which point there was no evidence of a road up there at all. The cliff, straight up, must have been 1,500 to 2,000 meters high. I said, uncomfortably, "That couldn't possibly be our road," only to find myself looking down a while later to the road from which we had just come. It was a long, steady, drive up that cliff from sea level to an altitude of 4,000 meters. The route was hair-raising, more often than not a one-lane road, muddy and cold. We just kept climbing—it felt as if we were never going to get to the top. The dramatic change in altitude caused headaches and nausea. Karina and Ben started to cough when inhaling and I had difficulty getting my fingers to move. I don't know how Ed manages to keep such a level head all the time. Fortunately, the van didn't have any problems, and this puzzles me. Why will it run smoothly at high altitudes on some occasions and not on others?

We met another vehicle only once and it was bigger than ours. We were on the inside, scraping against the rock cliff, while the truck inched its way past on the outside. I felt like vomiting—I don't know whether it was from fear of the truck going over the edge or from altitude. The situation didn't seem to cause any concern for the driver of the truck, who just eased confidently ahead. Soon after that minor obstacle we came upon a man and his young son filling potholes. They had set up a roadblock and asked for money. It may have been highway robbery, but it was an ingenious way to make a little cash.

Just when it felt as if the crest of the mountain was never going to come, the road leveled out. Although high in altitude we were no longer on the cliff and that alone made it easier to breathe. By huddling on the front bench-seat together so everyone could follow the road with their eyes we tried to prevent motion sickness on the winding descent. We had lots of space in the back, and on the 1,000-meter drop into Huaraz, Ed stopped to pick up a young family—a mom, dad and two young children about the same ages as Jake and Whitney. We didn't converse much but there was an awful lot of giggling going on among the children. As we entered the city of Huaraz, the man asked to be let out. He offered to pay for their lift but Ed refused; the huge smiles were payment enough.

Huaraz sits at an altitude of 3,091 meters, but after being up to 4,000 meters and coming back down, it was easy for us to acclimatize and body parts started to work again. I don't recommend going from sea level to above 4,000 meters in such a short time.

Meanwhile, snow-covered peaks and spectacular views of mountains surround us in Huaraz. Jake had his turn with diarrhea. Dayna was quiet too for a while, she didn't have diarrhea, but her stomach was bothering her. A couple of doses of grapefruit seed extract quickly took care of whatever it was that caused her discomfort. Despite the queasy stomachs, the kids still managed to clean up a plate of pancakes at a restaurant that caters to tourists. As most of us are struggling with altitude sickness or digestive problems, the thermal baths in Monterey were the visit of first choice. After feeling rejuvenated, we spent the afternoon exploring the city on foot.

In 1970, Huaraz succumbed to a 7.7 magnitude earthquake that destroyed most of the city. It has been rebuilt in a more modern style than the colonial cities we are accustomed to seeing. Our highlight was meeting a boy of about 10 years of age with four white, well-groomed alpacas. He makes money by having them available to tourists for photos, and needless to say, he made a fistful of cash from us. Alpacas are gentle creatures, and as we petted them, one gave Whitney a good kiss and she proceeded to give it a big hug back. It is easy to see how they become lovable pets.

We did a day-trip to visit a small part of the UNESCO World Biosphere Reserve, a short drive north of Huaraz. The park encompasses 3,400 square kilometers of the Cordillera Blanca above 4,000 meters, and includes two turquoise glacier lakes in the Hangunuco Valley. It is a glacial valley with its sheer vertical-drop cliffs. Waterfalls from the glaciers atop each side of the valley cascade more than 1,000 meters to the lakes. We were above 4,000 meters again, but none of us had the altitude symptoms we experienced after being in the Cordillera a couple of days. The kids ran, explored, and enjoyed themselves in the open space and when they were tired out, we started back to Huaraz. Being in natural surroundings helps us all feel better.

Nevada Huascaran Biosphere –Hauraz, Peru

As we drove past the monument of Christ overlooking Old Yungay, we discussed why it was there and I read from the *Lonely Planet Peru* book to help explain it to the kids: "It was here that the earthquake of May 31, 1970 loosened some 15 million cubic meters of granite and ice from the west wall of Huscaran Norte. The resulting alluvion picked up a speed of about 300 kilometers per hour as it dropped over three vertical kilometers on its way to Yungay, 14 kilometers away. The town and almost all of its inhabitants were buried. The earthquake also killed about 50,000 people in other parts of central Peru. Today the site is known as Campo Santo and is marked by a huge white statue of Christ on a knoll overlooking old Yungay. The path of the alluvion can plainly be seen from the road... At the old Plaza de Armas of Yungay, you can see just the very top of the cathedral tower and a few palm trees which are all that remain of the devastated village."

It made an impression—18,000 people were buried alive, absolutely everyone in the town at that moment.

We left Huaraz this morning after another pancake breakfast and watched the festivities of the Palm Sunday parade. A group of people was carrying a statue of Christ on a donkey, followed by a brass band and hundreds of people carrying braided and woven palms. Others threw rose petals onto the ground. It felt like Easter to us, too.

Easter Sunday, March 30, 1997: Lima, Peru

As we drove south through the desert, the mist over the ocean water indicated where the land-water line was. The fog simply does not move inland. It is a puzzling phenomenon to me.

We were playing funky kids' music and when a song called *Barnyard Boogie* came on, Ed snickered and told me to look in the back. I turned to see Tanya and Dayna standing with their feet on the middle bench seat, their hands propped on the back and bums bouncing back and forth in unison to the heavy country beat. I couldn't help but laugh before urging them to use their bottoms appropriately in the van.

As we approached the outskirts of Lima, we drove through miles and miles of shantytown, shelters built of cardboard, rocks, mud bricks, tin, anything that would protect from the sun. The shacks stretched over the desert as far as we could see in every direction, clearly accommodating thousands of people. It was the most disturbing thing I have seen so far in South America. My mind is full of questions. Who are the people that live in these dwellings? How do they survive? Where does their water come from? What happens to the fecal material? Is it an example of the rich suppressing the poor? Overpopulation? Is it people coming from the countryside with the idea of making a fortune in the city? I can't help but think there could be a better way. If the Incas, so many hundreds of years ago, had three times as much desert farmed and providing food than there is today, why isn't it still done?

Central Lima and the old city were a severe contrast to what we had just come through: going from shantytowns to Spanish colonial architecture, an island of prosperity surrounded by the reality of mass population and poverty. We picked up our messages at the South American Club where we were given a recommendation to a place where we could cook our own food.

It was my turn with diarrhea, but at least my body was cleaned out—constipation has been more the problem for me due to our diet. The kids took care of themselves for a day and Ed spent time with Liam, a Chiropractor from the United States who has a clinic here in Lima and a part-time clinic in Arequipa. Ed has made arrangements with him to work in the clinic in Arequipa until the Chiropractor that he hired takes over in May. It means five weeks in Arequipa and I like that idea. Liam invited us to stay in his house while we visit Lima. He's taking a four-day jungle excursion to Iquitos with another Chiropractor so we have his place to ourselves. Peter, the other chiropractor, is also from the United States. He has just graduated from Chiropractic College, was looking for opportunities outside his own country and has decided that Peru is where he will live and work. His real ambition was to go to Chile, as his fiancée likes the beach and he likes hiking in the mountains. But after looking into opportunities and discovering that chiropractic was not yet established there, he made arrangements to work with Liam.

We took the kids to the zoo to see Peruvian animals. The place has three sections for animals from the jungle, mountains and coast. The highlight was the condors. None of us realized how big they are, standing more than three feet tall. We drove around the city to get a feel for it and walked through the downtown area. Parque del Armour is a popular place for lovers to come and openly kiss. Ed was not happy—he said to me that it was not so long ago we would have been right in there with everyone else. I didn't know how to start with how I was feeling and remained quiet. Things haven't been good between us these past few weeks. We are staying in dirty, crummy hotels and eating food that doesn't nourish the body, and the kids are driving me crazy. I need to be well both physically and emotionally, to be open to the mood the people in the park were displaying. We are learning so much and enjoying the sites, but increasingly, we are not enjoying each other's company as a family. The kids fight a lot. I can't stand it, but I don't know how to improve the situation. Ed doesn't either; we didn't come up with any answers.

Tanya and Karina had a turn with unsettled stomachs and bowels this week as well. In our need to eat a greater variety of foods, particularly more vegetables, we have become less picky about what foods we eat. We simply have to let our bodies become accustomed to the bugs that affect foreigners, but not locals, and build up some resistance. Grapefruit seed extract is amazing stuff: the diarrhea hasn't lasted much more than a day for any of us.

Easter is a special time here. On Thursday we tried to visit the Plaza de Armas but there were so many people spilling out of the cathedral we barely got a glimpse of it. We didn't stay but went back again yesterday to send some mail from the International Post Office and even got to look inside the modest cathedral for a few minutes. It was built during the 1500s and has had a rough history from damage caused by earthquakes. The remains of Francisco Pizzaro, the Spanish conquistador who was instrumental in Atualpa's death, lie in the chapel there.

Ed is supposed to be in Arequipa to work by next weekend, so we need to move; it will take a few days to get there. We are in Pisco tonight and there are a lot of mosquitoes again.

April 5, 1997: Lima to Arequipa, Peru

We have had a fabulous week of sightseeing. On our first day out of Lima, we put a picnic lunch together and went to Paracas Peninsula National Park. Before arriving at the park we passed fishmeal factories where anchovies are processed, and the air smelled so bad that several of us came close to vomiting. It was a relief to move on. On the peninsula, from the cliff, we watched sea lions playing in the water and basking in the sun on the rocks below. The entire peninsula is sandstone desert with white streaks of salt running through the stone. We had a great hike on the peninsula but were in the open longer into the afternoon than what is recommended. Climbing back up the slope off the beach the wind began pushing us up. It was so strong on the plateau we struggled to open the doors of the van. The sand stung as it hit our skin and faces, making it difficult to see— afternoon winds are treacherous. Ed made arrangements for a boat tour to Isla Ballestas, the islands where a huge colony of sea lions live and give birth. While waiting at Paracas' dock, we watched fishermen bring in their catch of anchovies. So many of them in just one day, in one place—I don't know how the oceans keep up to humanity. Then again, they probably don't.

Jake was anxious to get going and when we finally did, he wanted to go fast. But shortly after the boat picked up a good speed he had had enough and wanted to go back. I was afraid we were going to have one of his scenes, but he sat on my knee and asked how deep the water was, why there was a whistle on everyone's life jackets, if there were sharks in the water, if the boat would sink, and all kinds of other questions that indicated insecurity. I assured him we were all fairly safe. I told him there were other boats with us and that if something did happen to ours and we ended up in the water, he should just keep blowing the whistle until someone pulled him out. Once he understood that the captain of the boat takes people out onto the water regularly to see the sea lions and that we were going to be fine, he calmed down. Sometimes ignorance is bliss, but knowledge is empowering.

The boats stopped at the far end of the peninsula to give us a look at the candelabra shape carved into the sandstone facing the sea. Fifty meters long on the slope, no one knows how it got there, how long it has existed, or what purpose it serves.

The islands are rugged, and caves and arches have been worn into the rock by the waves. They are covered with sea birds, penguins and thousands of sea lions. We were in awe of the abundance of wildlife and the sound of so many barking sea lions. Birthing time is January and February, and there are now many small pups. Mothers nursed little ones; some pulled their pups into the water, while others tried to get up onto the rocks. Two males fought before us, and when one pushed the other over the edge into the water he barked in victory. Guano (bird feces) covered the higher rocks. The ancient inhabitants of the area collected and mixed it into their adobe bricks to make the mud harden like cement. In fact, it is still collected today (by people licensed to do so) both for bricks and for use as fertilizer. After two hours of watching birds and animals we headed back with a lasting impression.

The village of Huacachina is for me the idealized picture of an oasis based on my childhood story reading of exotic lands. A small lake gives life to palms and vegetation amongst stark sand desert. We cooled down in the lake after Ed rented sand boards for the kids to slide on the dunes. Hundreds of feet high, the dunes protect the village from the strong winds of the desert. Although it was beautiful, whatever space the human species occupies becomes littered with garbage. To me, the reality of it is disheartening and depressing.

While climbing the tallest dune, sand slid out from underneath our feet, making it feel like two steps forward and one back. We took photos, lingered in the sun and sand, and "skied" back down. After dark we climbed part way back up and lay in the velvety sand to take in a bright sky of stars through humidity-free air. We think we have figured out the four stars that make up the Southern Cross constellation.

Ben got himself into another state over wanting to sleep in the hammock. Dayna gave in; it was supposed to be her turn. His demand was about more than just sleeping arrangements, but I don't know how to help him. He had a lengthy cry before sleep let him escape. When all was quiet, I listened to the crickets singing and the breeze rustling the palm leaves outside our window. It calmed my mind and gave me peace in the moment.

The following morning we had a brief visit to what are called the "Nazca Lines". The surrounding land is a flat plateau where immense line-drawn picture figures as well as straight parallel and crossing lines, stretch over 525 square kilometers. They could all easily be missed if not for the *mirador* or lookout tower that interrupts the flat expanse. We climbed to see the hands and tree figures visible from the top. The straight lines run for several kilometers, perfectly straight, as if surveyed, and the figures are so huge one would not know they were there on the ground except from the height. Flying over the plateau is the only way to truly appreciate the archeological puzzle. It is believed that the lines are about

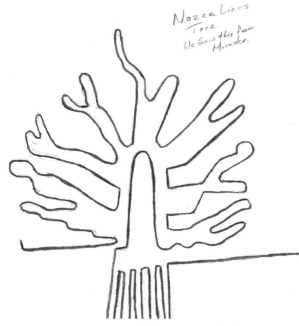

Nazca Lines
Tree
We Saw this from Mirador.

2000 years old. They were constructed simply by removing the dark weather-worn stones from the surface of the earth to expose the gypsum-laden, light-coloured soil beneath, but there isn't any evidence of who etched them into the ground or why. There are many theories but no definite answers. I find it all so intriguing.

We stopped briefly at Puerto Inca to visit the ruins of the ancient port. From there, a 240-kilometer footpath runs to Cusco, the capital of the Inca Empire at the height of its era. Originally, the path was set up with staging posts every seven kilometers and relay runners would cover seven-kilometer intervals, bringing fresh fish and messages from the coast to Cusco and the Inca kings within 24 hours.

We spent the night in Chala overlooking the ocean. The restaurant where we had dinner was empty on our arrival but before we finished was bursting with people who arrived to watch the soccer game. We enjoyed a refreshing walk on the beach and watched the red ball of sun set into the Pacific for the night. The kids went barefoot, much to my chagrin, as there is so much broken glass everywhere.

Ben had more issues over who sleeps where and again we gave in to him. All this unreasonable behaviour is driving me crazy. We slept to the gentle sound of waves. There is peace out there—we just need to bring it within ourselves.

The highway from Chala to Camana runs through mountainous desert hugging the coast. It is treacherous but beautiful, as cliffs drop to the clean, clear ocean below. After coming to several places where sand pours onto the pavement from the dunes above the road, Dayna said they need a sand plow. Drifting

sand is a common thing to see on the road, like drifting snow on a Canadian road during winter. As the road drops from the desert plateau into the valley of the Rio Camana, the small river creates greenery on either side as though a verdant line were drawn on the earth. This is common in the river valleys of Peru, but I still find it amazing that irrigation can turn something that appears to be so barren into something so productive.

Tanya contemplating a
petroglyph at Toro Muerto, Corire, Peru

We had a day before we were expected to be in Arequipa, so took a side trip to Corire. The clerk at our hotel gave us directions to see "the world's largest field of petroglyphs." More than two square kilometers, of light-coloured sandstone rocks speckled the sandy slope. The stone is extremely soft, almost chalk-like and easily scored, and ancient drawings were carved into any rock that had a flat surface. It was disheartening to see several of the drawings tampered with. There isn't much known about the carvings but archeologists believe they were created by the Wari culture about 1200 years ago. The stick-like figures are of birds, snakes, llamas, and the sun, while some are just designs. One stone in particular had several drawings that gave me the impression of a story about people moving. We would have stayed longer but our water ran out and the sun encouraged us to find some shelter.

Ben and I had another argument. Karina was using the bathroom and he opened the door nine times before I said something. I lost my patience and yelled, "Is it so unreasonable to leave her alone until she's finished and then it could be your turn?" Ed yelled at me to leave him alone and I yelled back that Ben didn't need to do that. I was in tears. We have had a wonderful week of seeing new, intriguing things, but my spirit is at the bottom and I feel as if I just want to give up and die. I was up early the following morning to write, but the only thing that came was tears.

When it was time for us to head to Arequipa, a truck transport blocked the garage entrance. While we were awaiting the driver's return, our hotel clerk intrigued us with his collection of artifacts. In one of the hotel rooms he had pottery, weapons, fabrics and a baby mummified at birth, all laid out on display. He has found a few of the articles himself but has purchased much of his collection from other people. He was concerned about keeping the artifacts from deteriorating and would like to put together a museum of collections from the area. However, he has been given no support for the project as yet. He continues to work on it.

Living Dreams

We found Hotel Nunez in Arequipa after a long searching ordeal, but it is at least comfortable. Ed and I have a single bed, Ben has one to himself, of course, while Jake is on the couch, and the four girls are in two beds.

My sleep was restless and now I am awake. I kept dreaming that the earth was shaking me up, trying to make me see something. The reality of physical shaking brought me back to consciousness. As I write, it is the middle of the night and I realize it was an earthquake and the vibrations were big enough to alert my senses and increase my heart rate. The others are not going to believe me.

Now that I am awake, the events of the week are going through my head. It is no way to live with our family always at each other and in such upheaval. The kids are fighting more than ever. I don't know whether they are acting this way because I am such an emotional mess or whether I am so down because they are acting this way. But I feel as if I have failed when they show such a lack of consideration for each other. Jake thinks everyone can be used as a punching bag. He needs somewhere to play and let that energy go constructively, but that isn't available to him in this situation. Ben can't seem to give at all, invariably aiming at getting more of everything than anyone else. He will rarely sit in the back seat of the van then complains it's not fair that Tanya always has a whole seat to herself. Tanya doesn't help, though she will let anyone but Ben sit with her.

It takes all my energy to cope with my own negative feelings. I feel like just another one of the kids. I can't seem to take charge and be the parent. I don't function well when I always feel less than good. My gall bladder is constantly burning; I need different food from what we are eating. We only put premium gas in the van so it will run properly but when it comes to our bodies we buy the cheapest to save money. Emotionally, I am at a dead end and no doubt the reason I am physically sick. We are in Arequipa for a few weeks. Maybe not moving for a while will give us a chance to change what is happening. I am hoping.

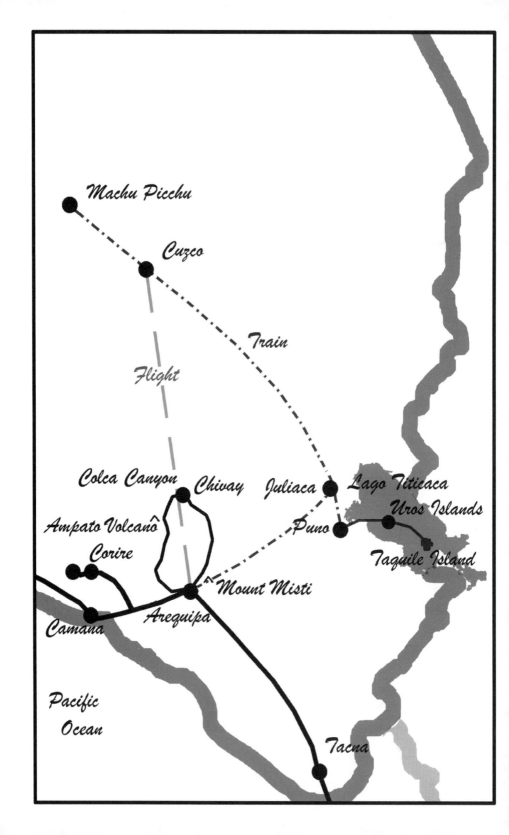

AREQUIPA, PERU

May 6, 1997:

Ed spent our first weekend in Arequipa (pop. 1 million) with Liam at the clinic while the rest of us did some exploring. We walked to Selva Alegra City Park on Saturday afternoon. A Peruvian boy, Reddi, about the same age as Ben, soon took notice of our group and followed us around. Every time Ben ran to the slide, Reddi ran to beat him. Ben enjoyed the interaction of someone new to play with and it changed the dynamics of our group. The kids just need space to run off their energy to keep them happy.

Sunday we walked to the Plaza de Armas and were lucky enough to get a quick tour of the famous white cathedral before the doors closed after mass. The church covers the full length of the plaza and constructed of sillar, a pearly white volcanic stone, from nearby mountains. The massive pipe organ spans the entire back wall. The ceiling is low for a cathedral, but all buildings in Arequipa are built according to height restrictions because of earthquakes. Despite the low ceiling, the light-coloured interior still gives a spacious feeling. Arequipa is known as the white city—most of the original colonial buildings and cathedrals are constructed of the same white stone. Because this stone is easy to carve, those buildings front and main entrance usually has an extensive display of intricate carved detail. It is unique to Arequipa.

In the plaza the kids fed the pigeons out of their hands and then wanted to go back to the Selva Alegra Park, which was crowded and chaotic. There were temporary rides for kids, a church group singing, vendors of all kinds of things, and people everywhere. We made our way to the slides but there were line-ups fifteen kids long.

A policeman yelled at a woman for nursing her baby on a bench while her other children were playing. She yelled back at him and refused to stop, flicking her hand and telling him to go away. Nursing babies in public is not as accepted in the cities as in the smaller mountain towns.

Children played at the edges of the pond attempting to catch minnows in their pails. When park police blew their whistles, the kids ran off but when the police left, they returned to hunt again. One policeman, who had become extremely irate with a young girl, pulled the bucket out of her hand and raised his hand to hit her when she tried to get it back from him. She lost her bucket. The park we enjoyed so much the previous day turned out to be awful: there were just too many people for our enjoyment and the kids asked to leave.

On our way back to the *posada* we met Ed, Liam and Carlos coming to find us. Carlos oversees Liam's clinic in Arequipa and wanted to meet us. Infatuated with the kids, he spoke with each of them; he has five of his own.

Carlos found our apartment for us. He also arranged for a family photo to be taken to include with the newspaper article about Ed and Chiropractic. His marketing worked so well that Ed was busy the day after it was published. A week later, Carlos arranged a radio interview that was also well received. It lasted twice as long as scheduled, with people calling in to ask questions. Ed was as busy within two weeks in Arequipa as he was in his established practice when we left home.

Our first week in the apartment felt long but we soon found a park to play in just a few blocks away. Ed comes home for lunch regularly, and has afternoon siesta hours, which gives us a break in our day. He brought a soccer ball home for the kids the evening after they told him about the dodge ball game they made up with shoes that morning. It gives them many more games to play.

We were invited to Tito's for lunch on Saturday the 12th of April. Tito owns and runs the medical clinic where Ed works. Sylvia, his wife, speaks English and is a bilingual executive secretary for a large steel company. What a house—it is huge! They served an elegant meal in the formal dining room with the employees catering to our every need.

Our family visits with Eduardo, Roberto, Sylvita, Sylvia & Tito
Arequipa –Peru

Tito and Sylvia have lived in her parent's home since they were married and she has inherited it. They have three children. Her father's death was a year ago, and she still misses him deeply. The children spent most of their hours at home with him and his passing has left a void in their lives too. Sylvia's mother is partially blind and cared for at home. Sylvia's full-time job keeps her away from home almost 12 hours a day, five days a week. Her two live-in employees run the house, so her biggest responsibility is making decisions and giving directions.

During tea and cake there was an earth tremor. Sylvia had a concerned look on her face and watched the lights; I felt only a small vibration. She said it was just a tremor, but is cautious when there are many people in the house. She then gave us instructions on what to do if a real earthquake hits: get outside and away from anything that could fall on you. or if you are stuck inside a building take refuge in doorways under lintels. It is supposed to be the safest place in a building during an earthquake.

Sylvia wants her children to have careers and visit other countries and cultures. She travelled throughout Europe and parts of South America before she married and would like to see her children do the same. Tanya and Ben were invited to sleep over and go to school with their kids for a day. They were to let us know when the arrangements were made with the school.

The following weekend Tito and Sylvia organized a tour to Piedras de Sembey for our families. We met the guide at 5:30 a.m. but we were the only people on time and waited more than an hour for the entire group to arrive. We have yet to learn the true customs of Latin America. Four vehicles drove toward El Misti, continuously climbing for almost two hours. With its snow-capped, perfect cone, El Misti stands at 5,822 meters and lies between the mountain Chachani (6,075 meters) and the volcano Pichu-Pichu (5,669 meters). El Misti has two concentric craters and Inca mummies have been found near them.

Little by little the sun crept down the mountains and eventually warmed the valleys. As we climbed, the road turned to volcanic stone gravel that breaks up into a substance with the consistency of talcum powder as vehicles drive over it. In some places the powder is several inches deep and the van slid in it as though we were in mud. The dust seeped into the van, clouding the air and coating everything; there was no way to stop it. On the upper plateau we drove on the north side of the mountain peaks that loom over the city—there is less snow on the sunny side—which is facing north in the southern hemisphere. This takes some getting used to.

We had a snack at Piedres de Sembey before our hike. A man in the group discovered a scorpion under a stone and carefully played with it while the rest of us watched. It was between two and three inches long and the same colour as the sand. Its tail curled up, ready to strike, but only when the stick was moved aggressively toward it; otherwise it searched for the shelter of a stone. After everyone had a good look to satisfy their curiosity, the scorpion crawled back underneath the stone and he was left alone. Jake, totally fascinated by the creature, exclaimed enthusiastically, "Wow, that's the first time I ever saw a scorpion!"

Our hike brought us through unusual rock formations. It rarely rains on the plateau, but erosion has been caused by wind, shaping and molding the stone into pillars, arches, giant mushroom shapes, and cones. One group of rocks is called the Castillo de Disney for the numerous towers of stone resembling Sleeping Beauty's castle at Disney World.

Walking was difficult above 4,000 meters in altitude. Karina was not well, Ben had a headache, and I had a nosebleed and headache. It took a tremendous amount of energy to get back to the vehicles. Continuing our tour we stopped to look for arrowheads on a flat expanse of desert, and managed to find a few. Our guide said that the area must have been a battlefield of some sort. Every year more arrowheads come to the surface.

We rinsed the dust off at the river and ate our packed lunch. It is a small river by Canadian standards—a creek—but it is clear, cool and clean amidst the dry landscape. While playing with the water—refreshing my face and watching the flow of it cleanse my hands, the water felt, almost sensuous. There in the stark landscape of high altitude, I had a sense of true appreciation of water and a realization of how precious it really is.

Our final stop was a small canyon with 5,000-year-old cave paintings. By this time, Karina had a severe headache and couldn't walk easily. I was disappointed not to see the cave paintings, but my own headache was so bad that I stayed with Karina and Whitney while the others did the hike. I lay down on the back seat and it took every effort I had to get back up when Whitney needed my attention. Karina didn't move a muscle the entire time the others were gone.

The road we travelled home on was so rough that I hit my head on the roof of the van when driving over an unexpected bump. I was miserable by the time we arrived back in Arequipa. Sylvia wanted us to come in for tea, but I refused, explaining that I felt too ill. I needed to go home and get into bed. However, the others wanted to stay, so my needs were set aside; I am still resentful about that. Sylvia took charge, washing the kids' faces and hands, and sent me to the upstairs bathroom to get refreshed. Alone in the bathroom I lay on the floor. It felt as if I was never going to move again and in fact didn't until Ed came looking for me.

The kids ate in the kitchen separated from the adults in the formal dining room. I was so disoriented, it was like I watching myself and everyone else from outside my own body, above the dining table. I've only ever done that in a dream or with conscious visualization, and it was eerie to have it happen involuntarily. Altitude can be really hard on a body and I went to bed that evening in the most pain I have ever been in my life.

Domingo, another doctor who worked at the clinic, invited our family to go on an excursion with his and his sister's families on Sunday afternoon. We toted along eleven young people, all in the same age range. He brought us to La Maison del Funadore, the home of Don Garci Manuel de Carbajal. He was a Spanish lieutenant who founded the city of Arequipa on August 15th, 1540, calling it "La Villa Hermosa de Arequipa." The Mansion, a colonial house with the original furniture and paintings, is now a museum. The panoramic views from the balconies are just as impressive as the historical building. Dinner was "real" Arequipa food, as Domingo calls it. Stuffed hot peppers, beef heart shish kebob, roasted potatoes and deep-fried pastries that melt in your mouth. The two older girls came to our apartment with Domingo after dinner to play cards. Domingo played some classic tunes on Ben's new pan flute and gave us a few tips on how to play. It is mostly practice, like any other musical instrument.

We needed more things to do while Ed was working, so Tito arranged Spanish lessons for us at a language school. After the first two days we found out that Liz Beth, our teacher, lives just a few streets away from us, so she made arrangements to come to our apartment for the Spanish lessons. She brought her games and the younger kids joined in according to their attention spans—a familiar home-school setting that created less tension than sitting in the class at the language school. Liz Beth came every weekday morning except for one of our three weeks together. She is in her early twenties and the kids, in particular Dayna, loved being with her. When Liz Beth had previous engagements made and couldn't be with us, Dayna was so disappointed she cried.

Both Ed's and my parents, concerned about our welfare, made us well aware of the hostage-taking at the Japanese ambassador's residence in Lima this past December. It is April and although many people who attended the Christmas party were released early in the siege, many were held captive for close to four months. We have been tourists watching the landscapes and looking for comforts on a continent with a suffering past. It is how Che Guevara, in his recently published *The Motorcycle Diaries,* would describe our adventures and us. He was killed in Bolivia 30 years ago, yet his revolutionary ideals and methods still live with those who do not tolerate, what they believe to be, an unjust society. The morning after the military stormed the residence and freed the hostages, I had my first political conversation in South America with Liz Beth. She arrived with enthusiasm and asked if we had watched the news last night. When she remembered that we don't have a TV she described what she witnessed on the screen. In her words, "It was just like a *Rambo* film—the army stormed in there, gunned down all the captors and not one hostage was hurt." It was filmed in gruesome detail and aired on public television within hours of the rescue. The government made its point demonstrating it would not tolerate such actions by rebel forces. She was happy the siege was over but not happy about the lives she saw terminated. Most of them were young university students her age. I asked about her impression of the rebel forces within her country. She thoughtfully expressed that some kind of reform is necessary for the people of Peru but she doesn't like the way the rebels are going about doing it. Violence is not the answer as far as she is concerned, but she didn't have alternative suggestions either. She believes the rebel forces are severely weakened now and there probably won't be much more violence of this sort. One of the most prominent guerilla leaders was among those killed in the siege.

On Thursday of last week Liz Beth arrived in a taxi to take us to her house and meet her mom, who invited us in immediately and gave the kids a drink of juice and me a cup of coffee. As we chatted she said she was so happy to meet the family that Liz Beth has been talking about. She is a busy woman; the front part of their house is a convenience store that she runs. It appears to do well, as they are a prosperous Peruvian family. Liz Beth gave us a tour of their home. Off the dining and living area behind the store was the kitchen, from which we stepped out into the back yard garden with its eight-foot walls. Along the left side and above the kitchen were six bedrooms on two floors that all opened out onto the garden. At the back wall we climbed two flights of stairs to the rooftop. This served as the laundry area, as well as home to a menagerie of animals: dogs, birds, guinea pigs, chickens and turkeys. The dogs were for guarding and barking at people on the street below. The feces are hosed down the drain in the floor. The birds are kept for their songs. The turkeys, chickens and guinea pigs are raised for food and kept in cages. The kids asked why they had so many guinea pigs and Liz Beth explained that guinea pig is a delicious, traditional food and has been since Inca times. Tanya replied, "My friends wouldn't like the idea of eating guinea pigs. They keep them as pets." Liz Beth was surprised. We told her that in Canada guinea pigs are pets and we play with them. She turned up her nose and shuddered at the idea.

She brought us back to the table to work with pictures and vocabulary, but that only lasted until her mom brought us another snack of cookies and lemonade made from lemons off the tree in the back yard. Liz Beth's mom showed us the different plants in her garden and gave us a bag of lemons to take home. At noon we prepared to leave and purchased a few things from the store. Liz Beth, her mom and I were chatting at the counter while Jake and Whitney were at the freezer studying the ice-cream and Popsicle display, chattering and giggling with each other. Liz Beth watched, listened and started to giggle herself. She has not had much success getting Jake to say an English word, never mind a Spanish one, but he was standing there at the freezer teaching Whitney to say, "*Cuanto cuesta para uno*?" repeating it several times. "How much for one?" Liz Beth told him how good he was at speaking Spanish and gave him a Popsicle. It was a fun morning and we enjoyed our time with her.

As promised, Sylvia arranged for Ben and Tanya to go to school for a few days. Ben had a sleepover with Edouardo, Tito and Sylvia's 10-year-old son, and joined his class for the day. The school invited Ben back for a second day, so he stayed with Edouardo overnight again. The following week he was invited back for three more days. He was happy doing something other than being stuck with his family and enjoyed himself with the boys, but he didn't like the restrictions in the school. His favourite part was English class where he was the center of attention and became the teacher for a few days.

Tanya spent only one night and day at school with Sylvita, Tito and Sylvia's daughter, and didn't show the same kind of enthusiasm as Ben. The only thing we could get out of her was that she spent a lot of time talking with a girl who spoke perfect English, her mother is Peruvian and her father is American. Tanya has had no desire to return.

We go to the park most afternoons to play and be outside. On one of the earliest days, three young boys about Ben's age were curious to see my English writing (I write at the park while the kids play). These boys looked at my journal, carefully turning the pages, and we had some communication, which is what brought the kids together. After the interest changed they all played on the teeter-totters and soon didn't have any trouble communicating.

The park has a soccer field with stands for spectators, swings, teeter-totters, a self-propelled merry-go-round, monkey bars and a won-ton wall. Won-ton is a Peruvian game similar to racketball but played outside against a single wall. Everything is freshly painted, and there is crushed volcanic stone from the surrounding area under all the play structures.

The kids enjoy being at the park, but always want me there with them. I need to get out as much as they do so going has become a daily ritual. I am always the only adult at the park, except for the one day that Anna Maria, from whom we rent the apartment, and her daughter, Jania, joined us. With her bit of English and my little bit of Spanish we managed to have a good conversation. She was particularly interested in the major appliances we have in our houses in Canada. She is tired of doing housework and really wants a dishwasher and a clothes washer. Dishwashers are almost unheard of in Peru and the common method of washing clothes in this country is by hand. It takes a lot of her time given that she works outside the home. Clothes dryers are unnecessary—when clothes are hung on a line here, they dry in less time than it takes to go through a drying cycle at home. She seemed overworked and restless with her life.

Although it is important to the kids for me to be at the park with them, they really never pay much attention to me once they are playing with the other children. One day Whitney commanded, "I want you to push me on the swing for five hours! I really don't feel like pumping." But even that only lasted a few minutes; she was always right in there with the older kids.

Remembering our trip up to Sembey, the kids and I talked about the same kind of stone that is on the ground in the park, how it was formed, and where it comes from. One evening I took Whitney's shoes off while getting her ready for bed, and a collection of fine stones fell out. She said, "Oh, I have volcanoes in my shoes, that's why it hurts." She has such innocent ways of making me laugh.

There are two girls who come to the park to play during the afternoons but it is only because Tanya, Dayna and Karina are there. Their mothers let them spend time with us to learn English. Peruvian girls don't tend to be out playing during the week, but on Friday and Saturday nights many young people are out to play on the streets until almost midnight.

Jorge, 16 years old, took an interest in our family. Once he discovered we were at the park daily he was there every day as well. He said he likes kids, has four younger brothers and sisters, and wants to be a pediatric doctor. Erika, his sister, sometimes accompanied him. He came to visit with us and practice his English, bringing along his Spanish-English dictionary to help find words he needed to say. In Peru, everyone in school learns some English. One day Jorge brought his guitar and played for us. He is learning English rock songs like *Hotel California* and Beatles tunes from recordings, figuring them out by ear. But his best playing, as far as I am concerned, is traditional classic Spanish guitar. His father taught him and he has that skill fairly well mastered. Often, he'll let Ben and me use his racket and ball for won-ton.

One day last week while the kids were playing on the monkey bars, I gave up trying to explain some moves on the bars to them and just got up the nerve to demonstrate. I could almost do the routine I did as a kid, but found out my stomach muscles are shot. I had to have Tanya help me get my hands back onto bar after hanging by my knees. I used to be able to bring my elbows to my knees easily several times when hanging from a bar—I guess six pregnancies took care of that, but I still showed the kids a few things they couldn't do. Jorge was shocked and asked me how old I was.

We do our food shopping at the local market. On our first trip to that unfamiliar territory, Ed didn't see a policeman's directions and was stopped. The policeman yelled at him (yelling seems to mean authority) and sent another policeman to take us to the station to pay a fine. We drove only a few blocks with the policeman in the van when Ed had negotiated and handed over the equivalent of 50 dollars U.S., as opposed to the threat of having the our vehicle confiscated. (When Tito found out the police had done this he was furious.) The policeman got out and we returned to the market, where the four-lane paved street is lined with semi-permanent stalls overflowing with food and articles for sale: anything and everything is available. We purchased mostly food, but we also bought a few dishes to have enough for everyone in the apartment.

Market days for us have been Tuesdays and Saturdays, and I found myself returning to purchase what we needed, mostly from the same two women. I was careful with the amount of food I purchased this week and told them we were leaving on Sunday. They were disappointed and asked where the kids were; they wanted to say goodbye. I called the kids over and everyone got big hugs. The market is as Peruvian as anything could be, we never did see another foreigner there. We must have been a spectacle arriving with the big van and so many foreign children.

Ben's birthday came and went and he is now 11 years old. He didn't think we were doing much other than making a nice meal and was pleasantly surprised when there was a new watch as a gift and a delicious chiramoya cake. (Chiramoya is a juicy, sweet South American fruit.) It took a while, but he got out of his pouting and had a celebration.

One afternoon during Ed's lunch break we visited the Monasterio de Santa Catalina, a cloistered convent located in Arequipa. It was built in 1580 and enlarged in the 17th century. Over 20,000 square meters in size, the monastery covers an entire city block. There are about 20 nuns currently living in the northern corner of the complex, while the rest of the monastery is open to the public. The architecture is fascinating—so much form and colour, predominantly of the Mudejar style, and characterized by vividly painted walls. The nuns have totally secluded themselves from the world for prayer. Never interacting with the outside world somehow doesn't seem right to me, but then again, seclusion for a few days now and then could be revitalizing. Touring with a guide is a fast, easy way to maximize learning when the kids are inclined to last an hour or so, as they did at the convent. Even Jake and Whitney said they enjoyed the tour.

Tito recommended we do an arranged tour of Colca Canyon. Maximo and Lise, our driver and guide, respectively, picked us up in a stretch Ford Econoline after picking up two other people; we then picked up four British women at a hostel. Our first stop in the mountains was close to Piedras de Sembey to look at the rock formations caused by wind erosion, a repeat for us but still intriguing.

We had lunch in a village that is so much like Nepal I found it baffling: the people, the buildings, the weather, the landscape, the altitude, a young boy running and pushing a hoop with a stick—the exact same game I'd seen there. Opposite sides of the planet, yet the places are virtually the same.

It was the third of May and the festival of Cruz de la Piedra was taking place. One village was in the middle of grand festivities with dancing, feasting and drinking in the streets. Lise took us to a bullfight but the bull wasn't really into it and was led back to the corral, which relieved the kids. On to what is called the amphitheatre, a huge area of terraced farming in a circular valley, resembling bleachers in a stadium when viewed from above. The variations of green alone are a feast for the eyes.

While taking in the sights Whitney managed to touch a cactus and a needle broke off underneath her fingernail, halfway down and visible through the nail. It hurt but not nearly as much as having to cut the fingernail short enough to pull the piece out with a pair of tweezers. There was some good screaming through the process but it was sudden relief when removed. It has been wrapped with a bandage and *Swedish Bitters* for a few days and is now well healed.

We were late arriving in Termas. The sun had set and it was dark by the time we walked the kilometer to the hot springs. It was a challenge but the thought of the soothing water enticed us all. There was something so invigorating about floating on my back in a pool of natural hot spring water looking at a sky full of brilliant stars. At four kilometers of altitude the thinner atmosphere allowed a cleaner view of the velvety black sky. It shimmered with more stars than I have ever seen when observing at night. There wasn't even a moon to fade them out. Exceptional moments in time for me—how could life possibly get any better?

It was even darker by the time our group was ready to head to the *posada* in Chivay for the night. Unfortunately, one of the British women had an extremely difficult time in the altitude. She vomited and had to keep stopping, feeling faint. It made for a long, arduous hike. Maximo had walked ahead with Jake on his shoulders and had been at the van for almost a half hour when we arrived back.

Jake got up in my arms, hung on tight and cried in relief when we finally got there. He was afraid he had lost us.

The altitude made it difficult for the British women to eat dinner, but we didn't have any problem cleaning the fabulous fresh trout off our plates. With full tummies, the kids relaxed, and most of them headed for bed. Jake had fallen asleep at the table. Ed and I had tea with the ladies and they asked about how we coped with the altitude. Our symptoms weren't nearly as severe as theirs and we assumed that having been in Arequipa for a few weeks had helped us acclimatize. I have certainly felt more severe effects before at lower altitudes.

We spent the following morning overlooking the deepest part of the Colca Canyon at Cruz Del Condor to watch condors in flight. The magnificent birds have a wingspan of up to three meters, weigh up to 15 kilograms, live on the cliffs of the canyon, and ride the thermal drafts in the mornings searching for carrion. Young birds are mostly black, while the mature ones have white feathers on their upper wings and a small amount of white around their head. They soared above our heads, rarely flapping their wings. One came over the edge so close he surprised everyone, and we ducked to get out of his path. Both Lise and Maximo said there were more birds than usual that morning.

As we sat on the edge of the Colca River canyon, and a great view of Mount Mismi, we were taking in the expanse with a 1,200-meter drop before us, mountains rising above our heads for another 2,000 meters and condors flying about with extremely close views of their flight. The whole experience left us in awe, humbled, feeling miniscule, yet empowered with every breath.

Lise explained that a few years ago a Jacques Cousteau crew discovered that Mount Mismi, across the river from where we watched the condors, is a source of the Amazon River, making the Amazon, not the Nile, the longest river in the world. She also claimed that the canyon is the deepest in the world and the terracing in Colca Canyon is even more extensive than in the Sacred Valley of Cusco.

After lunch in Chivay we were given an opportunity to walk through the shops and stalls that display hand-made alpaca hats, gloves, socks and sweaters. For our journey back to Arequipa, Maximo brought out a bag of coca leaves and told us we should chew some. He and Lise both took a good pinch in three fingers and put it in their mouths. Lise said, "We always offer coca leaves, because on the road back we go up to 4,800 meters and you will feel very bad. Unless you live at that altitude you feel it, and not many people live at that altitude." Coca leaves have been used for coping with altitudes since the beginning of recorded time. During the Inca era, runners and messengers used them for stamina. Ed, the kids and I all took some because of our previous experience at 5,000 meters, but the British women refused. Lise said to chew and suck the juice out, but don't swallow the glob of chewed leaves. It tasted like strong black tea and it was hard not to swallow the little pieces that came off the clump in my mouth. The kids just ate the whole thing. In a short time my headache was gone, I could breathe easier, and I felt normal again.

We were in the tropics and it snowed on us. At the highest point on the road, Maximo stopped to have us make a pile of stones in memory of our visit. The kids broke icicles off rocks and quenched their thirst. Lise showed us the moss that people from the lower villages come to collect and burn. It is a brilliant green, extremely hard, and thrives on the rocks. It burns hot and bright, so little is needed, but it grows only at a high altitude, takes a long time to mature, and there are concerns about it becoming extinct. It left a strong bitter smell on our hands.

Jake couldn't see the rabbit-like animals that Lise kept pointing out, so Maximo stopped the van. These well-camouflaged little animals are plentiful and almost impossible to see until they move. Maximo had a soft spot in his heart for Jake. He got out of the van with him and walked toward one to make it move. Intrigued, Jake couldn't get over how much they looked like—as he described it—"a rock on the ground." Maximo reveled in Jake's delight while they walked toward a few more. The British ladies appeared impatient. None of them was doing well and they probably should have had some coca leaves. Lise taught us a couple of Peruvian folk songs on our drive back to Arequipa and we discussed what we learned. It was a great weekend despite the difficulties of altitude.

I had a couple of rolls of film processed at a lab. The travel books say not to do this because the quality can't always be trusted, but I don't want to wait until we get back to Canada—it may be two years or more. The light meter on the Canon Ftb camera has stopped working, even with a new battery, and I wanted to see how I was doing calculating exposure off the top of my head. Both the transparencies and the prints are as good as anything processed at home, so we had the rest of them done as well. Only a few frames are not usable because of exposure, but I failed to recognize that the AEI camera worked only when it felt like it. The mirror stayed flipped up and I thought it was probably just a "sticking" issue. But I now understand that it was waiting for the shutter to open. There are many unexposed frames from that camera. The most peculiar thing about this is that most of the photos that didn't turn out are of people, so I have just a few of the native folks I found so beautiful and barely any of the seashore photos for which I worked at hiding the garbage. That's probably why they didn't turn out. The people pictures were usually "stolen," and those of the seashore were deceiving to what really exists. I have since done some soul-searching about my relationship with photographs. I may take them for the wrong reasons, like staying attached to the past or wanting them to fill something that is missing. I decided I needed to change my attitude toward the process. So I used the AEI at Santa Catalina Convent and every photograph turned out perfectly. I don't know what I did! This past weekend while using the Ftb at Colca Canyon, the light meter decided it was going to work. I was dumbfounded. Why were they both not working and now both working again? This whole adventure has practically been on faith alone; who am I to question the process?

We have learned so much during our time here in Arequipa, and a lot of it has been about ourselves. The morning after our trip up to Sembey, I lay in bed recuperating, all sorts of negative thoughts flying through my head. It felt as if it was time for me to get out of this family and that the kids would be better off without me—felt as if much of the time nobody listened to what I said or considered what I needed, Ed included. Somehow our goals for us as a couple and family feel like they have become different. I wondered if he really needs or wants me around. I was so confused and am not going to continue in our relationship half-heartedly. I don't seem to be any support for any of them. Tanya, Ben and Jake have been so unhappy and sometimes I feel like I'm the one who causes the problems.

Just when I was giving in to the thought that they would be better off without me, Whitney got up and began wandering around aimlessly with a forlorn face. I found a smile from somewhere within and told her to come get into bed with me, at which point her whole face lit up, the desperate look washed away, and I realized my perceptions about them not needing me were wrong. We snuggled and the happy little being that she always is returned instantaneously; my place is with them. It may be hard, but it's no excuse to cop out on them. I was in tears. We lay there hugging, arms around each other; she was the one consoling the hurt child, and I decided that I had to do my best to make this journey a better experience for the entire family.

Later that week, we had one of our toughest days. Jake broke the door on the buffet in the apartment and I spent a couple of hours gluing it back together. While I was doing that, Whitney knocked the television that Tito lent to us off the table onto the floor and it stopped working. I can fix a lot of things but televisions are beyond my area of expertise. I was at my wit's end. Then later that day, coming home from the park, Karina wanted to unlock the door. She put the key into the hole but not far enough before she twisted to unlock it and the key broke in the keyhole. It took some time but I managed to get my fingernail under the end of the broken piece and pull it out. We are fortunate that Anna Maria was at home; she found us another key. It felt as if the world was challenging and working against me. What a day!

Ed and I finally had a discussion about what was going on. He was not happy about the television and it caused some family tension. Jake jumped up underneath my head when I was bent over him and hit the bridge of my nose and eyebrow. It hurt so much it brought me to tears and it released the dam that was holding them back.

I told Ed that keeping the kids busy with constructive things to do is the biggest problem for me. If I were the only one waiting for him it wouldn't be so difficult, but it isn't any kind of life for the kids. I told him that Jake was like a caged lion, he doesn't have any place to let out his aggression constructively. We have been in the van and hotel rooms with no place for him to run and we are always telling him to be quiet. Now we are in an apartment where we still have to have consideration for the other family and be quiet most of the time. I also told him that I don't feel as if I am functioning as the mother—no matter how little is asked of me, it seems like too much. A lot of sadness was released, but no ideas for a solution came.

Tanya and Ben have had a difficult time getting along on this journey. They are always angry at each other. One day they got into a fight over something before Ed arrived for lunch; it stopped while he was at home but picked up right where they left off when he returned to work. Ben had so much anger in his face and had a fist up to punch Tanya. I ran, caught his arm and told them both to sit in separate chairs to cool down. The pattern they carry through repeatedly has to change. It was time to do something to help them understand their emotions and I thought it might be helpful for them to write their feelings down on paper. Tanya wouldn't take part; she left Ben and me at the table. I wasn't going to let her get out of this one, so we went to the bedroom as well and the rest of the kids followed. I asked Ben what he was feeling, and he said anger. What was making him angry? Tanya—everything is unfair. I always take her side and I never listen to him. Tanya said nothing and started to cry. I asked her what she was feeling but she wouldn't say a word. After a long period of silence, what eventually came out was that when she was at school, she and the girl who spoke English were put in a corner of the room during English class because they spoke English better than the teacher—Tanya was left with another bad impression of herself because of school. She hasn't had many positive experiences. Hurt feelings over being put down came out once we got started. Tanya told Dayna the school story but wouldn't talk with Ed or me about it. Dayna filled in some details. Tanya had a big cry. I attempted to turn that school experience around for her, explaining that it was the teacher who was inadequate. She should have had the girls helping in the class but couldn't see beyond her own limitations. Tanya heard me but I'm not sure it made much difference.

It then came out that Ben thinks I pick on him. We talked about why I act the way I do when I see what I think is abusive behaviour and what I lived through while growing up with my brother and sister, Clark and Jane. Clark had many sad, angry feelings locked inside of him because of how he was treated at school and he took it out on Jane, who was younger and smaller. When people are beat on, sometimes the only thing that gives them some self-esteem is the ability to have power over someone else; it usually happens to someone smaller. It is a negative chain reaction repeated in this family that has to change. It is why I stop Ben and Jake from using the girls as an outlet for aggression. They can't be used as a punching bag, verbally or physically. The aggression has to go somewhere else and not be directed at people or animals. Ben says it has to be that way for Tanya too, and he is right. She, too, needs to learn to express her anger without slapping or kicking when her temper flies. We need to learn the true reasons for these not so good feelings that cause the aggression.

We talked about hurt feelings and unresolved feelings, and what it does to us inside if the feelings are buried and not dealt with. When people feel good about themselves and have a positive self-image, it becomes infectious, and they make others feel good. People we come into contact with respond to what we put out, whether it be negative or positive. We discussed what happens to people when they are continuously beat upon by others. I used my sister Jane as an example, how for many years she had difficulty being a happy person. She moved from one thing to another, never really finding a content place in her life. She is happier now but that has taken a lot of emotional healing, an ongoing process. We discussed how unresolved feelings affect people, often physical health—our bodies are more susceptible to what bombards us from the outside if mentally and emotionally we are unhealthy. Our society is full of broken marriages, people with the inability to keep a job or desire to be an asset to society, people with feelings of low self-worth, difficulty being happy, while so many of us are dependent on outside aids to try to fix what is wrong on the inside. Even pursuits and activities that don't work out the way we would like can be positive experiences if we have a sense of self-worth. Somewhere, we need to find some compassion and understanding for the people we live with and with whom we come into contact.

Tanya said nothing and lay with her face in the pillow. Ben said he was frustrated with not having anything to do; he likes the travelling but misses his friends. Dayna said missing friends is not a big deal for her and she spoke for Tanya again, who apparently misses her friends too. Karina said she just wished everyone would stop fighting. Everyone cried and hugged. We decided we would be more considerate of each other's feelings. Above all, we learned that we needed to talk more when angry feelings come up and there was a definite increase in awareness of the feelings of others. I made a conscious decision to listen more. I have a tendency to block a lot out because I believe in letting them work things out on their own. They can't do it by themselves all the time. They need help more often than I have been giving it.

Jake has been unhappy over the past few weeks as well, and his paintings have shown it. They are happier now but I realized something was wrong when he shoved a painting under my face and said, "Here" and walked away. I replied, "Wow Jake, I see a black boy playing in the grass and trees." I thought he had painted the darker skinned children that he has been playing with here. He said, "Yeah, it's me" in a mournful voice. I was shocked; something desperate was going on. I ran to him, picked him up, held and hugged him while he cried. Neither one of us said anything. He stayed for what felt like an hour after he stopped crying and I asked if he was okay when he moved off my lap. All that came back was, "Yeah, just bored." Over the following days he painted the whole package of paper. One painting had four black children in it. But his more recent paintings have changed to rainbows, flowers and trees.

On our latest visit to the Plaza de Armas, after I'd had a long night of lying awake wondering what is going on, I watched the kids feeding the pigeons out of their hands and absorbed the surroundings, somewhat in a daze. The Plaza is the heart of Arequipa and a happy place. People are always curious about us and ask where we are from, how long we are here for, etc., etc. I heard the soothing sound of water flowing in the fountain; the fronts of shops in the plaza are protected from the street by covered sidewalks, I saw the beauty in the organization of the repetitive pattern of white archways. I felt consistency, seeing the same old woman there, as always, selling packages of seed to feed the pigeons. Water flowing, pigeons cooing, kids in delight and the bustle of the city surrounding us gave me a sense of being in the right place. I will just have to have faith there is a reason and be thankful. I sat and enjoyed the sun, and my spirits are better. I don't understand why I am unhappy so often. Many people would love to do what we are doing. I know I don't want to go home defeated; I want to be successful at this.

Friday, May 9, 1997:

I am sitting in the sun watching the kids in the park, enjoying the warmth of the sunshine, thinking about my impressions. The mountains are incredible. Blue skies are constant. We have had sunshine every day, but this morning there were a few clouds. However, it didn't take long for the sun to clear them out, leaving Mount Misti with a fresh face. It snowed generously on her peak overnight. One cannot ignore the mountains here and, as Sylvia says, if you get disoriented in the city all you have to do is find Mount Misti and you can figure out where you are. To the east of that special landmark, the mountains make a silhouette of a sleeping Indian who, it is said, watches over the city. Interesting that the people of Arequipa perceive the mountains as both male and female. From what I understand there is a sacred respect for the range that protects the city from the high winds of the *altiplano*.

On our trip to the Colca Canyon, Lise described with remorse last years removal of the remains of the young woman who was sacrificed high on one of the peaks in the area, by people of the scientific community. The story claims that the girl, (she was between 12 and 14 years old) gave her life as a gift to Pacha Mama and the gods of the mountains so they would be good to her people; and could live in peace. Although we live in a more scientifically based society, the fact that the well-preserved body on the mountain peak was removed does not sit well with the majority of people in Arequipa. The underlying belief system still has some hold on the people of the area. Lise expressed her feelings, explaining that she wished they would have left her in peace. She called the scientists "grave robbers" who were no better than looters looking for gold in other parts of the country. It was a wrong move as far as she was concerned and she felt that the mountain must be compensated in some way in that the girl belonged to it.

It is almost winter in Arequipa and people here are finding it cold. I find it hard to know how to dress. During the day it is so warm that I feel I should be in shorts, but as soon as the sun starts to get a little lower, the temperature drops dramatically and I need warm sweaters. Everyone here dresses in pants, sweaters and coats, and kids are bundled up even during the warmth of day. The air is dry; Jake's mouth is a cracked mess and all of us have dry skin. If we just took a little more care in putting some moisturizing cream on it wouldn't be such a problem.

One day while I was trying to get Jake clean I was thinking about why he is always so dirty. For one thing, he is always in shorts. At home when he wore shorts, he would spend half the day playing in the water so the dirt was washed off. The fine dust off the stone in the park here sticks to the skin like glue. Although it's warm, nobody swims because there really isn't a place to do that. Showers—well there's another story. Almost everywhere we have been in South America the showers are cold, and when the water is warm it is usually electrically heated and there is barely enough volume to call it a shower (this is a desert—we are so spoiled in Canada). Jake can't get a good warm shower so he simply won't take one.

We wash the dishes in cold running water, wiping them with a cream soap on a sponge and then rinsing them. That's okay for most things, but as soon as there is something greasy it is difficult to remove the oily residue. I boil water for the dishpan but I have to plug the drain with a cloth because I have never seen a plug for a sink. I guess it's all in what we get used to. I still like my hands in warm water to help me stay warm.

As I write, I am facing the main street on the opposite end of the park from us. A man has just walked past leading 11 cows from the pasture where they spent the day. The newer main roads of the city have been built with three to four lanes in each direction and a big grassy median in between. Arequipa has many farmed areas among the developed areas, so that cows are regularly moved down the streets in the grassy areas, in this city of a million people. Major traffic moves on either side of them.

In fact, there must be as many animals in this city as there are people. In the mornings while waking I hear roosters, chickens, turkeys, dogs and birds, particularly macaws. And so many dogs—on rooftops mostly—although some run freely. Dogs live on rooftops to keep watch and bark, and I believe they are extremely jealous when another walks by freely, roof top dogs go mad. The dog from across the street took a liking to me and is often on my heels when I am outside. He followed us to the park one afternoon, and there was so much barking from the rooftops we could barely hear ourselves talking. This gave us a good impression of how many dogs there really are. It is rare to see an animal dead on the road, wild or domestic, in that, the people of Arequipa make sure their animals are well cared for.

Tito has arranged a tour of Machu Picchu for us. However, we have had some difficulty figuring it out after he presented the itinerary and cost. Ed considered not going at all, but I refused to leave Arequipa without going to Machu Picchu, explaining that if we didn't do it while we are this close it would never happen. I don't understand why it has to cost so much when the travel books say it could be done on a fraction of what we have been quoted. Ed talks about driving to Cusco but it is not something either of us looks forward to after experiencing some of the roads that lead there. I am sure we could fly to Cusco and do most of the touring on our own, and it would cost barely half as much as the price quoted to us. Tito and Sylvia have Ed convinced that taking the local train and going without having things pre-arranged is not a good idea—they obviously have no idea of how we have been living these past three months.

At any rate, Ed has now found a different company and they have arranged a whirlwind tour at a price he can live with. We fly to Cusco Sunday morning. I am excited to visit the place that has intrigued me since learning about the Incas in elementary school. Without Ed having to drive, it will be a holiday for him too.

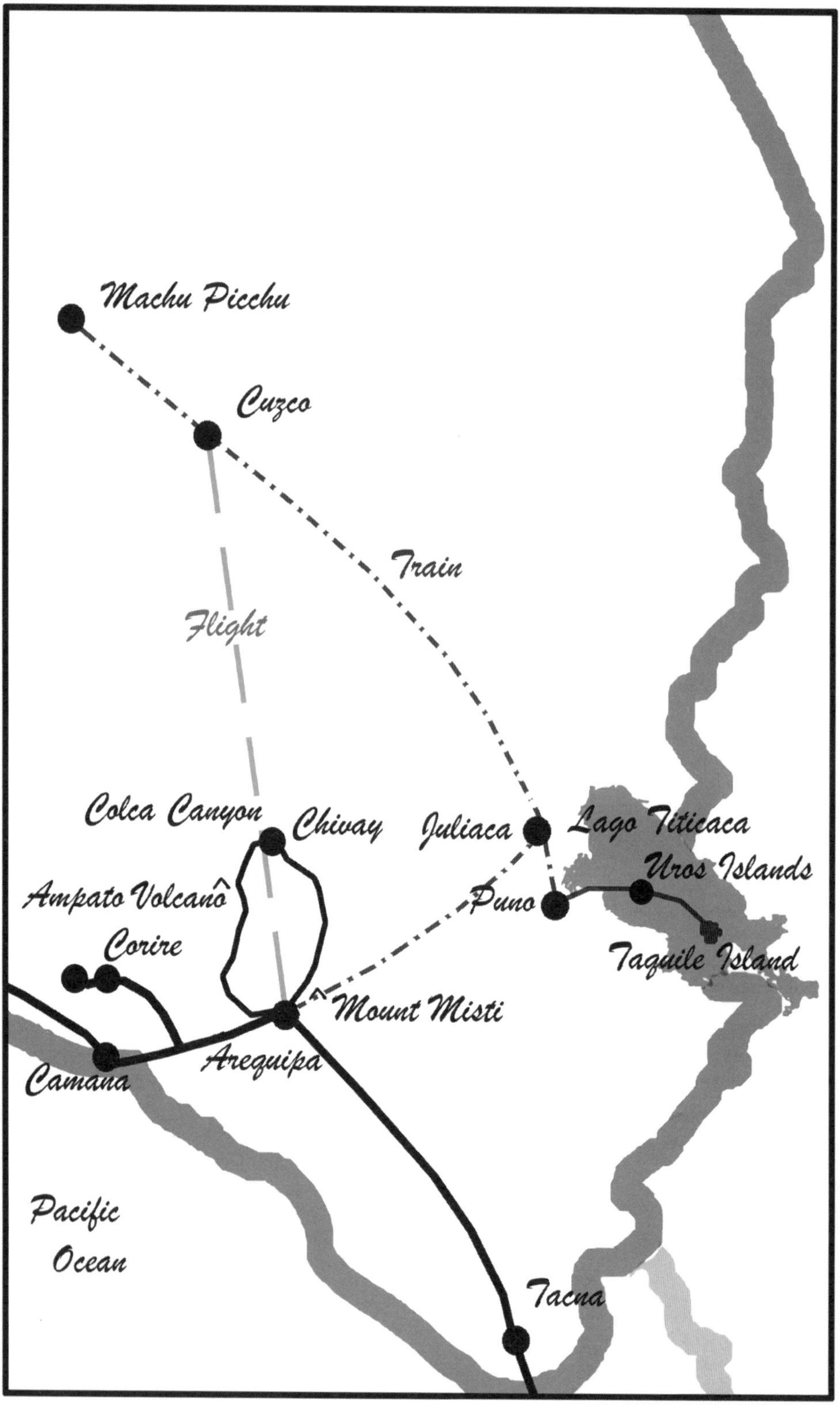

Machu Picchu

Cuzco

Train

Flight

Colca Canyon   Chivay   Juliaca   Lago Titicaca

Uros Islands

Ampato Volcano

Corire   Puno

Taquile Island

Mount Misti

Arequipa

Camana

Pacific
Ocean

Tacna

CUSCO, VALLE SACRADO and MACHU PICCHU

May 16, 1997: Cusco, Peru

A Mother's Day celebration full of pomp and circumstance with marching bands and parades filled the Plaza de Armas on our arrival in Cusco. Our hostel was located beside the huge square, where the celebration was taking place, and we found ourselves wanting to be amid the excitement. When eventually we went inside the hostel, we were promptly led to the dining room and given coca tea for the altitude. A grandmotherly woman served us and doted on the kids. She said it was delightful to have some children visit Cusco. She explained that it is tradition to have coca tea when you arrive because the city is at 3,300 meters and most visitors feel the effects of altitude; the tea helps alleviate the symptoms. After settling in to our space we spent the rest of the day walking, getting to know the city, and then made it an early night.

Our walking tour the following morning took us through another Santa Catalina Convent and Religious Art Museum, and two smaller cathedrals. We learned some history of the Inca-built walls that dominate the streets. The kids were intrigued with the famous "stone of 12 carved angles" and how the stones fit so snug that a piece of paper wouldn't slide into the space between them. The guide explained that when the Spanish conquered Cusco, the sacred buildings were torn down, except for the foundations. The tight-fitting, monolithic stones were impossible to move so the Spanish built their colonial buildings on top of the Inca foundations. It makes me wonder how the Inca people managed to build and place the massive stones together in the first place.

San Blas church made an impression on us as well. The finely detailed wood pulpit is totally hand-carved wood. And above it, sits the skull of the man who dedicated his life to creating the masterpiece.

The kids were happy that our afternoon tour was a bus ride, with visits to the 17th century cathedral, Santo Domingo-Coricancha, to Sacsayhuaman, Tambo Machay and Cusillyioc, all Inca archeological sites apart from the cathedral. We didn't have time to linger anywhere but all had interesting points to see. Again, the wood carving of the choir chairs and statues in the cathedral fascinated the kids. The most impressive stonework is at the Santo

Sacsayhuaman –Cusco, Peru

Domingo-Coricancha—Temple of the Sun. *Coricancha* in Quechua (the native language) means Golden Courtyard. Before the looting of the conquistadors, the courtyard held life-sized gold and silver likenesses of what was important to survival: llamas, babies, corn and a sun with inlaid jewels. However, the gold and silver was stripped out of the courtyard and melted down by the conquistadors immediately after they arrived, while the jeweled sun was removed by the Incas, and its fate unknown. When the Spanish first arrived, the Sun Temple was the site of ongoing daily ceremonies. It was also an observatory and a burial ground—mummified bodies of Inca kings have been found in the newer excavations. Current excavation also reveals some of the finest Inca stonework to be found from anywhere else.

The next stop was a site that had also fallen victim to the Spanish Conquistadors. The Incas envisioned and built Cusco in the shape of a *puma* (mountain lion). The ceremonial centre of Sacsayhuaman was created as the head and the saw-toothed wall simulated the puma's teeth. With the destruction of Inca sacred sites, Sacsayhuaman was used as a quarry to build the colonial city and homes of the Spanish conquistadors. Stones were removed from the site up until the 1930s before a government order stopped the practice; only about 20 percent of the original five-story structure remains. The largest stones are still in place—the tallest stands at 8.5 meters and weighs an estimated 361 tons. As monolithic as they are, all were carved to fit together perfectly. Ben was astonished by the size of the blocks and couldn't fathom how they were put together with just manpower. It does boggle the mind.

At Tambo Machay, known traditionally as the Inca Baths, spring water flows through underground channels to an opening in the Inca wall where water falls about five feet into a small pool. It gave the impression of an ancient locker room with showers and bathtub—still in excellent condition.

Our final stop was Cusillyioc—a ceremonial rock that stands on end where morning sunlight shines through an opening to light the cavern of the dwelling behind. By dinnertime we were on information overload.

Our following day tour of the Valle Sacrado—Sacred Valley—started with continental breakfast in the hotel. The kids have started to like *café con leche* and every day the same woman served us; she brought extra toast and jam that morning.

The first stop was Pisac Market where we had a close-up encounter with llamas. As a Mother's Day gift, Ed purchased a small painting of Cusco streets and a large, thick woolen blanket of extraordinary quality with a Chimu god on it. Ironically, while getting off the bus at the market, he had said, "We aren't going to buy anything right?"

The Inca ruin of Pisac was visible on the top of the mountain a long way before we arrived at the site. In the morning light, I couldn't help taking several photos even before our arrival. Jake and Whitney had fun, parking themselves in an Inca room and playing house while the rest of us listened to the guide. They had the whistle blown at them for climbing up onto a group of rocks when my attention was elsewhere. It was a great place for little people to climb and explore but it is understandable that it isn't allowed. Walking back to the bus through the grasses of the meadow on the lower trail, we were fascinated by numerous yellow butterflies. When we disturbed them they fluttered about our heads and then disappeared as we passed by. We are not made for tours—experiencing the butterflies was as important as the ruins but there wasn't enough time for such things.

We climbed through terraces and past classic Inca walls to the ceremonial centre atop Ollantaytambo, which provided a good overview. The Incas were a highly organized society and what they built is engineering mastery. Six monolithic stones carved of pink granite sit opposite the rising sun to reflect its warmth. A face carved in the mountain across the valley from the fortress sits at almost 4,000 meters in altitude on a sheer cliff. On the winter solstice (June), from a certain point in the structure we visited, the sun aligns with the eye at sunrise. The Princess Baths were engineered to create a whirlpool that separates the sediment before spilling over the spout. The spouts were designed so the water flow could be changed for different uses with just a touch of the water's surface. The most impressive accomplishment, though, was the fact that the stones used to build Ollantaytambo came from a quarry in the mountains on the other side of the valley. Each rock weighed several tons and was moved down the mountain, across the river and valley and up the mountain to become part of the temple and fortress. The Incas actually diverted the river course to move the rocks across the river bed then diverted it back, so as not to have to move them through water. The temple of Ollantaytambo was never completed and "weary stones" have been left where they were abandoned when construction stopped. Locals call these stones weary (*piedras cansadas*) because they believe the builders just got tired of constructing the temple, but archeologists date the construction to the arrival of the Spanish. Ollantaytambo was the fortress where Manco Inca—the Inca king at the time—held back the Spanish longer than they were held at any other Inca stronghold, even though the fortress was incomplete.

Our final stop was a church, but Whitney had had enough. She got into a snit and cried because I told her we would wait to have corn after our visit. We sat on the steps while she cried. Several children gathered around us wondering what was wrong. When I told them she was hungry, many of them started to imitate the sounds she was making—no sympathy. Whitney was curious enough about the children to stop making her miserable noise and then it became a staring match.

From our perch, the expansive vista overlooking the Sacred Valley was a sight to remember. The snow-capped peaks on the opposite side of the valley were a pastel pink in the setting sun and the Urubamba River was a ribbon of silver that stretched as far as we could see downriver to the west. The expanse of valley that lay below produced life sustaining crops for the Inca people, and it maintains its productivity today. The river irrigates the fields it flows through, making them the most fertile and productive in the mountainous region. The Sacred Valley— was "sacred" to the Incas because it provided the food that sustained the lives not only of the people from Cusco to Ollantaytambo but from long distances away as well. An interesting concept: land that produces food and livelihood is sacred. We certainly don't have that attitude in North America and it may get us into serious trouble in the future.

We each had a fat cob of corn to fill the gap after the others had completed their visit. We weren't fussy about corn in Ecuador, but it has now become one of our favourite foods. It was a quiet ride back to Cusco—Jake and Whitney fell asleep.

The following day as our train started to head for Machu Picchu, Dale, a man travelling alone and sitting in the seat across the aisle from us started to ask the kids questions. Not in school? On vacation? Enjoying themselves? Jake wanted to know why the train didn't just go; he said we weren't going to get anywhere when it just kept going backwards and forwards. Dale explained to him what was happening. The mountain is so steep the train can't just climb straight; it has to zig-zag, going a short distance, changing tracks, climbing a little more, back and forth up the mountain until it reaches the pass. He was entertained or amused by the kids and because he appeared to take an honest interest in them they liked him too.

It was a four-hour train trip. With time to think about our tours, Ed talked about how we could have done them ourselves in Cusco and it wouldn't have been difficult to organize the train trip to stay in Aguas Calientes overnight either. He said we would come back to spend a couple of days and have a longer visit. I looked forward to being on our own and learning about Machu Picchu at our own pace.

It was warm arriving in Aguas Caliente; and lovely amid the lush vegetation and by the rushing white water of the Urubamba River. Somehow, somewhere I hadn't noticed that the climate and vegetation had changed from arid cool desert to warm moist jungle.

Our bus climbed up the mountain on hairpin after hairpin turn. I was in awe of the sun spraying its morning light through the rugged mountains. I felt so good; I must belong among trees. We climbed for 20 minutes and arrived at the top, Machu Picchu lying before us. At the bottom, looking up, one would never know a city lies on the saddle of the mountaintop. Our guide gave us some background, both facts and theories. The people of the area knew there was an ancient city buried under the jungle and because of archeologist Hiram Bingham's questions and curiosity they brought him to the ruins. It was Yale University and the National Geographic Society that made it possible for him to explore the region.

From our vantage point we were shown that the lower part of the city was the industrial area, that the residential area was around the plaza, and the sacred buildings and temples were on the highest part of the mountain. Differences in stone structures marked the levels. The temples were built in classic Inca carved stone snugly fitted, while the residences and other stone buildings were put together more roughly. It is believed that the majority of the population was female of all ages. Of the hundred-odd human remains found within the tombs only five were male. Theories are that the city could have been a brothel for Inca kings, or a convent-like city. Whatever it was, the reason it is intact today and in such remarkable condition is because the city was abandoned and buried under jungle before the Spanish conquest. The Spaniards didn't know it existed and therefore didn't destroy it. The city is named Machu Picchu because it lies under the peak of the mountain of the same name. The mountain Huayna Picchu can be climbed to the peak, but one needs more time than the train tour allows.

Although we were on the top of a mountain we were at a lower altitude than we'd been at, making it much easier to breathe. At the caretaker's house, every one of the kids had to take pictures of the classic city photo. We found the "sacred stone" with many small stones around it. Another theory is that Machu Picchu could have been a place of pilgrimage because the stones found around the larger one have come from all over Peru. Jake and Whitney played in the quarry while we visited the "royal quarters" and the temple with "The Hitching Post of the Sun." The stone of which the shadow it created, was observed to track the sun, indicating seasons. It is carved such that on a certain day in March when the sun is at the zenith it casts no shadow what-so-ever—all four sides are bathed in sunlight. By the time we rejoined the group and boarded the bus back down the mountain, we still hadn't seen anything on the opposite side of the city. There was so much more to visit.

We met up with Dale again for the bus ride and he quickly started to ask the kids questions about what they learned. It didn't last—around the first hairpin curve a boy about twelve appeared at the side of the road, catching our attention with a sing-song voice, "Goooood Bye!" Dressed in Inca-period clothing, he waved his hand Inca fashion as we drove past him. After the next hairpin curve he was there again and did the same thing: "Goooood Bye!" The bus zigzagged carefully downward, while he ran straight down, meeting us at every stretch between hairpin turns. The kids expected him around each corner and along with Dale chimed in, "Goooood-Bye!" He was down that mountain as fast as the bus in his bare feet. He received a fine collection as the passengers stepped off.

Dale kept the kids entertained on our train trip back to Cusco and I asked him if he was for hire. Laughing, he said he thought our family was neat. He was impressed with the amount of history and geography the kids knew. They played "20 questions" geography. Even Jake surprised everyone with a few answers. It was 8:30 p.m. by the time we arrived back in Cusco with everyone worn out. Dale couldn't believe Jake hadn't slept the entire day.

It was difficult to move the kids out yesterday for yet another tour. We visited another church, the gate to the sacred valley, pre-Inca ruins, and saw clay roof tiles being made. The kids didn't have much enthusiasm left. All of them have been interested in visiting what is around them, but so much, so quickly, is hard to absorb. I know it is how people who have only a few days of visiting get the most out of their tour but I can't help thinking that it is almost like cramming for an exam. After it is over half of what was learned is gone.

We moved to a different hostel today. We were given one big room with seven beds. The unique thing about it is the two outside walls of the building are Inca-carved stone with trapezoid shelf-like indentations in the walls. It is a cold, mysterious atmosphere for sleeping.

This morning before breakfast Ed talked about not going back to Machu Picchu. He was figuring out how much things were going to cost and it appeared as though he had his mind made up even before consulting the rest of us. I confronted him with the fact that I had spent most of the day at Machu Picchu caring for Jake and Whitney, so they wouldn't disrupt the tour group that he had followed, and I didn't take time to absorb the surroundings. I was under the impression we would be coming back on our own and spending an entire day wandering the grounds. He told me to go back by myself and I guess I should, but it really is more fun doing things together. Ed has been adhering to a strict budget so we are able to spend as long as we can in South America. My logical mind says he is right about the finances, but what about what I was told and believed. I am terribly disappointed. Anyway, we bought train tickets to Puno for tomorrow.

May 17 to 22, 1997: Puno, Peru

On Saturday we were on the train to Puno at 8 a.m. It was a cold morning and when they served hot coca tea, we each took a cup. With the bumping of the train, Karina's spilled and burned her leg enough to make her uncomfortable for a while. After she changed out of her wet pants everyone settled into the trip. Jake made friends with Andre, a boy in the next seat, and they played together all day. It was a relief for both sets of parents. We had pencils and paper so they did drawings and played games. Tanya made origami animals for Andre and he just couldn't get enough of them. It created hours of imaginary games for the boys. At the end of the day Jake said, "I didn't even cry once today." A rare day indeed—he had fun, and noticed that it felt good.

While stopped in Juliaca for the connection to Arequipa, Ed made arrangements with an agent named Fernando for a hostel in Puno. Fernando met us at the station in Puno and led us to our accommodation. It was so cold all of us were shivering. Whitney had been wakened from her sleep on the train and was miserable. After the 12-hour trip I was tired too, lost my patience with her, and angrily told her to be quiet. She screamed at the top of her lungs. I covered her mouth with my hand, which of course just made it worse. I'm sure everyone at the hostel heard our arrival. She yelled, "I want Tanya" several times and would have nothing to do with me. Tanya took over and got her settled down. Ed was in the hall making arrangements for a tour to Isla Taquile in the morning. I tried to convince him that we had had enough, that it would be another early morning to get ready for, and we needed a break. However, he was told the Sunday market on the island was good, so the arrangements were made.

Our Isle Taquile experience took place on Dayna's ninth birthday and it was an experience. To start it off, Ed looked for his black bag but it was missing. He asked at the desk about it, thinking he might have left it there when organizing the tour, but it was nowhere to be found. He then left me with the kids and went to the train station to make inquiries. We needed to have the bags packed for storage and to have breakfast before leaving on the tour. I had a tough time getting the kids ready by myself. No one was enthusiastic and, with every obstacle I faced in our limited time I got angrier; I didn't want to go on another tour and was left with the preparations.

On our washroom trip before getting into the waiting tour group van I discovered I had started to menstruate after not having done so for the past three months. I have been in such an emotional upheaval even my moon cycle is messed up. The kids and several other tourists waited in the tour van for me while I found a clerk to let me back into the locked storage area for what I needed. I was consoled to know they wouldn't leave without me, they had the kids sitting in the van without parents and I'm sure they didn't want that responsibility. What a morning!

The van then picked Ed up at the train station; he didn't find the bag. Either we left it on the train or someone snatched it in the dark before we got off. Anyway, it is gone, and with it the *South American Handbook*, the *Lonely Planet* book on Peru, Ed's daily journal of Peru, the book with the daily expenses and mileage from the beginning of the trip, the information sheets on chiropractic that Ed had created in Spanish, maps, decks of cards, all the addresses of people at home, all the addresses of the contacts we have made in South America, post cards we picked out to keep and to send, our new pack of air mail paper—nothing of importance to anyone else, just valuable to us. I have something to be thankful for though—my journal wasn't in that bag as it usually was. I was writing when Ed packed it up and I stuck the book into my own pack when I finished. We still have one documented version of our journey and the addresses of a few people at home.

Lago Titicaca is the largest lake in South America. It is 170 kilometers long and lies at an altitude of 3,855 meters. Most people think that it is the highest navigable lake in the world, but there are others higher, because of its size, it is more famous.

It was a crisp morning and the sun was healing to my disposition of the moment. The water at the Puno docks was shallow, full of reeds out into the lake, and covered with

Lago Titicaca, Peru

algae, in all, pretty grungy looking. There were 24 of us on the boat tour. The guide held us prisoner with a long, drawn-out commentary. He repeated himself so many times that Karina asked why he kept saying the same thing over again. I was exhausted and didn't even care to listen. Just before arriving at Uros Islands he managed to grab our attention by performing a ritual of thanks to Pacha Mama and God, and then asked for a safe journey. The Quechua people use coca leaves like First Nations people of North America use tobacco in their rituals—as an offering to mother earth and the creator. All guides were given some to chew and some leaves were thrown into the lake for Pacha Mama.

The Uros Islands are called the floating islands, man-made from cut reeds laid atop the water amongst poles anchored into the lake bed beneath. Several small islands accommodate a community of about 300 people in reed houses built upon the floating islands. Some of us got wet feet in an area that needed more reeds— all these tourists must affect the rate of deterioration. Several of us watched a man build a reed fishing boat and when he needed it flipped, he had plenty of help.

During the two-hour trip to the island a man from Texas complimented us on how well the kids travel. He and his wife were in the same car on the train to Puno and had noticed the kids then. (Sometimes it doesn't feel like any of us travel well, so it was encouraging to hear.) He asked many questions about what we are doing and what the kids are doing for education. We are a puzzle to many.

At Tequile Island there was a long, steep climb up to the village for the lunch that was prepared for the tour group. I remembered reading in the *Lonely Planet* book, one reader counted over 500 steps. Most people find 500 steps a challenge even at sea level. Due to the thin air at this altitude, Whitney and I arrived at the top of the stairs last. Taquile Island is a quiet, peaceful place and the view of the sky, lake and mountains in the distance was invigorating. We enjoyed a delicious fish dinner and, as arranged, the tour boat left for Puno without us.

There wasn't a Sunday market, just two shops that sell all the same stuff at the same price every day of the week, with no bargaining. Ben liked the men's shirts but there weren't any in his size, so the two men in the shop said they would have one made for him by morning. Ed consented, and they took his body measurements. Everyone chose a beautiful wool ski-type hat. The fine wool is produced on the island and it is the men who knit the hats. We sat in the village square soaking up the sun and watching the children of the island play for much of the afternoon. Every child was dressed in red—it is believed that red protects children from evil spirits. We walked on the trails, discovering the island, and could see the mountains of Bolivia in the distance. Fernando told us that it was tradition to bring small gifts if we were staying overnight and that pencils and paper for the children were a good choice. But by the looks of it, that choice has been overdone; on our walk I picked up off the ground several discarded pencils and had almost as many to go back with as we had when we arrived. We will use them.

It cooled right down as we watched a rainstorm race toward us; we waited it out for two hours in the restaurant. When it slowed to a light rain, we ventured across the courtyard to our rooms. The only clothes we had were what we were wearing. Tanya got a wet shoe. I carried Whitney to keep her as dry as possible and didn't even look to see what Jake was doing. He walked with his sisters and wouldn't let Ed help him in the dark.

We had two rooms; one with two three-quarter-size beds, which smelled okay, had warm blankets, a dirt floor and a candle for light. The other room had four single beds, a wood floor and one solar-powered electric light, but it had a strong musty smell. I was disoriented again from the altitude and had another headache. I bumped my head twice during the day on low door lintels. I felt so discouraged, and now didn't even have a place to wash my hands.

We celebrated Dayna's birthday with the four small chocolate bars we carried to boost our energy when needed. We sang *Happy Birthday*, split the chocolate bars in two, and each had a half. That was it for the birthday celebration. It wasn't a regular birthday but Dayna enjoyed it. I sat on the bed in pain from the altitude, and so frustrated that I was on the verge of tears. I need to learn how to be as adaptable as the kids.

The kids needed to go to the bathroom but didn't want to. The toilet was a tin can—literally—outside behind a piece of plastic in total darkness. Necessity got the better of them—they became ingenious and went to the can as a group while Ed gave me a pep talk in the room. The kids were soon rolling in laughter outside. Ed said, "Listen to them, they are going to remember this day for the rest of their lives and they will laugh just as hard or harder about it 30 years from now." Dayna's

Children of Taquile Island

ninth birthday going to the toilet—one holds the candle, one the toilet paper and another, the plastic sheet that is the door so it doesn't blow in the face of the one sitting over the can. I started to laugh at them laughing; what Ed said was true—they will laugh for many years to come.

After each of us had a turn over the can, we played with the slush that started to fall off the tin roof from the rain that had turned to snow. At least our hands got washed off and I was thankful for that. After making sure the girls were settled snuggly, I bumped my head on the lintel again when leaving their room. Doors are barely five feet high in many of the dwellings and the altitude must have been playing with my senses. By the time I returned to the other room, the boys were settled and Jake was sleeping blissfully.

Just as I started to doze off, there was a knock on the door. Tanya was not well and felt like vomiting. We sat together outside in the cold until she finally did. She cleaned up, drank some water, and went back to bed. Ed was awake and asked how she was doing. I told him she was fine, but it felt as if my head was going to explode. For the second time, just as I was falling asleep, she was at the door. Again we sat outside until she vomited; she didn't drink water the second time. The cold air awakened my body and I couldn't sleep from listening to Ed's breathing. He didn't breathe for what seemed like more than a minute, gasped and breathed, and then repeated the scenario over and over again for as long as I was awake. When I couldn't bear how long he was going without breathing, I would give him a shake. He says the altitude doesn't affect him but according to what I have read, that is a symptom; he did the same thing the night we slept in Colca Canyon. When it started to rain hard again I found myself so thankful that the roof didn't leak.

We walked to the pre-Inca ruins the following morning and Whitney wanted to be carried. I had little strength in the altitude and made her walk. She yelled and screamed, wanting her way, and I let her do that because most of the time she just plays games with me. A couple of young girls were curious about the disturbance Whitney was creating and walked to the ruins with us. In their presence Whitney's tone changed and she walked the entire distance without another complaint. The girls hung around with us at the ruins and watched our crew out of curiosity. Ben asked if he could take their photograph and they gave him permission to do so.

It was a beautiful, sunny warm morning. The mountains of Bolivia were visible across the lake and the water was such a deep dark blue. Farm terraces created stair steps on the eastern slope of the island to the edge of the water. The brilliant green of new growth contrasted with the plots of deep, rusty red soil providing a true feast of colour for the eyes. It restored my enthusiasm.

We were at the boat docks by 1:30 p.m. and basked in the sunshine for almost an hour before realizing there wasn't a boat to take us and the other six people from a different tour back to Puno. The guide said a boat would be at the docks for us after lunchtime. Ed asked the captain of the one and only tour boat that visited to take us with them but they refused. He then asked a man from the island about how it was usually done. The man was surprised there hadn't been a boat to pick us up. Three men and one boy about Ben's age prepared a boat to bring the 14 of us back. They chose the last out of the 12 boats tied to the dock and had to move others out of the way to get to the one they wanted to use. It didn't move very fast and frequently needed to be bailed out from under the floor. The man doing the bailing was concerned. As we motored along, he looked at the sky to the east, the sun in the west and asked Ed what time it was. One young woman from France asked why he was so concerned. He didn't say anything but it wasn't hard to figure out: there were more storm clouds in the distance. It was after 3 p.m. when we left, a three-hour trip with a good boat, and the sun is down by 5:30 p.m. He played with the motor, which didn't sound good, and then took it out of gear while he worked on it, in the middle of the lake. Thankfully, the boat still floated. He put the motor into gear after revving it up and the boat travelled faster. He sat down content for the first time since we'd embarked, and the boy took over steering. It started to rain and Ben, to my surprise, offered the boy the jacket he wasn't wearing and the boy took it without hesitation and gave Ben a big smile of thanks; he was shivering. The rest of us were under the covered area but the station for the driver was at the back in the open. We offered him cookies too, which brought an even bigger smile. The last hour of the trip was in darkness. I don't know how, but our pilots did a fine job of landing us safely in Puno. Our hostel felt absolutely luxurious compared to the first night we stayed in Puno, the difference giving my perspective a serious jolt.

Our two days of Puno exploration turned into shopping days for alpaca jackets, sweaters, socks, hats and blankets, since there was such abundance on every street we visited. We put on our new pieces of clothing and took a whole roll of photos at the Plaza to send home. We must have been a spectacle—Ed heard one lady tell another, "Look, they are all wearing alpaca." Alpaca wool clothing is warm and comfortable for the climate; we appreciated it after feeling so cold.

Our overnight train to Arequipa was supposed to leave at 7:30 p.m. but we were informed of a problem with the track, and it didn't leave until 9:30. We then waited in Juliaca until we could get through to Arequipa. At Juliaca, when the rest of the passengers boarded the train, we were given blankets, the lights were turned off, and it felt as if we had been put to bed.

Our difficulty was that we only had six seats because of the full car. Since Whitney was on top of me and I was uncomfortable, I left her and Dayna to lie on the floor with the other bodies while there was still a little space left. Ed didn't like the idea of me on the floor, but I did manage to get some sleep. Our train didn't move until 5:30 a.m. and stopped a couple of hours later where an upside-down transport truck lay across the track. We were meeting the train from Arequipa at the blockage, trading passengers, and each train would return to the place it departed from. All passengers disembarked with their belongings when the train from Arequipa was due to arrive at the accident site. It was a frigid morning. Puddles were frozen solid and the tall grasses were frosty and stiff. Jake refused to put anything on over his t-shirt but we didn't get very far before the raw wind convinced him and he consented to some warm clothes. We do get some weird looks because of the way he chooses to dress, but I have learned not to argue with him. Sooner or later he will figure out that some of what I say makes sense. I am thankful we had the foresight to bring some food along; the trains didn't have food aboard and it was late afternoon by the time we arrived in Arequipa. The kids did really well. We may have had a long wait but we got to see the mountainous desert between Juliaca and Arequipa. It feels like we have arrived home.

Sunday, May 25, 1997: Arequipa, Peru

Tito and Sylvia have been extra good to us while we stayed here in Arequipa. Both of them were being adjusted when Liam came once a month but were glad to have more regular treatments with Ed. Ricardo, the chiropractor that was hired to work in the medical clinic with Tito, arrived this week. His parents are Puerto Rican, but he grew up in Ohio and studied chiropractic in the U.S. (Ed has kept in contact with Tito over the years. Ricardo married a woman from Arequipa and is still working in Tito's medical clinic.)

We had our last visit with Tito and Sylvia on Friday evening and it was just as much a birthday party for Dayna. She loved the hand-embroidered vest we found for her when we picked out Tito and Sylvia's thank-you gift. We hadn't been to that particular local artisan market before and we found the alpaca sweaters and clothing were less costly there than in Puno. There wasn't as much to choose from but it was still the same quality.

Ben spent the afternoon at the athletic club with Tito's boys, Roberto and Eduardo. He has enjoyed the social life he had with them and is not happy about moving on. I can understand how he feels—it is hard to establish relationships and then just leave them behind. Sometimes I wonder if what we are doing is fair to the kids. But then again, they are becoming more adaptable to whatever comes our way. Whitney, the poor kid, is dragged everywhere but is capable of sleeping anywhere when tired.

Yesterday, Ed returned the television to Tito—it had been in the repair shop—and took the van for a tune-up while the kids and I took care of the laundry. We had extra time before meeting up with Ed again, and Jake spent most of it doing the opposite of what I asked, generally on purpose to see how I would react. I don't know how to give these guys what they need these days. I took them to the park that we frequented during our first week in Arequipa to give them some space to run off the accumulated steam in their bodies. I laid a blanket out at the base of a tree to give myself a place to do the mending I was attempting to do earlier. Another mother and three children arrived shortly after, and the kids began to play together while their mother, Juanita, sat beside me. She spoke some English and between our little knowledge of the other's language we carried a conversation. Every South American person who asks about the kids is always concerned about their schooling. Most think the only place to get an education is in a classroom and when they find out that we do a little bookwork along the way, they think I am a teacher. So many people just can't conceive the idea that it is possible to gain knowledge and an education without sitting in a classroom. It is an unheard of concept to Juanita, a working mother who would like to spend more time with her children. After talking with her I had a glimpse of North American lifestyle seeping into Peru. She, her husband, and her family are living at a higher standard than most others of her country, but it is taking a toll on her happiness and what she feels is right for her family. I wonder where the true balance really is.

The mountains around Arequipa are so clear this morning; I won't forget how they dominate the city. We are an hour's drive away and the landmark of Mount Misti is still visible. There are snow peaks behind the first ridge of hills as we drive south. I guess we can expect these vistas for a long way yet.

Thursday, June 5, 1997: Tacna, Peru

Tunita had been to Arequipa each week Ed was there and when she learned of our plans to travel through Tacna she convinced him to stay for a while to treat her. She said she would set up a clinic for him to adjust others as well. We found Tunita's house easily but upon our arrival, couldn't find one of Whitney's sandals amongst the paraphernalia in the van, so she went barefoot. Tunita thought it was funny and nicknamed Whitney *zapatos*—shoes. Tunita's daughter, Maria, brought out a big bag of cookies and soft drinks for the kids. They devoured them while Ed and I spoke with Tunita. Upon leaving, the pockets of Jake's shorts bulged with cookies. I didn't know whether to laugh or scold him. Tunita laughed at him "just being a boy," and told him to keep them. (I'm sure she didn't want them back after they'd been in his pockets.)

With her help we found a place to stay, close to the Plaza, from where Ed could walk to work. We were in the central part of the city. Our place had two bedrooms, a large hallway with extra space and a decent bathroom. There were two beds in each room and we were given an extra cot. I made beds out of blankets on the floor for Jake and Dayna so everyone had a good space of their own to sleep. There wasn't much open on Sunday evening but we did find a place to have some dinner—white rice, chicken and soft drinks. "Back to this," I complained to myself.

Tunita arranged a radio interview for Ed on Monday morning and it worked; he adjusted 43 people that afternoon. Chiropractic is new to the majority of people in South America and Ed is surprised to get such an immediate, abundant response. Every day was the same for the nine days that he adjusted people in Tacna.

The rest of us spent the days mostly in the hotel room and meeting Ed for the mid-day meal at a restaurant. We had a television and the kids learned some Spanish, mostly because there wasn't any English programming available.

From our fifth floor window we could see sand dunes on the edge of the city. We went for a long walk in that direction, hoping to climb and explore, but discovered it to be a military zone where entry was strictly prohibited. I thought we might find something to do other than walking the streets for entertainment but it didn't happen.

By Thursday everyone was wild and I was getting to the point where I couldn't stand being with the kids. Jake drove me crazy and at one point I screamed at him to leave me alone. At another desperate point I yelled, "I'm going back to Canada and leaving you all here. I can't handle what is going on." I couldn't believe the words that came out of my mouth; I was as shocked as the kids were. All the emotional progress I made with them and myself in Arequipa took a giant step backwards. Since our visit to Machu Picchu, I have felt so angry. I went into the other room, shut the door and cried. After I cried myself out, I spotted the set of Wayne Dyer tapes on the desk. They beckoned me. I opened the cover, chose one of the eight tapes, and stuck it into the player. It began in the middle of the tape and the first words I heard were, "Do you ever notice how your kids seem to know how to push all the right buttons?" My ears perked up and my full attention was directed to what was being said. A few minutes later, Ben burst through the door wondering what was wrong with his mother. I was rolling on the floor in boisterous laughter over how Wayne Dyer described his relationship with one particular daughter and how she makes him look for new answers in himself. For me, it is my relationship with Jake. He always challenges, pushes and questions. He forces me to search for answers, learning more about my interaction with the world and myself than I would ever be aware of without my relationship with him. As Wayne Dyer says, they are here for a reason, for us to learn from each other, and we need to accept and enjoy the relationship. I have been given something new to think about again. I am not alone in what I am going through. I either learn to keep going with a healthy attitude or sink into the depths of despair and I really don't want to be there. I apologized to every one of my kids for my stinging words and we had a better afternoon than morning. There are so many things to be thankful for.

After our tough day Ben and Jake spent some time with Ed under Tunita's care, and that worked well for everyone—Tunita especially, who enjoyed the boys. She doesn't have grandchildren and looks forward to the day her daughters will provide them.

Tanya was bored and did three to five lessons of math each day just to fill the time. She found it so easy and I find it amazing how she has done no schoolwork for months, then sits down and flies through the book from where she left off. She completed almost a term of work in one week without assistance. Just living life has given her the knowledge she needed to do the math that was presented in the text. She has helped her father keep track of the daily budget, adding up what is spent and figuring out the average daily spending, as well as converting currency into Canadian dollars to relate value. It has kept her mind exercised.

Sylvia's friend Nora lives in Tacna. She and her husband Loe invited us to their beach house for Sunday. What a pleasant change for us as a family. We just need to live with nature to solve most of our problems. It was a cloudy, cool morning but the kids played on the beach and swam in the water anyway. Nora and Loe fed us a fabulous lunch of fresh fish and vegetables. During the afternoon we walked the beach, collected shells and sea urchins, and then the sun came out, turning everything hot and bright. We played soccer and all of us had a positive mood change. It was well after dark before we returned; everyone felt like staying.

Our visa for Peru expired today. We couldn't legally stay any longer. The people Ed has been adjusting wanted him to stay and it was difficult to say good-bye. This morning Tunita brought gifts for the children, our clothes from the laundromat (she took care of all our dirty clothes) and *empanadas* for breakfast. She got into the van and directed us to the highway that leads to Chile, and had a taxi follow us so she could get home. At the Pan-Am Highway we stopped. She hugged each of us with tears streaming down her face, and we left her standing beside the taxi waving good-bye.

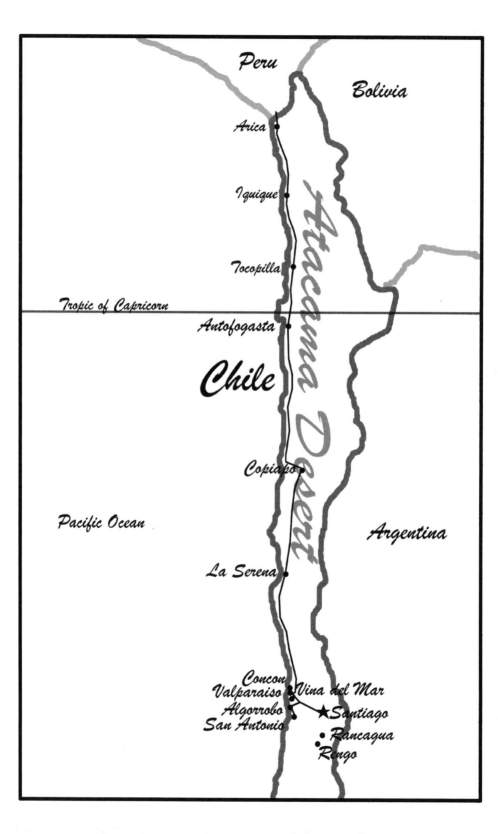

CHILE

June 8, 1997: The Atacama Desert

The Atacama Desert stretches south from the northern border of Chile for 1,000 kilometers, between the Pacific Ocean and Andes mountains, yet is barely 160 kilometers wide at its widest point. It is considered the driest desert in the world, with some areas having never recorded rainfall in 400 years. The Andes create a rain shadow, the altitude of the mountains averages between four and 6,000 meters. Any precipitation carried by the easterly trade winds falls on the east side. And the cold water of the Humboldt Current causes condensation over the Pacific Ocean leaving the western side of the Andes dry. Only when the ocean currents shift, bringing warmer water from the north to along the coast, does the desert receive rainfall, and that occurs more often in the southern part of the desert.

Our exit from Peru was fast and straightforward. We drove over a wide white line on the north side of which, in huge white letters, was painted the word PERU, the south side of which said CHILE. The kids, realizing that we had finally arrived in the country of our planned destination, cheered: "Hooray! We made it!" But it was a letdown when faced with the reality of the barren expanse of desert. The only thing standing out on the stark landscape was the grey strip of highway. At the isolated Chilean border check, which was several kilometers from the actual border absolutely everything had to be taken out of the van to pass through an X-ray monitor. The only other people at the border during our almost two-hour stop were border personnel. I am positive they kept us there just to have some company. They helped re-pack the van, asked about our journey, and on our map marked out interesting places to visit. They acted as information guides as much as border patrols. It was a long delay, but if we are treated like that everywhere in Chile, it will be exceptional.

The drive to Iquique was through desert without any vegetation at all, just the expanse of naked land. I wanted to take a little time to appreciate the intriguing landscapes. It is winter, so sunlight is low and shadows create depth on the landforms in shades of golden yellow against the clear, deep-blue sky. I suggested a stop to visit the Azapa Geoglyphs, but everyone else wanted to keep moving, so I didn't get my stop.

Our first night in Chile was spent at the first hotel we found in Iquique and it cost more than we have been accustomed to paying for accommodation. We visited the city the following morning only long enough to find a bank for some Chilean travel cash. While Ed did the banking, I watched the kids play at a children's park overlooking the ocean and beach. A feeling of comfort came over me: the new country felt different but comforting.

We chose to drive the lonely coastal highway to Antofagasta as opposed to the Pan-American Highway on the interior plain and stopped on a beach to stretch our legs and put our toes in the water. The air was warm, but the water was so cold it made my feet hurt. Combing for shells and stones, I flipped a rock over and a lizard ran out from underneath. It gave me a scare and I found I was wrong

about there not being a living thing on the desert. I wonder how even a lizard can survive in such an environment. What does he eat? There are so many things to learn.

Other vehicles and people were scarce until our arrival at the town of Tocopilla. We had a fabulous fish dinner, which even Whitney ate because I told her it was chicken. She has claimed she hates fish even though she ate it with enthusiasm until having heard Karina express her dislike for one particular kind. While eating she said, "This chicken is good but it tastes funny." When Ed told her it was fish, not chicken, she was thoroughly disgusted with us all for tricking her into eating fish. They didn't have anything else—the entire menu was fish and rice and her perception of not liking fish would have kept her hungry.

Tocopilla was originally established as a fishing village on a northwest facing cove. It was Bolivia's seaport before Chile took control of the area in the 1870s. What keeps the bustling little town going today is the fishing industry, the thermo-electric plant, and the saltpeter mines. It is also the terminal port for the nitrate railway.

A short distance north of Antofagasta, a sign indicated the Tropic of Capricorn as we travelled south out of the tropics.

We spent the late afternoon in Antofagasta looking for a hotel within our budget. It was a difficult task without our *South American Handbook;* we had depended on it more than we realized. Lacking patience with each other over where we were going to spend the night caused a trying evening but we settled on a hotel that provided two rooms with a community bathroom, at a price that didn't fit into our budget. We have to change our way of thinking here; this country costs more for everything. Gas is more money per litre than in Canada.

Our dark mood continued the following morning and we drove out of Antofagasta onto the Pan-American Highway, into the driest desert of the world, without food or water and having had nothing to eat for breakfast. It wasn't a very smart move on our part. Whitney continuously asked for food, knowing we had none, creating even more tension. She just needs to feel secure there is food and drink available at all times.

As we moved through copper mining country, south of La Negra, gigantic trucks used in the open-pit mines of the area were lined up along the highway. We were dumbfounded to see how huge they actually are. The wheels alone are close to ten feet in diameter—a man standing beside one wheel was just a little taller than the center of the hub. We have had a constant view of snow-peaked mountains on our left while heading south through the relentless desert.

After driving on excellent highway for two hours at speeds of 100 to 120 kilometers per hour we spotted a couple of tin-shacks. We actually saw the three transport trucks parked out front first. Ed zoomed past but took his foot off the gas after noticing the decrepit little sign saying *Restaurante* and turned around. Eggs fried in a layer of oil in individual pans (that were used as the serving dishes as well), white bread and *café con leche* filled the gap and it felt like abundance in the scant surroundings. I sat in the front seat for the afternoon, which doesn't happen often, but it does make a difference in how much nonsense from the kids Ed and I listen to. Sitting there allowed me to hear the motor running more distinctly and it didn't sound right—as if the muffler was starting to go, but the sound came from the motor. I mentioned it to Ed but it didn't concern him. The van was just tuned up in Arequipa and he was told it was in excellent shape for driving.

Further south, the river valleys had a little water in them and small strips of green from cultivation. Copiapó is an abundant fruit and vegetable-producing valley and grows several edible things I have never come across before. One in particular was a juicy fruit, but its flavor tasted like green beens. The Diaguita people cultivated the area intensely long before the Spanish arrived in the 1500s. Copiapó is a major fruit-exporting city, and thrives as well on the mining projects in the nearby mountains. We purchased some nourishing snack food of fruits and vegetables at one of the plentiful roadside stops and found a good motel at which to spend the night.

The desert continued south of Copiapó, where we started seeing shrubs and cacti which, as we travelled south, eventually filled the landscape. As we neared La Serena, clouds attempted to creep over and slide down the east side of the coastal range. The fog didn't have a chance as it was consumed by the dry air, creating an intriguing sight from the sunlit interior plain.

We arrived in La Serena on the coast under complete cloud cover. Our angels must be looking out for us; we found a comfortable *cabana* with a kitchen at a cost that wouldn't blow our budget. Jake said he wanted to stay forever. We found a market today and all of us appreciated eating our own prepared food this evening.

June 12, 1997: La Serena, Chile

We had a short break from the rain on Tuesday afternoon after an all-day rain on Monday. We watched movies, bought food and watched more movies. I have always said that people who watch television for hours on end are hiding from something they can't or won't face in their life. Every hour spent in front of the television is an hour taken away from time when kids should be playing creative games, reading a book, playing a musical instrument, doing activities outside, physical exercise or just plain playing. At home in Canada, television was reduced to some educational programming or selected movies we watched together on weekends only. We are managing the travelling, but something is really taking a toll on us, and television gave us an escape for a few hours.

It rained again almost all day Wednesday. The owner of the *cabanas* joked with Ed, blaming us for bringing the unsettled weather—it hasn't rained in La Serena since July 1992, five years ago. He doesn't like it at all. Imagine living every day under consistently sunny skies—a different way of life from ours in Canada.

While the kids were playing outside, a Canadian man asked Ben if we were really from Quebec. The license plate on the van parked next to where he lives in Chile piqued his curiosity. He is from Rouyn-Noranda, Quebec and has been working in the copper mines here for 10 months. He said there are many Canadians working in the area and living in La Serena. Down the beach there is a street that is almost all Canadian residents. He likes Chile, but barely speaks Spanish and was embarrassed to say so. He works in an English environment.

Jake has felt so comfortable over the last few days that he cried when he found out we were leaving. It has felt like we have had a home for a few days and it appears he needs that stability. It took longer than usual to pack; no one really wanted to move on.

Our day today was a mixture of rain and sunny periods. The desert is flooded with pools of water in the low-lying areas, while many streams have become raging rivers, overflowing their banks. The landscapes gave way to even more vegetation, much of it in bloom. The tall cacti have brilliant red flowers, and large areas of ground shrubbery are covered in small yellow blossoms. It is an El Niño year; a cycle that occurs about every four years that brings the rainfall that causes the blooming.

We drove through both Viña del Mar and Valparaiso along the ocean but found nowhere to stay the night. At the south end of Valparaiso, in a less affluent section of the city, we arrived at a dead end on the top of a hill, with no idea of where to go. Yet before us lay a sight to remember. The sun was a bright red ball falling below the horizon of the Pacific Ocean and from our perch we could see almost the entire city of Valparaiso starting to light up for the night. A bus and driver were waiting for something, or maybe he, too, was just enjoying the sunset. Ed asked him about accommodations. He explained that we would only find hotels in Valparaiso but he was certain there would be *cabanas* in Algarrobo about 50 kilometers down the coast with good, clean beaches. We wanted a place with cooking facilities so we kept moving.

By Casablanca the kids were complaining about being hungry and of course asking how much longer we were going to have to be in the van. It was a bustling little town for the time of night. We managed to find some *pan asado* and cheese to ward off the hunger. *Pan asado* is single-serving-sized, circular-shaped bread made of layered, salty dough, which splits in half or layers after it is baked. The fresh bread was absolutely scrumptious and stopped the hunger noises.

While driving the country road in the darkness toward Algarrobo, Ed made a comment about how much it looks like Canadian roads at home. The road continued through a residential area, down a steep hill lined with unlit buildings, and then ended. We sat in the van in the black of night with our headlights shining out into the wild waves of the Pacific Ocean, which appeared almost as if they wanted to eat somebody and were working hard at moving in on the town to do so. Ed asked, "Which way now?" Without any inclination of where we were, I answered, "Right." There were just a few apartments lit up in the tall buildings along the ocean, making it feel like a ghost town. We kept driving north along the ocean, finding more and more of the same—but no *cabanas*. Ed asked about *cabanas* at the one little *mercado* (convenience-like store) that had a light on. The woman told him to go to back to the end of the pavement but go right instead of left. She knew there was a place where the owners lived year-round. As we turned the corner, there was a sign, *"Castores Canadienses"* – Canadian Beavers. Ed said, "Well, I guess we're in the right place." We passed through the gate and down the lane called Beaver Street. Everything was dark. Only the main house was lit up and people were moving around inside. Immediately a woman came out to investigate our arrival and Ed made arrangements to stay the night in a two-bedroom *cabana*. While we moved ourselves in, the woman brought sheets and a pile of extra blankets. She spoke English with us. Her husband brought in a gas heater, set it up, and gave us operating instructions. The room has become comfortable and homey. We chatted long enough to find out that they had lived in Canada for 17 years and returned to Chile in 1989 when exiled Chileans were allowed to come back to their country of birth.

MIRASOL and ALGARROBO, CHILE

Friday, June 13, 1997: Mirasol – Algarrobo, Chile

It was such a sunny morning the kids were outside exploring their new surroundings when breakfast was barely over. Ed and I were enjoying a few moments of quiet when Tanya carried Whitney back screaming. She had run into the teeter-totter and cut her lip. After cleaning the cut, it was clearly visible the hole wouldn't stay together. She had to have a stitch. The woman we met last night took Whitney and me to the medical clinic in her car. Before arriving, she said she was going to tell the people in the clinic that we are her family from Canada, otherwise it would be very expensive. I replied, "Well, if you are going to do that, then I at least need to know your name." She is Christina, her husband is Aris, and they have a daughter Elizabeth, 10, and an older son, David, who is still in Canada.

We saw a doctor immediately and his first question was where Whitney's teeth were. (That was another accident. The chatterbox has accidents that involve her mouth. At 16 months old she fell in the bathtub and smashed her four upper front teeth, which were still missing.) Christina translated the doctor's assessment that the cut needed a stitch. He explained that he wouldn't do it, and suggested it would be better if it were done by a plastic surgeon. He recommended a doctor, whom his receptionist called to tell them we were coming. There was no charge for the consultation.

The clinic in Lleolleo (pronounced *jo-jayo*) was a fifty-minute drive south. What a tour of the coast! All the little towns have grown together, populating the entire coastline. It would have been difficult to find the Lleolleo clinic without Christina. She said that we would never find it on our own, and insisted on coming with us. She was more than likely right. There wasn't a direct road through any of the communities and no indication of which one to take to continue south.

Along the way, the unusual engine sound that hasn't seemed right to me for the last couple of weeks got loud enough for Ed to notice it as well, and for the first time he showed some concern about it.

At the clinic we were informed that the doctor wouldn't be in until 4 p.m. and it was just past noon. It was an unfortunate circumstance but we didn't want to waste Christina's entire day so drove back to the *cabanas*. The kids decided they would stay at the *cabanas* while Ed and I took Whitney back for her stitches. Another two-hour drive and a wait in the clinic did not appeal to them when they had a fabulous place to play. We purchased food for the weekend and Tanya said she would make a spaghetti supper for our return.

The doctor asked all the usual questions. Whitney was calm and didn't say a word during the visit. He said she would have a large white space on her lip if it weren't repaired. Putting two or three tiny stitches in would help it heal without leaving much of a mark. Usually the only way to put stitches in a child Whitney's age is to do it under general anesthesia but he thought it would be possible to do it with just a local. She was so "serene". (First impressions can be deceiving.) He was available to do them after his scheduled appointments, which meant another two-hour wait. We spoke with Whitney about the stitches and what to expect. She didn't like the idea and was apprehensive. Sometimes there is nothing like good old bribery to gain cooperation and I told her I would get her a treat after it was over—whatever she would like. Her eyes lit up—she decided to have something forbidden, and said she was going to have a Coke. Ed's eyes rolled. We've been buying soft drinks for the kids when there wasn't anything else, but never Coke. I just can't let them put something into their bodies that my father uses as a drain cleanser when the kitchen or bathroom sinks are plugged. Anyway, I told her she could have what she wanted, and that's what she chose.

Only one parent was allowed into the back room with Whitney so Ed stayed in the waiting area. I was supposed to change Whitney into the green clothes on the bed but she couldn't stand the idea of putting them on. She was to have slippers on as well, but the smock was all I could convince her into without creating anxiety. While waiting we discussed her treat and together we told the story of The Three Bears. It helped take her mind off where we were, and it worked until the nurse came in and put the big green slippers on her. That was it—she broke down, but the nurse scooped her up and carried her out of the room as Whitney yelled, "Mommy, Mommy!" maybe 20 times. I could hear the nurses talking to her in Spanish. She kept calling "Mommy" and when that didn't work, she tried "Daddy, Daddy!" several times at the top of her lungs. When that didn't get her anywhere either, she yelled repeatedly, "I want to put my clothes on and go home." "I want Mommy, where is Mommy? "I want to go home. DADDY! That tastes funny." Then a brief silence, followed by, "I'M GOING TO KILL YOU!" It was the loudest I have ever heard her yell. My initial reaction was shock, but also laughter and humour—not really funny, but it did make me laugh. She was obviously at a desperate and helpless point. I felt thankful the nurses and doctor don't speak English. There was no sound for several minutes until a normal voice broke the silence: "I can go home now?" The nurse brought her back, and she proudly showed off her new stitches, but turned sheepish and silent when I asked why she wanted to kill the nurse. She wouldn't answer, but I got a look that said, "Well, if you don't know you're pretty dumb." Anyway, we got her out of her funny slippers, into her own clothes and emerged from the incident. I had learned again that bribery doesn't work. When we met up with Ed he was talking with the doctor. The doctor then described the Whit as "valiant". Ed could hear her in the waiting area—valiant and loud. He did three stitches of fine work and pulled the slit together nicely. Whitney's eyes dropped as he shook our hands good-bye, appearing a little embarrassed by her previous behavior.

While driving back to the *cabanas,* feeling relieved that that incident was over and anxious about being away from the other kids for so long, a bang that sounded like a gunshot from the engine made all three of us jump off our seats. It was more than a simple muffler problem. At a main corner in San Antonio, just a block away from where it happened, Ed asked the policeman directing traffic if there was an open garage close by. We found ourselves continuing two more blocks to get the help we needed. The mechanics knew by the sound it wasn't the muffler and Ed did not feel good about how much it was going to cost, another $300 or more. Whitney and I walked to the bank machine while Ed stayed with the van. We were slowly working our way back when Ed came running down the street to meet us. The problem was repaired easily—the new spark plugs that had been replaced in Arequipa were not tightened properly and one had worked itself out of its socket. After being properly secured into place, the engine purred better than it had in a long time. I shudder to think of that having happened in the middle of the Atacama Desert—but it didn't.

It was 8 p.m. by the time we headed for the *cabana* again and we had told the kids we thought we would be back by 7 p.m. The table was set with the spaghetti supper waiting for us but the kids were nowhere around our cabana. We soon found them, worried, and at the main house talking with Aris. Christina had gone so far as to call the clinic in Lleolleo to inquire of our whereabouts. They were all relieved to have us back. It was a real Friday the 13th.

June 30, 1997:

I am on the beach this afternoon with all of the kids except Dayna. She is with Ed in Santiago looking for a house and clinic to rent. We brought a couple of blankets and packed a picnic lunch. It is not a swimming beach. People have disappeared in the under-current and never been found. Waves three meters high crash on the shore and there is only one swell at a time, not several rows of them behind each other. I could watch them for hours. When the wave rolling in meets the one retreating, there is a drastic increase in the height of the swell, but then, the wave loses momentum and doesn't roll up onto the beach as high as some of the smaller ones. Being with the elements feels so good and the kids are absorbed with playing in the sand.

We prepared to leave for Santiago on Sunday the 15th, but Aris and Christina convinced Ed to stay here until his work visa is in place and we have a house to go to in Santiago. Aris showed us a larger *cabana,* which was more comfortable for our family, and since it is his low season he gave it to us at a weekly rate. We are very comfortable and Ed is getting help with what we need to do to get started here in Chile.

That same afternoon we were invited to have a barbecue with Aris, Christina, their daughter Elizabeth, Christina's sister Maria and her husband Alberto, who live in Santiago. By the time the evening was over, Alberto decided he would sponsor Ed. When a foreign person wants to work in Chile, work visas are obtained faster and easier when they have a Chilean sponsor.

Securing the work visa, and temporary resident status, was a frustrating process. Ed first applied in Santiago, waiting two days before he saw an Immigration Officer, only to be told that because our address is Algarrobo, he was supposed to apply in Valparaiso and I had to be with him. The same thing happened again in Valparaiso, as Algarrobo is under San Antonio jurisdiction. After our second two-day wait, Ed explained to the woman at the visa office what he had been through and asked if she would at least go through the papers to make sure they were complete. She checked them over and after she found everything in order, she called the San Antonio office and made an appointment for us with an officer later that day. The immigration officer in San Antonio has a much lighter job; we were his only clients. Having lived in France for several years he spoke impeccable French and the process was more comprehensible for Ed, who is fairly proficient in Spanish now although, some things are still more easily understood in his first language. Ed will have a work visa and we will all have temporary resident status within eight weeks.

On Sunday afternoon last week I had enough energy to go for a walk with the family to the ocean and beach. Being there stimulated my senses after feeling as grey as the abundance of clouds in the sky. There was a crack in the clouds over the ocean where the sun streamed through, turning an area of water sparkling silver. I felt I was given the message: there is hope, there is light amidst the greyness and it will break through.

I have been physically ill for ten days since I last wrote, but I am capable of understanding now that it was just a reaction to what my emotions couldn't handle any longer. The morning Ed and Ben were preparing to leave for Santiago to start the work visa process, I felt feverish with aching muscles. I got up to use the bathroom and blacked out, ending up on the floor. It caught us all by surprise. Ed helped me back into bed and I stayed there until two that afternoon. Tanya and the kids managed their breakfast and lunch and made me tea as well. We were supposed to move into the big cabin that day but I just couldn't manage it. For several days I was terribly tired, my stomach burned and hurt so much after eating anything that it was just better to go without. I felt so angry at everything. My skin had a yellowish colour to it and Ed thought I probably had jaundice. After eight days of drinking only tea or hot water with a bit of lemon, I told Ed I needed to eat but just couldn't. On Thursday last week, while everyone was having dinner, I couldn't face the food and was going to bed to rest. As I was about to climb the stairs Ed asked if I wanted to get adjusted and to test to see if my problem was emotionally based.

Through his years of chiropractic experience he has learned that when a person has a condition that won't heal with care, alternative or medical, the problem has usually started with an emotional trauma. Until that trauma is recognized and taken care of—and that can only be done if the person is willing to face it—any outside therapy will not help something that needs to be healed from within. There is a technique Ed studied and learned to help find and release emotional problems that block the healing of physical ailments. He asked if I was ready to try it. It was time. I had not been well for months, and was taking its physical toll on my body and affecting our family.

Through muscle testing Ed found I was holding anger and resentment from three different times in my life: at four years old, 12 years old, and at Machu Picchu. The testing indicated broken promises for four years old and Machu Picchu, and disappointment for 12 years old. The anger at Ed for breaking his promise to me over Machu Picchu accumulated enough resentment that my body couldn't hold any more. The inner tension surfaced in gallbladder and liver problems, the organs associated with those feelings. Ed helped move the anger and disappointment out of my body with the necessary adjustments. I cried through the entire process and for a long time afterwards, but was able to sleep more peacefully than I had in weeks.

The following morning, before we went to the immigration office in Valparaiso, I managed to eat a little fruit for breakfast without adding to the burning sensation in my stomach. When we returned to the van headed for San Antonio, we found we had parked in front of a homeopathic pharmacy. Homeopathy hadn't even entered my mind to help with my condition, but since it was right before me, we went inside. The woman serving us asked what my symptoms were and gave me two remedies, one to reactivate the gallbladder and the other to relieve the discomfort. I took a couple of drops of both, my stomach felt normal immediately and I slept until we arrived in San Antonio. At the office, while talking to the Immigration Officer, the urge to vomit overwhelmed my senses and I just made it to the washroom. I didn't expect such a cleansing reaction so quickly; something was happening. I signed the papers that needed to be signed and left Ed to take care of everything else. I could barely leave the washroom. If I had known what was going to happen so immediately, I would have waited to take the remedies.

With a little of the right kind of help, it didn't take long for my body to move the toxins out. I had forgotten how effective homeopathy is when the remedy fits the ailment. After some rest I ate dinner. Ed's adjustments started the healing process and homeopathy sped it up. Now five days later, I am skinnier but certainly feeling normal again.

The kids have made good friends with Elizabeth and there is plenty of space for them to play here. Aris has made his *cabanas* an attractive, kid-friendly place for families to holiday. It has a pool, is within walking distance to the beach, and he keeps animals: three sheep, two dogs, several chickens, two ducks and a white goose. The kids have been feeding our compost and leftovers to the chickens, ducks and goose since we arrived and the birds have learned to expect it. We heard a knock on the door and expected a human visitor, but it was the goose tapping his beak, looking for handouts. He knew where we were and wouldn't leave until we gave him some toast. He has a funny character and is aggressive.

I didn't sleep much during the night that the tail end of the hurricane that did so much damage in Mexico and Central America hit us here in Chile. The rain on the roof was noisy and not a comforting sound like it often is to me. Many of the eucalyptus trees around us took a good beating from the wind and continuously scraped our *cabana*. Beside our *cabana*, one tree was bent right over, yet the roots remained intact. Broken trees and tree limbs were the only damage we were aware of in the area. The hurricane had lost its ferocity by the time it reached this far south, but still gave us a good storm.

Ed took us to Santiago to get our photos done for the visas and temporary resident applications. We had previously discussed the kids going to school just for the sake of learning Spanish while living in Santiago, so we visited the Waldorf School on the outskirts of the city. Ed spoke with a teacher and we were given a tour. The buildings are classrooms with outside doors, but no hallways. The grounds felt familiar and as Jake looked into the kindergarten classroom he exclaimed, "It's just like Lorraine's. Can we buy this place?" It had the same familiar feel to him that he was accustomed to at home. As we left, the teacher informed Ed of another Stiener Waldorf School in Providencia. She said she felt she needed to let us know there was a choice.

It is orange season. We stopped at an orchard on the way back and bought a 25-kilo bag. It didn't take long for the kids to make them disappear.

The kids have been great while I recuperated, Tanya in particular, who slipped into the primary caregiver's role so easily it is almost scary. She organized her siblings to take turns making meals and doing dishes. It is amazing what they are capable of when someone doesn't do it for them. Sometimes I think our North American society pampers our children too much. We don't give them the opportunity to be responsible people when they are young, yet expect them to do it automatically when they reach legal age.

We spent Saturday evening having another barbecue supper at the casino with Aris, Christina, Elizabeth, Alberto, Maria, their son Marcus, and his wife, who is another Christina, Christopher, their two-year-old son, and several other long-time friends of Aris. Christopher took to Jake and they became instant buddies. Aris had hot mulled, red wine with oranges for us to sip on after dinner, a Chilean winter beverage that warmed the evening. After all the play and a good dinner, the kids tired quickly. Ed stayed long after I had the kids in bed, and on his return he was full of stories.

Manuel, Aris' friend, is a quiet, content, well-read man. He enjoys the wine of his country and talking about his adventures. Both he and Aris were employed at the Palacio de la Moneda in 1973 at the time of the coup that ousted and killed the president, Salvador Allende. Manuel was a guard and had been present during the invasion. He survived the initial violence, changed into civilian clothing and escaped inconspicuously by just walking out of the confusion in the Palacio. Aris was off duty at the time of the coup. Everyone associated with the overthrown government was searched out and placed under arrest in the days that followed the storming of the Palacio de la Moneda. Manuel and Aris, as well as many other political refugees, found safety at the Mexican Embassy and eventually fled to Mexico. After Manuel learned how inadequate his military training had been for the kind of situation he found himself in, he promised he would never be caught so unprepared again. He and 12 other Chileans went to Cuba to train under Fidel Castro. Aris made a home in Canada. (Castro and Manuel became personal friends and on Castro's visit to Chile, he visited with Manuel.) Once training was complete, Manuel ranked as a General, and the Chilean troops moved to Nicaragua becoming citizens of the country, where Manuel's two sons were born. He led a family life yet with the unrest within the country, some of the Chileans became founding members of the Sandanistas. Manuel was one of the former leaders who caused the Americans some anxiety and in one standoff was even shot. When Pinochet pardoned exiled Chileans, allowing them to return without the threat of arrest, many did. Both Manuel and Aris's families returned. Manuel now lives a peaceful, simple life as a mechanic in the country he loves dearly. When Aris and Christina returned, they bought the piece of land the *cabanas* are on and have been building their business since. Manuel and Aris have remained close friends throughout the years. The people we meet!

Dayna liked the house in Providencia best and it is in a good location for easy access to public transportation. She said the bathrooms are really nice and the toilets have toilet seats (Dayna has always complained of the lack of toilet seats). The bedrooms have cupboards and drawers for clothes, something else she craves. (At four years old she gave me specific instructions, "I want my pants folded like this—so they will fit in my drawer like this—so it's not all messy".) She likes things in their place and likes to have a place to keep them. The house was acceptable; the things that are important to her are there. Ed says it is perfect for the clinic but he wants me to see it before he makes a commitment.

Wednesday, July 2, 1997:

I went with Ed to Santiago today. It is the first time we have left all the kids on their own for an entire day and they were just fine. Driving east toward Santiago the beauty of the countryside was astounding. The sun rose above the Andes and the pockets of foggy, low-lying areas glowed golden yellow in the new day's light. The clouds were lying on the ground and we had a clear view of the snow-peaked Andes east of the city. So many places on this earth produce exceptional moments, and this morning's drive provided one of them for me.

Alberto visited the house with us. My heart started to beat quickly, and I had a strong feeling of déjà vu. It felt as if I had been there before. The kitchen was small but it was better than everything else we had used in South America. The house was being painted and had newly renovated bathrooms. There is enough space for the clinic and good living space. It is also within walking distance of the Steiner Waldorf School.

At the agent's office where we made our offer to rent, Alberto told the agent we had three children. I didn't feel good about it, but something told me to keep my mouth shut. The agent said there were two other offers to rent and he explained what the owner expected, none of which sounded promising. I found myself getting tense so I sat back and shut my eyes and took a deep breath when I heard a voice say, "What are you getting so uptight for? This house will be yours, be patient." I sat through the rest of the meeting comfortably. We will be given an answer as to whether our offer is accepted by Monday of next week.

July 1997:

It is the end of July. The days have been long yet busy. I am getting better all the time and the whole family is getting better. My body mass is coming back. I got so thin when I wasn't eating that I could pull my jeans off without undoing them.

We got the house but not without haggling over it. The owner liked our offer because we didn't want to make changes to the place. He seems to want it rented but not used. We agreed to repair any damage we might cause and keep it in good condition. So we take possession the first week of August.

Christina, Marcus' wife, will be Ed's receptionist and has been busily promoting Ed and his services. Ed put information together about himself and Chiropractic, which she faxed to radio and television stations. She then made follow-up calls to be sure the information got to the person who could arrange an interview. Within the first two days, Ed was on a small Santiago radio station. The response was so good they wanted him back. During the second radio interview, a man listening to Ed while driving his car next to the station decided to go in and talk with him. He had wakened with a stiff neck that morning and could barely move his head. Ed adjusted him during the interview and it was a live testimonial. The skeptics shifted their opinion after the man had instant mobility and couldn't contain his excitement. It sounded fixed but wasn't. Ed couldn't have had anything more positive happen. He has done interviews at four radio stations, and after one of them a television station took notice and invited him to do an evening show that day. He was then noticed by Megavision and had an interview on *Domingo a Domingo*, a television program broadcast nationally and in some other parts of South America. The interview lasted barely five minutes which included the adjustments of two female models wearing miniskirts. The mistake they made was not announcing a telephone number where Ed was available. They regretted it—their own phone lines were so occupied all week with people trying to find out where his services were available they asked Ed to return the following Sunday. They even used his clip as a commercial to promote the upcoming show. During the entire second show, the phone number was displayed on the screen.

The TV and radio interviews have kept Christina's phone so busy she has had to take her phone off the hook to have a few minutes to eat a meal and doesn't have time to do anything else. There are over 500 patients booked, Ed is already busy for more than a month without a break, and the office isn't even set up yet. He is having an exciting time. It is what he has dreamed of, but he has had some panic too, not knowing how he's going to be able to help Christina with office procedures and to manage everything. Christina is a natural, though, and knows what to say and do almost instinctively. Ed came up with the idea of bringing Diane, his sister, to visit and to help familiarize Christina with proper procedures for the files and keeping financial records straight. Diane worked for Ed as office manager for many years in Canada until she semi-retired. She jumped at the opportunity to visit and is arriving tomorrow. Everyone is anxious to see her.

This past week Ed has been to Santiago every day and is now glad I insisted we should live there. He is tired of driving back and forth, as it takes a lot of time and is a long distance to commute daily. The coast is definitely nicer than the city but we need the city to support us. We can come here on weekends like everyone else does. That's what Aris has planned for us anyway. I would like that. I am going to miss the birds and quiet nights here.

I spoke with Dad and Mom early this month. Lee and Clif, my sister and her husband, are home from their trip to Germany. My sister Jane is having surgery on her back in August. She has been putting up with pain for four years and nothing has helped, so surgery is her last resort. She has lived with and taken care of Grandpa for a year now so he will be going into a home while she recuperates. He doesn't like the idea of being in a retirement home and is giving everyone a hard time about it. Dad and Mom are going to the east coast to visit with friends for two weeks. I told Mom I put my hand on a cactus by accident while walking down to the beach and she proceeded to tell me all the things I should do to take proper care of it and not get infection. It bothered me. Mom being Mom, it is her job, but it would do me a lot of good to know she has a little confidence in my abilities.

The kids have spent days playing outside, doing schoolwork and playing games with Elizabeth after her school day and we have spent several afternoons on the beach.

Tanya managed to complete her math program and asked, "Now what am I going to do?" I suggested she work through the grammar program but she turned up her nose. Ed explained to her that people who have an extensive vocabulary, write and do public speaking are the people who are most successful in life. Not much more was said but a week later she was working through the grammar workbook. More and more I'm finding that not pushing anything works best.

Mostly for something to do, she wrote out the story of Pegasus word for word from the tape. She asked how to spell a few words but generally they were the harder ones and all of a sudden her letter and sound reversals are not such an issue.

Ben hasn't done much in the way of "school work" but has spent so much time with adults speaking Spanish he is becoming fluent in his third language.

The kids are ingenious at occupying themselves and making up games. Not having toys creates space for the imagination. One morning there was so much laughter I had to find out what it was about. They each had a stick, formed two teams of three, and were playing a game of "get the shorts into the other's goal". The shorts were the pair Jake ripped and ruined on the barbed wire fence the previous day and the game lasted until the shorts totally fell apart.

Aris cleaned up the debris and fallen trees that the hurricane had left around the *cabanas* but left the one beside ours for the kids to play in. They have spent hours changing and remodeling it into a fort or house depending on their mood. Pieces of log made a table and chairs and of course they enjoyed tea and snacks in the little place they created.

Our *cabana* is beside the shelter for the sheep. They are let out in the morning and we don't usually see them again until dark. On Thursday the 17th they hung around all morning and were a terrible nuisance. The other sheep were bawling at the one named Sheena, wanting her to go to the field. She is the leader: where she goes the others follow, but that morning she stayed right beside the stall. She was in and out several times but didn't wander off. At noon Ed and the kids, except for Dayna, walked to the store to buy bread for sandwiches and while preparing lunch the thought came to me that maybe Sheena is going to have a baby. Just as this was in and out of my head Dayna ran in shouting, "Mommy, Mommy Sheena has a baby!" There was a reason she was hanging around. She is so thick with wool no one knew she was pregnant. The group of us watched the new lamb and mother. The lamb tried to nurse but couldn't find her mother's nipples amongst the matted wool and started to panic. With Aris and Christina gone for the day, Aris' maintenance man held Sheena down and I cut the excess wool away with a pair of scissors. Sheena didn't like the idea of us handling her and put up a good fight but "Little Dayna", as she was named, drank with enthusiasm afterwards.

The new lamb has made the last week and a half a little more exciting. The next day we were able to pet her. She has had no fear of us, is curious, and wants to sleep on the rug at our doorstep. It appears that she bonded with us, as well as with her mother, since we were all right there at her birth. She came into our *cabana* at every opportunity, much to her mother's despair. Twice Sheena came into our *cabana* looking for her baby, once when she wasn't even here. When the babe was snoozing on our doorstep and Sheena didn't want her there she b-a-a'd at her several times angrily, and when that didn't work Little Dayna was kicked and shoved so hard her mother knocked her off the step and shoved her around until she followed.

Little Dayna and Whitney have become buddies. I now really understand *Mary Had A Little Lamb*. Three days ago before the sheep were gone to the field for the day, Little Dayna came up to Whitney and gently butted her in the bum to more or less say, "Let's play." Whitney turned around, and jumped with both feet landing to the side to see if Little Dayna wanted to play the jumping game. Little Dayna copied her, lifting all four feet off the ground and to the side. Whitney would bounce and the lamb would bounce. They looked like a couple of "Tiggers" out of the *Winnie the Pooh* cartoons. The jumping jack game distracted the two little ones, taking them a good distance away from their mothers. Sheena and I watched our babies. I was in sheer laughter but Sheena seemed distraught. Hunger got the better of her; and she started to walk slowly toward the green field of grass. I got the impression she felt rejected and was giving up on her baby by the way she walked with her head down. Little Dayna was fully engrossed in the game and bounced alongside Whitney for several minutes, when all of a sudden she stopped, looking startled. She ran back and forth, searching for her mother but in her panic, couldn't see her. She let out a desperate cry of "Maaa". Sheena wasn't far. Her ears perked up and she called back as the lamb kept running from side to side calling "Maaa", wondering where she was. With each desperate call, Sheena called back calmly as if to say, "I'm here." She made herself visible to her lamb, and when Little Dayna finally spotted her, she ran as fast as her little legs would take her, gave her mother's abdomen a good bump and started to nurse. Whitney, disappointed at losing her playmate, sat beside me on the step and said, "I guess Dayna got scared being away from her Mom." "Yes, I think so, too, Whitney; babies don't like to be away from their Moms for very long."

During the past couple of days, Sheena hasn't had to go looking for her lamb. Little Dayna had enough of a scare and hasn't wandered away from her mother since. I found this change of behaviour in the lamb so dramatic after one seemingly little incident. Sheena, try as she might to make her lamb do as she expected, couldn't get the message across. Watching her give up and let her baby learn by consequences, confirmed my beliefs in the way the young of any species learn. When the lamb learned by what she brought onto herself, instead of what her mother was trying to force her into, she didn't have to be nudged, kicked or followed any longer. The lamb now makes sure she is beside her mother. I draw an interesting parallel to my own parenting here. It doesn't matter how often I try to get something through to the kids, it doesn't sink in unless they have a true interest or are motivated by specific related gain to learn what is being presented. Real reasons for learning. Pushing them in the direction I think they should go takes more time and causes more anxiety in both them and me than it is worth. It doesn't work; they learn what they need to for their own reasons, and sometimes it can be hard watching them deal with what they have brought onto themselves.

Sorting out confused feelings

My spirits have been up and down for several months. Some days I have felt very good, on others I have been at rock bottom, not knowing what is wrong. Being in such inner turmoil, then physically sick and in one of the deepest emotional lows I have ever experienced in my life, took its toll on the family. I had not been happy and the kids felt as if they were too demanding. Any little thing they asked overwhelmed me, and I didn't like being with Ed. Every time I was touched by anyone my skin crawled with angry feelings welling up from inside.

When physically sick and so tired it felt like I had given up on living, I spent whatever time I could in bed away from everyone. Everything seemed so senseless; I just wanted to disappear and the world to leave me alone. But it was the catalyst for turning my situation around. During the time spent in bed, alone and not asleep, my mind worked on how to change what was happening. I felt as if I needed to be away from every member of my family, which might be the only way I could come to terms with myself. I felt like a burden to Ed, another dependent like the children, and no more help to him than any of them. When going through how I would accomplish moving out of their lives and take care of myself financially, all I came up with were thoughts of recipes, stories and photos—were any of them really worth anything? If I put these together in a book it might be marketable but was not something that could be done quickly to reach an income that would support me. I needed to find something else. As my mind looked for alternatives, the idea of putting a book together kept coming back to me, and it wouldn't go away. I toyed with the idea of what it could be like—stories and photographs of our unusual journey. I had already written down several stories that were funny, described trying challenges, and what we learned from them. But I can't even write a paragraph without it causing agony, so how on earth would I ever put a book together? Plus, the only way it would be of any interest to anyone would be if we were truly successful, which wasn't about breaking up our family for selfish reasons.

I love them all, Ed and children. Why I wanted to leave was not because of them, it was because of discontentment in myself for letting the negative things I have experienced get in the way of letting me be peaceful and successful. Walking away from my family would be letting the dark side of life get between me and all that could be. All I had to do was take responsibility for my feelings, most of which come from a different time and place. I would have to accept that my success depended on learning from those experiences and using them to make every day better for myself and everyone around me.

After I sorted that part out in my head, Ed and I had a discussion about what I was feeling; he asked if I wanted to go home. I told him no. The way I feel about me has nothing to do with where we are. Being in South America isn't easy, but I arrived here for some reason and need to do whatever it is I am here to do and it is a good distance from all the things that created the darkness within me.

Leaving my family would only create more emotional damage in the people I love most dearly. It was not Ed causing my problems, nor was it my children; they just trigger something in me that I am discontent about. I can choose to continue to live in the same emotional rut I grew up in or make changes. The secret is: "now" is all I have and it will always be as good as I make it. That is my responsibility to me.

The interesting thing about this is that when I actually did take responsibility for my feelings and actions, it felt as if the universe was on my side again. Incidents like, Ed helping me discover the issues that needed to be addressed, and finding the homeopathic pharmacy by "accident" (is anything ever an accident?). I have now improved emotionally and physically and am again coming back to being a more functional, healthy human being again—I'm not fighting with the world and it is easier to live.

LIVING IN SANTIAGO, CHILE and SCHOOL

September 12, 1997:

It has been more than a month since I have last written. We haven't moved far but there have been many events.

Diane and her husband, Gilles, left on a teary departure. We sure enjoyed having them here with us. Diane helped us settle into both the clinic and house. She trained Christina in all new patient procedures, set-up, explained the filing system, and helped keep paperwork in order during the first weeks of confusion. It was a two-person job keeping everything straight given the volume of patients that came immediately. Christina mastered the task at hand quickly and took control of the office.

Diane helped me clean and paint the kitchen cabinets, by removing the ajoining door we turned the two small rooms used as food prep and eating areas into something more usable. This house is designed for an employee that is closed into a small workspace and not for the family lifestyle we are accustomed to.

Diane, the kids and I walked to the Steiner School to enroll the kids for the next four months and next year. The people at the school were going to discuss whether the kids would be accepted or not and call us back, as the classes are full. We didn't tour with Diane much until Gilles arrived, then it became a holiday for the two of them.

The van papers had to be renewed and the easiest way to do that was to leave the country overnight and return the following day. We ventured off to Argentina for the weekend. The closest route took us north from Santiago and east from Los Andes up La Cuesta de Caracoles, a series of twenty-nine hairpin turns that climb to an altitude of more than 3,000 meters on the moraine of Laguna del Inca. The lake is all that remains of the glacier, and the spectacular Tres Hermanas peaks lie behind it. This lake is unique in that the drainage is subterranean: groundwater flows in but there isn't a stream flowing out of it. We spotted six condors soaring and playing on the airstreams around the peaks. They never flap a wing.

At Portillo, the highway ran directly across a ski hill, but a long tunnel resembling a covered bridge had been constructed so that the road didn't intrude on the ski area. At Portillo, in 1987, the fastest-ever speed on skis was recorded at 217 kilometers per hour. Tanya and Ben were yearning to be out there.

We have driven through much of the Andes now and this road was impressive to us, but Diane and Gilles were stunned at how it was built. Gilles, being a warm-weather guy, didn't like the idea of encountering snow during August.

But crossing the continental divide and descending out of the mountains soon remedied that. In Uspallata the temperature was downright balmy. The drastic differences in landforms and temperature make it difficult to dress appropriately.

I actually drove the van one day when Ed was working so that Gilles could see the Pacific Ocean, Algarrobo and some of the coast. We bought *lagostinas* for dinner in San Antonio then came back to Santiago on the southern route. I have been nervous about driving in South America, vehicles are so aggressive, but Gilles made the comment that driving in Chile isn't any different from at home really. He was right, and I wondered what my problem was. This fear thing is something I am always working through. I did all right and driving shouldn't be the big deal I make it to be.

We took the *teleferico* up to Cerro San Cristobal. The statue of the Virgin Mary standing on the hill is visible from almost anywhere in the city and is an excellent lookout point to from which to gain an overall impression of Santiago. Gilles has a phobia about cable cars and the kids didn't make it any easier for him. The laugh of the week was about how he was such a wimp in the cable car.

When their departure time arrived, Diane wanted to know if we planned on coming back home. With the setting up of the house and clinic, we seemed so settled. We assured her we would but not for a year or two. Antonio and Maria drove them to the airport, but not before many hugs that were hard to let go of.

Peter and Amanda arrived three days after Diane and Gilles left. I liked Peter in Lima when we met him there. After graduating as a chiropractor, he wanted to work in Chile but didn't feel he could do it on his own. With the immediate response of so many patients Ed had, he called Peter, offering him a job. He and Amanda were on the bus shortly thereafter, leaving Lima, with their dog. They arrived Monday at 8:30 p.m. and Ed had patients booked for Peter the following day. They will live with us until other arrangements are made.

October 5, 1997:

The first day of school for Tanya, Ben, Dayna and Karina was meant for introduction. They were to be at the school at 10:30 in the morning and all were nervous. The children were outside playing at recess when we arrived, and Maria Eugenia, the principal, and one of the teachers, greeted us. The teacher asked which of the kids was in the third year and Dayna said, "That's me." He introduced himself as Angel (*ahng-hel*) and took Dayna by the hand when the bell rang, explaining that the class was going to do eurythmy. Ben went with his teacher, Bernardita, and Tanya with Carmen. Maria Eugenia took Karina and me to Karina's class. Everyone but Karina's teacher, Liliana, speaks English and Karina wasn't confident about going with her. I was not allowed to go into the class and she wouldn't be convinced to go alone. Liliana told me to not force her, to just bring her back in the morning. We waited for the others. They were to stay for only an hour but all were comfortable in the new surroundings and stayed for the next period as well.

Ben and I spoke with Alexandria, an English-speaking girl in his class, and then he gave me his sweater and went to play with the boys. While talking with Dayna about her class, Amelia, sister of Alexandria, dragged her mother toward

Dayna and me. Sheila is a Canadian from Vancouver and told me how excited her children were to have new kids in their classes. Frederico is in the *primero* year with Karina as well. We chatted a little but she had to leave to pick up a child in kindergarten. As she left I realized that life here is really much the same as at home. Sheila is an extremely busy woman, juggling the tasks of taking care of kids, being Mom the taxi-driver, a partner to a husband, and fitting in her freelance translation work amidst the activities of everything else.

Tanya was not enthusiastic after returning from her gym class. She said, "I did it all before." (That is not the purpose of a gym class.)

I tried to get the kids to bed early enough to be rested in the morning but it was an impossible task; they wanted to see their Dad. They were uneasy about returning to school. I assured Karina I would go with her in the morning. Whitney wanted to go, crying because she couldn't, and Tanya cried, wanting to stay home to work in the clinic with her Dad and Christina.

As it turned out the older three became absorbed in the playground of children from the moment we arrived at the gate. When the bell rang, I took Karina up to her class, where Liliana efficiently included Karina with the other children and closed me out. She did it so well Karina didn't even realize what had happened. A little while later, Liliana assured me Karina was fine. I don't know who this is harder on—them or me. During those minutes of waiting for word on Karina, the door to Dayna's class flung open and kids went running down the stairs with guitars, violins, cellos, drums, recorders, and chairs. I soon heard real music coming out of that class, and it sounded so good it almost brought me to tears. The kids have a wonderful opportunity to become part of it.

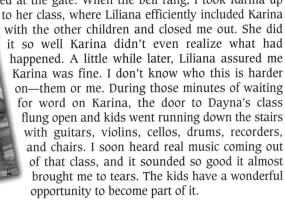
Karina –School Performance

As I waited for the older kids to finish their classes Sheila told me about the garden Dayna's class was building. It involved getting the entire group to the plot which couldn't always be done because they didn't have enough parents to drive. I offered the van to take kids and couldn't believe the words that jumped out of my mouth. I said it before I even thought about what was involved, realizing I had just sentenced myself to driving in Santiago. Everyone but Tanya was full of chatter about school on our walk home; she just didn't like it.

On Monday morning Tanya refused to get out of bed and get dressed. When Ed found out she had refused to go to school he said she was not allowed to do anything else either. She was to stay in her room. I told her what her father said. "Fine," she screamed, "I'll stay here forever."

As I was handing over the money to pay the school fees, it occurred to me that it was an awful lot to pay for the family turmoil it was causing. To say we had a trying second week is an understatement. Ed spoke with Tanya and explained that she is too young to work in the clinic legally during school hours. She agreed to go to school the next day, knowing she could be in the clinic afterwards. She and Christina have become friends and Tanya keeps the files in order for her. Bedtime has become a challenge. The kids need enough sleep to be up for school in the morning but they want to stay up to see their Dad, and we are not reading anymore.

Dayna came home with work to do that was different from what was assigned to the rest of the class and didn't like being centered out. We hadn't done cursive writing with her and she was given the task to learn. She cried, saying her work wasn't good enough, even though it was impeccable. Her perception was that the kids in her class were ahead and doing better, so she panicked, wanting to be able to do what they were doing. I explained she didn't know how to write in cursive—because instead of learning how in the past six months, she had been driving and visiting countries of the world. When she realized she probably knew more about some things than her classmates, she felt somewhat better, but still put pressure on herself to get to their level in the classroom.

I drove a van full of kids to the garden plot during the second week of school. I had thought I was going to pass on the driving but I did offer, and if I say I will do something I do it. Since the kids have been attending school, everything around us has been falling apart; we don't seem to have time for anything at home.

On the day I drove, Ed backed the van out of the driveway for me. That morning Tanya said she felt sick again as she had every day since school started. I told her I felt sick too, scared to drive, but we had to get over it and not let it stop us from doing what needed to be done. Ed helped plot the route to the school through the one-way streets on the city map. Ben was good support and kept an eye out for the street signs. At the school the van filled with loud, noisy, excited children grade three children and a group of five vehicles headed towards Sheila's new house, under construction, where a piece of ground was to be turned into a garden plot.

Part of the grade three curriculum is learning about plants and gardening and everyone had a shovel or hoe and started by clearing weeds and stones to work up the soil. Most of the kids—20 boys and10 girls—went at it enthusiastically keeping Angel busy. Whitney and I played with the bugs that stuck to our clothing. Sheila said they are called *pololos*—boyfriends, because they stick to you like a new boyfriend would. They are most abundant in October. She was once a journalist for CBC, does translating now, and would eventually like to get back into journalism but is busy with her children. I wondered if it is because she is Canadian that her life sounds like mine did in Canada, or is it really because no matter where we live it is the same kind of busy routine in our "civilized" society? She and her husband are building a beautiful home in the foothills.

As we worked the sun was warm and the air was clear. The mountains still had snow on their tops and were purple at the lower altitudes where there wasn't snow, which

Dayna with class & Angel building adobe shelter for the school's cow

created a pleasant contrast. I took in their majestic presence and found it invigorating.

Ed parked the van in the driveway. The gate leaves barely four inches of space for our wide vehicle. The challenge is stepping on the gas to get it over the ten-inch rise of the curb just when the mirrors are going through the gate, and it is even more of a challenge during the day when so many cars are parked tightly on the street around the driveway. Tanya refused to go to school again on Friday. She had a long face, acted angry with me, and wouldn't talk.

The second Saturday after the kids entered school, Ed had appointments to give adjustments in Algarrobo. It was an opportunity for us all to get out of the city and visit with Aris, Christina and Elizabeth.

We had lunch, and visited, then the kids and I went to the beach for the afternoon while Ed gave adjustments. We walked the trail through the fields. During this El Niño year, with the extra rainfall, we were told the spring flowers are more abundant than usual: bright orange poppies, lupines, chamomile, a cultivated watery plant with hot pink flowers, cala lilies gone wild, a type of narcissus tree blossoming, and so many that I don't know—the grasses were full of tiny flowers. A heady fragrance floated in the air. From the top of the cliff, the ocean was clear blue, dotted with white waves, and tame compared to what it was when we arrived.

We were lost in the elements of sun, sand, water and air; a hint of peace came and it felt good. The kids played while I lay on the sand and opened my heart to figure out what was going on. It is hard for Tanya; she is not as outgoing as I thought and is finding it difficult to adjust to the change. I would cry and be afraid too if I were put in a classroom in which no one spoke my language. New is hard enough, but the language too! I don't know how to make it easier for her. She has to work this out for herself. I feel torn up inside. I hurt for her and the others. Is it all worth it? I feel as if I should call it all off and then think I can't do that—I can't let her lose at this by just letting her quit. What is that teaching her? That it's okay to stop when it gets too tough? That's not right. I can't let her defeat herself before she even gets started. Karina surprised me. I thought it would be harder for her, but she has even gone to play at a friend's house for an hour one afternoon. The wind, sun, sand and sound of waves felt so good.

Ben tried to make a kite from his shirt and some stringy seaweed in the strong wind—it almost worked. It reminded me of a dream I had in July: I was flying a kite-like piece of clothing on a string. Ben ran up and pushed me; I lost hold of the kite string. "Ben," I said in a voice of disappointment. He laughed and thought it was funny; the kite flew off free. Ed just watched.

There he was doing in reality something similar in a dream I'd had recently. I started to laugh at what he was attempting to accomplish, (he always pushes physics) when Karina called out, telling us to look at the loose kite. It was making speedy headway, wildly flying away with the long string attached, and quickly disappearing out over the ocean. Coincidentally, Dayna had found a kite on the beach without a string or tail, but otherwise in perfect condition, and since Ben was trying so hard to get something to fly I suggested he retrieve yet another kite we saw stuck in the bushes on the side of the cliff to possibly put something together that could fly. The string of that kite was a tangled-up mess and the body of it was torn but the tail was in good shape. We stayed much longer than anticipated playing with kites.

All these kites making an appearance at the same time seemed too coincidental. As I cut off untangled chunks of string and tied them together to make another for flying, my mind drew comparisons. One with a string attached, broken free and flying wherever the wind takes it, kind of like us. Another without a string or tail and won't go anywhere unless it is fixed up to function the way it was intended, kind of like us. The third, broken but with the string attached, tangled up and stuck in the bushes; kind of like us. Ben used the tail from the torn kite, attached it to the good one and added string, piece by piece, from the one I untangled. It flew. We added length to the string, giving it more height in the wind. I came to the conclusion that all the mess we are in can be figured out. When Ben first gave me the string, I didn't think I would get even a short usable piece out of it, but little by little I managed to untangle the entire length and added it to the pieces of kite the kids found. Together, we made a good functional kite that was capable of flying high in the air and which we could keep under control. That could be done in our lives as well. Maybe I need to stop holding on and let them go through what they need to go through.

The third week of school was even more of a challenge. Whitney woke up each morning wanting to go to school, following me like a shadow, whimpering and afraid I was going to leave her behind. She cried to go and Tanya cried to stay home. On Monday, Tanya refused to go again. Ed spoke with her and she agreed to go on Tuesday, but Monday evening she stomped around, banged everything she touched and slammed doors just as Jake and Whitney were settled in their beds. Restraining my anger at her lack of consideration, I asked her to have a little respect for the others who are trying to sleep. We talked, but my anger at her being so unreasonable and not giving school a chance took over. I told her I was sick of the games she was playing with me. The kids told me she was happy whenever they saw her at school. She had her hands over her ears and I got louder, "You can't let fear get in the way of doing things; you won't do anything with your life. We are all afraid at times but we soon learn fear is only our imagination. The kids in your class have been asking for you. They want you there."

She kicked me and yelled, "Well, I don't want to be there!"

I lost it and, acting as if I were 13 too, slapped her back. Ed told me to leave and he spoke with her. "You gave me your word, Tanya. You can't go back on your word. It has to be worth something." I went to my room to cool off. One-way conversations are not communication.

She must have picked up on my uncertainty about sending her to school. Maybe it would be better for her to work in the clinic. She would still be getting language, math, and people skills, but in a real-life situation. She is very good at doing what the clinic demands, but then what about doing things with people her own age? Wouldn't she be missing out on a lot of fun? Does she really know what she wants? Is she old enough to make the right decision for herself? I feel guilty about sending them to school and I know I shouldn't. They are my children, my responsibility. Why do I feel as if putting them in school is running away from my responsibility? It's not so wrong—the majority of the world's children are handed over to other adults to be given instruction.

After I calmed down I apologized for slapping her and sat with her while she continued to cry. When she stopped sobbing, I gave her a kiss and hug, to which there was no response. As I left her I said, "Dad said you promised you would go to school in the morning. I hope you don't disappoint him. Try to get some sleep."

Tanya did go the following morning and came home with a note about skiing the following Monday. She was excited about the field trip and the week was better.

Wednesday was Dayna's garden day again. The sun was already strong at 8:45 a.m. and Jake, Whitney and I cleaned the worst of the garbage out of the van while waiting for the class. I moved the *libreta* and the crystal jumped off the dash onto the floor. I held it, shut my eyes and asked-asked-asked for the safety of all the little people I was driving around. I was not very focused or confident but stuffed the crystal into my pocket and drove. They were a noisy, rowdy group that morning but we arrived at the garden plot safely. I looked back at the mountains and made note of the receding snow line. The haziness obscured the crisp detail that was so visible the previous week. Jake, Whitney and I watched the kids prepare the soil with fertilizers. Some of the kids collected dry horse dung from other fields. Sheila asked if the three of us would like to walk to the field but Jake was content to stay with Dayna. Everyone, Whitney included, covered his or her hands with plastic bags and filled another with dung for the garden. When Whitney picked one up that was fresher than anticipated, it squished, surprising her. She jumped back, wondering what it was and made a comment about the smell. She figured out what to pick up after that and was proud of her contribution.

Upon our return, Jake had opened the last juice box and most of it was gone. Whitney took a drink, finishing it off. Jake was angry—he wanted it all after already consuming his own. I carried him to the van to get him away from the class while he took his fit. Sheila asked what was wrong and after I explained, a parent brought Jake another juice box. The squeaky wheel gets the grease, through yelling and screaming he got his way again, which really didn't teach him appropriate behavior. Jake has a way of getting around rules and discipline. I had a headache and didn't feel well. I just wanted to get home.

At the school, I parked in the dead end of the street, which was crowded with vehicles waiting to pick up children. The kids and I waited in the van for 15 minutes for an opportunity to get out of our boxed-in space, and when there was finally an opening, I slowly moved backwards. Ben watched while the intersection filled with cars again. I moved forward to let them through, backed up again, forward and back, slow and easy. Then I thought if I just went a little further I could be out. When I looked in my side mirrors there was clear space and I backed up more. I heard yelling and a crunch. Tanya yelled at me, "You hit a car!" I moved forward, jumped out of the van, and discovered I had smashed the driver's door of a very small car belonging to a woman from the school. The length of the car was barely the width of the van and I didn't see it. She got out, yelling at me in Spanish. I apologized over and over. Ben, my right-hand man at my right hand side, said, "Mom, Mom, what do you want to tell her?"

"Tell her I will pay to get it fixed."

The woman started to speak impeccable English. She was shaken up and I couldn't believe what had happened. After we both calmed down, we discussed the dilemma. As I was a parent of kids at the school, the woman didn't want to call the police, saying they make things too complicated. I told her I would pay for the damage, it was just a dented door. She decided to trust me, so I gave her my name, address and phone number and took hers. I was so wrapped up in how stupid I was for bumping into her car I didn't pay attention to anyone or anything. I got out of there safely, drove home, and even parked the van in the driveway. I had to hold some confidence for myself in driving. I told Ed what happened. He gave me an adjustment to help with the headache and by then it was so bad I felt like vomiting. Taking a cool shower I let my emotions go, angry with myself for being so stupid. I cried. Ed came in and said, "Gaye, it's not that bad." I yelled back, "Yes it is. I need to cry, let me do it, leave me alone!"

Bawling in the bottom of the shower with the water running over me I found myself saying, "Thank God it was a car door I wrecked and not a person." It was as if a light went on. That morning when I said my little prayer I asked for the protection and safety of the children. I gave no thanks when it is usually the first thing I do. All those children were delivered safely to where they were going, and back, and then I was given a reason to be thankful. A car door can be repaired, and it was definitely better that it happened to someone at the school than if it were a total stranger on the street. The police would have been involved. There is a positive side to this whole mess. With that little revelation in my mind, I had the strength to face people again.

I took a few minutes in the hammock outside to relax. I listened to the overall noisy hum of the city. So many people so close together interferes with my sanity. I do not like cities, and never really have—what am I doing here? Ed knew we should live in the country, but I insisted on the city so we could be together and part of the school but this is a quality-of-life question.

When Matta, whose car I'd hit, called, I asked how she and her son were doing and apologized again. They were both unharmed and fine. She called to say she would get an estimate on Monday. They were headed to the beach for the four-day weekend. I had the feeling while speaking with her that the main reason for the call was to check the phone number.

Pauline called from the kindergarten class that same afternoon asking me to bring Jake and Whitney to school Tuesday morning the following week. They were each to bring a pair of slippers and a piece of fruit to share for snack.

Amidst all the school turmoil, Ed told me that Antonio took the equivalent of two thousand dollars out of the business account. Being new in Chile, we are not allowed as yet to have a bank account of our own. All our banking is done through Antonio and he has access to our cash in the bank. When Ed confronted him with the fact that the matter was not even discussed, all he said was he needed money for his own business, there was some there, so he took it. Then Maria, who had started to help Christina, demanded Ed pay her more. Ed was not impressed and told her no, because she was already making a good Canadian wage for a position that, in Chile pays barely half what she was making. She was angry with him. There have been a few disagreements between Ed and these people over money.

Dad and Mom called to say hello a few days after the accident. Mom talked to the kids about school and asked how they were doing. I mustn't have sounded very good on the phone, as she asked what was wrong immediately. I told her it had been a rough three weeks and then asked her what the kids said about school. It was mostly positive. I told her about Tanya refusing to go and, by now, was almost prepared to say nobody goes to school. Mom said, "But Gaye, she has to try it."

"Yes, I know, Mom," I replied. "We made them promise to go until Christmas. I'm hoping they'll like it by then and want to go back in March, but Tanya would rather work in the clinic."

"How can you do that to her?" Mom asked. "She needs friends her own age. That was the best part of going to school when you were young."

"I am aware of that and I'm not doing that to her. She is not me. I can't live her life for her. Who is to say what was fun for me, is good for her? It's her life."

"But she still has to try it," Mom said.

I agreed. I told her we were planning a Patagonia camping trip in February and invited them to come along if they were planning to visit. She thought it sounded like a good opportunity and would look into flights. Dad got on the phone next. "What's this I hear about the kids not wanting to go to school? You tell them they just have to. They don't have any choice. They have been sitting around being lazy for too long. Gymnastics, swimming, skiing—they're enjoying their lives too much!"

I was choked for words and silent. Why does he say such things? Does he really think they sit around doing nothing all day, everyday? And what is so wrong with enjoying their life? When he has that attitude it still makes me want to do the exact opposite to what he is ordering, and I am supposed to be an adult. We didn't talk about school.

Dad is taking Mom to Grandpa's for a week but is not staying. He gets frustrated with Grandpa. Jane has not totally recovered from her disc surgery and can't take care of Grandpa alone. My brother, Clark, and Dad are going back to pick Mom up and bring the piano back. Grandpa told her to take it now—he wanted to be sure she got it. Life hasn't changed much at home—it continues with its usual ups and downs, little conflicts, competitions between brothers and sisters, parents and children, on both sides of my parents' families. Will we ever grow past all the garbage that holds us back from being fulfilled human beings and big, happy families? I'm glad I'm here now. I miss the seasonal rhythm of home but it is good to be away from the people for a while (not what I thought a while ago). I don't know why I let all those little turmoils affect my well being, but they do. I am going through enough unsettledness right now and it is just something else to weigh me down. I am here for a reason, possibly to gain a different perspective and obviously to be apart from what is going on at home for a while.

Tanya was excited about going skiing and had no trouble moving the morning of the ski trip; the trip was postponed because there weren't enough parents to drive and the students were promised they would be going on Friday. Tanya was not impressed but she did go to school every day the rest of the week.

Amanda and Tanya found an English second-hand bookstore that will exchange books, and they brought back some new reading material. This is a good thing. We did manage to get reading Laura Ingalls stories again. Dayna and Karina are enjoying them and it is hard to stop once settled in, but they need their sleep.

The day Whitney and Jake were to start attending school, Whitney was up, dressed and ready on her own. Jake wasn't raring to go but didn't complain, either. Pauline was at the door to greet us arriving at the kindergarten. The class is almost the same as the space Lorraine put together for our Tuesday and Thursday mornings at home. Jake whispered in my ear, "It's like Lorraine's." It was familiar and he felt good about that at least. The kids thought his gorilla slippers were funny, making him feel self-conscious—he just sat and observed most of the morning, hiding his slippers. I tried to explain when he chose them that big gorilla heads on the toes would not be suitable for school but he liked them and would not be convinced otherwise. He played only after he told me about his slippers and I told him not to wear them. Later, he took them home and no one saw them again, in the first hour he succumbed to peer pressure—he loved those gorilla slippers. Whitney sat on my knee most of the morning. The girls in the class were curious and they spent their time chattering to us in Spanish. Whitney played only while I sat close by.

The second day the kids felt more comfortable with the other children and I felt encouraged. I spoke with Carmen when picking up the older kids. She said Tanya seemed much happier, asked how the other kids were doing and then asked about me. She seemed sincere and concerned about how we were adjusting to life in Chile. My weeks of turmoil must have been showing—Pauline asked the same questions earlier the same day. The girls seem to be taking the whole experience in stride and Ben is more content than I have seen him in a long time. I am okay, all things considered.

The first week went well for Jake and Whitney but during the second week Jake lost what little enthusiasm he had. He didn't want to go despite being accepted to play with the other boys. Whitney wouldn't let me leave and was always checking that I didn't sneak out on her. On Thursday, while sitting in my corner of the room, Jake came up to me and said, "Mom, it is so noisy here I can't even think to play." My heart went out to him. He has always been an individual child who sometimes likes the company of other children, but needs lots of space of his own. Our home life has been falling apart since the kids started school. It has made me busier and had the opposite effect of what I wanted. Something didn't make sense. Jake and Whitney were regressing. Maybe that is normal progress, but at their age, to have me spending half my day in the noisy kindergarten for the next month didn't seem worthwhile, especially when from what I understand now we were doing just fine. We went home that day with no intention of returning. Eight days of school and dropping out. We don't have a very good track record.

The girls are not happy that Jake and Whitney don't have to go to school and say it's not fair. I told them they have to stay until the end of the school year at Christmas, like Tanya, then we will decide about next year.

October 30, 1997:

I must tell this little story:

Ed asked me to pay the hydro bill at the office in Los Leones. I put some cash in my pocket and went with specific directions on how to get there. I paid the bill and when leaving the office to head home, I spotted an English bookstore across the street. Curiosity got the better of me. I walked through part of the store and up a small set of stairs, turned to the right and over to a tall shelf. Immediately a book fell over and lay on its side: *Dreaming with the Wheel.* I flipped through it. I have been writing my dreams down for years but have never really done any specific studying on the subject. The book has contributing members and one of them is even from Quebec. The cost was 11,940 pesos. I had 12,000 in my pocket. I didn't think I should spend that much—$35.00 for a book that would be $15.00 in Canada. I put it back on the shelf, looked around and noticed that every book had the same inflated price. I didn't see anything I could justify spending that much on but was drawn back to *Dreaming with the Wheel*. It was meant for me. The subject is something I have been blindly working with for many years and all the circumstances that had to happen for me to get there just as it fell over was more "coincidence" than my spiritual mind would allow. I went home with 60 pesos in my pocket.

During mid-October while cleaning the windows on the doors between the living room and clinic I attempted to open them. They are sliding glass doors that roll into the wall. The track is rusty and the doors are always difficult to open. When one was partially opened I squeezed through the small space to push from the opposite side and as I did a vivid memory of a dream came back to me. While working at opening the doors, my mind started to race and remember. I went to my dream book to see if I had written down what my mind was retrieving. It was there, dated October 22, 1995: Ed brought me to a very fine house, well decorated, but not really my style. He asked me how I liked it a couple of times. He wanted to be sure that I was okay with the house. One room in particular had glass doors that were hard to open and too small to get through. I had a hard time putting the cat out. She had yellow spots on her then she turned all yellow. It took a long time to get through the doors when I was pursued by something. I don't know what I was running from, but it felt as if someone was chasing me.

I was a little dumbfounded when I read my notes on the dream. It really couldn't be clearer. Two years ago it told me about living in a house with glass doors. This house has fourteen of them and one set, in particular, is hard to open. When Ed brought me to this house, several times he asked if it was okay, if I liked it and if I thought we could live and work in it—like the dream. I have had vivid dreams all of my life, and in some of them that are still memorable, I was chased or pursued. Maybe I've been running from the fact that the spiritual world has been trying to tell me I should be using the information I'm given through my dreams. I have been avoiding it much of my life, mostly because of the fear of being seen as weird or ridiculous, and always in my childhood, when those dreams would stir up fear, I was told by my parents, "it was just a dream, it is nothing to be concerned about, go back to sleep." But it has never gone away.

Now as I am growing through the emotional repair that is helping me be a happier person, I've just had another dream that stands out in my mind and won't let go: There is a black family, with many children, in a dark blue van just like ours. They are driving backwards down the road. I am following, driving our van forward. The gravel road is rough, bumpy, and pocked with dried up mud holes that are difficult to avoid even when trying to go around. At the bottom of the hill, I am suddenly alone, walking barefoot in a clear, rocky-bottomed, fast-flowing stream, across which is an unfinished bridge not yet passable. There are salamanders around my feet. I have a clipboard and papers in my hands for writing.

Writing down my thoughts and feelings on the things that I am going through has been a way to heal myself. This dream has given me a little more insight into a bigger picture. I am driving the darkness out of my life, a rough and bumpy process that I cannot avoid. Water represents emotions and I am walking through them. I am getting well and my family is too. According to *Dreaming with the Wheel* the salamanders represent the part of us that desires the deep transformation of the fire element, life energy, and are a gift from the element of fire. All I know is that since July the fire in my spirit is coming back. Reflecting on the past few months, even that which felt wrong has had many positive aspects.

December 21, 1997:

By late October we had fallen into a good rhythm. Tanya settled in, not really happy but okay. The ski trip in the Andes was the start. She was one of just a few in her group who was a skilled skier and she helped teach the others who were on skis for the first time. She came home happier.

Ben –School Play

Ben settled in well. I believe he is the happiest I have ever seen him. Our relationship has improved. I guess emotionally I have stopped hanging on to him and trying to make him what I expect him to be. He seems to enjoy the interaction with many people and the freedom from me. He is responsible about whatever homework is assigned and makes sure it is done well.

Dayna has done relatively well but she kept asking how many more school days until Christmas. In her work she is a perfectionist; each page she wrote to catch up on her cursive writing had to be absolutely clean and perfect. When she made an error, it was as if she had let herself down. Angel gave her a workbook belonging to one of her classmates whose writing is flawless and if Dayna's work didn't look as good or better she cried. It just couldn't be anything less than perfect. Through the days she was in school I watched her put an awful lot of pressure on herself to meet those standards in everything she did. The problem was that she became troubled in trying so hard to live up to what she thought the expectations were and was no longer free to be who she really is. She was devastated when her beeswax crayons, which she kept so impeccable, were stolen. Angel picked out a set for her from the extras. At one time she had been a carefree, little person and I dislike seeing that disappear from her character. Does she really need that kind of pressure this early in her life?

Karina did alright—she didn't like the noise and chaos of the large class or being teased by the boy who sat behind her. She found it all tiring and would come home drained of energy. She did grow to love playing with the girls though; her friends made going to school worthwhile.

The one plus is that all the kids have learned some Spanish and I could not have given them that. If we'd been at home together we would have gone crazy without social contact, and they would not have the same level of language. I still feel that as long as we are living in the city of Santiago this school is the best place for them; and yet it is still a school with confining rules and a rigid curriculum without much choice for the child. On the other hand, there is so much music and art, and the teachers really know how to draw that sort of creativity out of the children. Plus, the place has a good atmosphere of a sort that only comes from harmony and cooperation among the people involved in organizing the environment.

I was not asked to drive again on Wednesday mornings and really didn't want to, but the kids didn't have enough parents to take them to the garden, and the activity didn't happen. During the second-last week of school Angel asked if I would drive the children to the country for the day. I had not driven the van since I crunched Matta's car door and I didn't feel confident about trying again. But I am the one who always talks about looking fear in the face and getting over it, so I couldn't refuse. We made arrangements for the morning.

The children piled into the van and Angel offered to drive and I let him, allowing my fear to take over. It was an easy out for me. The children spent the day building a shelter for the school's cow. The construction occupied them for the entire day. Angel had his hands full keeping everyone together and cooperating. It was a long day of measuring, sawing, hammering and weaving branches to hold the mud walls. Angel grew tired and I thought I should drive back; I could at least help out that much. I thought about the accident and how it was a lesson. I have been far more aware of giving thanks and was sure that nothing like that would ever happen again.

Five kilometers down the road, when the children were excited about something, I turned my head to look at what was causing the excitement and in doing so, somehow drove into the ditch. The kids screamed. I heard smashing glass and the van came to a stop. My mouth dropped open. "What happened?" I asked. It was as if I had blanked out. I didn't know what happened.

A post of the barbed-wire fence had caught the two windows of the passenger doors, smashing and ripping them right off leaving two open spaces with window glass all over the floor and ground. After taking note of each child and making sure they were okay we got out through the back and driver's side doors. A woman in a car drove up behind us and stopped to ask if we were okay with so many children. She let Angel use her cell phone to call the school and inform them that we were going to be late getting back. A tandem truck stopped and Angel made arrangements to have the van pulled out of the ditch within minutes. I swept the glass out of the van and, needless to say, Angel drove us back to the school.

Once the kids were safely returned, Angel apologized for the damage. I couldn't believe it. I told him not to worry about it. It was not his fault. It was my problem, not his or anyone else's. I was thankful the children were unharmed. The van can be repaired, but I don't think I'll ever live this down.

I drove home, and parked in the driveway again. Ed assessed the damage and I gave him the keys. I said "It is going to be a long time before I drive again." I lay in the bath and felt like drowning myself. Tears streamed down my face. I tried to find the purpose of it all by asking what positive thing could possibly come from this one? I was mad at God for letting me down, and then it dawned on me; I was being taught and re-taught some very important things.

*One — I was being humbled. It was arrogant to think and believe such things would not happen again and I was shown to not be so smug with myself.

*Two — Total present-time consciousness and giving total attention to my responsibility would prevent such accidents from happening.

*Three — The mind is powerful. Every person becomes what he or she thinks about. I manifested what my fears dwelled on.

*Four — I need to learn how to tell the difference between that inner voice that is there to help and the voice that paralyzes the life force from flowing.

I have a perfect driving record in Canada and here it is the total opposite. I better take my lessons more seriously.

Ed came in to talk. While he did not like what happened he is an understanding person, and told me not to be so hard on myself. How I deserve to live with this person I don't know. He is always there to support me when I need it the most. He was as thankful as I was that the only thing damaged was the van and my pride. I just wish I could be remembered at the school for something a little more positive.

Learning my lessons gave me the courage to go back to the school. It would have been very easy to just not show my face again. Before Tanya's class play the following evening, I met Ben's teacher, Bernardita, in the schoolyard. She said, "Gaye, you are a very famous person around here."

I replied, "I don't doubt it."

She said, "I'm not happy to hear you are leaving. I'm going to miss Ben in my class. He changed everyone in it and made it a better place to be. He's a special boy."

All I could say was "Wow!" I always question our methods of raising the kids and sometimes I think I'm totally messing everything up. But when I hear a simple comment like that, it helps me believe that maybe we are doing something right. I thanked her for accepting Ben in her class. I know he enjoyed being there.

Waiting for the play to begin, the huge palm tree beside the outside stage caught my attention. The wind was playing and the giant leaves were waving back and forth. I wondered if it was waving goodbye or if I should take it as a symbol of my constant uncertainty, swaying back and forth? The school had been a good place for the kids to be. There is so much offered that I couldn't possibly have provided for them. On the other hand, Ed and I are showing them the world, which, as Angel told us, is in keeping with Steiner philosophy. Just not in a conventional way.

The school decision was made easy by other things, in particular that we are decidedly moving out of the city. At least that is a positive step, and with what we save in tuition fees we can buy an awful lot of books and supplies to cover our needs.

The huge branches waved back and forth looking for their resting place. The wind slowed, and they settled, solid and strong. We have been wavering back and forth too, but it feels as if the wind in our lives is starting to settle a little, and our choices are becoming purposeful and clear. We will not be forgotten easily at the school, I made sure of that.

January 22, 1998:

The kids are happy about not going back to school and we spent a relaxed Christmas at Aris and Christina's, in "our" *cabana.* Having read Laura Ingalls stories again and learning about the Christmas celebrations of which Laura had such fond memories, we decided to use her family's traditions as ours this year. We set our breakfast table on Christmas Eve, and in the morning each of us had a couple of small gifts on our breakfast plate with a few pieces of candy. We had a wonderful breakfast and spent most of the day on the beach, then had a Christmas dinner of BBQ chicken, roasted potatoes, fresh green beans and salad. It was a wonderful family day together, not overly extravagant and so enjoyable. That is what Christmas is about for me, and the kids didn't suffer either.

I completed reading *Dreaming with the Wheel* then had this dream the day after Christmas:

I am a passenger in our van while we are driving down a major four-lane highway. There are bears along the road and we keep passing them. I say to Ed, "Look at them all. Where are they going? Why so many? What do they want to tell me?" Then I am walking on the side of the road to see them. There are chickens around my feet and one gets close. I don't like it and shove it away. The bears are gone.

As a young girl, I had a dream of a bear chasing me and awakened frightened. I went to my parents' bed but my mother put me back into my own, frustrated with how often I was in theirs, from being frightened by dreams. She left me in my bed but when I fell back to sleep the bear continued to chase me. However, this time it caught me and swallowed me whole. When I awoke out of that one, I had trouble going back to sleep, couldn't be where I felt safe, and resigned myself to the fact that I belonged to the bear now.

I get the impression that bears, both then and now have been telling me they have always been at my side, but I am afraid of walking that path with them. I am afraid of being the person I am supposed to be. *Dreaming with the Wheel* was written by Sun Bear, Wubun Wind and Shawnodese, all members of the Bear Tribe. Now they are after me in my reading and waking life, too. I am beginning to believe I have much to learn about what bears mean to me.

Throughout the month of December, Ed and Peter planned how to fire our sponsor family from their connection with the two clinics. Our sponsors seemed to think they should have control of the business, finances, and financial rewards. Ed arranged new legal sponsorship through our accountant Guillermo Martinez. He became a sincere family friend and since setting up the clinic, Guillermo became the most reliable resource helping us through Chilean legalities. Another sincere family friend, Luis, a medical doctor and he was the person who convinced Ed to find a new sponsor. Luis and his wife have been getting regular chiropractic care since September. He is also helping Ed set up another clinic in Rancagua; where they plan to have it operating in March after our Patagonia tour. Peter managed to get most of the patient files out of the downtown office without suspicion. He and Ed have rented a new space for the central clinic and, together, told Antonio and Maria they were fired.

As expected they told Ed he couldn't do that and were extremely angry when they were told there wasn't any choice for them, it was already done. From the looks of it Ed was not going to get back any of the money that was "borrowed", so he told them to keep it. The whole thing left some bitter feelings on both sides, but if the relationship had been one of integrity from the beginning, there wouldn't have been any need for confrontation. The situation made the children feel uneasy. We no longer have anything to do with Antonio and Maria and our relationship with Aris and Christina has become somewhat strained. They are related to each other, this is the worst of the situation.

After it was all settled, Ed and Peter worked out the details of the sale of the main clinic to Peter. There were many proposals back and forth until both were happy with the arrangements. Don, the new chiropractor, just arrived. He is taking over Peter's place in the central clinic.

Now, after the fact, I understand two dreams that were so vivid in early December: Our family was sitting in the van parked in a parking lot but cars blocked it in. There was enough space on the left side to get out but Ed had to back up and go forward many times before he managed to maneuver us out. He then drove toward the coast of Chile on Avenida O'Higgins. I picked flowers from the gardens on the centre median, took in the fragrance, and felt that everything was good.

The other was more complex: We were at Aris and Christina's *cabanas,* and Peter was with us. The kids were not happy with our looking around in an underground area; it was scary for them. There was a container of ice cream in a fridge set into the underground wall. It exploded, and what was left of the contents oozed out, making a sticky mess. Ed, Peter and I were sitting at a table talking with a medical doctor and I said to Ed, "Well, you can always tell them that your doctor said a break would be good for your health." The doctor had to leave. He said "See you in April." I wondered why April and realized that it was already March. At this point I lay down in the calm water of what seemed to be a fresh-water lake in order to wash the sticky ice cream off me from cleaning up the mess.

It tantalizes me to think that if I understood my own symbolism I would have a little more insight into the events of my future. The kids and I have been waiting in anticipation to move out of the city. It has been good living in Santiago and we learned much about life in the city, but it will be good to live elsewhere and have a family home-school life again.

January 27, 1998:

My grandfather has not been well for the better part of the past year. Mom called last week just a few days before they were to arrive to let us know that Grandpa had died. The funeral was the day before Mom and Dad's flight to Santiago. Grandpa planned it just right. He was so dependent on Mom being there for him and with the thought of her being away for so long, he decided to leave too. His passing does not come as a surprise to me. I said good-bye to him when I last saw him in Canada and did my mourning the Christmas we left. I knew I wouldn't see him on the physical plane again.

All month we anticipated Mom and Dad's visit. For several weeks the kids asked how many days till their arrival and Whitney counted down on her fingers. Then, on the 23rd, the day before they were to arrive, we imagined them getting on the plane at 10 a.m., then the five-hour wait in Mexico City, then getting on the plane to Santiago. We went to bed with three alarms set but in the end they alerted no one. I woke at 6:20 a.m., and they were arriving at six. We were out the door within five minutes and dressed during the 30-minute drive to the airport. I sat on pins and needles, knowing Dad would not like it that we were not there waiting for them. At the arrivals level at 6:50, he was on the sidewalk, hand on hip, the other on the cart of bags and a you're-in-trouble-looking face on. When I jumped out, the first thing he said was, "What's the matter with you guys, didn't you know we got here at six o'clock?" I knew he wouldn't feel safe. He is just not the kind of person to venture off into unknown territory; Chile—totally unfamiliar to him and a different language as well. Mom came out of the airport. She had been phoning to find out what the situation was but hung up when she spotted the van. After our reprimand, we were all glad to see one other and we spent the day catching up on news. Mom said it was hard to imagine her Dad not there in his house anymore. Generations do change and we got some good news too—Lee (my sister) is pregnant; the baby is due in August.

Mom and Dad are disappointed to learn the kids are not going back to school in March, but understand circumstances are taking us in a different direction and that this city is not the healthiest place to live. Ed, Ben, Karina and I have developed coughs since getting here. At first I thought it was because we were consuming more dairy products again, but on the evening I spent at Dayna's class meeting, realized it was more than that. I could not understand totally what was being said, and when the conversation turned into a discussion over some children that were causing concern, I slipped into a "half-here, half-someplace-else" state and noticed the coughing in the room. Indeed there weren't many people who weren't coughing, some more chronically than others. The serious air pollution is a major concern for people in Santiago, and the city carries many restrictions on vehicles, fires and factories. But this was the first time I had witnessed such a noticeable physical effect on the people. When I spoke of this to Mom she understood. She has always been concerned over Karina's tendency to asthma-like symptoms. Her breathing has been sensitive from an early age, but a healthy lifestyle has always kept the difficulties under control. So before we move, and we don't know where we are moving to yet, we will do some touring and forget about the little trials and tribulations we have been through in the past few months.

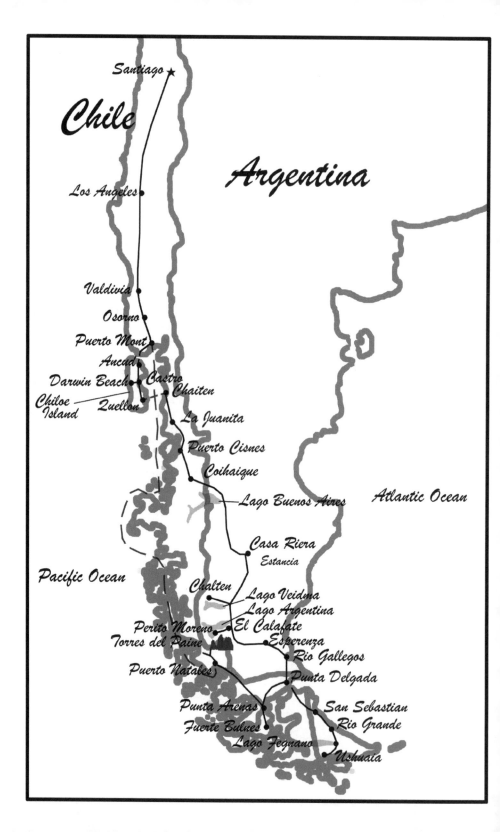

PATAGONIA CAMPING TOUR

February 1 to 4, 1998: Aboard the Puerto Eden

Puerto Montt is the gateway to southern Chile. It is the starting point for cargo ships carrying provisions to towns not supplied by road within the country and tours by boat or ship through channels and glaciers of the archipelago. The town was named after Manuel Montt, the president of Chile between 1841 and 1851. It was Montt who set in motion the German immigration program in 1848. He founded Puerto Montt in 1853 and the town was initially populated by German immigrants. It still has a large population of German descendants.

At boarding time each of the children hoisted their packs onto their shoulders, following the example of everyone else in the departure area. Whitney insisted on packing hers, too, and a tourist from Germany made a comment about how lucky she was to be a backpacker so early in life. (A symbol of freedom, I suppose.)

Our trek to the ship took us past the private vehicles waiting to board, as well as four kayaks sitting on the tarmac waiting to be loaded. We were among the last group of passengers carried to the upper decks by the cargo elevator, which was large enough to lift a transport truck. A group of four men, each wearing a fluorescent orange toque and speaking a mixture of French and English, were among us. "They must be on an expedition of some sort." Ed remarked.

Our rooms were compact, warm and comfortable but we quickly disposed of our belongings and got out onto the main deck, from where we had an excellent view of Puerto Montt as far as Volcan Osorno and much of the channel in both directions. We watched the loading of the ship until we noticed penguins playing in the water. They swam excitedly, dunking under the surface to reappear moments later, more often than not gulping down a fish. More penguins appeared, following the dark school of fish in the water. Jake was almost as excited as the penguins, which swam faster and faster as they fished and filled their bellies right there in port.

As I watched Jake watch the penguins, a hurtful memory surfaced. When Jake was two years old he watched the Omnimax movie *Antarctica* at the Museum of Civilization in Hull. Taking in the visual overload, he was so excited watching the penguins that he had to talk about it with me and wouldn't be quiet. Someone complained and we had to leave. Jake couldn't understand what the problem was and made an even bigger fuss as we left. Frankly, if he had been miserable I would have removed him, but his expressions were happy and he was asking questions, wanting to know more. We should all learn new things with such enthusiasm. At that moment on board, I saw myself as that complaining person, unable to see through a child's eyes. I watched the penguins filling their bellies in excitement and watched Jake again, fascinated by the sight, and realized that I need to let the child in me play more and look at things with wonder, fresh and new, and not let the burdens of life get in the way of being happy with the here and now.

Recently, I have found myself wondering why I had to come to the Southern hemisphere to work out my hurts, pains, anxieties, and illusions; but much of that is washing away now. Just before Dad and Mom arrived I found a *Northern Reflections* sweatshirt in a Ropa Americana store in Santiago and purchased it. It has a picture of a forest on the front and *Northern Reflections* emblazoned across the top. I believe I have been given the time and opportunity to reflect on my first forty years of life and the chance to make a few improvements on myself.

The school of fish moved, sometimes splitting into two dark masses and rejoining again. I couldn't get over how swiftly the penguins swam, wriggling back and forth, sometimes arching and jumping out of the water, only disappearing and resurfacing with fish in their mouths. Suddenly the fish and penguins were gone. It was high tide and tugboats arrived to remove the long ropes from the cement pillars that held the ship in place. The powerful little boats pushed and pulled our ship—a monster by comparison—aiming it down the channel until it entered waters in which it could navigate on its own.

The evening included a gathering at which we received safety rules and an agenda for the next three days. Marcelo, our director, told us of an area through which the ship would only be able to sail at high tide because water rushing in and out of the narrow channels caused strong currents that were capable of smashing a ship against the shoreline. He described the weather we could expect and warned that if the sun was shining, we should protect our skin with plenty of sunscreen. In the Southern hemisphere, the ozone layer is almost totally gone and skin burns extremely fast. He explained that the ship must travel into the open ocean around the Peninsula de Taitao. He joked about seasickness, while giving several suggestions for warding it off: don't drink much, especially alcohol, wear your bracelets, put acupuncture patches behind your ears or band-aids in a cross over your navel, take *Gravol,* and if all else fails lie flat on your back and don't get up. It was obvious he enjoyed his job. He was full of information, knew the ship, land, and waterways, and had a good understanding of the indigenous people of the south.

The kids and I sat on the floor and the man from Germany who had spoken to us earlier sat down beside us. I had two sleeping children on top of me, and Karina was asleep on Ed before Marcelo's talk was over. Ed carried Karina to bed, while I awaited his return to carry one of the others. Meanwhile, the German man had been filling his cup with wine and commented on how peaceful Jake and Whitney appeared. He asked about our family travelling and when I told him we had been in Chile for eight months his questions turned to information about wine. He and his group of friends had travelled to Chile to savour wines within the country in which they are produced. I told him I didn't know much about wine, as I had rarely indulged before coming to Chile, because of the way wine affected me. But wine is a Chilean way of life, and I have grown to like a little with meals and knew there were many good ones for which you didn't have to pay a high price. (For some reason, Chilean wines in Chile don't have the same ill effects on me as those back home.) He agreed and said he was shocked that one he liked so much—out of several he had tried—came out of a one-litre tetra-pak. There appears to be a European stigma about wines being packaged this way, but it is the way all table wines here in Chile are packaged. I am not a connoisseur, but the flavour doesn't seem to be too compromised and my newfound friend agreed.

Our first day gave us brilliant morning sunlight. We are not avid sunscreen users. My gut feeling is that all the chemicals that make up those creams are just as bad for skin as too much sun, and much of the hype is mostly scare tactics used to make pharmaceutical companies richer. The best defense, as far as I am concerned, is to let skin tan gently to give the best natural protection, and to stay out of midday sun. When that is not possible, we use sunscreen—sparingly—only on skin that is not covered with clothing. I sat on the top deck for a while but couldn't stay—the sun felt like pins and needles on my forehead and despite my use of sunscreen my skin felt as if it was about to bubble. None of us stayed out long. Even later, with a light cloud cover, the sun was hard to take. Tanya found it comfortable in the cabin reading, and Dad and Mom kept the others busy playing cards in the common room. We toured the bridge as a group but it was a re-run for Ben who had been up and wandering around early that morning, had visited the bridge area and spent time talking with a shipmate who gave him his own private tour.

Through Canal Apiac the land closed in on both sides. The islands were forested. I remember reading about the Southern Andes being lower and submerged and how only the tallest peaks remain above sea level. Well, that is what it looked like—mountains that had sunk into the ocean. In some places there were cliffs rising out of the water, while in others the inclines were gradual.

Ed and I spoke with Jim from North Carolina. We were not the only crazy people around—there were others who liked travelling over land and sea. A man in his fifties, retired from the American military, was doing a trip similar to ours through South America on motorbike. He had travelled North America first, west across the U.S., north to Alaska, east through every province of Canada, then southwest diagonally through the U.S. to Mexico and Central America and by plane to Venezuela to purchase his *libreta*. We met him on the ship, each of us now having made it through Venezuela, Colombia, Ecuador, Peru and Chile. He said his trip wouldn't be complete if he didn't make it to Ushuaia. He was planning on travelling the east coast and flying to Miami from Venezuela to complete his journey. All solo.

Instead of watching the movie that evening, I made my way to the cabin to organize and clean the cameras. As I walked, the floor seemed to fall out from underfoot, as we had now entered the open ocean. Jake was on my heels. "Mom, I don't feel so good." It didn't take him long to succumb to the effects of rolling water. Lying flat is the best remedy when you're able and I just got him snuggly into bed when Karina knocked on the door saying, "I don't feel so good." She lay down on a bunk but kept lifting her head. Once she was convinced to keep it level with the rest of her body the sick feeling subsided. Jake was another story. He was trying to vomit in the sink when Tanya escorted Whitney to the cabin and left. The door closed and Whitney said, "I'm sick." She was in bed and sleeping within minutes. Jake relieved his stomach of its contents and by the time I had him cleaned up and got him back into bed I had started to feel the effects myself. Ben popped his head in and said, "Mom, I just vomited". One by one they left the movie, came down, and climbed into bed. Dayna was next, which was unusual, as she hadn't been motion-sick since we left Canada. By the time we moved Karina to her own cabin, with Dayna, I was almost ready to follow Jake's example. With everyone down I lay in my bunk, letting the motion rock and comfort me. Lying flat worked. It was a blessing that we hit the ocean for our overnight sail.

By breakfast the following morning we were almost across the "Gooolfo de Pena", as it was written on the info board, and were headed for Banice Tarn and Canal Messier. The sea had calmed down considerably. A flat, grey sky and fine mist made the air damp and cold. We dressed in warmer clothing but Jake insisted on wearing shorts (of course). In the common room, Marcelo gave a talk on the indigenous people of the Patagonia, and then we watched a Jacques Cousteau film about the people of Puerto Eden. After the film, Marcelo explained that there is only one young woman, Marica Lousia, left in Puerto Eden who is of pure Owarquar blood. Her tribe has been absorbed into the dominant society.

Marcelo also informed us that there were four men on board representing the Cousteau Society who would be kayaking from Puerto Eden, where we were to arrive late in the afternoon, to Puerto Natales. He wished them well from the ship and crew. Theirs would be a long haul: a 600-kilometer research journey taking anywhere from three to four months. A test of true endurance, if you ask me.

We spent little time on deck the second day. It was wet and when the air dried out enough to enjoy being outside the wind at times was so strong, that it would hold you up while you were leaning into it. While sailing through Canal Inglesa and waiting to see the shipwreck, the kids started a game of playing in the wind. Before long they had almost everyone on deck playing their game and the roars of laughter were infectious. The fun stopped when the shipwreck came into view. There it was, tilted to its side, trapped on a mountain beneath the water and it hasn't moved for more than 70 years. We observed the pile of rusted metal that was once a seagoing vessel. It has been left as a reminder of how perilous it could be travelling through the straights and channels. A child died in that shipwreck, and it is said that his spirit protects mariners and fisherman. We were informed on our tour of the bridge that captains of ships that sail the archipelago have on-the-job training for many years before they are licensed to service southern Chile, and there are only a few who are qualified.

The ship stops regularly at Puerto Eden to provide supplies to the local population, and it was here that the Cousteau crew and their kayaks disembarked. When all four paddlers were sitting in their much smaller ocean-going vessels they saluted the crew and ship and headed off down the canal on manpower alone.

The passage from Puerto Eden to Estrecho Ancho reminded me so much of the Gatineau River it would have been difficult to tell the difference if I didn't know better. The channel the ship sailed was narrow and the hills were covered in trees. The mountains protected us from the wind and everything became quiet as the water calmed and the land closed in on us. The narrowest pass of the route was before us. In fact, as we approached there didn't appear to be any channel at all for the ship to pass through. Then the ship made a sharp turn to the left, at which point the water opened up into Estrecho Ancho. The wind picked up, and again it was raw, cold and damp. It is hard to believe a ship that size could sail through such narrow straits.

The length of day increased dramatically as we gained more southerly latitude. It being summer in the southern hemisphere, we still had full daylight at 9:30 p.m.

Our final day aboard was even cooler than the previous day, and Jake finally consented to some long pants for warmth. Several mountains to the west had glaciers on top, and small icebergs occasionally confronted the ship. We took refuge from the cold wind, and Marcelo entertained us and the other passengers with a film about pumas and another film about the wildlife of the Southern Patagonia. Both were informative about the animal life we could expect to see: black-necked swans, red foxes, grey foxes, guanacos, penguins, *lieveres* (Patagonian hares), condors and pumas.

By mid-afternoon the ship had pulled into the dock of Puerto Natales with the aid of two tugboats.

Passengers—we are a funny bunch, anxious to get on and anxious to get off, which makes me think about how most of us are always waiting for the next moment, the next day, the next week or year, myself included. What is so wrong with right now? Why are we always in such a hurry to move on to the next place? Why do we think it is going to be so much better someplace else or sometime in the future? It is an art to live in the moment. Being totally conscious of right now and enjoying it—is that possible or would it take away all ambition?

February 4 to 7, 1998: Torres del Paine Parque National

Since it was light until 10:30 p.m. we decided to head to Torres del Paine Park when we arrived in Puerto Natales. At the tourist information booth Ed purchased a detailed map of the Patagonia, completely informative right down to the location of every *estancia* (sheep ranch) and gas station on the highway.

As we left Puerto Natales and were driving along Seno Ultima Esperanza (Last Hope Sound), a flock of black-necked swans was resting and feeding along the shoreline. The pavement was short-lived, and as we traversed on the east side of the Andes, the land was desert-like, the earth dotted with dark grey-green bushes about knee high and scrub grass growing in clumps. The grass, coarse, stiff, and sandy yellow in colour, blended with the earth. When sunlight caught it from behind it glistened silver-white. The road wound and rolled along the foothills and gently descended into a river valley, at the bottom of which was a sign that translated to "Caution, dangerous cross winds." A moment later, as the van reached the flatter ground, we were pushed sideways by the wind, making it more of a challenge for Ed to steer. The river valley created a tunnel effect in which wind off the Pacific was funneled through at great speed into the *pampa* of Argentina. As the road turned west toward the Torres del Paine National Park, the land formation that draws hundreds of visitors each year was in distant but clear view. We spotted two foxes that didn't bother to make themselves less obvious. Hares darted across the road regularly, and several *nandu* (rhea birds) stood tall on the landscape or ran across it like five-foot high chickens.

For camping, the park ranger suggested Lago Pehoe where there are several hotels and *hosterias* offering excellent facilities and meals, but the least expensive starts at $60 (U.S.) per night per room with shared bathroom facilities. Chile has a gem of a tourist attraction, and they are making it pay for itself.

As we came around a corner, heading toward the campground, there was a herd of approximately thirty *guanaco*. They were on the road and on both sides: small ones nursing, others grazing, some lying down chewing cud and totally undisturbed by the presence of the van. The sun was low in the west and each one of them had a rim of backlight from our vantage point. Ed stopped. I quietly

Guanaco,
Torres del Paine National Park

The tight squeeze Torres del Paine National Park

opened the side door and took several photos. None of us said a word. Ed slowly moved on through, and those on the road just moved to the side to let us pass. Mom said, "How do you like that? In the first two hours of driving, we have seen every animal that we saw in the film this morning." But the kids reminded her, "not pumas," and although it would be great to see a puma we weren't really sure we wanted to meet up with a wild one.

Ed parked the van at the campsite office, and out the window to my right was a magnificent sight: the mountains called Cuernos (horns) backed with white cloud and bathed in late-day sun. It is understandable why the area is a protected park.

We set the tents up in a sheltered area but couldn't prevent them from bouncing around in the wind. We built a wind block around the stove but even so the flame blew out several times while we cooked dinner. We had a comfortable but noisy sleep, as our hexagon tents partially collapsed and bounced back all night.

We awoke to sunshine and blue sky with a fabulous view of the Cuernos reflected in the turquoise blue of glacial Lago Pehoe. The campground attendant said that the view was rare and if we were hiking in to see the Torres, we should go, as it is not often that they are free of cloud.

To get to the *hosteria* where the hike to see the Torres began, we had to cross a one-lane suspension bridge over the river, and it didn't look as if the van would fit. We felt defeated before even starting. We discussed walking the seven kilometers to the *hosteria,* but if we did that, Dad and the little ones would not have had the stamina to hike the mountain trail to the Torres. Just then, a small truck as wide as our van, carrying a load of wood, came up behind us. We laughed at the idea of him trying to get across but were soon proven wrong. One of the two men got out in front of the truck and guided the driver while the truck moved forward. The man on foot directed the driver a little this way, a little to the other, and forward easy. We heard a scrape, but inch by inch, without any space to spare, the truck moved across and the man on foot hopped back in and they were gone. If they could do it we could too. Dad guided Ed across after the rest of us walked the bridge. The side mirrors had to be folded in tight to the van. The tires ran along the edge board of the bridge and at one point part of the tire was partially off the floor of the bridge. It wouldn't be an exaggeration to suggest that there was even an inch to spare on either side of the van. The tires and hubcaps were scraped several times, but Ed made it. There were several Ford Econolines sitting in the parking lot at the *hosteria,* and the only difference from ours being that they were an extended length to seat 15 passengers. They were the park tour vehicles, and every one of them had several dents and scratches on the sides.

We had our picnic lunch before attempting the hike, and the kids started to play tag in the field. But they were soon back complaining about picky things in their socks—we discovered menace to be burrs the size of coriander seeds. Each one was a ball of barbs that rolled the fabric up around itself. They were difficult to remove without stabbing fingers and it took some time before ankles were comfortable for the walk.

Our hike took us along a rocky trail, across a footbridge over the Rio Ascensio, and up a steady incline for an hour and a half. It wasn't easy for Dad, and when we reached the top of our ascent, with a view of the distance still to hike he decided he had gone far enough. Ed, Ben, Dayna, Jake and Whitney were far ahead of us. Dad, Mom, Tanya, Karina and I stopped where we were, found comfortable places on the ground to rest, and had a snack. We lay basking in the sun, which for some reason didn't feel nearly as threatening as it had when we were on the ship. We didn't get a close-up view of the Torres, but the view up the Valle Ascencio was rewarding. When Ed and the kids reached our rest point, on their way back a while later, they too had a snack. They reported that the tops of just two Torres were visible. Unless we continued to hike much deeper into the mountains we weren't going to get a good close-up view. The walk back was downhill, easier on the cardiovascular system but harder on the knees. Pain or no pain, we always make it. Ed wanted to get back across the bridge in good daylight, so we didn't waste any time.

We prepared and ate a good nourishing meal consisting of the Chilean mainstay, bread and cheese, which, with wine, is the main late-day meal in this country. Our habits have changed considerably. In Canada I felt our family consumed a simple diet but have come to realize it was not as simple as I thought. Chilean people eat what their country produces and import very little food. In Canada, anything from anywhere in the world is available year round so our diet, like our lives, has become complicated by the multitude of choices. It does add variety, but I am learning that if we eat more of the foods that the land produces from the areas in which our physical bodies dwell, our bodies would be more able to function optimally in the surrounding environment.

The strong, cold wind discouraged us from moving out of the tents on our second day in the park and it was a battle to keep the stove lit long enough to boil some water for hot chocolate, cereal, and coffee. Getting into the van for the short trip to Lago Grey was pure refuge from the wind.

Charred dead trees, the remnants of fires set by ranchers to make grazing land for sheep, were scattered across the slopes to the east. The land was once an *estancia* and was claimed by the government as parkland. The trees have never regenerated; only small bushes dotted the landscape. Driving across Puente Weber, over the runoff from the Grey Glacier, afforded us another incredible view of the Cuernos, from a new angle. What a feeling of being small and unimportant—I was humbled. I am no match for the powers of nature but I can draw from it and gain internal strength. There isn't anything more perfect and beautiful than the earth in its natural state.

The information centre displayed photographs of wildlife along with characteristic data, samples of plant life labelled with pertinent information, and a relief model of the park, which is situated about 150 kilometers northwest of Puerto Natales, and covers 1,630 square kilometers. Its unusual rock formations have formed spectacular mountain peaks and sheer cliffs ranging in height from 2,600 meters to the highest, Cerro Paine Grande, at 3,248 meters. In contrast, the lakes in the region rest at levels of 50 to 200 meters. Several glaciers branch off the Patagonian mountain top, one of which, the Grey Glacier is accessible by boat tour within the park. The South African family we met on the ship from Puerto Montt, visited the centre with us. Since it was too windy for boats to travel on Lago Grey, they suggested we walk to the moraine of the glacier. They had done it the previous day, said it was well worth the hike and easy enough for the kids.

Dad stayed in the shelter of the trees and eventually went back to the van. I found myself disappointed that he had such a lack of interest even in relatively easy walking. He was the one who always took us into the bush when we were little to collect mushrooms or just for enjoyment. He took us on drives into the middle of nowhere in Northern Ontario to go ice-fishing and picnic on a frozen lake in January, or to the wildlife refuge to feed the ducks and geese—or to the garbage dump to watch the bears foraging. I am sure those experiences helped cultivate my adventurous spirit, but he seems to have little interest left in anything of the sort. I wonder what it is that has changed how he goes about his life. Maybe it is just age, although he really isn't that old.

Before our Patagonia camping trip I made each of the kids a simple windbreaker jacket from ends of Gore-Tex fabric that I found in the Ropa Americana section of Santiago. I was proud of myself; six kids each got a good windbreaker for less than $30 (Canadian). The kids were not crazy about them (too plain), but they appreciated them on our walk over the lakebed moraine. At the water's edge we were as close as we could get to the blue icebergs, of which looked as if it had been patiently sculpted and smoothed into shape from the mammoth Grey Glacier at the opposite end of the lake.

Ben, in his adventurous way, managed to pull a melting chunk of ice to where he and the others could haul it out of the water without getting wet. The kids always liked to suck on icicles at home and asked if it would be all right to do the same on some broken pieces. Glacial ice is as good and clean as it gets on the earth. If we couldn't consume it there, we shouldn't be able to anywhere in the world. We quenched our thirst the result being the next time I drank plain water; it was a disappointment to my taste buds.

The kids, Ed and Mom continued walking the shoreline and played in the stones while I took my time photographing the melting blue ice, when the sun came from behind a cloud giving depth to the shapes. However, it didn't take long before we grew tired of defending ourselves against the force of the wind, which was at our backs making the return walk much easier.

In the van we needed to get gas. I wouldn't even mention it except that in the park it was only available at the *hosteria* from 50-gallon barrels from which it was pumped by hand into five-litre wine bottles. From there it was poured through a funnel into the gas tank, an extremely time-consuming process. The price was so high that we settled for half a tank, which probably pleased the young man pumping the gas, who by then had a sore arm. At any rate, we had enough to do a little more driving within the park and get back to Puerto Natales.

February 7 to 12, 1998: Punta Arenas and Tierra del Fuego

It took a day to drive out of the park, and I didn't like leaving. It is a place where a person could easily spend several weeks hiking and camping.

We stopped at Otway Sound to see the Magellanic penguins en route to Punta Arenas. Again we bundled up to protect ourselves from the constant wind. A lady at the information centre showed us a map of walkways to the shelter for observing the

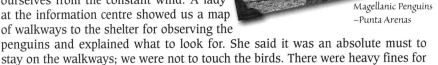

Magellanic Penguins
–Punta Arenas

penguins and explained what to look for. She said it was an absolute must to stay on the walkways; we were not to touch the birds. There were heavy fines for those who crossed the ropes to the beach. Then she said to go and enjoy.

It was a windy half-hour walk along the maze of ropes that lead to the lookout. In the beginning all we saw were grass mounds with burrows in them and no sign of penguins. We figured out why after spotting a fox intent on eating the penguin eggs and totally unconcerned with the people walking around. The field of grassy mounds went on as far as we could see the dull yellow ground foliage dotted with little black and white heads. From a closer vantage point we watched penguins waddling toward the beach, the lot of them giving me the impression it was hard work for them to be on land. Many birds rested on the stony beach, and we got to within three meters of some. It was afternoon naptime. Magellanic penguins sleep with their beaks tucked into their bodies and the only movement from those that were napping was their feathers ruffled by the wind. The penguins at Seno Otway were once a colony of thousands, but their numbers are declining. The wind soon made us want to find shelter, and the walk back to the van, straight into it was an arduous chore.

The road between Puerto Natales and Punta Arenas was at one time gravel only but is under improvement. The southbound lane is constructed of thick concrete, not asphalt, which makes for smooth driving.

Punta Arenas, with its population of 115,000, is the southernmost city of Chile. It was a busy stopover port before the opening of the Panama Canal. Today it is a center for the export of sheep's wool, hides and meat and is beginning to provide services for the growing tourism industry.

It was close to 9 p.m. when we arrived in the city and the first bed and breakfast we inquired at was too full to accommodate the 10 of us. When the woman who ran it found out we were a family with children and not a tour group the tone in her voice changed and she took us to another establishment down the street where Ed made arrangements for two nights. We were given two bedrooms with a total five beds, but the owner didn't mind us making a couple more beds on the floor.

The bank machine for foreign travellers was on the Plaza des Armas and while Ed and Mom went for cash, Dad, the kids and I strolled the square where a huge, ancient tree took up a good portion of the plaza. The kids together couldn't get their arms around the trunk, and each major branch could have been a tree itself. There is something about trees as such that attracts children, and the kids spent most of their time climbing the boughs.

Before arriving in Punta Arenas I read from the *SAH* to gain a little information about the city. There was a blurb that I read aloud to everyone:

In the Plaza des Armas is a statue of Magellan with a mermaid and two Fuegian Indians at his feet. According to local wisdom those who rub the big toe of one of the Indians will return to Punta Arenas. When we got to it, each of the kids took turns rubbing the toes and giggling. I didn't take the folklore very seriously but Dad wasn't too pleased with how the kids went at rubbing the toes of the Indians. They thought it was somewhat amusing and said they wanted to see if it would work.

We spent our afternoon at the Reserva Forestal Magallanes. The trees kept out some of the wind but even in the lean-tos where we cooked, the wind snuffed out the flame of the stove under our pot of soup. It was a pleasant afternoon of play in the forest, including a hike to the gorge of Garganta del Diablo (Devil's Throat).

Along a well-marked path through forest lush with plant life. At the edge of the gorge overlooking the Rio de las Minas and in the open, the wind was relentlessly strong and tiring. The views in every direction were incredible, but the kids were most intrigued by the trees that have been molded by constant wind, lopsided, every branch growing the direction the wind blew. Again, Dad insisted on staying with the van, instead of hiking.

After picking up our laundry we had a light evening meal in a restaurant. Jake and Karina had ketchup with their fries and had eaten a fair amount when Mom dipped a fry and ate it, and said, "Oh that ketchup is bad, you kids shouldn't be eating that." We asked for a new bottle but it was too late. The following morning Jake was too sick to eat breakfast but did drink some tea, only to vomit a few

The constant wind of the Patagonia molds the shape of the trees.
Ben, Reserva Forestal Magallanes.

minutes later. Karina didn't vomit but was feverish. Neither one of them liked the idea of taking grapefruit seed extract but it killed whatever caused the problem and they were as good as themselves again later that day.

The woman who runs the B&B was in no hurry to move us out, so we gave the kids a morning of recuperation. She kept bringing hot water for tea and coffee and more bread and jam for the ones who were eating. She was interested in our family, asked questions about the children and wondered if everyone in Canada had big families like us. She asked Mom and Dad about their family and asked if they had other grandchildren. She told us about her family. On the wall beside the dining room table hung a large photo of her late husband, and several others of her sisters, sons, and grandchildren. She was pleased that one son, and three grandchildren lived in Punta Arenas; she sees them often. She told us she had lived in Puerto Natales for 30 years, then Punta Arenas for 42, and hasn't been to many other places but learns about the world from the travellers that stay in her home while passing through. She is a healthy woman and gave the impression she missed her husband but content with her life, in fact happy and it was because she keeps busy. She didn't like the idea of not having people in the house, said she wouldn't know what to do with herself if she didn't provide a place to stay for "wanderers", as she called people like us.

The drive east along the Strait of Magellan was along the same sort of road as the highway between Puerto Natales and Punta Arenas: two lanes, one of which the eastbound side was cemented, so that vehicles both ways used it until they met another vehicle.

The *estancia* of San Gregorio looked like a ghost town: a row of buildings on each side of the highway, only two or three of which looked as if anyone might have been living in them. The deep blue sky made the day feel like autumn. The highway ran within sight of the water almost the entire distance to the ferry crossing from which we would cross to Tierra del Fuego. At the closest point between Tierra del Fuego and mainland Chile the strait is no more than six kilometers wide and land was visible in the distance across the water.

Ed backed the van into the high-sided ferryboat as directed. The vehicles were so tightly packed that only the driver's side door would open barely wide enough to let anyone in or out. Most people simply stayed in their vehicles. Only afterwards did I think about the danger of the situation. What if we had had to abandon ship? Abandoning the van would have been extremely difficult for my father. Ed escorted the kids to the top deck to watch the crossing, mostly because Jake was fascinated with the idea of visiting "the big island on the bottom of South America". On his return to the van, he claimed that it didn't look that much different from the mainland and asked why it was so special.

At Punta Delgado on Tierra del Fuego we took some time to secure the baggage on top of the van, and a familiar car drove up to the ferry launch. The South African family was returning to Punta Arenas. They were headed to Ushuaia but were turned back at the Chilean border. Their youngest daughter's passport had expired while living in Chile. A new passport had been issued, but there was no visa indicating that she was a temporary resident, like the other members of the family. The authorities would let them leave Chile but there was no guarantee she would be allowed back without the proper paperwork. Their only choice was to go back to Immigration in Punta Arenas to arrange for the proper stamps.

We set out onto Tierra del Fuego on a narrow gravel road. The dust was atrocious, the grassland flat and dry for as far as the eye could see. Tierra del Fuego produces most of Chile's oil and gas supply and we saw two fires in different fields where natural gas had escaped and was burning.

After an hour or so of driving we hit a huge bump and Dad yelled, "Ed, stop, something fell off the roof!" Ed brought the van to an abrupt halt, and while Ben retrieved the bag, the rest of us stretched our legs and had a chance to feel what the land was like. The silence was almost haunting—even the kids' screams as they fooled around were muffled. The only sound was the wind rustling the grasses. Time itself felt like it slowed right down.

At the Chile-Argentina border on Tierra del Fuego, Dad, Mom and Ed went into the customs office—*aduana*—to take care of the border formalities but Mom was quickly back out to search through her purse and belongings for her Chilean tourist card. She looked through everything, but it wasn't there, and she returned to say she didn't have it. The situation didn't take as long to solve as it could have, and the three of them were laughing on their return to the van. When Mom told the agent she must have lost it, the officer just said no problem, filled out another tourist card with the exact information from Dad's and the exit data, then told her not to lose this one, as it was important legal information. It may have been a case of the agent taking pity on Ed as when he found out Dad and Mom were Ed's in-laws from Canada, he said, "You must be crazy, if I brought my in-laws to Canada for a vacation I'd come back and leave them there." He made it as easy as he could for Ed.

Argentine *aduana* at San Sebastian was on a high plateau overlooking the sloping land and the Atlantic Ocean. The road along the eastern coastline is paved to Rio Grande and how luxurious it felt. Rio Grande has a population of 35,000. It too is a city that is a centre for trading in sheepskins and wool although the export of frozen meat is the main industry, and Rio Grande is home to the largest plant meat processing plant of its kind in South America. Everywhere around here, the gardens are filled with lupines in a rainbow of colours and roses of different varieties. Further south the land changed from flat grassland to hilly forests; the pavement ended, and again we were in the Andes.

The village of Tolhuin was a mess. A tornado had torn through the previous day and people were busy cleaning up the damage. The road continued through more forest and at the crest of a hill it opened onto a valley overlooking Lago Fagnano. At the campground, a sign on the main building said "Will be right back". We waited, taking in the beauty of the surroundings and the beginning of the sunset over the lake. We noticed broken trees and debris scattered throughout the campground. Ironically this was the first time we were in the open in the Patagonia where there wasn't a wind trying to knock us over.

We had the opportunity to walk around for only a few minutes when a white, beat-up truck rushed up the driveway and came to a skidding stop. A man about 35 jumped out, wearing work boots, jeans, sloppy shirt and jacket, and sporting longish curly brown hair, an unshaven face and full mustache—Roberto. Ed made arrangements to camp for two nights. Suddenly the sun demanded our attention. Warm light streamed through a break in the clouds, the water turned silver, the mountains to the west were grey silhouettes while those to the south were bathed in golden light. Roberto, in awe of the scene before the group of us, said we were lucky to see something like this—maybe once a month the mountains show their tops, and never as beautiful as today.

Roberto showed us around—this guy is a character. We asked about swimming—is it fresh water? He said, "Sure, it is fresh, very fresh, go swimming." Making fun of us he imitated the action of a diver then stopped as if frozen and walked like an ice block. A boat, large enough to live in, probably oceangoing, was grounded on the shore. It belonged to Roberto. Ed asked him how he got it there, and again he gestured, pulling on an imaginary rope, grunting and groaning, then said "hard work", but he never did tell us anything we could believe. The tornado had hit Roberto's campground. In relating the experience, he spun his index finger in circles spiralling toward the ground, made the sound of swirling wind with his mouth, then told Ed it was weird. Tornadoes never happen in the Patagonia. It's always windy, but there's never a twister and it's really unusual that there is no wind now. Roberto said that maybe the twister took it all away, and then he laughed.

Every campsite had an eight-foot windbreak set up to shield the tent from the strength of the wind, Roberto said we should put our tents behind them, so they wouldn't be blown away. At which point he had the children giggling with his antics and when they were in boisterous laughter, he really noticed them, counted them and rolled his eyes. He has two girls and two boys, who were visiting grandparents with their mother, about the same age as our three younger ones.

There was an outside kitchen area set up behind a windbreak, beside a fireplace with surrounding benches that Roberto had built from log pieces and planks. Worktables were huge cable spools, and Roberto apologized that there wasn't a sink; the twister had taken it away—just the sink, nothing else—and Roberto scratched his head as if wondering how and why. He told us to use all the firewood we wanted. There was a building with a bathroom and bathhouse and he had a fire on, heating water for bathing if we desired.

The kids played at the lake with the campground dogs and enjoyed the space. Then something happened among them and Jake was howling. When he's mad or something doesn't go his way, his cry is long repeated howls, in an irritating pitch that rattles the eardrums and ties a knot in my solar plexus. As he was walking toward me my body was working up its defense system. I haven't found anything that helps Jake change this in himself yet. Roberto was headed toward the bathhouse and of course noticed Jake's howling—who wouldn't? Roberto howled in unison and it took a few moments before Jake noticed that he wasn't the only one howling. Jake stopped suddenly, and I laughed. He looked at Roberto, wondering why he was making that sound. When Roberto stopped, Jake continued and Roberto continued with him. Again Jake stopped, looked at him and continued when Roberto stopped. Once more, Jake continued and Roberto imitated the sound. It was like a cartoon picture: Jake let out a piercing scream aimed at Roberto and Roberto went flying backwards with the volume. Roberto made me laugh but Jake's howling continued. Roberto shrugged, saying sorry, and continued on his way. Jake, extra mad, took it out on me and yelled, "You don't have to laugh".

"I'm not laughing at you Jake," I explained. "I'm laughing at Roberto. He is so funny; it's better than crying. It makes you feel better." I hugged Jake until he calmed down and asked what he thought Roberto sounded like, but he just looked at me. I said, "It didn't sound very nice, did it? It was a pretty good imitation though. So what's wrong, Jake, what started all this?" He couldn't remember. After his hug he walked slowly back towards the others, seemingly immersed in thought.

It was dark by the time we were organized, and Dad's fire gave off welcome warmth. We roasted the marshmallows we had found at the duty-free grocery store and the kids had hot chocolate. Then they started telling their grandparents about Chilean food customs. One of Ben's classmates regularly brought marshmallows to school, sliced onto crackers, with jam, for dessert. Apparently this is the most common way to eat them. Ben told his friends that Canadians eat them roasted on a stick over a fire until the insides are melted and they thought that was gross. Ben's next comment was, "It's a wonder they don't eat them with mayonnaise, they eat mayonnaise with everything." Gram said, "Now *that's* gross. But it's all what a person gets used to, isn't it?"

Tanya said, "Yeah, and Ben is getting more Chilean all the time—he even eats mayonnaise with hotdogs now".

Ben retorted, "That's because it's good, but not marshmallows."

It was a comfortable feeling around the fire having hot chocolate and family time after warm baths. We settled into our tents for the night, content.

February 11, 1998 was the day that marked the turning point in our journey. We reached the most southerly point we would travel with our van on the South American continent. The 120-kilometer drive to Ushuaia from Lago Fagnano was on gravel road under construction for paving. The first part was through forested Andes Mountains. The descent on the south side was a challenge. It had rained, and I feared we would not get through the mud slicks but Ed always manages to maneuver the van skillfully through.

Usuhaia, population 50,000, is a steeply sloped town on the edge of the

mountains that rise out of the Beagle Channel. Nobody was interested in doing much, but I insisted we at least go to the *Museo Territorial.* It provided a basic understanding of the history of Tierra del Fuego, displaying early photographs and artifacts from native tribes, samples of native clothing, plus pieces from settlers and missionaries that settled the area, model ships of the Fitzroy and Beagle, a room full of stuffed birds of the Patagonia, a room full of old books, and a display on beavers and what they have done to the environment. Because fur-bearing animal species were not naturally abundant in the area, the federal government introduced 25 beaver pairs in 1946. They thrived in their new habitat and a lack of natural predators allowed for rapid growth. The population is now estimated at between 35,000 and 50,000, ranging over 70,000 square kilometers. In 1981, hunting was authorized to control over-population.

It was not a large museum, perfect for a short visit, and we came away with a better understanding of the area plus a stamp in our passport saying, *Museum at the End of the World.*

We continued walking along the shore of the Beagle Channel and came to a sign saying, *Ushuaia Fin del Mundo* and thought we should take some photos for the record. There was a large group of people photographing one another in front of the sign, and I was asked to take a shot of a woman and her father who were from the U. S. It was the father's eightieth year, and his daughter was accompanying him on a tour aboard the luxury liner sitting in the channel. They started from Valparaiso, Chile, stopped in Puerto Montt, travelled through the Chilean archipelago to Punta Arenas, did a day-trip by air over part of Antarctica from Ushuaia, and will be stopping in the Falkland Islands and Bahia Blanca before travelling up the east coast to Buenos Aires. What a trip in the comfort of a warm cabin with food service. I was feeling a little envious and worse for wear, camping in the cold. The woman asked about us and said, "You're not on the ship are you? I would have noticed a family like yours."

Ed said, "No, we drove here. This is our turning point. We will always be headed back to Canada from now on."

"You didn't drive from Canada," she remarked.

"Yes, from Canada."

She was astonished, turned around, and told everyone from her group. We became instant celebrities and had several family photos taken. We were just tourists too, but our doing the trip independently at a fraction of the cost drew a comment that we are "brave". It isn't that unusual, lots of people have driven South America.

Tierra del Fuego is lupine country; I have only known lupines to be blue in Canada but in Tierra del Fuego, and especially Ushuaia, I counted 12 different colours. I kept looking for seeds, but spent blossoms are trimmed away so they will continue to bloom; I didn't find any.

It was a quiet ride back to our campsite. It felt kind of like the beginning of the end, and everyone was contemplating what that meant. We will always be headed north now.

The wind picked up through the night and both Ed and I awoke, alert to the tent bouncing over our heads. I lay awake listening to the rain and pondering Roberto's warning that the wind might carry us away, but it didn't.

February 12 to 18, 1999: Punta Arenas

Daylight arrived late because of the heavy cloud cover and everything was wet from the mist. Roberto invited us into his lodge before we left. He is an excellent wood craftsman and had hand built the interior of the house himself, including the furniture and art on the walls. The large main room had windows overlooking the lake to the west. An efficient woodstove kept the room warm, and around it sat several big inviting looking chairs. At the opposite end was a table that would have seated 30. Roberto said, "I didn't build this one, it belonged to my grandparents." One of Roberto's pastimes was carving pictorial motifs into wood. Several of these were displayed on the walls. Mom loves wood pieces and collects driftwood. She admired his work and he gave her a piece of the knotted wood from which he had made his coat hooks. We took photos of each other, signed his guest book and said our goodbyes. But it was hard to get away; he just kept talking. When we eventually did get away, Mom said, "I wonder if he's really as happy as he puts on. Sometimes people like that are sad inside and that's how they cover it up." I wondered if his family was really just visiting grandparents.

By the time we reached the plains the clouds had broken up and the sun had begun to shine. Jake fell into a long needed sleep just before we arrived at the ferry crossing. There wasn't any waiting, and we moved right onto the ferry. Jake enjoys boats, but he didn't stir when I gently tried to wake him, and he is always so grouchy whenever I do, that I decided to let him sleep for the sake of keeping peace.

Fifty more kilometers over desert plain when we got off the ferry, and we were at the Chile-Argentina border on the mainland. Dad, Mom and Ed went into the building to obtain our Chilean exit paperwork. Mom said the young woman who did the paperwork didn't stamp the passports with the exit stamp but no one acknowledged the process she remembered at the last immigration office. I find it odd that in these countries Ed gets all eight of our passports processed without them being matched up to an actual person.

On the Argentinian side there was a problem. Ed had to see the supervisor who wanted to know why Ed was trying to get into Argentina without Chilean exit stamps. After a lengthy explanation we were allowed to go back to Chilean immigration for the proper stamps and then we would be allowed into Argentina.

Once again Ed, Dad and Mom went into the building. This time it took much longer. Mom came out by herself and said there was a problem. The eight of us have a residence visa but Ed and I didn't have a *carnet* card that we are supposed to carry with us at all times. They could let Dad, Mom and the kids through but Ed and I might not get back into Chile if we didn't have the proper papers. Meanwhile calls were being made to the main office in Punta Arenas to ask about what to do with us.

When Dad and Ed returned to the van, Argentina was no longer a possibility and we were headed back to Punta Arenas to ask for a pardon from the government and to apply for a *carnet* from immigration.

We were running low on gas but were anticipating filling up in Rio Gallegos, Argentina, a short distance north on the highway, from the border of which we were just turned away. We had a 200-kilometer drive ahead of us with two gas stations indicated on our map between the border and Punta Arenas. The first one that was indicated had shut down and we were desperately hoping there would be gas at San Gregorio. The gas station was indicated as being on the west side of the *estancia*—ranch but not wanting to miss it and waste what gas we had left, we stopped to ask where exactly it was located. Ed knocked on the door of a house where there was a cat in a window. But there was no answer, just the sound of distant bleating sheep and the water of the Magellan Straight lapping the shoreline. We hung around, feeling the emptiness of the place, when a woman, who was the spitting image of my long-gone grandmother, appeared on the road. Ed asked her about gas and she looked at us skeptically and said, "This is the estancia; six kilometers that way you turn off the main highway to get gas". She seemed perturbed, probably thinking, "stupid tourists coming without gas," which was exactly what I was thinking.

Ed pulled up beside the pump and there wasn't anyone in the buildings, so we waited. Again someone appeared in the yard. It was almost ghostly. I wandered to stretch my legs. The evening sun was turning the landscape almost orange. Looking inland to the north we could see the geological feature called the Patagonian steppe, an abruptly rising plateau up to a higher altitude from the level of land we were travelling just a few meters above sea level. The warm light of the sun cast shadows in the drainage areas, creating visual depth. I had to photograph it.

With the tank full of gas we relaxed and were just back on the road, when Dayna yelled out, "Hey Mom, we rubbed the Indian's toes, that's why we are going back."

Ben said, "Yeah, it is—I rubbed all ten of them for all ten of us."

It was a little eerie. The Patagonia was giving us a taste of its mysticism. We wondered if the South African family rubbed the Indian's toes, too. Ed said, "Well I'm not taking you back to do it again, once is enough."

It was long past dark when we arrived in Punta Arenas, but we lucked out finding a place. Residencia Bulnes didn't have space for ten in the main house but the owner reluctantly mentioned a *cabana* in the back. It was a perfect place for our needs, and we told the woman we would stay two nights.

Ed and I were to be at the immigration office at 9 a.m. to see the person who was supposed to take care of us, according to arrangements made at the border the previous day. We went to the office and waited. I was thankful the children were with Mom and Dad. It was actually restful.

A custodian started to wash the windows of the waiting room as we sat there. The ceiling was about 15 feet high and the windows reached to the top. He didn't have a ladder and could only clean as high as 2/3 of the way up, then picked up his things and left. He didn't return and I couldn't but help think that no success ever comes with doing just part of a job.

Two hours after our appointment time we were asked to come into the office. Ed explained the situation. The agent was willing to help us out, but because we had broken the law, we first had to have a formal pardon from the Government of Chile before he could issue the paperwork for the *carnet*. Our choices were to go back to Santiago via Chile to have the paperwork done there or wait for it to be done here. Except that really we didn't have a choice, the only road to Santiago was through Argentina, and through Chile on the ship, we just came south on, didn't have a northbound vacancy until April. We tried to plan our trip going the other way around. So having the paperwork done in Punta Arenas was our only choice. It was close to lunchtime on Friday and the agent called the office from which the pardon would be issued and found out that there wasn't any way it could be done that afternoon. We were told to go to the Government Office on Monday morning and see Senõr Martinez.

The kids and Dad were happy with the situation—they had cable TV, and Dad was able to watch CNN to catch up on what was going on in the rest of the world.

On Saturday, we packed a picnic lunch for a day trip to Fuerte Bulnes, the farthest point south that one can drive on mainland South America. The road hugs the shoreline of the Estrecho de Magallanes, and the kids were intrigued by the ships and boats abandoned and beached along the shoreline. For most of the distance south it looked like a ship graveyard.

Fuerte Bulnes is a replica of the original fort that was erected on the site in 1843, similar to historical forts in Canada, this one with a view of the Strait in a strategic location. We walked the shore in the warm sun. Ed had a snooze on the beach and Dad had his in the van. Mom, the kids and I beach combed, finding shells that looked like mushroom caps. The largest pieces of driftwood I have ever seen lay on that beach. At one time many of them would have been magnificent trees. Some of them came up to my shoulder, in diameter.

Ben counted the ships on our return trip: there were 73 on the 58-kilometer stretch. Some looked as if they could be waiting for repair, but most were abandoned.

Sunday was a quiet day of hanging around. Mom, the kids and I walked to the water's edge. Mom, disappointed in what she found, said, "I can't believe the garbage on the beach and the sewage from the town pouring into the ocean. The smell of sewer is disgusting. It could be so beautiful but it's full of garbage."

"I know, Mom," I said, and told her I'd given up trying to find an ideal beach in South America. There have been few. Chile is much better than other countries we have visited but even here health standards are not always respected, if there are any. It has been a discouraging trip in that respect. I said, "We keep looking but have changed our expectations."

On Monday, at the government office, Ed spoke with a woman; Senõr Martinez, the man who we were supposed meet had started his holidays and wouldn't be in the office at all the entire week. The woman who was left in charge, let out a sigh of frustration. She was able to fill out the forms for the pardon, but that responsibility belonged to Senõr Martinez. The papers would have to be signed by another superior official, she was not authorized to do so. She would take care of it, but it would be Friday before the papers were complete. Both Ed and I were somewhat in a panic, Ed explained he had to get back to work. She let out another frustrated sigh and said, "Okay, Wednesday." The pardon had to be made out for each member of the family (even though it was just Ed and I who didn't have complete paperwork), and it was a lengthy form.

We celebrated Karina's birthday early, mostly for something to do. We managed birthday shopping at the duty-free market, got the cake into the *cabana* and the presents wrapped without her knowing what was going on. When it was time to decorate, she and Mom went for a walk by themselves. The others could barely wait for her to get out the door to blow up balloons and put the cake on the table. When she got back, she was surprised and then reminded us it wasn't her birthday yet. We had a fun evening playing cards and games together. Dad doesn't play cards much any more but when it comes to playing with his grandchildren he doesn't refuse.

Wednesday morning Ed and I were at the Government Office early. The same woman greeted us with a sober expression, but she did have our papers complete. As we signed the pardons Ed said, "It looks like you're the one who keeps this office running. We appreciate what you've done for us. Thank you so much." Her face softened, she smiled, and we had some conversation that wasn't so official. She was glad she could help and wished us a good vacation. It is amazing how far a compliment will go.

The two people who were working at the border last week were working at the Immigration office in Punta Arenas this week. Ed gave the papers for the pardon to the man who had turned us back. He looked through them, said they were complete, turned to the woman who didn't stamp our passports at the border, and instructed her to complete the forms we needed for the *carnets*. She started to type something, went to the man, touched him on the shoulder in a way that was more than a business relationship and asked a question about the form. With each new space that needed to be filled out, she had to ask another question and interrupted him several times while he was serving other people. When he was finished with the others, he looked at the forms, picked up the typewriter and brought us into the back office. There, he asked the questions and instructed her as to where the answers were to be filled in. He walked back and forth, leaned over her, touched her, and so on, as she giggled. I felt sorry for that young woman, who is not particularly good at her job, and was probably half his age. When he is past his infatuation she'll be history.

By lunchtime the eight forms were complete and the officer said we could pick up our *carnets* in four weeks. Ed told him that he was expected back to work in two, but that didn't matter. Then, Ed said the kids were supposed to be in school at the beginning of March, and pleaded surely there must be a way to speed things up; the man thought the situation over and decided he would forward the forms to Santiago. He then gave us papers to show the process had been started, so that we could cross borders for our return to Santiago. Ed promised to take care of things according to his instructions, thanked him for his patience with us and apologized for the work we caused, drawing forth a new amiability in the man. We shook hands and departed.

February 18 to 23, 1998: The Argentine Patagonia

On Highway 40, between Esperanza and Rio Bote, Dayna yelled out, "Hey Mom, Dad, look, it looks like Torres del Paine over there."

Ed said, "It probably is, it's not far away."

Tanya and Ben asked for the map and calculated that it was only about 70 kilometers away across the flat *pampa*. Jake asked, "If we are still on the big island how can we see Torres del Paine, Mom. Aren't we still on the island?"

I gasped and said, "No, Jake, we aren't."

"Then how did we get on the big land again?" I was amazed with his understanding of the geography. When I explained what had happened, the look of disappointment on his face was heartbreaking. He fell back into his seat and said "but I really wanted to see the big boat." I am always walking on thin ice with Jake.

Our campsite at Rio Bote had good facilities and the sun gave warmth to the air that made us feel like enjoying it for a while. Dad and Ed didn't let us do that; El Calafate was a 45-minute drive away and the Perito Moreno Glacier was beyond that. There was no time for lingering as far as they were concerned.

Canal Tempanos holds the runoff from the melting glacier and the water was as turquoise as the stone itself. The road wound between the canal and the mountain and we stopped to enjoy the view of the turquoise water, beneath the river of blue ice, between deep green mountains. Above the tree line the colour gives way to the greys and browns that rise to the peaks. The sky was an intense clean blue, and the last quarter half-moon hung above the frozen river. The road ended at a parking lot so close to the glacier we could hear the ice snapping and grinding. The 60-meter thick ice was on the opposite side of the canal and Dad was satisfied to stay where he was. But the kids were raring to go and were soon way ahead on the footpath which was no more than 100 meters from the glacier. The grinding, cracking sounds kept us alert and watching for chunks dropping off into the water. The kids, anxious to see more, kept us moving along the trail. Every few years the wall of ice closes off drainage of the canal, causing flooding and water pressure to build in the southern section. When the ice can't hold it any longer, it breaks apart, releasing the trapped water. Years ago the process happened about every four years; it now takes seven or eight.

At a good vantage point we stopped to just observe. The children, absorbed in the sight before them, soon asked questions. Why is the ice so tall? What makes it? Where does it come from? Why is it blue? How can ice be that old? Not much happened but something grabbed hold of our senses. Mom, Ed, Tanya and I continued just to observe while Ben and the others explored more. They were soon back with purple lips and tongues after snacking on the *calafate* berries that grow abundantly along the trail. Jake and Whitney's need for water, food, and a bathroom started to press. Ed said, "After that big piece of ice falls we'll go." They were satisfied to stay a little longer. I had the feeling Ed was right. I cleaned the camera lens and set up the photograph, prepared, and waited. As I looked through the camera to check the framing a sudden loud crack startled everyone. I jumped with the noise but collected myself and kept hitting the shutter as the enormous piece of ice broke away, crashing into the water. The wave it caused bounced back and forth between the shore and glacier. The new surface of ice left exposed was a deeper blue. When the waves subsided Ed said, "Okay, show's over, time for a picnic." Then the ones who were anxious to go earlier wanted to stay longer and see more.

The following day, we drove north on gravel road through intriguing landforms. From Rio Gallegos on the Atlantic Coast, travelling northwest, is like climbing massive stairs—flat for miles, across a huge expanse, with an occasional dip into a gorge that a river has cut out of the earth, then back up to the same level and eventually a mountainside to the next flat plain. There isn't anything gradual about the elevation differences—they are abrupt drops and climbs. Armadillos scampering across the road are a regular sight, as well as nandu (rhea birds) and wild grazing guanaco.

As we drove to Chalten the road followed the northern shore of Lago Viedma, at an elevation that is not much higher than the Atlantic Coast, according to our map. Before us, mountains peaked at 2,500 meters. At one point there was a small pool, pond or spring close to the lake but separate from the larger body of water. The odd thing about this was the contrast in colour of the waters, side by side, almost touching, meshed among the golden yellow brown of pampa grasses, rocks and dust. Lago Viedma was the rich turquoise of the glacial lakes and the small pool beside it was royal blue, similar to the colour of the freshwater lakes of the Canadian Shield.

Chalten is the same geographical form as Torres del Paine but its peaks are easier to see without hiking into the mountains. The peaks and cliffs are so sheer they don't hold snow.

We camped and bathed at the river. A short while later, a herd of horses drank and grazed downstream from us. Karina's patience and quiet ways allowed her to get close and pet a couple of them. When she came back to camp for dinner she had a few friends following her, and they remained to graze on the grasses around us. At sunset two "cowboys" on horses came through, rounding up the horses, one of which stubbornly refused to follow. The showdown ended within our camping area, where a few dishes got toppled before the horse would follow the rest of the herd. Dad said the horse wanted to stay with Karina.

We hiked to the glacier lookout in the morning, but Dad insisted on staying to pack up camp. I asked Mom why she thought he didn't want to see or do anything. She said, "He's with the kids, that's what he came for. He had no interest in coming to South America if they weren't here."

I wanted just to keep walking into the mountains, but the lookout was as far as we went. I felt weighted down with children, parents, lack of time, and cheated out of the opportunity. But one must be realistic and find balance; it is my family that enriches my life and to make those relationships good there has to be give and take. What I would like to do is just not feasible given the amount of time we have.

Dad had almost everything put away and lunch prepared on our return. Then we were back on the road. Gas stations are few and far between in this country and we stopped again in Tres Lagos to top up the tank. The sun was high, and the air was hot and still above the flat expanse of land. When paying for the gas, the woman at the station complained of the heat. She said it was unusual weather, almost scary. Something was not right, the *pampa* was rarely so hot, and she was baffled by the fact there wasn't a wind—apparently there is always a strong wind. It did make it easier to camp, though.

Throughout the *pampas* there were wide trenches dug out of the road about three to four feet deep, and covered with metal bars spaced about three inches apart. It took us a while to figure out that there was always a fence line on either side of the road where we were crossing them, and we eventually figured out they were *estancia* boundaries. The roaming sheep won't cross the grill and wouldn't be able to jump over it either. There are several kilometers between each one. It gave us a good perception of the expanse the *estancias* actually cover. Each *estancia* house is named and marked on our Patagonia map and many are small working communities that support more than a single family.

Several *estancias* provided camping facilities, so we chose to camp for a night. As we turned off the main road, there was a sign indicating the house was eight kilometers away, but we wondered at one point if it wasn't more than that. The road became a dirt track and descended into the basin of the Rio Belgrano. The track lay tucked alongside the ridge of the two different levels of land, where an expanse of yellow green and blues opened to our right on the river basin. When we stopped to open the gate, much of the surroundings appeared to be marshland with cattail like plants growing in the bogs. Several buildings in a row were tucked in close to the higher ridge of land, surrounded by tall eucalyptus and pine trees. The barns showed little activity. The main house was painted white, low to the ground, ranch style—one floor. Ed spoke to the woman within the fenced-in yard and made arrangements for us to spend the night. We were instructed to set up camp beside the house where there was an outdoor cooking area. We used the bathroom off the kitchen at the end of the house. While unloading our camping gear the excitement began and we soon understood why there was a six-foot fence around the house and "human area". Animals are free range—it is the people who are fenced in. Approximately 500 or more sheep were headed toward us. Four men on horses were in charge moving along outside of the heard, and three collie dogs ran around the sheep, moving them toward the barns and hold. The dogs worked the hardest, keeping the stray sheep with the rest of the pack. One of them shouted commands to the dogs, each of which was alert, ears erect and appeared to be having a lot of fun. Ben was on top of the van throwing things down and the rest of us quickly moved to the opposite side of the fence as the sea of sheep passed and was funneled into the hold at the barns.

By the time we had the tents set up, the dogs were playing with their seven puppies in the yard. The kids would like to have played with them but the man didn't allow it; they are working dogs. The puppies obeyed every word, even at their young age.

We used the bathroom in groups before settling into our tents for the night. The bathroom was opposite the kitchen and when Karina, Whitney and I took our turn in the facility, a late dinner was being prepared—mutton and fried vegetables all in the same pan, oily looking but it sure smelled delicious. It was a quiet warm night and the thick soft grass was comfortable for sleeping on.

I crawled out of the tent in the morning to face a young female lamb, white and clean looking, that had been clipping grass. The lamb spent its time eating until Whitney started petting her. She liked her ears rubbed and leaned her weight against Whitney until the two of them fell over on the ground. Whitney started to bounce around like she had with Little Dayna. Lambs can't resist and this one ran and jumped with her. Whitney got onto all fours and pushed her head against the lamb's head. It was as if the lamb said, "Hey, I know that game." Whitney butts the lamb, the lamb butts Whitney. It started out gently but each time it was the lamb's turn she backed up to get a little more of a run at it. They played until the little girl from the house called the lamb away by which time the game was starting to get rough.

The man of the house was preparing a large pan of mutton with potatoes on my morning bathroom trip. He had spots of fresh blood on his white T-shirt, and a wicked-looking knife (not really a kitchen knife) was sitting on the cupboard beside a leg of meat. Mutton may be just about the only thing they eat. I know it sounds funny but I couldn't get over how both he and his wife had body shapes similar to that of sheep—filled out and round on top of their legs. During our breakfast the sheep were herded out in the same manner as the night before—happy work-play for the dogs.

While we were packing up, the lamb came back with a bound. Ready to play with Whitney again, she jumped on all fours toward her, giving her a gentle bump. They played for a few minutes but it got rough again, and the woman took the lamb away, scolding her. She was a pet and was not supposed to do that. It was the last we saw of the lamb.

I found the woman of the house outside the back of the kitchen around mid-morning. Her employee brought tea for the two of them and sat down with her. I gave the woman the money we owed and chatted with what Spanish I could find in my head. She asked if all the children were mine and looked me up and down. I had the impression she didn't believe I had birthed them all. She asked where Quebec was. When I told her north of the States on the east coast in Canada, she looked quizzical. I'm certain she was unaware there was a country north of the United States. She told me there were about 700 sheep in the herd, more than I had estimated. I told her that here was so different from where I came from and thanked her for letting us stay the night. We managed to converse long enough that by the time we finished the final packing was complete and the van was at the front gate with everyone in it. I said, "Ciao and Gracias" again and ran to get in with everyone else.

It was north to Baja Caracoles, through *pampa*—50 kilometers of flat, dusty, scrubby desert, along gravel road, sometimes through muddy spots and extremely narrow roadways. Baja Caracoles sits at a junction with another dirt road. A new hotel, restaurant and gas pumps were operating, having opened just this year. In the past, it was necessary to carry extra gas in order to have enough to make it to the next service station. Once again, we had to pump the gas by hand, so we had a good break to stretch our legs.

Cueva de las Manos is a series of caves containing paintings of animals and human hands in black, white, green, red and orange, dating back about 10,000 years. To get to the site, we made the mistake of going the "shorter" route for the van off the highway, as indicated on our map and it involved a hike across the canyon for which we were totally unprepared. The only cave paintings we saw were through the telephoto lens of the camera, but the canyon itself was well worth the trip off the main road. We sat on the edge of it taking it all in and munched on calafate berries. It would have been a fabulous thing to do with proper preparations and if had not been pressed for time.

At the campground in Perito Moreno, a couple of young men came to talk to me while I was washing some clothes. They heard me speaking English to the kids and wondered if I had English reading material. I knew they weren't from North America and asked where they were from. Israel. I was curious. Other Israeli young people on the street in Santiago had asked me where they could get currency exchanged, another group for directions. I asked, "What does Chile and Argentina have to offer that attracts so many young people from your country?"

One young man did all the talking, "We have finished our service in the military, and most travel after they have done that to relax and let their fears go. Many don't go back to Israel—I don't think I will."

"I am a naive person when it comes to world affairs as such. It would be interesting to hear more of what you have to say," I replied.

The one young man who hadn't done any talking up to that point spoke with a bitter tone in his voice "Well, it's worse than you will ever see on TV." I asked them to join us for dinner but they declined, saying they had food for themselves but that they might come over later. I thought there might be a couple of books mixed up with the kid's stuff. I would look.

When I told the others I had invited them over, we had our own discussion about the Middle East. Dad is a constant watcher of news and doesn't really like the fact I don't stay on top of current events. It depresses me when I listen to bad news. There are probably just as many good things happening out there that we don't hear about and most of the time we are fed what the establishment wants the masses to hear anyway. It also takes a lot of time that, for me, is better spent raising kids who will make a positive difference in the world.

I dug out the books after dinner and dropped them off at their camp on my evening washroom trip. They must have been sleeping, so I didn't get the opportunity to talk with them again. I may not be able to do anything about what goes on in the Middle East, but making individual people's lives a little more pleasant, that much I can do.

I lay in bed thinking about how lucky the people of Canada are. The hardships we have to deal with are barely more than, say, a cold winter, and even winter isn't all that bad when we stop fighting it. I look at those two young Israelis in their early twenties, at the most, and think about the emotional repair work they will have to do before they can have a life. I am so thankful for my fortunes.

From Perito Moreno we headed west on a secondary road North of Lago Buenos Aires where the *pampa* slowly gave way to the rolling foothills of the eastern Andes. The road became a dirt track. I jokingly asked Ed if he was sure it was an international road. He said from what he read it was passable in summer and closed for winter. So much for sticking to main roads—but I did learn that a long time ago, didn't I?

Lago Buenos Aires is another turquoise lake almost surrounded by Andes in the north, south and west. The plain was still *pampa*, yellow and grey-green grasses and bushes. The road twisted and turned, climbing above the lake and rising into the mountains. At a fenced-in area three shirtless men were clearing and burning brush, and a short distance beyond that we came to a small white bungalow and a sign indicating the exit from Argentina into Chile. It was an opportunity to stretch our legs. The silence in the shadow of the mountains was profound. One of the guys put his shirt on and headed toward us. Exit papers were straightforward and we were told that the Chilean paperwork was to be done at the *caribinero* office in Puerto Ibanez after our descent out of the mountains. We continued to climb in altitude on a narrow gravel road. The colours were dull in the barren treeless landscape. The rock of the peaks closed in on us, giving a claustrophobic feel through the pass. As the mountains opened up on the west side, instantly the colour changed as the slopes were covered in green trees. On the descent, overlooking Puerto Ibanez, green and gold fields of hay and grains surrounded the town.

The *carabineros*—police—do the paperwork in Puerto Ibanez. It took much longer than anticipated, and involved several phone calls to Coihaique before the officials were able to figure everything out: tourist visas for Mom and Dad, our papers, us being temporary residents, and the van being a vehicle from North America. We still needed to go to the customs office in Coihaique to obtain the proper stamp for the van.

February 23 to 27, 1998: La Carretera Austral de Chile

The road between Puerto Ibanez and Coihaique is green and lush with forest that surrounds log homes and farms. By El Blanco the road was paved. Our maps didn't give an indication of such until north of Coihaique, and the smooth road felt luxurious after the past week of bumpy gravel. Ed was sailing along when we came upon a woman standing in the middle of our lane waving us down. Ed was about to go around but saw her hand wrapped up thickly with towels. He stopped. She had to get to the hospital in Coihaique. We shuffled our seating and gave her space beside Ben. The kids sensed something was not right, and no one spoke a word. She had just showered and gave off a pristine clean soapy fragrance—her hair was still wet. She and Ben were the only ones talking for a few moments, then, in chain reaction, Ben told his grandmother what had happened, Mom said something to the girls, and an "OOOOOOh" from one of them was the loudest noise of all. We let her out in front of the hospital about fifteen minutes after picking her up. The instant the door closed everyone started to talk, Ben said to Ed and me (who still knew nothing), "You know what happened? She was working in the barn with the cows and a bull stuck his horn right through the palm of her hand against the wall." We groaned. Not much wonder it was well wrapped.

While Ed and Ben finalized the papers for the van, Dad stayed in the vehicle. Mom and I walked to the pentagon-shaped Plaza de Armas with the kids. It is different from all other plazas we have visited, which are usually square. Children were peddling around in small, four-wheel cars that could be rented and of course the kids wanted to try it out. Dayna and Karina took off immediately, playing bumper car. It took Jake a few minutes to figure out how to maneuver his vehicle and he soon took part, while Tanya helped Whitney. Their 15 minutes were up too quickly.

We had our choice of camping spaces at the National Reserve, as there wasn't anyone else registered in the park. On arrival we were given a bathroom key, locations of campsites and strict instructions that we were to have no fires. We chose the south edge of the mountain, overlooking the town of Coihaique nestled in the valley of the Rio Simpson. We had a grand view of golden fields with a few blocks of deep green crops and the town itself with its squared-off streets, the rhythmic rows of buildings neatly lined up against a backdrop of the forested Andes, with their grey cliffs too steep for anything to grow on.

The kids explored and then played soccer until they almost lost the ball over the edge of the embankment—they ended their game. A rustling coming toward us out of the woods set our hearts beating faster. To our relief, the Park Ranger and his son came out of the bush on horses, wanting only to make sure we were settled and weren't making a fire. I don't know what we were so startled about— the only animal capable of doing us harm would be a puma, and those guys are not so clumsy as to be audible in the forest.

The next day was bright and warm, and the vegetation along the Carretera Austral was lush: tree-like bushes full of small red and purple flowers—blooming fuchsia, and nalca plants resembling oversized rhubarb with leaves the size of outstretched arms.

Salto Velo de La Novia was too impressive to pass. The falls were on two levels with pools below. It wasn't long before our crew was wading. Karina dropped a sandal and Tanya chased it before the water washed it away. She had a little swim in the cold water and Jake slipped on a rock and was totally wet too. Playing in the water filled the kids with happy, contented energy.

The Carretera Austral turned north to follow the valley of the Rio Manihuales. The road follows the river which flows along a U-shaped valley trough created by a long-gone glacier. The mountains on either side are gently sloped. It was a great geography lesson for the kids, as they could see the difference from a V-shaped water-worn valley easily after it was pointed out to them. The valley is pastureland for sheep and cattle and neatly divided by split-rail fences until it meets the rise of the mountains.

This is the area in which uncontrolled fires took place in the 1940s. Huge charred logs lay high in the mountains. *Chile: A Remote Corner on Earth* explained that a colonization law in 1937 granted ownership of land on the condition that the settlers clear-cut the forest to adapt it to farming. Fire was the main tool for clearing, and the fires were so great that smoke was blown as far east as the Atlantic Coast. The ancient forest never regenerated and it is a sad sight to see the damage.

As we drove north the effect of the fires was less obvious and the native forest flourished. The giant Alerce trees have tall limbless trunks with crowns that formed a ceiling above our heads. Green forest, snow-topped mountains, and streams of icy blue-green water are the best way to describe the area: rugged, untamed land with great distances between possibilities for human contact.

From its appearance, Lago de las Torres could have been situated in northern Ontario or Quebec just as easily as southern Chile. It was such a pleasure to see the forest and be amongst the abundance of greens and blues. The campground at the lake was closed but the warden said there was an excellent wild camping spot at the Rio Cisnes just before the bridge.

It was, as he said, a perfect place to spend the night. In my opinion it was the best place we have camped on this trip, certainly my favourite. Along the edge of the river, sat grey granite boulders. No wind, warm sun, and the river... the clearest, cleanest water I have ever seen, touched, smelled or tasted. The kids were drawn to the river, jumping from boulder to boulder, wading and exploring. It wasn't long before I heard, "Hey Mom, come see this—a log across the stream and balancing acts. I was soon in the water as well, up to my knees but able to clearly see my feet on the pebbles of the bottom. I bent over to caress the water's surface and was struck by a sense of déjà vu. Then as I drank water out of my hands, I remembered the dream in which I watched my feet walking in the water of a stream. It was almost the same. As I continued to drink my fill of the cold, refreshing water, I realized I was feeling happier and better all the time. It wasn't long before I had to get out and let my legs thaw out.

Ben worked his way upstream jumping from rock to rock and the kids and I followed. We could have climbed the rest of the day, continuing well into the mountains, with the river being a stony path deep into wilderness. We were gone an hour or more having left Ed, Dad and Mom to set up camp. When we returned, Ben and Dayna put their bathing suits on and swam in the pools. Jake and Karina were about to do the same, and I suggested that they go without suits so things didn't have to dry later. Karina turned up her nose and wasn't sure. Jake, the "no underwear" kid (he absolutely refuses to wear any at anytime) said, "Can we?"

"Of course," I replied.

He stripped down in no time and was in ultimate freedom. Karina wore her bathing suit. It wasn't long before we heard screams, giggles, splashes and Tarzan yodelling from Ben. Tanya, who hadn't been swimming, came back to get the camera, and a couple of minutes later there were screams and angry voices yelling her name. She returned rather quickly and put the camera back. They came back shivering, shaking and very clean. While we ate our dinner a truck went by, the driver honking his horn to say hello. It was the only vehicle that passed that evening.

During the night we were awakened by another truck stopping on the bridge. A flashlight beam crossed the tent a couple of times but the truck stayed where it was. I heard the other tent zipper being undone and Mom asking Dad what he was doing—clearly leaving the tent. Ed joined him, I didn't have to get up to figure out by listening that plastic water jugs were being filled and the truckers were soon on their way.

It took a while for me to get back to sleep thinking about Dad and how anxious he has been. He just doesn't feel comfortable anywhere other than at home. While driving toward the canyon of the Cueva de los Manos, he was extremely restless, then as I sat beside him on the drive back out he said, "I'm so glad you guys didn't go to those caves, this place makes me so nervous."

I asked, "Why does it make you nervous, Dad?"

"I don't know, it just does."

Dad is often intuitive about nature, but he has had this kind of reaction almost everywhere we have been, just fearful. I feel defeated, sorry for him in a way, and don't believe I am the person who will ever help him change. I just have to accept that.

I lay on the ground listening to the peaceful sound of the water running past, and thought about where it is headed. Water: its ultimate goal is to reach the ocean where it becomes part of the whole, powerful and strong. If each individual person on earth had that same ultimate goal spiritually, to be part of the collective consciousness, imagine the strength and what we could accomplish. The sound of the water soon carried me back into a restful sleep.

At daylight, I got up to relieve myself and realized there had been an overnight weather change. The previous day shorts and T-shirt were almost too much, but now it was cold and we dressed warmly, in wool socks, running shoes, pants, shirts, sweaters and jackets. It wasn't really raining but the damp mist made things uncomfortable. I made oatmeal and hot chocolate to warm us up and by the time breakfast was complete the heavy mist had turned to drizzle. By the time we were ready to move on everyone had wet stringy hair and damp clothing despite our jackets. We passed on the hike upstream. Ed stopped the van on the bridge to take our last look at the river and where we had camped. It was a special spot. Everything we had that would hold drinking water was filled again. Maybe the attraction was the purity of the surroundings.

The road continued to follow the gorge of the Rio Cisnes. At the landmark of Piedra del Gato, a massive rock wall, Ed told us that it was the only area on the entire Carretera Austral where there were fatal injuries during construction of the road. It was an incredible feat considering the mountainous terrain the road works its way through. At one point where the road was high above the river, we stopped to take in the sight of the green, rushing water that cut its way through rock channels. The mountains are covered in trees, which at this point, barely their silhouettes were visible due to the mist in the air. The sound of the river below was wild, not nearly as friendly as it was where we camped upstream.

Carretera Austral lined with nalca plants.

The road moved north from the Rio Cisnes, winding its way to a higher altitude, over another bridge, then back down to sea level at Seno Ventisquero. The cloud cover was heavy but where it cleared, we could see cliffs and several waterfalls draining the higher altitude. The top of the range is covered in a thick layer of glacial ice. As the clouds moved in and out we had glimpses of the Ventisquero Colgante, the Hanging Glacier, so-named because the ice cap, like a hat that is too big, overhangs the cliffs of the mountains, sending down countless waterfalls.

At Seno Ventisquero the road was closed for repairs. A small fishing boat pulled to shore with the morning's catch, and Ed asked the two men about the road. There was a ferry that took vehicles around the construction. They said just to wait, that it would be back and asked Ed if he wanted some fresh salmon. Ed, Ben and Dayna disappeared over the ridge with the fishermen to clean the fish. Just as the ferry was loading they returned with two five-kilogram salmon cleaned and ready for cooking. Ed was full of smiles and said they were only 2000 pesos (about $6.50 CDN). I couldn't believe it. "Two huge salmon—we'll never eat it all."

Both Dad and Ed simultaneously retorted, "We'll eat it."

Ed backed the van onto the boat. We were on the move immediately and were deposited back on land beyond the road repairs. Puerto Pugahuapi, on the most northerly point of Seno Ventisquero and our next gas station stop, was an interesting little place founded by four German settlers in 1935 with the anticipation that other settlers would follow. But the onset of the Second World War prevented that from happening. There were three impressive European-style buildings and many log houses along the street, a community with definite German atmosphere. The carpet factory is what gives the little town such importance. One of the settlers started it in 1950 even before road access, and it has produced and exported high quality carpets ever since. It can be visited but tours weren't until 4 p.m. so we didn't get the opportunity.

We arrived shortly after 1 p.m. into siesta hours and Ed pulled the van up to the gas pumps beside a trail bike whose owner had been waiting a while. A local person walked by and said, "The owner must be taking his dinner. He usually eats at the restaurant over there. I'll tell him he has some customers." After a short wait a man sauntered up to the station. Our gas tank was nearly empty, and he kept a close watch as he filled it. Twice he stopped to ask if he should continue. Ed said, "Yes, yes it needs to be filled." He watched nervously, as the amount of money we owed increased. He was relieved when it finally stopped and doubly so when Ed produced the cash. It is a big tank and takes a lot when empty.

We decided to look for a *cabana* instead of sleeping in wet tents and investigated the tourist centre of El Pangue. It provides fishing and canoeing services, a base for exploring and day trips to surrounding attractions. While waiting in the van for Ed and Dad to come back with a "yea or nay" we looked in through an expanse of windows into the formal dining room. The tables were set up for a first-class meal. Something didn't feel right. I'm not sure if it was me looking at crystal and china feeling like I wasn't up to standard, or whether it was the crystal and china in the surrounding setting. Dad and Ed came back with a "nay"—the *cabanas* were not equipped with kitchen facilities and guests were expected to eat in the dining room or order room service, something we weren't prepared to do when we had two huge wonderful fish that needed to be cooked and eaten. Just south of the village of La Junta, almost at the junction of the road that heads for Lago Verde and Argentina there was a group of *cabanas* for rent, some still under construction. The woman in charge was intrigued with where we had travelled and it took some time to answer all her questions. She gave us a *cabana* with six beds, kitchenette, full bathroom, and living space with a couch and a huge covered verandah. Ed spoke further with her and discovered that she and her husband felt that *cabanas* would be a good business in the area. The road to Argentina is in the process of being constructed to the coast, and when completed there will be east-west traffic as well as north-south.

It became a pull-ourselves-back-together afternoon. The kids put themselves to work without being asked and did a major cleaning of the van. Mom was surprised that the idea came from them. We rolled out the tents, swept the muck off them and hung them up on the verandah to dry out—the wet clothes, too. One by one we took hot, refreshing showers and together made a filling, nutritious dinner—lots of melt-in-your-mouth fresh salmon, fish at its best. Ed called the Navimag office for information on the ferry. It might not be running on schedule, as it was evacuating a coastal village threatened by forest fire; we would find out more in Chaiten. It was an evening of euchre, a game the kids are getting good at.

I awakened in the middle of the night dreaming that the tents hanging outside were flying away. I couldn't go back to sleep so decided if I was going to lie wide awake worrying about the tents, I might as well get up and bring them in. I moved in the dark, remembering that the keys were on top of the fridge, and got to the door of the cabana without a sound. I managed to find the keyhole but couldn't get the door open. Ed noticed me out of bed, flipped on a light and came to help; he couldn't get the door open either. If it's one thing I don't like about Chile, it is the locks and doorknobs. I have locked myself out so many times because the only way you can get in is to open the door with a key. There is never a doorknob on the outside, and on the inside there are always two locks and a safety bolt. If one had to get out of the house in a hurry and didn't have the necessary keys— you'd be trapped.

Dad turned on another light and said, "What's going on?"

I answered, "I had a dream the tents were flying away and instead of lying awake worrying about them I decided to bring them in, but it's impossible to get out this door."

He replied, "Well, we had better bring them in, then."

Mom was up too. She said, "It's a good thing there isn't a fire, we'd all be in trouble."

Finally the door released. One tent was rolling around on the floor of the verandah and the other was still draped over the railing but sliding over the edge to the ground. Both were dry, so we rolled them up and brought them in. Ben awakened and asked what was going on. Ed said, "The *bruja*—witch had a dream. We had to bring the tents in, that's all."

I wasn't sure I should take that as a compliment or an insult, but there wasn't a threat of the tents blowing away after we brought them in.

As we got closer to Chaiten the clouds broke up and let some sun through. Clouds are more common than sun in the temperate rainforest. But plant life is abundant; white and pink foxglove grows wild like bad weeds along the roadside, and nalca, whose leaves make great umbrellas, grow everywhere.

With the last two days of rain, the forest fire had been snuffed out naturally and the ferry was back on schedule. We booked passage to Quellon on Chiloe Island aboard the *Alejandrea* the following morning. Chaiten is a small, quiet town—at least it was on the day we were there. There is one paved street less than half a kilometer long. It is a town that accommodates in-transit stopovers: ships, planes and road vehicles.

At the tourist office there was a display of photographs and information about the protected forests of the gigantic Alerce trees. There is a Canadian company from British Colombia working with the CONAF (Corporacion Nacional Forestal) people to help preserve and regenerate the existing and declining native forests here in Chile. Western Canada and Chile have the similar climatic and geological conditions and are working together to find solutions to their shared challenges. Another shared ecological focus for the two countries is the puma or mountain lion as it is called in North America—mainly concerns around declining numbers and what can be done to prevent extinction.

February 27 to March 1, 1998: Chiloe Island, Chile

The ferry to Chiloe Island was delayed and we waited all morning. We played cards and snacked, but the kids couldn't sit in the van going nowhere the entire morning, so they went out into the rain, got wet and had fun. Dad sat in the van all morning disgruntled. He didn't think the kids should be playing in the rain.

The docking piers were on different levels. The lowest was slippery, and the slime on it indicated it was probably under water more often than not. The next pier was about three meters above it, then another sat three meters higher than that. I had a hard time believing the water levels differed that much and wondered how often the highest pier was used.

I went back to the van to get out of the dampness and read *Chile: A Remote Corner on Earth.* It helped my understanding. The difference between high- and low-water tide levels in the Corcovado Gulf is up to seven meters whereas on the Pacific Coast of Chiloe the difference is 2.5 meters. When the volume of water that comes with high tide moves into the shallow gulf the only place for it to go is up, hence the high level of the pier. Low tide leaves vast stretches of uncovered tidal flat. During high tide the ships move in and out. The constant changing currents can be treacherous for small boats.

It was close to noon when the *Alejandrea* made an appearance on the horizon. More people than I could imagine lived in town turned up for its arrival. We found a place to park ourselves in the lounge, and after the hunger gap was filled with Chilean hotdogs, the warmth and hum of the ship knocked everyone out for a quiet time.

The island of Chiloé is the most populated archipelago in Chile—rich in tradition and home to many myths and legends that are taken quite seriously by the inhabitants. It is an island of high tides on the inland side, which shape the peoples' livelihood. Rough seas and high constant winds make the western outer side a less desirable location to live. Chiloé is the island that Charles Darwin visited at least twice, and on which he found approximately 11,000 people bearing Mapuche names. Today the mixture of Spanish conquerors and Mapuche people has created a distinctive Chiloté population numbering close to 120,000.

The town of Quellon felt big after the previous few days, with its markets and paved streets. It is the southernmost port on Chiloé, has a seafood canning industry, and is where the Pan American Highway officially ends. The main street along the seashore was lined with wooden buildings that have shops on the ground floor and residences on the second floor.

When I purchased fruit and vegetables at the mini-*mercado*, I was greeted politely by the owner and was putting apples into a bag when Ben, Dayna, Whitney and Jake joined me. As each child came to help, the man found a bigger smile. He asked where we were from and was astonished when he found out we had driven from Quebec—he knew where it was. He spoke to Whitney and asked her about her teeth. She understood what he said but didn't have the Spanish words and replied to him in English. She is always willing to give any one who asks a good look and she lifted up her front lip for him to see. She spoke in English to him and he in Spanish to her; neither spoke a word of the other's language, but they talked to each other. Whitney didn't seem to make any differentiation between the two languages. As we left the man said, "God bless all of you and have a safe-good journey all the way home."

At one time the island was covered in forest, but cattle farming and logging has transformed the landscape. The rolling slopes are grazing land for herds of sheep and cattle, and are farmed as well with grains and vegetables. Transformed or not, the landscape is beautiful.

At a sign that bore an illustration of Charles Darwin, Ed shouted out, "Hey, do you guys want to go and see the Darwin Beach?"

The word beach sparked interest and they said yes.

Ed replied, "This is not just any beach, you guys, it is Darwin Beach—named after a famous anthropologist."

It didn't mean much until Ed started to explain, "You know, Charles Darwin studied the native people of Tierra del Fuego and the Chilean Coast during the early nineteenth century. What he learned gave him new ideas—from which he drew conclusions and presented the theory of evolution. It created a big upset in the churches in Europe. He was famous for his theories and he did a lot of research here. You can read his writings if you're interested."

Visiting the beach was enough for the time being. The road off the main one toward the coast was gravel, of course. The trees through the park gave way to the open expanse of the barren windblown coastline. The road turned into beach at Cucao, a quaint village on the shore of the open Pacific. A 1960 tidal wave washed the entire village into the sea, and it was rebuilt but without the architectural distinction of other villages on the island. When we arrived, the kids headed toward the water quickly. The beach, which must be 100 to 150 meters wide, is white sand on the landside, but where the waves break, it is stone. Mom and I started to catch up with Ed and the kids while Dad wandered off on his own. Sitting in the van was getting to him. My eyes caught sight of a little white ball with black specks sitting on the sand, and I picked it up. It was a stone the size of a marble, and almost a perfect sphere. I put it into my pocket. The kids were beachcombing and didn't make it to the water. I came across another larger, egg-shaped stone about eight centimeters long and so smooth. The original piece was from sedimentary rock and on the top and bottom were a series of perfectly shaped ovals in tones of grey. It couldn't be more beautifully shaped or polished if man had forced it. Where the water beats on the beach, the stones are shaped like balls and eggs of different colours, in sizes from a marble to a big fist. Excited kids had to show off their treasures. Ben said, "These stones have been here a long time."

Ed & Gaye –Darwin Beach, Chiloe Island

We camped on the beach instead of looking for a place to stay. Dad was discouraged but Mom liked the idea. A van that had crossed on the ship with us drove past, and like us, set their camp up for the night. Everyone but Dad ate dinner. I asked if he had diarrhea because I had stuff for it if necessary. He was just not feeling well and went for another long walk, some of the best medicine. When the kids were played out and it was close to dark, they had cookies and juice while we enjoyed a box of wine and the sunset over the Pacific from Darwin Beach.

The kids built a sand castle city in the morning and when that was complete we headed for the stones again. Ben brought a pail but Ed told everyone we could only bring as many stones as would fit in our pockets. We cheated and made a pocket of our shirtfronts too. I sat down and lined up the ones I had collected and admired them. What is it about stones? Every kid and even adults slip them into their pockets to hold, rub, feel—draw strength from. It must have something to do with their connection to ancient times. If only they could talk. We left the beach with a little extra weight.

Driving into Castro we had a good look at the *palafitos* (wooden houses on stilts above the water on the shoreline). They are constructed mostly to make full use of the seafront. At one time they existed in Ancud, Quemchi, and Chonchi, too, but only a few samples of the unique architecture are left in Castro.

The Mercado de Artisania on the waterfront was like a museum, a building full of hand-knit and crocheted sweaters in the distinctive Chiloé style. Stall after stall, women sat in their small spaces knitting and crocheting, waiting for someone to choose from their creations which were displayed to the ceiling. Beautiful warm garments perfect for the climate of the Chilean Patagonia most of the year and winters farther north. The Chiloé blankets were of excellent quality too—hand-woven on a loom from coarse, wool yarn, several kilos per blanket. Other stalls displayed high quality felt hats of varying colours or straw baskets in the unique Chilote style, used for carrying vegetables home from the market. Each of us came out with a new wool sweater, and we purchased a large, salad bowl hand-carved from a block of *rauli* wood—this from a range of woodcrafts that included dishes, canisters, spoons, candlesticks, etc., etc. Some pieces were decorated but most were left simple, showing off the grain.

Ed promised us a restaurant meal so that we could try *curanto*, a national dish typical of Chiloé. It consists of a pot of vegetables, seafood, chicken, beef and pork with dumplings, slow-baked all day surrounded by hot coals. Our waiter was a university student working to save for his education. He explained some of the area's food traditions and suggested a complementary wine to have with our meal. The *curanto* came in pottery dishes the size of a six quart soup pot, from which we dished into smaller bowls. Each serving was enough to feed two adults, and when we had our fill of the delicious concoction, we took our leftovers for another meal.

We had to see the church on the Plaza before leaving Castro. It was a typical Chiloé wooden structure, but distinctive because of its colours: orange, with mauve and white trim. The Jesuit missionaries persuaded the government to build churches and chapels for the native people, and on the archipelago of Chiloé there are still more than 150 such buildings. Even the smallest of communities has access to these, which were built from the same basic plan, entirely of wood, with individual characteristics. The first of them were constructed without using nails, only wooden pegs, and are still standing today two to three hundred years later. Nine are national monuments.

The other architectural feature unique to Chiloé is the shingles or *tejuelas,* on the outsides of buildings. German settlers introduced the style to the region, and with the abundance of wood, the shingles became a popular means of weatherproofing. It is the patterns created by the bottom edge of the individual shingles that give the buildings their distinctive look. We noticed several patterns and once we started looking for them we found that some were more popular than others. A simple straight cut on many buildings—mostly country houses, less time-consuming to cut and attach to a wall, similar to cedar shingles popular at home. Another common pattern was achieved with concave and convex cuts alternating repeatedly on the wall, creating a wave pattern. Another was a round cut creating a scallop pattern in the row. One of the most common we noticed was a straight shingle alternated with a shingle that had the two corners cut off, creating a three-sided cut.

Craftsmanship is of deep importance on Chiloé. Almost everything used for cooking, clothing, farming, fishing, and building materials is traditional. Some may say it is a backward, hard way of life, but there is something special about a community that is so self-sufficient.

We didn't know what Dad needed to improve his outlook but thought a bed for a night might help. We easily found a fabulous *cabana* in Ancud for a reduced cost— the fall term of school started this week and the majority of Chilean vacationers are home. There was a goat staked on the grassy hill behind our *cabana*. He is a character. He greeted us happily on our arrival, and when someone said something to him he would answer. It became a comical pastime carrying on a conversation with the goat.

The kids were hard to move in the morning, enjoying the luxury of something close to a real house. However, we did manage a visit to Fuerte San Antonio before leaving Chiloé. There wasn't much left of it apart from a few cannons. The views were good, as usual, at a stronghold but what held the children's interest most was a man at the entrance carving a piece of wood into what he called a *trauco*, a little manlike figure from Chiloté mythology, carved out of *rauli* wood, perhaps comparable to a troll in a children's fairy tale. There were several completed carvings on the shelves around the carver and as he worked he told us about the *trauco*. He lives in the forest, in caves and trees. He always carries a walking stick and will seduce young women or carry off young children who are wandering about without their parents. It's obviously a mythical figure created to discourage young people from going into a forest alone. However, I find myself wondering if such creatures would instill an unnatural fear.

March 1 to 8, 1998: Through the Chilean Lake District and back to Santiago

A German couple runs Camp La Herradurra close to Valdivia on the Rio Valdivia. Our accountant, who camps there regularly, recommended the place. We arrived as the sun was setting. The summer season is over, and the proprietors weren't particularly friendly but did give us a campsite overlooking the river. Two kittens turned up while we were enjoying some hot chocolate around the fire. The kids held and petted them, kittens and kids finding mutual comfort in one another and the kids wanted to take them with us. Ed told them they could have a cat and all the dogs they wanted when we got back to the property to live.

We were toured out. The extent of our visit to Valdivia was a walk along the wharf while our laundry was being done. The place does have interesting history, originally founded by the Spanish in the 1550s, deserted by the turn of the century to be occupied by Dutch pirates. It was reclaimed by the Spanish in 1645 and was the only Spanish settlement south of the Biobio River because of the strong Mapuche resistance. Capture of the walled city in 1820 by the Chilean Navy was instrumental in its liberation from Spanish rule. The city was destroyed in 1960 by a devastating earthquake and tidal wave, but it has been totally rebuilt. The original shoreline sank more than two meters during the quake, and the wharves we toured are rebuilt above structures beneath the waterline.

When returning to the campsite, Ed crossed the bridge to Isla Teja and made a turn in the wrong direction. We ended up on the Universidad Austral Campus at a dead end—but it didn't have such a dead look to it. On the other side of the fence was a group of rowers getting into their shells on the river for a workout. Ed said he didn't know what this unbidden reminder was about: to tell him there is rowing in Chile, too, or to make him realize some of the things that he was missing in Canada?

The kids wanted to try out the water slide at the dock of the campground. One thing we have found in Chile is that if it is cloudy, cool air off the ocean keeps the temperature from warming up. Despite that fact, the dock looked like a wonderful place for play, and the kids were determined to try it out. We watched river barges moving crates upriver toward Valdivia, along with many other boats moving back and forth. The kids figured out that there was a tide on the river. When they were exploring in the morning the water was moving out toward the ocean and in late afternoon it was moving inland. After discussing what they learned, they figured tides must occur on any river where it flows into the ocean. Cold wasn't a big enough word to describe the water, but Ben, Jake and Karina managed to get a couple of slides in before they started to shake. It was a cool night, and there wasn't any firewood around so we made it an early one.

We were in the famous Chilean Lake District and we should have been seeing some of what it has to offer, but everyone was tired of taking in new sights, and we were running out of time. Ed wanted to visit Villarica so we did a quick detour off the Pan Am to see at least the volcano and lake. I'm sure they would have made a more lasting impression if the volcanoes had been visible, but clouds blocked any view of the peaks.

We continued to the Los Angeles campground where there was no one but maintenance people and ourselves. We chose a grassy spot close to the pool and play structures. The kids swam in the pool, and four local teens joined in the play. Ben was soon back at our camp, almost in tears, insulted. He and the other kids were being made fun of in Spanish. Ben said, "They're saying that my nose is big and ugly and that I'm stupid and my hair sticks up; they're laughing at me and saying things like that about the girls too."

I didn't know what to say. The local youngsters obviously didn't realize the kids understood what they were saying.

"Ben, I can tell your feelings are hurt and what they are doing is not right, but are you stupid?"

"NO!"

"Well, that's good, it's important for you to believe. I bet they would be the ones feeling pretty stupid if you went back over there and started speaking Spanish to them."

"I'm not going back over there. I don't want to talk to them."

"Remember when we were living at the *cabanas* and you guys and Elizabeth were talking about people in English and not saying very nice things."

"Yeah."

"Well, there is a saying, what goes around comes around. You just got some coming back, didn't you?"

"Yeah, but I still don't want to go back to the pool."

Ed wasn't going to let Ben feel defeated. He said, "Do you want to swim in the pool some more?"

"Yes," he said hesitantly.

"Well, let's go, I'll go with you."

They went back to the pool. Ed talked to the kids in polite conversation asking them about themselves, school, etc. and Ben and Tanya started talking to them as well. There was an initial shock period for the young people, and after they all got over their embarrassment, they played together for a long while afterwards. So in all, everyone learned a little lesson from the situation.

We thought we were going to camp on Lago Rapel. It is a man-made reservoir for irrigation and hydro-electricity. It is a favourite regional getaway for the people of Santiago, located almost directly west of Rancagua, and it would have been close enough to the city for Ed to get to work. We searched for a suitable place to stay along the shoreline, but it just didn't feel right. Most camping spots or *cabanas* were asking a high price for the value. On the main highway we found a *cabana* in El Manzano with good rates, but the grumpy old man that greeted us, said the kids would wreck the place and he wouldn't have us. It was the first time we encountered that attitude in the 15 months we have travelled South America. After inquiring at 11 places we were discouraged.

Ed suggested we go back to Santiago. I didn't want to do that. Amanda and Peter had just gotten the place to themselves. Ed asked for another suggestion but I didn't have one. It was 8 p.m. and we had to do something. I agreed as long as we were out of the house in a couple of days. Ed called from Rosario to let them know we were coming. Peter answered and hesitated when Ed more or less told him. He had to ask Amanda if it was okay. Ed said he put Peter in a tough spot, Amanda wasn't happy, something was going on—more than merely our coming to stay at the house. Ed also called Luis, who agreed to have the receptionist change Ed's appointments to Saturday.

We arrived in Santiago at 11:30 p.m. and Peter let us in, but we didn't see Amanda. We spread the mattresses out in the upstairs rooms and made beds for the 10 of us for the night. There was an ominous, heavy feeling in the air.

Amanda was gone most of Thursday. We did our laundry and Ed made arrangements for us to visit a couple of potential rental houses in Rengo. Friday we left the kids with Dad and Mom to visit the houses and decided the Casa Quinta on the outskirts would be suitable—the kids would love it. Again on Friday, Amanda left early and didn't return until evening. Saturday after work, Ed arranged the details for renting the house. It needed a few repairs and we could move in on Saturday the 14th, a week away.

After spending the day being careful of what we said and did in the house, I convinced Ed that we should go to Algarrobo for the week. There was just too much tension where Amanda was concerned. Plus it would be a way for Dad and Mom to have a little time on the coast anyway. I made arrangements with Christina for Sunday evening after the weekend crowd left. We packed the belongings we needed for the week and left early.

We spent the afternoon at Cerro San Cristobal overlooking the city and visited the statue of Mary, mother of Jesus, visible from the windows of our Santiago house. Mom and I sat in the seating area while the kids played. I said to Mom, "Ever since we arrived in Santiago, whenever I look out the window and see her standing on top of the hill, I am always reminded of what she said in the dream I had when pregnant with Jake." Mom asked what dream that was and I was surprised I hadn't told her; I had told almost every one else.

Getting pregnant with Jake was a surprise and I wasn't happy about it in the beginning. I had just decided to home-school the kids and four were enough. But as soon as the schooling decision was firm in my head it was as if I wasn't given a choice, I was pregnant again. For most of the pregnancy I was mad at God for giving me more to take care of than I thought I could handle and just mad at the world in general. I didn't know how I was going to provide for everyone's needs. At about six months, I had a dream that changed my attitude: I was in the dining room at Mom and Dad's house. I went to the big window and was looking out over the back yard. I was sad, depressed and crying. Outside, the forest was green and lush; everything was healthy; flowers were blooming and the grass was a healthy green. Then Mary, mother of Jesus, floated down from the sky, stood right in front of me, barely five feet away, on the other side of the window. She was dressed in flowing blue robes, was pregnant, and held a small child in her arms, while another a little older clung to her legs. She stood before me, looking concerned, and said, "Be happy, it is the gift of life," then vanished.

I woke out of the dream, shaking. She was so real, bringing such a firm message. She not only changed my attitude toward the pregnancy but life in general. Life is a gift, every day every moment, and we are supposed to be happy. The really amazing thing about the dream was that when I first visited the hill with Diane and Gilles, the great statue took my breath away. It looks exactly like the Mary of my dream and every time I look up at the statue, her words ring loud and clear.

Ed spent the night in Algarrobo with us, then went back to Santiago on Monday. He stayed at Amanda and Peter's for the week while completing business.

Cerro San Cristobal, Santiago, Chile

LIFE IN RENGO

Tuesday, March 17, 1998:

So we are in our *casa quinta,* on the fringe of the small town of Rengo, a little more than an hour's drive south of Santiago and almost in the middle of the central valley. It is fruit country, not just for the grapes that produce the wines for which Chile is so famous, but for the oranges, lemons, apples, peaches, plums, pears, cherries and *kaqui* (persimmon) as well. The huge Dole fruit processing plant along the highway is busy with activity every time we go by. Fields of orchards and vineyards stretch across the flat plain until the landform changes to Andes Mountains to the east and the coastal Corderilla to the west, both a long distance away but still in good view.

Ed and I left the kids with Mom and Dad at the *cabanas* from Friday until Sunday so that we could pack what we took from the house in Santiago, shop for a fridge and washer, and pick up the new schoolbooks I ordered from Canada at the International Post Office. Just the duty is twice the cost of the books themselves. Tanya has already read two of the new books and Dad said this morning, "Sure is nice to see those kids reading." I had the impression he thought the kids couldn't read—there is still a lot of tension about this school stuff.

When I stepped out of the van at the house in Providencia, a black cat, about six months old appeared at my feet rubbing my legs. I picked her up to snuggle. She was a little scruffy but pretty, a few white hairs on her chest and one white whisker. After I put her down she followed me around. Ed seemed to like her and said, "If she's still around in the morning we should take her with us." She was around in the morning and even jumped into the van out of curiosity while we were loading it. Amanda said she was always on the street, didn't seem to belong to anyone and often hung around the house. She came in the van with us and the kids have decided to call her Jasmine. On Saturday afternoon while shopping for groceries, Ed was the one who remembered the cat food. He couldn't keep her secret either, allowing the kids to discover her, as we had agreed. Sometimes he is a real softy.

The kids ran and explored from the moment we arrived at the house. Jake came back from his lengthy investigation and said with sincere enthusiasm, "I really love this place." Karina has already hurt her back, scraped a leg and knocked the wind out of her self having fallen out of a tree. It gave us all a scare. She lay still from the aches and pains for most of yesterday but is up and moving around today. She will be fine and maybe a little more cautious when climbing trees.

Ed did a radio talk show in Rancagua yesterday morning. The whole concept of Chiropractic was so new and intriguing at the station they had him do a television interview as well. He was told it would be aired in the near future; they'll let us know when.

This morning I altered Ed's clinic jackets to fit. I'm still not crazy about them. In Chile every profession and every place of employment has a specific uniform. Ed says the jackets will give him more recognition as a practitioner when people are so conditioned to seeing professionals dressed as such. He's right, of course, but that doesn't mean I have to like it.

March 27, 1998:

We are becoming organized in the house. I managed to hook up the washer myself and got it working. But the taps didn't hold the pressure and leaked, so the guys who came to do the floor put new fittings on them. A couple of nice guys, they are employed during the day and every night last week worked here from 7 to 11 p.m.

While they were working on the floor one night two scruffy looking men showed up at the gate wanting food and a place to sleep. I gave them each a container full of food from the dinner we were having, but there was something ominous about them. It just didn't feel right to have them around for the night. Ben couldn't convince them to move on, so asked one of the guys who was working on the floor to help him get the message across, and the guy ended up yelling at them before they left. At that point, our worker brought his car inside the gate instead of leaving it on the road—he didn't have a very good feeling about them either. He told us to never let anyone like that in.

In the shed we found a chair with a broken cane seat, cleaned it up, and wove in cotton cord to replace the cane. As Jake says, "It's a really nice chair." On the same trip to the shed, Ben found metal racks that could be used for shelving. Three of the ripped-up floorboards fit perfectly on the racks, and we have a great set of shelves for our books.

Mom gave us money for Christmas to buy some furniture from Chimborongo, a small town about a 40-minute drive south of here on the Pan Am Highway. The shops are set up side by side, running parallel to the road for a good kilometer. We watched wicker weaving in progress and took all afternoon to look through the strip of shops. We furnished almost the entire house, buying a rattan table and chair set for the kitchen, a rattan loveseat with two matching chairs for the living room, lamp shades, a child's chair for Whitney, a wicker bedside table for Tanya, wicker blanket boxes for Dayna and Karina to store clothing in, a shelf for Ben and Jake for their bedroom, a shelf for my clothing, two wicker deck chairs, a woven straw mat, a laundry basket and a cat basket, all for about $450.00 (CDN).

So our house has been furnished in rattan and wicker, giving it a cozier feel and places to store the things we are managing to accumulate.

I picked some of the purple grapes off the trellis in the yard and made juice for which I hoped to make jelly. But the kids liked it so much it disappeared before we had a chance to make the jelly. Mom picked more and we did get to make six jars the second time. We are eating grapes all the time.

The kids have been getting into some schoolwork, mostly math, and Mom has been working with the girls, helping them with their reading. I know she thinks we aren't doing enough but we will have the time to turn our attention to books in the next few months.

The kids have been playing outside most days. Ben built a playhouse from the appliance boxes amongst the bamboo plants and the kids occupy themselves for hours out there.

Mom says she feels as if she is living in a convent. Given that she hasn't gone outside the gate for several days, and with seven-foot walls around our house and property, I can understand how she could feel that way. In Chile almost every home has at least a four-foot wall around it, especially in cities and towns. Dad is feeling a little cut off from the world too; we don't have a television, and he has asked for English newspapers to read. They are difficult to get here in Rengo, so he has been reading a few of the novels we have. This is not customary for him, and he is not happy with the situation. The kids look forward to evenings when Mom and Dad play cards, checkers and other games with them. It is good not having a television; we do things with each other to fill our time.

Ed spoke with his sister Lisa on Sunday. Our house in Wakefield was supposed to be sold to Pascal and Christiane on March 1st this year, but Pascal has informed us that it is too big for them, so they won't be purchasing it but will continue renting for the time being. So the house is still ours.

Ed had an interesting day this week. A physiotherapist, Raoul, who owns and works in the building where Ed has set up practice, has been working on introducing chiropractic in Chile. A group of physiotherapists have been studying together, and Raoul would like Ed to teach them how to do adjustments. Ed told him he wasn't licensed to do that, and if his group wanted to be taught how to give adjustments, Raoul needed to contact the World Federation of Chiropractic. Raoul said he would look into it. Ed did agree to talk about chiropractic philosophy with them. When Ed set up in the same building as Raoul, he was unaware there was a group of people working on becoming chiropractors in Chile, and Raoul did not know there was a chiropractor practicing in the country. I have a feeling divine intervention has put these two people together.

When Ed was running one morning this week he found what he said was a very nice-looking school and grounds a short distance from the house. Every one of the kids is adamant about not going to school. Ben said he would go if he could go back to the Steiner School in Santiago but that is not possible from here. I feel really torn with what is happening. What is the sense of us being in a Spanish-speaking country if we are still stuck in an English environment?

Dad and Mom's return flight time has changed, because the standard time change in Chile wasn't figured into it. They will be arriving home later than originally scheduled, which causes a problem for Dad; he has an eye appointment that he doesn't want to miss.

Ed did another radio talk show in Rancagua on Tuesday. He has now been asked to do a weekly interview because of the interest and inquiries the station has been getting, and it is making his clinic busier.

I seem to lose control of my family when Dad and Mom are around, and I haven't yet figured out how I let that happen. Mom gives the kids schoolwork, and Dad won't let them do dishes. The kids are supposed to be responsible for doing their chores and dishes once a day without being told. There is lots of tension between Dad, Mom and me. Mom and Dad have a lot between themselves as well, often talking with an antagonizing tone in their voice. It's nice to be with them but hard at the same time.

Mom and I had a discussion about things that happen in childhood which affect people and hold them back as adults, and I made the mistake of using myself as an example. I have learned I cannot talk about what has affected me negatively from my childhood. Mom feels threatened. I just want her to know why I feel discontent at times and why I do things differently with our children.

When Ed arrived home this afternoon Dad spoke with him about getting a TV and VCR for the kids after I had said no. Ed thought it was a good idea. Dad can't see what the kids are going to do with their time. I was looking forward to reading, writing, music, maybe even making a quilt with them, and I know they will be far less interested if they have a television. So we went shopping. Dad and Ed bought a TV and VCR while I ran my errands. Dad opened up, talking to me while Ed went to pick up the van from the car wash. He has many words when Mom isn't around. He tells me I can't isolate my family from the world, it's not right. They can't spend all their time reading books—a TV will give them something to do. I just listened and felt stunned. It feels as if he doesn't listen to or value what I say. He spoke about his eye. The surgery he had didn't work, and he'll have to have it done again to be able to see clearly.

I wish Dad could see that I want to live life differently from others. He gives us a TV? After thinking about what he said, I am a little confused about his ideas of us as a family. I really don't think Ed and I have isolated ourselves from the world. We have just spent the past year driving from Canada to Tierra del Fuego to learn about the world. What he really means is that he doesn't want us to isolate ourselves from *his* world. Then he said the kids couldn't spend all their time reading books. I really don't expect them to, but their reading of books—real books—is something that has just started to happen. They have just begun to discover the worlds they create in their minds through reading. TV robs them of imagination. I don't know what it will take to gain some acceptance of what I do from my parents. I am sure the pressure to conform it is the reason I rebelled so hard as a teenager. And yet, it is good for the kids and their grandparents to be together. But why does it have to be so strained? Why couldn't I have said no to TV and have my wishes respected? Why did I give in—because Dad had Ed on his side? In refusing the gift I would have appeared stubborn and ungrateful in my father's eyes? How do I make this a win-win situation? I am beginning to understand a little more of why the extended family is becoming a nuclear family in today's North American society and why in many families children and grandparents get cut off from each other. The middle generation wants to make changes, and grandparents do not always welcome it. We have the power to change negative emotional patterns that affected our childhood. I personally want to evolve beyond those patterns and give my kids a better beginning. There were many good things about how I was raised, but there is definitely room for improvement. Anyway we have a TV; I tried to go without but it didn't happen that way.

March 30, 1998:

We were supposed to leave for our weekend on the coast at 7:30 on Saturday morning, but everybody watched movies late Friday night, and we didn't get away until 9:00. We toured the coast and found *cabanas* in Concon for the night.

Our first stop Saturday was the house of Nobel Prize winner, Pablo Neruda. The Isla Negra house is atop a steep embankment overlooking the Pacific Ocean a five-minute drive from Algarrobo. Since last June, I have grown to love that part of the Chilean coast where I photographed hundreds of flowers. In his book of poetry, *Passions and Impressions,* Pablo Neruda wrote, "In Isla Negra everything flowers." The abundance and variety must have spurred the writing; it was his favourite home. Jake didn't want anything to do with the house then was absolutely intrigued by it. We had to tear him away from the ships in bottles—always the way. What a collector Neruda was! All his "stuff" made the house a museum. There must have been at least 500 ships in bottles, thousands of shells, stained glass windows, an insect collection, bowsprit figureheads and a narwhal tusk. I would like to collect such things, but they require a lot of work to keep clean and maintain. Neruda's friends called him a "spontaneous architect"—he added rooms to his houses to accommodate the growing collections and there were two such additions to the Isla Negra house. The guide said Neruda loved the ocean from the land, didn't like being on the water and called his house his ship. He became politically active as the communist candidate for the presidency in 1969 but resigned in support of Salvador Allende. He was granted the Nobel Prize for literature while ambassador to France and died just weeks after the military seized power of his country in September 1973. As a man for the people of Chile he left his four houses and all personal possessions for use as cultural centres.

But because of his political views the houses were vandalized, goods confiscated, and an irrigation canal was redirected to run through the Santiago house (La Chascona) in an effort to destroy and erase his memory. His wife Mathilde and a group of devoted friends persevered despite the political vengeance. They repaired the house and reorganized what was salvaged of his collections, preserving the writings and memory of his life. Today, the Isla Negra house is a museum of collections and La Chascona in Santiago houses the rare books, paintings, manuscripts and personal belongings that were saved. Both can be visited by the public.

Our *cabanas* overlooked the Pacific Ocean. Dad and Mom treated us to a fabulous fish dinner at a restaurant where Mom and I had locos on the recommendation of the waiter. (Afterwards, when I looked them up to learn what they were, found out they are an endangered species.) I don't understand why they were on the menu if that is the case.

All this time in Chile and Mom and Dad hadn't tried Pisco, so we ordered drinks of this distillate from the Moscotal grape, which comes in grades of 30, 35, 40, 43 and 46 percent alcohol. The different grades are said to have different perfumes, but it would take some experience to know the difference. It was served at the restaurant with Pepsi. How are you supposed to appreciate the taste of Pisco? I drank it straight; it is strong but has a distinct, flowery flavor of its own.

We drove back to Rengo through Santiago to change the return tickets at the airport but it couldn't be done on Sunday. It had to be during business hours. Just the way it is in Chile. Ed will have to do it tomorrow.

Professional sports are taken beyond serious here. Chino Rios, a Chilean, won the World Championship Tennis match yesterday afternoon. There wasn't a soul on the street until after the game. We were driving south through Santiago when Rios won. Everywhere people came flying out of their houses going crazy in celebration; a fighter jet did circles and loops over Santiago. It reminded me of last July when Chile participated in the South American championship soccer game. I was in the *cabana* with Jake and Whitney asleep that evening, while the others watched the game at the casino with Aris. All was quiet and peaceful until Chile scored and the silence was broken by the entire country cheering around me. The noise ground to an abrupt halt, then a few moments later the countryside was in celebration again, as Chile won.

Thursday, April 2, 1998:

Ed and I picked up our *carnets* (residence visas) in Santiago this week. We are now legal in Chile, as we had thought we were a few months ago. We also visited with Peter and Amanda. Don is not working out very well. Ed and Peter discussed firing him; he has an attitude problem, mostly, that is not changing—he swears at his patients behind their backs and has little good to say about anything. They are going to give him some more time. Amanda quit teaching at the international school; she doesn't seem to be a very content person, and is having a hard time living, period. I hope Peter can manage. He is such a good guy.

Ed changed the tickets for Dad and Mom. They left this morning to be home for Saturday. Dad was excited; he has been anxious to get back to Canada for a while.

Mom wasn't happy about leaving the kids a couple days earlier than anticipated and vice-versa.

So it was a teary morning but after we get used to being alone it will be really nice. Ever since we arrived in Santiago, someone has been living with us. I, in particular, am looking forward to some uninterrupted time with my children.

Bad news: Ben tripped on the cord of the computer and it fell on the floor. It was an accident and he felt distraught about it. The computer still works but there is a crack across the center of the screen.

Friday, April 3, 1998:

This morning, Ed was meditating, doing his "ohms". I was writing at the table under the light, listening to his hypnotic sounds when the light bulb exploded and broke off at the socket. Shattered glass fell over my writing and the table. He laughed at the mess and said, "I was asking for energy from the universe to help me help others." I get the impression he is being heard and answered. What a mess to clean up!

April 11, 1998: Easter Sunday

It has been raining daily since Dad and Mom left. Ed tried to get a video membership at two places instead of borrowing under Luis' name, but they wouldn't give him one because he is a foreigner. The Chilean people can be funny about some things. They just wouldn't trust us independently, from Luis with their movies despite our living right in their community with them.

Ed went to the chiropractic gathering last Sunday. A chiropractor from the States comes to Santiago to give classes to Raoul's group every two months. Ed spoke on chiropractic philosophy for an hour and felt his message was well received. He was again asked to teach adjusting but again he told them he couldn't do that until there was an arrangement made with the World Federation of Chiropractic.

Ben went with Ed to Santiago to help complete errands. He amazes me with what he takes on and is capable of doing. He was the one who went to the computer shop to discuss the repairs—and the possibility of scrapping the computer after learning it will cost more than $1000 (U.S.) to fix. It seems ridiculous, as that's how much the whole computer cost in the beginning. But parts have to come from North America, which means an inflated price. Ben and the sales rep discussed the possibilities of our buying another computer and it may be what we do.

Everywhere we went on Palm Sunday there was music and singing. Church bells rang all day. A procession of musicians and followers walked past the house carrying palm leaves and singing. The kids talked about Easter and how Chile has chocolate eggs in stores, as Canada does. Seeing their enthusiasm, I suggested that the Easter Bunny couldn't come without an Easter basket to put eggs in, so they have filled the week by giving the grape vines on the trellis an early pruning and collecting enough to construct baskets. They learned how to make baskets doing school activities with Lorraine at home and have displayed good recollection of their skills. They came up with six usable baskets that even have handles.

Ben cut a tree branch for an Easter tree. They blew eggs, coloured patterns on them with markers, and hung them on the branch, mostly for something to do. Our celebrations are different from what goes on here. Easter is a serious holiday and a quiet time for the Chileans, at least here in Rengo. The only busy place is the church.

Sunday, April 19, 1998:

Peter and Amanda's wedding was yesterday so we spent most of the week putting some decent clothes together for the kids who were excited about attending a wedding.

Ed went out yesterday morning and came back with a bicycle for Ben, since it was his birthday, and needless to say Ben was ecstatic.

We spent the rest of the day getting ready for the wedding and bathed one by one. Jake had to have two baths. The kids looked so good dressed up, a rare occasion indeed.

The Santiago house looked exceptional, decorated with flowers everywhere. Peter and Amanda were married beside the small pool they had installed in the back yard. Their Chilean friends were present. The ceremony was short with a fun dancing party afterwards.

Peter and Amanda met two Secret Service agents to President Clinton on Friday (Clinton has been in Santiago on business) and invited them to the party. They showed up, adding life to the party. Even after indulging in Pisco sours and having their tongues loosened they wouldn't say one word about Clinton. Secret Service means "secret" service and they are dedicated to their jobs. They showed the kids their badges, and one of them, Doug, gave all the kids some change, and Ben 2,000 pesos for his birthday. We discussed education, Doug, speaking about himself, said school was a waste of time for him and many other people he knew. He said he just wasn't ready to do what was expected of him as a student and wasn't interested, but now he reads everything and can't seem to satisfy his desire for knowledge. He said the kids were getting a better education than they would ever get in any school, then told them all how lucky they were to be having such an adventure. (They are not all convinced.) He couldn't believe we drove from Canada with six kids in a van and said, "You guys should be writing a book." Ed told him I was working on it. His eyes lit up, and gave me his business card, saying, "I want one when it's out." We found them as interesting as they found us. What a job they have; it must take a special kind of dedication.

We had a birthday supper for Ben today. He wanted lasagna, but there wasn't any in the grocery store as it is not a common thing here, so we made our own noodles and had homemade cannelloni instead. Everybody helped; the kitchen was a mess but we had fun together and topped off the day with cake and ice cream. He loves the bike.

April 23, 1998:

When I went to the window to get a glimpse of the mountains at 6:30 this morning, there was a spectacular sight in the northeast. The moon was close to new, with a perfect brilliant crescent but the full circumference was visible against a sky growing lighter with the dawn. Directly above the middle of the crescent were two planets as bright as the moon itself. They were the only nightlights left in the sky and looked liked diamonds. They appeared to pulsate bigger and smaller, while I stood there mesmerized by the sight. I left but had to go back to absorb it again and again until the sun blotted it out with its brightness.

April 28, 1998:

I have had to buy more blankets for the beds, with the nights getting so cold. These Chilean blankets are incredible: a mixture of thick wool and acrylic at a great price and they'll be wonderful during our Canadian winters as well. In fact, they should be available in Canada, given all the things we import.

The kids all wanted and needed some new clothes, so I decided it was a good time for them to learn how to use a sewing machine. Dayna often says she "can't" but both she and Ben have made themselves pajamas easily.

We did rubbings of most of the different leaves found in the yard. Jake got himself into a snit, expecting what he does to be perfect the first time he tries. What he did wasn't good enough for himself, so he wouldn't try again. I don't know how to help him understand that such things take a little practice to do well.

Dayna does school work diligently and wants me to give her assignments. A couple of weeks ago I explained to the kids that certain things "should" be done on a daily basis: math, reading, writing, science and drawing. She writes a page about something every day, is very good at doing what is asked of her and never needs to be reminded. She asks everyone else if they are doing the same. She is the kind of student the educational system likes but I would personally like to see her take a little more initiative discovering things on her own and thinking for herself, not just doing what is given to her. Her habits make someone else (meaning me) responsible for her education and the sooner she (or any other student for that matter) figures out they are responsible for themselves the better.

Ben loves the freedom the bicycle has given him. He runs errands, making a trip out of every single thing that needs to be done. We don't see much of him these days. After Ivan, Luis' son, is out of school for the day they go biking, play soccer, and go rollerblading. He is enjoying some time with friends like he did before we left Canada.

The mountains looked incredible during our drive to the city on Friday—a good illustration of "tone," which we were talking about when doing some art. Each layer of mountain in the distance was a different intensity of grey from the haze. I mentioned this living illustration to the kids and Tanya was frustrated with me for doing so. It is so easy to say something, however well intentioned, at the wrong moment, and it alienates us from each other instead of being a positive experience.

Dayna and I went to the English second-hand bookstore and found several books while the others visited with Amanda. We also found some crochet hooks big enough for little people's hands. We have a few more things to keep us busy.

Ed and Peter fired Don today. His poor attitude toward servicing people who came to him for care wasn't changing, even as Ed tried to help him out. Peter was adjusting an average of 40 people per day and the numbers had been reduced to between 15 and 20 since Don had taken over. He is good at giving adjustments; it wasn't that.

Christina called Ed early yesterday morning after she had received a phone call from a television station. Last night's show "Amigas e Amigos" was on health care and one of the scheduled medical doctors couldn't make it. They asked if Ed would fill in. The host was genuinely curious about Chiropractic, making the 15-minute interview informative and professional.

Last night, Ed stayed at the house in Providencia, since he started at the central clinic today, taking Don's place. He was late coming home this evening because the interview made him extremely busy. The phone didn't stop ringing and he had people standing out in the hallway waiting to see him most of the day. Ed believes in making Chiropractic available to everyone. What he charges for adjustments here in Chile is less than what he would charge in Canada but is affordable to Chileans and probably a good part of the reason why he is so busy. Ed said Don came to pick up his personal belongings and couldn't believe there was a line-up in the hall waiting. He thought people didn't accept Chiropractic here. I thought about that light bulb exploding—Ed asked for it, and he got it.

People came to pick and pack the *kaqui*—persimmon today. There were two truckloads from just the few fruit trees here in the yard, and I don't have the faintest idea of how to use it.

The older four kids climbed onto the roof of the house via the jasmine vines to sketch the mountains. Jake wanted to be on the roof as well and expected me to help him get there. I told him if he could climb up on his own like the others it was all right with me, but if he couldn't do it on his own it probably wasn't a place he should be. He tried but settled for drawing at the table with Whitney.

We went to a wool shop today and bought some wool to start crocheting the blankets the kids have decided to make. The project is ambitious, but the one thing we have these days is time, and right now it feels good.

May 9, 1998:

I am a little frustrated with the food. I don't feel like eating meat but there aren't many alternatives. "Whole grain" breads are mostly combinations of white and whole-wheat flour, and brown rice is never in the stores here in Rengo. The saving grace is that the market is full of fresh fruits and vegetables grown on local farms. Chileans produce most of their own food, and people eat the foods that are available in season. When we first arrived in Chile we ate celery until it wasn't available any longer. Never anywhere else have I tasted celery with such a naturally salty, delicious flavour. The same with broccoli, which is only available while in season. From January to March—in summer—there are cherries, peaches, plums, apples and fresh corn. In late summer and autumn, there are several varieties of grapes and fresh almonds and walnuts. Oranges and other citrus fruits are plentiful in winter but not as abundant on market shelves the rest of the year. Milk products, meat and bread are available year round. We are extremely fortunate in Canada to have such a variety of foods available to us throughout the year, but I am growing to believe that a more simple diet according to season, from food produced locally, is what our bodies require more than anything, in order to survive the climate where we live. Anyway, we are becoming less vegetarian here.

At the moment we are living in the heart of country that produces the wine for which Chile is so famous. Luis arranged a tour of Torreon de Paredes vineyard for us. It is only three kilometers away from where we are living, and because Larry Lederman, the Canadian Ambassador, and Patricia, his wife, joined our group we were given an excellent tour. Larry contacted Ed in October after settling into his new foreign post. Larry had had severe discomfort in his back, in Canada, before coming to Chile. One of Ed's patients was a personal friend of Larry and recommended to him that he look Ed up. He did, it only took a few adjustments for him to feel relief and Larry became an advocate of chiropractic.

Don Amado Paredes Cardenas bought and founded the 3000-hectare "Torreon" vineyard in 1979 at the age of 70. Two of his sons, Alvaro and Javier, a lawyer and architect, respectively, traded in their professions to run the operation when the wine business became an international operation.

Javier gave us the tour. The U-shaped colonial buildings have been restored, creating a wonderful atmosphere within the courtyard. Tile roofs and two-to-three-foot thick adobe brick walls help control the temperature inside and thus control the quality of the wine being produced. All the buildings have wide covered verandahs for protection from the summer sun and winter rain. One of the buildings has a turret or tower, hence the name "Torreon". Seventy five percent of the 150 cultivated hectares are sown with red grapes; the rest is for the white varieties. We were given a walking tour into a field, but it is late autumn, grape season is over, and the vines were bare. We were told there were nine varieties of grapes planted, each producing a different wine, produced and bottled on the estate. The owners are in the process of bringing new root stock from France, but it will be a few years before the vines start producing grapes and wine.

Chile has produced wine since the first Spanish Conquistadors moved into the country with Catholic priests who needed wine for sacraments. But production was regulated by Spain and vineyards were even ordered destroyed in an effort to keep up the demand for Spanish wine. After liberation, during the mid-1800's, the industry flourished when Don Silvestre Ochagavia visited France and brought back some of the best varieties of stalk along with an experienced oenologist to supervise his vineyards—all of which started a trend. Given Chile's fertile soil and a climate similar to the Mediterranean, the vines thrived, resulting in some of the largest and best established vineyards in the world. Indeed, it was only because of this transplantation that some of the finest varieties of wine grapes survived Europe's phylloxera plague (caused by the louse which penetrates the vine, eating and killing the plant). This is why, today, Chile is so strict in controlling what vegetation of any kind comes into the country.

Javier explained some of the theory that lies behind the wines that are produced at Torreon de Paredes. A good wine can only be made from top quality grapes and to obtain such grapes a rich, good quality soil is absolutely imperative. The environment is always taken into consideration, water and soil treated with utmost respect and care.

Yves, the oenologist from France, gave us the inside tour of operations. We were shown the last of the year's grapes laid out and aging to allow the natural yeasts to grow before the grapes are juiced. Then we were taken through the cellars and never-ending six-foot stacks of oak barrels lying on their sides. Being from Canada where we live with mildew growing in basements, I noticed a pleasant difference here in the cellars. They are dark but dry and clean—a necessary environment for a good wine. Yves loves his job. He carefully watches, smells and tastes the wines as they are aging and is the one who decides when they are ready to be bottled. Arriving back where we started from, we sampled both red and white wines and were given the opportunity to ask questions and purchase our favourites.

May 20, 1998:

It was a great day on the coast until we arrived home to find that we had been robbed for the first time in our lives. I walked into the house first, toward the bedrooms, where I discovered drawers pulled out and emptied. I yelled, "Ed, we've been robbed!" Everyone came running. All of our money was taken, right down to the jar of one peso coins we were saving for Rummoli chips. As we looked around the house, we discovered many more things were missing. Ed went to the police station to give a report and found out that our neighbour had called at 6 p.m. when he saw two young men climbing over the gate. The police came to the house and obviously scared the intruders off, so they didn't get to Tanya and Whitney's room. I feel so violated that someone would enter my home like this. We have a lot more than many Chileans and our clothing will be used elsewhere, I am sure. It's not so much what's missing that bugs me as the fact that my personal space has been invaded. They used our backpacks and must have filled all four of them. Ben was hit the hardest; almost all of his clothing was taken. The thieves were quite selective in other choices. I don't understand why they took the cheap Peruvian pottery and the camera but left the laptop sitting right beside it; they took costume jewelry but left my gold hoops. Monetary value was not the issue.

This whole incident is teaching us that we need to listen to our inner voices. Both Ed and I were given messages in the morning and yesterday. Ed put his earnings from Wednesday in his valuables bag, and his inner voice told him he should not leave the money in the drawer, but he did anyway. As we started down the road I remembered the cameras; something told me to go back for them but I didn't.

Two days ago I dreamt: I had in my hands the little pack of money Ed keeps in his drawer. I had to find a better place for this as someone was trying to steal our money. I had to put it someplace where it wouldn't be found. I was behind the wall; there were wood partitions and I thought that the money had to be hidden behind the surface of the wall so it wouldn't be found. Ed came and took the money from my hands and I thought, "It is not my responsibility anymore."

When I woke I told Ed of the dream. We learned the hard way. I'm glad Tanya and Ben were with us. It might not have happened if one or both of them had stayed but if Tanya had been here by herself as she was suggesting before we left, we might well have had emotional damage deeper than losing a bit of money and a few things. We will get over the loss of possessions and I am thankful it was a lesson for Ed and me.

May 31, 1998:

Luis and Maria Avelena have given us a German Shepherd puppy. Every house has a least one for protection and they feel we should be no exception. I didn't want to have a dog as we have enough to think about without the responsibility of that too. I told Ed, "It is not fair to the dog, to have it as a puppy and desert it when it is not convenient for us. You bring a dog home then it is ours, it goes with us wherever we go. We are not leaving it behind when we leave." Ed brought the dog home, a cute puppy and a family dog for sure the way things look. She has good character, her fur is soft and she is a roly-poly little ball. The kids have decided to call her Bess. Ed wanted to call her Serena because she is so calm and Chilean but Jake can't say that easily so "Bess" it is. We have been reading the Rose series of books. Almanzos' name for Laura is Bess.

Antonio and Maria have been having trouble financially with their own company since September and were suing Ed for wages they claim he hasn't paid them, but one visit with their lawyer set the lawyer and Antonio straight, the whole thing was dropped. They didn't like being let go of their so-called responsibility.

Last week I dreamt that there were many lizards and snakes being thrown at us but they never got close enough to do any harm. Ed was always able to turn them to stone in mid-air, and they fell to the ground.

Antonio and Maria have told patients we have left the country and have sent police twice to the offices reporting we were working illegally in Chile. The police never found anything over which they could shut the business down; the paperwork was legal, and so were we. Antonio and Maria are obviously not happy with us but if it had been an honest working relationship, with integrity, we would never have felt the need to move on.

June 5, 1998:

Today we have been in Chile an entire year. It is wet and cold and has been raining since I got up at 6:30 this morning. The dampness makes everything clammy. This house is concrete and the walls are full of deep cold. On warm, sunny afternoons when the windows and doors are open you can feel the cold draft rolling out of the house. Only 15 days to solstice and the sun will be on its way back. It won't take long for the earth to warm up again. I feel miserably cold in the dampness. Yesterday I wore a t-shirt, turtleneck, sweatshirt, Chiloé sweater, leggings, wool skirt and socks, and then my poncho on top. It wasn't until late in the day that I finally felt comfortable. This all sounds like complaining but I feel the need to put down what I am experiencing. We have a tendency to forget the not-so-nice things when it is convenient.

The box Mom and Dad sent arrived with Ed last night. It was like Christmas this morning; everyone got new old clothes and new old books to read. They sent two new games, videos, and we had a breakfast of peanut butter. I'm positive that was Dad's idea—four pounds of it. He missed eating peanut butter when he was here. It was a good day for the box to arrive and the kids have been busy playing games all morning. With the weather so cold and the house so difficult to keep warm, we can see our breath in every room except the living/dining area where the fire is. The winters may be a lot colder in Canada, but they're definitely easier for me to cope with.

June 12, 1998:

Ed bought a gas heater, and what a difference it makes. Because of the robbery, the kids don't feel safe in the house any more. However, it looks like Ed will be setting up a clinic in Vina del Mar and that we are going to move again; they are happy about that. I have always wanted to live beside the ocean, so the coast will be good for a while. The robbery gives us a valid reason to break the lease. Blanca won't be happy we are leaving but she misled us by not telling the truth about the other robberies, even when asked. It was the police that told Ed the previous tenants were robbed four times. This house attracts all kinds of not-so-fortunate people and robberies.

Thursday, June 18, 1998:

When Lee, my sister, said she would take us up on our offer of a bassinet from Chile as a gift for the new baby, another trip to Chimborogo to purchase a bassinet and a project with purpose was set in motion. The gift grew. It started with making a crocheted baby blanket, bumper pads and mattress. Then I decided to make a couple of fitted sheets for the mattress and two receiving blankets. I made the bumper pads differently from what I'd anticipated in the beginning and had enough material left over to make a baby quilt to go with the bumper pads. I asked Ben if he wanted to give the baby the pillow he made in school and he offered it willingly along with the pillowcase. Tanya was making a pillowcase with a frill but it ended up being a pillow filled with leftover fibrefill from the quilt. Dayna made a pillowcase for the feather pillow and embroidered on it. We bought a Chilean baby blanket to add to the package. The bassinet is more than complete. Lee won't need anything else for the baby's first bed and won't have to do the work in a hurry now either. It gave us a meaningful project to fill the time on our hands. Ed and Ben took the huge box to the Post Office this morning.

June 21, 1998: Winter Solstice – Southern Hemisphere

I now understand why the winter solstice is celebrated the way it is in both hemispheres. In Inca times June Solstice was the time of celebrating the return of the sun. Inti Raymi is still a major festival. I can picture Sacsayhuaman in Cusco—a special place that will hold thousands of people for the festivities. Anyway, I like the fact that the sun is returning. I feel like I have been cold since I arrived in Chile. We missed the hot part of summer this year by going south.

June 25, 1998:

A woman named Joan phoned last week. She is a Canadian from Toronto, has three children and was home-schooling in Canada before they moved to Chile in January. She enrolled her son in the Waldorf School in Santiago but found school to be too much change all at once and took him out. She had contacted the Steiner School as well and was in touch with Sheila, who gave her our phone number.

We made arrangements for the family to visit today. She seems as discontent as I was last year at this time, feeling out of her element and looking for a place where she and her family belong. Her husband, Juan Pablo, is Chilean and they are living with her in-laws. She feels it will be better at least when they have a place of their own. Pax, an outgoing confident boy, is Karina's age. He and Jake got along really well, guy stuff. Joy is just a few months older than Whitney and quiet. It took her a while to warm up to us but she did eventually get into some play. Maria is a little more than a year old with an ever-smiling round face, and dark hair and eyes. She played but stuck close to Mom.

We had a good afternoon. It is the first time since we left Canada that I have spoken about education with someone who has similar thinking to my own. Joan is a certified school teacher and saw many not-so-positive things in the school system in Canada. Like me, she is struggling to find good alternatives and was doing well in Canada. Home-schooling is not a sane idea to the Chilean people. Joan did find a home-school community but they are expatriates, not the right kind of group for someone who is here indefinitely and needs to make a life. Well, we didn't solve any world problems or come up with answers but we did have some good discussions. The children got along well, and Whitney has already asked when she can play with Joy again.

June 28, 1998:

The kids have spent many long winter evenings, as well as a few rainy days, crocheting while I read stories and novels aloud. All have been working on their blanket projects more diligently than I expected. Ben completed his today and it looks good on his bed. He is proud of what he has created. The girls' projects are coming along as well. Every square of Dayna's is absolutely perfect. Karina is making a patchwork throw from the ends of balls of yarn, as well as squares the others aren't using. Tanya's is coming along but slower; she is interested for a while but has several things on the go. Each piece is a true expression of its maker.

July 4, 1998:

So it is the big American Holiday—Peter and Amanda are having a salsa party tonight and I don't have any desire to go. Everything has turned inward for me. The *Dagoli* sweatshirt with the "Creative Spirit" on it that I found before we left home reflects what I am doing now. I wear it almost constantly. Since leaving, many creative ideas and capabilities as well as the time to consider or practice them have surfaced in my life. I have been spending uninterrupted time with my kids, writing down our experiences, taken hundreds of photographs, many of them good and now with doing the art course in the kids' school program, I have found I can actually do pencil sketches that aren't all that bad. I have been sewing and making clothing too, something I didn't have time for the last few years in Canada. I enjoy having time to do things such as what we did for Lee and the new baby and I didn't take the time to make it happen that way in Canada. I am also enjoying the time I have with the kids, and the reason we have it is because Ed is doing new things in his profession as well. The dream I had last week summarizes these thoughts:

I am in a room similar to the dining room at home in Canada. I see snails on the buffet. Their shells are made of gold, and their babies are on their backs. In the corner there is a clock on the wall with a pendulum. The pendulum moves very fast, and I put my hands on it to slow it down, but there is so much friction it catches fire. Ed gets the fire extinguisher and puts the fire out.

July 4, 1998: Letter home to Ed's family

Dear Lisa, Pierre, Diane, Gilles, Gert and Ben,

Hello.

I know when Ed talks on the phone he doesn't volunteer much information about what is really going on, so thought I would write. We are doing very well. The kids and I are catching up on the schoolwork of the last couple of years back home. There wasn't much time left for the basic 3 Rs the last little while. They don't have any way to escape it now. Either they do some schoolwork or they are bored out of their minds.

Tanya was way behind in everything when we left but the last few months she has managed to advance to the level she should be at in Canada in reading and math. But she will still only write what she absolutely has to. I am concerned that if she doesn't make an effort to stay in touch with girlfriends at home they won't be so interested in continuing a relationship when we return. I have talked with her about it; she is aware but hasn't taken any action. She may have to learn the hard way. There is value in writing. The time on her hands has turned her to books, though. She discovered she can escape into another world and has read everything we have. We found a second-hand bookstore and have lots to read now, as we make regular trips there. She sleeps less at night, though. In the morning, the book is on her face and the light is still on. I feared she would never read for enjoyment but it is not a concern any longer; maybe writing will take the same path. I bought her a pair of jeans last week and they are the same size as mine.

Ed is working so much that Ben has become the man of the house. He is an exceptional kid and takes care of everything, goes to offices to pay the bills and does shopping for groceries by himself and any other errands that need to be done. It has improved his language skills as well as giving him meaningful things to do; otherwise he is causing trouble with the others. He is fast at his schoolwork and always does it first thing in the morning. He reads and writes what he needs to in order to get by and in math, the grade six textbook was so easy for him he skipped the first half to get to where the work was more challenging. It is a challenge for me to keep him busy with constructive things to do.

Dayna is still the organized person she has always been. She knows what she has to do for schoolwork, does it, and then asks the others if they have done theirs for the day. She's getting better at reading, is working in the grade five math book and always writes something. I haven't been too successful in getting her or any of them to write home, though. They just keep saying, "What am I supposed to write?" I'm not going to do it for them; it has to come from them. Dayna and Karina have been sharing a bedroom for the past few months and her organizational skills are rubbing off on Karina. I can always count on her to do what I ask of her and more; she likes things about the house tidy and spends much of her time keeping it that way. Although she is growing she is still short—Karina is almost as tall as she is. She doesn't like me saying that.

Karina is working hard at reading. She struggles much of the time, wanting to be able to do what the older ones are doing. She reads at Dayna's level but works hard to be there. She, Jake and Whitney play well together when not interrupted by the older ones. She bounces back and forth between the two groups, fitting in equally well in both. She likes playing euchre and the four older kids spend several evenings a week playing while waiting for Ed to get back from Santiago at 11 p.m. Many nights I go to bed and leave them playing. They seem to be freer to have more fun when I am not around. I lie in bed listening to the nonsense, laughter and screams of "You're cheating!" I laugh. I know which side of the family that comes from—a true Chicoine household.

Jake, well what can I say? He is still his moody self. Can't stand to lose when he plays any kind of game. He won't have anything to do with any kind of schoolwork, but he draws and draws—crayon drawings: mountains, trees, deserts, rivers, the ocean, everything he sees around him with several interpretations. Most of the time he is content to play by himself, skips better than anyone else, does ninja dances on the front yard, and doesn't like it when anybody is watching. So I watch once in a while when he is unaware. He looks so happy, but when he sees me or someone else he puts a mad face on and pouts. I am starting to think it is just mind games he plays with us. He sits on my knee and will cry on my shoulder that he is bored, gets his hug, and is off playing again. He just needs to recharge his batteries with hugs, but I sure wish he could do it without so much crying attached. He doesn't have to make life so hard for himself. There are other times he can be so thoughtful and generous. He is good at keeping the bookshelves in order and tidying up in the living room, but he always has to do it himself, without me suggesting it. I'm not sure I will ever figure this guy out.

Every once in a while Whitney still claims she is boss. She is a Wit all right, always adding her opinion to everything. She drives Ben crazy, doesn't back down from him at all, and blames everything that goes wrong on him even when it isn't his fault. She's out to get him for something. Her other brother she caters to hand and foot. She knew how to tie shoelaces a long time ago, would do her own, then Jake's as well. Jake was finally embarrassed enough to learn, after the others teased him, but it took him a while to get control of his fingers. Whitney is almost reading and has a memory like a photocopy machine. After reading a story a couple of times she knows it and can dictate it word for word. If Dayna or Karina are stumbling on a word and she is familiar with what they are reading she will often tell them what the word is. That doesn't do much for their egos but I don't ever remember her making an error when coaching her older sisters.

It has been good in many ways for us to be by ourselves the way we are for a while. We have become a closer family and the kids are better buddies. They get along much better than they used to. I know it is selfish of me but I am really enjoying having the time alone with them. There aren't any interruptions from the phone or friends pulling them away when they are focused on something. We just had too much social life at home. (And people think home-school kids don't have a social life—if they only truly knew.)

The house we are in right now is called a casa quinta, a country house without a farm. It has a ceramic tile outdoor terrace in the middle of the U-shaped building. Bedrooms and living area each have French doors that open onto it, built for outdoor living. The gardens and vegetation on the property are lush. When we arrived, the geraniums were as high as my shoulders and flowering abundantly. There are three huge jasmine vines that have been blooming profusely ever since we arrived and I find myself wondering if they ever take a rest. Every day I breathe in the jasmine and it fills my senses with its heavenly scent; when the sun warms the blossoms the fragrance is amplified. Just today another type of tree has bloomed, spilling its scent into the air. There are four tall trees with flowers, a bright goldenrod yellow—the flowers even look like goldenrod. We have lavender, periwinkle, irises and daffodils all over the property, but we will miss the blossoming of the daffodils, as they bloom in August. There is a gigantic trestle of grape vines, of both red and white grapes. We have been enjoying avocados off the trees in the yard, as well as figs. Figs are absolutely decadent ripe off the tree. There are about 30 kaqui trees. The fruit is very tart and hard to eat before totally ripe. The gardens, vegetation and trees make it worth being here, and it has felt as if we have had a real home for a while.

Ed works three days a week in Santiago. We didn't plan it that way—it's just how it worked out. It has improved our financial situation considerably but it is too far for Ed to travel every day. He enjoys the work but there are a few things that bother him. It is hard to trust most people to keep their word; they will tell you anything if they can't tell you what you want to know. It is frustrating. There are so many possibilities for Ed here. Vina is the next place for a clinic, then possibly Brazil for a while. We take one day at a time.

When looking at the "big picture" of this whole adventure, I get the impression that it may be beyond our control and we are just making choices from those that are sent in our direction. We will end up back in Canada when the universe decides that it is right.

Meanwhile, there is a group of people here calling themselves a Chiropractic Association, and there isn't a licensed Chiropractor among them. Ed has become diplomatically involved trying to get them set in the right direction.

Lisa, I know you are holding all the responsibility for the house. We were supposed to be free of that by now. I don't know how to express my gratitude to you for what you have done for Ed and me. As far as the taxes are concerned that is not your problem, they just have to be paid. We knew it was coming. Ed thought it would be more than that. It just takes away the comfortable cushion that was sitting in the bank for emergencies. There is always something that makes us reach beyond ourselves. It is true, the money could have paid the trip home, but the taxes need paying and we still have work to do here.

We will be home most likely in the year 2000. I know it sounds a long ways off, but when you think of what is between here and there, now and then, I sometimes wonder if it is enough time. On the other hand, we can't keep the kids "prisoner" for too many more years. Not that they are really suffering so much. We are learning more than we ever could have in the lifestyle we were living at home.

Well, the kids need some attention. This is Ed's night in Santiago. He doesn't come home until tomorrow evening and they sometimes get moody. We are well and enjoying this time-out phase of our lives. For me it feels like a chance to let my first 40 years digest, so I'll be able to take in the next half in peace. It is not all a bed of roses, but there are many good things happening for us.

So I am sending all of you my love, our love, we think of you often and at some point we will be together again.

Love,

Gaye.

Saturday, July 18, 1998:

Amanda went to the States for three weeks and Peter came to spend a night with us. He wanted to ask Luis to deliver a baby for a woman from whom they plan to adopt the child after he is born. Luis won't do it. He says what they are planning to do is illegal. In Chile there is a law stating that a couple must be married four years before they are officially allowed to adopt a child. They have been married barely four months, and plan to get around the law with a private adoption.

Wednesday, July 22, 1998:

For a month now we have been looking to rent a place in the Vina del Mar area and we did find one in the city if stuck for alternatives. But I really don't want to live in a city again if I can help it. I am a lucky person to have the choices I have. Ed called the agency to say we would take the condo we visited on the weekend but it turned out no animals are allowed so we were looking again. He lined up a couple of places to visit on Wednesday morning while he was in Santiago on Monday. Ben and Dayna wanted to visit potential houses too so asked if they could go to Santiago on the bus by themselves to house hunt with him. Ed liked the idea of having help choosing a house, so the two of them took the bus from Rengo to Santiago at 3:30 p.m. At 6 p.m. Ben called from Ed's downtown office, having made the subway connection easily. They seem to be too young to do a two-hour bus ride and transfer onto a subway in a city of five million. I'm not sure I'd feel okay about them going from London, Ontario to Toronto and taking the subway downtown. I don't understand why it feels as if they are so much more capable of doing it here in a country where even the language is different. At any rate, they found a duplex. Dayna says it's okay, Ben says we could live in it and Ed says if the other was good enough than this one will be okay too—it has more yard space. It will have to do—Blanca wants us out of this house on Sunday. We are cutting it a little close.

July 24, 1998:

We went to the fabric store yesterday afternoon to buy the wool I have desired for several weeks. It is high quality wool from the Biobio area in the south. It's almost like felt and is used for making the classy wool winter coats I see everywhere. I purchased three meters of royal blue then said good-bye and thank you to everyone in the store. They knew us better that most in Rengo. We gave them plenty of business and they showed genuine interest in what the kids created, and wore, out of the fabrics they supplied.

As I closed the gate after Ed left this morning, there was a family washing forks in the stream. I said, "Buenos Dias" and the man asked for food. I looked them over—a family travelling, two men, one woman and three children. For some reason I felt compelled to give them food so gave them a block of cheese and a loaf of bread. They were extremely thankful and moved on. Later in the afternoon the two boys were back, asking for a container (I figured out later) to make tea. We didn't give them anything. I couldn't figure out what they wanted. I went outside the gate to see the thin line of the setting moon, at which point the boys came back again wanting milk and sugar for their tea. I did give them that. They appeared to be spending the night under the overpass of the railway track. I am full of questions about what they are doing, where they are coming from, where they are going and do they even have a home, but that was the last I saw of them.

The moon set tonight at about 6:30 behind the coastal corderilla in the west. It followed the sun south from where the sun dipped below the horizon. It is a new moon. It rises farther north than the full moon and sets further south than the sun right now. I am finding all this interesting to figure out.

Another move and another new moon.

LIFE IN CONCON

July 26 to November 21, 1998:

Con: The Mapuche tribe's word for water.

Concon is the name of the town we have moved to located at the mouth of the Aconcagua River where it flows into the Pacific Ocean. Concon translates as—where two waters meet. This river's drainage system begins at the tallest mountain of the Americas, Aconcagua, standing at 6,959 meters.

On July 23, a newspaper article reported that a dead whale had washed up onto a beach in Concon, a small community 16 kilometers north of Viña del Mar. This is where we found our condominium, and I believe I had a dream on July 14th that told me what to expect:

I was looking out over the ocean from a window of the house I was living in. A whale was coming up onto the beach. I was afraid he would get stuck and wouldn't be able to get back to the ocean. The kids and I started out to see him while many more whales were coming towards the beach. From halfway down the hill we watched them play in the protected pool on this side of the rocks. It was a long set of steps down to the level of the beach. Dolphins slid on the sand slides and played in the pool with the whales. On the shore there were two North American native men—older, grandfather-like—who brought me out onto the water on a small, flat wooden raft, to be with the whales. They wanted me to learn what the whales had to teach. The water current was carrying us a long distance from shore. I looked back at the whales and dolphins playing in the protected rock pool with the kids, I was concerned for the whales; I feared they would not be able to get back to the main part of the ocean. Then I wondered how on earth we were going to get back to shore without paddles. The men were sure of themselves and expected me to have their same calm sense of knowing. Just when I was starting to feel concerned about us on the water, the current started to move the raft back toward the shore. The kids played with the whales and dolphins in the ocean pool and on the sand slides when I was out on the water. I wondered how the tides worked and hoped when the high water was here again the whales would be able to get out of the pool and back to the ocean where they belonged.

August 12, 1998:

Moving day was July 26. By the time the girls and I had cased the new house the moving truck was unloaded. It was going to work well and the bonus was that we were just a five-minute walk down the long stairway to the beach.

Our property manager, Mauricio, must be in his sixties. He's a bright, happy man with a square-ish weathered face, a full head of white hair, and a salt-and-pepper mustache. No taller than I, he dresses in well-worn, good quality woolen clothing. And he is a talker. He showed us how the gas supplying the house works, the keys, the alarm system and the calafon water heaters. Calafon water heaters are connected to the hot water tap. A gas fire heats pipes to heat the water as it passes through them while the taps are open. There are many different types and everywhere we have been they work a little differently. Here in Chile all eight of us can take a hot shower consecutively and we don't have to worry about there ever being enough hot water, since it's heated as we use it.

Mauricio asked me several times if I liked the house. He seemed to be worried that I wouldn't want to stay. Dayna did a good job of choosing the three-story condominium. There is a small front yard in the shape of a triangle because of the way the two streets meet. We are fortunate to have any yard, as the other condos didn't. The Chilean way of life is different from what we are used to in Canada. People have someone live with their family to cook, clean, maintain laundry and gardens and even this small house has a room next to the kitchen to accommodate an employee. Mind you, the room is no bigger than what will fit a single bed and a walk space but it is there beside the bathroom and kitchen. This is a country where there's a big difference between the people who have and the people who don't, although that appears to be shifting some. It is common for people who are better off financially to have domestic employees, and those employees often become like family members when they stay for long periods of time.

The first floor has the living and dining area together, and a small functional kitchen no more than nine by nine feet, with the employee's quarters beside it. Out the back door, off the kitchen, is the laundry area, which is about the same size as the kitchen. It is enclosed by three, eight-foot-high concrete walls with five rows of clothesline strung from one side to the other. Upstairs are two full bathrooms, three small bedrooms and the third floor loft. Modern buildings take into consideration the cool winters; this house has two built-in gas space heaters. Everything is compact and functional and our big family fits into it comfortably.

Ed stayed in Santiago during the first week we lived in Concon. He was busy working at the central clinic and in Rancagua. He did another television interview on Chilevision television station and picked up Melanie and her partner Clayton at the airport. Melanie is a chiropractor from Canada who has come to take over Ed's position in the central clinic and at Rancagua, making it possible for him to set up the clinic in Viña del Mar.

The kids and I spent Monday settling in, and it didn't take any one of the kids very long to make his or her own space a comfortable corner. These kids have learned to adapt to new surroundings easily, making wherever they drop their belongings home. When evening arrived we turned the space heater on and there was no more seeing our breath while getting into bed.

Tuesday morning the kids did some exploring and then asked me to go to the beach, Playa Amarilla, with them for the afternoon. I was given a tour as they excitedly showed me every set of steps they'd discovered leading to the beaches from atop the hill we live on. As soon as their feet hit the sand they were into building sand castles and left me to my thoughts. Sleepiness came over me in the warmth of the sun and the gentle sound of waves. I lay down on my stomach with my solar plexus in direct contact with the sand. My thoughts drifted and I thanked God for his blessings, the time I have to spend with the kids, and for the inner peace that has come back into my life. It was my solar plexus that held the knot of discontentment, the ache. I thought about what I have learned here in Chile, the mistakes, the blessings, and how naive I am in so many ways, about the geography we have been learning and what makes Chile so unique. And then

I thought about earthquakes. There hadn't been a quake since November last year—a long period of time to elapse without one occurring. I thought to myself, "I would like to experience a real earthquake, not just a little shaker underfoot."

Jake interrupted my inner world, "Mom, I have a really sore tooth." I brushed the sand off my hands, looked into his mouth and found a white fistula on his gum, some kind of infection. He needed a dentist. I told him I had clove oil for the pain; we would put a *Swedish Bitters* compress on it to help kill the infection when we got back to the house, and we would have it taken care of by a dentist. Sitting in the sand, sun and surroundings we carried on a conversation, dreaming about buying the house for sale that overlooked the beach. I said, "If we buy a house on the beach, I want that one on the point." It is luxurious looking, with Spanish arches at the front and the best location overlooking the ocean. Everyone picked out their favourite but all agreed that the one on the point had the best view. Almost all homes in this area have a great view since they are built on the slope, row upon row, up the mountain.

Ben watered the gardens when we returned. The single copper pipe with a tap for the garden hose stood perpendicular to the ground without support, two feet high. It snapped off when he tugged on the hose, creating a geyser that flooded the yard. He ran to the break and covered it with his hand in an attempt to stop the water from being wasted. Holding it back took all his strength while I found the vice grips to turn off the main valve. The water stopped flowing from the break in the pipe but it meant no water to the house either. There are stiff fines on water bills for using more than what is allowed per dwelling. Ben saved what he could. We have become more conscious of how much we use and how wasteful we are with the water. It is a precious commodity here.

Ben suggested we call Mauricio and he was at the door in 15 minutes. Together we plugged the hole in the pipe with a cut-off end of a wooden spoon and a rag so we could turn the water on to the house at least. I asked about a dentist for Jake and he looked in Jake's mouth so inquisitively that I began to think he was a dentist. We also needed hooks to replace the broken ones for the clothesline so I asked about a hardware store. He tried to explain but neither Ben nor I knew the town, and because I wasn't able to understand much of his Spanish, he was frustrated, so Ben went with him. When Mauricio brought Ben back, Ben knew where the "best" hardware store was, and they had arranged a dentist appointment for the following afternoon. An hour later Mauricio called to tell us a plumber would be at our house first thing in the morning to do the repairs.

We did manage to settle down and read after the excitement, yet I still felt uneasy. Jake's tooth, another house with water problems and my inadequacy with the language makes it difficult to stay in control of my environment. I still depend on Ben and he is growing impatient with me. After I read the kids to sleep I did some reading for myself and had a glass of white wine to help relax.

I was startled awake by a loud bang, like something had smashed into the windows. I was sitting bolt upright before I knew it. An earthquake: the rumbling of the earth and vibrating windows didn't let up after the initial bang. Because it was more than a little shaker underfoot and I felt like it was never going to end, I jumped out of bed and ran to the kids' rooms yelling, "We have to get out of the house." They didn't hear me. Ben was up and yelled something back, but we still couldn't hear one other over the noise the quake was creating. I yelled about six inches away from his ear, "Get Jake and bring him outside." I started up the stairs to get the girls but the quake dropped in intensity as quickly as it started. The windows stopped rattling but the floor still shook. No longer feeling the desperate need to get out of the house we went back to bed. As I lay there the windows started rattling again and then the quake dropped in intensity as abruptly as it did the first time. Areas of city lights went out in sections until there wasn't even a glow from Viña-Valparaiso. I lay awake, feeling the bed vibrate off and on. I dozed uneasily and woke when my body relaxed, feeling the ground still. Then I awakened again to the city lighting up in the distance.

I had wanted to experience a real earthquake and I have now. I better be careful what I ask for. I don't think I want to experience that again. I can handle snow, ice and cold at home with more confidence.

My wine glass was on the floor after falling off the night table. Most of the books had fallen off the shelves, one glass on the edge of the sink had fallen and broken, and one window pane had cracked—other than that, there was no major damage that we could find. All windows in this house are made up of small panes no larger than 8 by 10 inches. I now understand why.

The plumber fixed the outside water pipe and put a connection for hot water on the calafon for the washer. Teasing, he asked me how I liked the quake and informed me that it measured 6.1 on the Richter scale and that the epicenter was in La Serena, farther north, where it was even stronger. He said he has experienced stronger ones. About ten years ago he was on the beach in Viña del Mar when an eight-point-something hit and he said the dry sand was bouncing 15 centimeters in the air. I told him 6.1 was strong enough for me. I still felt rattled. He also said a man died last night when the wood structure he and his family lived in collapsed. In Chile, because of the earthquakes, there are strict regulations about how permanent dwellings are built. Wood frame is unacceptable, the reason why proven last night.

The plumber asked what brought our family to Concon, and after Ben explained what Ed does he said, "God works in mysterious ways, I am going to go see him." He has severe pain in his lower back and down his legs and hasn't found much relief with anything he has done. He was willing to try something different.

The dentist just looked at Jake's tooth; he wouldn't do anything until the infection was taken care of and gave us a prescription for it. Jake said his tooth felt better yet the dentist didn't do a thing. Sometimes Jake gets lost in the crowd and just needs some extra attention.

Ben took Dayna and me to Santiago. I say it this way because it would be much more challenging without Ben and his language skills. We met Melanie, and Ben went with her to the immigration office to help with translation for the completion of her paper work. Dayna and I did birthday shopping for Tanya and Whitney, then visited with Amanda. An unwed mother has agreed to give up her baby in a private adoption if Amanda and Peter pay her medical expenses. Amanda asked every question she could think of about taking care of infants and appears to have nervous feelings about the whole idea. Because of a medical condition, she was told she would never have children and is so happy she is going to have the opportunity to be a mom. Both she and Peter are looking forward to the baby being theirs in September.

With the clinic handed over to Melanie, Ed was feeling anxious about not working and not having cash flow coming in. But that was the way it was when Peter took over the Santiago clinic too. Melanie told Peter she wasn't confident about going to Rancagua and cancelled Saturday. I don't know who was angrier—Ed or me. Ed would have gone if he had known that was the case. He is concerned about patients losing confidence in the people they come to for care and not getting the service they are promised. He works so hard at setting these places up for people like Melanie to get a good start and she cancelled out. That's what irks me.

Ed visited the radio station in Viña yesterday to discuss the possibility of doing an interview, and there was a half-hour spot for him on a health program today— another "coincidence". Calls have started and he is once again booking patients before the clinic has been set up.

August 13, 1998: 15th wedding anniversary

We spent the afternoon on Playa Negra as a family sharing it with only eight other people. We wandered the rocks looking for the different sea animals we have discovered but there weren't many to be found when the tide was high. The kids were not able to show their Dad the starfish and other sea animals they had known were around and asked why the water was high sometimes and low at other times. It was a question for which we were all looking for an answer.

Mauricio recommended a restaurant and when we got there found we were expected without having made a reservation. The waterfront building on the north end of town appeared to be like any other building from the outside but the interior floor was earth, covered with loose stone and shell. Dinner tables surrounded the circular fireplace with its glowing warm fire and, it being a winter evening, we sat close to it. We had good conversation over a dinner of congor eel, rice, asparagus, winter salad and a soup made from *zapallo*, the staple squash of most South American countries.

We discussed the kids and how they were coping with everything that was going on around them. Dayna, Karina, Jake and Whitney seem to be doing fine. Dayna says she misses family but is happy she doesn't have to go back to school. Being in a foreign country affects the younger ones less; it seems their environment isn't as important as being with their Dad and Mom. Tanya and Ben need more than that now. Ben has become an outgoing young person and after having had such a tough beginning has said he isn't ready to go back to Canada yet. It is just Tanya. Ed and I have both noticed that she is not her happy usual self and is lacking something. It may be her age—13 to 14 can be a tough time for any young person.

Ed told me he wasn't going to set up any more clinics; this was the last one. His plan is that we work and live in Viña-Concon until we've saved enough cash to take us home. Having the van in Chile is causing concern that we may have to pay customs more than the van is worth to keep it here after two years. Ed is not prepared to do that and feels that the way we are living is no real life for the children on a long-term basis. He is hoping to move on by next June. Peter and Amanda are planning to stay. For the baby to be legally theirs they have to give the mother four years to decide whether she wants to keep the child or not. They won't be able to leave the country if they want to keep him. Ed is hoping Peter will buy him out of the business.

The food kept coming and plates leaving; when we had eaten everything we ordered, the waiter offered a liqueur on the house and asked if we had a preference. Ed told him to surprise us. We were given a Chilean liqueur, Arauacano, made from herbs the Mapuche people of the south use to aid digestion. It had both a bitter and sweet taste, taking away the feeling of being full—it tasted like sweet *Swedish Bitters,* also excellent for digestion.

August 14, 1998:

There have been small earth tremors every day since the 6.1 quake two weeks ago. Last night I awoke feeling the bed moving underneath me. I don't know whether I am paranoid about earthquakes or just aware of the earth, but my body feels the earth trembling and I am alert. I was in and out of consciousness every time the bed vibrated. Ed snored through it all. Having lived my life on the Canadian Shield, I'm used to solid rock under my feet that doesn't shift with the frequency it does here. I'm not sure I will ever get used to this.

Today's feather.
Aug 15/98

Seagull?
All shades of greys.

Jake is always bringing me feathers.

White at the edges where the sun catches it.

August 27, 1998:

Ed did another radio interview about Chiropractic. It was only supposed to last five minutes but people started to call asking questions and the show ended up running for 50 minutes. Ed had adjusted Pablo, the radio host, the day before and he said that he had slept the best he had in years, for the entire night, which was unusual for him. He was so impressed with the positive effect the adjustment had on his body his excitement was caught by anyone who listened to the program.

Ed also did an excellent TV interview and demonstration of Chiropractic two days ago. The Santiago clinics received many calls but there were fewer in Viña and Ed is feeling discouraged. He needs to remember that Viña is a fifth the size so the number of calls is proportionate. Not only that—in the month we have lived in the Viña area, it is easy to see that people are more relaxed, take life easier and are far more conservative than the people of Santiago. It takes more effort to get them excited and curious about something new. All these facts are of no comfort to Ed, who is eager to be busy again.

September 10, 1998:

I had an extremely vivid dream this morning, and told everyone at breakfast: We were moving and had a pile of belongings in front of the main glass doors of the place we were moving into. I put the keys in the door and felt the apartment was small but we would manage to save money. There was a couple beside us in a hallway who had just moved into the place beside us. That place was represented by a set of doors and there was another place represented by another set of doors we were responsible for as well.   At one point I was on a higher piece of floor looking down on someone we seemed to be holding captive in some way. He wanted to go but I wanted him to stay. I resigned myself to him not being happy if he stayed so told him to just leave. He did. I had the impression this person was Peter.

The kids didn't like the idea of us moving again. They love it here at the beach in Concon.

September 12, 1998:

The day was cloudy and windy when Amanda and Peter visited—certainly not sunbathing weather, but there were fabulous waves to watch crashing on the rocks. We bundled up in sweaters and jackets to walk down to the beach. Ed and Peter kept walking and the kids followed them. Amanda, Tanya and I talked about babies while propped on rocks that we considered "ours" and watched the waves. The woman having the baby is due on the 28th of September according to the doctor. An ultrasound places it at another date, while the midwife predicts yet a different date. Meanwhile, the mother wants to be induced now in order to have it all over with. Amanda is not comfortable with the uncertainty and wants to know when it will be. She asked me about labour and what giving birth was like. I said, "Painful—your body just takes over and pushes the baby out. But nature has it all figured out. When that baby is in your arms the pain is all washed away by love."

I told her I wasn't a very good example of what it is like for most people. With chiropractic, heredity, and my belief that my body was capable of giving birth easily, the girls were born within three to four hours, Ben in 45 minutes, and Jake—I woke up in the middle of the night and just pushed him out. I barely had time to waken Ed. All but Tanya were born full term at home, entering the world quietly, gently and easily, at healthy weights, and without interference. Ed caught the babies and the siblings were present for the birth of the younger ones. Aunts, uncles, grandparents, family and friends were together and I feel the birth of our children at home bonded our immediate family as well as extended family in a way that wouldn't have been possible under other circumstances; real birthday parties. I almost said, "It's a wonderful experience to go through," then remembered the reason they are adopting is that she has been told she would never get pregnant because of her medical condition.

For most of the year that I have known Amanda she has given me the impression that she is not a happy person and has trouble coping with anything that takes effort to overcome. But the prospect of having a baby to take care of has given her new life. She does seem to be nervous, but definitely happier and excited.

Peter was having nervous father feelings too. Over dinner we teased him about how his life would never be the same. Say "so long" to full night's sleep, and so much for the pick-up-and-go life for a while, and on and on about the realities of having a baby. Ed and Peter always banter back and forth in fun but Ed had the advantage on this one. When Peter started to shake his head saying, "Stop, stop, tell me no more. It can't be all that bad," Ed assured him, "It's not bad, most of the time it's fun."

September 25, 1998:

Anna Maria, the receptionist for the Viña clinic, produced a well-organized Chiropractic Information night at Quinta Vergara. She sent invitations to government people, radio and television stations and placed public announcements in the local newspapers. It was the first time, in our entire life together, that any of Ed's ideas for promotion of the clinics didn't involve preparation from me. We arrived early to pull the last details together, but the kids were not much help and Ed asked me to take them out until the reception started. We found a children's playground, which occupied them until we walked the trail of the botanical garden. It became a mini-journey into the wilderness and we found ourselves within a grove of pine trees similar to the white pines of home. The soft pine-needle forest floor and pine scent gripped my senses, reminding me of home, and it was the first time I had real pangs of missing Canada. We enjoyed the natural surroundings longer than anticipated, and a glimpse of the outdoor auditorium was all we had time for while racing back to the reception.

Ed gave an "Introduction to Chiropractic" talk, an explanation of the profession in North America and what he was offering here in Chile. Pablo, the radio station host, and Larry Lederman, the Canadian Ambassador, each gave short talks and enthusiastic testimonials about chiropractic. After the information was delivered, the evening was topped with champagne, pisco sours and hors-d'oeuvres for the guests.

Pablo was a wealth of information and full of life. He and his wife are learning to do the *Queca* together, feeling the need to carry on Chilean traditions. The *Queca* is the traditional folk dance for courting couples—a dance that features handkerchiefs used in a flirtatious way. Pablo said they have found some new life and fun in their marriage learning to dance together.

He also gave me an extensive commentary on the estate we were on. The Palacio Vergara is a mansion constructed in Venetian style. Blanca Vergara, the granddaughter of a rich merchant and ship owner named Alverez, had the impressive building constructed in 1908. Alverez acquired the estate from the Carrera family in the 1840s. Today the mansion houses the Museo de Belles Artes and has rooms available for social gatherings. The main floor of the building has been preserved as it was originally constructed. Averez's wife Delores Perez was intrigued by plants of the world. She started the botanical garden with her son Salvador who brought exotic varieties to her from the Far East and Australia. She introduced many species and a number of them thrive today. Blanca, Salvador's only daughter and heir, married Jose Francisco Vergara. They continued the tradition of looking after and expanding the well-established gardens. Quinta Vergara is now municipally owned. The outdoor auditorium is used for concerts and ballet during the summer months and is where the International Song Festival is held in February every year.

An excellent newspaper article inspired by the evening reached even more of the population, and the clinic in Viña is growing as a result.

September 28, 1998:

The baby boy, Zachary, was born September 22nd and as of the 23rd, he belonged to Amanda and Peter. Four days later Amanda phoned. The umbilical cord had fallen off and Gilda, their housekeeper, said it was too soon. Gilda was also telling Amanda that a doctor had to check the baby next week, he has to have an immunization shot, and he has to have cow's milk formula, not soy. I explained the umbilical cord would be fine as long as it wasn't bleeding, which it wasn't. After listening to her uncertainties I explained that our kids didn't have any of that, and they grew up healthier than most kids I know but if she felt it was necessary to have a medical doctor assure her he was developing properly, then she should go ahead. As far as the soy formula was concerned, I explained that it really depended on Zach and how well his digestive system did. Soy base is just as good being formulated to give a baby the nutrients he needs. Cow's milk formula costs less than soy in Chile, and the Chilean people are big users of dairy products in the belief that we need them to stay healthy. That is where Gilda was coming from with her comments. This was a touchy subject. My attitude is "breast is best" and I gave Amanda my spiel on milk. Cow's milk is meant for calves, cat's milk is meant for kittens, human milk is meant for the babies we give birth to. If we give a mammal milk from a different species, there are always health issues and compromises. If Zach is content on the soy formula then don't change anything. It is not worth the screaming an infant will put you through."

Everything is so controversial. I recommended that she use her instincts to do what she felt was right for her and Zachary. New mothers are always in a vulnerable position wanting to feel capable in their new responsibility, and when receiving conflicting information from different sources, it can cause a lot of anxiety. Amanda just needed to be reassured that they were doing all right.

October 4, 1998:

Larry Lederman invited us to a family day on the *HMCS Winnipeg*, one of the Canadian Navy's "State of the Art" patrol frigates. The vessel was in Valparaiso for training and exercises with the Chilean Navy and U.S. Coast Guard. While in port the crew and officers entertained Canadian families living in Chile at a Sunday afternoon barbecue. So we got to socialize with some Canadians for a change and took a tour of a Canadian Naval ship. So halfway around the world in a country other than our own we learned about the Canadian Navy.

We were greeted and saluted by sailors on duty and directed to the barbecue being held on the open space of the helicopter deck. The kids returned from the table where the food was laid out exclaiming, "Mom, there's relish, we can have relish with hot dogs!" They were excited over a food condiment not available in Chile. The "American-style" relish available here, is not really relish and nowhere near the same kind of flavor we were accustomed to at home. So the kids smothered their hot dogs with "Canadian relish" and found a place to sit down to savour something they hadn't tasted in a long time. They reminisced about Canada and summer days at home when hot dogs were a fast, easy lunch between swims off the dock and then asked when we were going home. A little thing like relish... they are home-sick when reminded.

While the kids and I ate hot dogs, Ed met the captain, spoke with a few people and hooked up with a member of the crew who agreed to give us a tour of the ship. The *HMCS Winnipeg* was the ninth of the 12 new ships recently built for the Canadian Navy by the Saint John Ship Building Company in New Brunswick. The second group of six ships, including the *HMCS Winnipeg,* has the ability to defend against aircraft, submarines and other ships. Each was fitted with state-of-the-art communications, command and control systems. We were escorted down a set of interior steps to what became a maze of doors with ten-inch thresholds, opening and closing behind us as we passed through them. All could be locked and sealed off from fire and water. Several fire stations insure quick efficient control of fires. We were shown the operations room, the communications systems, the cafeteria, a comfortable dining room and a bar. It was explained that the ship was designed to accommodate a crew of mixed gender. The fact that few people are required to keep her sailing allows for more spacious accommodations and comfort. The boat has a waste storage and disposal system, so only grey water is flushed into the sea. Back on the upper deck we were shown four radar systems, the Bofors gun and missiles, and then told that as impressive as it all is, the ships owned by the drug cartels of Colombia still have more missiles aboard than the Canadian warships. The Canadians have strict orders to stay out of conflict with them.

A sailor, who introduced himself as Angus, interrupted our tour to hand out information pamphlets about the 12 new warships of the Canadian fleet and one specifically about the *HMCS Winnipeg*. Speaking mainly to the kids, he opened up the colour brochure to show them the emblems of the fleet and pointed to "the best one". He asked if they saw the buffalo's head in the helicopter hangar. He said it is their symbol. Jake shook his head yes, scanned the emblems on the bottom of the poster, and said, "I like this one".

Angus replied, "Ah, that's a beaver—buffalos are strong," while standing up and puffing out his chest. Karina, chuckling at his antics teased, "Beavers are strong, too, they can move trees and they're little."

"You guys must be easterners", he said. "You're no fun." Then in a more serious tone, he said, "Enjoy your tour," and was gone.

On the bridge we were shown the instruments for steering and controlling the ship and found ourselves drawing comparisons to the Navimag ship we travelled on in February. This one had the same navigational instruments but was far more "sophisticated". Back at the helicopter pad we were served ice cream while our guide kept talking. He couldn't tell us enough. The crew has a well-deserved sense of pride about the high-tech modern-day warship they sail. I feel a little of that pride myself.

October 16, 1998:

Amanda phoned again on Thursday. Peter was in Puerto Montt for the second time in the past week. We were unaware that he had been there before but both he and Amanda were there to register Zachary as if they were the birth parents. The people at the registry office suspected something and Peter was asked to return. Being the honest person he is he couldn't continue with the deception through the questions that were being asked of him and told the officials what they attempted to do. Amanda was in a bad state of mind. Peter called her from Puerto Montt, saying they hadn't put him in jail but there would be an investigation and that they may let him return to Santiago.

On Friday after Peter arrived home he consulted with a lawyer who gave the pair a gloomy-looking scenario. Peter phoned Saturday morning to speak with Ed, who was in Rancagua for the day, so I spoke with him. The lawyer said there would be no way out of being charged. There was supposed to be an inquiry the following Friday for which Peter and Amanda were to be available. I told Peter, "If I were in your situation I would be getting out of the country as soon as I could. Babies are very nice to have but maybe this isn't the one."

He replied, "We really thought he was".

"Peter, leave him here. He will be taken care of; he will have a home. The Chilean authorities won't go after you if the baby is still here. If you still have your passports and it is certain you will be criminally charged then you should go before they do charge you."

"That's what Lynne said, too, but that's not what we want. We want to keep Zachary."

"Well, even if you aren't charged is there any chance that you might be able to keep him?"

"No, not likely."

"Then why take that chance? You should just go. We'll figure something out here."

He said they were going to speak with another lawyer and would call back later. Tanya was hanging around listening to everything I said. As I hung up the phone she exclaimed, "Do you realize what you just did? You made your dream come true." She recalled my dream before I did. "I didn't make it come true; it was telling us what was to come."

At 5 p.m. Ed was still not home when Peter called back. They had been told so many different things. Peter was in a bad emotional state. I could hear both Amanda and the baby crying in the background. He asked if I would come and say good-bye. They were probably going back to the States in the next couple of days. I left the kids expecting their Dad home soon that evening and took the bus to Santiago to spend the night with Amanda and Peter.

It was hard to believe everything they had gone through. I am dumbfounded by the fact that these two people, who have so much common sense, managed to get themselves into such a fix. Both of them looked the worse for wear and Amanda had a sick stomach with vomiting. Through the evening Zachary was a peaceful little boy and eventually settled for some sleep.

I was up early and thought I would go so we could spend a day on the beach as a family, as we had planned, but Peter was up with Zachary and asked if I would take care of him while they tried to get a few hours of sleep. I spent the morning feeding, cuddling, burping, walking, and changing him and was flooded with maternal feelings again. While walking Zachary around the house it dawned on me how full the place was. If they left in a hurry they wouldn't be taking much with them and I didn't look forward to cleaning it out.

Monday was a holiday. Tuesday they consulted with another lawyer. Wednesday came without a ray of hope and no possibility of keeping Zachary. They were on a plane back to the States that evening, leaving Zach with Gilda, their housekeeper. Amanda arrived back in the States wondering why she was still feeling sick and vomiting, only to find herself pregnant. After we received that news I understood the dream that occurred just after my visit with them:

Ed and I were standing on a bridge overlooking a beach area. I saw a large female spider crawling on sand that slid out from under her feet. She walked over shells and mushrooms and when she did they were magnified through her body to a larger size. Then it seemed there was a baby inside the spider and she was gone. I saw the spider again and followed her. She hid where someone's things were close to a tree at the base of the trunk in a hole like an animal house underneath. A woman came up to me and pulled me away because she thought I was there to steal the things on the ground. I said, "No, look, now the spider has two babies inside her." When I visited Amanda and Peter for the last time, Amanda was about two weeks pregnant and unaware of the fact herself.

(In the weeks that followed Zachary was placed with a Chilean couple that had been waiting to adopt an infant for ten years.)

October 23, 1998:

Monday, five days after Peter and Amanda left, there was a message on the answering machine at the Viña clinic. A chiropractor named Steve Flinn from the States, whose wife Pamela is Chilean, had called to find out about practicing in Chile. His mother-in-law had sent them the newspaper article from the Quinta

Vergara information night. On Tuesday he called the Viña clinic again. He and Ed had a lengthy conversation. He was under the impression that it was illegal to practice chiropractic in Chile, which is why they had not come here. Over the phone he made the decision to come to Chile and is contemplating the purchase of the entire business from Ed. It has been their dream to live in her homeland for several years.

It had looked like we were going to be in Chile longer than two years but miracles never cease. This might explain another dream, on which I saw a bridge spanning a city street where our family is standing, looking down. There were two young men who looked like tourists walking on the street below. They walked toward the bridge and were at the end of it coming toward us. We got off and moved to the side to let them pass. They were going the direction we just came from.

(A few months after we left Chile, Steve had an associate from the States join him.)

October 22, 1998:

I needed to come to terms with moving back into the city for the final duration of our stay in Chile. In the back of my sketchbook, as I sat alone on the beach after the kids had had enough and gone home, I wrote:

Playa Negra, Playa Negra
I enjoy you so much I need to say it twice.
We watch your water that is so cold.
The kids still manage to play in it though.
You have taught us so much about the ocean.
Mad sea days and days that are truly Pacific peaceful.
So much about the shells you collect in your rocks.
And then your rocks—they too, have so much to say
Orange, pink and yellow granite with ribbons of black in between.
Your sand doesn't know whether it wants to be rich sandy gold or black.
Black mostly I think.
You hold so many mysteries.
Will I ever know the answers to anything?
Low tide hopscotch, paddleball and more
Many Chileans make a soccer field of you
You hold so many treasures and have given us plenty
What more can I say?
The treasures have been so much more than shells, stones and feathers
You gave the kids and me a place to discover new things and each other.
Treasures that will last a lifetime
For me, special times
Although the kids may not think so
I know they will many years from now.
From the beach in Florida where I remember telling God I needed to understand so much more
Today I find myself saying as I sit here alone

I understand so much more
Yet know there is more to learn
But I thank you, Thank you! Thank you!

November 19, 1998:

We made arrangements to move back to our house in Santiago at the end of November. The time spent in the sun with the sand, rock and waves has given me the ability to let go of the ache in my heart and body. I am positive with the events of the past few weeks, that this is the beginning of the end of our stay in Chile and the beginning of our journey home.

By September the kids and I were settled into a routine of reading, writing and arithmetic in the morning, lunch and a daily afternoon visit to the beach. The first thing we did each day was hunt for shells in the rocks and low-tide days were the most rewarding. At first everything went into the pockets but we learned to be more selective in what was brought home. During the lowest tide we found fleshy pink starfish clinging to the rocks, there were too many to count in some places. Another similar animal called *sol del mar*—sun of the sea, with many tentacles, clung to the rocks as well but was more camouflaged than the starfish its colours similar to its surroundings. Underneath stones we found *lapas*, jointed crustaceans similar in appearance to turtle shells. They don't like the sun and use suction to keep themselves stuck to the underside of rocks. *Potitos*, spongy, slimy, volcano-shaped creatures about the size of a fist, also adhered to the rocks. They were purple, blue, green or brown. In their tops they have a hole and if touched, squirt water. There were several *locos* (the endangered species), similar to abalone but smaller. *Choritos* (small blue mussels) blanketed the rocks. There were so many we forgot we were walking on them most of the time. *Flores del Mar*—Sea Flowers, hung on the undersides of rocks where the water covered them at a high tide. They are small, colourful watery creatures similar to upside-down daisies. We soon learned where the crabs liked to hide and would watch them scamper away to safety when we came close. Occasionally one would get washed up in the sand and would bury itself quickly to avoid being spotted by a gull. Once we knew what to look for, we found crabs were more abundant than we were originally aware.

Curiosity about the tides got the better of us. Playa Negra became our playground as well as a study in which we recorded the water level and moon phases to see if we could make any connections. This created a need to go to the beach every day. The new moon of August 21st was our start day. At 3:30 p.m. all play stopped to pace, measure and record the waterline distance from the wall of the road above the beach. Everyone sketched the moon phase and all have discovered that the moon rises in the sky during the day up to the full moon and at night after the full moon. Staying in Concon until the end of November gave us three moon cycles to make observations. We never really did figure out whether the moon pushes or pulls the water but after observing and graphing three moon cycles we did recognize patterns. Full Moon and New Moon had extreme low and high tide levels whereas the level changes were not as great during quarter moons. What we found so incredible was the amount of sand rearranged on the beach. We chose rocks to sit on from which to make consistent observations, then two weeks later found them being buried little by little. One mad sea day and the rocks were all higher out of the sand than when we started making observations. This happened twice during the three moon cycles. Dayna made the observation that the sun was in a different place in the sky in November at 3:30 than it was in August at 3:30. Just being curious about one thing brought on discovery of other things too.

The beach collected driftwood close to our favourite place for parking our afternoon paraphernalia. Jake's favourite pastime was searching for pieces from which to make swords and lances. We read two versions of King Arthur and three versions of Robin Hood while in Concon. His mind was full of the battles of Arthur's knights and the trickery of the Merry Men of Nottingham. Every stick that was the appropriate size became a sword. He fenced and played out imaginary battles with the air for hours on end. He charged down the beach, pole-vaulted and long-jumped. He practiced running across the sand and up the stone wall four steps before jumping back down; he still doesn't like anyone watching him.

On Playa Negra the sand is black from volcanic rock that has been broken down. The rock formations captured our interest. The pink crumbly granite didn't get smooth with the action of the water. Crystal pieces the size of glass beads washed off. Between the cracks of granite is black volcanic rock. At Playa Negra one can see how, at one time, the earth had cracked open to relieve pressure from below the surface, and between those "cracks", lava came up from underneath, filling in the spaces. It is clear that lava pushed up through wherever it could and cemented the granite back together as it cooled. Tanya came to the conclusion that the volcanic rock was softer. It was more worn down by the waves; the black sand grains were smaller and always lay on top of the lighter coloured sand. The contrasting grain colours created patterns in the sand as the waves retreated. When we started to really look at the rock we found bright green areas in the granite, deposits of the copper that Chile provides so much of to the world. The more we looked the more we saw and started to understand the stories the rocks told. We beach-combed for rocks and found several different types. Karina found many that caught her eye then proceeded to put them into groupings that were alike and brought all of them home. We found one that had a white quartz stripe through it, although at one time the stone had been broken and the strip of quartz had shifted. The two white lines of quartz were originally one and didn't line up. All came to the easy conclusion that an earthquake shifted it.

When the sea birds were abundant we would watch them fish out on the ocean by diving from the air. Some days the flocks would make an area of the ocean dark; other days they wouldn't be there at all. They flew counter clockwise direction above the water in such abundance I wondered how they didn't run into one other. They circled and dove from high in the air, splashed into the water, and flew back up into the air following the school of fish. One afternoon when Ben was the water with the boogie board, a lone cormorant dove in a few feet away and brushed his legs as he swam past, giving him a good surprise. When pelicans, another abundant species here, took to the air in a group the kids noticed they flew in V formations like Canada Geese. Sandpipers scampered in and out with the waves, sticking their 10cm beaks continuously into the sand, feeding on... something. There were six hawks in the Concon area that came to the beach to feed on the seafood only when there was little human activity. They landed twice when we were the only people on the beach and were not moving around.

One quiet early morning I settled for a walk on the sidewalk above the beach in order not to disturb the birds. I counted 12 different species resting on the rocks and sand with beaks tucked under wings. Most of them I had never seen before. A special morning, cool, quiet, peaceful, the water unusually calm, the sun giving a golden colour to the rocks stretching into the water—one of those moments that sends me into future days with a peaceful energy and when a camera or sketchbook would never match what etches into the soul.

Bess loved beach afternoons. She got down there and ran in circles out of excitement, chasing every bird she saw even if it was 50 meters off the ground. It took us all to wear her out. She chased the ball when playing paddleball. We couldn't throw a stick far enough or often enough. And if someone was trying to read, usually Tanya, she would walk over top of her and lie on the book. It often made Tanya take a break from reading. If Bess wanted to play, nothing would stop her from using her resources to get our attention. She'd pick up someone's hopscotch stone and run off with it, or Jake's swordstick which looked like a good object for a tug-of-war game. She would dig in the same holes in the sand as the kids, wondering what they were looking for, or dig a hole of her own and throw sand over everyone else. She is like another two-year-old in the family. On the days when a dog friend (a stray that liked Bess and hung around our house) would go to the beach with us, the two would run and play together, giving the rest of us a break.

We played paddleball and hopscotch when the tide was low, leaving firm wet sand perfect for drawing on. When the kids were played out on the beach but no one felt like going home I would read books and stories aloud to them.

One day we had to find a new place on the beach to park ourselves. The tide washed up a dead sea lion and left it on the rocks where we did our tide and moon records. We watched the man on beach patrol tie a rope around the decaying animal and drag it to the water. He knelt down before the ocean and sea lion, said a prayer then dragged the animal into the water. He swam out past the pool within the rocks and into the current of the deathly cold water and swam back to shore after releasing the sea lion. We watched quietly when Whitney came out with "Now the seal is where he is supposed to be."

Sea lions were another thing we learned a little about. A small colony lives on the rocks about halfway between Concon and Viña. Most of the time, several bask in the sun and swim around the rocks they use for rest. One old, partially blind male (his eyes appeared to have cataracts) found himself a place for handouts at the fishing wharf in Concon. In doing so he attracted attention to the fisherman as well as business, I'm sure. When we bought a meal of fish the kids would go right up to the sea lion to feed him the heads and bones that had been cleaned off for our dinner. He was so confident he wouldn't be harmed that one Sunday morning he was up the ramp sitting close to the tables that are used for cleaning fish and begging. The fishermen seemed to like him.

Another place the kids enjoyed while living in Concon was the sand dunes, which must cover close to 10 acres. The wind shapes and changes the sand in drifts and patterns, creating ripples and waves on the gigantic hills. We would drive to the base of the dunes and climb to the top. The kids would run and jump over the edges into the soft sand below, dig, play and move the dry sand around, and drag each other through it. One would sit on the peak of a dune and the others would dig several feet below, taking away the support and causing a landslide with the one sitting on top riding down. They loved to roll down the hills and make sand angels. Their hair, ears, pockets and underwear were always full. In one "valley" between dunes Ben found the sand was not so soft. Then after rubbing and clearing the loose stuff away he exposed hard but breakable layers in different colours. It was hard but could be broken up. What he found made a lasting impression: sandstone in the process of being formed—always something to learn, even in play. Every kid loves a sandbox and this was the ultimate. We didn't go often enough for the kids' liking.

It didn't matter how hard we tried to leave the sand where it belonged, it always came home with us. Some days the floor of our house looked like the beach. One afternoon before I let Whitney into the newly cleaned house, she had to have the sand removed from her skin. Her feet, knees and damp clothes were covered. We took her shorts off and brushed her skin with the soft broom. She laughed, "It tickles." I laughed and said, "You know what, I used to do this to the kids in the winter time at home. I made them stay outside and would come out with the broom to sweep the snow off their clothes before I'd let them back in the house."

Her eyes sparkled as she said, "Really?"

"Yeah, when they made angels in the snow it would even be inside their clothes, just like the sand."

"Can we go back to Canada so I can play in the snow?"

Right at that moment I felt as if I had been depriving this little Canadian girl of something truly Canadian. She was so young when we left Canada she didn't remember snow.

"We'll be back to play in the snow. It will be a while but you'll have your chance."

The earthquake we experienced in July raised more questions about the earth. Why earthquakes happen and what can happen when an earthquake occurs in the ocean. We discussed the plates that make up the earth's crust and the evolving process of what is happening to them. The kids now have a clear understanding that the Nazca plate is moving underneath the South American plate, and when it does we feel it as an earthquake. Ben marked down on the calendar every time we felt the rumbling and shaking of a tremor. One day Dayna got out of the water saying it didn't feel safe. Soon after, the beach patrol said, "The kids shouldn't play in the water for a few days. There have been a lot of earthquakes, and it is unpredictable by the rocks, just until the water settles down from the quakes." We heeded his warning. The rocks stretching into the ocean created a protected pool braking up the gigantic waves but with the earthquakes there were unpredictable currents.

There was a quake the day Ben stayed at home to make up some forms for Ed on the computer. The computer shook and blanked out a moment. On the beach the rest of us didn't feel anything, yet one wave came up unusually high, wet our towels on the dry sand, carried several pair of shoes away, and wiped out the hopscotch game we were playing. Karina said, "What was that? One wave like that when the water is way over there, that's weird." It wasn't until Ben asked if we felt the quake that we realized we had experienced a small tidal wave.

The days in Concon were a gift that will last a lifetime for the kids and me. The beach was a live science classroom, a gymnasium for yoga and sports, as well as a place to relax and read; we had uninterrupted time together to absorb and learn from our surroundings.

Friday, November 20, 1998:

The last week of our four-month stay in Concon has been one of mixed feelings. Moving back to Santiago means spending more time with friends, but we leave behind the spaciousness of the beach. Each workday in Santiago, Ed took a load of our belongings into the city. We plugged the holes we made in the walls and painted the door that Bess scratched up. The kitchen was so small we took off the door between it and the dining area the day we moved in, but when Tanya and I tried to put it back up we didn't succeed and left it for the guys. Afterwards, Ed and Ben worked at it unsuccessfully as well. When we looked at it more seriously the hinges didn't line up. They were closer together on the frame and above the doorframe was a wide split in the ceramic tile. We concluded that the earthquake moved something; we left the door off.

Our last day on the beach was pleasant. I had a month to grow accustomed to the idea of moving, and with all the "coincidental" events that have happened, I have faith enough not to question why. It is the next step of our journey through South America. As much as I loved the time we have spent here at the beach, I no longer feel the need to hang on. I walked up the 152 steps away from the beach today and didn't need to look back.

Saturday, November 21, 1998:

My 42nd birthday and we moved back to our house with the glass doors in Santiago, Chile. Another end and another beginning.

EDUCATION:
WOES AND TRIUMPHS

February 1999:

I don't know when I will ever start to feel confident about the way we are raising and schooling our kids, but that insecurity has started to shift during this southern hemisphere summer.

Last year when I realized that the Steiner School in Santiago was going to become part of our drop-out-of-school history too, questions in my head needed answers: What is my education objective for my children? What do I expect of them? What do I want for them? What might they want for themselves? What is really important in life? And as I was brainstorming my ideas, I wrote them down in the back of my journal:

- *Children who grow up in a secure and healthy environment.*
- *Happy people, peaceful from within themselves.*
- *People who are capable of understanding and working out human relationships in a positive manner.*
- *People who have the capability to be self-sufficient and resourceful.*
- *Children who are capable of solving problems and to think things through.*
- *To grow up to be people capable of supporting themselves and their dependants in a job and lifestyle they choose.*
- *To grow up with a sense of being responsible for their actions.*
- *To become a positive, contributing member of community and society.*
- *Children that develop in spirit, mind and body equally.*
- *Children who are reliable people with integrity, when they say they will do something, they can be trusted to do it.*
- *To grow up with a set of morals acceptable to our society.*
- *They have to be able to read, write and have a basic understanding of mathematical principles.*
- *I want to spend my time with them while they still want to spend time with Ed and me.*

And the next questions were: *How do we accomplish those ideals? How do they obtain those skills? And am I being unrealistic?*

Conventional schools say that reading, writing and arithmetic, along with knowledge of other academic subjects, are what is important. But to have those skills doesn't necessarily give a person the proper tools to be a fully functional human being in our changing society. There are many highly educated people who have a hard time getting anywhere in life because they don't have "people skills" or know how to communicate. The ability to build healthy human relationships with family, friends, co-workers and acquaintances is just as important for success as being skilled in your vocation.

In my search for a school for the kids, before a home-based education was much of a consideration for our family, I learned about Waldorf Education based on Rudolf Steiner's philosophy. It advocates development of body, mind and spirit with instruction in the arts in balance with the scientific. The curriculum in every Steiner School around the world is basically the same. Ideally the philosophy advocates reverence, respect and responsibility in every aspect of living and learning. When we learn about anything from a reverent point of view, respect will fall into place. Once we have respect for anything—person, place, thing and ourselves—a sense of responsibility is developed. When each person in the world becomes a responsible human being, the world becomes a better place in which to live.

If these virtues are developed along with reading, writing and arithmetic, I believe a young adult will have what is needed to take him in any direction he chooses with the capability of being successful and creating a better world for himself and everyone else. As I sorted this out, all of a sudden the conventional 3Rs seemed such a small part of the big picture but nonetheless an important one.

From watching the way my children have learned reading, writing and arithmetic, I have found that until children are nine or 10, formal instruction for academic subjects is unnecessary unless they are begging someone to teach them something in particular. I always found a great deal of resistance to any type of writing unless it involved titling a drawing or writing something down that had relevant meaning in the kids lives. I struggled with teaching the children reading at a young age, unless I was reading to them, and with arithmetic when it came to putting numbers on paper. What we are experiencing in our own family is what my instincts were telling me long before the kids even started school.

So what is really important until children are "ready"—and for some, it may not happen until they are 12 or older—is that they do anything available to them to develop their bodies, learn what they are capable of, how far they can push themselves physically, and how to gain control. They need to move, play games, do sports, gymnastics, etc., etc. to develop gross motor skills. They need to sew by hand, crochet, knit, and fold origami—anything of the sort to develop manual dexterity. It is a must that they be allowed to play in and with the elements of earth, air, fire and water. They need to learn how to use, work with, and respect these so that an understanding relationship develops with the life-giving resources.

To make a positive contribution, children need to work within the family in any chore they are capable of. This develops their self-esteem, giving them a sense of value and belonging. They need the opportunity to paint, draw and express themselves on paper in any way they see fit and this will eventually slow down and become writing. They need to be read to—as much as they can stand it—and eventually they will not be able to wait for someone to do it for them any longer. When it comes to mathematics, any little person can figure out how many cookies each will get when given a plate full to divide between a group of friends. Living life teaches mathematical skills, and if kids have the opportunity to work with "math manipulatives" as toys, first, eventually written expression will follow.

Children need to be children first, free to learn through play until they make the conscious shift to formal learning on their own—and that means they don't spend time in front of the television. There is a quote from Plutarch that has always stuck with me: "The mind is not a vessel to be filled, but a fire to be ignited."

When I realized in Tanya's first grade of school that school really wasn't a good place for my children, education became a huge dilemma in my life. Remembering my childhood experience and seeing the pattern being repeated for her did not sit well on my conscience. In Quebec, a child must be six years of age by September 30 to be in grade one. Tanya turned six in mid-August, making her one of the youngest in her class; some children were close to a whole year older. By October my happy little girl was turning quiet and withdrawn, but a wonderful thing did happen. Being in a French school with many English children enrolled, a French immersion class of 14 children was created with a young, enthusiastic teacher. The difference was night and day. The kids received more individual attention and Tanya was in a happier environment. Yet as the year progressed she was always tired, didn't pick reading up as quickly as her classmates, and she wrote many of her letters backwards. The teacher was concerned; at that time, the Quebec system dictated that a child was to be a capable reader by the end of the first grade. It was just not happening for Tanya. She was being labeled dyslexic and a slow learner. I had confidence that all she needed was time. She spoke many of her words backwards when she was a toddler—would say, for example, crutch gib instead of big truck, and eventually straightened that around. My gut feel was telling me that the same thing would happen with her writing, given the opportunity, in a way that would not make her feel inadequate. She doesn't have to go through school being labeled a slow learner. My own lack of self-esteem and confidence took a long time to grow out of and I still catch myself at times calling myself slow. It created a long-lasting pattern that was hard to break free of.

It is extremely important for children to grow up with a positive self-image throughout their formative years so that they have the ability to become fully functional adults. Between these ideas and the failure of teachers to address the inappropriate moral behavior of the children, school didn't feel like it was the right place. It should have been a better experience for her than it was for me. My children don't have to go through school being emotionally handicapped by a formal institution and by adults insensitive to children's real needs. It is extremely difficult for one or two adults to meet the educational and emotional needs of just a few children—how is it possible to do that in a class of 25 or more, whether the people are trained to do so or not?

Now after eight years of home-schooling I am finding facts that back up my instincts. A book Joan gave to me to read just recently covers my ideas well. *Making It Up As We Go Along* by Chris Mercogliano is the story of the Albany Free School and validates my beliefs. Kids need a sound, safe environment to develop the spirit within themselves, to learn who they are and find a direction that has meaning and interest. They need to learn how to function and integrate with others, which doesn't happen easily until they have a positive self-image. When they do, the child's natural abilities unfold and the "school stuff" works into their lives more successfully. In the introduction Mercogliano states: *Some may wonder, how can kids learn to read write and solve complex mental problems amid all of the messiness, noise, turmoil, and play? Do they achieve the same competence as students in conventional schools? Absolutely. With one caveat: provided that the parents of children whose natural motivation has already been* damaged by the anti-learning tactics of conventional schooling or by too many anti-life messages from the surrounding environment are willing to back off long enough for the necessary inner repair work to take place. Almost without exception, kids who have spent any significant length of time with us—with permission to learn according to their own rhythms—find themselves at least on par with their peers if and when they enter a traditional classroom situation. Many discover they are way ahead of the game.

And from his conclusion: *We do bear an important message, one based on decades of hard earned experience—and one that many still find hard to embrace: Children learn best when they do so for their own reasons, when they are respected as intelligent, responsible beings, and when they are free to move about and question within living, loving, exciting environments that are not sealed off from the outside world.*

Another impressive read about children who were actually home-schooled, not just free schooled, is the story of the Colfax family *Hard Times In Paradise*. The four Colfax sons showed society and the school system that it is possible to gain an education without attending school. Living their life and supporting themselves came first. The "school stuff" was incorporated as needs and interests developed. When the boys decided that university was what they wanted to do, they focused their education on that goal. The three older boys each attended Harvard. During our second year of home-based education, I met Drew Colfax at a home-schooling conference in Ottawa, where his parents spoke. I had the opportunity to have a short conversation with him and he made an impression on me, appearing to be a confident young man with an excellent sense of self-direction. He became my mentor, embodying the expectations I had for my children.

So now after all my indecision and turmoil over our children's education in the past eight years I am starting to see results that are positive and give me confidence enough to stop wondering what we are doing.

Tanya, just 14, is doing the job independently that she wanted to do a year and a half ago. For the past six weeks she has replaced Christina and Monica, the receptionists in the two clinics, while they have taken their summer vacations. Ed has just realized how well it has worked out and from the comments his clients have been making to him about her, how good Tanya is at what she is doing. They have asked who the new girl is, and when he tells them she is his daughter most are pleasantly surprised. One woman wouldn't believe she was only 14. Ed pointed out to me that she was doing the full job competently by the second week. That involves receiving and acknowledging people by name as they come in the door, having their file ready to go, being courteous—doing it with a smile, keeping files in order so they can be found easily, answering the telephone, giving information about Chiropractic, booking appointments, collecting payment and balancing the books at the end of the day. (There were only two occasions on which she didn't "balance".) This was servicing 60 to 80 people per day. To top it all off she was doing it in Spanish, a language she could barely speak a year ago. Essentially running the clinic while Ed concentrated on giving adjustments. Tanya enjoyed being busy, liked the responsibility and the people she came into contact with. Her whole well-being improved; she became a happier person, with her self-image and self-esteem becoming more positive. She found a purpose and a direction to put her energy into something that was a meaningful contribution to others. For her there was the financial reward as well. For me it is encouraging to see her blossom, to watch her bright eyes full of enthusiasm, to see her accomplishments and know that if she is capable of that at 14, she is well on her way to being a self-sufficient young woman. She already has enough basic skill to be in the "real world" and work a "real job" that will support her when necessary, yet still has plenty of time to hone those skills. If she continues to put her energy into an area where it has meaning for her, she is capable of becoming a skilled person in any career she chooses.

Ben is 12 and he felt that spending the summer in Santiago was not going to be much fun. When at the *cabanas* for Christmas with Aris and Christina he spent time with David, Elizabeth and other people his own age. He enjoys being with people other than his family; he wants and needs more freedom and independence.

He asked me if he could work at the *cabanas* for the summer. I told him that it wasn't up to me; it was Aris that employed people to work there. He said, "But you said we were going to do school for the summer." And I replied, "Well, Ben, if you can land yourself a job for a few weeks then school stuff can wait until the job isn't there any more, but I'm not asking—if you want a job, it is between you and Aris. You have to ask him." He did ask and he did get a job for his room and board and the opportunity to be at the beach and *cabanas* for the summer. He has immersed himself in a Spanish environment and is expanding his third language.

Now it is the end of February and Ben is still working at the *cabanas*. He, another boy his age and David, Christina and Aris' son, keep the grounds of the *cabanas* raked clean, they collect and dispose of the daily garbage, and they clean and maintain the pool. In his spare time, Ben goes to the beach or swims in the pool with his friends. As far as I am concerned it is a wonderful way for a boy his age to spend his summer. It keeps him busy at the beach and he is taking the responsibility for himself seriously.

On Wednesday evening, Guillermo, Ed's accountant, was here to finish up the year-end paper work. He was at the *cabanas* for the weekend, saw Ben and said he appeared to be doing well. When Guillermo was talking to Aris about Ben, Aris praised Ben's work and said he was really reliable. If he gives Ben instructions to do something, it gets done the way he expects it done and he doesn't have to think about it again—a quality every employer looks for in an employee and one that makes him or her stand out from others.

The kids are doing great, enjoying their life and getting an education that does prepare them for the real world—they are a part of it. All I need to do is keep things in order for them by being the facilitator. A dream eight months ago told me this precisely: In that dream, we were living... someplace. The kids and I were on our own and on our way somewhere? We stopped to see Ed but he was busy in the clinic and we couldn't see him. Next, we were rock-climbing a steep mountain cliff. There were many loose rocks along the way, making the climbing difficult for me. The kids were ahead, moving easily and quickly. Drew Colfax was leading and took each one of the kids by the hand as they reached the plateau at the top. I struggled on. Although there was just a small distance to get to the top I felt stuck. I looked down, thought, "Oh God, what a long way down" and felt paralyzed. There was a voice inside my head saying, "Don't look down" but I looked again. The voice said it again and I wondered, What on earth am I doing here? I was so afraid I couldn't move. After I stopped looking down I continued to climb; I couldn't go back. When my hands took hold of places I could hang on to, the feeling came that it really is okay, it is safe and the kids are already there, I just have to keep going. Eventually I made it to the flat area at the top. I found our clean laundry, folded it and put the clothes in order.

I need to relax and enjoy the life direction we have chosen for ourselves. It is working.

Sketches that appeared in the back of my sketch book after a visit to the National History Museum Santiago, Chile. Nobody has laid claim to them as yet.

OUR LAST WEEKS IN CHILE

March 20, 1999:

It is the equinox and many things have developed in the past three months. We are running out of time here in Chile and will be leaving within the next month. Tanya is ecstatic, as are the others. It is just Ben—he has settled into Chilean life nicely, enjoying being here and not so sure he is ready to move on. I, too, have mixed feelings. It has taken me two years to be able to converse with people in Spanish and just in the last six months I have started to feel comfortable here, liking who I am and where I am.

Ed is glad the end is in sight. It has been rewarding and fun for him, but he works long hours and is ready for a break. A group from the World Federation of Chiropractic will be visiting in two weeks; after that we are Chilean history. If we were to stay until June, we'd have permanent resident status, but have a foreign vehicle in the country that is a dilemma. We do need something to take us home, so we are moving before it becomes two years.

How things have worked out for us is truly—I am reluctant to say coincidental—revealing may be the word I am looking for. Steve and Pamela visited in January, liked what they found, have purchased the business from Ed and have been here for the past two weeks gradually taking over just as legal time for the van in the country is running out.

The last couple of weeks have felt like autumn. The really hot weather has passed, days are warm with autumn light, nights are cool, kids are back at school; all those things that happen in September in Canada are happening here in Chile now. I walked past the bakery today and it had autumn leaves in the window for décor.

It has been a different summer for us, not seeing Ben for two months and with Tanya working. The younger ones and I spent a lot of playtime with Joan, Pax, Joy and Maria. I thought we would wander and learn more about the city, but that was not the case; most of those hot days we spent inside. The concrete houses that I have complained are too cold for winter are perfect for summer; this one in particular feels air-conditioned during the hot afternoons. So we have found things to do right here.

Dayna has become the gardener and sweeps the sidewalk on a regular basis. (In Santiago each household is responsible for keeping their part of the sidewalk clean.) This city is on the desert, but you would never know it because of the vegetation. Wherever there is vegetation, someone is watering it daily. Dayna took on the watering responsibility as well and never misses a day.

Karina has become a cook and salad maker and helps make a good part of the meals these days. She would probably do more if there weren't so many other women in the household. She is an avid reader now, just because she doesn't have much of anything else to do.

Jake has found a corner in the basement of the house. He always needs to find a space of his own to hammer, saw and create without interruptions. He has built himself a playhouse under the steps, torn it apart, and remodeled it I don't know how many times. He spent many hot afternoons doing that this summer. He didn't like having a bedroom to himself while Ben was gone and is much happier with his big brother back in the family circle.

Whitney still likes to be boss and complains about how everyone tells her what to do. She can't stand it when Dayna gets after her to pick up her clothes and make her bed, or when Tanya is in bed trying to sleep and tells her to go play somewhere else. But when it comes right down to it she really does have a lot of influence on the family. She is the reason everyone has a pair of roller blades to themselves. We were just going to buy three pairs and share them but she wanted a pair of her own and wouldn't come out of the store until I suggested she take her argument up with her Dad. She did get her own pair of roller blades, which meant we had to buy two more pairs to make it fair. So, to say the least, we have spent many evenings at the park roller blading and she has never looked back.

It has been a chore getting everything in order for moving on, but the end is in sight. We are set up for camping this time. It will be much better to cook our own food. Ed made arrangements to visit the largest observatory in the southern hemisphere, El Tololo, east of La Serena. It will be a trial run for the camping gear.

April 6, 1999:

We have been at the seashore south of La Serena and have had an interesting past few days. We checked in at the university on Friday afternoon to confirm our visit to the observatory Saturday and then continued the drive into the Valle de Elqui. When Santiago had its first rainfall of the season on Thursday, Valle de Elqui, which has clear skies 360 days a year, had clouds. There were still some clouds on Saturday, but we visited El Tololo nonetheless.

An association of universities of the United States, Brazil, and Chile run the observatory. It has 14 telescopes, including the largest in the southern hemisphere with a focal length of four meters, and they are in the process of building another twice as long. Just the mirror of the four-meter telescope took three years to build. The views of the mountains alone were well worth the trip. The observatory is at 2,200 meters leaving less atmosphere though which to observe the heavens. The location, on the highest point of the area until deeper into the Andes, is a perfect perch for viewing the layer upon layer of peaks toward the east too.

At midnight we visited the town of Vicuña, where the observatory has a small, 12-inch focal length telescope that we had a chance to look through. We had a mini-course on southern hemisphere astronomy, learning about the southern sky. Jake was exited about looking through a telescope to see the moon but was intimidated by the group of people until I picked him up and convinced him to have a look. His fascination and excitement returned, exclaiming, "Wow, just like the real pictures." The moon was so clear every crater was visible. There was a bit of a commotion when our turn was up. He was intrigued and wanted more time to satisfy his curiosity.

Outside, another volunteer oriented us to the compass points, how to find the south, tell time and season; he pointed out the closest star to earth, and where the planets and constellations are. The grouping of stars that has been my second reference after the Southern Cross was high in the sky. I have called it the kite constellation—four stars in a diamond shape and two more for the tail, prominent at the sky's zenith during winters in the southern hemisphere. I found out that if I include a few more stars it is the constellation Scorpio; the astrological sign I was born under. It is the one thing I've watched the sky for anytime I've looked up in the past two years. Maybe I have looked to the stars for answers, but all I know is that when I see the star-kite flying in the sky it is a reminder to fly with it.

Despite dressing in our warm clothing for our midnight adventure, we froze. I still haven't learned to prepare for the temperature extremes on the desert.

However, we had pitched our tent on top of long grass and I had the most luxurious sleep I have ever had in any bed in my entire life. I woke feeling comfortable and well rested. It is said that the Valle de Elqui is a magical place; maybe that is part of the reason for my restful sleep. The deep blue sky and sunshine were good for my soul.

While we were packing up to head for the beach there was a group of children playing around the four-foot-deep natural pool. I knew they were there in my peripheral vision but didn't really take special note of them, assuming they had come for a swim like several others had that morning. Out of the corner of my eye I saw one "dive" in and a few moments later when another called out a distressed, "Mommeee!" I looked and saw a little person in the water bobbing up and down. The word caught my attention—I call it the "mommy reflex". Anyone that is a mother knows that a scream of "mommy" grips your innards and doesn't let go until you are satisfied the problem is taken care of. Ed and the kids were packing the van at a closer distance to the pool but didn't notice. There wasn't any time for words or thought (for that matter); I ran past them all, jumped in, scooped him out of the water and stood the boy up on the edge. He immediately started to scream. While pulling myself out of the water everyone else arrived. The father picked the dripping little guy up and ran away with him. I didn't even get to see what he looked like. Ed and the kids were stunned; it was all over before they realized what was going on. I don't even remember throwing my sweater and shoes off; they were lying on the ground en route.

The incident changed the process of the morning. The kids didn't swim the day before and had a bet on who would be the first in. They never dreamt it would be their mother. They had a swim. To tell you the truth I never would have put my toes in if there hadn't been someone in need. I should change my attitude; it was refreshing. Since my hair was already wet I washed it at the sinks. While walking back to our campsite I met the parents and found out the little guy was fine, just frightened. The mother was in tears blaming herself for not watching him and I was "thanked a million." I encouraged her as best I could to not feel so bad. I know it is hard to keep them all safe all the time. I was glad he was okay.

South of La Serena we found a campsite on the edge of the beach under palms. There is nothing like the elements to bring out the best in us. Grey mornings on the beach are disappointing and cold to get up to, but it cleared yesterday and we had a wonderful afternoon. Bess thought it was the best thing that had happened since Concon. She ran with another dog at the campsite and didn't stop until dark. The beach had a shell on it we hadn't seen elsewhere and we spent much of our time combing the sand. Today was cloudy again, and it didn't promise to clear up, so we set to packing after a hot breakfast.

The beach tired everyone out, and it has turned into a quiet ride back to Santiago. Bess isn't moving; she is stiff from running yesterday. It was a good trial run for camping; we are carrying far too much stuff.

April 15, 1999:

Our last days in Chile have been somewhat hectic. We had planned to leave by the end of March but it didn't happen. Every move we have made in Chile was on a new moon and circumstances have kept us here until the next one as well. There must be more to the moon and stars than we will ever know.

Ed had a busy weekend with David Chapman Smith, his wife Sira (a chiropractor from Brazil) and David's group of people from the World Federation of Chiropractic. Raoul, Steve and Ed escorted them anywhere they were going. They met with people at the Ministry of Health, as well as the only Chilean chiropractor, who has been in practice for several years but has been quiet about it, and with the group who have been studying chiropractic together. It looks like something will be organized for Chile; it will just take some time.

We have been staying in "our *cabana*" at Aris and Christina's since the house in Santiago is empty of all furnishings. The kids enjoyed our last days with Elizabeth, playing until all hours of the night. Aris and Christina have been generous; we were their guests this time. They have been sincere, supportive friends to us here in Chile. We had Playa Grande almost to ourselves, as we did during our first weeks here 22 months ago. I sat on the beach Saturday afternoon, watched the waves and remembered a recent dream, January 8th, 1999: I am watching the waves of the ocean from the beach. The waves are shaped like tall, skinny fingers. The ripple of white water on the top looks like it is waving goodbye. Then we are climbing the mountains of Chile going toward Argentina. The people of Chile are cheering us on saying, "Ole! Ole! Ole!" as we are leaving. They too are saying good-bye.

As much as I am going to miss the time spent on the beaches here, it is time to go. But I don't know what we are going to do when we get back to Canada.

The kids stayed at the *cabana* by themselves overnight on Tuesday while Ed and I went back to Santiago to clean the house and put Bess on the plane to Dad and Mom. Regulations are that when an animal travels on its own, the temperature in the destination country must not be an extreme difference. So the authorities finally allowed her to fly out on Wednesday morning.

At 7:30 this morning the sun rose over the mountains and spilled its yellow light, warming everything it touched. What a day it promised to be. We arrived in unsettled weather with unsettled emotions but are leaving in life-giving sunshine, more at peace within our family and ourselves. I in particular am at peace within myself. I am thankful for the time we have had in Chile, we have learned so much. There were lengthy good-byes with Aris and Christina.

Tanya & Elizabeth before leaving Chile

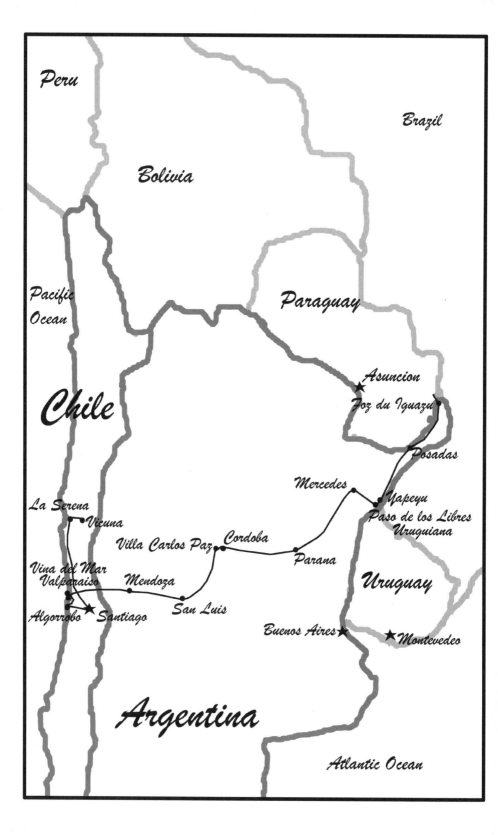

ARGENTINA

April 18, 1999: Mendoza and Portillos

At 5:30 p.m. we were at the border. The officer looked at the form for the van and in a joking manner said, "You aren't leaving any too early are you?" It was true. It was the last legal day for the van in the country. It didn't act up at all on the climb up La Cuesta de Caracoles. It had overheated when Ed and I tried to go to Larry and Patricia's on Tuesday evening, so we went back to the house. Ed brought it to Manuel on Wednesday but he couldn't find anything wrong. Ed and I were both baffled; there was coolant on the ground. Anyway, after listening to us express our concerns about getting up and over the Andes, Jake said confidently, "It will make it," like his voice was coming from someplace else. The van has kicked up a fuss every other time it climbed that route but this time it worked without a sputter.

Ken's directions were perfect. He is an American chiropractor working in Mendoza. Ed was not at the house when he came to Santiago in the summer but he left his phone number and told us to visit when we came through. Our afternoon visit was short as he had patients so we explored the city.

What a city Mendoza is! While walking the streets we got a look at the ceramic-tiled sidewalks. It appears that each house or building tiles the sidewalk adjacent itself, which creates an interesting variety of patterns. The tiles underfoot led our eyes to the houses and main doors. Many of the doors were a work of art, most were made of wood, many had wood carvings on them, and not one of them was ordinary.

A huge park and well-planned cultivation has made the city green. They boast that every street is lined with trees, and it is true. All the streets have a deep gutter between them and the sidewalk and mature branching trees that create overhead tunnels. The gutters, which are part of the complex irrigation system that keeps the trees watered and healthy, are sometimes full of water. Like Santiago, Mendoza is on the desert. When we crossed the Mendoza River the kids talked about the dried up riverbed and how the river was barely a stream. Then a minute later while crossing another bridge, we discovered rushing water at least 50 times the volume of the actual river, in a man-made canal. The river had lost its natural route and been put to work irrigating much more than city streets. Fields and fields of grapevines produce a selection of good quality wines. The desert area has been turned into cultivated country producing for, and supporting the lives of thousands of people.

During dinner and our evening visit with Ken, he mentioned he had friends that rent out a mountain cabin in Portirillos. We thought it would be a great place to spend Ben's birthday so made the arrangements. The cabin is quaint and comfortable tucked in off the road, surrounded by trees and backed by mountains and a stream. The kids were so attracted to the stream they forgot the cabin and were gone for hours exploring as soon as we arrived. We spent Ben's birthday today hiking in the area. It is autumn – April autumn leaves—different from

Canada but not really; it could just as easily have been an October afternoon in the Gatineau Hills. A clear, crisp, blue sky and bright yellow trees with leaves crunching and swishing underfoot making the head feel light; it was invigorating. Ben had a good day—the stuffed stomach from a fabulous birthday dinner and excellent strawberry cake alone put a big smile on his face.

April 20, 1999: Carlos Paz

When coming back into Mendoza from the mountains yesterday Ed was driving the same speed as the other traffic at 100 kilometers per hour in an 80 zone. The slower speed limit is unreasonable on the freeway and traffic travels much faster than what is posted. Ed was stopped along with 12 other vehicles and was asked to get out of the van. He was shown a book in which the fine was listed as 400 pesos. The police officer proceeded to tell him he didn't have to pay if Ed would give him some cash. Somewhat taken back, Ed asked how much—50, 100, 150?—it wasn't enough. Ed didn't give in. The policeman spoke with his partner and when he came back he told Ed to leave. The whole situation impressed upon us that the police in Argentina are corrupt. We saw others stopped at the same time as us, leaving only after cash had been handed over.

On our arrival at Ken's to return the keys to the cabin, Ed put the papers that he had taken out for the police, back in order and noticed that his International Driver's License was missing. He was sure it was given back along with the stack of passports but it just wasn't there. We had to give up looking; he still has his regular Quebec license and we are hoping it will be sufficient. We weren't going to go back to the police.

It was dark when we stopped for gas in Lujan. The owner and his son spoke with Ed at length about our travels. They were full of information. The son had travelled in Brazil and they discussed some details. We ended up staying, setting up the tent and using the garage's bathroom and water. It worked out well but Tanya was appalled at the thought of sleeping in a garage lot; the others didn't mind at all. It was just as good as anything; the bathrooms were clean and it was free.

Today was pampas, free-range sheep, goats and cattle on miles and miles of flat grassland. Some of it was cultivated and there were many slough-like areas until we climbed the ridge of mountain that jumps out of the plain west of Cordoba. It felt as if we were back in the Andes.

We are at a campsite on the man-made lake, Lago San Roque at Carlos Paz. We have had the entire place to ourselves, since it is off-season, and the kids have enjoyed it immensely. After arriving, we hardly saw Jake and Whitney who were happily playing. They found Styrofoam, sticks and plastic bags, made sailboats and played on the edge of the water with their creations, hardly taking time out to eat.

After dinner Jake was sitting at the lakeshore with the dog that had befriended us; the two of them were looking out over the water in the dusk. I watched Jake talking to the dog; shortly after he sat on my knee and sadly confided, "I miss Bess."

The kids made up a game of "kick the plastic bottle", like North American football, then tried some gymnastics. Jake's cartwheels are taking over his walking; he even cartwheels down the city streets. The others are trying to get him to do some flips and a back-walkover. With some proper instruction it wouldn't take him long to learn.

The wind has picked up significantly tonight and the sound of the wind-blown trees is loud, yet peaceful.

April 23, 1999: Tapeyu

The land on the east side of the Cordoba Sierras is flat; it holds more water than the west, and *estancias* dot the landscape. Cattle and goats grazing are a common sight and *gauchos* riding their horses. They were usually dressed in traditional clothing: a sombrero with the front turned up, a belt that holds everything needed, always a colourfully striped saddle blanket and a faithful dog keeping up to the horse. They were usually moving groups of cattle alongside the road.

We thought we would camp on the west side of Rio Parana on Wednesday but found ourselves crossing and going through the tunnel toward the city. The Rio Parana at that point is a wide sprawling river; the land it travels through is flat with several channels of water creating islands. The road skips from island to island by bridge over waterways and marshland, and then a tunnel plunges underneath the main part of the river where large vessels travel upstream. We travelled 36 kilometers from dry land on one side to dry land on the other. Farther south from where we crossed the river and its inclusions the river is twice that wide. I looked back to see the red sunset at our back while crossing the expanse and it was especially beautiful when reflected off the water of the marshes. The big red ball slowly dropped below the hazy horizon.

Last night and this morning we experienced mosquitoes that were unbearable for the first time on our travels; they were worse than in the forests of Canada in the spring. We couldn't linger anywhere, and pulling pants off to use facilities gave them opportunity to feast. Even the morning sun didn't discourage them, we packed up quickly and moved out without breakfast. The Parana River and marshes are obviously a breeding ground.

Police stopped us three different times yesterday and Ed's Quebec license was accepted without mention. The problem was that at one point Ed hadn't put his seat belt back on after stopping from a previous check. We usually wear seat belts but sometimes get careless; it is not a common practice in South America and we have become lazy about it. The policeman asked him to get out of the van. Again, Ed was shown the fine in the book, 400 pesos but the cop would let Ed go if he paid him 100. These tactics doesn't create a very good impression of the Argentine police force. The "fines" appear to be inflated values just to make a pay-off more appealing to the one being charged. (The Argentine peso is equivalent in value to the American dollar.) Ed paid him the 100 pesos. Back on the road he said, "Let's get out of Argentina, I don't like it here. It's expensive and the police are just licensed crooks."

After studying the map and discussing options we decided to head for the Brazilian border. As we were making that decision Ed pulled to the side of the road again because there was a truck on our tail flashing his lights and wanting us to stop. My reaction was "Oh god, now what?" Two men got out of the truck and walked toward the van. The driver was a big burly guy, the other had partially balding curly hair, not as tall, and a big grin on his face. We didn't know what to expect. Ed jumped out of the van and the smaller man asked, "Are you guys really from Quebec?" in English.

Ed cautiously answered, "Yes."

The man exclaimed, "Wow, I'm from Chicago! You drove here?"

Ed replied yes with relief in his voice and we began a lengthy visit. Paulo—Paul—introduced himself and his cousin Juan. Juan owns an *estancia* close to Mercedes and Paul has been visiting family for the past three months.

Juan pulled a container of mate (mahtay) out of his truck and we shared an Argentine tradition on the side of the road. *Mate* is tea that is carried everywhere in Argentina with a thermos of hot water. It is ritual shared amongst friends and family. A cup, always made of a gourd, is filled with the herb and hot water is poured over it. The first person drinks all the tea through a metal straw that strains the tea while drinking it. The gourd is then filled again with hot water for the next person. Then again for the next until all within the group have had a cup. It's bitter stuff though.

Paul asked so many questions wanting to know about our trip. He spoke with each of the kids, asking if they spoke Spanish and liked what they are doing. They all said yes (for the record) but are glad they are on their way home. He told me he was envious of our travels. He wanted to come here for a year then shortened it to six months, then four and said he was not looking forward to going back. He enjoys the calmer life here.

He told us about the *estancia* he had visited yesterday and its elderly owner. "The Old Gaucho," as he called him, is 70 years old, on his third wife with five children; his previous wife had 13 and he had a wife before her who had three. He laughed as he spoke of him, so full of life, still running his *estancia* and living like he is still 30. He said, "That's a man who knows how to live."

After he asked about my background he told me he had brought 400 rolls of film with him and hasn't used half of it. Ed had been talking with Juan while I spoke with Paul. When it was time to move on, Ed asked about a campsite and Juan gave him directions to the Gaucho Gil grounds. I was about to close the side door when Paul was back with his hand in a bag. When he pulled it out he dropped a handful of rolls of film into my lap, put his hand in the bag again then thought better of it and dumped the entire contents on top of what he had just dropped. He said, "I'm not going to use it all and you will, so you might as well have them. It's good film; I'm not giving it to you because it's bad. I know you will use it. Good luck and God Bless. I wish I were going with you."

I was speechless and barely got a mere thank you out before he was gone. Thirty-three rolls of colour print film left in my lap—what a gift. They waved as we went our separate ways.

Gaucho Gil was a healer; people came from all over Argentina to see him. The campground was his home and it is the location of a yearly festival in January that attracts up to 60,000 visitors. The campground was adequate but garbage was strewn everywhere and there appeared to be no effort to clean it up. I must be South Americanized—it bothers me but I can ignore it now and function without the negative effects depressing me so much. As that thought occurred to me, I wondered if that is what has happened to us as a human race? We have serious negative effects on Mother Earth but we just turn our back and don't look at them because it's too much work to take care of them. I can't let it depress me, but I need to care enough to do something about it.

We had several trials today. For some reason, at the Argentine border, our vehicle came up in the computer as having had an accident in the country. An officer looked at the van but was more taken back with the kids playing around it. He of course found no evidence of an accident but the confusing thing was our complex 17-digit-letter Ford identification number came up as being a Mercedes Benz. It took four hours to clear up. Ed spent the morning talking with Silvero patiently explaining what happened with the police in Mendoza and about his International License. He decided we were legitimate, took the accusations out of the computer, and gave us our exit papers.

The next challenge came from us failing to do our research. We need a visa to enter Brazil and it was not possible to obtain one at the border because we were not born in South America. We went back to Argentina. Ed parked the van in the no-man's land between countries and our crew showed up on the doorstep of the *aduana* again. They were surprised. Ed explained the new situation. Silvero suggested we take a bus to the consulate and leave the van parked where it was to avoid the paperwork. We did exactly that.

It being Friday afternoon the consulate was closed until Monday morning. Back at the border Ed talked to Silvero again. He was willing to leave the paperwork as it was and told Ed to take the van back into Argentina, and that if we passed through on Monday at his border station we wouldn't have problems. We were reluctant to have the van in the country when it was already signed out, given the experiences we have had with the police force. We went back to plan A, Iguazu Falls via the Argentine side. Ed humbly asked if they would complete the paperwork for the van and allow us full re-entry into their country. Ed has always talked with every border control person in a friendly manner; it paid off. It was as if Ed and Silvero had become friends. Silvero told Ed that there would be a campground at Tapeyu and if we had any trouble at all when we did try to leave the country to have the border control call him. We were thankful he was an understanding human being; he could have made it much more difficult for us. Win some, lose some, live and learn, what a day. We are still in Argentina.

We found the campground in Tapeyu on the Uruguay River. A new owner just took charge and the facilities are run down. He didn't give Ed a fee; he just said to give him what we thought was good. Since we were paying between 10 and 15 pesos in other places Ed asked if 10 was okay. He was pleased. Ed said, "I guess we were supposed to stay a little longer. This man and Silvero have given me a better impression of the Argentine people."

We have found refuge in the tents early tonight. Although the mosquitoes are not nearly as bad as in Parana they still chased us inside.

April 25: Puerto Iguazú

While Ed was making arrangements for a camping space at Cataratas de Iguazú the kids discovered several butterflies that had smacked onto the front grill of the van. After they peeled them off and laid them out, they let Ed drive into the grounds. There were 13 that were still in good shape and all were not dead. Two revived and flew away after their shock. Meanwhile, there were dozens of butterflies in many different sizes and colours fluttering about our heads, the most intriguing of which was the large, shiny, peacock-blue one we tried to follow. Jake decided he wanted to keep the dead butterflies so as carefully as we could, without destroying them more than they already were, we taped them into his book with wide clear tape.

We made good use of the pool for the rest of the afternoon. It was nothing short of paradise, as we soaked up the sun surrounded by tropical plants.

Monday, April 26: Cataratas de Iguazú

First things first: we needed a visa for Brazil. It took some talk, and it wasn't easy—Portuguese is different enough from Spanish to make listening and understanding a chore again. At first the officials were only going to give us a 12-day visa. Ed explained what we have been doing and what our plans are. He told them in a calm, diplomatic voice that we knew they issued 90-day visas and that was what we were hoping for to give us sufficient time to travel through Brazil. The man had a disbelieving look on his face but discussed the situation with his supervisor. When he came back, he asked us to show them proof that we could support ourselves while in the country. Ed gave him the letter from Larry along with all the credit cards we had. (Larry Lederman, the Canadian ambassador to Chile, had written a letter explaining our intent to travel back to Canada by road and it was the only time on the journey that we actually did use it.) After a lot of chat in the back they decided they would issue a 90-day visa. It took almost two hours of patient waiting but we got what we needed.

The next four hours were spent exploring the World Famous Cataratas de Iguazú on the trails of the park. The falls are truly immense—there are no words that will ever describe them sufficiently. *Guazu* is "big" in the language of the Guarani people—they named it accurately. The *SAH* describes them: "There are rapids for 3½ km above the 60 m precipice over which the water plunges in 275 falls over a frontage of 2,470 meters at a rate of 1,750 cubic meters per second"

Butterflies added to the magical atmosphere, fluttering about, following and landing on us. Karina managed to entertain one for more than an hour until it decided it was going to stay beside the falls when we started to move away. There are about 500 species in the area. The different kinds, colours, sizes and patterns were impossible to keep track of. We noticed few birds other than vultures and parrots; the butterflies were so prominent.

The trail of bridges over fingers of the river above the drop gave magnificent views of the water fall. On one side of the bridge there is a quiet river gently easing its way through the forest, but on the opposite side the water plunges into a deathly 60-meter drop where half the water ends up as mist that breaks the sunlight into brilliant rainbows.

The lower trail brought us halfway down the precipice along areas where, during wet season, a higher water level would make viewing from that point more difficult. The vegetation was lush and green, growing profusely wherever it clung. Grasses, ferns, flowers (so many orchids) and trees thrive in the environment.

Standing extremely close to Salto Bassetti, we received a cooling shower from its spray. Listening to the roar and feeling the power of the thundering vibrations of just that small part of the falls touched every cell of our bodies, taking us all into an invigorating mind space. When we finally tore ourselves away, we left feeling cleansed and light-headed.

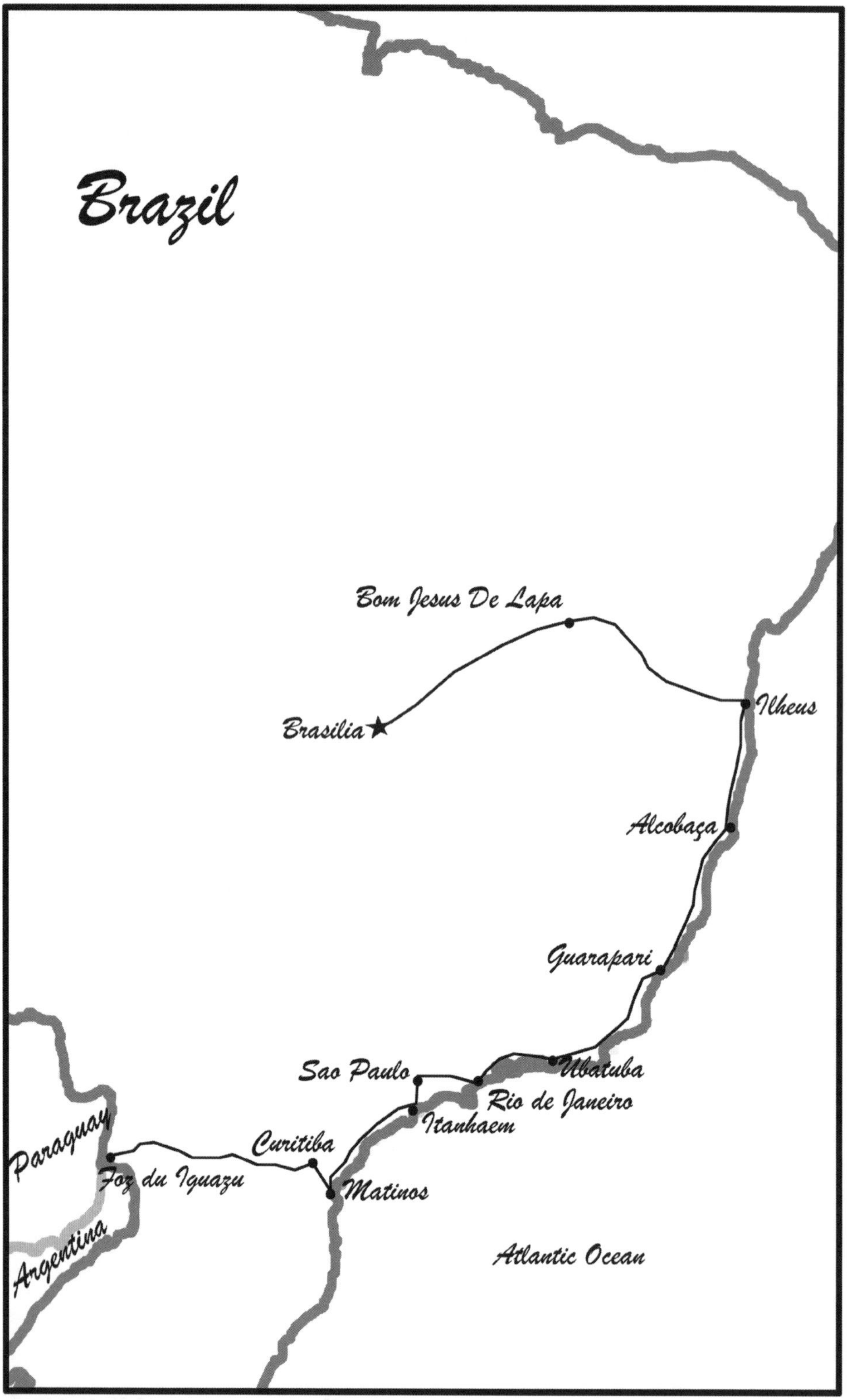

Brazil

Bom Jesus De Lapa

Brasilia ★

Ilheus

Alcobaça

Guarapari

Sao Paulo

Ubatuba

Rio de Janeiro

Itanhaem

Paraguay

Curitiba

Foz du Iguazu

Matinos

Argentina

Atlantic Ocean

BEACH HOPPING BRAZIL

Tuesday, April 27, 1999: Iguazú, Brazil

Crossing the border was straightforward—it did take three hours but only because we had a foreign vehicle. The man in charge was gone for lunch and nobody else knew how to process a North American vehicle. We had a wait, but entertainment too.

While at the Argentine *aduana* office, a man was almost knocked off his feet as he entered the building, by a goat. In the aftermath, the man moved inside but the goat stood at the door looking in. He was reluctant to follow but made it difficult for anyone to enter or exit without getting close to him. Where or to whom the goat belonged was a mystery. After another man stopped the goat from doing the same thing to him an *aduana* officer took his billy club, wrapped the strap around his small horns and led him away, tugging in the opposite direction. He was dragged to the field away from the buildings. That was the end of Billy—I'll call him—for a few minutes.

We found a bench in the shade close to the Brazilian *aduana* building to wait. We talked with the woman from the vehicle office until she became occupied with her duties, and then we noticed that Billy was back—on the Brazilian side this time.

He walked alongside people and gave most a good sniff; most people walked well around him. When people weren't paying attention, he butted them with his head and made them notice. One man kicked Billy in response and Billy looked at the man as if to ask, "Hey, what was that for?"

A woman in a mini-skirt showing off her long legs, and unaware of the situation, stood and waited. Billy noticed, trotted towards her excitedly, put his nose on a leg and took a good sniff. She noticed him then, looked down, moved back, spoke to him and gently patted his head. Billy had found a friend. All of a sudden his disposition changed, he held his head high, puffed out his chest, had more control of his mannerisms and it looked as if he was standing guard over her. It was not long before her male partner had his business complete. He took the woman by the hand and shooed Billy off as they walked toward their car. Billy was glued to them, getting excited and running from one side to the other, wondering where they were going. They stopped, the man shooed him off again, turned his back on Billy, and continued to walk away. Billy wasn't going to take that—he saw his chance, ran with head down and butted the man smack in the behind lifting him off his feet so that he landed on his derrière, well ahead of where he was hit. Was he mad! The woman wavered between shock and laughter. The man got up, seemingly unharmed, and ran after Billy. Billy knew better, and didn't stick around. He watched them from a distance. The man opened the door for the woman, who by then couldn't contain her laughter. When the man took his place in the driver's seat he sped off angrily, squealing the tires on the pavement. Billy started to follow but stopped and stared down the road as if wondering where she had gone. When he decided she wasn't coming back he turned his attention elsewhere. There were more people. By this time he was a little more aggressive, butting anyone who wasn't paying attention. He started to pick on another man from the *aduana* and butted him in the leg. The officer pushed him away and Billy went at him again; they struggled back and forth. The kids were laughing. Whitney noticed Billy had an erection and asked what it was. The officer had his hand on Billy's head holding him back so he wouldn't be bumped again while backing toward the door of the building. When he was inside he closed the bottom half of the door. Billy continuously banged it with his head until he ejaculated on himself and the ground. There was a look of surprise from the goat, like he couldn't figure out what had happened. He looked down between his two front legs and turned in circles like he was looking for where it came from. The kids had as many questions as the goat. Billy soon found himself wearing a bucket of water that had been thrown out the top half of the door. While rolling in laughter, all I could think of was that he must be a teenager; so much energy and he didn't know what to do with it. In the confusion of ejaculating and trying to shake the water off himself, Billy was caught off-guard, found a rope around his neck and led away once more. We didn't see Billy again but the whole show was something we'll never forget.

We are camped at Hostel International. After we settled in we enjoyed an afternoon swim at the pool. The kids were a happy bunch today but I am afraid we disturbed the group of six German tourists. They left soon after our arrival. None of them had smiles on their faces and all of them ignored my hello. I had the impression they were annoyed with us for bringing our kids. Anyway, that is their problem, we are paying customers too, but it made me think about how we have been received in South America by the people we have come into contact with. The people who have been the most intolerant of us as a family have been North American and European tourists.

It being autumn, the sun is setting noticeably earlier, and it is cooler in the evenings.

April 30, 1999: Foz do Iguazu, Brazil

We visited the Brazilian side of the falls yesterday and were greeted in the park by raccoon-like animals called coati (*nasua nasua*). They are ring-tailed, have long noses, dog-like fangs, and are inquisitive and real beggars. After the kids and animals checked each other out, we walked the trail. The Brazilian side faces west and the series of falls were bathed in morning sunlight. White water pours over the escarpment where it has worn down the basal rock. The rock faces and cliffs on the escarpment that are not submerged in water, are lush with green ferns and palms that are always wet. Birds cling to the rock cliffs in between the falls. The kilometer-long hike along

the north shore of the Iguazú River brought us to falls after falls. The Garganta del Diablo (Devil's Throat) appeared before us, white and roaring. From the platform we watched the *vencejos* (swifts)—hundreds of them—fly through the waterfall to and from their nests behind the falls. A visit to the tower gave us an overview of the area, but from the ground it is impossible to see the falls in their entirety. I was humbled by the beauty and power.

The *coatis* sniffed out our lunch soon after we started to eat. They are not shy animals; we had several beggars at the van door, and one tried to jump in. Ben lured them away with a sandwich so we could close the doors.

Our next visit was the Itaipu Bi-national Generating Station—the largest hydroelectric power plant in the world. Because there's an average of 1,500 visitors per day, an organized bus tour is the only authorized way to visit. We were driven around the premises with short stops at strategic places for viewing the technological wonder, but the film at the visitors' center in Paraguay was far more informative.

- April 1973 – Brazil and Paraguay agreed on using the Parana River as a source of hydro-electricity.

- 1975 – Construction began with the digging of a diversion canal to drain the original riverbed for construction of the main dam.

- October 1982 – The diversion canal was closed. It took 14 days to fill the reservoir. The waterfall, Sete Quedas—almost as big as Iquacu, as well as 1,350 square kilometers of land, were submerged.

- 1984 – The generating station started producing power, providing energy to 89% of Paraguay and 25% of Brazil.

The lake that was created by the 7.6-kilometer dam is 170 kilometers long, with an average width of seven kilometers in the Parana River valley. The film showed that the water level in the lake is maintained at a constant 220 meters above sea level, guaranteeing the safety of riverbank residents. It was designed for leisure activity, commercial fishing, irrigation, a water supply, and hydro-electricity. The film also demonstrated that the environment was taken into consideration. Archeological and historical articles were removed and preserved, plant species unique to the area were transplanted, attempting to save them from extinction, and during the filling of the reservoir, teams of people in boats scanned the area, rescuing and relocating trapped animals. Trees have been planted along shoreline areas and a fish migration canal was built to maintain the fish population. They say that Itaipu is "one of the most successful enterprises in the social environmental aspect".

I came away feeling lost and wondering how man could live without doing such things. A waterfall almost as large as Iguazú is gone; it is difficult for me to conceive of that.

Today at the pool with the kids, Ed met a woman, Olga, from Colombia. She and her husband have just travelled by boat and bus through the Amazon basin of inland Brazil via Manaus, Puerto Velno, Cuiaba, Campo Grande and here. They are from a small beach area on the outskirts of Santa Marta and she said she would help us arrange transportation of the van and ourselves to Panama through a friend who is a travel agent. She gave Ed the name of the *cabanas* beside her house and told him to call her when we arrived.

May 1, 1999: Matinos, Brazil

Two days ago I had this dream, it keeps coming back so I had better write it down: I am flying through the air looking at the earth from above. I fly from place to place, enjoying the freedom and sense of flight. While flying from one place to the next I started to analyze how I was able to do this and doubted my ability. I was falling from the air until I heard a voice, "All you have to do is keep your faith. You will fly and always be safe." My faith in my flight returned to my body, I felt peace, and continued to fly. The next place I landed was in an autumn-winter tree. The air was warm but the tree didn't have any leaves. I held onto a branch with two hands; one hand faltered and I let go but the tree caught and held me.

Our drive to the coast from Iguazú was over rolling hills and green farmland. We stopped for gas and lunch at a modern roadside stop. The waiter who sat us down was curious about our crowd. Ed told him we were from Canada, had driven to Tierra del Fuego and were on our way back. He didn't believe Ed and was not convinced even after Ed showed him the licence plate on the van. Nonetheless, he was proud to introduce us to Brazilian foods, explaining the selection of rice, beans, cooked vegetables (many we didn't know), salads, and several chicken dishes. Then he said we really must try their Brazilian national dish: cow stomach in gravy. There were plenty of comments from the little people and I was glad he didn't understand English. The price of the food was calculated by weighing how much was on the plate. Ed took one serving of the cow stomach, telling the kids we couldn't insult him. We filled our plates with an excellent variety of foods. Everyone had a couple of bites of the cow stomach and Ed ate the rest. We have changed our eating habits in the past two years. It was different from anything the kids have ever eaten and I'm impressed that they tried it at all. The flavour was good but they found the chewy, slippery texture not so desirable.

Ed prepared them. "This man is going to ask how we liked the cow stomach and you have to tell him it was good, okay?"

Jake said, "That's lying, Dad."

"Well, sometimes a small untruth is alright, when somebody's feelings and impressions are on the line. He'll be really happy if we tell him that it was good."

Sure enough, when he came to collect the dishes, he asked. Eyes shot back and forth and the kids did tell him it was good but not with the same kind of enthusiasm that apple pie and ice cream would muster up.

It was another gas station night outside of Guarapuava. It was a decent place. Tanya was not impressed—she got moody and wouldn't talk to us.

We were moving with the trucks early the next morning. We found a route around the city of Curitiba and were in Matinhos early in the afternoon. When faced again with a left-right decision at the ocean (this time it was the Atlantic), we took a right by chance, mostly because it was good luck the last time, and it worked again. The main road runs parallel to the beach, and it was easy for us to see that the area is a getaway for the people of Curitiba. Small streets between the road and ocean are jam-packed full of cottages and some more permanent-looking homes.

The first campground we found in Brazil was a Camping Club do Brasil—CCB. After reading about camping in Brazil, Ed thought we should find this club's listing of their campgrounds in the country. He made arrangements for two nights stay and purchased a membership for our family. If it goes as planned we may be camping most of the time we are in Brazil. We now have a list of all CCB locations, which are fully guarded night and day. They are equipped with a canteen during peak seasons, as well as washroom facilities: showers, sinks and toilets, dishwashing sinks, and an area for doing laundry. There is a wide, white sand beach across the street from this campground, and since it is off-season, we have the place to ourselves. There are three tent-trailers parked here but they are closed up tight.

Ed and I left the kids to set up the tents as best they could while we went to purchase some food. Ed had difficulty getting the van to start for our return; it choked, sputtered and stalled. After many tries, it did go 20 minutes later but kicked up a fuss. We have heard about alcohol in Brazilian gas. Maybe that is the case, and neither one of us like the implications.

By today, we have had two days of enjoying the beach. Yesterday the ocean was calm and we had great swimming, but the surf was much stronger today. Jake tried to go out deeper to be with Ben and Ed, but got caught in a side current and was being pulled away. He tried swimming and yelled at Ben and Ed but they didn't hear or see him. When I saw him drifting sideways I went after him. A man on the beach noticed Jake as well and started to run but Ben noticed, got to him first and used the current to get them both into shallower water farther down the beach. It was a scare. Jake just wanted to ride the waves with Ed and Ben like he did yesterday. Today, however, the ocean was much more of a challenge.

On the brighter side, there have been three kittens hanging around; they are about three months old. One is pure black and has taken up snoozing on our couch (a bench out of the van) for the night. The girls in particular like him and of course are calling him Jasmine. The tidbits they feed him are encouragement for him to stick around. A large rat-like animal walked along the top of the wall and up into a tree; he didn't look like one that would be good to get to know. It wasn't a rat, though, as the fur was different. We watched him come and go. His eyes glowed in the dark. He wasn't concerned about us at all and went on about his own business.

May 5, 1999: Itanhaem, Brazil

Itanhaem is a similar beach to Matinhos: flat and wide. On this beach there are delicate pink clamshells with white rays reaching outward. They are so fragile that it will be difficult to get a couple of them home in one piece.

Ed called Eduardo, the Chiropractor in São Paulo, to make an appointment for an adjustment and directions on how to get to his clinic. He also called home, since he hasn't been in touch for several weeks. Ben, Ed's father, has had a heart attack and has been in the hospital a few days. He is doing all right now but it was a trying time for everyone at home. We have had a quiet couple of days taking in what it means. Now it seems as if we aren't going to be home soon enough.

May 8, 1999: Ubatuba via São Paulo

As it moves inland and northward toward São Paulo, the highway is a complex engineering wonder! It increases in altitude in a drastically short distance, as well as zigzagging around river gorges, reservoirs, mountains and cliffs. At one point it hangs off the edge of a cliff in two levels (one level for each direction) that starts and finishes with tunnels on either end of the span. After climbing the mountain we were so high up we could see the ocean.

Before arriving in São Paulo we passed another sight that left an impression. Six police cars with flashing red lights were escorting a bus. Curiosity caused many questions and as we overtook the entourage we had a few answered. Each police car carried four heavily armed men. The bus was full of men, one to a seat, and handcuffed to the bar of the seat in front them; two guards stood at the front of the bus—each with a machine gun. It was a live picture of something we have only ever seen in movies. Whitney asked if all those guys were "bad guys". I said, "Yes. I think all those guys have probably done something pretty bad." As she observed the scene before her, she said, "I don't think I want to be a bad guy".

Eduardo gave us excellent directions to his clinic. The drive through São Paulo seemed short, considering it is a city of almost 20 million people. It is one of the fastest growing cities in the world and the largest in South America. It has been rebuilt through history with a high concentration of skyscrapers, leaving little of what was originally built in the 1900s and earlier. It is a modern, bustling city.

Eduardo and Cheri greeted us warmly. Ed got his long-needed adjustment and we had a tour of the clinic. Cheri and Eduardo met in Chiropractic College in the States. He is Brazilian and she is American; they married and practice together. Eduardo gave us directions out of the city. Passage is straightforward and easy if you know where you are going. One thing we noticed while driving through the huge city is tha. São Paulo has much less garbage strewn on the ground than other South American urban centres—either that or we didn't go through the worst of it. Just north of the city we crossed the Tropic of Capricorn where a sign stated "Officially Entering The Tropics."

What a road to Ubatuba!! It was easy going until we got to the Serra do Mar (Great Escarpment), and once again the land drops from 900 meters to sea level almost immediately. There was a sign indicating "Dangerous road ahead. Steep hill. Check your brakes before descending."A magnificent view unfolded before us: blue ocean for miles in several directions: east, north and south—and a long way down. Our descent was hairpin after hairpin turn. Ed drove with the van in low gear and the brakes on constantly. The road clings to what little edge there is. Ed took it really slow and at one point had to back up on a hairpin to be able to make the turn. The brakes were hot. There was sign after sign, "Ouch brakes," "Use low gear," "*Frenos*," "*Frenos*," "Brake repair 2 km," "Just 1 km left," then, "Ah, you made it," At the bottom there were brake repair shops aplenty. Viewed from the bottom, the escarpment is a wall of rock rising from the sea. We descended into tropical vegetation again. The plateau above is a different landform and climate zone altogether.

Ubatuba is a beach town; bathing suit shops line the main street. The CCB campground is an incredible spot on the beach. Another black cat has been hanging around and the kids have been playing with him. He is fat and well taken care of and likes the attention the kids are giving him. Tanya says Jasmine is following us whether we like it or not. She was particularly upset when I said Jasmine didn't need to go to Canada. Tanya wants me to feel some remorse about leaving the cat behind, but the cat wouldn't have survived the 20 hours in a cage on airplanes without going mad. She had her own mind, and didn't belong to us; she just stuck around because we gave her food. She didn't like being held and went crazy when she couldn't get outside. She had a good place to go: Aris was more than pleased to have her join his menagerie. Otherwise I might have consented to sending her home. I will not feel guilty.

What a storm last night! Lightning, thunder, strong winds, pounding rain and we managed to stay dry inside the tents. The storm littered the beach with clamshells that look like butterfly wings. Each is a mirror image of its complementary half and has its own unique colours of identification in yellow, orange, pink, purple and blue. They intrigue me; there are so many I filled my pockets. Each time I hold a shell I have collected it takes me back to where I picked it up.

May 9, 1999: Rio de Janeiro

It was an interesting drive along the coast. Mountains are closer to the water than on the southern coast where there is a stretch of land at sea level before it climbs into the sierras. One town gave us a good indication of the universal presence of television. The highway climbed a hill on the outside of town, which populates the slopes down toward the ocean. We had a view of rooftops and satellite dishes. At least every third house had a large satellite dish on the roof, creating a rhythm of geometric shapes, of ellipses breaking up the rectangles and parallelograms that the series of clay tiled rooftops created.

Ed had our route planned so we could get to the CCB at Recreio dos Bandeirantes without going into the city of Rio. He thought he would give himself a break and we would visit Rio by bus. But that's not the way it worked out. Somehow we missed the highway south before Rio and when we realized it found ourselves entering the city from the northwest. We tried to figure out a game plan while driving; the outskirts just didn't look like a place we should stop. Before we knew it we were in downtown Rio de Janeiro and at Baia Guanabara amongst dense city that sat wherever it could between dramatic peaks and deep blue water. There was a sign for Leblon. We knew it was the general direction we needed to go, so Ed took the exit. The coastal highway took us to the southern part of the city and we drove along the Copacabana Beach area of Rio, one of the most densely-populated areas in the world: 62,000 people per square kilometer. I can't imagine living like that. It is not much wonder the crime rate is high. Put too many animals of any species in a small area and they fight. We may be a thinking species but we're not always superior, are we?

We made a giant U-turn—into Rio from the north and out of Rio from the south. I find it odd that this was the one city Ed decided he wasn't going to drive in—had researched city tours and buses so he wouldn't have to do that. We don't always get to do what we plan and often find we are more capable than we think—or want to be. A gas station stop after moving out of the city centre where we posed a single question: "Do you know where we can find this place?" We showed the attendant the CCB brochure and he gave Ed clear directions and just five minutes away. We shook our heads in disbelief—no searching, just a tour through Rio de Janeiro without a decent map and we found where we were going mostly by instinct; we saw a good part of the city on our own.

CCB Recreio dos Bandeirantes is across the road from a white sand beach and it is a large campground. It took us a while to find a tenting spot we could agree on. It just goes to show that with more choice comes more indecision. Then, while setting up tents, we decided to move again. Ed unknowingly stood on a fire ant hill, and after his experience we moved a good distance away. Several people have warned us of fire ants and we have always been on the lookout for them. But on a tropical grass lawn they were tough to spot. Any type of disturbance to their territory and these tiny little red creatures swarm by the thousands faster than you would believe. They attack and sting the offender, leaving a burning sensation on the skin. A single sting is bearable but usually several hundred ants sting at once. Ed's foot is covered in tiny red dots and there are several up his leg as well.

We headed for the beach after setting up. There was a strong surf, not good for swimming, but we spent our afternoon watching the surfers and walking the beach. As we prepared dinner the kids spotted monkeys running along the electrical wires and through the trees. People fed them bananas and mangoes. It wasn't long before the kids were feeding them out of their hands. At dinner another young black cat visited us. The girls fed him morsels of food, encouraging him to stay and he too made himself right at home.

In the evening, when a campground attendant turned on the lights, the light we had moved under was not working, and he suggested we move our camp next to the one that we had just moved away from. Ed told him we had some experience with fire ants there and would like to stay where we are. He replied, "It's for your own protection. It makes it easier for the night watchmen to spot anything suspicious." Ed asked about changing the bulb and was told to talk to someone at the office.

Ed and Ben went to the office and came back with Miguel, armed with a ladder and new light bulb. They changed the bulb but it burnt out when it was turned on so the problem was the fixture. Again we were told we should move. Ed asked about the danger of theft. The attendant said it didn't happen often, but was more likely in a spot where you can't be seen easily. We didn't want to move tents and sleeping gear again so we put our kitchen belongings in the locked van for the night. Miguel accepted that and invited us to the canteen to visit with him and his friends. One of them has a couple of kids.

Miguel liked Ben's Canada hat, which Larry gave him, and asked for it. Miguel served Ed and me a stiff drink of cane sugar alcohol with pineapple juice, and the kids had Coke. Whitney's eyes popped open and let out a giggle. She knew I wouldn't say anything. Miguel knocked Ben's hat off and put it on his own head. He wanted it badly but the problem was Ben was not willing to part with it; he needed something to keep his hair under control and the sun off his head. It became Miguel's. Jake and Marcus, a boy Jake's age, played in the sand together. The rest of us got into good fun playing table tennis. Miguel gave Ed ideas for visiting Rio and said it was an easy city to drive in. There are plenty of things to do but the kids were only interested in going up the cable car to Pão de Açúcar

(Sugarloaf Mountain). That made it easy. If they aren't interested, it's a waste of time, money and energy.

The cat had hung around all morning. When the girls were fixing up the tent they let him in to play and he has made himself right at home. On returning from our walk, we found the cat had managed to get into the tent and was curled up, sleeping amongst the sleeping bags. We wired the zippers shut to keep the cat out for our afternoon on the beach but he proved to be a Houdini cat: once again, on our return he was curled up on a pillow.

Miguel invited us to meet a Canadian friend of his who was having dinner at the cafeteria. Gerry, from Winnipeg, teaches English here. Except for the 40-degree heat in summer, he enjoys Rio and has been living here for nine months. We talked about how easy it was to live without walls around us in Brazil. For the first four months, a tent in the campground was his home, and he said he didn't feel the need for much more than that. But now that he is in a small apartment he likes having his own shower.

We discussed law enforcement in Brazil and he sounded a little cynical when he told us about a man getting out of jail and being back on the same beach—this beach, five days after he killed a man in front of several witnesses. He said, "Some things just don't make sense. The guy is obviously guilty and yet he's on the streets." It doesn't make sense to me either.

Gerry asked many questions about our journey and his only real comment in an envious tone was, "Your kids are so lucky". We chatted a while but Gerry worked early the next morning, so he didn't stay long.

The cat was sleeping in the tent again. The girls put him out several times but he kept crawling back in and didn't take the hint. Even they complained he wouldn't let them sleep; it wasn't just Ben. Ed got up, grabbed the cat, slapped him and threw him away from the tent. The girls then complained that Ed was mean. Ed can't win. He assured the girls the cat was okay, he saw it running away after it landed.

The cat is definitely okay. This morning he sat next to the safety of a tree and watched us. There were monkeys everywhere this morning. The kids fed them and the cat, too, and the cat took it as permission to come back. He was in the tent hindering the sleeping bag roll-ups and on top of anything that was being packed. He was a regular nuisance until he spotted monkeys. The monkeys were getting daring on the ground, retrieving food people left out for them. The cat spotted one within sprinting range and watched with ears perked up, then suddenly took off when he thought he had a chance. The pursued monkey had a cheering section. Every monkey in the trees must have been screaming; the noise was wild. The one in danger made it to the safety of a tree and lit to the top. The cat attempted the climb but thought better of it. The monkeys' scolding of the cat afterwards was comical; several monkeys even came halfway down trees to scream at him. It was only when the monkeys let their voices be heard that we realized there were so many in the trees above our heads.

"The combination of a dark blue sea, studded with rocky islands, with tumbling wooded mountains and expanses of bare gray rock, which surround the city, is very impressive. The city sweeps 20 km along a narrow alluvial strip between the mountains and the sea."

That is a perfect description, in the *SAH*, of what is viewed from the top of Pão de Açúcar. The city of more than five million sits anywhere it will cling to dry, somewhat horizontal land. We lingered much longer than we expected, taking in the visual contrast of deep blue ocean and city amongst mountains; the constant hum coming up from below was a good indication of how busy it is. The strip of Copacabana beach lined with highrises overlooking the ocean was clear from our perch. To the north, Baia de Guanabara hosted cargo and passenger ships, a yacht club, and the span of the bridge crossing to Niteroi on the opposite side. It is easy to understand why the city was established where it was; it is a huge, naturally protected harbour.

Pão de Açúcar was a popular place to visit. There were so many tourists that Whitney asked, "How come so many people speak English here?" She was just not accustomed to hearing so much English spoken from people other than us.

Wednesday, May 12, 1999: Guarapari, Brazil

It rained intermittently on our drive northeast, and I found my energy dropping. I have grown so accustomed to sun and blue sky that grey skies are going to take some getting used to again.

Several things caught our attention between Rio and here. Vultures were in noticeable abundance. It was impossible to look to the sky and not see them circling. Twice we saw a line of fence posts with one vulture on each post—twenty or more lined up looking like a row of statues. We passed a road kill and it must have been fresh; we couldn't see it for the vultures having a feast. Towns don't look as prosperous as those south of São Paulo. We drove along the coast, and what struck me about the landscape was the mountains to the west. They are irregular humps and bumps with sheer cliffs exposing the grey rock, but on the flatter tops, they are heavily forested. One formation reminded me of Torres del Paine. They are no Andes, but driving through the Brazilian Highlands is as challenging. There were so many sugar cane fields—green field after green field.

Guarapari campground is on a little cove. What a spot! The cove is protected from the rough seas by a small opening in the rocky coastline and on the inside is a small, gold sand beach.

Ed and I awakened to the kids yelling Ben's name, and he was in his best annoyingly fun form the rest of the day. He rolled over top of everyone in the tent for a start and didn't let up. At least at the beach he used his energy pulling the younger ones around on the boogie board in the water, and when he was hungry I convinced him to make tomato sandwiches for everyone. He brought them to the beach for lunch. We swam more and watched the fishermen. A man came with two little girls Whitney's age; they played all afternoon, not together but curious and they watched each other with deep interest. Ed, Tanya, Ben and Dayna discovered the rocks to be a perfect spot from which to dive. We watched sand crabs hunting for food and found a few new shells. We think a crab pinched Karina's foot in the water. Whatever it was, it left a good scratch on her arch.

The kids are doing well with our travels these days. We have had a healthier lifestyle camping in the past few weeks than we have had since arriving in South America. We're eating almost total vegetarian again since leaving Chile, and my excess weight or water retention—whatever it was—has slipped off my body. But that was probably the wine; we haven't had any since leaving Chile, and we were having a little every day while there.

We made supper together tonight: whole grain rice and stir-fry vegetables in ginger and garlic. Brazil must grow ginger; it is so fresh the outside skin scrapes off easily. It is so good to eat ginger-garlic combinations again. I'm sure it has something to do with how healthy everyone is. Nobody is having digestive problems anyway.

May 16, 1999: Alcopaca, Brazil

It was a long day's drive to Alcopaca, and making a wrong turn in Vitoria made it even longer. We had a harder time in that small city than in Rio de Janeiro.

As we reached the state of Bahia the mountains moved inland. The land we travelled was flat and the air temperature increased dramatically. We need a proper road map, as the one we have is not accurate. The road to Prado off BR 101 turned out to be gravel—dirt and mud in many places, yet it was marked as a main road. The closer to the ocean we got the worse it got and I was so thankful it didn't rain. The coast road marked as a secondary one was paved and in as good condition as BR101. We were pleased at that.

The first CCB campground after we left Prado didn't look inviting. The beach was hard to get to and the facility didn't offer water or electricity. That's all right when we are prepared, but we weren't. Ed wanted to stay. I know he was tired, but to unpack everything and have to put it all back to move in the morning seemed like wasted effort for the gain. I convinced him to drive to another CCB about 40 kilometers away; it, too, is on a beach and has turned out to be worth taking the extra time.

While setting up the tents an argument broke out over who would sleep where. Tanya and Ben often have a difficult time with each other. Tanya, almost 15, is getting annoyed with sleeping in the tent with her younger brothers and sisters. She is doing exceptionally well, except when she and Ben have a clash. But the friction probably wouldn't be much different even if we were in a house and living a "normal" life.

Oh, dear God, how am I ever going to go back to that life? I can't even imagine it. I feel stuck in the middle, as if I don't really belong here, yet I don't want to live the life we left behind in Canada either.

Before crawling into the tent for the night Whitney, Karina, Jake and I walked to the water. From the beach the sky was absolutely clear and full of stars. We looked to the south to find the familiar southern hemisphere constellations over the Atlantic Ocean. When we faced north, I exclaimed in a voice that startled the kids. "Look, we can see the Big Dipper. It's upside down and looks like it will take a big scoop out of the water".

Karina said, "Yeah, what's so special?"

"Well, Karina, it is a group of stars that most people in the northern hemisphere know even if they don't know any others, and we haven't seen it for two years".

Jake, taking in what I said, ran up to tell the others we could see the Big Dipper. Whitney asked if that meant we were home yet. The rest came to the beach to see the Big Dipper on the horizon. It took some pointing out and drawing dots on the sand for Whitney, Jake and Karina to recognize the constellation, but they figured it out.

The sky was clear to the north, and a brisk cool wind came from the south carrying clouds that slowly blocked out the Southern Cross. When our view diminished we headed back to the tents to read for an hour or two. It wasn't even seven o'clock, and the sky had been completely dark for an hour.

Being in the tropics, Tanya said something felt different and she talked about the warm summer-like weather, but the sun disappears so early. In both Canada and Chile in summer when the weather is warm there is sunlight until nine or ten in the evening. We are not accustomed to this total darkness before 6 p.m. in the hot weather. Another thing I noticed in the tropics is that there are only a few minutes of twilight; it is light while the sun is above the horizon and dark when it drops below it. There is less than a half hour transition time.

It rained most of our second night here and it was a real thunderstorm for a while. The heavy wind mixed up the wires on the poles, which caused the transformer to blow and short out the electricity. It didn't make a difference to us until the sun went down for the evening.

Jake, Whitney and Karina played in the space of the campground all day. They just disappeared. Jake and Whitney both said they were hungry early in the morning, but by the time I had some breakfast ready they were so engrossed in play they had forgotten about being hungry. When I mentioned to Ed that there was food ready but they didn't want to eat, he said, "Well, it just means what they are doing is right on purpose." Total focused attention, child's play—child's work; what they were doing is important to them and their development. They were really hungry when they took a break.

Given the opportunity and outdoor space to play, it is amazing how they occupy themselves for hours. Sticks make batons, guns and poles for vaulting. Palm leaves make houses and hideouts as well as brooms for sweeping out the created spaces. Sticks, stones, balls, ropes, strings—the best toys. They played pirates, house, swords and heaven only knows what else; their imaginations are so free.

I wonder how that gets lost in so many of us adults. Why is it so hard to let the imagination run free? I have realized I am boxed in, for example with the sketching I have learned to do with the children; I try to make what I am drawing look real. Why it is so hard for me to let the abstract in?

While I did laundry the kids found a coconut palm and managed to pull off a coconut. They poked a hole in it, drank the milk from the inside, and used the empty green coconut as a ball for a game of hot potato and a careful game of soccer. They have learned to make something of anything.

I find myself so thankful we are not staying in hotels or *posadas* and eating in restaurants for our journey home. With the camping, although the surroundings change, the kids still sleep in the same sleeping bag in the same tent with our own familiar belongings and consistently eating our own familiar cooking. I believe it is contributing to maintaining a healthy mental attitude.

I prepared our dinner in the daylight and we ate early. The kids were into their own things and Ed was reading. I had a walk on the beach alone, enjoying the natural sounds of birds and ocean, and beach-combed. When I noticed dark clouds heading in our direction I turned back; our belongings needed to be put away. I was concerned about not having light to read by earlier and thought we should go to the village to purchase some candles. But to save on gas and a trip just for candles, we decided we could manage with the one flashlight that still worked. Beach-combing, I saw what I thought was a candle in the rubble of shells and seaweed at the high wave line. I removed the seaweed and found a white eight-inch candle a little bumped up from the ocean but otherwise unused. I sat for a moment; it was too much coincidence for me to accept as coincidence. Everything is right on purpose. I looked to the sky and said, "We are going to need this, aren't we?" I said thank you to... whomever as I cleaned the sand off and continued back to camp. A short distance further along I found a partially burnt candle and then another. They were more than likely remnants from a ritual on the beach connected to the Umbanda religion Gerry told us about. I left the partially burnt candles where I found them and did some contemplating over the unused one I picked up. Many mysteries can be attached to such articles. Gerry told us if we came across anything of the sort to be sure to leave it untouched.

Umbanda started to take hold of the people of Brazil in the early 1900s. Its roots are African spiritual traditions, native Brazilian traditions and Catholicism. It has become a fusion of practices and rituals from a time when Catholicism tried to convert the native peoples. Rituals often take place beside a body of water and are performed by a medium. It is believed there is a hierarchy of spiritual guides who will help identify the root of conflict and unhappiness. Through dancing to drums and chanting, the medium learns from spirit guides how to counsel those who request guidance and protect them from spiritual attack. There is an evil counterpart practiced, but Umbanda works for the good and it is widely practiced throughout Brazil.

I dropped the candle into the pocket of the van door and put things in place for the night. I told the kids we could finish our novel when camp was cleaned up. They liked the idea and were getting ready when there was a smash in the tent. It was dark; we could barely see a thing. Tanya yelled, "Stay back, there's glass all over." She was trying to hang up the flashlight at the top of the tent when it slipped out of her hands to the ground below. The front glass and bulb shattered and what light we had was out. My hand found the candle in the door of the van and the matches from the pots box. Tanya asked, "Where did you get the candle, I thought they were all gone?" After I explained where it came from she said, "Sometimes I think you're weird." We cleaned up the glass, set the candle up in a safe place, and the kids settled into their places. Ed snuggled up beside Jake to help him feel secure; no light was a problem for him. I sat beside the candle and read aloud. When Ed's wristwatch beeped 9 p.m. only Dayna and Ben were still awake. We opted to finish another time.

It took all day for the transformer to be repaired. We were going to leave but the weather improved after another drenching shower early in the morning. We spent the day drying things out and gave the van interior a good cleaning and reorganization. We did have some beach time but no swimming; the unsettled weather made the waves look too unpredictable.

May 24, 1999: Ilheus

When Sira and David were in Chile, Sira told us to use her house in Ilheus for as long as we wanted and here we are. Sira was originally trained as a medical doctor in Brazil and practiced for several years. When she learned about chiropractic she packed up her family of boys and moved to the States to study chiropractic. She returned and set up a chiropractic clinic. Her son, Iury, has since become a chiropractor as well, and together they practice in several locations. When Sira and David met during a business trip they became inseparable. Sira now lives most of her time with David in Canada, making frequent trips to Brazil to ease Iury's workload and oversee the business she started. Aside from the presence of Epifonia, the caretaker, her house is empty for most of the year.

Epifonia let us into the house on our arrival, and shortly after Iury arrived to greet us. He showed us around, told us to make ourselves at home, and said that Epifonia would help with anything we needed. Epifonia lives here and is paid to take care of the house, gardens and dogs.

We had intended to stay just a couple of days but there have been a few developments, and Ed is going to help Iury out in a clinic for a while. They want to hire a chiropractor to work in the clinic in Brasilia and there are a couple of prospects but no one definite as yet. Iury has been working at the clinics in Ilheus and flying back and forth to Brasilia to treat patients.

Ed spent a morning in the chiropractic office, during which he and Iury gave each other an adjustment. Iury asked Ed if he would stay to work for a while after speaking with Sira about the situation, and they made tentative arrangements for Ed to work. Iury was going to help us find a cottage on the beach while Ed worked in Brasilia. It wasn't exactly what I had anticipated for our time in Brazil and it caused some inner turmoil, but I decided we would be fine. My concern was for Ben. A year or two ago it wouldn't have been the same, but he is 13, as big as I am, and rushing into adulthood. Although not really rebelling, he ignores much of what I say; he looks to, wants to be with, follows and respects more of what Ed says. I know I wouldn't have a problem with him but Ben seems to need Ed's presence and the example of an adult man.

For two days we felt unsettled with the arrangements and everyone felt irritated about something. Thursday morning last week I was up early to have some reading time. I opened the book and the first words I saw were "*When you come to a fork in the road, take it.*" Yogi Berra. It was a loud and clear message. An opportunity had opened up for us to get to know what inland Brazil is like, not just beaches. At that instant I decided we should be going to Brasilia together. With that settled in my head, we have had more peaceful days, Ed feels better about the move, and everyone is happier. Our only dilemma now is where do we live in Brasilia? There is a bachelor apartment available for the chiropractor that works in the clinic, but it is insufficient for our family. Anyway, we will find something and plans are that we will head for Brasilia Tuesday morning. It will take two days to drive there.

Iury's cousin took Ed and the van to a mechanic and had everything repaired that needed repairing. Ed is happy he waited until we arrived in Ilheus. It took a whole day, and the van is running well again at a reasonable cost; knowing people makes a difference.

We are enjoying the comforts of a house. The kids have said they like the travelling but are anxious to be in a house again. I wonder why I am so tossed between these feelings. I want to live simply and with less. Life is so much less complicated with fewer things and stuff to think about. My mind is freer to be on the spiritual journey that keeps my soul at peace. Yet I enjoy the comforts of life. I like a comfortable place to sleep and a place to keep the fewer clothes I've become accustomed to, clean and dry. I like working in a kitchen where I can create a real meal. I like a bathroom with hot water to bathe in and a comfortable sofa to sit on to read a book or occasionally watch a movie. And I definitely like hand-made artistic creations where one can see the thinking of the creator. But all that stuff takes upkeep; if something breaks, it needs to be fixed and it all needs to stay clean. The piles of clothing we accumulate need to be laundered, mended and some things ironed. Everything we use steals time in little bits and pieces. And when we let life get full of more things, comforts, electronics, etc., etc., there is less time and space in our lives for children, parents, extended family, friends, co-workers and most of all—the self. What happens to time to be truly with oneself so we are open to listening to the voice of our creator? It is the one thing I personally lose out on. Time alone lets me talk with God, give thanks sincerely, let my thoughts run free, and listen to the world. Time allows the solving of life's daily dilemmas in a more constructive, loving way and gives me the inner peace that carries me onward. When that inner peace is there it doesn't seem to matter what I am faced with; I can usually get through and out on top. Is this the reason that the great spiritual leaders of the world have been people who live with so few personal belongings? Things distract the mind from what we are put on this earth to seek and do. So how do I create and have an environment for our family that is comfortable but simple? How much do we really need and where do we draw the line between necessity and the simple desire for more? It is important to find a balance.

All this thinking about a house has made me feel that having one of our own again would be all right. In some ways the responsibility is more than I really care for. But then again I see a little person like Jake who seems to need the consistency of a secure place and surroundings, knowing where he is going to sleep and what he is going to do tomorrow to keep his mental attitude stable. I have the responsibility of providing the kids with a stable home environment so they will grow up emotionally, physically and spiritually well. But I still don't understand why we feel the need to park ourselves in one place and collect a whole pile of stuff to hang up around ourselves. Home should be wherever the self is and nothing more. We come into this physical life with only the soul and it is only the soul that leaves. We don't take anything with us apart from how we have developed that soul while journeying on earth. I am feeling so much confusion. Anyway, what is right for our family will happen, just like it always has. *Que sera, sera.*

Apart from swimming in the pool the kids were looking for things to do. Time on our hands always turns into something and these guys seem to understand that when they have time, they do some math and reading. Dayna is frustrated with her math these days but she is working a year ahead of what she would be in school. I keep telling her to take a break, but in no time she's back into it. Her ambition is to catch up to Ben, which keeps him moving. I find it amazing that if I let go, don't push, and have the attitude that it doesn't matter how much schoolwork gets done, they take the responsibility for doing it themselves. Tanya has been somewhat moody this week and hasn't stepped outside the gate since we arrived on Sunday but has kept herself occupied. She has been figuring out our six three-dimensional puzzle cubes and drawing out the solutions on paper. It is complex work and she spent two days at the kitchen table doing it. What she created has given Whitney a challenge too. Whitney figures out which puzzle piece lies in which of Tanya's drawings.

Epifonia introduced us to the popular Brazilian breakfast food, couscous. A coarse corn meal cooked in a steamer with young, fresh coconut added—not the dry stuff we are accustomed to in Canada, and we have enjoyed it all week. It is extremely economical feeding the eight of us with a nutritious food for less than one Canadian dollar. The kids said maple syrup would make it extra good (we do miss our maple syrup).

On a free afternoon last week, Epifonia showed us some beaches to the south. There are miles and miles of white sand beaches. Nothing beats Brazilian beaches; they are the best in South America from what we have encountered. We stopped at a *cabana* managed by one of Epifonia's close friends and spent an hour there. *Cabanas* here are palm leaf roof shelters where one can purchase water, soft drinks, and beer or cocoa water. They are a regular fixture along the beaches in this country where it is easy to dehydrate if you're not always replenishing the body with fluid. What a construction! It is a roof on stilts that provides relief from the sun. It is made up of palm leaves tied together in thick bunches then tied to the roof frame in the same manner as shingles. Not only is it waterproof, it insulates from the heat as well.

We went shopping to purchase a few pieces of clothing appropriate for the climate and found flip-flops and shorts for the ones who are growing out of what they have.

Shika, the housekeeper, has been spoiling us. She prepares a fabulous midday meal every day and won't let me help with the dishes. She washed our white clothes and they are *white*—it has been a long time since that was the case. The secret is a couple of tablespoons of bleach in a washtub and soak the clothes in the water in direct sunlight. Apparently it doesn't work if they don't soak in sunlight. I don't really like the idea of using bleach but it is a way to use much less if it is being put to use. Everything is so clean.

I do eat less when I am the cook though, I don't take the time to make as many different dishes at each meal. But this kind of life could be too easy to get used to. I have had time for being with the kids, sketching, and writing. It was a real holiday having someone else doing the everyday things for a while and a comfortable reprieve from camping, but we are on the move in the morning. I think Epifonia and Shika would like us to be staying a little longer; they have invited us back. We have added to the work they have to do around the house, but it is certain we have made it a livelier place as well. Sira and David aren't here much.

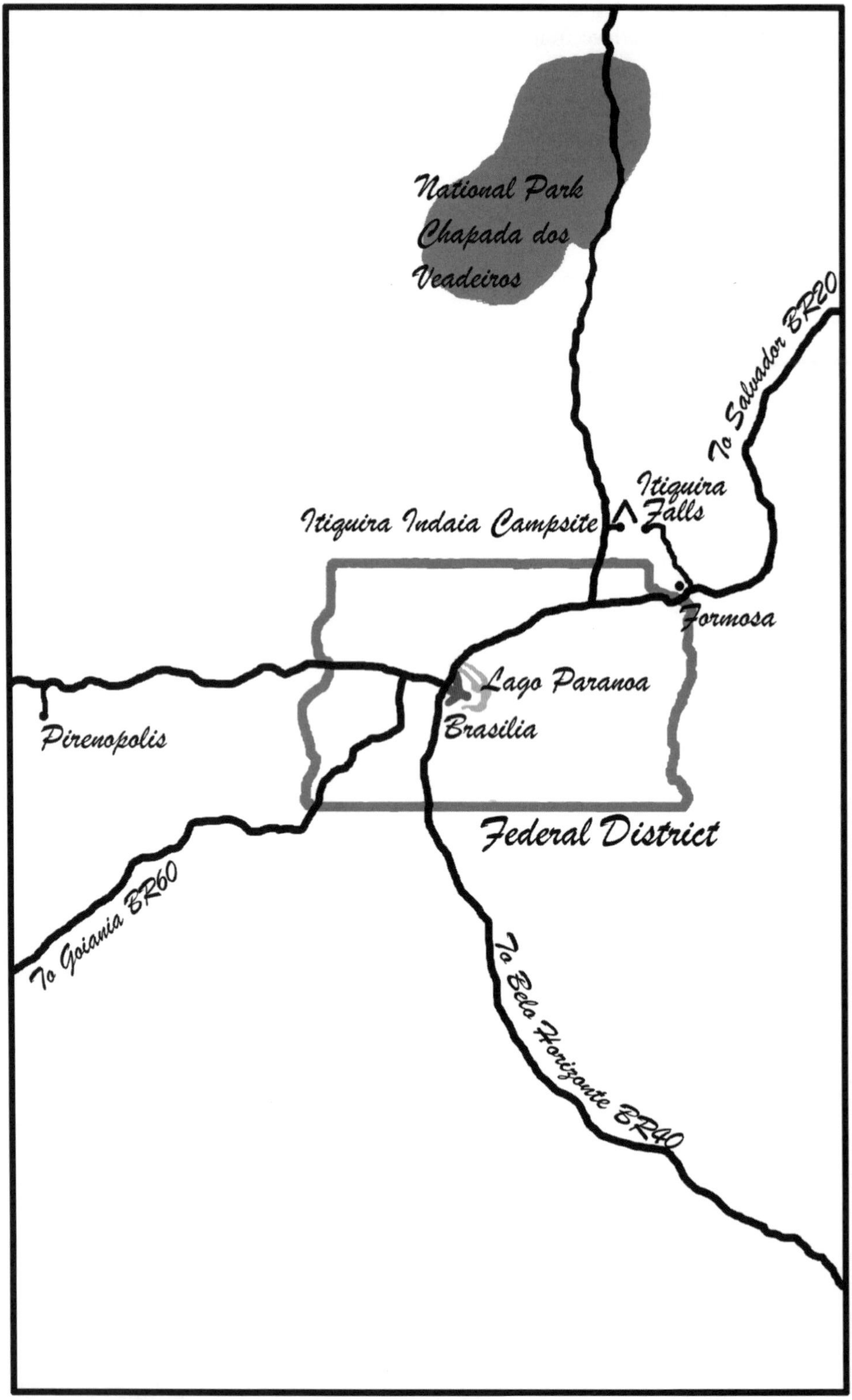
National Park
Chapada dos
Veadeiros
To Salvador BR20
Itiguira
Falls
Itiguira Indaia Campsite
Formosa
Lago Paranoa
Brasilia
Pirenopolis
Federal District
To Goiania BR60
To Belo Horizonte BR40

BRASILIA CITY INTERLUDE

May 26, 1999: *Ilheus to Brasilia*

Our route took us through Itabuna, Vitoria da Conquista, Brumado, and Bom Jesus da Lapa—a long day of driving. The land turned from lush, jungle-like foliage and farmland on the coast to dry sierra. Where there are small rivers it is green, with some cultivation, but as we travelled further inland, even that was less evident.

Bom Jesus de Lapa is a halfway point en route to the capital from the coast and is set up for "overnighters". It is also a sanctuary and pilgrimage spot with a church built into the unusual rock formation, a short distance from the Rio San Francisco.

We took advantage of the truck stop on the east side of town. Tanya has a problem with truck stops. They put her in a bad mood but they really are the best place for overnighters. Always free, always guarded, full facilities, and clean bathrooms are always available. (What more could we ask for?) We set up only the large tent and three slept in the van for the night.

When I made our evening meal a young indigenous girl, about eight years of age, hung around and watched us. She disappeared for a while but was back with a plate asking for food when we served ours. Ed filled her plate and again she disappeared. A short while later I spotted her with her mother at the far end of the truck stop. We had eaten all we needed and there was food left so I brought another plate of food to them. The daughter spoke Portuguese but the mother was difficult to understand. They were travelling somewhere, and on foot until someone was kind enough to give them a ride. I watched them from our camp. The two young women snuggled up tight together in a couple of blankets on the concrete floor against the wall of the building that held the sinks for truckers to do their washing up. I had many unanswered questions.

Shortly after dinner, a large motorhome pulled in beside us towing a small car. The couple who owned it ate at the diner. On their return the man saw our licence plate, knew of Quebec and was full of questions. He visited with us but his wife went into the motorhome. We talked while standing in the middle of the parking lot until he invited us to have a beer with him. He bought Ed and me a beer and soft drinks for the kids. Marcelo is a retired lawyer and didn't have any financial concerns. He and his wife have four grown-up children and several grandchildren. Three of their children live in Florianopolis and they have chosen to live there as well after having spent 22 years in Brasilia. For the winter, they take their motorhome inland and north. Caldes Novas—a spa and hot springs—is their destination this year, but they are taking their time and enjoying the stopovers. They were going to visit the sanctuary here in Bom Jesus de Lapa before visiting friends in Brasilia. Marcelo says they are in no hurry for anything these days. He gave us exact directions to the CCB, it is where they will be staying for their time in Brasilia.

As he asked and learned more about our travels, family and plans, Marcelo encouraged Ed and me, saying that it may feel hard at times with what we are doing, but when we are his age we will never regret one moment. They were good words to hear; sometimes we do wonder what on earth we are doing. After our drinks he invited us to visit with his wife, Marianna. We climbed into the motorhome, and every one of us fit with room to spare. We had an inside tour; the home lacked nothing, right down to VCR, TV, CD stereo system, full kitchen, clothes washer and queen-size bed—the place sleeps six comfortably. Marianna was delighted to have us; we chatted about children and grandchildren. Marcelo said they visited a different pilgrimage place a few days ago where he bought ribbon wrist bracelets, in which he gave one to each of the girls and me. We were to make three wishes while putting them on; we aren't to tell anyone what the wishes are and we have to let the bracelets fall off by themselves; otherwise the wishes won't come true. It became a late night of visiting, but we seemed to have so much to talk about.

When we crawled into the tent, the cocoon of blanket covering the two young women by the sinks was unmoved from when they first settled. As we lay snug in our sleeping bags, I thought about the people around us sharing the overnight space: indigenous people with nothing, affluent people who have far more than they need and hauling it around, truckers, some alone, some with a driving partner, some with families, some whose trucks are their homes and then there is our family. What a contrast. The one thing we had in common was that everyone was moving in the morning.

The remaining drive to Brasilia took us over continuous arid, flat land. It was desert-like, but occasionally a cotton field changed the landscape and there was one unusual tract of tall cultivated pines. The sun must bring out the oils in the trees. The heavy aroma of hot, dry pine attacked the senses, reminding me so much of home.

The BA 349 had been recently paved, and Ed took advantage of the smooth pavement. We were at the campground by mid-afternoon and it was a big disappointment. It does not live up to CCB standards. There is one flat-roof, brick building, housing the office and facilities, and a rectangular, paved parking lot. Dishwashing sinks and clothes washing tubs are at the back. There is only one functional bathroom, with one shower for both men and women. The camping area is dry dusty ground, a little dry grass and very few shade trees. We didn't feel too enthusiastic about staying but without any other choice we found the flattest place we could, close to light and electricity and set up the tents.

While we were cooking dinner, the people who live in the more permanent-looking tents arrived. There were children. One inquisitive, forthright boy came right over and started to chatter, asking all kinds of questions. Names, how long we were staying, what we were eating, did we have toys? It didn't take long before we met Adrianna, the mom, Juan, the dad, Lira, the ten-year-old daughter, and Iyago, who would turn four in June. They are gypsies and live in the campground during the winter months while selling comforter and sheet sets in markets and on the roadside. They said it was a good business. We were having our dinner, so they didn't stay long. Adrianna dragged Iyago away but he wanted to stay. After we ate, the kids played ball together and spent the evening getting to know one other.

Thursday, May 27, 1999:

We joined Ed for the afternoon to see where he will be working for the next few weeks. He spent an hour with Iuri to learn clinic procedures while the kids and I waited. Iuri and the ladies were impressed with the patience of the children. They were on their absolute best behavior and have proven once more that they have it in them when necessary.

Carmen, Sira's sister, and office manager to the clinics, lives in Salvador with her family but comes to Brasilia regularly to take care of the business of the clinic. She has a daughter, Roberta, just a little older than Tanya, whose ambition is to live in Canada. Carmen said she would love to get to know Tanya—they could do many things together—and invited Tanya to spend time with her family in Salvador. Tanya wasn't so sure.

While Carmen described the things they would do in Salvador, to make the idea more appealing to Tanya, I recalled the day Tanya and I were sitting in the back seat together. We were talking about the country and the different language. She said, "You know Mom, I have a good understanding of Spanish. Portuguese is so close I would like to learn it really well too. It would be fun." She sounded sincere in her ambition. I replied, "Well, we'll have to find some way for you to do that."

It never ceases to amaze me how the cosmos works when sincerity, intention and ambition come together. I didn't even have to think to create that opportunity for her—life on purpose. When these tentative arrangements were coming together neither Ed nor I said anything. It was Tanya's decision. As Carmen talked, it seemed that Tanya was going to refuse, but Carmen kept talking and said, "If you don't like it, I can put you on a plane back to Brasilia." Tanya's face lit up; she was convinced. Carmen was going to discuss it with the rest of her family, to make sure Tanya's stay wouldn't conflict with other arrangements they had made. Tanya was going to go for a short period of time, whatever the case.

The Weekend of May 30: Indaia-Itiquira, Brazil

Itiquira campground appears to be the most attractive one from the photographs on the CCB brochure, and the kids have been anxious to check it out. The afternoon drive northeast took us over sparsely treed, dry, rolling hills. Once we were off the main road, the single-lane earthen track dropped in altitude into the valley of a small river whose source is a spring. It flows north to empty into the Amazon. Along the river, jungle flourished. It was an instantaneous contrast in vegetation from the grassland we drove through from Brasilia.

Stepping out of the van, we found ourselves singing the tune *When You're Living in the Jungle* from a kids' tape we have along. It begins with a myriad of jungle sounds that weren't any different from what we were hearing live. We giggled in excitement and commented on the squawking sounds of birds, which was overwhelming. It didn't take long for the kids to find the man-made pools. But what makes these different is the fact that the spring constantly fills the pools with fresh water and overflows back into the stream. There is a huge adult pool and a wading pool for younger children. Like all other CCBs there was a canteen (and a bar at this one) open for business. We may be in the forest, but we don't have to rough it if we don't want to.

After we pitched camp the kids and I walked the trails through the bush. Gnarled vines in the darkness of thick foliage sent Ben swinging and singing again. He couldn't resist a Tarzan howl. We found ourselves at pools where the water springs out of the ground and feeds the river. (One kilometer away is the Indaia water bottling company). Unusual bird sounds were coming from the trees above our heads, and we investigated. Moving as quietly as the group of us could, we briefly observed four large, blue and yellow birds with long tails, in close proximity. Then they flew off, squawking at us for disturbing them. We were told they were araras.

Saturday morning we were awakened by the noisy chatter of a huge flock of parakeets feeding on the blossoms of the eucalyptus tree under which we were camped. I lay with my head out of the tent to watch the excitement of the little green birds and was showered with pieces of the delicate yellow flowers, like a gentle snowfall. Without warning, the entire flock flew off, and it felt too quiet.

We hiked along the river to see the rapids, falls and pools, but didn't swim. We were overly cautious foreigners with a lack of knowledge. One of the campground workers said we had walked to Indaia Falls. Itiquira Falls is 160 meters high and three kilometers downriver. Since we had to return to Brasilia Sunday, we decided to come back here for the holiday weekend to do the hike. It was a great campground from which to explore.

The Weekend of June 6: Itiquira, Brazil

Our second weekend visit started with Whitney yelling out, "Hey, look at the toucan!" Sure enough, a long-beaked bird was flying on our right. When I asked her how she knew it was a toucan she said, "Duh, Mom, everybody knows what a toucan looks like."

"Duh, Mom," I said. "You haven't seen one before."

"Well, just because I'm five doesn't mean I don't know what a toucan looks like."

And she did. It was definitely a toucan. She was pleased with seeing the first one and reminded everyone about it all weekend. To get a rise out of the Whit, Ben said he saw it first and every time it has been mentioned since, it works. The argument doesn't stop until Ben backs down, laughing at her for being so stubborn.

It being a holiday weekend, the campground was full of people taking a break from the city. As foreigners with a different licence plate we became celebrities. Ed spoke with a man who was camped close to us, and it wasn't long before everyone seemed to know our business.

The hike to Itiquira Falls was our plan for the weekend. We took a day, packed a lunch and did the eight-kilometer hike that we had attempted on our previous visit. It doesn't have to take that long, but we have little people, and everything takes almost twice the time. If we account for and respect their needs, life is much less stressful.

We left the campground with our packs on our backs. Whitney and I stopped to retie a shoe before we even got out of the campground. A woman ran up to me and asked if we were going to Itiquira Falls, and I gave her an affirmative answer.

She said it was a long way and dangerous, looking at me with concern. I told her I knew it might be long, but that we had been on hikes before and it is not a problem. She seemed to think we were crazy. Her body language was telling me the kids should not be going, and I felt she was almost angry with me for taking them. The others had gone on ahead, and I told Ed about the woman's concern when we caught up. He said I had to consider where it was coming from; many people won't walk a few blocks to the corner store. And after thinking about it, it was true; she wasn't exactly a picture of fitness or health and probably lives life in total safe mode.

The first part of the trail was a little confusing. Ed asked a group of people at the base of the Indaia Falls if they knew where the trail to Itiquira Falls was. They said it was impossible to get there from here—we knew it wasn't and knew we wouldn't get lost if we just followed the river, and did just that. It was slow going walking through the tangled jungle. Ben was the trailbreaker, and just when the girls were getting frustrated he called from ahead, "I found the trail!" The river kept dropping. It never just flows calmly along on level ground. When we caught up, Ben said, "This is where we should have crossed the river the first time. The trail probably goes through the field at the top and then comes down to the river." Walking was much easier on the worn path and we soon arrived at a set of falls nearly 100 meters high. Several people were rock climbing the cliff beside the water. Following the trail, we crossed the river again to go around another cliff and in a short distance, we crossed it again, walking along a series of rapids that dropped in stair-steps, with yet another river crossing. We gave up taking shoes off and left them on to protect our feet from the rocky bottom. The day became so warm that a dunk in the rushing water was refreshing. We could hear Itiquira Falls and kept walking until the noise of the water was behind us when we found ourselves on a cliff above a 200-meter direct drop. We were so high, the view stretched before us to where the horizon starts to curve away. On the edge of the cliff was a dangerous spot for anyone not using some good sense. In the parking lot below, the cars were the size of ants. We kept walking but didn't get a glimpse of the falls as the trail started to work its way down to the park below. The girls protested, including myself. We were told the falls were visible from the top. If we walked all the way down, it meant three steep uphill climbs to get back to the campground, plus all the other easier walking en route. Ed and Ben were not easily convinced that it was too far for Whitney, but they did give in reluctantly and we didn't see the falls. As it was, Ed ended up with Whitney on his back for half the trip.

The woman who scorned me for taking the children into the forest seemed surprised to see us back safe and in one piece. She asked many questions. All I could tell her was how beautiful the river was and how much we enjoyed our day. She shook her head in disbelief. I wanted to tell her that hikes through forest with nothing but natural sounds around me puts my soul at peace and that it is a wonderful thing to do with the kids. It gives them a natural understanding, appreciation and respect for the beauty of the earth. They witness geography and botany first hand. I wanted to tell her that hiking is an excellent way to keep fit, that on such endevours the kids learn what their bodies are capable of and in the end feel a sense of accomplishment. The children learn so much more, intrinsically, than we can imagine. Many people have difficulty conceiving what we have accomplished on our travels and where we have taken the kids; she is one of them, just more vocal than some.

The man Ed spoke to, and his wife, brought their two daughters and several friends camping for the weekend. So there was a large group of young people in their early teens hanging out, and they invited our guys to play volleyball, speaking the English they had learned in school. Both Tanya and Ben have been fast picking up Portuguese and, with a little knowledge of each other's language, the group didn't have any trouble communicating. We didn't see much of any of the kids the rest of the weekend.

June 22, 1999: Tanya's Departure

It was arranged that Tanya would fly to Salvador with Carmen after Carmen's next work week in Brasilia. That was today. Tanya left with Ed this morning to spend the day in the office until her flight left at 7:15 p.m. It was the only way we could arrange the trip without Tanya having to take Brasilia's public bus system by herself for the first time. At breakfast she was excited about flying to Salvador. For me, the reality of her not being with us started to sink in. I said, "I'm going to miss you, your help, your meals, and all the care you give Whitney and Whitney is going to miss you; that is for sure."

She said, "Ben won't."

"Probably not nearly as much as Whitney; you are just as much a mother to her as I am. I'm going to have to be a full-time Mom again."

Tanya burst into tears, "I'm going to miss her too." I started to cry as well and said, "I didn't mean to make you cry, I was just trying to figure out what it is going to be like without you."

Sometimes I can make things worse than they need to be. Ed looked at the two of us and said he and Tanya better go before Tanya changed her mind. We hugged long and tight. I said, "Be wise, think about what you do before you do it. I love you". Tanya shook her head yes and got into the van without another word. She couldn't speak for fear of dropping more tears. My big little girl, not even 15 yet and doing her own thing; it's getting to be time. I have to learn to let it be that way, support her when she needs it and let her go when she needs to.

As I wrapped Iyago's birthday gift at 6 p.m. this evening, a jet took off overhead. I ran out from under the tarp to watch and said, "There she goes. That's Tanya's plane." I mumbled under my breath while the lights of the plane took my first-born daughter away, "Be safe Tanya, God take care of you." Tears welled up in my eyes again. "I guess we did give you wings, you are flying away. I just didn't expect it so soon."

The Weekend of June 27: Pirenopolis, Goias, Brazil

Ed befriended Angelo, who came for treatment at the clinic. Angelo is a middle-aged man in fairly good shape. He has long, black, kinky hair that he keeps tied in a half ponytail, and the frames of his glasses are the same colour as his hair. He was born in Argentina, and met Adriana in Brazil. They married and have made Brazil home after having lived in Argentina for four years.

Angelo comes from Pirenopolis once a week for treatment, stays overnight, and has another adjustment the following day before returning. He invited our family to visit Pirenopolis for a weekend and arranged for us to stay in an empty house that belongs to the mother of a friend. We took him up on the offer.

Pirenopolis is a quaint, interesting place. Rio des Alvas runs through the centre of town. There are several quarries in the area, and the houses, sidewalks and streets are built from the discarded pieces of stone that aren't transported out for commercial use. The stone is white or pink and comes apart in huge slabs similar to slate but far more attractive. The town glitters—the crystals sparkle as they catch the endless daily sunlight. Pirenopolis was established as a colonial silver mining town and has been declared a National Heritage Site. Jewelry shops line the streets.

We had refreshments and visited after arriving Saturday morning. Angelo speaks his Spanish and Portuguese so articulately that I understood almost everything he said. I actually joined the conversation. Ben was embarrassed by the way I spoke; Ed just shook his head. What came out was a mixture of Portuguese, Spanish and the odd French word when my mind needed one that wasn't English. It is interesting how the mind works when it comes to languages and mine is a muddled mess of knowing a little bit of three that aren't English. Ed gave me heck and told me to straighten them out. Angelo laughed and said, "No, no, it's okay, I understand what she is saying". In some things I am hopeless but at least I have started to speak about more than just food shopping. Ridicule immobilizes people; we should all learn to hold our tongues if it isn't a positive statement. Anyway, we got along great.

Adrianna, Angelo's wife, is a dentist and worked for the morning. Antonio, their son, who is nine, tried to get the kids outside to play, but it was cooler inside. Angelo showed us his house: small, comfortable and homey. Oh the Brazilian life... living in houses built for protection from the sun more than anything. A tile roof sits atop concrete walls, between which is a large air space. Angelo called it natural air conditioning; it creates circulation and prevents the inside from becoming a stuffy hothouse and from collecting mildew. They have mosquito nets over the beds but we were told they were really only necessary during the wet season. The kitchen was half outside. The sink and clean-up area were on part of the back verandah, and Angelo said they brought the stove out as well during the summer months when it is very hot. The wide, L-shaped verandah runs the length of the house and around the kitchen. The kitchen has two outside doors: one leads to the sinks and utility area, the other to where the big wood dining table sits in the open air under the tile roof. In the space that is left under the protection of the roof, there are hammocks strung between support posts and the wall; a great place for afternoon siestas. Off the verandah is a productive vegetable garden that is meticulously taken care of. Angelo says winter is the growing season; in summer everything rots and washes away with so much rain.

Angelo brought us to the house he had arranged for our accommodation. He was participating in a chess tournament and had a match in the late afternoon. The area has several clean, rivers and waterfalls. He suggested a hike to natural swimming pools and invited us to come back for supper at six.

On a scorching afternoon it was great to enjoy some water. Our hike took us upstream along a series of seven different *cachoeiras* (waterfalls), each with deep, ice-cold water pools at its base. We cooled down and continued to walk the well-worn path. The end of the trail brought us to a large pool enclosed in smooth rock. The waterfall above must have been 40 meters high, and people were diving from the top. Ben asked if he could try. My instant reaction was "No way," but I was choked for words and couldn't believe he would even consider trying. This young man is going to do all kinds of crazy things in his life and he has to be able to make decisions for himself. If I do his thinking for him, what he takes on is my responsibility. He needs to figure out what he is capable of and be responsible for his own actions, be they life threatening or not. Ed didn't think it was such a great idea either but wouldn't hold anyone back from a physical challenge. He, too, stumbled on his words. I found myself saying, "If you think you can dive off that cliff into the freezing water and come out of it alive then do it. But I don't know what I would do if something happened to you." Something inside me let him go at that moment. I don't have control over his life and he might as well figure out that it is he who lives with the consequences. Why give myself ulcers trying to make him someone he isn't, or hold him back from being someone he can be?

Ben seriously considered his challenge. He watched how the others were taking the plunge while we sat for what seemed like forever awaiting his decision.

The water was so cold it was almost impossible for me to get into, yet so clear and clean it was drinkable. The kids had been swimming despite the cold temperature; I don't know how they do it. I forced myself to swim, didn't dunk my head, and still came out light-headed. For a country that is so warm, the water is unbelievably cold. Such a contrast—figure that one.

After everyone cooled down and was ready to go, Ben still hadn't made a move. The pressure was on and much to both Ed's and my relief, he came out with, "I guess I won't do that today." If we had said no, we would have been arguing the rest of the day.

Angelo asked the kids if pizza was okay. Kind of a silly question, and he knew it; they were ecstatic. Adrianna was home. A soft-spoken, well-proportioned woman, she too had a head of kinky dark hair, but shorter than her husband's.

Ed adjusted Angelo before dinner and then we had a great party. Julia, whose mother's house we were staying at, came for the evening with a couple other friends. Angelo ran a pizzeria before they moved to Pirenopolis. He made the best pizzas we have ever eaten anywhere, and they kept coming for half the evening. Then a mountain of peanut brittle, homemade from fresh Brazilian peanuts and winter sugar, was set before us. Around a fire in the backyard we enjoyed a hot ginger drink, made with sugar cane alcohol, and we felt nothing more.

On Sunday morning Angelo took us to another river and more *cachoeiras*. On an escarpment, at a lookout, we had a view for many miles in every direction. Two rock quarries, where stone was being cut out of the hills, broke the smooth lines of the rolling landscape. From our vantage point, we could understand the land formations that make up most of central Brazil—rocky hills and escarpments, creating breaks from the expanses of red dusty plains that are desert-like at this time of year. Strips of lush green jungle indicate rivers originating from underground springs.

We hiked along the river and four different waterfalls before we reached another little paradise. We spotted toucans which, like parrots, must flap their wings hard to keep airborne. We spent the morning soaking up the sun on a small beach opposite a 10-meter waterfall, on a huge pool of ice-cold water. The overflow works its way downhill over rapids and more falls. This river would be called a stream in Canada, yet it supports a lush forest on both banks. The kids swam and dove off the rocks. I forced myself into the water again—I couldn't let these wonders pass me by. The kids were preoccupied in sand play while the guys were talking. I absorbed my surroundings: the sound of the water falling, the blue of the sky and water, and the green of the trees is always so healing to my soul. My hands and feet couldn't stop caressing the warm velvety sand—and the sun; where would we be without the sun? It gives every living thing life.

On our return, Ed adjusted Angelo, and Adrianna fed us another traditional midday meal before heading back to Brasilia. They gave us a weekend we will never forget.

Brasilia Campground People

Brasilia campground becomes a temporary home to many people at different times, and it was our residence as well. The people we had the opportunity to get to know made the experience most memorable. We were a small community that came and went during the day, often getting together in the evenings for fun and chat. Living an outdoor life beside others doing the same, we had little privacy so we all got to know one another fairly well.

The Gypsies

The people we lived beside were two families of gypsies selling their wares and living in tents. The fathers are brothers. We got to know Ricardo, Francesca and Mayara more so than Juan, Addriana, Iyago and Lira. These two families still speak their traditional language of Homoneise and live in a traditional way. Both spend their days on the sidewalk, parking

lots or roadside selling sheets, blankets, comforters and pillows in matching sets, from the backs of their modern, full-size pickup trucks. Ricardo explained to us that there is a factory in São Paulo run by gypsies, which sells only to gypsies. Their products are of good quality and can't be purchased in stores. During the Brazilian winter when the months are cool they have a good business—in fact only work six months of the year, spending the summer fishing and living in the state of Mato Grosso.

Ricardo is sociable, outgoing, needs to know everything that's going on and volunteers far more information than we would ever pry for. He gives the impression that he is a happy person and loves his life, in particular his family. Francesca is a quiet woman most of the time and is always trying to gain weight; she is on the thin side. Ed said she reminds him of Olive Oyl, Popeye's girlfriend in the comic strip. Mayara could get her screaming. Francesca admits she has no patience whatsoever. She does all the selling. Ricardo does the child rearing. He would like to have one more child but Francesca says she would go crazy, that she doesn't know how to handle even one. She seems to know what she is capable of and has drawn the limit. Their daughter Mayara is three-and-a-half and a handful—adores her dad and torments her mom. She would like to be a tomboy and get dirty but her mom keeps dressing her up and expects her to stay clean. She doesn't have a left hand; her arm appears to be amputated just below the elbow—she may have been born like that. We don't know what it was and with everything Ricardo told us he never did speak about it. She gets along great, though. She has a beautiful round face, a thick head of dark curls, and is basically the same shape as her Dad—rounded out. He waits on her hand and foot. As an activity one windy afternoon, I had the kids make hand held windmills from paper, but by evening the breeze had died down and Mayara still wanted her windmill to go. Her father put her in the truck with the windmill out the window and drove around making it twirl until she finally fell asleep. She is everything to him.

Given our living conditions, it was impossible to hook up to the Internet, so our computer was something we were just carrying around and not using. It took up space in the van and was becoming more a burden than anything. Ed asked Ricardo if he would sell it for us. That was as far as it went—we swapped for comforters, as the nights were becoming much cooler. After Ben taught Ricardo how to use it, we saw less of him as he discovered the world of computers. I don't think Francesca thought it was the greatest idea; she has had to take care of Mayara more. On one of their three-day trips to São Paulo for stocking up Ricardo came back with an electric generator so he could use the computer in Mato Grosso while fishing.

In the other gypsy family, Adriana is more sociable than Juan, who is not a happy man. He is on anti-depressant drugs and sleeps most of the days as well as nights. He is hardly ever seen and takes little interest in anything. It is easy to tell when he is awake though; samba music blasts out of his truck loud enough for us to get into dancing at our campsite, almost as if he needed to drown something out—maybe Adrianna.

Adrianna has her hands full holding her family together with the role of mother and father most of the time. She is a strong character, somewhat controlling, perhaps because she has to be because of his personality. She is a bleached blonde who might reach 5'2" with a voice three times the size of the woman herself. She has out of necessity left her daughter Lira in charge of Lira's younger brother, Iyago. The one thing I won't miss is the "Liiii – ra" in her deep nasally voice, which can be heard a long distance away. Lira is beckoned, Lira runs. Lira and Iyago spend much of their time with us (we have a tendency to attract kids wherever we go).

Iyago is a difficult child to deal with. He never lets Lira do anything without interrupting. Lira is between Dayna and Karina in age and they spend most of their spare time with one other. Lira does not go to school but does do some book work; she can add and subtract complex questions with efficient skill, knows the value of money, and can read efficiently. Her mother speaks three languages and she urges Lira to learn as much English from us as she can. When I asked Lira what she did all day while they were out she said she took care of Iyago and studied when she could, while her mother did the selling. I asked what her Dad did and she replied, "Oh, he sleeps in the truck." He is the driver moving them from one place to another.

Lira's time with us may have been something of a reprieve. She learned the recorder easily, playing with the girls, but each time she had one in her hands Iyago would pull it away. When he was given one of his own to use, he wanted the other one because it sounded better. After watching what was happening I made some rules: Iyago was not to take the recorder from Lira while she was playing. He found the consequence of being sent home unbearable the first time it happened, but soon figured out what was expected. Lira learned to play some tunes and soon figured out some familiar pieces from her own background. Karina gave Lira her recorder as a gift when we left; she was so happy when Karina put it in her hands, there were tears in her eyes.

Adriana took little responsibility for Iyago except to tell Lira to dress him, shower him, take him some place, play with him, etc. Then she would give Lira heck when Iyago got into trouble, which is not fair to Lira and is frustrating to watch. Iyago is a bright but mischievous child, manipulative of his sister, but they were doing extremely well under the circumstances. By the end of July, Adrianna told us she and Juan had saved enough to purchase a small house. She thought being settled in one place might help Juan, and was looking forward to living in a house where Lira and Iyago would have the opportunity to go to public school. I give that woman a lot of credit—she really was trying to do what was best.

Iyago loved the truck, and whenever he could, would try to figure out how the door handles worked, the wipers and washers, the headlights—would try to get the hubcaps off or open the hood. He took every opportunity he could to figure out how things worked. Juan kept the truck locked up tight; otherwise Iyago would be into the precious stereo and compact discs.

It was fascinating to see how Ben took to Iyago and vice-versa. Ben could somehow keep him out of trouble, would wrestle and play rough with him. Iyago just needed a male figure—or someone—to take an interest in him.

My guess is that Ben must have recognized something of himself in this little guy. Ben still laughs hard when he tells the story of the windshield wipers. One morning while preparing the truck for a day's work Juan cleaned the windshield with the wipers and fluid then left the truck running unattended. Within two seconds Iyago was playing with the controls as his father had just done. He turned the windshield wipers on, tried the different speeds, found the washer fluid and squirted it liberally, trying the wipers and fluid together. How come the wipers go back and forth? He climbed up onto the open door to grab the driver side wiper while the other continued in its fury, he then pulled it over the edge of the windshield and hung onto it. When he let go, the wiper flipped back and forth but not on the windshield. His eyes popped open when he realized he had done something that was not going to go over too well. At this point, he turned the wipers off, took his seat and looked as innocent as he could while waiting to go out for the day. Moments later when the family was in the truck, Juan turned the wipers on to give the windshield another cleaning and the wiper flopped off the edge of the windshield. He attempted to put it back into place using some force and it broke right off. He looked at the wiper in his hand, frustrated, and threw it into the back of the truck, while Iyago sat with the most innocent look on his face. And since they were leaving for the day, we didn't see anything more.

Lira and Iyago ate with us often, and it didn't take long for them to figure out that we are mostly vegetarian. Our getting to know Adrianna and Francesca came from them wanting to know how to cook without meat. Iyago and Lira ate fruit, vegetables and salads the way I prepared them but wouldn't touch them at home. I had a regular visit from the ladies in the evenings to taste the late-day meal and find out how it was prepared.

We had our differences, though—they wouldn't let their children play in the sandy dirt. Our kids spent hours building houses, castles, roads and towns in the open space of the campgrounds. Adrianna and Francesca didn't like their kids getting dirty and had a fear of what they called a "bijou", a bug that gets under a toenail, making it sore and sometimes causing the nail to fall off. I was shown that Iyago had one under a toenail, but they wouldn't do anything to take care of it other than prohibiting him from playing in the sand. Whitney was the only one of the kids that picked up a "bijou." However, a dunk in *Swedish Bitters* and a compress overnight was all that was necessary to kill it. There were some hard feelings over the fact that I wouldn't keep the kids out of the sand. I simply wouldn't and couldn't cause that much tension in our family. Kids need to play in and with the elements. It is important that they have that opportunity and that we as parents allow them to do so. I am sure that it is half of Francesca's problem with her expectations of children. If she could have just accepted the fact that Mayara needed to play, and could have let her be dirty for a while, child rearing wouldn't have been such a struggle.

They were an interesting group of people.

Fachema and Pablo

Pablo is an air force pilot from Recife, and was on temporary assignment in Brasilia. He and his wife Fachema lived in their motorhome at the campground. They have three grown-up children. Fachema gave me the impression of being a happy woman. She was always smiling and always willing to help with anything whenever called upon. She loved children and became a surrogate grandmother to Mayara.

Two days into our stay, Fachema came to say hello and said that she didn't speak much English but if there were anything we needed she would be willing to help with whatever she could. When Jake scraped the end of his big toe off playing soccer barefoot, Fachema came home that evening with a bottle of Sanitivo, an antiseptic she had purchased for us. She said it was the best treatment for anything that needed to be disinfected.

She was a motherly person and always sincerely concerned about everyone's welfare. She and Pablo left an empty space in the hearts of several of their neighbours when they headed back to Recife at the end of June. Mayara, in particular, had a tough time saying good-bye and had to be dragged out of the motorhome the morning they left.

Rogerio

Rogerio is a big man with light-coloured hair. He is of German descent and in his late twenties. He is from São Paulo and living in Brasilia while studying at the university to become a customs agent. The course is offered only in the capital. He is in class every day of the week, at the campground evenings only, and goes back to São Paulo every weekend. For the six month period of his program, his home here is a small two-man tent and a table under a large blue tarp.

He travels back and forth to school on a motorcycle that won't start unless the wheels were moving. It is too heavy to push by himself unless the motor is running. Each morning, he and someone else—usually Ricardo—push it to the top of the small incline on the pavement in order to push it down to gain enough momentum to turn the motor over. Ricardo often leaves before Rogerio does, so most mornings they start the bike and it sits idling until Rogerio is set to go.

Rogerio usually eats his evening meal before coming back to the campground for the night. But one evening he sat with us and I offered him dinner. He said, "No, no, please, not someone else." Then he explained that the evenings when he and Ricardo jam together on their guitars, Francesca won't let him leave until he eats something; he couldn't say no to her and it has happened so often he's gained weight. He likes to play guitar and socialize but said he didn't want everybody to feel like he needs to be taken care of because he is a single guy on his own. I offered, but didn't push it.

One evening, together, both Rogerio and Ricardo got to telling us about the wildlife and laws. The one law that is common knowledge is that if you are caught killing any species of wildlife it is automatic prison, with no chance of getting out until a trial, which can often be years away. They laughed and said penalties are not as severe if you kill a person. A murderer can get out on bail but it's not so for an animal killer. But the poaching continues, and payoffs to "authorities" are always a way to get out of trouble if caught. I wonder where the integrity of the human race has gone.

The evening Rogerio and Ricardo spent with us was the catalyst for us to consider immunization against yellow fever. Immunization has its place, but to a certain extent is just a way for drug companies to make billions of dollars per year. Most of the time, natural immunization, gained from contracting non-life threatening diseases, is the best way for the immune system to build resistance. Childhood injections went against my instincts, yet Tanya did receive the first few. After she was born there was pressure from everyone around me. They said, "If she gets one of these diseases you will be sorry." So she received the first three and after each we had night after night of crying and screaming; I stopped the process with her. When Ben was born, I had enough understanding and confidence to ask for the DPT inoculation but without pertussis, the vaccine that has caused brain damage and sometimes death in many children. Even this didn't feel right. Ed found the books, and we informed ourselves thoroughly. With inoculation there are positive effects as well as risks whether you choose to immunize or not. We chose to trust our life processes and do what felt right for us as a family—not what society dictates through scare tactics. The rest of the children didn't receive those inoculations. Ricardo was stunned we were not immunized for yellow fever, at least, and Rogerio informed us that we would not be allowed into Venezuela travelling over land without such immunization. It was for this reason that Ed asked for more information at the public health clinic. There are still some cases of yellow fever throughout the Amazon basin in people who are not immunized. Of those who contract the disease, statistics are that one in six dies. It was those odds and the issue of returning to Venezuela after being in Brazil that made us decide to immunize for yellow fever since we would be spending a considerable amount of time on our travels through the Amazon.

The government provides inoculations for yellow fever free of charge in Brazil. We just had to make an appointment at the clinic to have it taken care of, which we did.

As Rogerio was a student of *aduana*—immigration and customs, and our three-month visa time was about to expire, Ed asked about extending our visas and the inevitable paperwork that would be required for the van. Rogerio told us that we would have no trouble extending visas for another three months but the van might be a different story. He went to his supervisors and asked what could be done to make the process go smoothly. Questions back and forth went on over a four-day period; then Rogerio said he would take care of things. A few days later he arrived with three copies of a typewritten letter that needed nothing more than a date. We were to bring it to the *aduana* office when the time came. (When the time did come the letter produced the official papers within 24 hours, and Ed was told if he wanted another three months just to come back.) Rogerio saved Ed a lot of time, trouble and running around.

Rogerio liked playing chess with Ben. He said he could tell Ben was a thinker and that it was fun to watch how quickly his skills improved. Ben never did win, but he enjoyed playing with someone who was a challenge.

Rogerio and Ricardo spent many quiet evenings strumming guitar, laughing, singing and creating a happy calm in the night air. When Ricardo obtained the computer it happened less often; he and Rogerio were often glued to the screen. I'm not sure we did them a favour.

The Hippies

Ricardo calls the group of three young people camped far away from everyone "hippies". They are somewhat a reminder of what the sixties were like. They arrived in late June and were still at the campground when we left. The couple—a man and a woman who was much older than he—slept in a large tent, while another young man had a small tent of his own. They were from Pirenopolis and made jewelry and sold it on the streets in Brasilia. They were always at the campground until mid-afternoon making pieces, then were gone until late in the evenings. Everyone called them "the hippies". They kept to themselves, although we did know some things about them. The single man, for example, had lost the thumb and index finger on his right hand. He still managed to make jewelry, do wood carving and sell on the streets. Of course it was Ricardo who found out what happened. The man's hand was caught in a *caldo de cana* machine, and it crushed his thumb and finger. A *caldo de cana* machine presses sugar cane, pulling the tough stalk through extremely powerful gears to release the juice. Fingers wouldn't have a chance.

I never did find out their names. The kids watched them make jewelry on many occasions, and were the only people "the hippies" interacted with. We did end up purchasing a stone necklace for each of the kids at bargain prices. It was one of the very few times I ever spoke with any of them. The woman was aware of the tension concerning the kids playing in the sand and told me it was natural for them to want to play and touch the earth, and that I should let them play in it. Of course I agreed. She also offered a whole lot of other encouragement that I didn't totally understand. She obviously had observed what was going on.

Lilianna and Andre

Lilianna and Andre are a newly married couple in their late twenties. It is a mixed marriage: she is of Portuguese and native decent, and he is of African descent. They live in a camper of painted white plywood that at one time fit on top of a pickup truck. The box sits there under the trees across the parking lot from us, propped up on stilts off the ground, and a set of steps to reach the door.

Lilianna had consistent shoulder pain that Ed helped relieve. One evening while Andre was working late, after Ed had treated Lilianna she visited, had tea, and told us their story. They met while travelling separately, joined up, and travelled much of southern Brazil and Argentina on a motorbike together. They married without either of their families knowing about it. They didn't have a place of their own, and when Andre started to work they attempted to live with his family until they could support themselves. His family did not welcome the marriage, and living with them didn't last. Friends gave them the thing they live in and they moved to the campground.

Andre is off to work early each morning in business attire, on his motor bike, and returns in the evening, turning the bike off and coasting in quietly to surprise Lilianna. It is refreshing to see young love; they appear so happy.

Andre likes to keep fit. He has a muscular body in excellent shape, and took to the idea of rock climbing. He and a friend purchased ropes and equipment, and on several weekends they used the abandoned concrete water tower on the campgrounds to practice. They fastened the ropes to the top and practiced going up and down. Ben watched with interest and was given the opportunity to try. In the beginning, Lilianna was reluctant to attempt the ropes but with Andre's encouragement she figured it out.

Andre doesn't want Lilianna to work; she says she would but that's the way he wants it, and she likes not having to. They were living at the campground when we arrived and were still there when we left.

Katarina, George, Pao and Morgan

One afternoon two old, beat-up cars drove into the parking lot. A family of four got out of one, a single man out of the other. The five walked around solemnly, looking and taking things in. The family was well dressed. The dad had a dark tan, was tall and big around; his silk shirt stretched at the buttons, ruining the weave. He seemed to enjoy showing off his jewelry—he had several gold chains around his neck and a ring on almost every finger. The mom had long, blonde, curly hair down to the middle of her back. She was slim and was dressed in a pleated mauve skirt with a jacket to match over a white frilly blouse. She wore dark sunglasses. Nothing was out of place. The couple appeared so mismatched to me. Their daughter, about seven, was a beautiful miniature. But the boy, a couple of years older than his sister, was too thin and looked more like mom than dad.

The other man was balding, as round as the father, but shorter, not nearly as well dressed; he walked beside the big guy, giving the impression of being a sidekick. They wandered around aimlessly until the kids gravitated toward us, and Pao, the boy, picked up a set of bow and arrows the kids had built. He didn't say anything, just ran away and started to play with them. Morgan, the girl, stood and stared. The big man, George, walked up to our table as if he owned the place, sat down and asked many questions. Where are you from? Why do you stay here? How long are you in Brazil for? Do you like it here? Who lives in these tents? If you were to set up a tent where would you put it? Is it safe? Have you ever seen snakes? What religion are you? Where did you get the table?

Ben asked if they were going to camp. Tension was evident on the woman's face, and she seemed angry when she was faced with the idea of camping. She had been silent the entire time but now she blurted out, "Me, and the earth don't get along with each other." I don't know if that was their main conflict but certainly it was an area of contention.

They sat at our table and took up most of our afternoon talking about what to do. George said they would camp temporarily until they could find a house to rent. When they left our table, the men walked around while the woman sat in the car; the kids were into everything, pulling our things out and leaving them lying in the dust. They were obnoxious.

George gave the other man some directions and the man pulled a tent out of the car trunk. The kids and I thought, "Oh no, this does not look good." When the tent was rolled out on the ground, the woman stepped out of the car and screamed at the two of them. The tent was returned to the trunk. The kids were called to the car and they drove off, leaving our belongings spread out around the campsite. We breathed a sigh of relief.

The following morning the two cars were back, one man in each. They set up a large tent that had seen better days, left for the afternoon and were back in the evening. George slept in the tent alone and his sidekick used his car. George showered and dressed as if he was going out for the evening while the sidekick threw himself together. They got into one car and were gone until late evening. That continued for several days. Then one night the sidekick didn't return and never did come back. Two weeks went by and there was no sign of the family either. George continued to come and go daily. Then one Sunday mom and the kids showed up for the afternoon and again the following Sunday. Both times Katarina spent the afternoon sitting in the car.

One evening George returned earlier than usual and spent time talking with Rogerio and Ricardo. Ricardo, in his inquisitive way, doesn't hold back when he wants to know something. It turned out that George and Katarina had owned an elite restaurant; they went bankrupt and lost everything but their personal clothing. Katarina was having a hard time adjusting to the lifestyle change. For now, she was at her parent's house, but they wanted her out. They are looking for a house to rent but are having a tough time finding a place after going bankrupt.

One weekend on Friday, Katarina and the kids arrived, took down the tent and left for Itiquira for a few days. When they returned they set the tent back up and stayed.

Their routine changed: George had work, and the kids, no longer attending school, were at the campground daily. It took a long time for everyone to get used to them being on the site. There weren't any laid-out rules at the campground but everybody respected everyone else's space. The tents were our homes and that was understood. Ricardo, taking it to extremes, would even "ring" an imaginary doorbell when he came to visit. Pao and Morgan didn't take privacy into consideration, and their parents didn't give them any guidance in that respect. Our kids are capable of befriending almost anyone, but they found these two a challenge. Everyone at the campground did. Pao and Morgan would take belongings and toys without asking and would leave them someplace, or take them home. It became a tough situation and all of us had to create some boundaries, to the point where Ricardo even yelled at the kids one evening to get the point across.

Katarina was extremely meticulous. She washed clothes for hours, even with the water shortage. She scrubbed Morgan's white shoes daily—with a toothbrush—and spent the rest of the day watching television and hiding in the tent. We have no idea where the television came from. Not a happy woman. They were still there when we left. I wonder how they are doing and if they got their life back together.

The Visitors

Ricardo says Brazilians rarely stifle their curiosity and he himself is a good example. He knew something about everyone. Being foreign campers in Brazil, we were used to the curiosity and being stared at. But while living at the Brasilia campground we experienced the ultimate nosiness.

One afternoon two motorhomes as large as transport trucks rolled into the grounds. They had all the conveniences, right down to an automatic washer and dryer in the storage areas underneath. They parked a short distance from our campsite, facing each other, creating a private space between them. Three couples—friends in their late 50s (Ricardo had found out)—were in Brasilia on political business. While they were setting up, two of the women kept staring in our direction. When their set-up was complete, they set their chairs up facing our direction and watched our family. It went on most of the afternoon. When Ed returned from work the two women couldn't handle it any longer. Without invitation they just walked over and sat at our table. They introduced themselves, but I didn't catch their names, I was so taken back by their boldness and the rudeness of the earlier afternoon. When they sat at our table, we were in the process of putting a dinner together and were ready to eat. Even so, they asked many questions, wanting to know everything about the trip, kids' school, Ed's work. Ed was so annoyed he told them only the bare minimum. When they left, I'm sure they didn't have much more information than what they had previously gained by observing.

After breakfast the following morning, the kids sat down to the table with their math lessons. I took the dirty dishes to the rear of the building to be washed. Twenty minutes later, as I came back with the clean dishes, one of the women was at our table going through Tanya's work. When she saw me returning she left before I made it to our camp. The kids complained; she had gone through everyone's books. Tanya said the woman turned the page on which Tanya was reading a question. She glared at the lady, who asked if she was disturbing her. Tanya said, "Well, I am trying to do my work and can't if I can't read the questions." They all left a couple of hours later for the rest of the day, and left for good the following morning—to our relief. It was an extreme case of curiosity and obnoxiousness. In our interactions with most people, the curiosity usually comes with friendliness and a willingness to help if necessary.

Campground Workers

The "chief" (as everybody called him) and five employees ran the office and grounds. The "chief" had a hard job. He took over as boss two months before we arrived and was attempting to bring the run-down grounds up to CCB standards. It had been a municipal site for up to 3,000 campers on several acres, but it has been unused and was grown over. The chief has a heart of gold. When we asked to use a decrepit picnic table at the back of the main building, he had the workers build us a new one. Why he did this no one knows. Supplying picnic tables to tenants is not CCB policy.

Maria, a short, round woman, always wore her thick, black hair tied on the top of her head in ringlets, an "evening" type of hairstyle. She always looked well taken care of and was the only employee who didn't live at the campground; she worked six days a week from 7 a.m. to 4 p.m. She cleaned the bathroom twice a day, cooked the midday meal for the campground staff and washed their clothes as well.

Four men lived in the "barracks" behind the main building. One young man whom we didn't see much of was the night watchman. He went to school during the day. When he slept was a good question.

Raoul, another young man, filled in wherever and whenever there was a need, usually when the others had a day off. He built our table. He and Ben often kicked the soccer ball around, which sometimes ended up as a full-fledged game involving anyone who wanted to play. Raoul and the other maintenance man (we didn't get to know him at all) were installing a water reservoir tank when we left.

And then there was Reise (I'm not sure of the spelling), an older black man with greying hair. He doesn't seem to have a family but has found a niche here. He spends his days raking the dry grasses and keeping the grounds clean. The vegetation was under his care—he watered the trees in the mornings and tended the vegetable garden that he planted. We met regularly at about 5 a.m. at the water faucet. He filled his buckets for watering plants and I filled the kettle for my morning fix. He always had a big smiling face and a "Bom Dia" for me. He

The Statue of Candangos, Representing the people who built Brasilia

appreciated everything Maria did, and she, in return, was fond of him; he helped her in any way she needed it.

Learning about Brasilia

We spent our free weekends exploring Brasilia, the capital city. It is newly constructed although the idea of relocating the federal government there from Rio de Janeiro originated in 1823. The move served three purposes: to create a capital away from the threat of naval attack, to develop the heartland of the country, and to build a small city with a small population, making it easier to control uprisings. Every government from 1823 on supported the concept, but it wasn't until Juscelino Kubitschek made an election campaign promise to a common citizen that the city started to take form. After he was elected president a competition for proposed plans was set into motion. The submission of Lucio Costa, an architect and urban planner, was chosen, and construction began in 1956. The city is designed in the shape of a bow and arrow, some say a bird or airplane, but it was conceived from the bows and arrows of the original peoples as a tribute to the history of the country.

To provide the necessary water supply, the first thing constructed on the arid plane was the reservoir. The arc of the bow (residential areas) parallels the U-shape form of what has come to be known as Lago Paranoa. The president's official residence, Palacio Alvorada, sits on the shore with the city to the west. Once the federal district was established, the city was inaugurated as the capital on April 26, 1960 and has grown continually within the guidelines of the original plans.

The arrow (the major traffic thoroughfare) runs east-west, creating north and south sectors. The streets are well planned—we never found ourselves stuck in traffic even at the busiest time of day, in part because public transportation is so efficient. The city centre where the bow and arrow intersect, is dominated by public and government buildings. The main city is restricted to accommodating 500,000 residents. No construction other than what was originally planned is permitted and some fear it may create what is referred to as the "Petrified Capital of the Sixties". Certainly, the plan has been proven to be somewhat limiting and several satellite towns have sprung up in the past forty years to support the two million people of the federal district. Nonetheless the modern architecture and unusual layout of the city are interesting to explore.

During the first weekend we spent in the city we chose to go up to the observation platform at the TV tower to get an overview. The shape of the bow and arrow is not distinguishable even from that high off the ground, and while we were there, trying to make some sense of the shape, the Nazca lines and figures came to mind.

We did not get an exciting impression of the city from the perch above the ground. The most intense colour came from the red soil upon which the city was built. Otherwise, the carefully laid-out structures looked as if it was overly organized—maybe the city was too well planned.

A weekend handcraft market sprawled at the base of the TV tower, attracting visitors in true South American style. We were intrigued by the creations and purchased a cotton hammock to hang in the pines beside our tents. We also found a small square basket with a handle and its inside quartered into four sections. It is just what we need to store and control our mess of utensils. An abundance of tie-dyed light clothing suitable for Brazilian heat, monopolized the market, but ironically, it came from Indonesia.

We wandered the Praca dos Tres Poderes, where the main government buildings stand, and admired the modern architecture, which was designed by Oscar Niemeyer, Brazil's leading architect. In my opinion the most outstanding building is the cathedral. I don't even dare call it a building—it is a piece of art. The circular dome and structural supports represent a crown of thorns and the ceiling is of magnificent stained glass. It is unusual, eye-pleasing and functional. The kids enjoyed getting a good look at some of the sculptures for which Brasilia is noted, and all agreed that "A Justica" was their favourite.

The colourfully dressed guards in front of the Palacio do Planalto puzzled Jake. They never moved a muscle, and he asked if they were real people. When I confirmed that they were real, he asked, "How can they stand still that long, and how can they wear those big jackets in this heat?"

The two things Jake cannot relate to: standing still and wearing clothes.

I asked, "How would you like that job, Jake?"

He was quick to reply, "No way, that would be the most boringest job in the world."

When I informed him there were guards like that in front of the Governor General's house in Canada he said, "Well, I'm not going to be one. I just can't wear all those clothes."

He knows himself. His questions were valid. These guards were dressed in red jackets, black trousers, tall leather boots and hats. That same afternoon we drove

Brasilia Campsite

around the lake to learn how big it actually was and spotted several emus nibbling the grasses at the Palacio do Alvorada. Jake, still caught up in the fact that the guards wore so many clothes, barely acknowledged the huge birds.

July 2, 1999: Living Simply

Yesterday morning, while having my coffee and sitting in the quiet of the morning, I considered my thoughts and feelings of the recent past. I live a paradox. And so here we are for the past month and a half living much more simply than we ever have before. Our campsite is our home. We have comfortable beds to sleep in; a two-burner stove creates all our meals; two metal barrels and a door make a food prep area; three wooden crates are our cupboards. We have a picnic table that is the centre of our "home" and the seats out of the van are our "couches". Cardboard boxes hold our books and our basket of toiletries, keeping them out of the dust on the ground. We share the bathroom with everyone else—I don't have to clean it or get after someone else to do so. I never sweep the "kitchen". The wild birds love the toast crumbs and food scraps that fall on the dirt floor. We do dishes in the sinks provided or in our dishpan. We have just enough dishes for our family, so dishwashing is never a big job. We have few clothes, so it takes just forty-five minutes to wash by hand the dirty things from the previous day. And the clothes are much cleaner than those we washed in the washing machines we owned in Canada and Chile. After our minimal chores are complete, I read to the kids during the heat of the day under the tarp that protects our worldly possessions from the afternoon sun. I have time to spend playing cards and games with them. We have been writing and taking the time to talk about the compositions, so that we can turn them into decent pieces of work. The kids do at least two lessons of math each morning. The campground has acres of unused land, and the kids are free to roam. They play soccer, volleyball, and paddleball, plus all kinds of other games they make up. Behind our tents there is dry, sandy soil that serves as a sandbox. The kids have very few manufactured things to occupy them: four decks of cards, a chess set, checkers, a game of Boggle, travel Battleship, origami, Rumicube, a tangram, some puzzles and a small box of Lego that all fit into a games box, tucked under one of our "couches". With fewer possessions, the kids occupy themselves with what is available around them, and they explore and learn about their surroundings.

When we first arrived in Brasilia we read *Robin Hood*—again, which spurred the construction of bows and arrows as toys. Once everyone had a set, the competitions began, which led everyone to attempting to figure out how to build better bows and arrows for winning the competitions. For the past three weeks Ben has been improving his designs figuring out what construction is stronger and what arrow flies most accurately—quite sophisticated. He found a stone shaped like an arrowhead, which led to a day of searching for perfectly straight sticks for the shaft. When he tied the "arrowhead" onto the end of the stick, the arrow wobbled in flight. Then it was a search for feathers and, after experimenting with several feather positions, he got the arrow to fly through the air with more precision and land close to where it was aimed. With trial after trial and error, he came up with an arrow that actually worked.

Is living simply, and with less, good for them? When I see things like the arrow construction, my instincts tell me "yes". Ben has been extremely occupied in some positive work, spending whole days thinking the construction through, then building the apparatus and making it work. He has figured out his own lessons in physics, how weight and balance work together as well as learning aerodynamics. After the arrow flew and stuck into a tree, he said, "Hey, that's neat—a simple thing like a stone, a stick and feathers." He didn't give what he worked on much thought afterwards, but the knowledge he gained by working through the process will never be lost. He mastered his challenge and moved on. My challenge is providing an environment that creates such learning opportunities and challenging his abilities. What I found so amazing was that simple things like a stone, a stick and feathers could keep that boy so preoccupied for the length of time it did.

The same kind of circumstances would never have arrived living the life we were accustomed to before we left. We were too busy running from place to place and trying to keep our own place in some kind of order.

I find myself enjoying the rhythm we have fallen into and not feeling so bad about where we are anymore. In the beginning I didn't like it at all. Living like this is good here now, but I ask myself how long would it be before everything becomes a burden here, too? Then again, inner peace has moved into my soul, and not much is a burden when that is the case. Right now our daily cost of living averages out to ninety *reais* per day. That includes the gasoline for our gas-guzzling van as well as dentist appointments, food, appropriate clothing for Brazil, and camping facility fees. That is less than 100 Canadian dollars per day for our family of eight. It is a good life we live. Our travels have given us experience unequaled by anything we could have done in Canada in the same time period.

Everything in life is a matter of choice, isn't it? I just need to choose to live more with less in order to give me the time I need and want for my family and myself. Then again, living with less is much easier to do here in the tropics. Outdoor life and sleeping on the ground is much harder to enact during a Canadian winter, where a warm shelter is necessary for survival. I have a big challenge ahead to keep my Canadian life simple. Will living simply be possible in Canadian society, where we are so conditioned to "keep up with the Jones" and fit in? In a way, I am fearful of going back.

July 3 to 18, 1999: Itiquira, Third Visit

Ed had a week's holiday, as Sira was at the office, giving us an opportunity for our third visit to the Itiquira campground. It was a peaceful week, since we were one of only two groups of patrons, yet we accomplished little "schoolwork." The kids complained of how hard it was to get into work when their father was around. Ed has a tendency to give them different assignments that do not necessarily result in them progressing through their books. We found ourselves listening to inspirational tapes and doing more physical activity than usual.

Ben gashed the palm of his hand on the wooden bridge and the cut could have used a couple of stitches. Ed disinfected the cut and wrapped it in sterile bandages to pull the gap of skin together. Since Ben didn't like the idea of stitches and promised to take proper care of it, we decided to save ourselves a long trip to a medic. (It healed well without a problem.)

Cashueras de Itiquira, Brazil

We attempted to picnic at the falls, where the rock climbers were climbing the last time we hiked but but after coming across three snakes on our short walk we decided not to hike through the jungle. Other than at the zoo we hadn't seen a live snake in Brazil; we don't have any knowledge about tropical snakes. Sometimes ignorance is bliss, but it can also be a serious detriment. We went back to the small falls, picnicked, sunbathed and played in the rapids and water close to the campground.

Alone, without anyone around but us, I took my bathing suit top off to soak up the sun. The kids exclaimed "MOM", surprised their mother would do such a thing. I told them they could, too, but it was just Whitney who joined me. With the kind of weather we've been experiencing even a bikini can feel like overdressing. What is the sense? Clothes are for keeping warm and, while living in such a climate, they are not necessary. Dressing is just a response to our so-called "civilized society" saying we have to cover up our bodies. I lay down on the warm smooth rock and found myself thinking about how much I love the earth and its wonders. The earth, she always feeds my soul.

July 6, 1999:

Ed and the kids were into a game of cards by the time I had the supper dishes cleaned up, and no one wanted to join me on a walk. I couldn't believe how much warmer the air was as I moved away from the trees, up and out of the river valley. A sparkling clear sky and the chirping of crickets in the grasses created a peaceful night. But there was sadness in me: our journey was going to end within the next year. The end always means a new beginning and it always takes me a while to warm up to new beginnings. I have a real apprehension about returning to Canada. As much as I want to, I don't want to and I don't understand why. I looked to the stars. I'm not going to have the southern sky to enjoy much longer. Scorpio was already at the zenith of the sky, and the Southern Cross had twisted around sideways from pointing due south. My kite and the cross are the dominant constellations. I asked myself why am I not ready for this mid-life interlude to be over—what are we going to do when we get home? And it felt as if it was time to find some answers. While I stared up at the heavens, the legend about the creator hiding the answer to the purpose of life within the human species started to flit through my head, and I understood, I have the answers, I just have to have the courage to face them.

By Friday we needed some fresh vegetables, juice and bread, so we combined a day trip to the Itiquira Falls Park before a food-shopping trip in Formosa. From Formosa toward the park, we dropped in altitude onto a flat plain. Driving the highway and looking to our left, we could see a rock escarpment that jumps straight up out of the plain. From five kilometers away, we could see the Itiquira Falls as a vertical white streak against the rock in the sunlight. Ed teasingly said, "Okay we've seen it, we can go back now." The kids protested and Ed laughed. He wanted to get a close-up view as much as anyone else.

At the base of the falls, we were up against a 200-meter perpendicular, sedimentary rock wall. It was hard to believe we had walked along the ledge at the top a few weeks earlier. We spotted people up there; they were hanging over the edge, looking at the falls, shouting down and waving. From our point of view it appeared that they were defying the law of gravity while viewing the water tumbling over the edge. So, it was possible, but precarious, to see the falls from the top. From the bottom it was apparent that the flowing water had cut the V-shaped cleft in the rock ridge, creating the valley we walked through. The river plunges 158 meters, without interruption, to the smoothed-out pool on the lower plain. Much of the water becomes airborne mist and never reaches the pool. It moistens the surroundings and makes the vegetation lush. On either side of the falls, ferns cling to the cliff and sway with the energy of the water. We sunbathed and swam; Ed soaked his foot in the cold water. Thursday, while playing Eenie Inie Over, he twisted it during the excitement of catching the opposing team— mainly me. (We are not as young as we used to be.) The cold water helped alleviate the swelling. Food was not allowed in the park so we stayed as long as our stomachs would allow.

In Formosa, Ed called the office to get an update and spoke with Sira for only a moment. She was busy with clients and said, "Here, talk to Jason," leaving Ed to talk with someone he didn't know. Jason was looking into working in the clinic and taking over from Ed. Sometimes you just hit it off right with certain people. They had a lengthy conversation and Ed invited him and Renata to the campground for a visit.

July 11, 1999:

Jason had met Ian and Emma (the British couple we met in Venezuela) while surfing in Ecuador. They told him about Ed heading for Chile to set up practice.

Jason was in Santiago twice looking for Ed to possibly work, but he never did locate us. So now that both of them had circled the continent, they had an opportunity to talk. Early Saturday afternoon Jason and his female friend, Renata, a Brazilian, arrived at the campground. We talked all afternoon, through dinner and well into the evening. Jason, an Australian and a serious surfer, has travelled much of the world. He met Renata in Europe. At present, he has a full-time clinic in Lima, Peru and is looking to set up in Brazil in order to change their long-distance relationship into one in which they can see each other more often.

Renata studies languages and speaks several of them. She is a tall, blonde-haired, beautiful woman with an Aussy accent. My first thought when we met was, "I thought you were Brazilian." To my inexperienced ears she could have passed for Australian, but that has been Jason's influence, and the result of having lived in Australia for a year. I described my first impression of her and she said she knew what that was all about. When she lived in Europe, no one would believe she was Brazilian.

There was no shortage of things for us to discuss. Jason and Renata are avid travellers and travelling was a subject of conversation to which even the children could contribute. Although we compared our experiences of Asia and Australia, Brazil was our main topic, and we recommended our favourite places to one another. Jason and Renata visited Cuiaba recently and told us of their tours into the Pantanal (*SAH* calls it one of the world's greatest wildlife reserves). Their guide could call *araras,* and the birds would come extremely close out of curiosity. They saw several different birds (there are 300 species in that area) as well as snakes and alligators. (Alligators out-number the human population five to one in the Matto Grosso States). The tour guide stopped their jeep when the road was blocked. An anaconda was stretched across the road, head and tail in the vegetation of either side. They touched the snake and were told by the guide when anacondas are stretched out as such they are unable to spring and catch anything or even move very fast. The guide and Jason lifted the tail together. Jason put his hands together to make a circle said it was this big around—volleyball circumference. The kids, in awe, came out with "Coooool!" One tour company showed them a series photos of an anaconda crushing and killing a calf by constriction and swallowing it whole. Jason said there was another photograph of an anaconda with the shape of a man in its belly. It is believed he was a fisherman that went missing—great stories. Matto Grosso is where Ricardo goes fishing in summer, and he's concerned about bijous getting under toenails. The kids were convinced they wanted to visit the Pantanal, to see anacondas. Renata said, "If you do go bring lots of insect repellent; the mosquitoes are vicious. They bite right through your clothes." After they left, we read in *SAH* about the Pantanal. It is a vast wetland, home to species similar to the Amazonas, only more easily viewed than in the dense jungle. It is an area where 300 bird species, 230 varieties of fish, and a large variety of snakes, alligators and mammals thrive, and only a small area is a protected park. Hunting anything is punishable by four years in prison, and strict licence laws regulate fishing. Rainy season is December to March, dry season July to October. *SAH* mentions that campers should be wary of snakes, piranhas, killer bees and *jacares* – alligators. "The inexperienced are cautioned not to strike out on their own."

We discussed the possibility of visiting the area but Tanya isn't with us, and it's a two-day drive in each direction to see birds we see here in Itiquira, get eaten alive by mosquitoes, and see snakes—albeit man-eating ones. Ed and I were not convinced. Dayna complained, "But we are here now". Ed told her she has lots of life ahead, to put it on her own goals list.

Chiropractic and its development in South America was another topic of conversation: what is happening in Chile, Peru, Argentina and Brazil, the difficulties in getting anything going, and the willingness or unwillingness of the governments to recognize chiropractic as an independent profession. There is a lot of work to be done, and it is going to take many dedicated people to bring it up to international standards.

Both Jason and Renata asked about the kids and their education. Jason asked if there are any budding chiropractors. Ben said he was going to be one and Dayna said she was as well, and was planning to go to college with Ben. Jason told Ben that when he finished college and wants to work someplace that he'll help him set up in Brazil if he wants, especially if he's into surfing. The Brazilian coast would be a great place to live, work and play.

We asked Jason and Renata to stay overnight with us, but they opted for the little hotel about ten kilometers away. They came back for breakfast and as much of Sunday as they could squeeze in. They laughed as they described their overnight accommodation. It was a hotel that rents rooms by the hour, and they had a difficult time convincing the clerk to let them stay all night.

Jason and Renata both told us that up until yesterday neither one of them thought much about having children. Their idea was that kids were a lot of work, cost a lot of money, and they thought travel would be almost impossible with them. Visiting with us helped them see things from a different perspective. It was a wonderful compliment to our family.

Ed and Jason traded long-needed adjustments. It is difficult for Ed to get good regular care when there are so few chiropractors in South America. We took photos, exchanged addresses, said good-byes and promised to keep in touch before they had to leave for São Paulo.

July 12, 1999:

This morning, after a night full of dreams that dealt with my apprehensions about returning to Canada, I understand my fear. It will be a test to see if I can be all I am aiming to be. Is it possible to maintain and hold the changes I have made in myself in the past two years when I go back to where I came from? I believe it has been easier to break away from the negative patterns of the past by removing myself from the familiarity of life in Canada. Talking all this over with Ed this morning, he smirked and said, "Got to be careful what you ask for, don't you?" I guess I was ready, I asked, and answers came. It's not always that clear and easy to understand. God works in wonderful and mysterious ways. It is so good to learn, grow and find a few answers to great questions.

July 12, 1999: From Dream Book

This week, I used an idea that came to me based on examples provided in *Dreaming With The Wheel*. I asked my spirit keepers to allow dreams to come through that would give answers to what I need to deal with before I go home. That was a week ago. Since last Monday I have been dreaming about my family. Not my brothers and sisters but Mom and Dad's families as far back as grandparents and their brothers and sisters. The dreams have been numerous, four to five per night, and the only two people who are noticeably absent are my two grandmothers. There is only one I will put on paper as they are liable to be misinterpreted, and I have caused enough hard feelings within my family by letting others know what has caused my hurt feelings.

Dream — July 8, 1999: On Baba and Gedo's farm in the centre of the large circle of land created by the barns and the house, there was a wagon. (Baba and Gedo are the Polish words for Grandma and Grandpa.) Gedo was on the wagon and my father and his brothers were around it. Gedo was using a whip, lashing out at his sons, hitting them and telling them to get pulling the wagon.

I know Gedo hit and abused Baba at times, but I am unaware that he ever beat his sons. Nonetheless, I wonder what happened in his life that caused him to be the way he was? It comes from a long way back.

So now what do I do? One morning last week I read in Guy Finley's book *The Road to Good Fortune*, "Walking away from the heartaches you don't want in life gets easier each time it gets clearer to you who you no longer need to be." That statement jumped off the page at me. I no longer need to be the person my family tried to make me be. It is okay to be who I really am and live what I believe according to natural law. I no longer choose to be the victim of my hurt feelings from the first 20 years of my life. All the pain, anger and injustice which I allowed myself to feel victimized by, has haunted me for the second 20 years of my life. I had many troubled times, reliving negative experiences each time one of my children or someone else triggered a memory. It happened again this week after a lengthy break from such occurrences.

The children were verbally putting each other down, not really arguing but pestering one another. When one asked that it stop and it didn't, I started to get angry inside. It was a feeling I hadn't experienced in a long time and that I didn't know how to work with in a constructive way. Many times in the past when I have been angry in this way I have ended up hitting somebody. I knew I had to remove myself or it might happen again. I got up to do the dishes. The behaviour stopped for a few moments while the kids went to play on the swings and in the sand, and then it continued. I need to learn how to intervene in a constructive way, but my mind was in no positive place at that moment. Someone ended up crying and feeling hard done by. Ed was there and had no comforting words for the one who was crying. I couldn't handle the rage that built up inside me, and a string of angry words came out in a loud yell aimed at Ed: "He has no right to do that to his brother and sisters. They have all asked him to stop. Why is it so hard for him to respect another human being's request? It's abuse and no one has the right to do that to another person. I get so mad when this kind of stuff goes on I could strangle someone."

I cried and I continued to cry the entire time I did the dishes. I didn't hear another word from the kids or Ed. They stayed away for fear of another blowup. It was the hurt child inside of me I was crying for and I had a difficult time stopping. The rage and the memories of the incident that caused it were there inside me as strong as the day the anger found a place in my body—I started to understand. I took a shower and let my thoughts dwell on the true reasons for my anger. Once again, because of my children I have learned about my own behaviour. I shut my eyes and let the comforting water wash away the anger and visualized it flowing down the drain.

Ben was upset, and the others looked at me as if to ask, "Is my Mom back?" I felt I owed them an explanation of what happened but when bedtime came around I couldn't manage one. If I tried to talk more tears came. I just had to hug and kiss each of them, make sure they were okay and tell them I loved them.

Two days later there was verbal abuse back and forth again. When it gets mean, anger starts to take over and often a physical fight will start. As far as I am concerned if one person is making himself feel superior at the expense of another, verbally or physically, it is abuse. It degrades the other. I am hoping to help the children find compassion and respect for others and be loving, considerate people. There isn't room for such behaviour when we value and respect others, and that can only happen when we are free of the emotional garbage that creates disrespect in the first place.

I heaved a sigh of disappointment and hoped I could help them understand what they are doing to each other. I intervened. It was the moment to tell my story.

"Hey guys, you know the other day when I got so angry and cried a long time, you know what it was from? It wasn't because of you guys, it was because of me."

They thought I was mad at them. "It wasn't about your fighting with each other as much as what you reminded me of. My reaction was an over-reaction because of what I lived through when I was your age."

I had their full attention. "When I was growing up we lived at Baba's house for almost a year while Gram and Grandpa's house was being built. One of Grandpa's brothers tormented me endlessly and I hated it. I hated being in the house when he was home because all he did was bug my aunt and me. He stuck his tongue in my ear, he tickled me until I cried, he pulled my hair, poked me with his fingers, teased, bullied and all kinds of things that seemed as if he was being mean for the sake of being mean. He did it to me less than he did it to his sister and I remember lots of fistfights because he wouldn't stop. One day when he wouldn't leave her alone after being asked and pleaded with, a fight started and I got in on it. I hated what he was doing to her and I hated him doing it to me, too. My anger let loose and my fists pounded him with all the strength I had, but Baba pulled me away. I remember his face just laughing at me with no understanding of how much I hated what he was doing, and him, at that moment. If I had had the means to kill him I might have, being out of my mind with livid rage.

"So the other day when you were bugging the kids, Ben, it was as if I was the victim again. Do you see what I mean—that it wasn't you guys as much as it was me? When I recognize the same kind of thing happening to one of you I become the victim that I didn't grow out of, my anger gets directed toward the tormentor, and it becomes a dangerous situation. All I am trying to say is that I would like you guys to understand that doing mean things to each other will often cause life-long scars. I don't want any of you growing up with emotional damage, because it causes dysfunctional adults who abuse children and other people and even become murderers. Most people learn to live with emotional damage, yet have trouble developing positive relationships with the important people around them, and have difficulty being happy and successful. Fortunately, things can improve when we understand where the trouble comes from. I got mad at your Dad because he didn't have sympathy for the victim; he didn't come to the victim's defence. The adults in my childhood environment were not aware of what was going on and how much damage the abuse was causing. They were unaware of how to get to the core problem that caused my uncle to be the way he was—if they saw it as a problem at all. When we don't know how to deal with difficulties we usually attempt to bury our feelings and hope the problem will go away. So nothing changed and the problem continued to have an effect on another generation of lives as well—us. I got mad at you, Ben, when you wouldn't stop bugging the others when they asked you to—my uncle never stopped until somebody felt really bad and cried or on the rare occasion that someone bigger stopped what was going on. I refuse to carry on the negative behaviour patterns that have come to me from generations back. Once we understand the root of problems, it is easier to forgive and when that happens it is easy to have compassion for those who created the situation in the first place. They are the ones being tormented by emotional garbage that causes them to live their life the way they do. I want you guys to be able to grow up as self-actualized people who know no limits to what you are capable of doing. If you grow up without so much emotional trash, you'll have a headstart on doing whatever you choose to put an effort into. You know the difference in me when there is or isn't something gnawing away at my insides. It doesn't have to be that way for you."

With awareness of our feelings and where they come from, we can change the patterns we grew up with into something much more positive and healthy. That's what I'm working towards here—the negative patterns of alcoholism, drug addiction, divorce, sexual abuse, violence, and something as simple as food-eating disorders can be improved. Show me an emotionally well human being and I can show you a person who doesn't have room for the abuse of any of those things in their life. I know I'm not perfect and I don't expect that the kids will grow up perfect either, but no one ever gets anywhere without aiming and working for it. (The several days after I told my story were the most peaceful that we have lived with one other.)

July 18, 1999:

Ed had use of the clinic apartment this week. The rest of us stayed here at Itiquira doing math and writing during the morning, taking afternoon walks to the river and enjoying the swimming pool in the quiet atmosphere. Nighttime reading was *Talking Earth* by Jean Craighead George. The kids were immersed in the story and found the things Billy Wind makes and uses from nature fascinating. Karina asked, "How does she make palm leaf mats by weaving them together."

I replied, "I don't really know, but weaving is easy. You know how to do it, so I guess you would just weave the leaves together?"

The following day Karina was breaking leaves off a palm tree and I told her to stop, that if everybody did that there wouldn't be any leaves left. She was disappointed with me but our policy is always to leave a place we have visited unharmed and as clean or cleaner than when we arrived. The next day she dragged a dried up branch of palm that she found on the ground back to our campsite. She said, "I didn't break it off a tree" and gave me a mischievous look. She broke the leaves off and attempted to weave them together, but had a difficult time. She quit; they were just too dry. She really wanted to make a palm leaf mat and gave the others a notion that they wanted to try as well. They convinced me there was an abundance of palm trees and leaves. Palms grow profusely in the area—I was being unreasonable, and it would give them something to do. They spent every unoccupied minute throughout the week weaving mats. At first they used the whole wide leaf. It was fast and easy and wove a large mat. The following day it had dried out and left spaces so they attempted making another one, this time tighter. Then they peeled the big vein out of the centre of the leaf, making thinner strips with which to weave. It was a challenge to keep a square but they discovered that the thin strips made a nicer-looking mat. We ended up using the first big ones for ground mats in front of the tent doors (they kept the interior of the tents cleaner). They made several smaller mats, and Ben made a small box with a lid. The campground people, accustomed to seeing more of the kids, came to ask if everything was all right. They were delightfully impressed with what the kids were creating and couldn't have cared less about us scoffing some leaves.

On Tuesday a motorhome arrived occupied by a man and his two young sons taking a holiday together. They parked a comfortable distance from us and the kids had someone their own age to interact with. Thursday morning the father invited us to walk to Itiquira Falls with them but I declined. I would have enjoyed the walk again but wasn't sure I could manage if I had to carry Whitney back. Ben jumped at the opportunity to get out of a math lesson and was gone. The four of them were back much sooner than I expected. Ben was excited and said, "Hey Mom, remember the tree we saw those guys hanging off when we were at the bottom, well I hung off it. Was it ever neat! You can see right to the bottom, and we waved at the people just like we waved to people at the top last week".

My stomach did a flop and I was relieved he was back.

He said, "It's really not dangerous, Mom, the tree doesn't hang over the edge. It probably just looks like it from down below". The man commented on Ben's good physical condition. They did a fast hike back from the falls in one hour and eighteen minutes—uphill.

I said, "That's good to hear but you should give that compliment to Ed. He is the one that encourages the fitness in the family and makes sure the kids are active." (He keeps after me too, but I'm one of those people that go at it off and on—not a good example to the kids.) He was interested in what we were doing for the children's education. Ben told him a little about our adventure, so his curiosity was up. He asked if I was a teacher—everyone asks that. For some reason I felt defensive, so put on airs and said not an elementary school teacher but I did teach photography part-time at three different community colleges as I moved around in my career, if that qualifies. Then he wanted to know about that. I told him that before I started having babies, photography was my trade and I taught it. After babies started coming all I did was practice my photography on them, but my main work was as a darkroom technician, and I have a little experience in many areas of the trade. Now I'm just a jack-of-all-trades—wife, mother, photographer, teacher, writer, cook, laundress, and seamstress—main ones—you name it. If it needs to be done and I feel like doing it, I probably can. He laughed but it is no laughing matter, and not always an easy job. He asked what the kids did for school. I explained that I really only expected them to do a lesson in math, a little writing and some reading most days. While travelling, the kids are getting history, geography, science and a third and fourth language through our discoveries and contacts in the countries we've been visiting. He shook his head and said, "Wow, you can't get a much better education than that."

I asked if his boys were on school vacation this week. "Yes, we all are, I'm a Phys. Ed teacher, and we decided to get out of the city for a few days." This explained his comments on Ben's physical condition and education. He learned his English in the States. His wife is American, but living here they speak Portuguese most of the time. He would like his boys to speak more English but they don't. They lived in Miami while the boys were babies, but both the teacher and his wife have better jobs in Brasilia. He asked about Ed's work, and when he found out Ed was a Chiropractor he wanted to know the phone number of the clinic. Having lived in the States, he had experienced the benefits of Chiropractic and was happy to learn there was someone in Brasilia. He wanted to get a treatment himself and send some people he knew who could use help as well. I told him Ed would be here on the weekend and he could talk with him then.

He said, "I'll miss him. We're going back to the city tomorrow; we have plans for the weekend."

That same afternoon Ben and the kids were at the pool with the boys. Jake was the first to return, "Mom, Ben cut his toe. He's coming back." Ben walked slowly and he had his headband wrapped around his toe; it was soaked with blood by the time he sat down. His big toe slipped into a hole in the ceramic tile getting out of the pool and when he pulled it out it was bleeding. He just wrapped it up; he didn't want the other kids to see what he had done. I got the first-aid box and unwrapped his toe. Everyone's reaction was the same, "Oh yuk, Ben". My stomach did a flop as the toe gushed with blood. Ben didn't realize it was as bad as it was either. I poured disinfectant over it and the bleeding slowed down. I cleaned the debris off of the toe and the second time I poured disinfectant over it Ben let out a scream. There was a chunk of skin scraped off the top of his toe from the toenail down three centimeters long and two centimeters wide almost to the bone. While I was trying to figure out what to do next the cut started to bleed hard again. I didn't have any non-stick pads left; we had used them all on his hand, but we had to stop the bleeding. I wrapped it in gauze and ran to the teacher to see if he had any bandages but that was a wasted effort. The only thing I came up with was a mini-sanitary pad; it was wrapped and would be sterile. When I got the pad out Ben yelled, "I'm not wearing that". I calmly replied, "You don't have any choice. We have to keep it clean."

At that point Ben couldn't stop shaking and his face was white. He may have been in some shock, but he had been swimming too. Dayna pulled out some warm clothes for him, Karina brought him a couple of blankets and I gave him a few drops of *Rescue Remedy*. The shaking stopped almost immediately. After he had some warm clothes on, I wrapped the toe and taped it as tight as he could stand to stop the bleeding.

Ben is always quick to resume where he left off after an injury and shortly after his ordeal he was up walking around. I said, "Ben, you have just forced yourself into a chair for the next day or two. Give your foot a chance to do what it needs to do to heal or it will bleed more. No swimming, no volleyball, no soccer and if you're looking for something to do with yourself, your pile of little-used books are sitting right there." He complained, of course, as any 13-year-old would, and asked if he could at least go to the bathroom. I said no, in a kidding way, but he believed me and whined, "What am I supposed to do?"

"Don't take me so seriously, Ben. Of course you can go to the bathroom but that's the only walking for a day, and I guess you can get out of doing dishes for a few days."

Dayna and Karina complained that it wasn't fair; he hadn't been helping with dishes last week either because of his hand.

Ed arrived Friday evening with fresh vegetables and cold beer for the weekend. There aren't any patients booked on Monday so we have one more day here. When we unwrapped Ben's toe for Ed to take a look it was still clean but needed to air out. Staying wet wouldn't allow it to scab over and build new skin.

Ed said, "Good one, Ben, almost to the bone. I guess you're not doing anything for a while are you?"

On Saturday morning the girls who Tanya and the kids got to know during our previous visit to Itiquira returned for overnight. They were happy to see us and jealous of Tanya being in Salvador. We were camped close to each other for the weekend. Ed and I got to know the parents—Wilton and Marina—while the group of kids disappeared together. He has a high-ranking job in a Brazilian phone company and speaks English well. He said Bell Canada has helped restructure and update the Brazilian communications system, and he has been part of the reconstruction since the beginning. He talks to people in Canada regularly for systems support. By the time Saturday evening rolled around he gave us his cell phone to call family at home in Canada, and we talked with Tanya this afternoon. They had lived in Africa for a year and knew how important it is to keep in touch.

Marina is a stay-at-home Mom. She cooks and does her own housework in a five-bathroom house. This is unusual for their social status in Brazil. They have four daughters, two in university (Fabian, 21, Vanessa, 19) and the two who are with them this weekend, (Denise, 13, and Karini, 12). They are special people. The first weekend they were here they had a girl about four years old with them, as well as four other teenage girls. Marina said she takes care of the little girl—her daughter's namesake—Vanessa, often. The mother is single and needs help.

Wilton is in excellent physical condition and loves to play volleyball with his girls. The girls are on a Brasilian swim team as well as a volleyball team—an active family.

Ed told them about chiropractic and adjusted everyone. Marina has had neck and shoulder pain for a long time and felt an improvement immediately. Ed adjusted her twice more on the weekend and she couldn't get over how much better she started to feel.

Marina looked at Ben's toe and she too thought it should be allowed to dry out. She said not to cover it but to disinfect it from airborne bacteria three times a day. It made sense but in Brasilia, it would be difficult to keep an open injury clean.

They told us the weekend of July 31st is an annual celebration and party at the campground, which they help to organize. They came this weekend to set up their tent and start preparations (it is still two weeks away). They left today and will return Friday. Marina will be staying the entire week before the fiesta, but Wilton will be back in Brasilia for the work week and will return again for the weekend party. They invited us to be here for it.

At the pool yesterday, Ed looked at the hole Ben cut his foot on. He said, "This great big pool and that little hole not much bigger around than your toe. What are the odds that your toe would get in there without you putting it in? You better ask yourself what message you've being given. Two bad cuts in two weeks.... something!" (It took five weeks for the skin to rebuild and close over the hole left in his toe. Ben was careful to keep the wound clean. Open worked best and he disinfected it several times a day.)

July 19, 1999:

While packing to return to Brasilia we heard an unusual sound that continued for some time before we realized where it was coming from. A pair of toucans sat in the tall eucalyptus above our heads. It was the first time we connected sounds to these birds. The birds were content to be in the tree until I had my hands on the camera, as soon as I aimed it in their direction, they flew away. We have seen a few flying in the wilds, but never sitting long enough that we could get a good look at them. Their beaks are as long as their bodies.

July 22, 1997: Brasilia Campground Again

At 6:15 a.m. I moved away from our camp to face the rising sun. I shut my eyes in meditation and let peace become a part of my body as the sun warmed my face. I became aware of the contentment in my life, and then heard a "whoosh" sound close to my left ear. Wings? I opened my eyes to catch what was passing but missed it. Then there was another "whoosh" on the same path and I found myself in the presence of a black toucan with a multi-colored beak no more than two meters away. In fact, a pair of toucans sat together in a pine in good view. It was the first time I had spotted toucans at the campground. Either it is mating season or toucans, parrots, araras and parakeets travel in pairs. Watching the two of them, I felt I was being touched by something special, mates travelling the same path. I had something to ponder... is that what Ed and I are doing with our lives? Ever since we started spending time together in 1980 we have travelled the same path. We have similar ideas about where we want to end up, and when both of us put our energy into the same goal we have usually accomplished it. Travel in Asia, the children, then travel with the kids in South America. I am thankful this man is my partner, and I like sharing the same path. My place is beside him. As partners we make each other's lives richer, more fulfilling, and fun. We have different jobs and both are equally important to providing a healthy, happy life for us as a family.

Since we left Canada, we have had no choice but to hold together and travel the same path. The drastic step that took us on this unusual path has taught us to depend on one another again. In this, we have found a relationship that has developed to a higher level. No doubt this explains the four different dreams I have had in the recent past about Ed and I getting married again.

Dream, July 3, 1999: Ed and I were in a room with several other couples, all of whom were about to be re-married. Everyone was on a bus, and the bus driver was driving extremely fast as if we were late for an appointment or event. Ed and I were at the front of the bus. The highway was curvy, hilly, and we travelled over rough road. As we came to the last hill the road opened out onto a plain where the driving got much easier. To our left were beautiful mountains and on the tops of them were many different kinds of houses and castles. Some had turrets, some were like those the Incas had built, and others were like the houses built by the Pueblo Indians of the North American southwest. I was in awe of the beauty. The bus started to fly.

Dream this week: Ed and I were getting married again. Many of Mom's family were at her house for the wedding. Aunt Freda, Verna and Mina arrived in a car driven by Uncle Bill. The room was full of family ready for the wedding at 2:00 p.m. I decided it was time to get dressed and when I was almost finished, Mom came in to dress as well. Jean was there but Ruth wasn't; I wondered why. Then Mom was gone. It was well past 2:00 and I was still trying to figure out my hat. I was wearing the same dress I was married in originally but the veil was not right. It was pinned to a hair band but it kept falling off. I tried to make it right, but it just didn't work. Then my headpiece was a baseball cap, forwards, backwards then covering my face. Then it was a pilot's hat with thick ear muffs covering my ears; I was satisfied with that. Mom came to tell me to hurry up, as everyone was waiting. I replied, "Well, they will just have to wait." Ed was patiently waiting for me; he knew I would be there when I was together.

This explains much of what has been going on in my head this past month or so. Try as I might to be what is expected of me by previous generations, I can't be. I just need to do my own flying, and I may need to wear earmuffs to get through some of the interference that has come from generations past. Ed knows the person I am capable of being, and waits for me to be that person.

In Anne Morrow Lindbergh's book, *Gift from the Sea,* she discusses bi-valve shells. Joan gave me a copy as a gift when we left Chile. I had read it before but was thoroughly enjoying my re-read and getting much more out of it during our northbound beach-hopping along the Brazilian coast. The beaches of the southern part of Brazil were littered with shells shaped liked butterfly wings. They reminded me of what she referred to as "Double Sunrise". Each side of the shell was marked with the same pattern of colourful rays spreading outward from the hinge to the edge of the shell. One half suggests the golden yellow sun rising, the other half a perfect reflection. As a bi-valve shell grows into a mature animal it builds itself in rings that grow from the hinge equally on each half. I find the shells symbolic. The halves are joined at the hinge, and that hinge is the delicate part of the shell; if you wish preserve it as a unit. When the joint is strong, the shell is almost impossible to penetrate. If it isn't carefully taken care of, the hinge breaks and the shell becomes two pieces. When two people become life partners, if that partnership isn't cared for and respected it is susceptible to being broken. The halves of the partnership must grow simultaneously if they are to achieve maximum strength together; if one side grows without the other, imbalance is created and weakness in the relationship has an opportunity to develop. When both halves grow together the hinge stays strong, providing protection from predators.

I really feel that removing ourselves from everything familiar in Canada for this period of time has helped Ed and me as partners. We forced ourselves to depend on each other and follow the same path. In doing so, both of us have grown as individuals and learned so many new things. And as partners we have grown together. My hope is that we can go back to Canada and give what we have to offer, and that it will come from two people who can count on one another for love and support.

Friday, July 23, 1999: Brasilia Campground Fire

There were many new visitors at the campground during our last week in Brasilia. One bathroom facility to accommodate us all before the onslaught was ridiculously inadequate. Now there was twice the demand on the scarce supply of water, which was running out in the afternoons. We had to wait until evening before it came back. Ed suggested that he take us back to Itiquira for our last week in the Brasilia area. He would camp out of the back of the van and use the clinic facilities. The kids jumped at the idea. We love it there. Before he left for work that Friday morning he gave us directions to take the tarp down, put the seats in the van and pack up as much as possible.

We had all day and decided to leave the tarp up until after the intense heat of the afternoon sun. There was a strong gusty wind, which was unusual in the early morning—it didn't usually pick up until later in the day. It gave the day a strange beginning. While I cleaned up the breakfast dishes, the kids tried to do some math but complained that the pages of their books wouldn't stay still. I said, "Don't bother guys, there is something unusual going on. Why don't you just go play?" And they did.

We didn't have any clean towels left and only a few clean clothes. I didn't think I should use valuable water to do laundry, but since others at the campground didn't seem to take water into consideration and the wind would dry the clothes in less than an hour, I decided to wash a few necessary things. Every so often, while doing so I got a whiff of smoke, but there wasn't a fire to be seen. Dayna walked up to me with a solemn look on her face and quietly said, "Mom, I think I started menstruating." She had just turned eleven; I hadn't expected this for at least another year.

"Wow Dayna, the beginning of being a grown-up girl. How do you feel about that?"

She cocked her head sideways and said, "It's okay I guess".

"It's too bad Tanya isn't here, you would have someone more your own age to talk with."

Being a private person about personal matters, she just wrinkled her nose at me. I said, "I guess I should stop and help you get fixed up." When I returned with the clothes Maria saw me rinsing them out and frowned. I don't know what the frown was for, as I was simply doing laundry. When I told her it was Dayna's first time her expression changed and she said something I didn't quite understand but it did come across somewhat sympathetically. When another whiff of smoke reached us, Maria said there was too much wind and she didn't like it.

With a sharp crack, a hot gust of wind took us by surprise. Startled, I jumped and turned around to see the tarp billowed and ready to sail. As the gust subsided the tarp sagged, blanketing our "house." The wind had put a three-meter rip in the tarp. Ben said, "Well I guess we aren't waiting until later anymore." We spent the next hour wrestling and freeing the tarp from where it was tied down over our "house." We attempted to fold it in a wind that wanted only to carry it away, and settled for rolling it crudely, and shoving it into the back of the van to prevent it from being carried away.

I went back to the laundry and finally got it hung up. The kids wanted noodles for lunch but the stove wouldn't stay lit so they settled for mustard and lettuce sandwiches. By then the smell of smoke was constant. There was a fire somewhere, but we couldn't see it on a walk around the grounds. The conditions were perfect for a good grassfire.

While I was packing our "kitchen" into the crates, Jake, Whitney and Karina came running from the opposite end of the grounds yelling, "Mommy, Mommy, there is a fire in the field." Everyone at the campground gathered along the fence line to watch the fire. I arrived to see a small tree in the distance explode into flames. The fire was still a good distance away, and there was little concern about it heading in our direction. Adrianna said it wasn't dangerous, that firemen would come to put it out. I asked, "Has anybody called the fire department?" She didn't know. We were downwind; each gust of wind brought it closer.

I called the kids and told them to come with me, but they resisted, wanting to watch the fire. I made somewhat of a scene and insisted they come with me. Again Adrianna said the fire wasn't dangerous. But back at our site we prepared for the worst. Ben, Dayna, Karina and I un-pegged the tents and attempted to move the big one with everything inside, to be sure we could drag it to the pavement should the need arise—we could. We packed everything else sloppily but quickly to be prepared to move in a hurry if necessary. Ben disconnected the gas and put the tank in the middle of the paved parking lot. I instructed the kids that if the fire got into the pines on our side of the parking lot the safest place for them to be would be on the block of pavement or in the building; there would be no stopping that kind of fire. I gave instructions to Jake and Whitney that if the fire got close they were to go into the building and stay there until I could come and get them. The building is brick, and there is pavement and gravel all around it; they would be safe there. Jake was panicking already and asked, "What about you, Mom? What are you going to do?"

I replied, "I'll just be away from you long enough to get the tents moved, okay?" He was satisfied.

We went back to see how far the fire had advanced. Everyone was still just standing there. The wind kept pushing it closer. When we could feel the heat, Lilianna let out a scream, breaking the trance everyone was caught up in. All of a sudden everyone scurried as it moved in.

The three campground workers realized their thin wood cabin could go up in flames. They grabbed their rakes and pulled the dry grass away from the cabin. One of them hacked off mango branches for beating the fire, and as it reached the cabin, the three of them managed to snuff out the flames. While attention was on saving the cabin, a pile of scrap wood further down the fence line caught and turned into a bonfire. The fire continued to move toward the tents of the people who arrived two days ago; the campground workers moved it. Lilianna carried her belongings out of their "house." Ben disconnected and moved her gas tank onto the pavement and did the same for Katarina who was cleaning out her tent in a mad fury. I asked if I could help. She said, "Yes, yes." The girls and I helped her move their clothing and mattresses into the brick building. Jake was on my heels, scared and crying, Whitney sticking close to him. After carrying an armful of clothes into the building I stopped, took Jake by the arms, looked him in the face and said, "Jake, stay right here. Whitney, stay with him, you will both be safe here."

In a calm, big-sister tone of voice Whitney said to Jake, "You stay with me here, okay?" I wonder how it is that she managed to come into this world after him. But then again she always lets him go first. Why would I think it would be any different coming from the spirit world?

The workers managed to beat out the flames before they got to Lilianna's and Katarina's dwellings and the two small tents were easily moved onto the pavement. When everything was moved that could be moved, everyone took to beating the flames which continued to eat their way forward. The water barrels that Maria had been filling every morning were quickly emptied (the precious water). At that point our tents, as well as Adrianna's and Ricardo's, were not in danger. Everyone beat the fire or carried buckets of water to spread on the ground in front of it. Adrianna told me not to let Ben get close to the fire. He was beating it out and keeping it back as much as anyone else. He knows what he is capable of. Another heap of dry grass caught fire. Raking the grass back and wetting the ground in front of the fire slowed it down enough to beat out the smaller flames.

The campground chief arrived back from his outing, stopped his car in the middle of the lot, picked up a fresh cut branch and started to beat at the fire too. My arms ached from carrying pails of water. Ben and the chief furiously beat at the fire in the grass pile at the fence. Several buckets of water slowed that particular part of the fire down to bring the last of it under control. But other sections of fire were getting ahead of us. A couple of pines started to burn, and the fire was at the base of a few more—it looked hopeless.

Then, for some unknown reason, the wind just stopped as if someone had turned it off. The air hung thick with smoke and there was a lull for an eerie moment— then the wind started to blow again. But by the grace of God, it did an about-face. The flames didn't have much fuel left, and the big part of the fire in the field moved north away from us. As long as the wind kept blowing in that direction the campground was out of danger. Jake and Whitney felt safe enough to help stomp out the small flames that were left and had fun doing it.

A group of four firemen showed up and walked through the field behind the fire. They caught me by surprise, dressed in black fire duds, masks and each carrying a long pole with a chunk of flat perforated rubber on the end for slapping out flames. They looked like four *Darth Vaders* coming over the rise amid the lingering smoke. The campground people cheered them on in sarcasm, arriving when the worst was over. In actual fact, they don't try to put out big fires. All they attempt to do with fire in the open is control the edges. They don't have equipment to drown out such out-of-control fires in the countryside and a grass fire of this sort encourages the re-growth of vegetation. They just kept walking, following the fire. We really could have used their help a little earlier.

We gathered together, laughed and talked. There was no great damage, just a good portion of scorched ground on the one side of the parking lot and two burnt trees. We were lucky the wind changed directions when it did. The chief patted Ben on the back and thanked him for his help. We laughed about how dirty we were and joked about the water running out. At least we all smelled the same. Juan stumbled out of his tent and surveyed the situation; he had slept through the entire afternoon and fire. The chief attempted to move his car to his parking spot but the car had a flat tire, which was curious.

The campground's one shower was kept busy that afternoon and, miraculously, the water held out. Dayna took the clothes off the line and put them right back into the washtub. They were dry but full of dust and they smelled of smoke.

Ricardo and Francesca were shocked when they arrived home for the evening. Adrianna filled them in on the events of the day. After being told the story, the people in the two small tents were thankful to have had their tents moved; the ground was scorched where they had been set up. Ed returned after dark and asked what the smoke smell was. He got the story in pieces from the kids. Karina said, "I bet Tanya is really happy; she is in Salvador today." Karina strained her arm carrying pails of water. Dayna said, "We stayed in Brasilia one day too many." I had no dinner ready, everything was in chaos and the way things were packed and stowed, they wouldn't fit into the van. The tarp was down but only because of the wind. We were exhausted. Ed bought us a take-out supper at *Carrefour*. Ricardo and Mayara visited. Ricardo wanted to hear Ben's story and Ben gave him a play-by-play of the events of the day. He laughed as he told Ricardo about Juan sleeping through the disaster. Ricardo shook his head, and sadness took over his face. He doesn't like watching what is happening to his brother. Ricardo can't even talk to him any more. He said they are going separate ways at the end of August; he can't help his brother when he doesn't even see that he needs help. How does one reach another in despair when the other is unaware of what is happening to him and how it affects his family? There has to be a way.

Everything smelled of smoke but we slept out of sheer exhaustion.

July 24 to 29, 1999: Itiquira, for the fourth time

During our last week at Itiquira, there were more people at the campground than we had ever shared it with previously. Marina and the girls noticed our van immediately as we drove in. The girls followed us along until we stopped and gave the kids hugs as they stepped out of the doors. They seemed sincerely happy to see us. The girls are on their school holiday and this is the week that leads up to the weekend fiesta. Several families are staying the entire week.

On Sunday morning Ben got arguing with Marina's girls who didn't believe we had hiked to the Itiquira Falls. But Ed assured them we had. Moments later Wilton was dragged over to talk with Ed to learn about our hike—the girls wanted to do it. Wilton told the girls that he didn't have time to do it with them, but they had all week, and Ben could be their guide. They were happy at that prospect but it didn't sound like such a great idea to me.

Marina is a busy woman. Several small groups of family and friends have been coming and going all week. They would set their tent up to reserve their space, spend the night and leave in the morning to return on Saturday. Marina fed everyone who came to set up, and as the parents left, Marina was left in charge of even more kids. The circle of tents around her large one kept getting bigger.

As Ed was leaving Monday morning he told me to be sure to tell Ben that if he takes the girls to the falls he is to use common sense and no hanging off the tree or being a daredevil. I felt the same way, not confident that a group of eleven-to fourteen-year-olds should go to the top of a 200-meter cliff on their own. I said, "I wish you had told him, Ed; he respects your opinion more than mine. When it comes from me he just thinks I'm being an over-protective mother."

"Well, tell him I said he's to be careful then."

As if that makes any difference—it would still be coming from me. As it turned out, Marina didn't think it was such a great idea either. Being responsible for several young people that aren't her own, she wasn't going to let them go without an older escort. The girls argued with her, and Marina threatened rather loudly to go back to Brasilia immediately and forget the fiesta. The subject was closed. She was right. If it had been just Ben and her two girls I would not have had the same concern either. The larger a pack of wild dogs gets, the wilder and more dangerous they become. Somehow, with kids, logical sense and sanity gets lost in a crowd.

After the issue was set aside, the kids settled into doing other things together. Denise and Karini are good at including the younger children. They played volleyball, football, swam at the pool, learned each other's card games and played snooker at the canteen. After dark they sang songs around the fire, and played flashlight tag and hide-and-seek until the wee hours of the night. I didn't see much of our guys except during meals. It was wonderful to watch the interaction. Our kids' Portuguese improved and the others picked up a lot of English.

By Wednesday afternoon I decided I needed some activity and asked the kids to walk to the Indaia Falls with me. Ben was not pleased but came anyway. While walking the trail before it dropped into the valley of the river, we were above the trees in the river valley. We could hear noises of cracking branches and rustling leaves in the still air. After settling our belongings at the pool of the falls, the tree sounds seemed to surround us and I grew curious as to what was causing them. When I watched more closely I spotted a monkey and exclaimed, "Hey, look at the monkey." Once we knew what to look for it didn't take long before we'd spotted more monkeys than we could count. They had large bodies with brown-black fur around black faces. They were about two feet long, not including the tail, which was much longer than the body. We watched them forage for food, breaking branches off and eating the bark and blossoms. They weren't concerned about us and weren't shy. Two of them came within 20 feet, as curious about us as we were about them. Dayna put half her banana on the ground. One monkey came part way down the tree, cautiously scouted the area, jumped down, snatched the banana, jumped back up and ate it in the safety of the tree. Through the tops of the trees, after almost an hour of foraging in our vicinity, they crossed and continued downstream, and were gone. Ben said, "Okay, time to go; we saw what we came to see". He was glad he came after all.

July 29, 1999:

I lay in bed listening to the morning symphony of birds, picking out the individual sounds, and thought that I'd better write them down; I would never remember them all.

1. A large black bird with a long neck that makes a warble sound deep in its throat.

2. A small bird, chickadee size, that is mostly red, has peacock-like crown feathers, and has a high singing voice.

3. A brown bird, robin size, whose whole body moves when it chirps and calls.

4. I don't know where they come from, but there are blue jay-like scolding sounds in the mornings—wake-up calls. Whatever birds make them don't really sound like jays, but they have the same scolding attitude.

5. There is another bird that could be a type of robin, but its breast isn't red. It is around looking for crumbs, but I haven't heard it say much.

6. Parakeets chirp, squawk, and chatter back and forth. They are the same colour of green as the sun in the palm leaves. They are curious and inquisitive. The wild ones will stay and, as Ben says, "watch you as you watch them." They give the impression that they are happy birds.

7. We don't get close to wild parrots at all; they are an elusive bird. However, we do see them flying from a distance and hear their noisy squawks. There are two at the campground that are pets of the workers; their wings are clipped. They have the run of a large part of the place, but they don't fly. During the weeks when we were just about the only people here we got to know them. Once they learn to trust you being around they can be comical to interact with, mocking and repeating your sounds and actions. I don't know who was mocking whom one afternoon. When the kids went to say hello to the birds, the birds started to lift their legs and wings demonstrating what the kids were trying to get them to do on a previous visit. The birds started it and got the kids going. They appeared especially to enjoy mimicking laughter, and bouncing their heads while doing so.

8. I call it the Yellow Bandit, a plentiful bird about the same size as a blue jay. It is yellow with brownish-black wings, a black Zorro mask over its eyes, a white stripe above that and then a black-brown cap on the top of the head. This is a common bird, and we have seen it all over Brazil (maybe a flycatcher of some sort).

9. There are mourning doves every day, morning and night.

10. There are two owls here. They hoot back and forth some mornings before daybreak. It sounds like stereo when we are in the middle.

11. Often a peculiar sound comes from a distance. At first we thought it was a bunch of puppies crying, but it was at the zoo where we connected the sound and bird. I still don't know the name of it, as the name wasn't posted on the cage, but it is a large grey bird with a white stripe between its eyes. We haven't seen these guys in the wilds.

12. There are always woodpeckers pecking at the coconuts to get to the oily-tasting insides.

13. Araras or in English, macaws. We are told there are 13 pairs in the area. Everyday I get a glimpse of them flying back and forth. They squawk while flying, alerting others to their whereabouts. They fly with greater ease than parrots and much higher in the sky. The macaws in this area are large birds with lemon-yellow and sky-blue plumage, and tails three times as long as their bodies.

14. We have seen only a few toucans here in Itiquira. They make a peculiar sound. The kids say they sound like pigs grunting, and I almost agree with them but hear more of a similarity to a low croaking frog. The park attendant says there are six pairs in the area.

15. Oystercatchers, at least that was what Mom called them when she was visiting in Chile. They're a gull-like bird with brown and black markings on a mostly white body.

16. On our walks to the river there are always white egrets in the fields with the cows. They are a common bird all over South America.

17. There is a creature whose sound is like bubbles being blown into a cup of liquid—maybe a frog or tree toad of some sort. I hear it often but haven't figured out who the creator is.

18. Hummingbirds aplenty, the same as in Chile: green and black with a white breast.

19. I call it the South American Chickadee because of its character, but it is more sparrow-like. It is not afraid to get close to human beings and often cleans our "floor" for us. It is a small brown bird, no more than three to four inches long. Its song reminds me of a cardinal—can it ever sing!

20. There is another bird here that lives in Chile as well and I know it is a sparrow but I don't know the type.

21. There is a bird about the size of a robin but completely black. It is not very special as far as appearance goes but it, too, sings a beautiful song. It is not around much until later in the day.

22. There is another sound I haven't placed—like a kitten crying. I hear it often but there aren't any kittens around.

23. In the mornings as the sun is rising, before the wind picks up, there is a buzzing sound. The first time I heard it I thought we had camped beside a bees' nest, but investigation revealed nothing of the sort. When really listening I noticed it came from all around me, and the only thing I could figure out is that it was millions of insects busily going about their business. I hear it only on mornings when the air is still and there are fewer birds to drown it out.

Parakeets at Itiquira

There are so many parakeets here in Itiquira, and I have had plenty of time to observe them this week. Sometimes they fly in a flock of 200 or more and are extremely noisy with their cheery sounds. Right now almost every palm tree has a pair residing in it. This is definitely mating season. Several times we have had male parakeets fighting over a female on the ground beside us—once on top of the tarp, once right in our living space beside us while we were having breakfast. Two days ago a competition ended with two birds in one palm tree and four in another engaged in some kind of staring match. The four chattered and scolded the other two. The pair patiently waited for the four birds to leave, and when they did I witnessed the mating of parakeets. It surprised me to see how gentle and loving they were with each other, rubbing heads and bodies together, "kissing" with their beaks. The male got on top of the female several times with caresses and kisses in between. It went on and on in a display of true affection, not just survival of the species. It affirmed my belief there is more to the animal world than what modern-age man will ever take the time to understand.

When the sound of a Toucan came through this morning, I jumped out of bed but missed him. They are tough birds to get a glimpse of—he got me up anyway. I made my morning fix of Brazilian brew and found a spot to wait for the sun. I had time before the kids would be up. It is so good to have an hour to talk with God, and this morning all I could say was thank you, thank you for our time here, thank you for the monkeys we saw and photographed in the wild yesterday, thank you for so many encounters with different birds, thank you for keeping Tanya safe and giving me the opportunity to grow. I feel no need but to be thankful. I am content here right now, but I am a little cut off from reality, or am I not? There is the reality of the city and there is the reality of nature, both are real in different ways. My reality is that wherever we live, I still make meals, do dishes, laundry and schoolwork—our daily routine doesn't vary that much. So why does it feel so much like paradise when we are camping, sleeping on the ground and reducing our belongings? It just goes to show that paradise can be anywhere if there is inner peace. Itiquira is a special place, though; it kept calling us back.

Sira and Carmen wanted Ed to work a couple more weeks while arrangements were being made for someone to take over. Carmen offered the rest of us accommodation at their cottage in Barra Grande, but to get there we will have to miss out on the fiesta at Itiquira. There are many disappointed people, but it couldn't be worked out otherwise.

On Thursday evening Ed was back, and Marina came to be adjusted. We had the opportunity to talk. I made a remark about this week not being a holiday for her. She agreed and said she had already cooked ten kilos of rice and had called

Wilton to bring more food and beer for the weekend. They thought they had brought enough when they came. She just laughed. She was pleased with how well the kids got along and said she wished we were staying for the weekend. She didn't stay long, as she had more food to prepare.

I see myself in Marina and her family. She is living the life that we—I—left behind in Canada: a huge house to take care of, mother to more than her own, involved in community, always taking people in and being social with everyone. I look at the way she goes about her life, she appears to be a happy person and I think, "Yeah, I can do it again". I am almost ready to get involved in life again, on a smaller scale than what we left, though. I still need to keep some of myself for me. I don't know whether she does that or not, I should have asked her that and if she doesn't, how does she stay so sane and happy?

Friday morning we took our camp down and packed things up. While trying to load the interior of the van we worked around 11 young people sitting inside not wanting us to leave. The kids traded jewelry and hats and took pictures of each other. With the final packing complete I went to say good-bye to Marina. She was sweeping out her tent and had food on the stove. I gave her a hug and said it was great to get to know her. She hung on and said the same. I didn't think I was going to cry leaving the Brasilia area, even though I grew to enjoy it so much. But when we parted she had tears in her eyes and that was the straw that did it for me.

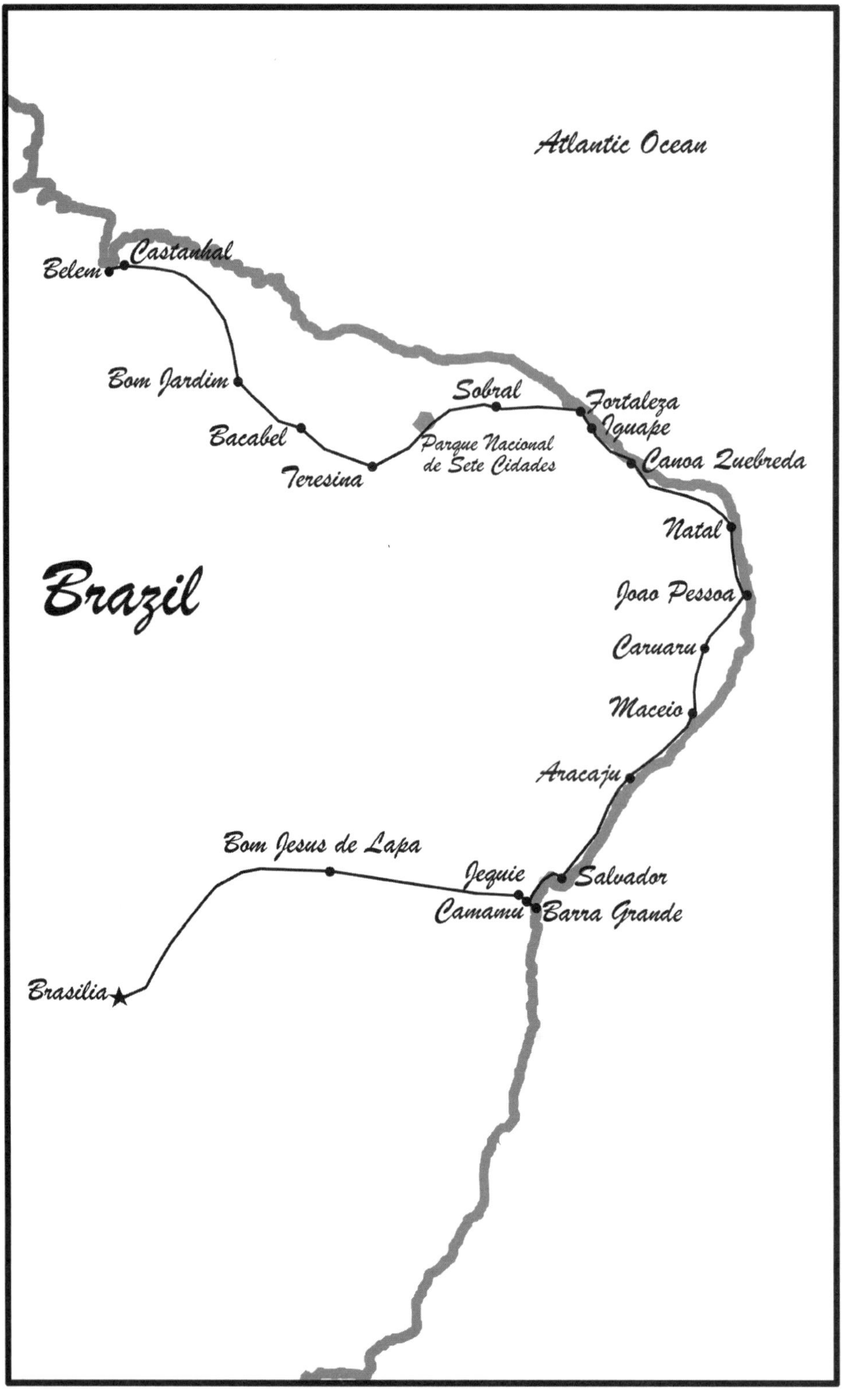

Atlantic Ocean
Castanhal
Belem
Bom Jardim
Bacabel
Teresina
Sobral
Parque Nacional
de Sete Cidades
Fortaleza
Iguape
Canoa Quebreda
Natal
Brazil
Joao Pessoa
Caruaru
Maceio
Aracaju
Bom Jesus de Lapa
Jequie
Salvador
Camamu
Barra Grande
Brasilia

BACK TO BEACH HOPPING

August 1 to 15, 1999: Barra Grande

We backtracked on the same roads that brought us inland, another overnight stay in Bom Jesus de Lapa, and we were in Jequie by 1:00 p.m. Saturday, July 31. Señora Borges, Carmen and Sira's mother, welcomed us with open arms. She immediately set her employees to work preparing a huge meal, and then sat us down in the living room at the opposite end of the house to wait for the meal to be put on the table. She talked, asked a few questions and talked some more. The kids were impatient but managed to sit until food was served. The Señora seemed to be a lonely woman. Her husband had recently passed away and her children are gone with families of their own. We had a wonderful dinner and were not allowed to help clean up. She gave us directions to where we could purchase the food we needed for the coming weeks in Barra Grande, and we set out to do so. Carmen arrived that evening and the following day we stayed for the midday meal to celebrate her mother's birthday.

The land between Jequie and Camamu, cultivated country, is situated in the Atlantic coastal rainforest. Almost anywhere, palms, bananas and clove trees (the fragrant spice) grow. Cacao trees are beneath them. The latter get a stronger start to their 25- to 30-year lives under larger trees. Cacao requires year-round mean temperatures 18 to 32 degrees Celsius and plenty of rainfall. Dry soil results in poor production and damaged trees. The coast of Bahia state has those perfect conditions. The cacao tree originated in Brazil and has been used as a food in northern South America and Central America for more than 10,000 years. At one time Brazil was the largest producer of the cacao bean but it now ranks fifth in the world and barely meets its own market demands.

We stopped at the edge of a farm to get a better look, and it wasn't long before a man appeared, wondering what we were doing. Carmen introduced us as if she knew the man, informing him that we were Canadian and had never seen how cocoa grows. A huge smile spread across his face; he was more than happy to give us an education. All he wore was a pair of pants cut off just above the knee, and flip-flops. He appeared to be in his fifties. His deeply tanned skin had a leathery look, yet every muscle in his body was finely toned without an ounce of fat. He located his machete, searched through the plants and cut a few pods off to give to us. A whack of the machete opened up the cacao pod and revealed neat rows of seeds individually encased in a thick, white membrane. The seeds are what produce chocolate, but they aren't good to use or eat until mature, fermented and dried. He and Carmen both showed us how to eat the

Cocoa Man

Abandoned canoe and kids. Barra Grande, Brazil

sweet pulpy insides of the pod and leave the seeds; it was a tasty treat. The farmer loaded us up with chocolate pods. We took several photos and said our thank-yous and goodbyes before continuing to Camamu.

Before we reached the ocean, the sky dumped rain on us, and sunshine broke through intermittently. The coast and inland Brazil have opposite wet seasons.

Carmen arranged a private boat to take us and our heap of possessions across the bay to Barra Grande. As we arrived at the dock, the sun dropped below the horizon. It was barely a 15-minute walk to the cottage but by the time we got there it was pitch dark. There is no in between here—either it is daylight or the dark of night. I need to know why that is. The first thing we did after opening the cottage was put an evening meal together, then Carmen showed us how to put the beds together complete with mosquito nets tucked under mattresses—we wouldn't be able to sleep without them.

Early Monday morning, Carmen was on her way back to Salvador and Ed to Brasilia for another two weeks' work. Our first day in Barra Grande gave the rest of us a clear blue sky. The cottage had been closed up tight. In the daylight we could see it was a haven for spiders, bugs and mildew. We cleaned and aired everything and by the end of the day we were nicely settled in a comfortable space. Rain fell almost all day, every day, of the week after that. The few clothes we washed didn't dry; they just mildewed and had to be washed again. The week could have been a disaster, except for walks on the beach between downpours and finding some really fabulous shells.

Karina, whose breathing is so sensitive to some stimuli, was having a hard time with the mildew. She actually sounded asthmatic. I didn't know how to deal with that and feared I was going to have to move us all out before our two weeks were up. But a couple of days later, with the house opened up, the mildew receded and the breathing problem eased.

The house was full of mosquitoes finding refuge from the rain. Every time a wardrobe door was opened, it disturbed them and they flew out in a cloud. We woke up daily under nets blanketed with the little creatures but surprisingly few bites. During evenings, before we hid under the nets, the only way to avoid being bitten was to cover up in loose-fitting clothing. The mosquitoes would bite right through tight clothing. In all our travels, this place and the Rio Parana in Argentina are the only places where we encountered mosquitoes as bad as they are during spring at home. Once we figured out how to deal with our environment we were fine.

I am glad to say that my latest search for head lice reveals that we have them conquered. When I discovered them on Whitney's head a few weeks ago, I went through everyone's hair, and it appeared to be a female problem. Dayna, Karina Whitney and I all had them crawling around on our scalp but I found none on Ed, Ben or Jake. It seemed a little odd when everyone sleeps in the same tent all the time. Ed asked Carmen what was used in Brazil to clean them out of hair, and she put my mind at ease. Her first comment was, "It's a wonder you haven't had them before this with the way you have been living." Apparently, head lice are a common affliction in Brazil and not many people are lucky enough to go without an infestation at some point. It was encouraging to hear but we still needed them cleaned out of the hair on our heads. We spent an evening at the apartment in Brasilia where Carmen attempted to do just that with the product we purchased for the purpose. It was costly, smelly, not very easy to use and had to be repeated a few times to be sure the little creatures were eliminated. When we were working on our second treatment at the campground, Adrianna saw us struggling with our problem. She came over and told us to use plain white vinegar as a hair rinse once a week and we would never have them in our hair. Every one of us has been using plain white vinegar as a hair rinse since. A quarter cup of vinegar in a cup of water: rub it in and rinse it out, or you can use it straight too. Those of us who were infested experienced a warm sensation all over our scalps when rinsing with the vinegar the first time. We anticipated the same sensation the next time we rinsed but it never happened again. The warmth must have had something to do with all those bugs dying. One bottle of vinegar cleaned all our heads out at a fraction of the cost of the single use bottle of chemical made especially for the purpose.

My grandmother used vinegar as a hair rinse often and similarly I often received a vinegar rinse as a child. It was probably a lice treatment then too. You have to eat raw garlic when you have a cold, you have to eat garlic and onions all the time to keep your blood clean, you have to eat pickles and vinegar to not get worms, and vinegar was the best thing for hair (no matter how much screaming was involved in the process of applying it). There is truth to "old wives' tales". Vinegar makes hair soft and, shiny and loosens the tangles after washing. I wonder if I can come up with a fresh scent vinegar.

We are several days out of Brasilia. I am sitting here on the porch watching the never-ending rain, reflecting on our time in that city and looking forward to seeing Tanya again. Her absence has created some new dynamics and understanding within our family. The truth is, Tanya is doing well, she is happy and having fun. I miss her but our family still manages to function, just differently. She has been attending school with Roberta and loved being the centre of attention—finally a positive experience. The girls and teachers wanted to get to know her.

We have spoken with her a few times, and she would have nothing to do with coming back. Even a car theft right under her nose didn't make her feel insecure and want to come home. One evening while attending an event at the school, Roberto (Carmen's husband), Carmen, Roberta and Tanya stepped out of the vehicle they had just parked. Three young men, one with a handgun, came up to them, took the keys and left the four of them standing there as they sped off with the vehicle. It unnerved Carmen and Roberto, and they did lose their car, but no one was harmed. Tanya said it happened so fast she hardly realized what was going on until the car was gone. The incident only sunk in afterwards, but she still felt content enough to stay right where she was.

She left an empty space here though. Whitney mentions her the most and as I think about it, I miss her companionship, her smiling face and messy habits. I miss how much help she was with Jake and Whitney, taking care of them and being their second mom when I got to my wit's end. Now I can see how much of an example she is to her sisters. They have had space to grow up and take on more responsibility in her absence. It has been interesting to watch the changes we were more or less forced into. Nothing ever stays the same, does it? It is important to grow with the changes.

The one thing I don't miss is the love-hate relationship she and Ben have with each other. Our life has been more peaceful in that respect. I remember listening to Adele Faber and Elaine Mazlish speak at a conference once. They are the authors of *Siblings Without Rivalry* and *How To Talk So Kids Will Listen and How To Listen So Kids Will Talk,* two valuable books that started to give me ideas of how to gain cooperation and to communicate more effectively with my children and others. One comment that stands out in my mind was that parents need to realize that some children will never get along, and all we can hope to do is help them live in the same house together. I accepted that then, but now as I have grown and understand more about life and relationships, I feel there is more to it than that. It can be better. When reading parenting books and doing study groups with other parents I realized that we as parents create most of the rivalry that happens between our children. Today, I recognize when I am careless and do such things, but in the beginning I was unaware of what I was creating. Those study groups came long after the damage had been done between Tanya and Ben.

Ben claims that Tanya hates him, that I hate him, and that I always take her side. Tanya says Ben just always bugs her and won't leave her alone. Ben would like to have a different relationship with Tanya and be able to do things with her, but she says he bugs her too much. It doesn't matter what he does; he just bugs her. They don't dare sit in the van or at a table beside each other. More often that not, if they are in close proximity, they end up in some kind of argument.

I am able to understand now that it was probably I who created this situation. When Tanya was born, the moment I laid eyes on her I felt that she was what I was living for. Suddenly my life wasn't so dispensable, and there was valid purpose for me walking the earth. I was awed by the miracle Ed and I took part in creating. I didn't want to be separated from her and went into the new relationship with a devotion I didn't know I had. As she grew, we read and played together. I talked to her all the time about everything, whether she understood or not. She is the only person I have let hear my inner thoughts and feelings.

Then Ben was born and I had another little person who demanded almost 100 percent of my time. I loved him as deeply as Tanya and was ecstatic when he was born, but resented not being able to carry on the same kind of relationship with Tanya that we had before Ben came into our lives. I was totally unprepared for the change. He was a demanding baby and it was difficult to do anything else other than hold him to keep him happy. I told Tanya my feelings. If we were reading and Ben woke up and interrupted us I would say, "Boy, it's hard for you and me to get time together." I remember one night while Ed was working late, I got angry with her for not leaving me alone to put Ben to sleep so she and I could have time together. Tanya was barely two years old; it was an unreasonable expectation. Why wouldn't she resent him for taking me away from her, especially since I reinforced her resentment by saying the wrong things about Ben?

Some psychologists say that by the time a child is two or three he or she already has an ingrained impression of what the world is like. When it comes right down to it, I'm positive it was I who gave Tanya the attitude that her brother bugs us and interferes all the time. I regret not taking the time to learn more about human relationships before the children were born. They are doing well, but with more effective parenting life could go more smoothly.

Now, after possibly finding the true reason for their difficult relationship, maybe I can help them both. With a little understanding of where their hard feelings come from, possibly they will be able to forgive me for my errors and clear some of the tension between themselves. I know when I have a better understanding of what is going on I can change how I am, and that understanding is always the first step. If I want my children's behaviour to change, I must change my own actions, words and behaviour first. I look forward to being with Tanya again. I may only have a few years left before she really has a life of her own. I'd like them to be good ones.

On the rainy days, which took up more than half of our two weeks, we baked cakes and cookies, played card games, read three novels aloud, and the kids spent hours at schoolwork just for the lack of something else to do. We spent the sunny, days exploring, and enjoyed them immensely. The cottage is on the bay side. We walked the beach to the ocean side a couple of times; I even swam. The beach was a wealth of sea creatures and the best shell-picking beach we had ever set foot on. Dayna found a 10-inch spiral but it had a live animal in it. She didn't want to throw him back. Ben found a sea turtle skeleton and every one of us found large unusual shells and washed-up chunks of coral the size of softballs—some even larger. Pieces of black coral littered the beach. On two occasions, at a high-tide swamp, we watched white herons and discovered them to be graceful birds despite their lanky proportions. Coconut trees were plentiful and Ben pulled a few down daily to have some coconut water.

Bira, our neighbour, is a fisherman. He is gone before sun-up each morning and is back by 10 a.m. with his catch. Barra Grande is a fishing village that is quickly becoming an attractive place to holiday. But because it is accessible by road only during dry season it is saved from too many outsiders coming in and changing it too quickly. The fishermen here build traps just off the beach; tall poles are secured into the ocean floor to hold homemade fishnets. The nets are made from the casing that wraps a new coconut branch. As the leaves open up, the casing breaks away and falls apart into stringy fibre. The fibre is twisted into strings

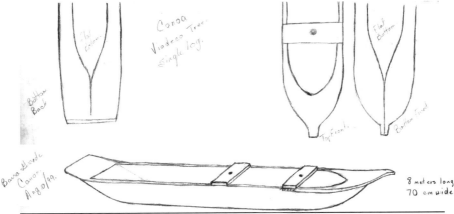

and tied together to make nets. Bira spent many of his non-fishing hours in his hammock twisting fibre into strings.

After living with the people in this village and observing their lifestyle, it didn't take long before I thought that these "poor" people—and there are many who likely feel life should be better—have an enviable lifestyle. I thought, "Wow, what a way to live!" From what I have observed, they have food to stay healthy, and live a relatively simple lifestyle. What is the sense in living a stressful life to make more money and have more things? These people live mostly with what the immediate environment provides and are close to their families. They work, yes, but in a place where most of us in Canada dream of spending a week's vacation in winter. Commuting to work is a stroll down a white sandy beach and a ride in a dugout canoe. What a life! I don't understand how or why the human race has managed to complicate life so much.

Rainy days are hard to take after growing accustomed to the blue, sunny, rainless skies of the desert. They put a damper on everyone's spirits. The kids fought more and the whole family seemed to be out of sorts when it was raining. The kids didn't like being away from their Dad. Neither did I, and when I realized that the separation was the original plan while Ed was working in Brasilia, I was thankful it didn't work that way.

On Tuesday of our second week, when it had rained all day again, every one of us was feeling down and moody. The parakeet's wing Whitney found in Itiquira, and which she asked me to keep in good shape for her, fell to the floor from between the pages of my journal. I picked it up and really looked at it; delicate but strong and beautiful, the feathers fold and fit together perfectly. It is impossible for anything to fly without two healthy, strong wings working together. Ed is my other half, on whom I depend, and I missed his presence terribly. Just when my tears were about to fall, a blackbird let out the cheeriest song behind me. I turned to see him sitting on the peak of Biras' house. Behind him, against black raining clouds, were two full arcs of the most vibrant colours I have ever seen in a rainbow. I shouted excitedly, "Two rainbows guys, come and see." They rushed out of the cottage. We watched the brilliance of the colours grow and fade in relative proportion to the intensity of rain and sunshine. In awe of the phenomenon, Karina asked, "What makes a rainbow, Mom, how does it work?" I explained that white light splits into the colours of the spectrum as it passes through the water droplets. It was a lengthy explanation to help her understand, and as I was providing it, all kinds of interesting ideas started to fly through my head.

The previous days of rain "dampened our spirits" when there was so little to do and we expected to be spending time on the beach. When the sun was out everyone was happier. It is sun and rain together that make a rainbow. Hard times and good times together create our lives. It is the rain in my life that has brought forth growth, and has made the sunshine so truly appreciated. Is a rainbow an illusion or reality? It is a real thing, but it could be considered an illusion. We can create a rainbow under the proper circumstances, yet it is impossible to take hold of it, apart from how the light registers on the mind. Is life an illusion or reality? It depends on how we choose to see it. Pain, joy, tears, laughter, sadness, happiness—are they illusions or realities? All of them could be one or the other and all are a matter of how we personally choose to perceive, interpret and deal with those feelings. We can live the illusion of sadness or we can live the illusion of happiness, but we can also live with both together in balance. Darkness is the absence of light; it takes happiness to know sadness and vice-versa, and the idea holds true for any opposites. When we know both and we choose to use both we radiate the realities of life, touching all those we come into contact with.

I felt like a lifeless single wing not getting anywhere, but decided to change how I perceived the illusion I was living at the moment. How can I expect the kids to be happy and capable of coping if their mother is an old grump? Life can be warm and bright or can be dampened and dark, but we can't have life on earth without both. I found a pot of gold right there among my own illusions.

Our last three days in Barra Grande were perfect beach days, full of sunshine. I decided to act like cheery sunshine, and that's what we got from nature. The power of the mind... is it possible???

August 15 to August 22, 1999: Salvador, Brazil

Roberto and Carmen were at the dock as planned to pick us up the morning of the 15th. The distance between Camamu and Salvador is about 120 kilometers, but we took the better part of the day to get there, enjoying the sights. We visited more *cachoeiras* and watched rock-climbers testing their skills alongside the falls. We stopped at a rubber plantation to observe the tapped trees and see how the latex is collected into pails. It is basically the same principle as collecting maple syrup. A diagonal cut about 18 inches long is made in the bark of the tree and a pail catches the latex that seeps to the bottom of the scored bark.

The Bahian Women who fed us a meal of acaraje

Rubber is another reminder of unfortunate industrial developments of the past. The rubber tree *hevea brasiliensis* is native to the Amazon rainforest. Long before the European discovery of the Americas, the Amerindians of the rainforest were making use of the latex for waterproof containers and footwear. As the diversity of the product was recognized, the demand for rubber grew rapidly, creating an economic boom in both Belem and Manaus. Brazil attempted to maintain control of the industry by not allowing export of seeds or seedlings. But as supply could not keep up to demand, Henry Wickham smuggled 70,000 seeds to Britain in 1876. They were propagated and seedlings were shipped to British colonies in tropical Asia, where plantations were quickly established. It was the beginning of cost-effective production. Rubber was still being collected from the wild in Brazil and although plantations were attempted, many didn't survive because of leaf rot that infected the stands of trees. In Asia, without natural enemies, the trees thrived. By the time the Brazilians had planted stands of trees in other states, away from the diseases that afflicted them in Amazonas, Asian production had taken over the market. Today, Brazil produces enough rubber for its own demand and is aiming at joining the international scene again.

From the ferry that took us across Baía de Todos os Santos—Bay of All Saints—we had a delightful view of Salvador, the port and the lighthouse on the point. For two centuries, Salvador was the capital of Brazil, until Rio de Janeiro became the economic power in 1763. Salvador is the third largest city in Brazil. Roberto explained, "In Salvador you could go to mass in a different church 365 days a year and not visit them all." The kids counted 18 steeples, easily picking them out on the cityscape before our approach to the dock. Roberto took us the long way around the city just for the opportunity to see a little more of it before arriving at his and Carmen's home late in the afternoon.

Roberta and Tanya were at an afternoon concert in celebration of Tanya's 15th birthday, and Carmen had the evening arranged. After the girls returned, we talked of the events of the past two months over birthday cake and coffee. Tanya and Roberta have had a wonderful time together and I am afraid Tanya is going to feel a pinch getting back into the tent with her younger brothers and sisters; she paid little attention to us.

Ed flew to Salvador Wednesday evening. It was his last day of work in Brasilia and our spread-out family was reunited. We spent two days learning about the historical city and one day enjoying the beach.

The city is divided into two levels by a 175-foot escarpment that is mounted by the Lacerda elevator which provides easy pedestrian transport up and down. The lower city is a modern commercial district amongst the docks of the port. The Upper City, Pelourinho, is the historical centre, named a World Cultural Centre by UNESCO. The colonial buildings were in grave disrepair until the 1990s when the Bahian state government funded the restoration of some of the finest colonial architecture in the world. The buildings and shops that line the cobbled streets are a feast of colour for the eyes and give one the sense of being taken back in time.

Our day of touring with Roberto began with Forte Santo Antonio on the tip of the peninsula. Fortification commenced in 1583, and although the ramparts were improved at the turn of that century, they were still not enough to enable the residents to fend off the Dutch in 1624. The Portuguese reclaimed the city within two years, and construction of what now exists started afterwards. We strolled the path around the fort, visiting both the lighthouse and nautical museum.

The old customs house was transformed into the Mercado Modelo—an artisan market where each stall is filled to the brim and overflowing with hand-made crafts and articles used in *umbamba, candomble* and other rituals. It is a touristy place with friendly, patient shopkeepers. The building burned to the ground in 1984 and was rebuilt in the same 19th century style. We shopped briefly and as we exited the building, rhythmic music captured our senses and drew us to the games of *capoiera.* Mesmerized, we watched the acrobatic skills of the participants demonstrating the Afro-Brazilian dance-like martial art.

Salvador is known as the most African city in the western hemisphere. For three centuries it was the major centre of the slave trade from western Africa until the practice was abolished in the 1830s. Although dominant society attempted to suppress African religions and customs, the people managed to maintain much of their culture. Customs were integrated and adapted in the New World.

Capoiera was initially developed by the slaves as a way to resist their oppressors and keep their culture alive. It is a dance in which two people demonstrate the skill of attack and defense, showing the movement without completing it, which means it doesn't focus on injuring the other player. The overall movements match the rhythm played by the *beteries*—the group of musicians and singers. The latter drums, (*atabague),* tambourines (*pandeiros)* and *berimbaus* an instrument made from a wood bow and a steel string with a gourd attached for resonance. It has a unique sound. A slow rhythm corresponded to highly controlled movements, while faster rhythms allowed for more circular momentum and bigger air movements. While standing there watching the guys perform, I couldn't help but think that it was much like break dancing, only to have Roberto tell me later that break dancing evolved in New York City after the first school of *capoiera* was set up there. I could have enjoyed the music and watched them for hours.

August 22 to September 18, 1999: Aracaju, Brazil

The name Aracaju is a combination of two words: Ara—from *araras*, the bird, and *caju*—the cashew tree. Aracaju is a friendly place and as safe as any North American city of the same size. The population is a little more that 400,000 and the people are far more laid-back than in other large Brazilian cities we have visited. It has a wonderful climate, no hurricanes, tornadoes or earthquakes—just beach weather all year round. This city sees rain and wind, but it is the wind that makes the heat bearable and keeps the bugs in hiding. The rain keeps everything green, lush and growing. The city, and our campground, is located on a fabulous beach that continues until it fades on the distant horizon in both north and south directions. The dry sand feels like velvet, the coast is flat and shallow, and waves break 15 rows back—the kids say it is like Sauble Beach in Ontario, except bigger. When the tide is out offshore the beach must be 100 meters wide. The people of Aracaju care for, make use of, and enjoy it. On weekends, it is the recreation centre, where soccer, volleyball and footvolley tournaments are held. It is certainly a focal point for activity.

Ed contacted Camargo (the brother of a patient he treated in Chile) the first evening we arrived. Camargo visited shortly after the call, and the two of them have enjoyed each other's company since their first meeting. One year ago Camargo decided to learn to speak English and he is now fluent. He is always anxious to practice and has spent several evenings visiting and talking with us. He runs a silver reclamation business, has jewelry made by artisans, and sells it. He spends much of his free time keeping fit and is in excellent condition like so many people here in the body-beautiful country of Brazil. Camargo made our stay in Aracaju worthwhile. He picked up Ed the first morning we were here to introduce him to people at the health food store and the yoga centre, and then took him to radio and television stations. Ed's first radio interview was that afternoon. Gladstone, the director of the Yoga Centre, invited Ed to talk to the yoga classes about Chiropractic and offered Ed the yoga centre as a base from which to give adjustments while in Aracaju. The first few days he adjusted several people. By Monday of the following week he had adjusted 37 people and it continued daily. Ed loves helping people live a better, healthier life and the money he makes is always a reward; he is reluctant to leave.

Aracaju would be an excellent city to settle in but we are leaving Saturday; we already extended our stay to the 18th because so many people have wanted Ed's service. We are running out of Brazilian visa time and have only five weeks left to get to Venezuela. Ed has made some good friends, met some wonderful people and has adjusted many. But it has become four long weeks for the kids and me, and it is increasingly hard to wait for him. It feels as if our life has been put on hold here the last while. We have had enough of a time-out and are ready for interaction with other people. Part of the problem is that we have read every one of our books at least twice. The kids keep working at their math and writing, but it feels as if it's time to do more than that.

Sergipe lived in his tent-house in a corner of the CCB campground we are staying in. He is an elderly widowed man from Rio Grande Sur who spends his winters in the north. It gets wet, damp and cold in the south during winter, so he migrates north to live in a more desirable climate. He does a little work for the municipality and keeps himself busy with his visitors coming and going. He has taken us under his wing, tells me not to make dinner, and treats us often. He finds it amazing that the kids do reading, writing and math without being in school. (Home-schooling is a difficult concept for him.)

The first weekend at the campground, Nor and Sergipe came to visit. Sergipe brought Nor to translate even though Ed can get by in Portuguese fairly well. At one time, Nor lived in the Chicago area; he had done a trip similar to ours 20 years ago, but when he landed in Brazil, he married a Brazilian woman and stayed. He loves it in Aracaju and teaches English as a career. He says he doesn't make as much money as he could in a bigger city but the lifestyle here is good and he doesn't have to worry about crime. He has since divorced, but Brazil is his home. Sergipe kept asking questions. Through Nor he wanted to know everything, then invited us for a barbecue dinner that first evening. Nor came back, bringing with him Francisco, a young man about 20 years old. Nor met him 15 years ago as a child selling ice cream on the beach and instantly liked him; he was a humourous, quick thinker and still is. Nor semi-adopted him, and Francisco learned to speak English. Francisco and his partner are Brazil footvolley champions. Footvolley is a two-person team sport that combines beach volleyball with soccer moves—the ball cannot be touched with the hands or arms. He played the following day and invited us to watch his game on the beach. Volleyball with soccer moves—that takes some skill. After being intrigued by this new sport we purchased a foot volleyball and the boys have been practicing at the net Baxinho set up for us. Several times, Francisco has come for the boys and taken them out to practice on the beach.

Baxinho, the caretaker of the grounds, has befriended Ben, who is fascinated by Baxinho's coconut tree-climbing skills. He has two ropes, each with a loop to support the foot at the bottom. The ropes are tied to the trunk, leaving about two feet of length from which the foot loops swing free. The slipknot around the trunk is loosened, the rope is lifted higher on the trunk, and the knot is pulled snug against the tree again. The ropes are moved alternately, one supporting the weight of the body, then the other until the coconuts are within reach. The ropes are flexible supports to work from while cutting down the crop. Ben watched carefully as Baxinho tied the knots for climbing, then he constructed a set of his own. It took a few tries before they partially worked. Baxinho found what Ben was trying to do comical and gave him some pointers; it wasn't the ropes that were the problem, it takes skill and coordination to get them to work.

Baxinho easily climbed the tall palms, cut the coconuts down and trimmed off the dead branches. When he took a break from his chores he got out of his ropes, sat in the middle of the palm leaf foliage at the top, chopped open a coconut and drank the sweet water while enjoying the sights from his perch. Needless to say he did that on days with little breeze. One afternoon while the kids were kicking the foot volleyball around, the ball came to rest in a tall palm up there with the coconuts. Ben attempted to climb the tree with great difficulty and barely got halfway when Baxinho displayed another skill that awed us. He climbed to the top of the coconut palm using just hands and feet. The bottoms of his feet were against the trunk, knees splayed, arms wrapped around the tree. He worked his way to the top hanging on with feet and hands alternately, pushed the ball out of the tree and shinnied back down. This, too, takes practice and is a desirable and useful skill in a country where coconuts are a staple food.

We became consistent coconut water drinkers here in Aracaju. It is a fluid that is made for the heat and we spent many hot afternoons drinking the water from fresh coconuts and eating the green coconut (which is slimy and took some getting used to but now tastes delicious to us). Often it is all a stomach needs, in that it is filling, cools the body down, and quenches thirst. It is a perfect food for the climate and probably nutritious as well. We don't dehydrate drinking it, anyway. One afternoon Ed came home from the market with 50 large green coconuts in the back of the van. When Baxinho took a look at our heap he said, "You guys must really like coconuts." They were gone within a few days and Baxinho, realizing our appetite, now had a place to dispose of the excess coconuts the campground was producing. We never had to buy another. Boxinho pruned his trees, the campground attendants used what they needed, and the surplus was ours.

We spent most mornings doing bookwork, then enjoyed the afternoon on the beach. But the closer we get to equinox, the stronger the sun grew. This week we have turned our rhythm around, having beach time early and staying sheltered under our tarp for the afternoon. This beach has been the most enjoyable in Brazil.

The Niko monkeys visit daily. They travel through trees, on power lines, fences or whatever is en route but they rarely touch the ground. We fed them bananas once and they have been back regularly for the treat. They could easily become pets— such curious little guys. Once they learned to trust us they grew bolder, going for bananas without invitation and scurrying through our "house". They climbed and sat on top of the tents curiously looking inside. When ignored they would make sure we noticed them, sitting on the van seats close to our shoulders, staring. One afternoon we discovered they weren't vegetarian. One of the monkeys caught a lizard by the tail but the lizard dropped the part that was caught and escaped. The monkey ate the tail then looked hard for the rest of lizard, which was long gone and well hidden. They were a group of five, two males and three females, one of which is probably an older baby; she is smaller than the others. This past week the group has been reduced to four. Something happened to one male (maybe chased off by the other) the two of them didn't get along so well. It has been interesting to observe the personalities and interaction of their group.

Whitney needed a tooth repaired while here, and she surprised me with how she has overcome her traumatic early experience of teeth and dentistry. The evening of the appointment she was somewhat tired from our day on the beach. While waiting her turn, she put her head on my knee and asked if it was okay if she fell asleep in the dentist chair. I said I didn't think the dentist would mind as long as she kept her mouth open. Half way through having her tooth repaired the dentist and assistant were quietly laughing. Whitney had fallen asleep with her mouth open. I couldn't believe what I was seeing. It was my lifting her out of the dentist chair that wakened her. Never have I heard of anyone voluntarily sleeping through dental work.

Time spent in Aracaju has been good. We have been restless, but most of that comes from not having enough new books to read. Finally I can say we are becoming a family of readers, and we miss it when books are not available. We are on the move again tomorrow.

September 18, 1999: Maceio, Brazil

Palms, palms and more palms, pregnant and drooping with coconuts almost too heavy to hold any longer—cultivated fields of them amongst green, wavy fields of sugar cane. North of the San Francisco River the road hugged the ocean again. Tropical sea-green water looked inviting, but as we neared the city of Maceio, it turned black and the beaches were covered in garbage. Where a soccer game was being played the trash was raked into heaps on either end of the goal lines. The only place where there was no garbage was in front of the shops and bars where people have taken the time to clean up their part of the beach. What a simple concept. If every one of us truly took care of the space we occupy at all times the human species would have a more positive effect on the planet that gives us life. Our North American society doesn't see the reality of garbage. We just toss out everything we don't want or need, bring it to the curbside, and a nice big truck just rolls it off... someplace. Here, the problem is more difficult to ignore.

The CCB North of Maceio was a disappointment, being the first place we'd been in Brazil where garbage has been left where it falls in such abundance. We were unenthusiastic while setting up the tents, although the facilities of the campground itself were excellent. A motorhome that we saw leaving Aracaju yesterday morning is here today. We had said hello to the owners occasionally in Aracaju, but today we chatted with each other. The owners are a middle-aged couple from Rio de Janeiro who have been travelling for two and a half months in Brazil. They were planning to go to Natal and farther north but are discouraged and thinking of going back to the southern part of the country. They don't like the strong wind and rain, but it is tolerable when the beaches are good.

Ed planned to move on in the morning and called Maricia, the friend of Roberto, to ask if we could use her cottage. She gave Ed directions without hesitation.

After dinner I decided to walk the narrow beach, despite the garbage. Without the garbage, it would be exceptional—white sand lined with palms. Ed refused to come; Karina, Whitney and Ben joined me. Beside a crab hole we discovered broken eggshells and upon closer inspection we saw that they looked like eggs we saw at the sea turtle conservation area south of Aracaju. Karina asked, "Would a crab eat turtle eggs?"

I replied, "I don't know, Karina, but from all the shells outside the hole it might be a pretty good assumption."

It spurred several questions. We wondered if there were more turtle eggs in the sand on this beach. Southern hemisphere spring is laying season so it was a good possibility. Whitney remarked, "We shouldn't be walking here, then, we could be walking on them."

Ben replied, "They have lots of trouble surviving, don't they? Even the crabs eat them."

"It is true, Ben, but the crabs are a natural predator. It is man moving into their environment that is the biggest problem."

I picked up some of the broken shells and we headed back to the tents to show the others.

We enjoyed the sound of the waves, at least. I thought about the sea turtles, the beaches and the ocean. Those huge, gentle creatures have been living on the earth for the past 350 million years and it is only during the last 100 or so that they have been decreasing in numbers.

September 20, 1999: Playa Carneiros

Yesterday we saw sugar cane as far as the eye could see. Around every corner and over every hill we climbed there were green wavy fields of cane. We have had *caldo de cana*—sugar cane juice—on the beaches and have chewed and sucked the juice out of the cane as well. The kids wanted to stop and cut a few down to snack on. Ed said it would be stealing and didn't stop for them. Dayna complained, "As if one is going to make any difference."

He said, "It is still stealing."

She retorted, "People have stolen from us."

"That doesn't make it right, Dayna."

Shortly after that conversation we hit a pothole (one of many on these northern roads) and popped a hubcap again. Tanya and Ben both saw it roll into a cane field. Forced into a stop, we had our opportunity for a good look, tromp and feel of the sugar cane plants while searching for the hubcap. They were almost twice our height. Discouragement set in quickly—the leaves scratched, leaving tiny cuts on arms and legs, creating a terrible itch. Ed persevered, found the hubcap, put it back on, and no one even thought of cutting a piece down.

Confused with directions in Tamandaré we ended up in an area with luxurious homes. My expectations of Brazil are always being surpassed.

At Carneiros, and on the right track, we drove through four-lane road construction and a classy condominium development; it is another fishing village becoming a modern resort town. When our directions brought us to a grassy path everyone burst with excitement over what opened up before us. The cottage sat adjacent to a private white sand beach lined with tall coconut palms on the bay of the Rio Formoso. The water was clear sea green, shallow and calm, protected from the open ocean by the sand bars of the delta. Ed made arrangements with Pedro next door, and we are to stay two nights.

The kids noticed the cottage was built the same as the Barra Grande cottage, but no mosquito nets could be found, so it was an easy decision to use the mattresses off the beds inside the tents.

Lost in the elements again Jake built a sail boat from coconut husk, sticks and a plastic bag. The intensity of his interest drew Ben in and they built one with a keel to help it stay upright.

We found another different kind of shell on the beach, many of them, but hermit crabs occupied most. The kids became frustrated trying to find some of the one- to two-inch spirals without live animals in them. While in our hands there was no indication of a creature inside. We brought five into the cottage and put them on the table. When we lost patience and didn't watch them for a period of time they walked off the edge and scurried away to find a hiding place. They did this a few times without being noticed until they were on the floor. It was as if they had radar, and only moved when no one was looking. They were comical little creatures, and we did put them back at the water's edge when we lost interest in them.

Whitney was not well yesterday but looked much better when she crawled out of the tent this morning. Ed asked how she was doing and she said, "Good, I broke my fever. I'm not hot anymore." The statement came out like she was in charge of her fever and made it go away. This little person is so capable of being in control.

Ben and Jake continued with their sailboats, but when Ben found a piece of driftwood he decided a dugout wouldn't sink and spent the rest of the day carving a toy boat.

There is an older man living here outside the cottage. He uses the outside sink and cooks what food he has by fire in the backyard. He has a bad cough and doesn't appear to be very healthy. He makes baskets to sell and has made three little ones today. He slept on the verandah of the house last night with his back against the wall and a single blanket covering everything, including his head, to fend off the mosquitoes. He appeared at the door asking for food when I made our first meal yesterday and we have fed him every time we ate today.

September 21, 1999: Caruaru, Brazil

I gave the man food for the day before we left and he gave me one of his baskets. I thanked him but he shook his finger at me and said, "No, no, I thank you."

I now have a container for the shells I picked off the beach here, and it even has a lid.

All the flip-flops were on the verandah overnight but when it was time to go Tanya's were missing. We came to the conclusion that the man must have taken them. We never did see him with anything on his feet. Tanya said, "I don't mind, I should have given them to him, but now my sandals are packed in my bag up top." He was managing without shoes period; she managed the day.

Barely 80 kilometers inland, the vegetation changed dramatically; there was no more sugar cane and the fields became desert-like grassland. In Caruaru Ed called Butch and Andrea from a phone booth and five minutes later Butch was at the corner. Somehow, without knowing where we were headed, we had managed to arrive within six blocks of his office. Camargo said Caruaru would be a good place to purchase some necessary clothing, and Butch, Camargo's close friend and associate, would be happy to entertain us for a while. So here we are. Butch took us to the *feira* (marketplace) and what an experience it was. Caruaru is known for its markets: *Feira des Artisanas* (artisans), *Fiera do Troca-Troca* (barter market), *Fiera do Gado* (livestock), *Feira de Antiguidades* (antiques) and *Feira de Sulanca* (clothing), in which we spent the morning. The *Feira de Sulanca* alone occupied several city blocks, with stall after canopied stall—a crazy busy place with clothes, clothes and more clothes suitable for Brazilian life. We each found a couple of garments to replace what we'd worn out or grown out of. Butch walked around, leading us from place to place, haggled the price when it came to buying, and wasn't shy about telling the vendor the price was too high. I have a hard time doing that when prices are already so much lower than what I was accustomed to in Canada and Chile.

We were shopped out by noon and Butch invited us to his house for the midday meal. He showed Ed the upstairs and offered two bedrooms for the night. He expected us to stay and it appeared he would have been insulted if we hadn't. We accepted, and Butch told the kids to put bathing suits on to have a swim in the pool. Butch and Andrea have three employees that do cleaning, gardening and the cooking of meals in a house smaller than the one we left in Canada. While changing into a bathing suit, I was much aware of my bare feet on the carpeted floor; it has been a while since we have been in a real house. I rejoined the group to find a beer waiting, with Guarana, and nonalcoholic beer for the kids.

What a meal! Plain rice, rice with vegetables, shrimp mayo salad, spaghetti dish, mashed potatoes, colho cheese, ham and cheese lasagna, steamed vegetables, *chouchou* (a tropical vegetable), green beans, onion and tomato salad, and a platter of beef in a delicious sauce with olives, then two different cakes for dessert. After we had eaten as much as was civil, we were asked if we would like to sleep a while—afternoons are much too hot to do anything. Ed and I took our hosts up on the offer while the kids watched a movie and had cookies and ice cream. We were planning to go to the artisan market but it didn't happen. At 7:30 p.m. we were served another meal of soup and salads. We were still full from eating earlier. While enjoying the cooler night air and having a chat, Carmargo called to check in on us. He wants to see us safely through Brazil and tells Ed to keep calling to let him know where we are.

Butch explained that June, July and August is rainy season but they haven't had any rain at all this year. The population of Caruaru is 250,000, and city water is severely rationed. Each household receives water once in 20 days. (This house has a full swimming pool of fresh water.) Butch and Andrea purchase a truckload of water weekly. We noticed water trucks on the road this morning and now know why. Andrea made up a bed for each of us with fresh linen that felt absolutely luxurious. Ed wouldn't let any of us take a shower even though we were told we could if we desired.

Checking out Rocks –Joao Passoa, Brazil

September 24, 1999: Joao Passoa, Brazil

Andrea and Butch had their employees make a fabulous breakfast of melon, papaya, corn couscous, plain scrambled eggs, scrambled eggs with vegetables, two kinds of cheese, fresh buns toasted with butter, crackers, fresh orange juice and all the coffee I could drink. After that, the huge cake the kids had enjoyed the previous day was set on the table, and they managed to clean that up too. They must think we eat an awful pile of food, and we did at their house—it was different from what we are used to, and scrumptious. I am afraid we may have appeared gluttonous, but both Butch and Andrea enjoyed watching the kids eat. Their son is a selective eater. It is a good thing we don't eat like that every day or I'd be a two-ton Annie. I enjoy good food but my body sure feels better when I eat simply. A sincere thank-you came from all the kids, without prodding. We were overwhelmed with hospitality.

Our route took us on what is called the Marijuana Highway. Butch warned there would be police checks, and we were stopped within the first 10 minutes. Within 10 more minutes we were stopped again, and this time the police officer was almost hostile. Ed gave him the papers for the van, his passport and license. The cop looked at them for an extended period of time then decided to check it out on the computer. We waited at least 15 more minutes, the kids'anxiety developing as they began to think that we had a problem. Ed assured them there wasn't anything to worry about. When the officer returned with the papers all he said was "*bom viagem.*" It was the coldest exchange we had with any Brazilian. A highway patrol car stopped us again. Two police officers with rifles came to either side of the van. They told Ed to get out and open the back doors. They wanted to see our cargo. At least they were a little more amiable. Ed laughed while explaining that we are Canadians passing through, and that our cargo is six kids and baggage. The cops faced several young heads peering over the seats out the back doors, and were somewhat surprised. They took a half-hearted look, realized we weren't what they were looking for, and told Ed to move on. Another time-consuming police check outside Campina Grande was the fourth in less than 100 kilometers. The highway stretched through desert covered in cacti. I don't know how marijuana could possibly grow in the area. Closer to the coast the land turned from dry yellow-browns to green again.

The CCB Campground at João Passoa is on Ponta do Seixas and the farthest easterly point of the continental Americas at longitude 35 degrees. After studying maps we realized we now have an east-west trip to Lee and Clif's in San Diego, California, that is farther than the distance we travelled from Ottawa, Canada to Santiago, Chile.

At 5 a.m. almost everyone at the campground was active. It is the best part of the day in this heat. I found an intriguing feather on the ground close to our campsite, pale yellowish-grey with a black section two-thirds of the way from the base; I put it with my collection of "junk". I happen to like feathers, stones and shells.

An attempt to enjoy the beach at mid-morning was cut short because the sun was just too strong. Shade is important, and we stayed under the protection of our tarp until late afternoon.

I didn't even have to remind the kids—they just did schoolwork with the unoccupied time on their hands. Laundry didn't take long at all but, then again, we are not wearing much these days.

As the sun set, a group of birds settled in a palm tree beside our campsite above where I found the feather. They are larger than robins but smaller than crows, with a black stripe across their long tail feathers. They have blue jay-like tufts on the tops of their heads, pale yellow abdomens and brownish wings. It was one of their tail feathers that I had found. On a midnight bathroom trip I counted 11 of them lined up, huddled and sleeping together. They couldn't possibly have gotten any closer to one another. Heads and tails faced the same direction down the spine of the palm leaf.

The full moon was at the zenith. Through the tent without the fly, I watched it move across the sky. I'd like to know why I spend the few sleepless nights I have watching the full moon and what it lights up. Thoughts just kept rolling through my head, and I felt as if there were bugs crawling all over me. Ants are always crawling everywhere. I find them on me, on others and in everything we own. As I crunched one between my fingers the thought of home came up. Oh Canada, how nice it is to live without bugs for a few months of each year. There is never a break from them here. My mind did eventually give in, even with the ants, and sleep came.

Breakfast was over by 5:30 a.m. this morning—life does change. By 8:30 the kids had completed their math and were playing volleyball. Ed spoke with the campground caretaker and learned about a section of beach two kilometers south where we would find small caves and lagoons. We took a walk.

Yesterday this beach was one of the most beautiful we had set foot on in South America. At 9 a.m. this morning, the tide was low and at the top of every receded wave line was a row of oily black globs of tar with barely a clean area on the white sand. My heart sank. Despite the disastrous look of the beach and the reek of oil in the heat, there were still many people sunbathing. Yesterday we discussed walking to the colourful rock cliff; we didn't let the mess stop us from going today. Whitney and Jake didn't wear shoes. Their feet and legs were covered in tar and before long the bottoms of our flip-flops were caked with a thick layer of the stuff. The campground beach area was in good shape compared to what we discovered farther south. The oil smell was stifling in places and tar blobs were impossible to avoid.

Ed asked a fisherman on the beach if it happened very often. The fisherman said no but it does once in a while and pointed to two oil tanker ships on the horizon. He said, "It comes from those ships. It is common practice for empty oil tankers to fill their tanks with sea water and flush it out."

We discovered the cliffs to be clay, not rock, in purple, red, orange and pink; the clay was hard but it broke under pressure. The shore was the same colourful clay and looked like a marble floor in steps. This was intriguing and would have been more so if we didn't have to be so careful of where we walked.

Beyond the cliffs, we visited the small caverns amidst a tropical paradise: a lagoon lined with mangroves. On the clean sand above the wave line, we soaked up the sun. If we'd stayed, high tide would cut us off at the cliffs, and the girls grew anxious, not wanting to wade through water full of tar and oil. So they headed back, taking Whitney with them. The boys, Ed and I lingered. Our walk became a hot one and by noon the tar globs were melting into the sand from the heat. As the sun broke the tar down, the tide washed away the disintegrating oily stuff. By four in the afternoon the tide was receding again and the beach was almost clean. Nature does heal itself—it is unnatural interference that is the problem.

It was a chore getting the muck off our skin and shoes. While I was carrying Whitney on my back for part of the walk, she painted my legs with her feet. Another camper saw us struggling to clean up and told us to use cooking oil on a cotton cloth to wipe it off; it worked well but the dish cloths we used were a write off.

September 26, 1999: Lago Bonfim (Natal)

Ben left his flip-flops in the grass outside the passenger side door of the van, but he got into the driver's seat, drove to the gate and didn't remember them. They are a necessity of life in this climate. Otherwise it is bare feet, and the hot ground is hard on the soles.

The road from João Passoa took us through desert with some of it cultivated in sugar cane that was being harvested—one cane crop was being burned. (I was told weeks later that sometimes this is done to drive snakes out of the fields before harvesting.)

Our tour of Brazil depends on where the campgrounds of the CCB are and the closest en route is on the fresh water lake of Lagoa do Bonfim, 15 kilometers inland. The Brazilians call the water sweet, not fresh, but the sweet water, too, is a sea-green colour and palms line the shore. The air here is fragrant with a light, jasmine-like perfume. The tree that is so plentiful, aside from the palm, is in flower: small, delicate, red-pink striped, star-shaped flowers in clusters. The kids were drawn to one that called, embraced and held children so easily. Before we knew it all six of them were within her boughs above the ground. What a spot, what a tree!

We are camped underneath the grandmother of all trees in the area. It would take three people to wrap their arms around the trunk; her crown is at least 20 meters in diameter. The huge bottom branches have grown almost parallel to the ground. Dayna, Ben and Karina strung hammocks up amongst the boughs to sleep in. We discovered that the trees are cashew nut; some are blossoming, some showing the beginnings of a new crop, some ready for harvest.

There is a menagerie of animals here: chickens, geese and cats. There are many *nikos,* the same monkey we grew familiar with in Aracaju, and the kids fed them our bananas the moment we arrived. Animals obviously like us, given our impulse to feed whoever and whatever comes around. Ed and the kids were exploring while I prepared dinner. I chopped the cilantro ends and vegetable discards for the geese and chickens and threw the compost makings on the ground about 100 meters away from our camp, because the birds had been hanging around begging. I came back to the stove to continue preparing our meal when the cat looked up at me and gave a mournful cry; she saw me feed the geese. She is pregnant. I gave her a bowl of rice with a little butter on it, away from the campsite. I came back to five monkeys lined up sitting on a bough of the tree above the stove, all pleading, red-brown eyes looking at me. I said, "Oh no, you guys already ate all our bananas, you're not getting anything more." They squealed and scampered off through the trees as if they understood what I said.

The kids played and swam in the lake most of the day. They say they like swimming in fresh water better, it makes them feel cleaner, and they don't have to take a shower after.

We fed the *nikos* again today. There were more of them this time, two mothers with tiny babies clinging to their backs, the babies' tails wrapped tightly around the mothers like ropes, holding them securely in place. This was a different group from those that were here yesterday. This type of monkey does not seem to be shy of humans at all.

The soccer ball disappeared but it is partially our fault, in that it was left it in the grass away from our campsite.

Great Beaches in Brazil

September 27, 1999: Canoa Quebrada and Iguape

The coast is green but it soon gave way to desert-like plains as we moved inland. Now that we know what cashew trees are, we see them everywhere. Most of them are in full blossom and some are bearing fruit. Wherever the land is blessed with a little water between Natal and Mossoro, there are orchards of cashew trees. They're one of the best shade trees, with their wide branches stretched out horizontal to the ground. They cover and require a lot of space. Most of the land is desert-like savannah, rocky with some hills to the south. I didn't expect Brazil to be so desert-like.

Highway 304 travels close to the north-east coast again, within six kilometers of Canoa Quebrada, and since Canoa Quebrada was recommended as a place to visit in the *Rodavia Praias* and *SAH,* we did some exploring. Off the main highway, near the ocean, we drove through acres of huge, rolling, sand dunes. Ed parked beside a restaurant in the village, next to a tourist bus, and there must have been 50 dune buggies waiting to take passengers out onto the dunes. We strolled another incredible beach of white sand.

Canoa Quebrada (translates to Broken Canoe) originated as a fishing village but is turning into a tourist and resort town. There are furnished houses to rent for 15 *reais* per day and many *posadas* with accommodation as well. The main street is lined with artisan shops, and a few mini-markets sell food. At the ocean the main street gave way to deep sand and beach. We had a challenging moment turning the van around when we couldn't follow the dune buggy ahead of us on into the sand.

We have seen so many different beaches now that they don't make such an impression anymore, or maybe we are just seeing so much so fast that it is difficult to appreciate everything. Ed and I thought it would be a great place to stay but the kids didn't. It is usually majority rules and we were out-voted. The village attracted "hippie-like" people and felt like something out of the 60s, a little too passé for our kids.

The road continued northwest along the shore, according to the map. To our right, rolling sand dunes cut off any view of the ocean. It was just one big beach.

Iguape was originally a fishing village but has become a popular retreat from the city. As we walked around town we discovered that the permanent dwellings were

---

not as prosperous as the weekend homes, but people are not starving or living in terrible conditions either.

The campground has full facilities and a swimming pool with a towering water-slide, every kid's dream. But it was Monday and the pool was closed for maintenance after the weekend crowd. A walk on the beach helped to cool us down, but the surf was so strong that swimming was out of the question. The ocean was shifting and changing the beach; the palm roof *baraccas* (bars) were half buried in sand.

The pool was well used the next day. Jake and Whitney used the slide after getting over their initial apprehension of its height. Both of them are good, capable swimmers now.

Ben set up a sleeping hammock outdoors and that is where we all should be—the tents are suffocating.

September 29, 1999: Forteleza visit, Sobral and Parque Nacional Ubajora

At 7:30 a.m. we entered the city of Fortaleza where a temperature sign said 27°C. There were billboards and signs everywhere urging people to put garbage where it belongs and to recycle. It is having an effect; the city was very clean.

Butch, in Caruaru, recommended we buy hammocks in Fortaleza for our Amazon boat trip. Fortaleza is known for textiles and there are thousands to choose from. At the Mercado Central we purchased three 120-string, 100 percent cotton hammocks, and each is a piece of art. The four-story market building was jam-packed, full of textiles, hammocks and fine linens. We found an exquisite cacao fibre tablecloth to fit our big table at home, for 85 reais. Ed gave the vendor two 50s and he tried to sell us another for 50 *reais.* "Cheap," he said. We didn't need another one; I told him no and he brought the price down to 40 and I still said no thanks. I didn't need or want another tablecloth but he said he needed the money and put the tablecloth in the bag. Ed took it out and told him he wanted his change. The price came down to 30 but Ed didn't give him any more money. He was either really desperate for cash or we paid too much for the first one. He put the tablecloth back into the bag and said we could have it for 15 *reais.* To get out of the tough situation we took it for that price. I'll pack it away and one of the kids can have it when they have a use for it. (How I end up with a house full of things.) We moved out of the market quickly after that, with more than what we went for.

We have left the ocean behind and will be travelling on inland roads now for the next few days. To say it is hot is an understatement. It must be 40°C. The wind blowing in the window is like having your face on a forced-air heating vent. There are more cashew orchards dotting the desert-like land, and it is goat country. Many are wandering free in herds on the road and in the fields. West of Sobral is hilly, rocky country, the rocks having been moulded into unusual shapes by the wind. One tall column reminded me of the Statue of Cerro San Cristobal in Santiago.

At the Serra do Ibiapaba the road started to climb, and 15 minutes later we were still climbing. Not far from the top the van hesitated and backfired. Ed stopped, and we let it cool as much as the heat of the day would allow, put fresh water into the radiator, and continued. Almost on the plain at the top it started to choke and hesitate again. It just didn't want to go any farther. Ed stopped at a modern and well-equipped gas station. When he asked for permission to cook supper and give the van a rest, the owner said to camp overnight if we wanted. Then he suggested that we move behind the wall into the parking lot for a little more privacy, use the showers in the washrooms, and watch TV in the restaurant if we liked. *Fica vantagem*—direct translation: take advantage. Our unfortunate circumstance worked out all right.

The owner's daughter was about eight years old and intrigued with the foreigners. Her father said she thinks we talk funny. Ed told her the kids could speak a little Portuguese and really liked to play. But being shy, she sat, watched and listened. I gave Whitney some Canadian flag pins to give to her. They created a grin from ear to ear and helped break the ice enough for them to talk a little, but it didn't last. The girl was either shy, or girls here don't play soccer; she wouldn't play with Whitney. We did take advantage of the showers, as the heat is stifling, and we needed to cool down to sleep.

October 1, 1999: Teresina

Through the night, Karina vomited up what little she had eaten for supper, and then went back to sleep. This must be some kind of flu bug; the kids are taking turns succumbing. It lasts about 24 hours. It was so hot I slept naked all night without covers. I've never done that before anywhere.

By 7:45 a.m., we had arrived at the Parque Nacional de Sete Cidades in sparsely populated country. Ed purchased tickets at the information center to see the rock formations but was told we were not allowed to camp. We thought we would stay the night, but the camping area is closed. If we had made it the previous night as we had planned, we would have been turned away.

I don't know the reasoning behind the prohibition on going into the park without a guide, but it is not allowed. Sete Cidades is named for seven different rock groupings, unusual formations caused by wind erosion. The trails are sand, the rocks are sandstone towers, arches, and animal shapes. In one area with a different type of rock, there are ancient paintings estimated to be 6,000 years old—hands with six fingers and stick figures of people. All of it was fascinating but the intense heat inhibited our enthusiasm.

Shortly after resuming our trek toward Teresina, Jake screamed in surprise, causing us all to jump. An insect, maybe a preying mantis, between 12 and 15 centimeters long, crawled out of hiding and perched himself on the top of the van seat between him and Ben. Startled, Ben jumped into the front seat. Jake laughed at him for being such a wimp. Once he knew what it was Jake opened the back window and moved it out. It was the largest insect any of us had ever seen.

The sun's arc is moving south and we are moving northwest. We will cross paths at some point soon and will be on the north side of it again. By the time it returns north we will be north of the Tropic of Cancer. We have been on the south side of the sun for more than two years.

Teresina is the second hottest city in Brazil: the temperature regularly hits 42°C. I don't know which city is the hottest, but this is hot enough.

The *Camping Clube do Nordeste* wasn't really open for overnight camping, but it had a swimming pool and water-slide open to the public. We were allowed to camp but were told there wasn't a vigilante at night. Ed asked if it was safe. The caretaker laughed and said, "Nobody is going to touch you here." We are finding the northeast states not at all as they'd been described by people in the south. The main roads are good almost everywhere and the people are helpful and friendly.

Needless to say, since it was 40 degrees we spent what was left of the afternoon in the pool. It could have been more refreshing, but when the temperature is so hot, how could we expect the water to be cool?

There may be two messages in yesterday's difficulties. One: we should only be driving four to five hours a day as we had planned in the beginning. Two: I need to keep my faith constant. Why is it so hard to stay in a faithful state of mind 100 percent of the time? The next thing I need to learn is how to connect messages from my dreams to real-life situations as they are happening, not just after the fact. The van stopping where it did gave us a decent place to stay for the night. My dream of flying from place to place told me that all I have to do is hold on to my faith, and the force that is carrying us along will safely get us where we are going.

We spent the day in the pool, in between reorganizing and eliminating what we don't need. We were carrying too many clothes for Brazil and the tropics, too many blankets, souvenirs, rocks and shells. We all reduced our clothing again, and we cut the tarp in half. It was the right size while living under it for longer periods of time but cumbersome for quick set-up and breaking camp. We gave half of the tarp and the box of clothing the kids have outgrown to the campground manager, and put together two boxes of warm clothing, blankets, books and souvenirs to send to Canada. After we completed our reorganization, we did laundry together at the outside shower stalls, and, needless to say water fights were the order of the day. How could we do laundry like that in this heat and not have a water fight?

October 2, 1999: Teresina to the state border of Maranhao – Para

Ed spoke with the kids about this being a long part of the journey. Belem is almost 1,000 kilometers away, and there are only small villages and no campgrounds between here and there. He asked for their patience during the drive; if the van didn't kick up a fuss we were going to go as far as we could each day. They understood—the anticipation of seeing family at Christmas has given them incentive to keep moving.

Yesterday's travel took us through dry grassland with a few fields of mango and cashew trees alongside small rivers. There are many riverbeds in this area that don't have water in them these days but these ones did. As we passed through Bacabal, the main highway bisected a market where one stall was overflowing with flip-flops. Both Ben and Tanya found what they needed. I wonder how long these will last.

The land turned greener north of Bom Jardin, and the sky became cloudy for the first time in several days. The afternoon was cooler than what we have been experiencing and it felt so good. The van worked well but it was a long day for Ed—we put almost 700 kilometers behind us.

Just before the state border we stopped at an Esso gas station. It was a truck stop, with a luncheonette and restaurant, a repair garage, gas pumps of course, and a parking area to accommodate transport trucks spending the night. The buildings were open on all sides but fully covered by a roof. Ed filled the gas tank and asked permission to stay overnight in the parking area. It was equipped with tables, sinks, television and lights. There was a separate building for washrooms and showers, with attendants who clean and take care of them 24 hours a day. Brazil takes care of its truckers with clean, well-equipped roadside places where they can spend the night, and this is an excellent one.

Ed had the oil changed and we chose a spot for the night. Just as we parked under the enormous roof that covers 16 transport trucks, it rained so hard for an hour that we could barely see 50 feet away—refreshing after the hot dry days we just came through. We had our dinner and washed the dishes in the sinks provided. The kids played soccer and then cards before dark. A group of curious children hung around. One boy boldly asked me if Whitney was a boy or girl, while Whitney and Jake were playing soccer. (They play soccer together endlessly and the skill level is close to even.) The boy mustn't have thought a girl could play football that well, or maybe that she shouldn't have been playing at all, but he was definitely surprised at her capability when he got in on the game. She doesn't hold anything back.

As the evening wore on monstrous transport trucks moved in and surrounded us. Cooking equipment is built into most trucks, and the drivers prepared their own meals. A variety of delicious aromas filled the air for most of the evening.

There were two vigilantes carrying guns who kept watch over the grounds during the night. Dayna, Karina, Whitney and I were playing Rummy when one of them stopped to say hello and watch our card game for a few minutes. He used his rifle as a support to lean on. Whitney was unaware of him until he spoke, and then she gave him the once over from gun up. She whispered in my ear with a quiver in her voice, "Mom, he has a gun."

I whispered back, "I know, he watches the place to make sure nothing bad happens overnight. He's a good guy."

She replied, "Oh," and concentrated on her cards again.

The luncheonette had fresh, homemade, crusty buns first thing this morning. We indulged ourselves and had toasted buns with banana conserve, corn couscous and hot chocolate, a satisfying Brazilian breakfast.

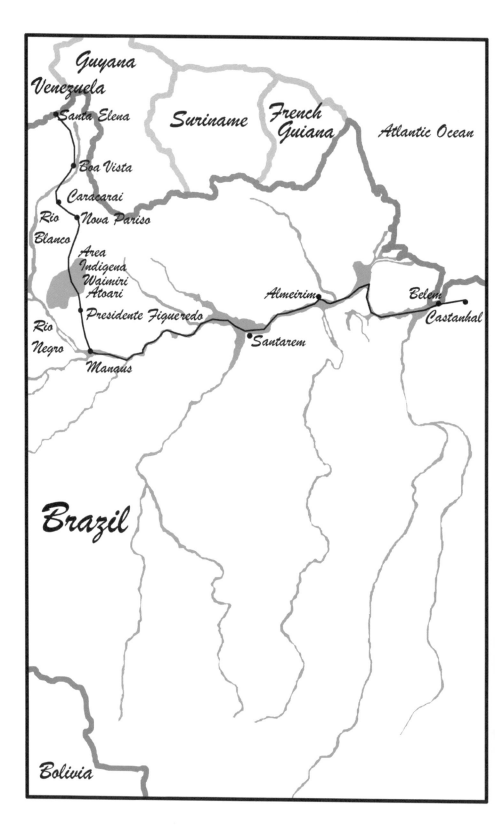

THE AMAZON

October 4, 1999: Castanhal

The campground we found here in Castanhal is a ranch, orchard, picnic area, *cabanas* and overnight camping space. What makes it a popular spot are the two swimming pools and large pond with paddle boats.

After choosing a spot, Ed and I left the kids to set up the tents while we purchased food. While driving back into the campground, trees that I recognized as Brazil nut caught my attention. After all this time in Brazil it was the first time we'd seen and recognized them. While concentrating on the trees Ed said, "Look, Gaye." His tone put fear in the pit of my stomach, but I was soon awed with what the kids had accomplished in our short time away. All I could say was, "Wow!" The tents were up, beds were made and the "kitchen" was set up, ready to cook the food we had just brought back. We have become a real team.

It didn't turn out to be a great a spot, though—the fire ants were biting. By evening everyone had little red bumps and a burning sensation all over their feet and legs. I gave in and put shoes and socks on. Despite the heat, my toes needed protection.

Ben found people to play football (soccer) with. Dayna, Tanya and Karina played volleyball with two girls about the same age as them and made friends. Their dad and mom visited and asked if our older girls could go out for dinner with their girls. Ed said it would be okay and they came to pick them up at 7:30 p.m. Five girls and the mother were seated on blankets in the back of the pick-up truck, laughing excitedly as they left. The dad asked Ben if he wanted to go to but he refused—too many girls. (It won't be like that in a couple of years, I'm sure.) They had pizza in a restaurant, a tour of the town, and were back at 9:30 full of fun.

I spoke with Mom on the phone for a few minutes this afternoon to let her and Dad know of our whereabouts. We needed to know the address of the hotel we are to meet them at in Oaxaca and let them know we are sending home two boxes of belongings. I told Mom we were going into Belem tomorrow to organize our Amazon River trip for Wednesday or Thursday. Mom expressed her concerns about bugs and germs on the Amazon and told me to be careful, to take care of the kids. She told us to be careful in Colombia, as it is not a safe place right now, and advised us to take care in Panama too. I was really looking forward to talking to my parents for a few minutes but got off the phone thinking, "This is what I'm going back to?" I know she was only expressing her concerns, but I'd like to know why it is I feel as if they think I can't handle what I take on in my life? And why do I let it get on my nerves that way? Maybe I overreact, but sometimes I think Mom has not come to terms with her children being adults.

Just yesterday we listened to "Barbara Coloroso's" tape *Discipline, Kids are Worth It* in which she speaks about giving kids responsibility and how most parents just tell their kids what to do all the time yet expect them to think for themselves. And, most parents continue to do that throughout their children's married lives as well. We have to give our children the opportunity and power to make choices at an early age so they will learn how. The comment that really struck me was, "Some of you will never be free until your parents die." I know exactly what she is talking about. Mom herself told me about the difference in Jean, her sister, since Grandpa died. In Mom's words, "Like she was set free. She seems so much more peaceful." I don't want it to be that way for me. How do I be the free self I need and want to be without being 10,000 miles away from my home, family and friends, when a 15-minute conversation brings up so much turmoil in the pit of my stomach? I know she is just being a mother but when can we be friends, and how do I change our relationship so that it can be friendship? Is that a change I am capable of making? I know with the kids' behaviour if I want to see a change in them I need to change how I think, act, talk and respond to their actions. Can it work the other way too? They are my parents and I want to be accepted for the person I am, not for who they expect me to be.

While I sit here thinking about this I remember even my grandmother coming home crying from a visit with her mother. I was about 10 or 11 years old and spending the summer on my grandparents' farm. Her mother lived in the village in an apartment. A couple of times each week we would spend a hot afternoon hour or two with my great-grandmother. One day in particular I remember well. Grandma had on a pair of shorts that looked like a skirt and a top of the same pink and white check pattern. Because it was a pair of shorts, it was higher above the knee then Grandma's regular dresses. The first thing her mother said to her was, "Well, aren't you getting a little daring in your old age?" Grandma showed her that it was a pair of shorts but it wasn't good enough. I don't remember what else was said that afternoon but I do remember leaving not long after we arrived, not getting any cookies and Grandma driving home in tears. She cried most of that afternoon. I couldn't figure out what was so wrong with what Grandma had on; I thought she looked pretty. Is this a learned behaviour we pass on to our children from one generation to the next? It is certainly evident in this family for four generations.

There may not be much I can do about the receiving end of the generation line but there can be many changes in what I pass on. God help me be friends with my kids. I must let them be who they need to be and accept the fact there will be things they will do differently from what I think is best. They need to know they have control of their own lives, the power to make their own choices and rejoice in or suffer the consequences accordingly. They need my love, support and acceptance without me undermining their confidence, belief and the faith they have in themselves. From what I see in life, it is people who believe in, and like themselves, who are capable of making decisions without doubts or fear attached that live happy, successful lives. I sure hope I am capable of giving that to my children.

The kids wanted to stay and play in the pool for the day, so just Ben went to Belem with Ed and me to make arrangements for our boat trip. Like Santiago, Belem is a city of five million people and influenced by Mary, mother of Jesus. The name Belem derives from *City of Our Lady of Bethlehem*. The six-lane street leading to the central city has a centre median of flower gardens and is congested with smelly buses. The downtown area streets are lined with tall mango trees, creating natural tunnels that keep the pavement underneath significantly cooler.

At the tourist office the woman made phone calls about boats travelling up river to Manaus but much of the information she gathered conflicted. She told us the

Festival of Nazare was on the twelfth. It incorporates a procession of two million people on the weekend. People come from all over this and neighbouring states for the festivities. So most boats with upriver destinations, were leaving the week after the festival to return celebrants to their homes. It occurred to both Ed and me that if we could leave this week conditions on the boat would probably be less crowded.

The Basilica de Nossa Senhora de Nazare in Belem is the home of a sculpture of the Virgin Mary that was purportedly produced in Nazareth during the early years of Christianity. The history of the sculpture incorporates stories of miraculous events. While the sculpture was kept hidden from the Moors it made its way to Spain, Portugal and eventually Brazil in the 1700s. It was lost during transport in the jungle and found again a century later by a homesteader. A shrine was built to house the sculpture of the Virgin, and soon stories of more miracles circulated amongst the population. Today, on the second Sunday of October, a copy of the sculpture is carried from the basilica to the cathedral along with a 380-meter rope weighing close to a ton. According to traditional belief, anyone who touches the rope will receive a blessing from the Virgin Mother if they are faithful. Two weeks later a procession returns the statue to the basilica. The interim is Cirio de Nazare—Festival of Candles, a celebration period in Belem.

The woman gave us a map of the city with directions to get to the Enassa shipping company and said we would find other such businesses in the area as well. Most travel options were for the week after the festival and it takes five days to get to Manaus. If we didn't leave until after the festival we would have been left with only six days to obtain a visa for Venezuela and travel another 950 kilometers before our Brazilian visa expired. We felt we needed to give ourselves a little more time than that to move out of the country.

While leaving the Enassa office, no further ahead, we were bombarded by people selling fares on various boats. A man named Ronaldo caught our attention, saying there was a passenger boat leaving tomorrow night and that the van could go on a barge at the same time. He took us to his office. The dates were good for us but before we paid anything we asked to see the boat—it is a long distance to Manaus. It was livable, the bathrooms were half decent; we were shown the kitchen, everything was clean and there was staff for maintenance. We decided we could manage for the five nights and days of boat travel and hung our hammocks up to reserve our space. We paid the fares at the office (there was no charge for Jake and Whitney), and then Ronaldo took us to the shipping company to complete the arrangements for the van. I didn't like the idea of the van going separately from us. The man in the office gave Ed a business card and on the top left in large typeset were the letters TLC. What immediately came to my head was tender, loving care. Those were not the words the shipping company used and a stupid thing really to put my mind at ease but for some reason it did. Then after Ed spoke with the agent we were convinced that the company really did care about providing good service. It cost 500 *reais* as opposed to the 450 that was originally quoted but our van is longer than most in Brazil and takes up more space.

Ronaldo then helped us complete our errands in Belem, directing us to a bank and the Central Post Office. While Ed took care of the banking, Ben and I each took one of our bulky 20-kilo boxes and stumbled through the doors of the Post Office, dropping them as soon as we were inside. There were three line-ups with 30 or more people in them and it looked as if we were going to have a long wait.

A uniformed woman came up to us and said we needed to purchase tape from the vendor outside but as soon as she saw I had some and that the boxes were going to Canada she led us to a wicket ahead of everyone else waiting in line. I still don't understand why she did that and it didn't appear to be a problem; at least, I didn't notice any looks of contempt.

Ronaldo then directed us to a welding shop to have the roof racks repaired. In less than an hour we were putting the box back onto the top of the van with the reinforced supports. Ronaldo took a bus back downtown and we were on our way back to Castanhal with everything complete. Ed offered to pay Ronaldo for his service but he said, "No, tomorrow when you are on the boat." He trusted us, and wanted us to trust him.

We were gone all day and I was concerned that it would be long for the kids alone, but the girlfriends were at the campground again, after school was out for the day, so ours had playmates.

October 10, 1999: The Amazon River

Ronaldo was waiting at our agreed meeting place and directed us to the *Nielo Correa*. He and Ed dropped the kids and me off late in the morning to board while they brought the van to the TLC Shipping Company. Left alone, we set up the remaining three hammocks alongside the others and organized the bags neatly underneath, claiming our space.

It became a long afternoon of waiting. The novelty of hammocks on the boat soon wore off and the only entertainment came from watching the cargo being loaded for upriver destinations. A chain of men loaded absolutely everything aboard by hand. Laundry soap, dish soap, Quaker oatmeal, canned milk, boxes of juice, macaroni, crates of eggs, hand soap, a truckload of boxed crackers, chocolate milk boxes, a door, boat motors, beds, motorcycles, gas stoves, champagne glasses, nails, sandals, mail, sacks of dried shrimp and flour, copper and plastic pipes and many different kinds of boxed cereal, just to mention a few things, and it all went onto the bottom level.

On Ed's return late afternoon he said, "I don't think we have anything to worry about. They went through the van thoroughly, made a detailed inventory and said they were responsible for everything listed."

Ronaldo made sure we had sufficient space for our hammocks and departed after Ed paid him for his help and direction. We appreciated his assistance; it was faster figuring out travel plans and navigating in another big unfamiliar city than doing it on our own.

The passenger's floor was tight with hammocks by the time darkness fell. The riverboat, perhaps 10 meters wide, accommodated three overlapping rows of hammocks 18 to 20 inches apart. To say the least, it was cozy. Our early arrival had given the eight of us a place together and I was thankful for that.

A cheer of "*cabo*"—finished—came from the guys loading the cargo. They looked like a bunch of painted ghosts from the flour dust glued to the sweat of their bodies and walked with less spring in their step, but still had enough energy to laugh and joke about their appearance. The last of the cargo was barely tucked into place before the boat pushed away from shore. As the lights of Belem faded into the distance we all settled into hammocks and fell asleep easily for our first night on the Amazon River. Whitney, firm about not sleeping strung in the air, was content with her made up bed on top of the packs. She snuggled down into the middle and we didn't hear from her again.

Ben and Whitney were up before the 5:30 a.m. breakfast bell, exploring the riverboat, and were the first to arrive at the dining area for hot milk, bread and coffee. (Brazilian coffee is made so sweet I can hardly drink it.)

Travelling through the narrows revealed palms and hardwoods with vines climbing tree trunks and an abundance of aninga arum flowers. The latter looked like giant calla lilies as tall as banana trees and created jungle to the edge of the river. Only where a stream emptied into the main artery did we get a glimpse of a small dark tunnel under the thick foliage.

For hours it was much the same on either side of the river. When the kids lost interest and were acting up I urged them to at least do some reading or math, which to my surprise they actually did. As we inched past small wood houses, women and children paddled to the riverboat in canoes in hope of someone throwing them food or clothing. I excitedly told the kids to come see the people, different canoes and houses. Ben quickly retorted in a frustrated-with-his-mother tone of voice, "Mom, you told us to do some math, and that's what we are doing."

I replied, "That's when there wasn't a lot to see and you were causing trouble. You're on the Amazon River you can do math any time. Come see the people." They climbed out of the hammocks to take in their surroundings again, and it was Ben who brought to my attention that the people living along the river were wearing similar clothing to any other Brazilian and didn't really look that different. They may not have looked that much different but I am sure the abundance and variety of food that the levels of society are accustomed to differs extensively.

Almorco, the noonday meal, turned out to be better than expected: rice, Brazilian *macaron* (cut-up spaghetti in a small amount of tomato sauce), the satisfying mainstay of Brazilian beans (Brazilians know how to make different kinds of beans appetizing in a variety of ways) and chicken cooked in the orange-coloured coconut oil that I have only experienced in Brazil; all tasty and filling. Coffee and cookies were available in the late afternoon and supper was the same as the mid-day meal with a different type of beans.

Tanya became instant friends with a young woman named Maria, beside her hammock. After Maria discovered that Tanya could translate the words of English songs she enjoyed, Tanya spent most of the afternoon translating songs. Ben spent the evening talking with a group of young men on the third floor, playing cards and dominoes. The young people beside us were a group of forestry students travelling to Manaus after studying in the Belem area. One woman, Dasney, had a turtle with her. She showed the kids and let them touch his back. Mario, the older student whose hammock was beside Ed's, was intrigued with Whitney's spunk and convinced her to play cards with him. She is growing out of being so timid with strangers.

Just before dark the eight of us found ourselves enjoying the evening meal peacefully together while watching the water of the Amazon River move slowly underneath us. I cherish those moments. It was a less troublesome day than I anticipated, and the kids did really well despite the tiff over sharing what was left of our mangoes.

The river and vegetation changed during our second day of travel. Once we were out of the delta and narrows and onto the main part of the river, there was no sight of land facing west. The vegetation became sparse, no more palm trees, and the terrain inland from the water's edge was flat and meadow-like with grasses. To the north in the distance, we could see highlands, and the south was as flat as Saskatchewan, the humidity causing the horizon and sky to fade together.

Throughout the day we encountered people in small fishing boats with triangular sails, held in place and adjusted by hand to catch the breeze. Occasionally we were able to hear parakeets over the hum of the engines in the sparse trees while the boat travelled close to shore. White herons and *manguares,* as Mario called them, blue heron-like birds, often stood in the shallows searching for a meal. Brazilian cormorants were plentiful on the river and easy to spot.

During our short stop in Almeirim a small group of people disembarked while several others from the village quickly unloaded the cargo that was being left behind. I noticed the boxes of champagne glasses and thought about the anomaly of small villages on the Amazon, and such luxuries. Vendors had enough time to come aboard and peddle their wares. We purchased, and proceeded to devour, a large bag of the best homemade banana chips we had ever eaten and would have purchased seconds but the boat departed before we had a chance.

Being an unusual group of foreigners we gained a measure of celebrity status. The ladies from the kitchen were extra courteous to us as a family. After our huge *almorco* and snacks of fruit and cookies late in the afternoon, only Whitney, Ben and Karina went to eat dinner. One woman who served the food came looking for us, wondering why we hadn't come for dinner. Ed tactfully explained that the food was good but one heavy meal in a day was enough when our bodies are so inactive.

The kids found friends and occupied themselves most of the day, giving me the opportunity to read Arthur Hailey's book *In High Places.* For the afternoon I was lost in words reminding me of Ottawa and home. Ed relaxed and enjoyed the travel without having to be the one to move us along.

Ed and I discussed what was happening with the children, how well they are doing with the different environment, and found ourselves wondering if we had come directly from Canada and done the Amazon trip what our impressions might have been. It would be interesting to know if everyone would have settled in so easily and stayed as healthy as we are in the tropics. Right now we live, eat and sleep as the majority of the population of Brazil and it suits us well.

Mario had a bottle of Vermouth and asked Ed and me to join him for his nightcap. He has been studying the Amazon jungle for several years and has recently come out of the forest after spending a year with an ancient bush tribe, studying plants and trees in the jungle. He is older than the other students and took an interest in the children. Like others we have met on our journey, he was concerned about the kids' education and their not being in school. But it didn't take him long to realize it wasn't doing them any harm. He thinks they are mature and sociable for their age and totally agreed that math, reading and writing could be learned anywhere, anytime.

Before being fully conscious of my surroundings this morning at dawn, I dreamt of touching and admiring the patterns on two pieces of pottery standing side by side. I awakened docked in Santarem at 4:30 a.m., to the sound of workers unloading cargo.

We ate our bread, tomatoes, avocado and juice from the cooler, and again the same women from the galley came to ask why we hadn't come for breakfast. I explained as best as I could that we had a little food with us that would go to waste if not eaten up and I really preferred coffee without sugar. She replied, "Okay, tomorrow I'll have *cafe almargo* for you." I was surprised she would make a special pot of black coffee without sugar for me.

All cargo stayed in Santarem, and the unloading continued the entire day. Ed and the kids went for a walk to visit the town and Ed called Camargo to let him know how we were managing. There were so many people coming and going, selling food, clothing and souvenirs, and others disembarking, that Tanya and I decided to stay with our belongings. After finding a bathing suit store with great deals, the others were back within an hour and Ed took Dayna and me to purchase bathing suits. The only one I had was so worn Ed was embarrassed to see me in it. They do get a lot of wear in this country. Dayna found one immediately, and I chose suits for myself and both Tanya and Whitney, since theirs were in much the same shape as mine. Not one of the suits cost more than eight Canadian dollars, leaving me to wonder how a store so far away from manufacturing companies could sell such articles for so little.

On our stroll back to the boat we discovered an interesting artisan shop overflowing into the street with straw baskets, hats, pottery, masks and all kinds of other handmade articles. A large pottery *chicha* jug standing three feet tall caught my attention. I loved it but decided it would be just too much trouble to get it back to Canada in one piece. Above it on the shelf my eyes rested upon a smaller version. As I reached out to lift its lid to see if it was glazed on the inside, making it useful as well as beautiful, I remembered my dream and looked no further. The lid, a kind of hollow stopper the shape of an inverted pear, fit into the opening of the jug and alone could be used as a small vase for flowers.

The shopkeeper was dressed in a fine white linen shirt of a sort that is popular daily attire for businessmen here in Brazil, but there was a roughness about him that didn't seem to fit the clothing. While paying for the pottery Ed noticed bottles of ginger liquor on the shelf behind the counter and asked if it tasted like ginger. That was an open invitation to pour some drinks and before we knew it, we each had a full shot glass sitting before us. We savoured it while chatting with the shopkeeper, and needless to say he made another sale.

On our return Mario and the kids were sitting lined up along the pier with fishing lines in their hands. Mario had hooks and Ben contributed our line. With the hope of a catch, Mario had a unique way of occupying the kids.

It is at Santarem that the Rio Tapajos drains into the Amazon River. The water is clear, clean and warm, whereas the water of the Amazon is muddy and opaque with silt. There was a swimming area on a small beach in the clear water within sight of the pier and several people from the boat took advantage of it. The kids were in the water all afternoon having fun with the forestry students, making pyramids and diving. Being the lightest, and capable of diving, Jake was the top of the pyramid most often. While Ed talked with a British couple who boarded I decided to join the young people and cool down once more before the boat departed. By that time the bottom of the river was stirred up and there was something about it that didn't feel right. I didn't last long. Just as I was getting out, giving into my uneasiness about being in the water, Dayna screamed in agony and brought her foot to the surface with a bleeding mark on her arch. Grimacing in pain she said, "It's really stinging!" Limping toward the boat she cried, "Now it's in my knee."

Seeing her in fear and pain triggered panic in me as the worst scary thoughts started to run through my mind. But that ever-guiding voice popped into my head saying, "You are not going to do Dayna any good if you lose it; keep your head together." She couldn't walk. I squatted for her to climb onto my back and as I carried her toward the boat we met a group of forestry students returning as well. A big guy with lots of muscle scooped her up and had her in her hammock within minutes.

News travelled fast. As Ed poured Sanitivo on the wound to kill bacteria, Dasney appeared. She looked at it, recognized it as a sting from an *araia* and immediately cleaned and squeezed it to bleed out the poison. She said it had to bleed.

Dayna's crying attracted a lot of attention and everyone gave his or her advice. People argued over whether the wound was really caused by an *araia*. An older woman sitting on the bench confidently said that it was. In the confusion I asked Ed to ask her what would happen if it were an *araia*. Is it dangerous? Will it pass? Everyone quieted while she explained that for a day or two it would be painful but not dangerous. She urged Ed to take Dayna to a doctor to give her some relief. I knew it was painful—Dayna only cries, otherwise when her feelings are hurt.

Another forestry student went for the vessels's staff nurse and when she took a look at the wound she too said it was an *araia*. So she, Ed, Dayna and I piled into a taxi and 10 minutes later arrived at the local clinic. Even the taxi driver was sympathetic. The nurse knew the taxi driver and the people in the clinic by name. Everybody knew everybody. The nurse called to someone through the locked emergency room door and explained what happened. Both a doctor and another nurse came out from behind the bolted door, looked at the wound and confirmed that it was *araia*. The doctor explained to Ed that only one of us could go into the emergency room with Dayna. Being more fluent with the language he went with her to help her understand what was going on.

Anxiously waiting outside, I asked the nurse what time the boat was supposed to leave. She said four o'clock and it was already 4:10. I must have had a look of concern on my face. She chuckled and said, "Don't worry, they'll wait." Dayna's comfort was more important.

Twenty minutes later everything was complete and I could tell by the look on Dayna's face she had some relief. Barely one minute in the taxi, and the driver's cell phone rang. He stopped the car to answer the boat captain inquiring about how the young lady was doing and how long he thought we would be. Our driver gave his assessment, saying she looked much better and that we would be there shortly. He folded up his phone and continued to drive.

I asked Ed what the clinic staff did and how much it cost. With a gleam in his eyes he said, "It was just like a John Wayne movie and a rattlesnake bite, only she had the benefit of a local anesthetic. The doctor gave her three injections and when I saw the knife I told her not to look. He made an incision in the bite, bled it, cleaned it up, made it bleed again, cleaning it thoroughly, closed it up and bandaged it. He gave her a tetanus shot and some anti-inflammatory drops for the poison that was left in her body. He explained that when an *araia* stings it opens the skin up and injects venom that moves into the blood stream immediately. That was why she could feel it up her leg so quickly."

Again I asked how much it cost. He replied, "Nothing. He just gave us the drops, said *bom viagem* and we left. Nobody wanted anything."

Either it was a public facility where no one paid or they were being really nice to us. I asked Dayna how she was doing and she said it was just her ankle that was sore.

She was a famous little lady on the boat where almost everyone was curious and concerned over how she was coping. She rested in the hammock with a circle of people around her, now able to enjoy the attention. Dasney and her boyfriend Philippe asked how she was and then we heard some real stories of the jungle. Philippe had a clean-shaven head and an amusing way about him—he makes everyone laugh. He knew how painful Dayna's sting was and lifted his foot up to her face to show her the scar where an *araia* got him. (Ed looked *araia* up in the dictionary and learned that it is the Portuguese word for stingray.) Philippe was doing research in the jungle when he was stung and didn't have the benefit of medical attention. It took three days for the pain in his leg to subside. We talked about some of the insects here and I complained about how itchy and bothersome the puss-filled blisters from the fire ants were. Fire ants are a minor irritation, according to Dasney. She told us about the time she and Philippe disturbed a nest of bullet ants, which are three centimeters long and extremely fast moving, hence the name bullet ants. Before they knew what happened these ants were on their arms and neck stinging like a swarm of bees. The itch lasted for weeks. Philippe rubbed his bald head and said he got ticks of some sort, not lice, in his hair and couldn't get rid of them so shaved his hair off as a last resort. He has also had malaria three times and survived. Ed, joking with him, asked if it was part of their curriculum to experience all this and if they got extra credit. Everyone laughed, Dasney in particular, and she said Philippe got top marks in that category. Dayna was much better, she relaxed and laughed at the stories, too.

After the evening meal Mario pulled out his vermouth, and Ed opened our ginger liqueur and we passed some evening hours on the river chatting. Mario spoke about his research identifying plants and some of the medicines that come from them. Ed told him, "Gaye is a *bruja* too. [He likes to call me a witch.] She makes medicines from plants in Canada for all kinds of things." Mario told us of some of the remedies he had with him. I wish I had understood more of what he was saying. I was missing the opportunity of a lifetime to learn some valuable information. Ed translated what he could for me but even he doesn't have the vocabulary to understand it all.

I met Rosa, the cook, in the morning just before both of us were about to take a shower. She said she would have coffee ready for me soon. There were only a few people moving around before 5 a.m. and I enjoyed the sunrise with my small pot of *café almargo*. I gave thanks and wondered what I had done to deserve such special treatment when I didn't ask. The humidity of the air filtered the sun, creating a magnified, red-hot ball breaking the horizon. The temperature increased dramatically the moment the sun lifted into the sky. I couldn't resist photographing it; I wanted to remember the incredible moment.

After Mario finished his breakfast he dug around in his bag and sat beside me with two big bottles of "medicine" and a chunk of compressed plant. He wrapped the compressed plant in a leaf and gave it to me, *breo branco,* used for headaches and as a bug repellent when burned. He then put some of each of the liquids into two smaller bottles and gave them to me. *Agua jatoba* is a tree sap used as a blood purifier internally and a disinfectant externally. *Oleo de copaiba* is used to fight infections—two drops in water or tea to take internally, or used directly on a wound. It won't irritate the skin. Mario then proceeded to pull out a bag with 46 different kinds of seeds he had collected, labelled and classified from trees he had researched in the Amazon forest when learning from the tribe with which he spent a year. He has tree-planting ideas and is in the process of requesting money from the government to put his project into action. I knew only two out of the 46: mahogany and pau darco. The first because of the beautiful wood and the second because the bark of this tree has become a common herbal remedy for several conditions in North America as well as South America; I have used it successfully for female problems. He gave me a wood sample, a seedpod from the jatoba tree that could be used as a rattle, and a small piece of amber he had collected. He loves the rainforest and has a deep respect for the trees and plants. He said his family lives in São Luís and can't understand why he wants to live in Amazonas and work in the forest. He hopes they'll understand someday.

The entire portion of the Amazon on which we travelled was inhabited, sparsely in places, and the scenery was much the same. We were always seeing people and fishing boats on the river. I'm not sure what to think of the houses which are built from what the surroundings provide. Most are constructed like board boxes with square holes in the walls for windows; some are painted and all have dry palm leaf roofs. Every house is on stilts and all have docks out into the water. In the small amount of forested area, houses were set where a tiny piece of jungle had been cut out. There were many groups of both types as well as individual dwellings. All had one or two canoes sitting at their docks. Believe it or not, there were several homes with satellite dishes mounted on their roofs or off to the side. In the evening after sunset the blue lights of televisions glowed out of some of the houses. So the people are not as poverty-stricken as what my North American eyes might make me think. In this climate one needs shelter from the sun and rain and the houses would be unlivable hothouses if glass were put into the windows. We have been finding this out for ourselves. Sleeping in the tents has given us shelter for the night, but in the past few weeks it has been difficult to breathe inside them, even without the fly attached. The answer is hammocks slung in the open air under shelter from the rain.

People in general are fairly environmentally conscious. On the boat organic garbage gets thrown into the river where it is often gobbled by fish as it hits the surface. Most plastic and paper is put into the trashcans. It seems to me that it is the older generation that resists using them. I witnessed an elderly couple dump a box full of plastic bags and several soft drink bottles into the river, despite the fact there were garbage cans everywhere on the boat. A lot of education is necessary yet.

Our fourth day on the river brought us into sparsely treed land, on both sides. Farm after farm had laid claim to the riverbank. I grew tired of barnyard, cattle and goat odours carried on the wind. As this was the dry season, the banks were four to five meters high and eroding. Wet season is May and June, when the river overflows, and when the houses built on stilts are put to the test. It is hard to imagine the

Amazon River houses

volume of water in this river, given the expanse to the opposite bank.

Our boat travelled upriver, hugging the shoreline, where the current caused less resistance. Riverboats travelling downriver were always in the middle, taking advantage of the propulsion of the current. The trip from Manaus to Belem is two days shorter than its opposite. There were many islands on the section of river we travelled yesterday, forcing the boat to maneuver from one shore to the other.

Several times during the day, we caught glimpses of pinkish-orange fish, almost eel-like and possibly two meters long. One of the crew told me they were called *bota* and are a plentiful creature in the river.

During the evening the kids played chess, checkers and cards with their acquaintances, and one young man kept losing to Ben at chess. The laughter and fun was infectious.

Late in the evening, Ed was long asleep by the time I stopped reading and found Whitney on the (increasingly) dirty floor. After I put her back onto her "bed" I realized that Tanya and Ben were not in their hammocks. Nor were Mario, Dasney or Philippe. I found them all on the upper deck where Mario was entrancing a group of eight with stories of his adventures and spiritual findings in the jungle. Tanya said, "You should be listening to this, Mom—this guy has spooky stories to tell." But I didn't join their group; I misinterpret too many words and wouldn't have got much benefit.

There was a new moon and the stars were extra bright for the hazy tropics. I found the Big Dipper close to the northern horizon and enjoyed losing myself in the sky for a few minutes before stretching out in my hammock.

The boat travelled along the north bank for many hours during the afternoon today and we continued to see houses and farms. The rocky clay of the banks appeared to be similar to that in Joao Passoa: grey, white, red, pink, purple, yellow, and orange. East of the mouth of a tributary we passed, the water turned to clear dark yellow much cleaner looking than the muddy opaque grey we were accustomed to. As we crossed to the south bank, there was a distinct line where the waters of the Amazon and tributary met but didn't mix.

Having seen several more *bota* today spurred Tanya into telling me about Mario's stories from last night. Indigenous people of the Amazonas believe *bota* are capable of shape shifting. Tanya and Ben listened to a story that mixes myth and imagination: *botas* like beautiful young women and have a hard time staying away from them. Occasionally, desire overwhelms a *bota* and when he cannot resist the temptation any longer he will transform himself into a handsome young man and come to shore to entice a young woman to be his own forever. The woman who falls under the *bota's* spell will see and hear only the *bota*. She will follow him away and never be seen again. As Tanya was relating this to me, my mind drew a comparison to the story of the mythical Qallupilluit of the north. Qallupilluit live under the sea ice and like to have people to come live with them. Out of respect for these mythical creatures, children are raised with a "healthy fear", which protects them from venturing out onto unpredictable shifting sea ice unaccompanied by adults. But in the case of the *botas*, I don't understand why young women should be "protected from going to the river alone—there must be more to the story.

Another story Mario told last night came from the tribe he lived with. It was about a young woman saved by her grandmothers from a *bota*. There was a family of women, four generations, living together. A *bota* had eyes on the youngest of this family. The mother of the young woman went to look for her daughter after she had gone to the river to fetch water and had been away longer than she should have. She found the girl at the river's edge talking to a young man. The *bota* saw the mother coming for her daughter and caught the mother up in his deception as well, in that she wanted the girl to marry a strong young man who would take care of their family. The grandmother of the young woman grew concerned and went to look for her daughter and granddaughter. She was too wise to fall into a *bota's* trance, and when she saw her granddaughter talking to the transformed creature she rushed home to consult her own mother. The old woman, knowing the ways of the *bota*, gave instructions to wet the fish-man down. This would break his spell and he would become a fish again. The grandmother did this and saved the girl and her family from becoming part of the *bota's* world.

When I heard this, my mind started to speculate. It made me think that maybe the story had grown out of some inappropriate match made by a mother. Maybe the mother thought her daughter would never find a husband because of her family, and it was the grandmother who convinced the mother that the match was wrong, saving the young woman from marrying someone not suited to her. I will likely never know, as stories vary depending on the storyteller. But no matter how much they are distorted, the underlying message usually stays intact. What came to me out of this one was the wisdom of elderly people and their ability to see what is really happening when younger people head into situations or actions without thinking them through. It is just my interpretation. But I love myths and legends that bring out perspective on the trials and tribulations of life. When I read such stories to the children they are always willing to listen, and in the last two days, we have seen several of the creatures that are featured in the folkloric stories we have heard.

Mario has taken us under his wing. He is going to help direct Ed through Manaus, take him to the port to pick up the van, locate the Venezuelan consulate, and find a place for us to stay a few days.

We are docked in Manaus tonight and almost everyone has disembarked. There are about 15 other passengers camping out with us on deck. Anyone who didn't have lodging in the city was welcome to stay on the boat overnight.

October 14, 1999: Manaus, Brazil

Mario, Ed and Ben left to retrieve the van shortly after Mario arrived in the morning. The rest of us waited. We read and played games while the heat grew more intense. The boat staff prepared around us for the return trip to Belem, and everyone kept asking how Dayna was doing. One worker said it couldn't have been *araia*; she would have been in more pain for much longer. After he left Dayna told me she still had sore muscles in her leg and hip—she just doesn't complain.

Finally, at 2 p.m., Ed, Ben and Mario arrived back. Ed said, "We have bad news. The van didn't leave Belem until Saturday and won't be in Manaus until Thursday morning." The barge was docked in port without our van on it. When the TLC agency brought the van to be loaded, the barge was full; but it did leave Saturday. Meanwhile, this caused some confusion for us. The guys had rented an apartment in Manaus for four days on the basis that we would have our belongings to cook our own meals.

Ed asked Karina to fill our water bottle with the water we were drinking on board the boat. Mario had a mini-bus taxi waiting, and we loaded our belongings. Ed asked me if I was sure we had everything. I checked the floor and under benches. Discouraged with not having our kitchen supplies for the apartment and angry at the shipping agency, I got into the taxi with everyone else. When the taxi stopped at the port gate, I glanced over the heads. "Karina!!! Karina's not here!" Ed exclaimed, "Oh, shit!" Tanya's mouth dropped. I started to panic. Before the taxi driver could figure out what was happening, Ed jumped out of the van and ran back to the boat. I jumped out after him feeling absolutely nauseous and like a stupid, uncaring mother. How could we all get in and not miss her—how did that happen? I couldn't believe it. As I walked in circles in worry, Mario directed me back into the mini-bus, which had been turned around, and we were driven back to the boat. Karina was with Ed and had a big smile on her face. It hadn't been long enough for her to panic. She got into the taxi with the full water bottle as if nothing much had happened. I gave her a desperate hug and asked if she realized we had left her behind. She said no. The nurse fortunately had taken charge and Karina understood she was to just wait. When Ed arrived, he calmly said, "Come on, Karina, we're waiting for you." Ha! We didn't exactly wait for her. We were on our way again, this time with everything and everyone. Ed said he felt as if we were missing something when we left. How can we miss a kid? Tanya, trying to make us feel better about our stupidity said, "Mom, it's easy to miss Karina, she is so quiet when she is with us you hardly know she is there." It is true, but no excuse. Karina has the type of personality that is quiet when there is chaos around, makes few demands on others and always waits patiently for her siblings to have their turn first. It is an admirable quality, but it appears to have just worked against her. Maybe this little incident was intended to bring to my attention that I am the one who needs to create change in the family dynamics and be sure to place Karina's needs in front of the others more often. I need to help her be a little more assertive, so she is not always taking the back seat to others.

The apartment is a neat place, run down with things falling apart but it doesn't have any odours. We have managed fine. It is within walking distance of *Zona Franca* and food markets, and we get around easily on foot. Manaus is a city of a million people, but it doesn't have a big city feel to it. A couple of amazing facts: It is 1,600 kilometers inland from the ocean but only 32 meters above sea level, and the average yearly temperature is 27°C, making it the hottest city in Brazil.

Mario took us to the food market, helped us move in, and stayed to visit. After he left we showered to cool down. At 8:30 p.m. the temperature was still 40°C and the air was so still it was almost impossible to sleep.

We had a lazy get-to-know Manaus day, walked through *Zona Franca*—the duty-free area—and met Mario for the midday meal. In the artisan market Ben found a blowgun and exclaimed, "Hey look, guys, just like in the movie *Jungle to Jungle!*" It was decorated with a "spooky" face whose mouth was made of piranha teeth. Every one of the kids watched in fascination as the woman demonstrated how it worked. She blew a dart into the grass beside her stall. Dayna was totally taken with the whole apparatus and exclaimed, "Coooool, can we buy it?" Ed rolled his eyes and replied, "Only if you can get it for five *reais.*" The woman obviously took a liking to the kids or she wanted to make a sale, because she gave it to them for five *reais* as opposed to the seven she was asking. Now they have a blowgun with bamboo darts. We listened to an Andean music group in the square until it was time to meet Mario for dinner. I love the mystical sounds of *quenas* and pan flutes. Being closer to Colombia, Ecuador and Peru again there is an Andean influence here.

For us to have our main meal of the day, Mario chose an economical restaurant with excellent food. After dinner, Karina got up to use the washroom, shook her finger at me in jest, and said, "I'm going to the bathroom now, don't you forget and leave without me". We laughed. I am glad she has a sense of humour about what happened and I am not sure I will ever live this down.

During the afternoon black clouds rolled in churning in the sky. If it were Canada we would have been in for a whopper of a thunderstorm but as Mario explained, it is dry season and the threat would likely pass. It did, although it brought some welcome cooler air. The temperature may have dropped to 33°C so at least it was easier to sleep.

Since the *Zona Franca* is a duty-free area I thought I might be able to purchase another camera body for a reasonable price, but cameras are not a popular item here. Stereos, televisions and music are more a priority for Brazilian people. They do love their music. Tanya found a Walkman for a good price, is happy to be able to listen to her own tapes. After Mario had finished school for the day, we met him at the same restaurant he brought us to the day before and had tasty *asado frango*—barbecued chicken. We discussed the heat. With the temperature soaring above 40°C, Mario said, "I don't think I have ever experienced such heat. If we just move out of the city the temperature drops 10 degrees." He told us the trees, where they exist, keep everything cooler, but in Manaus where it is practically all pavement or concrete it is much hotter. The absorbed heat continues to radiate long after the sun is gone and the city never has a chance to cool down. Mario doesn't like living in the city, but this is where his school is.

Being so hot we decided to hide out for the afternoon like everyone else; the city streets were especially quiet. Ben and Jake were in the apartment first, the rest of us well behind, when we heard screams, laughter and several bangs on the floor. They surprised and chased a three-inch cockroach looking for a meal. He got away.

Later we tried to go to two museums. One was closed for renovations and the other closed at five, so we missed both but visited Mario's friends. He calls them his second family and home. We had afternoon coffee and sweets with Theresa, the mother of Mario's friends, yesterday and she asked us to come for the midday meal today.

Mario said he didn't have to be in school this morning and would help Ed get around the city with the van. They left early and were back sooner than expected with the van in the same condition as we had left it. We organized ourselves for travel tomorrow and then had dinner at Theresa's.

Theresa is another amazing woman. When she invited us for dinner yesterday we refused, feeling that feeding our crew would be too much of a burden, but she absolutely insisted we come. She had an abundance of all basic Brazilian foods ready for us, prepared as deliciously as what any gourmet restaurant could offer. Her entire house is barely as big as the kitchen of the house we left—a square built of cement blocks, divided in half, one half divided in half again with fabric curtains to create three rooms. One quartered-off area was a bedroom; the main door opened into the other quarter and held a well-worn couch, one chair and a television on a metal stand. The kitchen at the back was well equipped. The dishes of food covered the table so we ate wherever we found a spot. Theresa has two sons, both in their twenties, and they, as well as many of their friends, including Mario, find refuge and food under her roof. During our visit, people came and went to say hello and have coffee. Two woman friends had dinner as well. I am beginning to think we may have been the attraction.

After dinner, Mario took us to the zoo to see the animals that are found locally. It's a small zoo, but the two female jaguars have adequate space, and it is possible to get extremely close to them. We came up to the barred and chain-link fence to see huge cat paws extending out the bottom of the enclosure, batting the waving grass. The jaguar at the fence looked at us with interest in her eyes. Mario immediately pulled off his hat and started to play with her as one would play with a kitten and a string. He played and teased the cat for several minutes. The other cat found this interesting and came over to play also. Soon there were four giant, declawed cat paws poking out the bottom of the fence. Excited, the cats would growl like puppies playing tug-of-war. When the play slowed and one cat had the hat between her paw and the cement wall into which the bars were secured, Mario petted the giant foot. Curiosity and wonder got the better of me and I drummed up enough courage to do the same. I have always wanted to touch a giant cat; I had the opportunity and did. I looked into her eyes and it was as if she gave me permission to touch her. Dayna did for a moment as well, but when Jake attempted, he moved too fast and startled the cat, causing her to jump back and swat at us. Mario played with the cats again and when the cats finally got the advantage he almost lost his hat under the fence. He hung on, but it came back minus a chunk, as one cat had managed to grab onto the hat with her teeth. Suddenly the cats weren't so passive and there were growls and snarls over a small piece of hat. One got the chunk to herself and the other in frustration grabbed the chain link fence with her canine teeth and made an indentation. That ended the play. They moved away from us.

They are magnificent animals. My heart aches for them in captivity; it's not where they should be—but then again they certainly aren't going hungry, either. It is still not right for them, though. They are grand wild animals that should be living in the forest.

After visiting the zoo we drove up the Rio Negro to swim before sunset. Dayna said she was not going to swim no matter what anyone said. Mario told her there weren't any *araias* in the water this far upriver. She was not convinced. The water felt so warm it was barely refreshing, clean but dark. One person on the boat, describing the water of the Rio Negro, said, "Take a glass of water out of the river and you would swear it is *Coca-Cola*." A good description: in the water, half way to your knees, it is hard to see your feet. Dayna managed to overcome her fear enough to get wet.

I watched Ed and the kids swimming and playing in the water and took in the surroundings. On a beach on the Rio Negro in the heart of Amazon territory northwest of Manaus, bars and restaurants stretch along the shoreline. There was a four-star hotel with all the frills amongst condominiums and high rises. There were people using rowing shells, Sea-Doos, motorboats and water skis. It didn't look or sound any different from a commercialized Muskoka lake north of Toronto. Mario and the kids

Mario & Kids
−Rio Negro Beach, Manaus, Brazil

made a sand castle. We took one last swim to wash off, and just after sunset we went back to Theresa's. She insisted we come for *ajanta* (supper) as well. Where the weather is cooler, *Ajanta* is usually a bowl of soup and coffee but in Manaus it is a sandwich and cold soft drink, usually *Guarana*, made from *guarana* fruit, found mainly in Brazil, and the best soft drink I have ever tasted. (available only in Brazil.) It seemed that Theresa didn't want us to leave. She loved the kids and enjoyed having them in her house.

In the short time it took to walk back to our apartment we were covered again in sweat. Mario stayed a short while and had a ginger liqueur with us. We exchanged addresses and promised to keep in touch. He told Ben to come back to plant some trees and go fishing with him in the jungle. Ben said he would for sure someday. Mario said he didn't like good-byes so gave us all a quick hug and left abruptly.

The sky is filled with lightning again tonight, but no rain.

October 15, 1999: *Presidente Figueredo*

Today it started to rain shortly after sunrise and didn't let up until noon. The temperature dropped to a more reasonable 25°C and it actually felt cool. The kids fell asleep: the highway, grey sky and cooler temperature knocked them all out. Ed and I watched the land pass and enjoyed the peace. The scenery looked familiar. I said to Ed, "If I didn't know better I could almost swear we were on Highway 17 between Ottawa and Sudbury."

Ed laughed, "That's just what I was thinking." Bush to the edge of the road, cleared spaces with modest houses and farms, a restaurant here and there, ponds and low lying areas where swamp has suffocated the trees, leaving the skeletons. The grey highway stretched and rolled up and down through the green; the vegetation is different though.

There was a campground marked on the tourist map at kilometer 110 north of Presidente Figueredo. It is in the process of being built, but we were invited to stay and enjoy it anyway. Any facilities feel like a privilege. The roofed hammock and tent area was furnished with picnic tables. The washrooms were incomplete but useable. Our host showed us the path to the stream and falls. He said to bathe there if we wished and explained that if we continued on the trail it would take us to the rapids. We settled our belongings under the roof and made a vegetable supper. It was so good to eat vegetables after eating white rice, beans, macaroni and meats for the past week and a half. The darkness fell, and the forest revealed a big difference between here and the forest of Canada: the sounds of tree frogs, crickets, screams, howls and growls (probably howler monkeys).

Tanya and Ben started to talk about Mario's stories again and wondered if there were jaguars here. Ed, attempting to reassure everyone, said jaguars more than likely stayed in the deep forest, and there probably wouldn't be any here.

Ben, Jake, Dayna and Karina said they were sleeping in the hammocks, so we set up only one tent. Ben let out a growl to tease the nervous girls. Dayna and Karina, after listening to the night sounds, decided that they were not sleeping in the hammocks, so Ed and I inherited them. The trip to the washroom before bed was undertaken as a group; no one felt confident about going by themselves in the unfamiliar surroundings. Ed put a machete beside Ben and one beside himself. He felt wary. Jake settled into his hammock long before everyone else and was into a deep sleep almost immediately. He relaxes and sleeps where the rest of us aren't as secure, yet a simple cloudburst will send him into a panic.

The girls took much more time than usual to settle in the tent, talking about every sound that pierced the night. I lay floating in my hammock, listening to the jungle. There were so many unfamiliar but peaceful sounds.

I awakened through the night, cold from the damp air, out of a dream about talking at length with my lifelong friend Lulu. October 15th is her birthday and it felt as if I had had a really good visit with her. Here I am in the Amazon forest, Amazon translating as "friend zone." There is something magical about the forest and river here and the dream seemed to deepen my connection to her.

I retrieved a sleeping bag from the van and crawled in with the girls to warm up enough to sleep again.

October 16, 1999: Nova Paraiso

Last night, we slept in the open and didn't hear a single mosquito. Ants, yes, but we are not bitten. In the morning, there was an ant trail (the larger size ants, the kind that are impossible to crush) leading to and from Ben's shoes and hat, which he had left on the ground underneath his hammock. As he shook out his shoes dozens of ants fell out along with pieces of shoelace. Surprised and in a complaining voice he exclaimed, "The ants! The ants have chewed my shoelaces all up. They cut one into three pieces and the other one in two. These crummy ants, I'm sure not going to miss them when we leave Brazil!"

He tied knots in his laces so he was able to wear them and when he put on his hat, it too had been chewed and shredded. "My hat I got from Denise in Itiquira, they've ruined it!"

I consoled him in a teasing voice saying they must have liked the taste of him. The Whit had to add her opinion of course and said, "Ben's shoelace from his foot? Eating that, they should all be dead."

How could I not laugh? He asked, "How come they did that?"

"I don't know, Ben, maybe it has something to do with the laces being cotton; maybe it is a food for them." He spent the next twenty minutes sewing his hat back into a wearable state.

We had a good discussion over breakfast. Ed asked the kids, "Do you guys realize we drive over the equator today? Today we will be back in the northern hemisphere."

It got us reminiscing about Canada, and now we have a few anxious kids. The one good thing about being together like this is the amount of uninterrupted time that we spend in real conversation with each other. We have discussed and learned so much and are enjoying the travel this time, the kids all being three years older. It's so much easier now that they almost take care of themselves.

We enjoyed the morning, with a bath in the river and a walk in the jungle. The latter was short—given our limited understanding of the plants and animals of the Amazon, we were cautious. I actually felt fear and realized that almost everyone on earth fears what we don't understand. It's a primal survival instinct, but it also boxes us in and holds us back from doing things that could expand our knowledge and quality of life. This is the reason for elders, teachers and mentors. I wouldn't have any trouble walking through this forest with someone who could teach me about it, but alone without knowledge I'm vulnerable.

The land we travelled over to get onto the Warmiri Atroari Native Reserve has been totally cleared for cattle farms; no forest whatsoever remains. The 120 kilometers of highway through the reserve revealed terrain no different but the trees and vegetation would swallow the road if given the chance. Private vehicles are allowed to pass through during daylight hours only, without stopping, and there were frequent signs to remind users of the fact. The few people we saw, carried guns and they did not look friendly. It was clear that if you were not part of the tribe that lived on the reserve you were not welcome. I can understand the reasons why. It is easy to see the devastating effect non-native people have had on the forest outside the protected area. Through the reserve the temperature of the air was cooler. Trees are perfect protection from the sun and create a livable temperature amongst them. It wasn't hard to know when we were out of the reserve—the landscape was once again the same dry cattle farming terrain.

While the kids and I were talking about the reserve Ed abruptly slowed the van and in an astonished voice exclaimed, "Look guys!" A wild spotted jaguar jaunted across the highway in front of us no more than 30 meters away. We were breathless. Maybe our caution last night and this morning wasn't as foolish as we had thought.

The equatorial monument was on our left minutes later. It is like a huge hockey stick propped on a twenty-foot rock. The temperature was so unbearably hot the kids didn't want to stop but I insisted. From September 21 to March 21 the shadow falls on the north side of the monument; from March 21 to September 21 it falls on the south side. And for two days a year it casts no shadow except directly underneath where the monument doesn't touch the ground. The sun travels east to west directly over the "hockey stick". We took some photos for the record—another reminder of distances travelled.

Again, in Nova Paraiso, without dipping into our pockets, we found overnight accommodation at the station where we stopped for gas. *Fica vantagem* is an expression we are getting to know well.

October 18, 1999: Boa Vista, Brazil

We were on the road early the next morning without breakfast and waited for the ferry at Caracai to cross the Rio Branco. Ed didn't want anything to eat from the *barraca* but I purchased two tapioca crêpes for each of us along with *café completo* for everyone as well, he enjoyed these too. (*Café completo* is coffee that is half cow's milk sweetened with raw sugar.) The crêpes were the epitome of "stick-to-the-ribs" food, but tasty. It only took a few minutes to cross the river despite the current trying to sweep the boat away. A bridge under construction upriver, within view, will render the ferry obsolete in a year or two.

It being Sunday the wild camping spot recommended on the river was not so wild—well, it was wild with people (they arrived by the truckload). Dayna was reluctant to swim in the river and the black flies drove us crazy. It would have been impossible to have a comfortable night being constantly bitten, so we moved to the public park north of the city and had more space and privacy. As we left, two more truckloads of people arrived.

While in the city, Ed prepared for our border crossing, changed half the *reais* we had left, exchanged the 20-litre water bottle for a full one, and had the roof racks repaired again. One support repaired in Manaus was coming apart. He also purchased a new tank of gas for the stove. When we had arrived in Brazil the fittings had to be changed to Brazilian standards. If we run out of cooking gas in another country they will have to be changed again. The rest of us did laundry, and I had time to complete the jaguar sketch I started yesterday. I have wanted to sketch a jaguar for a long time and it has just been since touching and seeing them that I've felt like I might be able to accomplish it. My jaguar sketch turned out really well, as far as I am concerned.

We will be in Venezuela tomorrow. I have enjoyed Brazil.

The Equator –Brazil

Caribbean Sea
Puerto Cumerebo
Riohacha
Santa Marta
Baranquilla
Maracaibo
Cartegena
Macuto
Caruao
Valencia
Caracas
Puerto La Cruz
Ciudad Bolivar
Panama City
Venezuela
Panama
El Dorado
Santa Elena
Pacific Ocean
Bogota
Guyana
Colombia
Ecuador
Brazil
Peru
Pacific Ocean
Bolivia

VENEZUELA & COLOMBIA, THE SECOND TIME AROUND

October 21, 1999: Boa Vista, Brazil-Venezuela border to Ciudad Bolivar

The road climbed 1,000 meters in altitude, over 50 kilometers, to the Brazil-Venezuela border. Our visas were in order, so the paperwork for the passports was completed quickly and our 30-day van permit was produced in 20 minutes. It was a shock shopping for vegetables, fruit and bread in Santa Elena, Venezuela—everything cost twice as much as in Brazil. We started to think Venezuela may not be as economical as it was when we were here three years ago, but we had a pleasant surprise purchasing gas. Only half the tank needed to be filled and it cost the equivalent of $12.00 Canadian. A half tank of gas in Brazil cost $60.00. Ed left the gas station with a huge smile on his face, as gas was our biggest expense in Brazil.

Driving north the terrain changed to grassland again. The expanse of La Gran Sabana is covered in yellow-green grasses, with trees and green vegetation lining rivers that have created hollows, gorges and canyons. Cascading waterfalls are abundant, with excellent places for swimming in the clear, clean water—some of which places have rock formations of jasper and crystal.

The higher altitude gave us some welcome cooler air. To our right from the northbound highway, in and out of cloud cover, we spotted Monte Roraima, Kukenan *tepui* and Turuani *tepui*, each with their sheer cliffs and flat mesa tops. (*Tepui* is Spanish for "flat top".) The plateaus atop these mountains are among the oldest landforms on earth. The highway creates the eastern edge of Parque Nacional Canaima, which covers 30,000 square kilometers of the country. It is one of the six largest parks in the world. Within its boundaries is Angel Falls, the highest waterfall in the world, plunging 979 meters, 800 of which are a direct drop.

Mount Roraima and Kukenam with their flat mesa tops. Venezuela

We were told at the military checkpoint that we could camp almost anywhere; we just needed permission from the native people where we chose to stay.

San Francisco de Yuruani on the river looked like a good spot and Ed asked permission to camp. It was not only granted but we were told to use the community toilet and drinking water from the spring uphill. Everyone uses the river for bathing and washing clothes. We were invited to make ourselves at home for the night. There was an abundance of black flies again and upon close inspection we discovered that they are not much different from the black flies we live with in Canada during spring. They leave a little itchy red dot and, for many, a white welt around the bite.

Setting tents up was a challenge between torrential downpours. One flexible pole for the large tent needed to be repaired. Ben set the tarp up but the wind changed direction and blew it down. Whoever had set up the small tent hadn't pegged it down properly and the fly ripped almost the entire length on three sides when a gust of wind tried to carry it away. I was caught in the tent during the most vicious part of the thunderstorm while the others found shelter in the van, but this ended up being a blessing as I managed to keep the sleeping gear dry and out of the stream that started to flow under the tent floor. We moved the large tent out of the water drainage path after the storm let up; you would think we'd have learned to pick better spots by now. I prepared dinner by candlelight while it rained again. The saving grace with the rain was that it forced the bugs into hiding. They had driven us all into pants, socks, and long-sleeved shirts. The kids settled happily into their tent, which despite the rain it was still dry. Ed and I slept in the van, as the third downpour had soaked our sleeping gear in the torn tent. Shelter is so important to keeping life running smoothly.

I crawled out of the van to relieve myself in the night and experienced the intense quiet that engulfed the land. The clear sky was a sea of brilliant stars, and there was a peacefulness that made everything feel right. We would never know peace if we didn't have some rough moments to teach us the difference, would we?

After things were dried out and packed in the morning we ventured off to the falls to clean ourselves up. The river dropped 30 meters in two stages; it was clean and clear with a gravel rock bottom. We let the waterfall be our shower and thoroughly enjoyed the experience. We contemplated staying another day but the flies changed our mind.

Ben and Jake explored the rocks on the higher level. When Jake came

Playing and climbing in the falls at San Fransico de Yuruani, Venezuela

back, leaving Ben sitting at the top, he said to Ed, "Ben cut his ankle, but it's no big deal."

Ed asked if it was bad and got a "maybe" reply from Ben. Ed told him to come down and get it bandaged. Ben said, "I'm trying to stop the bleeding."

"It won't stop in the water, Ben, you have to get out."

He climbed down while blood poured out of a deep cut on the tight skin of his ankle. The wound needed a stitch. We were a long distance from a medic, but Ed said he would do it; Ben was not happy with that decision at all. I fetched the first aid box and sewing kit. We disinfected the needle, fishing line and our fingers, and Ed told Ben not to look. He picked up the skin and attempted to push the needle through but the needle punctured his own finger with the eye of the needle. It was Ed that let out the yelp of pain. It hurt Ben but he took the situation well and laughed at his Dad. I handed Ed a thimble out of the sewing kit to push the needle through the skin. It worked, the knot was tied and the cut bandaged and all was complete with little complaint other than the first yelp from Ed.

The area is dotted with Indian villages where the dwellings are round structures with straw roofs. The abundance of waterfalls is a major tourist attraction, and we stopped at Quebrada Arapan and Kami Falls, each an exceptional sight to behold. Kami Falls drops 82 meters, in an area where lush green vegetation clings to the cliffs. Local people wear clothing fully covering their bodies, even in the heat—a necessary protection from the flies. It is the tourists who walk around with exposed skin covered in welts. The kids didn't linger. All were back in the van finding refuge from the *puri-puri,* as we learned they are called.

San Fransico de Yuruani, Venezuela

I asked to stop at Danto Falls before descending off the escarpment, but no one else wanted to venture into the flies. The escarpment and cliffs are fascinating. If you can stand the *puri-puri* it is a geological wonderland of adventure. For 50 kilometers as we descended off the escarpment, we were swallowed by thick jungle with an occasional glimpse of the lower plain stretching out in the distance. Ed made the comment, "I'm sure glad we're going downhill on this one." The van was running rough. He was sure it would never have made the climb. After a few minutes of sailing on lowland plain, a look backwards revealed a rock cliff supporting green vegetation anywhere it was able to cling, and several waterfalls tumbling over the edge.

On the north side of El Dorado at the Rio Cuyuni, Ed caught sight of a sign for camping and since it was late afternoon we stopped. The camp area was a couple of modest buildings with several tables and chairs set up around a "kitchen." Each table bore a table cloth and plastic red rose in a vase. There was a man, presumably the owner, standing at the BBQ-fireplace cooking (smoking we found out later) large pieces of fish. Dayna immediately exclaimed, "He looks like the bad guy in the movie *Anaconda*". He was wearing army bush duds and rubber boots. He introduced himself as Yan and greeted us like long-lost friends. Loud squawking noises drew our attention to three scarlet *araras* in a skeleton-like tree. *Araras* is a suitable name because the noise these birds make when not squawking, sounds like a-ra-ra rolling off the tongue. When Whitney pointed out the *araras,* Yan told her they are called *guacamayos* in Spanish. He told us one had a hurt wing and stuck around because he fed it. The other two stick around because they are too lazy to hunt for food. We said hello to the birds and they squawked at us as if we were intruders, which I guess we were to them.

Yan told us that he and his partner are building *cabanas* and a restaurant, and explained that they have cleared the space themselves. He pointed to the opposite bank of the river and said that when they started it looked like that. The other side was dense bush to the edge of the water. More deforestation and we are supporting it just by being here. There has to be a way to live without removing so many trees from our earth. Jake asked Yan if there were snakes here. Yan's eyes lit up as he said yes and told us to follow him. He showed us his pet anaconda, picking him up out of the huge laundry tub full of water and snake. Yan said he is almost four meters long. As Yan raised him, his head hung over the edge of the tub and he appeared to pay no attention to his lower parts being picked up. His eyes stared straight out at us. Jake asked if he was dangerous and got a quick reply: "Nah, anacondas are only dangerous when they're hungry, twice a year. It's the type of snake that bites that you really have to be careful of."

Yan is Swiss but has lived in Venezuela for 25 years. He said it is too cold in Switzerland in the winter, and he likes it better here. He told us he was in Montreal for a few months a long time ago but it's too cold there, too.

It threatened rain again. Ed and kids were hot so they swam in the river. I had no desire to swim—there was something about the water I didn't like. It was a red-brown colour from the iron content and with so much silt it was not clear. There are many gold and mineral mines in the area. The town of El Dorado, a few kilometers north, is one of the many small towns that were established during the gold rush. Although the gold supply is largely depleted, tours are available to see the mines. Ed bought some cold drinks from Yan and had more conversation with him. The kids hung around, finding his stories interesting, and kept an eye on the snake. Yan, sensing Jake's curiosity and uneasiness, reassured him that the snake wouldn't be dangerous for us, but, the little dog they have here, was vulnerable, as were any of the ducks or turkeys. (That's probably what they are for—snake food.) Tanya came to tell me what they had been talking about. Just up river there is a high-security prison, where Venezuela's worst prisoners are sent—there was a movie made about it. Then Tanya told me Yan said there was no reason to be concerned because nobody has ever escaped and if they get caught trying they're shot dead, no questions asked. The *SAH* says the prison was made famous by the movie *Papillon* and is in use again, since renovations have been completed. When Ed returned he told me Yan and his partner had a black jaguar hanging around for a long time and that it had become a kind of pet. They fed him fish they caught, but when the machines came to clear the forest he disappeared. Yan knows he is around; he still hears him once in a while. Ed says I should see the fish Yan caught: two 20-kilo *paraya*, smoking over the fire.

The rain started and we sat in the van for close to an hour. Jake asked all kinds of questions concerning prisons and bad guys. Listening to the stories caused some concern about his security, and he wanted to know what the movie was about. So as not to spook him any more than he was already spooked, I told him I didn't remember. Dayna made the comment that the snake was too scary for her liking; he reminded her of the snake character Kaa, in the movie *The Jungle Book*. She said it seemed as if he was trying to hypnotize her. She didn't like the snake's eyes, that's for sure.

Yan lay in his hammock for a rest after the rain. As soon as he shut his eyes one of the macaws flew out of its designated tree and into a tree next to the kitchen. Yan told the bird to get back to his tree, in a pleasant voice first, and when he didn't respond, he scolded him, telling him to get back where he belonged. The bird flew back to his tree squawking. We were amazed at the understanding and conniving of the bird. Yan said the birds wait until he is asleep and then help themselves to whatever is left out in the kitchen. They know they are welcome in camp if they stay in their designated tree. A few minutes later, the other macaw flew into the tree close to the kitchen. The bird perched himself behind a branch, thinking he was hidden. Cautiously, he poked his head out on either side to see if Yan was watching, looking for an opportunity to fly down into the kitchen. Yan let out one word and the macaw flew squawking back to his tree, as if complaining about being caught in the act. It is obviously a game they play often. Yan said they like fish, and he would give them some but not before it was done. They are impatient. I took photos of the macaws. They really have characters of their own. The one with the hurt wing sat on Yan's arm and let us pet him while perched there, but when he sat on the railing he wouldn't let any of us come near him. He has befriended and trusts Yan.

Yan asked if we would like some fish. How could we refuse? He was generous, giving us almost half of one of the 20-kilogram fishes. It was nothing short of absolutely delicious and the supper I made was barely touched.

Having said our good-byes, and on the road again in the morning, Jake said, "I liked that place but Yan looks too much like the bad guy in *Anaconda*."

As we arrived in Ciudad Bolivar late in the afternoon, it rained again in torrents. At a gas station Ed asked if we could pitch camp in the overnight lot for trucks. Daylight was gone by the time the rain slowed, and the walled lot looked like a lake: there was not a dry spot to pitch a tent. We finished our book, *Shadow at Hawthorn Bay,* using the flashlight, and slept on the floor and seats of the van, we settled in well under the circumstances.

October 25, 1999: Puerto La Cruz

Two major things have gone on in the past few days. First, the van is not working well, and second, we have decided that we are going back to our house in Wakefield.

When Ed awakened on Friday at 5:30 a.m. he decided to move immediately since we were all in the van. It choked and hesitated and didn't want to go but finally did after a couple of minutes of complaining. We crossed the only bridge over the Orinoco River in the dark. We passed El Tigre by 6:30 and were at Anaco by 7:30 a.m. Just as we were talking about being at the Caribbean Sea and beaches by 10:00 the van started choking and backfiring. Ed managed to pull it to the side of the busy road before it stalled. It could not be coaxed to start again. He tried to flag down several cars to hitch a ride back to Anaco, without success, but when the kids and I got out onto the side of the road a car stopped almost immediately. When the man and woman found out we were Canadian they took Ed right to a garage and towing service to make sure he got a fair price. The tow truck and Ed were back within 30 minutes.

It took four hours for the mechanic to find and fix the problem—a valve that regulates the gas circulation. The Caribbean was an hour's drive away, but as we arrived in Barcelona heading toward Puerta La Cruz the engine started to cough and choke again. Ed pulled into a place where he could stop just as it stalled again. After it cooled a little it started and took us a few more kilometers before it stopped for the third time. At an auto parts company close to where we were stranded, Ed asked about a mechanic and was given directions to "Tony's".

There, Ed and Ben were told our problem could be any number of things: fuel pump, the electronics module, or anything electronic. When parts get hot they expand and can prevent the fuel from getting to the motor. He would have to check it out on the computer. Unfortunately it was Friday afternoon and the garage still had a lot of work to do before the end of the day. But if we wanted to bring it in on Monday morning Tony would be happy to check it out then.

We drove barely two kilometers before the van was choking and backfiring again. Ed walked back to Tony's to ask if he would recommend someone else who might look at it that afternoon. The first place Tony recommended didn't analyze Fords. At the second place the man who received us didn't even look at the van and said it was the fuel pump. They couldn't do it Friday but would Saturday morning. He also said that the mechanic who changed the valve shouldn't have—it wasn't necessary; the problem was the fuel pump. Ed was not convinced by this person, looked at me and said, "Okay, now what do we do? Should we go to the beach?" We'd slept in the van last night, hadn't used a bathroom all day, and all we had eaten were empanadas and the previous night's leftover cookies. Our ice water was sustaining us. I said, "I don't want to go anywhere with the van like this. It could leave us anywhere. Why don't we get a room for tonight, take a shower, get a half-decent dinner and a good night's sleep. By the look of the clouds it is going to rain again when it's time to set up the tents."

Ed was not convinced. "I don't like this guy. He didn't even look at the van and says he knows what the problem is. I think we should go to the beach for the weekend and get Tony to fix it Monday."

The van went to Tony's but we didn't go to the beach. The girls wanted a room for the night, and the boys said to camp. Females are the majority in this family, but it still took a downpour before Ed consented even to looking for a room. While driving toward the beach Ed asked if there was food for supper. I told him we could make do with what we had, but we had no extras. He pulled into the parking lot of a grocery store. We sat there while it rained. There wasn't a sound from anyone as we let our tough day get the better of us. Dayna said there were lots of places to stay along the street we had just driven along; she had been watching for them. Ed gave in to make the girls happy; he didn't feel like setting up tents in the pouring rain again either. He and I walked the street to look for a place for the night.

We found the villa we are in right now, with the help of another Tony, at a travel agency, where we asked about accommodation. After visiting hotels, it was a great price by comparison. Everything was under control at the van when we returned, but we worried the kids we had been gone so long. At least their stomachs were full—they kept the hotdog vendor on the street busy cooking hotdogs for them between downpours. We purchased food for three days and met Tony after he closed the agency to bring us here; we had to be signed in. By this time, the van sat for almost three hours and cooled right down. It ran so smoothly driving to the villa you would have thought it was brand new.

The "Villa" is a middle class community of row housing on a Caribbean beach. Our angels have been working for us again; there is everything we need and more.

Saturday was a "pull-ourselves-back-together" day. Yesterday was Ed's 45th birthday and he says he's not getting older, just better. I'll vouch for that and love him more every day that passes. Can't live a long life without adding numbers to our age, can we?

He called Lisa at home to let her know of our whereabouts. The situation is that Christiane and Pascal still don't want to buy the house but would like to continue renting for three years and move back to the city when their son is ready for school. Ed told Lisa that since they don't plan to purchase the house and they will eventually move we don't have much choice. We need a place to live when we return to Canada. Ed had Lisa tell Pascal we need our house for May 1, 2000; he can stay in the clinic but we need the house.

The kids are happy about going back to the home they left. I am not so sure, it's not exactly what I had planned for our return. There must be something incomplete that I need to do, or Wakefield is the home where I, we, our family, belong. I think about the morning sunrises across the Gatineau River, the beauty of spring, summer, autumn and even winter and the changes we watched take place overlooking the water. It would be good to go back to the familiarity and rhythms we lived in that house. But it will be a challenge not to let myself get caught in the "busy pieces of me everywhere" kind of life I left behind. So the test is to put me back in the same life we lived before, stay sane and make it work this time.

Birthday dinner was a happy time. The anticipation of going back to our house made the children extremely excited, and already there has been an argument over who is going to have which bedroom and who is sharing with whom.

They were talking about what they are going to do when they get home. Karina asked if we still have our piano. Tanya told her it's at Diane's. Dayna said she is going to learn how to play piano when we get home. Karina too. Tanya said she's going to do violin again, then thought about it and came up with, "I bet if I had basic books and tapes I could teach myself if I wanted."

I said, "I bet you could teach yourself absolutely anything if you wanted and had the resources." She stopped to think and it was as if a light went on in her head, "Hey, yeah I can." What she doesn't realize is that, with a few resources, teaching herself is exactly what she has been doing for the past several years, and that she is becoming a competent young woman who now speaks four languages. I hope she understands the value in that and builds from it. But it has to be her choice. All I can do at this point is lay out ideas she hasn't come up with, help her obtain the resources, and support her wherever she chooses to go in her life. Ben just listened; he is excited to be going back to Wakefield but isn't making plans as yet.

Ed took the van to Tony early this morning and before the kids got up I spent some time letting the reality of going back to our house sink in. At moments I am excited; at other moments a sick feeling takes over in the pit of my stomach. I never feel comfortable with changes until I am well into the change, and then I don't want things to change again. I just feel if we go back to that house we will likely never leave it again. But like Ed says, "Is that really so bad?" I would just like a less busy spot to live, but then again I am the mother of six children; how can I expect life to be less busy?

After lunch I said, "We are going to the beach for an hour and everybody is coming, no excuses." Every one of them complained that it was too hot to go to the beach. It took some effort to move them out. Dayna didn't put a bathing suit on, and I made her go back. She says she doesn't like swimming in the water; there are too many animals, but at the beach she was the first one in. They wanted to go back to the villa within 20 minutes, but I insisted we were staying for an hour. Dayna complained, "But why, Mom?" I said, "Dayna when you are 30 and in a job that gives you only two weeks vacation per year you are going to say to yourself I should have enjoyed those beaches in Venezuela and Brazil when I had the chance."

She grumps, "No I won't—how do you know?"

"Dayna, you'll find out. Just enjoy where we are right now."

When the designated hour was up everyone but Karina and I headed back to the villa. We hunted for shells and listened to the gentle lapping of the waves. Puerto la Cruz is a vacation and working city. Sailboats and yachts are anchored in the bay, ocean-going ships are in and out of the port, and the stark grey Chimanas Islands, with cliffs that look as if they have been chopped straight down with a machete, are the backdrop for it all. The area is priced toward tourism; it is not what we are used to.

When we had had enough sun, Karina and I wandered back to find Tanya and Ben throwing things at each other. Both were out of control, angry and yelling over something. For all the words Tanya knows, she forgets to use them when anger builds. Ben went upstairs to get away from her and she sat on the couch steaming. Her voice came out like a growl through clenched teeth: "I'm so sick of living in this family." After a few minutes of cooling off I asked her if she was tired of travelling. She said, "Yeah, I just wish I were at home."

I asked, "What would you do with yourself if you were at home?"

She said, "I don't know".

I replied, "Well, I'm not so sure it would be that much different unless you really knew what you wanted to do with yourself." She just sat in the chair and it was the end of the conversation.

Tony checked the van on his computer and everything seemed fine. He spent four hours running the van, doing tests, changing the brakes, cleaning the spark plugs, changing the oil and doing a general tune-up. He thought that possibly the problem on Friday had something to do with the motor cleaning itself out after the other valve problem. If we have difficulties again we have to get the van to a mechanic, so that it can be put on a computer when the problem is occurring. That's what we wanted on Friday, but it didn't happen and now we are supposed to continue without the real problem being fixed. I don't feel good about this. We leave for Caracas in the morning, as nobody wants to camp on the beach.

Thursday, October 28, 1999: Macuto, Venezuela

We followed an oil pipeline along the seashore for most of the day and passed a major oil refinery. The route inland again was through a low-level, heavily treed landscape with hills and mountains to our left. The van ran as smoothly as new for several hours until we arrived in Guatire. Then it acted up again. The kids were extremely patient on Friday, and on Tuesday they just resolved themselves to waiting. The one comforting thing is that when the van cools down it moves. Ed asked about the location of a mechanic and was given directions, but the van stopped two blocks away from the garage. After a 20-minute wait it started, and then coughed and sputtered into the shop. The mechanic didn't have a computer to check electronics but checked other things and found both the gasoline filter and the air filter clogged. The parts were changed, he tested the van on the road, and it worked like a charm. We were 20 minutes away from Caracas, and he told us we had lots of time to get to Macuto before rush hour.

We were just above sea level; Caracas is at an altitude of 960 meters, a climb of almost one kilometer over 30 kilometers of highway. We started through rugged mountains covered in lush, green trees. Ed said, "Hello Andes, you really are beautiful, aren't you?" and the van replied with backfiring, and began hesitating again. Ed pulled into a gas station before the engine stopped. We waited. Fifteen minutes later, Ed wanted to leave. I said, "We should not go anywhere until the van is cold. Give it a few hours rest and drive to Macuto after rush hour. It will take us that far at night when it's cooler." But Ed wanted to get through the city before rush hour. "If we go a little at a time, stop and let it rest, it will get us there." We rarely argue but we had a difference of opinion and I am the cautious one. Caracas is a city of four million people in the mountains. What if it stopped on a bridge or on the edge of a mountain with no shoulder or in a tunnel during rush hour? Tanya and I traded places. I sat in the back and said no more. My gut feel said the fuel pump should have been changed on Saturday. There was a hum in the van that sounded like a small motor trying to run—unsuccessfully; both Dayna and I could hear it while sitting at the gas station. Ed couldn't hear anything. He went maybe another half kilometer before the van stalled again on the busy highway in the sun. We waited a half hour and went again. It moved but coughed and sputtered with every inch it climbed. At a sign that warned of a tunnel I couldn't keep my mouth shut and yelled "Ed, don't you go into that tunnel. You don't know how long it is and the road is really busy!" He pulled onto the shoulder. Tow trucks travel the highway looking for business and two slowed down but without a response from us didn't stop. Another tow truck, undeterred, stopped ahead of us. The man spoke with Ed, telling him it was rush hour until 9 p.m.

Ed decided to have the van towed to the Macuto highway where driving was downhill from there to Pension Guanchez. When the van was hooked up he said, "*mucho pesado*"—lots of weight. So there we were, being towed again. The volume of traffic increased dramatically, bumper-to-bumper traffic crawling along, just like in Toronto. The van was reflecting what we are all feeling. On the road, tired out and looking for the energy to keep moving. Some days I feel it would be nice to be in one place for a while, but I know when we are back in our house I'll be wishing I were on the road again. We had a relaxing drive through Caracas and got to look around. It took almost two hours to get to the La Guaira freeway, 12 kilometers from where we were towed. The van ran perfectly again. Ed's comment was "The van runs like a woman—it only works when it wants to." He was making reference to me, continuing our tiff, but the van was working and I could laugh. Some days I work hard, others I say "to heck with it." Within a half hour we pulled into the driveway of Pension Guanchez and the van didn't cough or sputter once.

Both Tanya and I looked around and said the same thing. Either we are really South Americanized or there has been a lot of fixing up done. Pablick was so happy to see us. Ed asked if there was room. Pablick said, "The whole house can be yours." He told us to bring our things into our house. He was so pleased that we could talk to him now. He teased Whitney and said, "Three years... everyone's bigger." He gave us the bigger, quieter room across the hall from the one we had three years ago.

Ed said, "Either this place feels like luxury or our comfort tolerance has really changed." Interesting how our perception is based on where we come from. It is not much wonder there are so many differences of opinion in the world. Everyone comes from a different background even within the same culture and most of us fail to recognize and accept that.

Ed and Ben spent the morning trying to figure out van repairs and came back with another story. The mechanic listened to the van's history of the past week and said any one of the things that were changed could have been causing the problem and it could be one of a few things not checked yet. The fuel pump or electronics module are two other possibilities. He suggested changing both. There wasn't a fuel pump in stock anywhere in Caracas but the module was changed. Ed started the van and asked if I heard the hum. He never did hear the different sound it was making. I didn't hear it but it was not as hot as it gets after several hours of driving.

We went without breakfast, anticipating the midday meal at Pension Guanchez. The meals we were served here on our first visit have come up in conversation several times in the past three years. At 9 a.m. two men walked into the main entrance of the house with a huge slab of fish of some sort on their shoulders, maybe shark. It was lunch. Whitney refused to eat the fish. Pablick asked her if she wanted some chicken and she sheepishly shook her head yes. Fifteen minutes later Pablick brought a half breast of chicken that had been pounded to a thickness of barely a centimeter and sautéed on both sides. It spilled over the edge of the dinner plate. Whitney's eyes lit up. She gave Pablick the biggest smile she owned and said *"gracias"*. It was a sincere *gracias*; convincing Whitney to use the words please and thank you has been a challenge. If she didn't have Pablick at her beck and call before, she does now. He is totally spoiling her and likes to make her smile.

Ed found out the room was double the cost and midday meals triple what we paid in January '97. We were just assuming prices were similar.

Ed took everyone but Ben to Caracas today to start the process of getting the *libreta* for Colombia, as the other one has expired. It wasn't necessary for Brazil and Venezuela, so we had travelled without one, but Colombia requires it for vehicles that aren't South American. The kids didn't want to stay here again today with so little to do and Ed was willing to take them along. What a treat for me.

Ben and I walked along the beaches and streets we had visited three years ago and discovered that the whole area was in better condition. There was some garbage, but there were people out picking it up. No more smelly heaps, and places are repaired and painted. Everything looks better.

At 4 p.m. Ed and the kids were back and the van worked without any problems. Ed commented, "What a place to put a city, the poor trucks." The airport and shipping port are both on the coast at sea level and the major part of the city is in the mountains. There were several disabled trucks and cars stopped alongside the highway—it is tough getting up that high in such a short distance. Ed didn't think the van was going to make it. The temperature gauge went more than half way up, then it went right back down, but it hasn't done that before.

At the office to purchase the *libreta* Ed was informed that because the van was more than five years old it needed a vehicle inspection. The agency sent him to the other side of the city to the Government Vehicle Inspection Station, where people typically arrive at 4 a.m. to obtain a number, in the hope of having their turn that day. It was going to take days, so Ed went back to the office for the *libreta*. In the middle of Ed's explanation Dayna piped in, "So Dad told a lie, Mom, he told the lady they wouldn't inspect the van because it was from Canada." Whatever the case, the lady believed him and started the papers for the *libreta*. Not only that, she surveyed all the kids and said, "Since you were here before and waiting, if you want to wait a little longer I'll prepare it for you now." Twenty minutes later he had the papers that were supposed to take three days, along with a refund for the *libreta* from three years ago. The whole thing sounded a little confusing to me but I wasn't going to question the outcome. Some days are easier than others, and today was one of the easier ones.

Otto, a mechanic and Pablick's friend, who we met the last time we were here, came for a visit. He couldn't get over how much the kids had grown. (Kids do that, especially in three years.) They discussed the van, and he thinks since it made it up the hill and worked fine today that the problem is likely solved. Otto has a cottage at Caruao and offered it to us. It is not on the beach but close to it. We took the opportunity. It rains every day and in torrents for an hour or two. Keeping things dry while camping is a challenge. So we have a cottage for a few days, and will travel during the week from now on, in the event that we may need a mechanic again.

Word is out that we have returned. People that Ed adjusted three years ago are back and being adjusted again tonight.

No one had been at the little cottage for a month and the jungle was moving in. The place was on a plot of land that at one time was cleared and replanted with fruit trees. Everywhere, there were limes, lemons, mandarins, oranges, navel oranges, another kind of large orange and bananas. We explored and ate our fill of citrus fruit and bananas. The night sounds of the jungle were different from those in Brazil. Crickets, frogs and toads were so loud and distracting that it was hard to sleep. They were so much louder than in daytime it makes me wonder where the creatures hide during the day; we rarely see any.

I awakened with the sounds of the jungle changing to the sound of rain. Gentle at first, but the distant rumble of thunder gradually crept closer until it surrounded us. Ed woke up as well. I said, "I could really enjoy this if I thought we wouldn't have trouble getting the van out of here." He told me to enjoy, it's not going to be a problem. The lightning and thunder felt as if they were trying to say something. One bright strike with an instant sizzling crack wakened everyone but Dayna and Whitney. The bathroom light we had left on went out. Mother Nature gave me the impression she was angry, and I felt at her mercy, yet a sense of peace was present with the faith of knowing it is God and Mother Nature who are the only forces truly in control of all life. The rain was so intense for so long, even Ed said if it didn't stop soon we were going to be swimming out.

We spent a leisurely afternoon lying on the beach and swimming. Fishermen came in with the day's catch and Ed asked about purchasing fish for supper. The curiosity of the kids created some amusement for the fisherman and they were more than accommodating, letting us touch and observe the sharks that were caught. One fisherman opened a shark's mouth to reveal four rows of sharp triangular teeth and the kids were nothing short of awed. Jake said, "It's not much wonder they can bite legs off."

Our laundry from the previous day didn't dry and the clothes smelled of mildew so they had to be washed again. The day felt like a steam bath with so much moisture in the air. Considering that it was the rainy season and we were in jungle-like forest, there were surprisingly few mosquitoes.

Otto said to take what fruit we wanted, that it was just going to waste, so the kids filled bags with lemons, oranges and mandarins to take along. We won't need to buy any for a couple of weeks.

Otto and Pablick both mentioned returning to Macuto through Higuerote. The road is longer but there aren't as many mountains—the only killer was the one we didn't make it up on Tuesday. When we got there, the van kept climbing and so did the temperature gauge. I held my breath in nervousness. The altitude leveled out and when the temperature gauge followed suit, everyone but me cheered. Kidding, Ben said, "See, Mom, that wasn't so bad was it? You can relax now."

I told him I would relax when we were at Pension Guanchez. At that moment, almost at the La Guaira freeway, we heard a backfire. Nervously I blurted out, "It's doing it again!" Ben, in denial, said, "No, it was the truck beside us." But he was proven wrong. The van coughed, sputtered and backfired again. Ed pulled into a rest stop off the freeway and turned the engine off. He was so discouraged, as were the rest of us. On the positive side, Ben said, "Well, we made it to the top anyway, it's downhill from here." This was true.

The day was cloudy and cooler than usual so after an hour's wait Ed turned the van on and drove to Macuto problem free. While eating our evening meal in the room there was a knock on the door. Ed answered it to find Oswaldo, two women and a boy about ten years old. Oswaldo's sister was adjusted the last time we were here and she brought a friend whose son has had a problem since falling out of a tree a few months ago. Nobody has been able to help him with the limp and pain in his leg. Ed brought the table out to the balcony and adjusted the boy. Immediately the limp was gone, along with most of the pain. Ed always attracts a crowd. Many of Pablick's 11 brothers and sisters were home for the weekend and after they witnessed the results, Ed adjusted them all, including Pablick's mother. She couldn't raise her arms to comb her hair and after her adjustment she could reach her head. She thinks Ed has been sent from heaven. Oswaldo patiently waited his turn, telling me that we have to come and live in Venezuela, that Ed could make lots of money—but we are going home for now.

Otto showed up too and asked if we had a good weekend. He checked the van and is almost sure the problem is the *bobina,* the pick-up coil. Tomorrow Ed will have that changed too. He called Daniel, a patient of his in Wakefield and a mechanic at the Ford dealership where we had the van serviced at home. Ed wanted to discuss the problems we have been having with the van. He came back from his conversation feeling assured we are not doing repairs for nothing. Everything repaired was probably necessary and Daniel recommended changing both the pick-up coil and fuel pump to have the problem covered.

It was late by the time everyone left. Meanwhile, Oswaldo had brought some pastries for us from the *panderia*—bakery—and the kids cut them up so everyone could have a taste of each. It was difficult for them to wait for their Dad. One piece was missing icing, and when Tanya confronted the younger ones Whitney yelled back, "I didn't do it, the knife did!"

They were giddy. They pushed three single beds together and everyone but Tanya was on them. Not used to so much sweet at once, they couldn't sleep, even though it was midnight. Tanya and Ed were frustrated with their foolishness. There is nothing like a pajama party, except, it was hardly a big deal here, in that they all sleep in the large tent together all the time. The one consolation I have always had when having difficulty getting babies to go to sleep is that no one can stay awake forever, and it still holds true.

Ed and Ben were gone for van repairs again this morning. The mechanic who worked on the van today changed the pick-up coil only and said if it were the fuel pump it wouldn't go at all after it quit. There still wasn't a fuel pump in the city to fit the van and Ed was convinced that it was the pick-up coil after seeing it cracked and burnt. We will try again.

During our midday meal, Pablick's mom walked by dancing and waving her arms above her head. She is so happy and feels so good. Pablick calls her the big boss, and the big boss said we don't pay for this two-day visit. She has invited us to stay longer, but Christmas is coming and we need to be moving on.

The kids spent the afternoon playing hide and seek in the huge house and no one minded. As a matter of fact Whitney was finding the best hiding places with help from Pablick himself.

When I returned from food shopping for supper Ed was adjusting the crowd. With Tanya's help I spoke with Pablick's mom. I have enough language to shop and get around, but when it comes to full-fledged conversation I still don't have the vocabulary. She had 13 children but lost two at birth. Her husband was 30 years older than she was and died six years ago at the age of 101. They have lived in this house for 55 years, the children grew up here, and the place has been a *pension*—rooming house—all through those years. She told us her husband's family was from Spain. She has children in Spain, Sweden and the U. S. but most are in Venezuela. She has 18 grandchildren, but her only granddaughters are in Europe. She visits once in a while but doesn't see them often enough for her liking. As she spoke there was a longing in her voice. There seems to be pain in these grandmothers separated from their grandchildren; Graciela in Ecuador spoke the same way. It makes me think about our guys being away from their grandparents. Anyway, we are on our way home, and the days of feeling guilty about what should and shouldn't be will soon be gone. After everyone left, Pablick and his mother invited us downstairs. They gave us three pieces of Venezuelan pottery, a beer mug, small dish and a candleholder. Saying thank you and telling her that I have been collecting pieces of pottery from every country we visited made her happy that her choice pleased me. We have some special friends here.

November 2, 1999: Macuto to Puerto Cumerebo

Even Whitney managed to pack her belongings this morning. Only one sock was left in the corner and one shoelace hanging in the bathroom where she washed it. She decided to leave some rocks behind, saying they made her bag too heavy to carry. Pablick and his mom gave us sincere hugs and told us to be sure to come back. It was a long good-bye.

Morning rush-hour traffic in Caracas took patient waiting as we moved at a snail's pace to get to the freeway leading to Maracay. The mountains were covered in pine forest and a blanket of cloud engulfed us as we climbed out of Caracas. Then the sun returned as we descended the south side of the Andes. The Caracas-Valencia Freeway is like a park on the lowlands, one of the prettiest and well-kept highways I have seen anywhere. This morning, the Andes on our right caught clouds moving in from the sea. The peaks had hats. We travelled in sunshine on the south side, viewing green rugged mountains below the cloud line with the morning light playing in and out on the juts and water-worn valleys. God's creations are hard to beat.

From Valencia we crossed through the peaks going north to the coast again. We thought we were going to have to climb the wall of Andes once more but the terrain fooled us. The road made zigzagging turns east, west, north and south, all through valleys, making the crossing the first low pass we had encountered. It felt extremely unusual.

On the coastal highway there were sandy beaches, *cabanas* and row upon row of cultivated palm trees full of coconuts against the blue-green of the Caribbean Sea. Inland and northwest the land turned to scrubby desert with cacti, while to the south the blue-grey Andes still loomed in the distance. So many different landforms in a small area.

We found our camping spot here in Canema. It being off-season, the pool was closed and the grounds were not taken care of, but we were welcomed to stay. This is a family-run place, and the owners have been hospitable to us, even cleaning the bathroom before we used it. After the tents were set up, we walked the beach to release some pent-up energy. Between washed-up garbage and muddy-looking water, the shore was not inviting even in the heat. The sand was crawling with crabs. As we walked forward, they ran away and then scurried back into the walking space we left behind us, as if we were some kind of infestation from which they needed to stay a safe distance. I find them comical creatures to watch, walking sideways and backwards all the time; there must be some reason for it.

We should have had a crab dinner but had beans and rice. When the electricity was turned off for the night, the sky lit up with billions of stars. It is hard to sleep in the heat. The tents are suffocating; we should be using hammocks.

The van is working as good as new. All the work that has been done in the past two weeks is the first real repair work on our journey, other than fixing worn-out brakes; all that travel over three years and only two tires of the original four had to be replaced. I now feel that the van will get us back to Canada.

November 3, 1999: Puerto Cumerebo to San Rafeal de Mojan

We drove through scrubby countryside all morning with the Andes to the south and another oil pipeline along the road for the entire distance. Jake asked what it was for. We discussed Venezuela's oil riches, where the oil comes from, what it is used for and where it goes. Oil rigs dot the lake and gulf on either side of the eight-kilometer bridge over the Lago de Maracaibo bottleneck. General Rafael Urdaneta Bridge is the longest pre-stressed concrete span in the world. What a structure!

At the Colombian consulate, it was confirmed that there isn't a ferry running between Colombia and Panama. There was at one time, but the two countries cannot agree on terms of moving vehicles back and forth. It will not be dangerous for us as tourists travelling through, but we were warned to drive only during the day, and we need to purchase insurance in Maicao. If short-term insurance isn't available there, it will be in Riohacha.

It has been raining profusely here. In the town of Mojan half the streets lie underwater and many have unseen potholes. We hit a bad one that knocked us all sideways. We stayed at Posada Sueca on the shore of the Gulfo de Maracaibo. We were told the area was not the safest for camping but sleeping in air-conditioning will be a treat. When we arrived the gulf was swollen to the brim and splashing over the concrete break wall. The passenger side door on the van wouldn't open because the roof rack gave way when we hit the pothole that knocked us all sideways. While emptying the van and box, working our way around the water lying in the lower areas of the parking lot, the lady that signed us in mopped the floors of our rooms for us. She said there was three centimeters of water on them this morning, because the water level was so high in the gulf.

The owner arrived while we had the driveway blocked to unload. He welcomed us and introduced himself as Paolo, from Switzerland. He spoke English, was very friendly and patiently waited while we finished unloading. Ed asked him why he chose to live here. He explained that he married a woman from Maracaibo; he likes it better here than in the big city. He said we could swim in the lake if we liked. He added that it is just a little muddy from the rain but everyone swims in it anyway. For some reason I asked if there were *araia* and he answered yes, but said they shouldn't bother you if you stay active in the water. That decided the swimming issue. For sure, Dayna wouldn't go in, and the others probably wouldn't either. It looked too dirty after the rain anyway. He said rainy season is usually over by mid-October but it is November and still raining as though it were mid-season. There was a tone of tiredness in his voice—he seemed tired of the rain like I get tired of the snow by mid-March when there are still a few more weeks of having it on the ground. It doesn't matter what we have to live with or where we live, the seasonal changes, even in the tropics, come with most of us looking forward to them.

Ed had the racks repaired again and said the next time something happens to them our storage box is going to be history; we will get rid of stuff and sit three to a seat so we have room for the camp gear. Ed was back within a couple of hours and the kids hadn't left the air-conditioned room; the heat is getting to us all. We washed ourselves from the barrels of clean water provided (the running water was contaminated from flooding) and slept well in the air-conditioned rooms.

Thursday, November 4, 1999: Mojan to Santa Marta, Colombia

It hasn't rained since yesterday morning and the water is drying up. We were on our way quickly this morning only to be held up by six police checks within 51 kilometers. These police were not friendly, and each stop was time-consuming.

North of Mojan the land is swampy. I have never seen so many herons in one place. They have white bodies, black beaks and orange feet and appear smaller than white herons—maybe they aren't herons, but close relatives. At one point an entire flock of hundreds took flight in front of us. Ed slowed the van to watch the striking contrast of white wings against the deep blue sky.

The highway was built on gravel about three meters above the natural elevation of the land. It must have cost a fortune. The landscape was at a lower level than the highway for 30 kilometers and was covered with floodwater on both sides. The area was flat and the blue sky blended into the water on the horizon with the grey ribbon of highway cutting through it. The small box houses of the native people sat on small pieces of elevated ground surrounded by water.

Crossing the border wouldn't have taken as long if our timing had been better. But we had to wait for two busloads of people to pass first, and the heat was getting to us. The mean temperature of the area is 28°C. Tanya asked, "Is there such a thing as being sick from heat?" She was miserable, grumpy, barely able to tolerate it any longer, but wouldn't wear a hat either.

I answered, "It's called heat stroke but I don't think any of us has that." Heat rash is the annoying problem that all of us except Jake, Whitney and Ed are dealing with. It comes and goes and is bothersome. Tanya said, "Oh, it would be just right in Canada right now. I could even wear a jacket."

Ed bought short-term insurance at La Privasora in Riohacha. He had a tough time finding a bank machine that worked. It took him and Ben two hours of searching while the rest of us waited with the van. Even when we were parked in the shade, the heat was tough to take.

The landscape was green and mountainous from Riohacha to Santa Marta. Fifty kilometers to the south the altitude is 5,800 meters. The flatness of the La Guajira Peninsula that we passed through yesterday, is an intense contrast to the majestic mountains of lush, green forest jungle.

At Rododera, a young teenage boy heard Ed ask the gas station attendant for directions to La Guajira Cabanas. The boy explained that he lived close to there and offered to direct us if we would give him a ride. Five minutes later we arrived and he walked the rest of the distance home. Ed rented an apartment with nine beds, a kitchen-living room and a pool outside, all for 50,000 *pesos,* which is about $43.00 Canadian. The kids were ecstatic. They cooled down in the pool while Ed and I stocked up with food. Standing in the checkout line waiting to pay, I suddenly realized I was ill. I had had a headache most of the day but at that point every muscle in my body ached as well; my pulse felt as if it was exploding throughout my body. Ed and the kids had to prepare their own food.

Thursday, November 4 to Sunday, November 14, 1999: Cabanas La Guajira

We have been here for 11 days and most of them were good. Olga, the lady we met in Foz de Iguazu, visited us. She took over and brought Ed to a friend who sold him airline tickets at a Colombian rate, not tourist rate. On Wednesday, Ed and Olga made arrangements for the van to be shipped to Panama. They found Seaboard, the same shipping line we used for the Miami-Caracas journey, to be the most honest. The paper work is only 300,000 *pesos* instead of the 700,000 *pesos* that other agencies were quoting. We will end up staying in Colombia a little longer. The van leaves from Barranquilla on November 19. Ed, Tanya, Jake, Karina and Whitney fly on the 20th, while Ben, Dayna and I leave on the 21st. We couldn't get eight seats together on one day until December. The van will arrive in Colon on the 25th.

All these arrangements have taken Ed several days to get straight, and we have been two weeks longer in Colombia than anticipated. But it has been recuperation time for me. Ever since we arrived in Santa Marta I have been down with fever and body ache. When there isn't a fever it is as if there is nothing wrong, but everyday the condition has put me down for several hours. No energy. Everyone we asked about it says it is nothing to be concerned about, just take aspirin and Vitamin C. It is a common ailment here. Probably dengue. Fever and body ache are the symptoms, and it usually takes weeks for it to move out of the system. I am feeling more myself today, this afternoon anyway. It has been a good place to have some down time.

While the kids were swimming and playing in the pool, I watched them. I have been thinking about Christmas with anticipation and reservation. It will be good to see family again. The reservation comes from not wanting the same kind of strained relationships I've had with them, and I honestly don't want to continue that kind of relationship with anyone. There were tears I could not stop, but after a time something happened; there was a relief in my body and I felt different. I must finally be ready to make the necessary changes in my own attitude and am feeling capable of doing it. Somehow I know it will be different and the changes will be positive.

The kids have been doing well with me flat on my back for most days. With schoolwork, swimming in the pool, cable TV and card games, they are keeping themselves busy. All of them have become nicely tanned, have a good natural protection from the sun, and are looking really healthy.

We decided not to go to Cartagena this week. The country's beauty pageant is taking place and the city is full of festivals. It would be difficult to find a place to stay. So we are here until tomorrow.

The cabanas are undergoing major renovations for Christmas. Everything is being cleaned and fixed and I think the owners would like us out; we are the only tenants. It is a family-run business. The mother is the boss, a beautiful woman a little on the obese side, but with very good looks and peacefulness about her. The father works away from the *cabanas* and restaurant during the week; they have two boys in their late teens, and a girl about nine.

There has been a lot of rain here as well. We have beautiful sunny mornings, but every day it rains for a few hours. Ed asked Luis, the owner of the *cabanas,* about the landslides we saw on television. Luis said there was so much rain just last week alone that there were 37 landslides in the area. The mountains are evolving—even Mother Earth doesn't stay the same. Luis told Ed it is the rain in the mountains south of here that causes most of the problems. There has been lightning every night with power disruptions. The river beside the *cabanas* swelled and flash flooded within hours a few days ago. It flooded a house on lower ground beside us, although there was very little rain here. The following morning the river was a creek again. The extremes are hard to believe.

We took the kids to visit the museum in Santa Marta on Friday. Dayna complained about going, but they thoroughly enjoyed it. We learned about Tairona culture and the lost city Cuidad Perdida, that covers 400 hectares on the Santa Marta range. The Taironas were one of the more complex and organized native groups of pre-Colombian America. They were advanced in agriculture, metallurgy, and engineering, and displayed an outstanding level of environmental management. There was a good display of gold artifacts in the vault. After visiting the museum the kids compared the city to the Inca culture. They felt the local culture was as well developed, and that people had an equal number of skills, but their culture existed long before the Incas.

Jake's birthday was this week. We managed to make a decent cake with pineapple filling and the natural thick cream they have here. I wonder why we don't have the same quality of cream in Canada; it is so much better than the stuff we have at home. Jake was happy with a tasty cake and some money of his own to spend.

This turned out to be a great place to spend our extra week; the pool made our stay resort-like and the rest has done us all some good. We are ready to continue.

November 16, 1999: Cartagena, Colombia

The police stopped us before we reached the outer limits of Santa Marta. One friendly young policeman said, "Quebec—I have friends in Montreal." Ed, making small talk, said, "We live close to Montreal, just a short drive." Then the policeman asked for the papers, where we were going and where we were coming from. He and his partner looked the documents over and told Ed they would have to have their superior look at them. The older policeman came to Ed's window and asked where the permit was for the tinted glass on the van. Ed told him he was unaware that it was necessary. When we entered Colombia, the agents at the *aduana* checked the van and didn't say anything about a permit for tinted glass. He explained that we didn't have one when we first came through Colombia either. The policeman did not like the challenge, told Ed to get out of the van, and wrote a ticket saying, "If you want to give us 50,000 *pesos* we'll let you go." Ed, already discouraged said, "I'm trying to get six kids back to Canada and you ask that much." The policeman changed his tune. "Okay, 30,000." Ed paid the 30,000 so we could leave and told the younger and obviously more conscientious officer, "You know this isn't right." The young man dropped his head and looked the other way. Ed got back into the van and we left. The older policeman was just looking for money and he found some. More highway robbery.

The drive from Santa Marta was wet and windy, making it a challenge to keep the van on the road. The highway was washed out in one place with just a little more than one lane left of what hadn't slid down the hill. We experienced this in Colombia the last time we were here as well.

The lagoon west of Santa Marta was abundant with white herons, blue herons and egrets. The area is flooded out right now, having experienced a hurricane. People are wading through water everywhere, but the birds are thriving. The ocean was moving in on the town of La Boguilla east of Cartagena. We drove along the beach and even through the tops of waves to find the campground recommended, but under the conditions we opted instead for a modest room with a kitchenette in Cartagena. The Caribbean looked like Algarrobo in winter: with dark water, waves threatening, splashing over the concrete barrier, flooding Avenida Santande. It stormed hard most of the night, with lightning and thunder. We did a bus tour of the city during the afternoon to see historical sites but it felt like a mistake. We could have done it on our own and enjoyed it more. Never a tour again—please remember.

November 17 to 21: Baranquilla, Colombia

Normally the box is waterproof, but hurricane force winds managed to drive the rain inside. Our sleeping bags and clothing got wet on our last road trip, so now everything is packed inside the van for our drive back to Baranquilla.

At another landslide a car must have been trapped, as there was a broken windshield on the ground when we passed the clean up. It is flooded everywhere. Low-lying houses are filled with water and people are wading through them, salvaging what they can.

In Baranquilla, Ed found an apartment with a kitchen, living area, beds for everyone and two bathrooms. We shopped at a supermarket across the road and found tahini, canned chick peas and whole-grain pita bread. There are whole-grain loaves on the shelves and whole-grain rice too. Colombia has more healthy food available than three years ago. We made hummus and thoroughly enjoyed it. The kids watched a movie, and Ed and I let them put themselves to bed. We actually spent some time talking to one another without questions and interruptions. I asked Ed how he was really doing. He has had a cough and it has been hanging on for a few weeks, but he said he was fine. I asked if he was tired of driving. He said it's not the driving as much as dealing with the dishonest people who are just after money. He is not looking forward to the corruption in Central America, where we have been told it is worse. We still have to find a way to get new van ownership papers, for Canada while in Mexico, and insurance reinstated for the United States and Canada. Ed's mind is so full of concerns and issues that need to be taken care of, it is not much wonder he looks tired. I haven't been much help, being down with ache and fever over the last while; it has added to his responsibilities and concerns.

On Thursday, Ed and Ben went to Customs at the port, waiting from nine in the morning until two in the afternoon for one man's signature on papers for the van. It was a ten-minute job. Ed talked to another officer for most of the morning just to pass time, and when he tired of waiting told him that he and Ben were going for a walk. The man said, "No way, nobody goes for a walk around here. You'll find a gun at your head as soon as you step outside the gates." They didn't go for a walk. When the necessary signature was obtained they went to the Seaboard office to complete the shipping papers and the photocopy shop for copies of the papers for me. We need proof we will be leaving Panama to be admitted into that country, since we will arrive on one-way airline tickets.

Jake and Whitney played hide-and-seek, tag and all kinds of other running-around games in the apartment. The traffic outside is so noisy here it doesn't matter how loud the kids get they aren't disturbing anyone.

When Ed got home, he noticed his black bag missing while sorting papers. We searched everywhere but it wasn't here. I asked him to go through the afternoon in his mind. He thought he might have left it at the photocopy shop. The airline tickets were in the bag. If it wasn't there we would have more paperwork to deal with. Ed's head was so full of things to take care of, he wasn't thinking clearly.

He went to the copy shop at 8 a.m. the following morning, but the woman was not helpful, telling him to come back at nine when the woman that served him was in. She wouldn't even look for the bag in the back of the shop. Ed told her that I would be the one retrieving the bag, as he had to take the van to the port. The bag was sitting on a chair behind the counter when Tanya and I arrived. What a relief. She gave it to us and kept talking. I was just plain thankful and didn't understand or even hear much of what she said. We have been shown that there are honest, helpful people in Colombia too.

Ed drove the van into the shipping container and the storage box just fit inside at the end of the van. If we had built the box one inch taller it wouldn't have fit. Ed closed it up, sealed the container, and he will be the one who opens it in Panama. Under the circumstances it should be intact. Otherwise, Seaboard is responsible. All of Ed's work paid off—it only cost 140,000 Colombian *pesos* in port fees (about $100.00 US), much less than the 700,000 we were being quoted by brokers on top of the $950.00 US for the ship.

Ed, Tanya, Karina, Jake and Whitney left this afternoon, and the rest of us moved into a hotel room for the night.

November 21, 1999:

My 43rd birthday and these are my last hours on the South American continent for a few years. What can I say? I have enjoyed getting to know the land and people. I have learned so much about this different way of life and myself, and it doesn't feel so foreign to me anymore. All I can do is give thanks for the wonderful people we have met and the new things we have learned. I will come back. So much of South America feels like a part of me now.

Sunday evening and Ben, Dayna and I are still in Colombia. The plane was full; we didn't confirm our space so didn't have seats. I called Ed to let him know and he is not pleased. There were several empty seats on yesterday's plane, so we could have all flown together. I had better be sure I want to go tomorrow. Maybe it is my reluctant feelings that have kept us here.

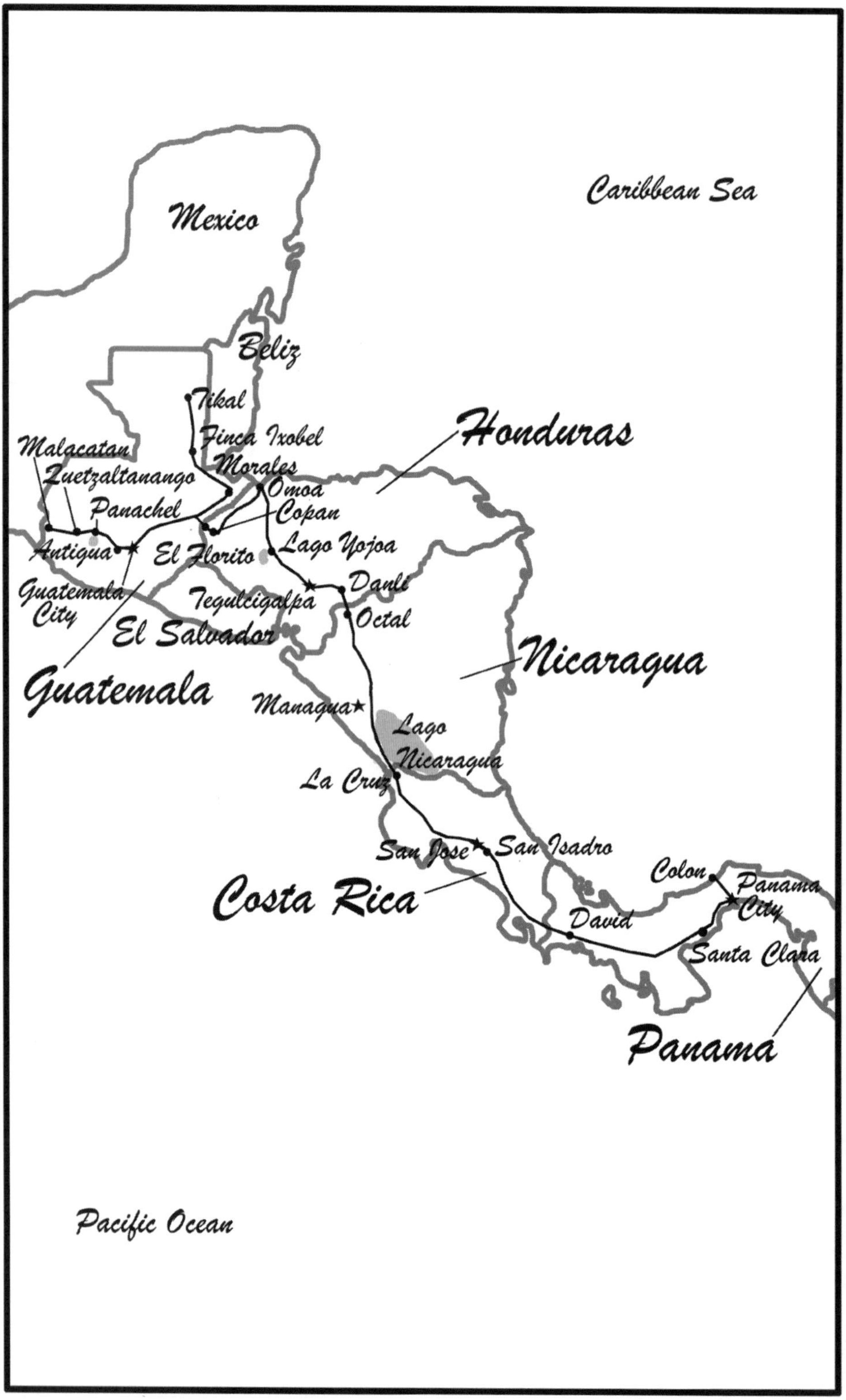
Caribbean Sea
Mexico
Beliz
Tikal
Finca Ixobel
Honduras
Malacatan
Morales
Zuetzaltanango
Omoa
Panachel
Copan
Antigua
El Florito
Lago Yojoa
Danli
Guatemala City
Tegulcigalpa
Octal
El Salvador
Nicaragua
Guatemala
Managua
Lago Nicaragua
La Cruz
San Jose
San Isadro
Colon
Panama City
Costa Rica
David
Santa Clara
Panama
Pacific Ocean

CENTRAL AMERICA

PANAMA

November 23, 1999:

We made it today after not being able to get onto a flight until Tuesday. Either we were not properly informed, or reserving space on the flight a few days in advance slipped Ed's mind. Whatever the case, the result was that Ben, Dayna and I were stranded in Colombia. We had a ticket with a date, time and flight number but we needed a "reservation" as well. Not being experienced air travellers we were unaware of the way things should be done.

On the way to the airport in the taxi this afternoon, I was filled with nostalgia. Watching the shops, stalls, and people as we passed them evoked images of what we have experienced on the continent of South America. The shops along the streets have metal rollup doors protecting the storefronts. It almost appears as if nothing exists behind them when they are down and padlocked at the sidewalk level. It is the same in every larger town wherever we have been in Latin America.

Most people have dark hair and dark, beautiful skin. City women are dressed in tight-fitting clothes and high-heeled or platform shoes. In Santiago they were always dressed up—even wearing nylons in the summer heat. The men have their macho ways, although there is evidence that that is starting to change some.

It was picture memories of places, mostly, that popped into my head. Algarrobo Beach, the Andes, the death-defying road we took from the Pacific coast to Huaraz, the lakes we visited in the mountains. Arequipa, Cusco, Machu Pichu, and Lago Titicaca, the *altiplano* of the Andes with its different ecosystems, the people of the *altiplano*, each group having its own style of hat (so many well-made felt hats, especially in Ecuador). The easy-going feeling of Puerto Mont, Chiloé Island and the houses on stilts over the water. The crystal-clear streams, rivers and glaciers of Southern Chile, Torres del Paine—the rock formations, Playa Negra and ConCon, Ushuaia, Lago Fagnano, the endless miles of pampa in Argentina, the turquoise glacier lakes of the Patagonia, the smog of Santiago—and on clear days, the incredible views of the wall that separates Argentina and Chile. Discovering the length of desert on the Pacific coast from Ecuador to La Serena in Chile. The Atacama Desert, with its total absence of rain. The noise of Santiago and Jake walking down the street with his fingers in his ears. The outdoor concerts in Parque Bustamante at Christmas; listening to Handel's Messiah from the back porch of the house was the highlight. The kids, roller-blading in the park—that park made life okay in the city. The El Tololo Observatory and the Valle del Elqui. Colca Canyon—that was something else. The condors, Foz do Iguazu, the butterflies, the beaches of Brazil—all so different and so many good ones. The Amazon not being what I expected, the heat of Manaus and Teresina, the jaguar we saw jaunting across the road in front of us. Looking into the eyes of a jaguar and petting her paw. Itiquira—we had so much fun there. There were so many nights I admired the brilliance of the southern sky at Aris and Christina's *cabanas* and many other places. Aris and Christina themselves—they were so good to us.

Watching the kids in the pool in La Guarjia, the three big ones with the three little ones on their shoulders and the competitions of dunking the other teams; they made me laugh so hard and they had so much fun together that evening. The Gran Sabana of southern Venezuela—the unusual mountains with flat plateaus on top. The beautiful mountains of Colombia, something especially different about them. I will always remember the Andes Mountains on the drive between Rengo and Santiago. We had such spectacular sights in the cool winter mornings of June and July, when the bands of mist created layers of the jagged tops. So many pictures run through my head, so many places we have visited, and now they are all in the past like a dream come and gone.

There are many memories and thousands of photographs to jog the memory when it fails. That's the reason I like a good photograph—a way to remember what it was like, the people and places that made impressions. Life moves on quickly, and many times I take a photograph because I want to fully appreciate the moment. Many of us don't know where the days, months and years are going, never mind the moments. When I am 80 and asking myself what have I done with my life I will have many photographs of what has been important to me—my family, people and the beauty of the earth. So now we are in Panama, and I feel as if we are almost home.

November 29, 1999:

By the time Ben, Dayna and I arrived, Ed had to spend the days preparing the paperwork for moving the van through Customs, and therefore we didn't see much of Panama City. Walking to the grocery store a couple of times was enough to learn that it is a Spanish City with a strong American influence.

Ed and Ben took the bus to Colon to pick up the van on Thursday, as instructed by the office here in Panama, only to return without it. The van wasn't unloaded off the ship until Friday. Back in Colon, Ed and Ben went to two different offices each, twice, because of incomplete instructions and information. Once the paperwork was complete, the container was opened and checked, complete with a dog-search for drugs, and then it was fumigated before Ed could take possession of it. Ed and Ben were back in Panama City with the van by 4 p.m., and we prepared for travel again.

The only excursion we had planned was a visit to the Panama Canal. The section we toured was the Miraflores Locks, but the film and relief map in the visitor's centre gave a good overview of the geography and history involved.

It began in 1881 when France first attempted to build the canal under the direction of Ferdinand de Lessep, the engineer who successfully completed the Suez Canal. It was soon apparent that a sea level canal like the Suez would be impossible to build and the Panama Canal had to incorporate dams and locks to cross the divide. Building costs soared and the death toll from yellow fever and malaria was rampant. France's financial resources ran out, and in 1904 the United States purchased the rights to complete construction of the canal at a price of $40 million. Their first mission on the project was to eliminate the diseases causing so much death and to build a better standard of living for the workers. William Gorgas' success in helping to control yellow fever in Cuba gave way to the theory that it was the mosquito that spread the disease. Eradicating the mosquito population, quarantining anyone who fell ill, and tracking down all possible sources spreading the disease, eventually brought yellow fever under control. Construction was slow until George Gothals, a military engineer, took charge in 1907, and the canal was completed seven years later, $23 million under budget. The most difficult portion of the canal to build was through the Culebra Cut. Landslides off the mountain had to be continuously excavated, and dredging of the canal is still done daily to keep it from filling in. Approximately 80,000 people worked on the construction during the 34-year period and an estimated 30,000 died from disease, mainly yellow fever. The man-made Catun Lake created by the dams is 85 feet above sea level. It takes eight to ten hours to traverse the 50-mile canal and ships do not use their own power but are towed by train-like engines through the locks. It costs a ship an average of $45,000 (U.S.) to cross the canal but it is always more economical than travelling around the continent of South America. The voyage from New York to San Francisco is more than 11,000 kilometers shorter. The canal has been under American jurisdiction since 1904 but Panama will be taking control on December 31, 1999, five weeks away.

After gaining all that historical knowledge, we crossed the Bridge of the Americas—the only non-swinging bridge connecting land on either side. It is a graceful structure arching across the water at the Pacific entrance to the Canal.

We stayed at Santa Clara last night, in *cabanas* on the beach, and enjoyed a couple of hours of late afternoon sun. The wind came from the northeast and the water was calmer than most Pacific beaches we have set foot on. We discovered another kind of shell: pink scallops with dark pink-red markings. There was a wonderful view of the sun rising over the Pacific this morning. There are not many places on the Americas where it does that.

While travelling towards David, there were five police checks within 27 kilometers, and 18 in total today. All police were friendly; their aim is to encourage safe driving. Ed was stopped for passing another car and not getting back into the right hand lane before the dotted line ended. The policeman asked him to get out of the van and come to talk with him. Ed did and the kids, not being as intimidated by police officers as they have been, were right behind him. The policeman had our entire family staring at him in curiosity. He was polite, and urged Ed to take care driving and to slow down "for the kids". Ed liked the effect we had on him—there was no ticket issued or any talk of money. He made the comment that if we had been doing what we did today everywhere, we might not have had to hand out so many pay-offs. I'm not so sure that would have been the case, though. The police in Panama have been much more conscientious than the people Ed paid off.

COSTA RICA

December 2, 1999:

The Pan Am Highway to San Isidro reminded us of the mountains of Colombia— rolling highway through valleys and mountains green with a variety of vegetation. It is the first time we have seen fields of pineapple cultivated in such abundance. The road, as rough as those in Colombia, kept us alert watching for fallen rocks; there were several landslides being cleaned up. We passed one place where stones were trickling down from above and bouncing on the pavement.

Finding a place to stay within budget was almost impossible. The hotel we picked out in San Isidro was twice the cost listed in our book. Ed asked about camping in the area and the woman said if there was any it would be toward Rivas. We headed in that direction along the road to the Chirripo National Park and La Amistad International Park, where one can visit cloud forest and alpine environment on the plateau, lakes of glacial origin, and a variety of flora and fauna, or climb the Chirripo peaks, the highest being Cerro Chirripo Grande (3,820 meters) in Costa Rica. La Amistad International Park (193,929 hectares) has the largest area of virgin forest and biological diversity in the country. When we didn't find public camping we stopped to inquire about *cabanas* but the woman didn't want us to cook our own food. She was sympathetic to our situation and called the tourist office to inquire about camping in the area and relayed the message that there wasn't any. Somehow that was hard to believe. When Ed suggested we continue to San José she told him the road was called Cerro de la Muerte (Hill of Death) for a reason. It climbs from 750 meters to 3,479 meters and back down to San Jose at 1,200 meters and takes more than two hours to drive. We decided to leave that challenge for a time when there would be sufficient daylight. She may have been sympathetic but she wasn't giving many positive alternatives either.

We went back to San Isidro and found Pension Jerusalem. The woman was pleasant to talk to and gave us three rooms with space for all of us at a price that put a smile on Ed's face. The place was clean, more than I can say for some places we have stayed.

We were on the road by 5:30 a.m. yesterday. We thought it was 6:30, but the time changed at the border the previous day and we were unaware of it. It was a steady uphill climb from the moment we left town. We had rain, fog, limited vision, and it became cold. The people who live on the mountain were wearing winter jackets and toques. Nalca, the same big leaf plant that grows so abundantly on the Carretera Austral, grows along the road here as well. We had the feeling the world had closed in on us amidst the cloud cover, when there was a sign indicating 3,019 meters, then a short while later another saying 3,479 meters. The descent began, and the temperature increased again.

At the Nicaraguan Embassy in San José, Ed inquired about entry visas to Nicaragua. A visa is not necessary for Canadians, so we headed for the border.

On the downhill stretch to the Pacific Coast, we went from cool, comfortable air to hot and humid again. Likewise, the land changed from forest to farmland and, closer to the border, became desert-like.

Just before La Cruz we spotted a sign for camping at Hotel Las Colinas and headed towards the opportunity to sleep in the open air and cook our own food. It was a beautiful spot with a *posada* and a large space for camping. The woman in charge spoke English. There was a pool, and she told us to choose any spot we liked; the place was ours. Jake, the girls, and I set up the tents and "kitchen," while Ed and Ben shopped for dinner. It was so good to be in the air. The kids talked about how much they missed camping. It had been a few weeks, and this was much more pleasant than the hotels we have been staying in.

We had a happy evening with talk of the upcoming Christmas holidays, getting back to Canada and memories of home. The kids somehow got onto the subject of which snowsuit was going to fit whom, and Ben said, "I'm not wearing Tanya's old one this time." They laughed, and Dayna said she didn't want it either, explaining that it's pink and green and she hates pink. Whitney, listening to the bantering back and forth, piped in with, "What's a snowsuit?" There was instant silence and a burst of laughter. She looked at everyone, wondering what was so funny. We were surprised with her perfectly valid question. Having just turned three when we left she didn't know what a snowsuit was. She doesn't remember much at all about the country in which she was born.

After a quick decision to swim before bed, everyone but Karina jumped into the pool. She retrieved the flashlight while everyone teased her about being chicken. A moment later she said, "I knew something big jumped into the pool," and then aimed the flashlight at an extremely large frog. Then we found out who the chickens really were—did they get out fast! Using the long-handled net, Ben caught the frog four times before it could be convinced to stay out. It was at least eight to nine inches from nose to tail—the biggest frog we have ever seen. They swam after the frog headed in a direction away from the pool, then went to bed content and tired out. Kids really need the outdoors; what a difference in their behavior—these guys anyway.

Jake grumbled about moving on. He wanted to stay and swim in the pool for another day. Ed said, "Jake, if you want to be with Grandma and Grandpa for Christmas then we have to get there." Incentive for us all and Jake was more cooperative.

Before packing up, I took out what few dishes were left in the box and then the cloth that wraps them up to keep them clean. Crumbs accumulate in the bottom of the box and I decided to shake it out. There between the cloth and box was a three-inch black scorpion. I figured out why I didn't like the idea of walking around in the grass; something didn't feel right. Our angels are still taking care of us—I chose *this* morning to clean the box out and I'm sure glad I didn't pack a scorpion into the van. I showed everyone what I found then turned the box over to knock it out, back in the grass. Everyone walked around more cautiously and put their shoes on. After always checking shoes before putting them on, wherever we have been, I found one in the dishes box. They do like little hiding places.

NICARAGUA

December 3, 1999:

The new immigration office at the Nicaragua border is under construction and up to international standards and the border we were warned about being the most difficult to get through was as straightforward as any other.

A strong east wind knocked the van around as we drove along side Lago de Nicaragua on our right. The volcanoes of Concepcion and Madera, perfect cones outlined clearly against the sky were surrounded by deep blue lake water. The Pan-American Highway headed due north. Volcan Santiago was in good view from the highway, throwing so much smoke and ash it looked like a Canadian forest fire. Intrigued, Ben said, "We have seen lots of volcanoes, but none as active as that."

Bridges are in the process of being rebuilt after being washed out by the floods from the hurricane in 1997. One bridge on the Pan-Am was closed with no alternate route indicated. It took us a half hour of asking directions and making wrong turns through Estelli before we found the temporary bridge.

Fields of amaranth were being harvested as we travelled through the lowlands. There is more evidence of poverty in Nicaragua than in Panama or Costa Rica. The highway rose in altitude and the air became cool again. The mountains were covered with sparse pine forest, different from the jungle-like vegetation of the lowlands. Where people inhabit the slopes, there are cultivated banana trees. For some reason, pine and banana trees look to me like an unusual combination. What would the people of the tropics do without the banana, such a basic food?

We arrived in Ocotal in the late afternoon, and that was the extent of Nicaragua for us.

HONDURAS

December 6, 1999: Omoa, Honduras

The kids were getting extra grumpy so Ed decided to take a rest day in Danli after crossing the border into Honduras. Travelling long distances on too many consecutive days takes away everyone's better humour. We purchased enough beans and tortilla-makings for everyone to have their fill, and all we did for the day was eat, watch television and sleep.

On the road again the kids bickered back and forth, even with me sitting in the back. Jake took another fit—I don't even know what caused it. They need a few days of activity, not television.

We camped at Las Renos Posada on Lago Yojoa. Ed paid to stay overnight but our hosts were not exactly helpful or friendly, and then we had to pay a dollar each for the use of the pool. Ed said if he knew for sure there was someplace else we could set up our tents we would have left. Anyway, the lake was beautiful, and the kids were outside. Ed and Tanya went searching for some dinner (the kids were getting to Tanya too). After the tents were set up I sent them all to the pool with enough money for a swim. I didn't go; I needed a few moments of quiet. When they were at play I faced the lake and took a few deep breaths, letting the blues and greens of nature calm my soul. Hills frame the lake, which was the same intense blue as the lakes of northern Canada in autumn. The marsh along the edge was alive with long grasses, plants, and birds: white and blue herons, flycatchers, a hawk and several other species unfamiliar to me. I need nature as much as the kids do; it keeps us all in touch with whatever it is that brings out the best of our personalities. Some days it is hard to give thanks to God, but it is so much easier when there is natural beauty to soothe the soul.

Ed and Tanya came back with fresh bass—the specialty of the area. The enticing aroma of dinner cooking brought the kids back shivering, hungry, and with changed attitudes.

It turned out to be a good evening with all of us getting into more great conversation. Tonight the kids wanted to hear about how mischievous they were when they were little and Jake was the winner in that category. Infatuated with tools and how they work, before he was even two years old, he kept us alert in the house, using screwdrivers and wrenches on everything. No light switch or plug cover ever kept a screw for long. The patio door handle fell off in my hand regularly—the screws holding it together, no matter how often replaced, were always gone. When I found a pile of washers sitting on the floor underneath the table I discovered the wrench wrapped around the last nut on the underside. The tabletop was barely attached to the pedestal. It didn't matter how high the handsaw was placed, Jake managed to get his hands on it. He used it on furniture several times, once destroying the fabric on the arm of a sofa. The only place the saw was safe from Jake not using it under supervision was on top of the warming oven above the hot woodstove. One spring morning I came down the stairs from doing laundry to discover Jake had pushed a chair up to the stove and was standing on top of it with the saw in hand. I exclaimed, "Jake, what are you doing?" He informed me of the facts. "It's not hot, Mommy, don't worry." As if that was what I was worried about. Tools started to go missing, and when Ed found the level on the shore of the river he did a serious search along the bank and found a hammer, the pipe wrench and several screwdrivers in the water. When Jake was old enough to understand he had been into mischief, he just got rid of the evidence. A few things have mysteriously disappeared, and I am sure they are resting at the bottom of the river. Ed and I had the kids in laughter describing Jake's antics and our despair. They crawled into their familiar places in the tent, laughing, happy and friends again.

I was up before the sun to listen to and watch the birds. There must have been close to a hundred white herons roosting in a tree. One at a time they wakened and flew upriver. I tried to photograph them but there wasn't enough light. I watched, resigning myself to the fact that there are some photos that just have to be part of memory alone. I heard footsteps behind me. I whispered, "Good morning, Whitney," and put my index finger to my mouth. She whispered back, "Mom, why aren't you using the video camera, you can get the birds flying and hear all the sounds too." She was right. The exposure wouldn't have been the same challenge either. Kids can be so profound at times. More often they see the bigger picture where an adult mind is so boxed in from life-long conditioning. How does that get trained out of us?

Moving toward Omoa, along the roadside, people had set up fireplaces and were selling boiled corn on the cob out of huge pots. We couldn't resist. It was boiled with the husk on and peeled when ready to eat. We have eaten so many different kinds of corn in so many different ways with so many different textures and flavours, but that corn was sweeter than fresh August corn on the cob at home. Our single cobs disappeared quickly and we made a second stop to purchase enough to satisfy everyone's palate.

We camped at "Roli and Bernie's Place" close to the beach at Omoa on the Caribbean side of Honduras. Roli recommended a higher section of ground to put the tents on, showed us a fridge, laundry facilities, and bathrooms and showers. He had a few basics for sale and told us there were bicycles and sea kayaks to use if we liked. He gave us a gate key so we could come and go as we needed. The kids were into table tennis, badminton, chess and the other games that were set up in the yard. Ed and I had a hard time getting them to help with the tents and it was late afternoon before we made it to the beach. The water was warm and clean; and on the sand, there were pebbles and stones that we discovered to be pumice. Jake and Whitney made up a game of throwing stones into the water and watching the waves float-race them back to shore again. Although we had a good swim, there were so many sand flies they drove us off the beach faster than we would have liked.

Roli spent six years driving the world. He left his home in Switzerland 10 years ago with his van and drove to South Africa. He shipped the van to Singapore, drove through several Asian countries, then Australia; shipped it to Peru, drove South America, Central America, to Alaska and back. Ed asked him of all the places he had been why did he end up in Honduras. He said Honduras is easier for a foreigner to settle in legally, and after six years of travel it was where he lost interest in moving so much. He would rather have been in Africa but he is a tour guide and translator for European travellers and there is more work available here. He has run the rooming house for four years now and said he is starting to have itchy feet again. It is good to talk with other adventurous people; they don't think we are so crazy. He was a wealth of information and was full of suggestions on how to use our time efficiently in Guatemala.

As Jake requested, I read King Arthur again and there weren't any objections. The kids settled quickly, and I had read barely 15 minutes when every one of them was sound asleep. There is nothing like fresh air and activity.

When Roli gave Ben, Dayna and Karina each a bike to ride, Jake and Whitney were upset that they didn't have one. (He didn't have bikes small enough.) Tanya, being sensitive to the younger two, took Whitney for a walk to the beach. Jake was invited but, being his hard-to-get-along-with self, decided to sulk. It is so hard for this boy just to go with what comes his way; he could enjoy himself more if he didn't put up such a fight all the time.

It rained off and on all day, so the ground is mushy underfoot tonight, and absolutely everything is damp through and through. If the weather allows us to do laundry tomorrow we will stay, otherwise we will head to Copán.

December 8, 1999: Copán Ruinas and Copan – The Mayan City

Roli came to visit first thing in the morning and said, "I guess it's not a wash day, is it?" He was on his way into Pedro de Sula and wanted the gate key before he left. He wished us the best with the last of our journey and was gone. Ben packed the box and did it under the tarp so the contents would stay dry. The tents and tarp were the only things that were packed wet.

The road to Copán Ruinas rolled through tobacco fields amongst hills and valleys. The kids were lulled to sleep again, and it was a quiet morning for Ed and me. By the time we arrived in Copán Ruinas, the rain had stopped and there was blue sky, making our afternoon of visiting more pleasant.

Taking a rest at Copan

We followed Roli's suggestion and have been staying at Los Gemelos Hotel. It is clean and has a large protected parking area. We visited the museum on the town square first, as he suggested. It was a good introduction to the ancient city of Copán. In one shop, on our wandering through the streets, a woman was infatuated with Whitney and was impressed that she was speaking Spanish. She gave Whitney a friendship bracelet, which left the chatterbox almost speechless. She did remember to say *gracias* without being prodded and it earned her a hug as well. In another shop we watched a woman doing some extraordinary weaving. She used a technique that creates a pattern or picture on the front of the fabric but not the back. All of us, including Ed, who usually takes little interest in such things, were in awe of the creation. We bought a piece of her work.

Today we visited Copán, everyone thoroughly enjoyed the 1,200 year-old Mayan city. Copán is called the "Paris of the Mayans" because of the artistic work among the ruins. Countless hours went into carving stone sculptures. History and art together created an esthetically beautiful city. What it must have looked like in its prime! We went from *stalae* to *stalae* looking at the sculptures. (*Stalae* are rectangular pillars of stone on which are carved historical picture stories.)

We climbed stairs on the pyramids to get to vantage points for overall viewing and observed the hieroglyphic staircase in awe. Every stone (there are more than 1,250 of them) bears a sculpture that relates a piece of history. Only the bottom 12 steps were found intact; the rest were scattered and put back together, as would fit.

At the top of the steps to the east court, Ed learned about Copán from a caretaker, Eduardo. He gave as much information as any guide, and then asked Ed if we were interested in seeing the Sepelturas in the afternoon. They were four kilometers away and the fee for it was included in the entrance fee into Copán. He would bring horses to the hotel and take us there on horseback. Ed was not so sure, but Karina promptly reminded him that he promised another horseback ride where everyone had his and her own horse, so the decision was made.

Meanwhile, the west court included two sculptures of dancers with jaguar masks on a pyramid wall. I said to the kids, "The person who came up with drawing Tigger in the *Winnie the Pooh* cartoons must have visited Copán. The sculpture is in the same position and has the same face that Tigger does in his bouncing story." The kids recognized the similarity too and Tanya, intrigued with the idea, said, "Hey yeah, look, the ears are exactly the same." As much as they enjoyed exploring, the kids were anticipating the horseback ride and were ready to go after five hours of walking through the ruins.

Eduardo came to the hotel at 2 p.m. with the horses as he said he would and there were two small ones for Jake and Whitney. They mounted theirs first and had big smiles on their faces. Eduardo walked, saying he would stay beside the little ones. When everyone was set, the horses were anxious to move. They knew where they were going and headed out of town. My horse liked to be in front. As much as I tried to hold her back to be with the others, she was determined to be well ahead. Ben kept yelling, "Mom, I want your horse". He likes to be the leader, and his horse was not cooperating. The horses had a break while we toured the Sepelturas on foot. Eduardo showed us two different trees that were important to the Mayans. The leaves of the first one have been used for hundreds of years for stomach and liver ailments and are still used today. The second one was used for building ancient structures. He broke open a seedpod and showed us the sticky gum oozing out of it. The gum was an important ingredient in Mayan mortar because it hardens when exposed to air; it looked similar to milkweed gum and extremely sticky.

The Sepelturas were interesting but not as spectacular as the main city. Eduardo explained that what is left of the buildings is believed to have been the residences of the king's family and tombs.

When Jake and Whitney got into a tiff over the water bottle, Eduardo took the hint, and said to us all that we had seen almost everything there was to see and he thought the kids would rather ride the horses. The kids' enthusiasm returned, and we headed back. He was right.

While Whitney was waiting in her saddle for the rest of us to mount securely, her horse decided he was ready to go and took off in a gallop. Eduardo ran to catch up but couldn't. I yelled, "Whitney, pull back on the reigns hard and say 'whoa!'" The horse galloped about 150 meters before he had his head almost yanked off and Whitney displayed her ability to be "Boss." She did what needed to be done and the horse stopped almost as fast as he took off. Eduardo caught up, took the reigns from Whitney, impressed with her control. She came back smug with herself and not nearly as shaken up as the rest of us.

Eduardo said it would be a nicer ride along the Copán River. I opted to give him my horse, took an hour for myself and walked through the village. I wanted to see weaving and pottery without people waiting and telling me to hurry up. As I passed a shop, a young man asked if I would like to ride horses tomorrow. I said, "We just did this afternoon, thank you anyway." I continued to walk and browse the shops. A little while later he was on another street corner watching me. As I walked past him the second time he joined me, saying, "Why don't you come on horseback with me tomorrow? You are beautiful, I'll show you around."

"I told you, we already rode horses this afternoon."

"Who is we?"

I looked him in the face and said, "My husband, our six children and me. They are still riding and will be back soon."

A stunned look took over his face and all he said was, "Oh!" I kept walking and didn't see him again. It made me think about how vulnerable women travelling alone can be in Latin America.

GUATEMALA

December 13, 1999: Finca Ixobell

Climbing the Temple in the great Plaza –Tikal, Guatemala

We followed Roli's suggestion and crossed the border into Guatemala 10 kilometers from Copán Ruinas through the village of El Florido. It was construction all the way but easily passable.

We headed north at Morales and found Finca Ixobel easily. The place is a working farm, but also a guest house with shelters to set up hammocks. Camping is also available on the grounds and the farm is a popular destination with foreign travellers. We gave ourselves a rest day.

Jake enjoyed the space and lost himself in the natural elements. Sometimes I fear this boy may have the makings of a hermit. Being outdoors and alone brings out the best in him. I saw him only when his stomach said "food". At the house we found Scrabble and Monopoly games and purchased some homemade, whole-grain bread. Whole-grain bread is a rare find in Latin America, and we savoured it. After laundry we played games.

Our family at Tikal Ruins, Guatemala

We met a couple, Frank and Peggy, who had driven from New Mexico. Ed had questions about driving through Mexico, and they were interested in driving farther south, so they had several questions for Ed.

Frank gave us a book to look at, *Camping Mexico*. It was just what we needed to find campgrounds easily. When Ed returned it, he ended up talking a long while again. Peggy told him to take the book, since they weren't camping. Ed promised to mail it back from California on our arrival there.

At the Tikal Ruins, we camped across from the visitors centre. Our ambition was to be at the ruins by 7:00 a.m., Roli said that if we wanted to see animals we needed to be there early, so that was the plan. As the night closed in on us the natural sounds of the environment took over. Howler monkeys interrupted the peaceful sounds of insects and toads with their growling and intimidating noises. It sounded like deep jungle.

We were at the Tikal entrance just as it was opening. No more guided tours of such places. By reading the guide book and visiting what really interests the kids, and letting them explore and move in their own time, we were all happier and we got so much more out of the experience. As I write this down I'm reminded of an aspect of the kids' "regular" schoolwork. When they are not obligated to sit, listen and write, and have the option to pick up learning material and put it down when they are interested, they absorb more and it stays with them. Each child, at any level, takes in and holds what his mind is capable of grasping. It takes a short amount of time for the child to build from what he or she has learned, when the child does it for his or her own reasons.

The energy of the kids has been positive since they enjoyed Copán so much and they anticipated another interesting day. And had one. Several trails and roads through thick jungle made the map essential. Tikal is an ancient city that covered more than 16 square kilometers judging by what modern-day man has mapped so far. We visited and climbed many structures—not nearly all of them, but several of the main temples and buildings.

In "Group G" of the structures the kids climbed any steps they could find. They discovered a tunnel and were in and out of the rooms until someone called to see the spider monkeys. Ed kept us moving, reminding us there was a lot to see. We were in awe of the rear of Pyramid One before we even arrived at the Great Plaza. We climbed on, and walked alongside, the Central Acropolis into the Great Plaza. What a place! When standing on the Plaza floor, your voice seemed to stay within the Plaza and come back to your own ears. There are two great pyramids on the east and west sides, with two sets of massive rambling ruins: the Central Acropolis to the south and, opposite that, the North Acropolis. The Central Courtyard displayed several *stalae* and mantels. We climbed to the crown of Temple II overlooking the North and Central Acropolis. Ben and Jake were up and down the steep steps without much thought. Ed said, "You guys should save some energy; there are lots of pyramids to explore, yet and Temple Four is the highest. You want to be able to get to the top." I held Whitney's hand while we carefully walked down the steep incline. Once we were within a comfortable distance—for me—to the ground, I let her go; she took off and went twice the speed we'd been going. I was holding her back from getting where she wanted to be, and as fast as she could get there—I wonder how often I do that in other endeavours.

At the North Acropolis the kids found a tunnel leading into an area with masks on the walls. It was dark, so we used the lamp of the video camera until we thought we heard bats, which prompted us to make a fast exit. We laughed at ourselves for letting our imaginations get the better of us. After we all felt safe in the daylight again, Ben said, "Let's go back," but "uh-uhs" came from the others. That was the extent of our delving into the unknown. We climbed more. Ed read information from the guidebook whenever there was curiosity and I photographed at every opportunity. The kids explored, telling us to come see this, come see that, everyone finding something different that caught his or her interest. The Central Acropolis buildings were built on top of other buildings; there were more structures underneath the main platform of the massive complex and, in total more than a dozen earlier versions, one on top of the other. The Mayans just kept building another building on top of what was already there, which was why our footsteps created a hollow sound on many sets of steps. It was noticeable on Temple II as well.

We continued to the Plaza of the Seven Temples and the Lost World Complex, climbing up and down steps. No one lost any interest but all the kids talked about how sore their thighs were getting. At another structure, Dayna said she wasn't climbing it; she wanted to save her legs for Temple IV. She sat beside Ed and said, "For such short people you would think they would have built their stair steps a little smaller." Ben climbed another structure and said, "What a view up here." That was it, she was gone and all of them were on top, enjoying the sights of the archeological structures around them. They were slowing down though.

The mound of Temple IV is covered in vegetation. The climb is up ladders and stairs, which end above the canopy of the jungle. It is just the top of the pyramid that had been cleared and restored. From the top, the roof combs of each of the other great temples and the South Acropolis were the only things that stood out from the jungle as far as one could see. The view gave us a healthy appreciation of the expanse of city that once existed. It is impressive how the jungle overtook and buried the buildings in just a few hundred years. From the lofty perch of Temple IV, overlooking the prolific jungle, something gave me the impression the earth would continue whether man does or not.

After a visit through the ruins classified as Group H, the kids had had all they could take. Tanya and I wanted to see the Temple of Inscriptions and did that on our own while Ed returned to camp with the others. The Temple of Inscriptions is dated at 766 A.D. and consists of panels of hieroglyphs rising from the bottom of the pyramid to the top of the roof comb, as well as on the sides. It is the number of glyphs that make the edifice unique: the carved stones out-number the plain building blocks.

Tanya and I were handed sandwiches the moment we arrived at our torn down and packed camp. A stop in Poptun replenished our vegetable supply. Ben found marshmallows to toast on the fire he was planning to make; there is firewood to burn at Finca Ixobel where we have returned to camp.

Ben spent today preparing for his evening campfire when the hatchet handle broke. Mishaps like that are never a problem for Ben; he just found a piece of wood and began shaping it to make another.

To give us a headstart in the morning, we decided to pack the tents and use our hammocks in the campgrounds' circular hut if it wasn't occupied. I was returning from the farmhouse and office this afternoon, after requesting use of the shelter, when Ben was shaping his axe handle. I heard him yell, "That stupid bird!" The scarlet macaw that had been hanging around all morning didn't like Ben or what he was doing. Ben, working with a continuous chop, chop, must have irritated the bird. It flew down, clawed Ben's shirtless back and left big scratches. Ben went back to what he was doing. The macaw came screeching down at him again. Ben turned to defend himself and the bird came at him several times. Ben had the machete in his hand and hit the bird with the side of the blade to protect himself. The bird backed off, seemingly unharmed, and flew into a nearby tree. That was when I heard Ben yell, "That stupid bird!" They kept a wary eye on each other all day and the bird has stayed away. Ben kept the machete hooked to his belt just to indicate to the bird he wasn't going to fool around if he came at him again.

The girls didn't like the huge spider that had made a home in the outhouse while we were at Tikal and have complained about walking the extra distance to the other facility. It is another huge hairy spider similar to the one Ed smucked in Ecuador. We left this one alone.

Ben's work and ordeal came with a reward. Our campfire after supper made our evening special. After all these months of camping it is the first real campfire we have had. But then, of course, in most places we have camped wood is a scarce commodity and not used in such a manner. Our eyes were drawn to the heavens again. Everyone found the familiar constellations and looked for the visible planets. They found Mars, Venus and Jupiter easily. Tanya, with her knowledge of stars, told Whitney that you could see Saturn sometimes but it is easier with binoculars and that you couldn't see Uranus or Neptune without a telescope. Whitney, being her forceful self, claimed a bright star as being Uranus. They argued back and forth with Whitney being stubborn and Tanya not giving in to her foolishness.

While preparing for bed, Karina was not willing to make the long trek across the grass in the dark to the outhouse so moved away from the sun shelter but not out of the light. With her back to us, she dropped her pants, squatted and relieved herself on the grass. There is nothing like being mooned, but it was Whitney who had the last word, hollering out, "Now we can see Uranus!" How could we not laugh? She had us all in tears and Karina will most likely be a little more discrete about where she relieves herself.

What a different atmosphere in the circular hut. Eight hammocks are slung from the center support pole to the outer walls. We make an eight-pointed star. Whitney has overcome her dislike of sleeping in a hammock.

December 16, 1999: Antigua and Panachel, Guatemala

We stopped to purchase food in the market of Rio Dulce and while walking through I noticed the lack of height of the men and women. They must be of pure Mayan descent. It has been concluded that the Mayans were a shorter race of people than we are today because the doorways of the ancient buildings are so low. In that market I felt tall. I am five feet, four inches in height, and hardly anyone was as tall as me. I noticed one woman who was no more than four feet tall.

Quirigua is a small-scale Mayan site; it is said to have been the stopping place for travellers between Tikal and Copán. The buildings are of the same style as Tikal, but what has made Quirigua significant is the picture stories in *stalae*. One shows the decapitation of a Copán King. An hour to visit was enough, and a perfect break from a long day of driving.

The Atlantic Highway, along the Motagua River valley, connects Guatemala City to Puerto Barrios and is the main highway of Guatemala. The terrain became more mountainous at El Progresso and we started to climb. Guatemala City is at 1,500 meters, not terribly high, but still a gradual increase in altitude. The van started to choke and cough and once again it stalled. Everyone knew the routine and resigned themselves to a long wait. Ed put octane in the fuel line but the engine still coughed, sputtered, and hesitated. On the outskirts of the city a mechanic told Ed that the spark plugs and wires were worn out. Ed purchased spark plugs but wires to fit were unavailable; at least the plugs were changed. The process took close to two hours and the van worked without complaint through the city. The route to Antigua took us up and through San Lucas Sacatepéquez, rising to 2,100 meters and back down to Antigua 43 kilometers away at 1,500 meters. It was another tough, steep climb for the van and it complained again. We stopped at another mechanic's shop, but there were no new suggestions. Since it was downhill to Antigua, we headed for the city. It is a treacherous road built with emergency exits running uphill on the inside of the mountain. One thing I can say about Guatemala, where they have taken time to build a highway, is that they have built a very good one.

It was too good to be true easily finding a hotel that indicated parking and camping space available. It was closed for renovation. After an hour of searching for another, we decided on a reasonable place with hot water showers and seven single beds in two rooms. It was clean, and we don't ask for much more than that. The *posada*, decorated for Christmas, was lit with candles along the stairwell. So simple, yet elegant. Protected parking for the van was unavailable but the ladies at the desk said it would be fine on the street out front; the police patrol the streets night and day. They suggested a restaurant around the corner, and when we had had our fill of tacos, the down-in-the-dumps mood affecting our crew improved significantly. Ed said he would find a mechanic in the morning.

I wakened first and was writing when the van alarm broke the peacefulness of the morning. It sets itself off, so often it is more of a nuisance than anything. I put some clothes on, grabbed the keys and met Tanya in the hall, coming to tell us about the van. We went together to turn the alarm off and check things out. A police car arrived just as we did, pulling up to the rear of the van where a window had been broken. I asked Tanya to fetch her Dad to talk with the police. They spoke with me but I didn't understand everything and told them to talk with Ed; he was better than I at Spanish. The driver's side, rear door window was shattered and marks in the paint indicated a screwdriver or something of the sort was used to pry underneath. There was glass on the ground and all over the cooler inside the van. Ed arrived with the rest of the family. He was thoroughly discouraged with the new situation he had to deal with. The police told him it just happened, as they patrol the streets and were by here no more than an hour before, and everything had been fine then. After checking the van, it appeared the inside had been untouched; everything was still in its place. Wouldn't you know, the day I curse the alarm system for going off again, is the day it pays for itself. Since nothing was stolen the police didn't need a report and left. The women were right about the streets being patrolled, but not that the van wouldn't be touched.

The kids and I emptied and cleaned the van of glass while Ed asked about mechanical work at a garage. For the problem Ed described they recommended he have the van checked on a computer, which would be available in Guatemala City only. It was also the only place to find a new window. Ed and the boys, armed with maps and a general idea of where to go, headed for Guatemala City.

The girls and I walked the streets to get to know Antigua. The native people were beautifully dressed in their woven and embroidered fabrics. (More so the women than the men.) Most men wear jeans and North American style clothing with cowboy-type hats. We savoured the beauty of the handwork in the artisan market. Every piece is a work of art and we purchased two weavings. The woman who sold them to us showed the girls and me several pieces she was working on, gave us a demonstration of how it is done, and showed us the difference between machine-woven and hand-woven. There is no comparison in quality. Often in other cultures machine weaving appears to be better quality but the skill of the Guatemalan women here is superior to all. The work takes time, yes, but anything that holds real beauty and function takes time, skill, and patience to create. The

Guatemalan women clothe themselves in their own art and wear it with pride. Our modern day society seems to care more for a collection of clothing, as opposed to fewer items of higher quality, beauty and usefulness. I would be willing to bet that any one of these women, dressed as such, may have only one change of clothing. Their handmade finery is what they wear all the time, and they always look beautiful.

The market was full of foreign tourists and an occurrence I witnessed helped me understand the not-so-friendly attitude we have been experiencing from many people. An American woman had chosen a weaving similar to what we purchased, which takes many long hours of labour to create. This woman wanted to trade a colouring book and crayons for the piece of work, but the Guatemalan woman refused. She had a young child with her and was almost tempted but expected more for the weaving and said so. They haggled back and forth, but she stood her ground and the American woman left in disgust. I was dumbfounded with the attitude that was displayed. Why is it so difficult for some people to treat others fairly? There was no value comparison.

We looked at rugs, place mats and all kinds of "modern-day" things made in traditional fashion that people wanted us to buy. They were quick to give a price for anything you showed any inkling of interest in, and if you didn't respond the price went down. In some cases it went down by half, just by not saying anything. More than half the battle of not obtaining too much clutter in a house is resisting the temptation to buy something that isn't essential, even if it is a great price.

The girls and I visited the centre square decorated for Christmas and on our travels discovered several church buildings in ruins throughout the city. They appear to be just about the only buildings that haven't been restored from past earthquakes.

The guys stopped in San Lucas Sacatepéquez, to ask the same mechanic, where we stopped last night, about where to have the window repaired. The mechanic was on his way to the city to pick up parts needed for a vehicle and was not only full of suggestions, he drove our van into the city to test it out, brought the guys to a shop to have the window repaired, and brought them along to pick up the parts he needed—for our van as well. It was a relief for Ed. Moving around in a large city you don't know, when you must find a particular place, can be overwhelming. There wasn't an exact window but a Plexiglas copy of the other was measured, made and mounted. It won't open but we have a window again.

The mechanic replaced the electronics module that controls the gas intake, but Ed still didn't find spark plug cables to fit. With all the driving the mechanic did with the van today, there wasn't any evidence of a problem, and he offered to buy the van; he loved how smooth and comfortable it ran. We still need something to get us home, though.

I called Mom to ask her to bring some new books to read, the next math text for Tanya, a Scrabble game, maps of Mexico and the States for the last stage of our trip, and tent repair shock cord. I told her unless there was a major disaster we would be at the airport to pick them up. She told us to be careful on that mountain road to Oaxaca, it was a bad one; it felt as if she still didn't have confidence or faith in us driving after all the distance we have been.

We decided to head to Panachel. While packing, Ed couldn't find the leather bag he bought in Brazil, with his writing and work in it. He said, "So there was something stolen yesterday." Ben replied, "No, Dad, it was on the seat beside me when we drove to Guatemala City." That was the last time anyone remembered seeing it. Ed realized it was probably stolen when the window was being repaired, the only time the van was out of his sight. It is gone and this is the second time his bag has disappeared with his work and papers in it. (Maybe he is being told he needs to take some time off.) We are not having a very positive experience in Guatemala. It feels as if we are seen as people to take advantage of and are just not really welcome, wherever we go here.

The mountainous, narrow road was fascinating through the small villages. Each village has its own style and variation of clothing. While passing through one little town, I noticed every woman's blouse was red, different weavings, but the basic colour was red. The last part of the road before reaching Lago Atitlan was treacherous with little habitation. The van coughed and choked, and we thought it was going to give out again but it didn't. As we rounded a corner at the height of the road, the view of the lake overtook us. Ed stopped to savour the beauty. The water changed from turquoise to deep blue, forest green, and silver before our eyes; algae in the water cause the colour changes. It is a mysterious lake—the water level is continuously dropping, despite the fact that water flows into it and it doesn't have an above-ground outlet. The road must be 1,000 meters above the lake. From our perch we had a view of its entirety. Four volcanoes create the skyline south of the lake, holding the water within the valley they create. Around the next corner from where we stopped was a Mirador and picnic area. Ed stopped again saying that it looked like a great place for lunch. Several villages dot the shore around the lake, and the town of Panachel was to our right. It was a downhill drive from there. Mountains give any vehicle a good workout: if not the motor pulling the vehicle up, then the brakes heating up and wearing out on the descent.

We easily found the campground on the lake but it is Boy Scout camp weekend and we were turned away, even though there was plenty of space available. The only other campground we were aware of was on the lake as well. It is part of a hotel complex without access to water or a bathroom, and expensive. Given the events of the previous day, and the *Mexico and Central America Handbook* saying the homes of temporary foreign residents are prone to theft, we didn't really want to leave the van or tents unattended for any period of time. We looked for a hotel again, lucked out and found one with a kitchen facility for use by patrons, and protected parking. The latter was a tight fit for the big van to get into, though. No one would ever steal it easily with the maneuvering it took to get through the gate from the narrow street.

Panachel is known for its fabrics and textiles. The market overflows with handwork, textiles, clothing and crafts. Ed told the kids that since it is Christmas they could each have 250 *quetzals* to spend on clothing of their choice. They chose jackets, backpacks, vests and t-shirt souvenirs. Welcome or not, we still spent money.

Ed and I discussed the van situation. If we have any chance of having it repaired in time to get to Oaxaca by Tuesday it means we must be in Quetzaltenango tomorrow.

December 19, 1999: Quetzaltenango and Malacatán

Ed, concerned about how the van was going to manage the mountains in its lame state, asked a bus driver about the road to Quetzaltenango. The bus driver said it was a 1,000-meter climb from Panachel, but once up there the road is less mountainous and in good condition. He told Ed to take it slow, adding that there were signs indicating the direction to Quetzaltenango.

We climbed and climbed. The van choked a little, but we reached the levelling off point, above 2,000 meters, without having to stop. It was cool and clouds covered peaks that soared above us. Every bit of the highland plains that could be cultivated was. Fields were abundant with cooler weather vegetables: broccoli, cauliflower, cabbage, onions, and potatoes.

Ed found a mechanic on the outskirts of Quetzaltenango and discussed with him everything that had been replaced and repaired. The mechanic thought it was all probably necessary. He listened to the motor; it would have to be put on the computer to find the problem. He couldn't do it Friday and told Ed to be there at 7 a.m. Saturday morning. Ed asked if it was possible to find the parts needed. He replied, "It's not always easy to find what we need but we can usually make something up that will work." We laughed and felt encouraged. The Guatemalan people are ingenious at repairing things with what they have, which is evident from the amount of "old clunkers" on the road.

Quetzaltenango is at 2,335 meters, and it is cold. While Ed had the van at the garage Saturday morning, the kids and I tried to do some schoolwork, but the kids were rambunctious with Christmas around the corner. The anticipation of seeing family had them excited. We lay in our beds and talked about what we will do when we get home. I still wonder about that one. The kids are looking forward to returning to Wakefield.

Ed was back by mid-afternoon. The mechanic couldn't find anything wrong. He just tuned the van so it runs efficiently while advising that with cables in the kind of shape ours are in, the engine might still miss once in a while, but it shouldn't be a problem. So the problem is still not repaired.

We headed for the market to find Jake a pair of running shoes. Again, he has grown out of his shoes and needed something warm for his feet. The markets were full of decorations for the Christmas season. Brightly coloured dyed sawdust in yellow, orange, red, blue, and green is in almost every stall. (I don't know what it is used for.) The moss from trees, thousands of candles and nativity scenes carved of wood were on display on street after street. To me, it is pleasantly different from the plastic, tinsel and artificial lights in the department stores of North America.

One street was closed off for Christmas festivities, turning it into a promenade lined with food stalls and stands for groups of singers and dancers. We stopped to watch a group performing on one of the stages. Tanya said, "If this were Brazil it wouldn't be just the people on stage dancing, everybody would." The crowd observed without participation or enthusiasm. The Brazilians are a fun-loving people who don't let anything get in the way of a good dance. The cultures are so different.

My observations as I watched the dancers on stage drew some thoughts. Three of the four dancers put energy into what they were doing and they looked as if they were enjoying themselves. The fourth carried through with the choreographed motions but was missing the same kind of energy. Her lack of passion for what she was doing affected the group, making their performance less than excellent. I found myself wondering if she even liked being where she was. I mulled the word "passion" in my head. People who are passionate in what they do are people who have purpose, and more often than not, are highly successful. When we do something we like, it holds our interest and becomes a passion. When we go at something with passion, we have a tendency to put everything we have into it, with outstanding results.

I have had the opportunity to meet and talk with two great photographers: Roman Vishniac and Yousuf Karsh, and with both, the impression I received was a loving passion for their work. That passion spilled over into other areas of their lives, so life itself became a passion. I thought of Pablo Neruda as well. From reading his work, visiting his home and learning about his life, I know he too lived with passion. Nothing held any one of those people back from living his vision.

While listening to the music and watching the people dancing, questions ran through my head. Am I a passionate person in what I do? In some areas yes, and where there is a yes it is usually in the areas of my life where I excel. So how do I go about other areas of my life with the same kind of passion and enthusiasm that produces excellent results? How do I instill that passion in the children? How do I help them find what they can be passionate about so they're not just going through the motions of life, but really living, loving, laughing and learning with passion? I know every one of us on this earth is born with a purpose; finding that role and living it with passion will create success. Passion, passion, passion.... I will have to remember and work on that one. Living, doing and being an example are far stronger than words.

Today, we travelled at an average altitude of 2,500 meters until the villages of San Pedro and San Marcos, where the highway started to descend. From there, it dropped to the lowlands at 366 meters in 53 kilometers, a 2,000-meter drop. The air temperature increased and we were forced to peel off our warm clothes again. As the road dropped in elevation, twisting back and forth, the grimy smell of hot metal and grease let us know it was the brakes that were given the workout today.

It is downright hot again in the dirty town of Malacatán and people are not friendly at all. We looked for a place to stay for the night and at two places in particular, where there wasn't a soul, we were told there wasn't any space. We were under the impression people just couldn't be bothered with us. The rooms we are in cost more than half our daily budget, although they provide a refuge until we leave in the morning. The kids were comfortable in the rooms watching television, while Ed and I found some dinner for the crew.

While waiting at the stall for our hot tortillas to be made, we met two very young missionary women and got into some conversation. They were somewhat discouraged with how they were being received. They have been working in small towns of the countryside and said there is a lot of poverty. People are not as friendly or receptive to them being there as in the bigger towns. I told them I could understand that; it's not just them. To a certain extent the towns folk just don't want any of us here. The girl with darker hair asked, "Why do you say that?"

"We interfere too much and that has happened throughout history. The people who lived in the Americas before Europeans arrived were living a life that provided for their needs. They survived, thrived and had a spiritual life in rhythm with the earth. Then Europeans arrived and told them how they were living was wrong and tried to make them live a life that was beyond their self-sufficient understanding. All of a sudden they needed resources from outside their own abilities, to live up to the new standard. So instead of living a "better" more prosperous life, they were barely able to survive, and it is still happening."

Ed started to look at me as if to say, "Gaye, shut up."

"Many of these native peoples have had enough, are starting to make changes and are rejecting what the dominant society is feeding them, which means the people too."

Our meal was ready. Ed said, "The kids are waiting to eat, we should go." He didn't let me talk any more.

Walking back he reprimanded me for being so opinionated. I told him, "It is okay to voice my opinion once in a while and maybe they need to hear a different perspective. Not saying or doing things doesn't make changes to a world that needs improvement."

Feeling that he was stifling my female voice—at that moment it felt like that same male-dominated power that has caused many of the problems we are faced with today—I went on voicing my opinion to him, whether he liked it or not.

"The way I see it, Ed, God is our father and Earth is our mother. If we have a spiritual life and a physical life, we have a whole life—holy life, one is as important as the other. Both are equally necessary for life as we know it. Men seem to resent the fact that they come from a woman and need women; it has been a power struggle throughout history. Why does one have to have power over the other? Why can't we be true partners and reach a higher level of being together? For 2,000 years women have had their importance in the world suppressed, and we have had wars and disharmony all along. Our world would be much different if our governments had equal representation from both men and "true" women—not women acting like men. Women would never send their creations into war and destruction willingly. Today's society places little importance on mother earth and what she produces unless it pads the bank account, and because of it we are destroying her. Just think what would happen if the people living on the outskirts of Lima embraced Mother Earth and moved to a place where they could work in harmony with her, grow their own food and raise animals. There isn't any reason why it couldn't be done now when the Incas cultivated so much more of the desert three to four hundred years ago. Combine a spiritual life with working with the earth to provide for physical needs, and one has a real life. We are just too disconnected from respect for the earth and that balance. In Africa 40 years ago, nomadic people were living off what the land provided and where it was provided, and then they moved to allow for regeneration of the land. But government and encroaching "civilization" forced them into a farming culture on land that was incapable of supporting such lifestyle. The people starved. And what does the world do? Blame it on the weather and the earth. It is the lack of following natural law that really causes that type of thing to happen. Earth peoples all over the Americas had that figured out long before the white man came, and they are taking back the right to live in a way that empowers the creator, Mother Earth and themselves. It is probably the kind of thing those two young women were coming up against and I was just trying to give them a better understanding of where the not-so-good feelings might be coming from."

Ed, shaking his head at how I go on, said, "I agree with most of what you say, but you don't have to rant about it. Who says they would even listen?"

"Well, maybe they wouldn't, but not voicing what I had to say wouldn't even give them a chance to hear a different perspective. They are really young women with a lot to learn before they can become true teachers, especially within a society that places so much value on experience and learning from elders who have that experience. It's not much wonder they didn't feel welcome."

We prepared to cross into Mexico and are glad we are moving out of Guatemala; we have been left with a less than favourable impression of the country. Ed asked for the American cash I had to figure out if there was enough to pay the fees at the border. I don't understand why fees for crossing borders in Central America always have to be paid in American dollars and not the currency of the country. That should be illegal, especially when we are not American and have to purchase American dollars. We have not had to pay people off to allow us through as we were told might happen, and I am thankful for that—we haven't paid anyone off for anything in Central America. Are we lucky these days, is it different here, or are times changing? It is a pleasant surprise; borders are becoming more standardized.

USA
Mexico
Gulf of Mexico
Sayulita
Puerto Vallarta
Barra de Navidad
Manzanillo
★Mexico City
Playa Azul
Acapulco
Oaxaca
Tehuantepec
Tonala
Puerto Escondido
Tapachula
Malacatan
Guatemala
Pacific Ocean

December 20, 1999: Tonala, Mexico

Malacatan to the border was a 10-kilometer downhill ride. When the van achieved more speed than necessary and the brakes were a must, our ears were assaulted with a grinding sound from the front wheels. We had obviously worn the brakes out yesterday. Discouraged with the challenges we have had to face in the past few days, Ed let out a deep sigh, "Is this van ever going to give us a break?" This getting to a specific place on time is putting us under a lot of pressure; travel like this should not be done on any kind of schedule if one plans to stay sane.

We attempted to get a headstart on the day, arriving at Guatemalan customs at 7 a.m., but it didn't open until 8:30. We were first in line; exit processing was fast. We needed to do some haggling at the Mexican border to obtain a 180-day visa, as they only wanted to let us stay for 30 days. After an explanation of our travels and our intent to stay until the end of February, and when the immigration authorities were assured the kids were home-schooled, we were given three months.

All signs are bilingual, English and Spanish, and the surroundings feel more North American all the time. As we left the Mexico-Guatemala border behind, what seemed like a never-ending line of vehicles waited to enter Guatemala: school buses, trucks and cars. Taking a closer look we noticed that the license plates were from California, Arizona, New Mexico, Oregon, Washington—every one of them had a western states license plate. When one of the kids noticed a car inside a bus we watched more closely. Every vehicle large enough was loaded with fridges, stoves and other appliances. Cars were inside buses, a truck pulled a boat and trailer with fridges inside the boat, and trucks and cars pulled second cars. The buses with cars inside had had their entire backends cut off and welded back on. Old North American school buses are the vehicles used for public transportation in Guatemala and I was dumbfounded at what was waiting for entry into Guatemala: discarded and unwanted things no longer used by the people of North America. If these things are so useful to the people of Guatemala, why aren't they useful to the people who purchased them new? Is it because we always want new and flashier things to use and show off? It is because we don't take the time to maintain or repair our vehicles, appliances or clothing. We have become so much a consumer society we don't even use and consume what we purchase anymore. I believe if we shopped less, repaired and fixed more, many of us would have fewer financial difficulties and there would be much less waste in the world in general. The line-up brought to mind Chile and the *Ropa Americana* stores on Bandera Street in Santiago, where decent pieces of clothing could be found for extremely low prices. We purchased Northern Reflections sweatshirts and shorts, jeans and t-shirts from Sears. There were heaps and heaps of clothing from Goodwill and other such stores with the store tags still attached. Most of it no one purchases because it isn't useful to anyone. It must go by the shipload from Canada and United States.

Those are two examples I have run across personally, and I know for certain that North American discards are ending up in South and Central America. I don't begrudge the South Americans making use of what can be useful to them, what bothers me so much is where it's coming from. Why do we use these countries as a dumping ground? Why should they have to deal with our garbage when they have enough of their own? Something is not right here. What kind of a society have we become? We can't be bothered, we don't have time, something else looks nicer, it has to be better or the absolute best. It is good that when we no longer need or use something that we pass it on to someone who will put it to good use, but we should not become so arrogant to think that discarding things is okay because they will be passed on. If we ourselves cannot make good use of this stuff, can someone else really either? I am as guilty as the next person of purchasing too much and ending up with so much stuff in the house that it was driving me crazy. And now I'm going back to the same house. After living with fewer material possessions these past three years, I sure hope I can go back and live with less desire to fill empty spaces. Many times we try to fill empty spaces in our hearts and minds with material things and we bring something else into the house, yet the empty space is still there. I seem to have fewer empty emotional spaces—being away from home for a while has given me a different perspective. But trash, trash, trash—it's a global problem. All we have to do is stop purchasing the trash and the companies that are producing it might take notice. It has to be a conscious decision, though, and it really begins with each one of us changing our own attitudes and habits. It is something else for me to keep in mind and work on.

The Ford dealership in Tapachula didn't have new brakes but rebuilt what we had and put them back on. They didn't have spark plug cables either, but Ed was informed they are stocked in Oaxaca. The dealership didn't find a cause for the engine's hesitation and choking. Ed was not pleased, as the price of the repairs was high, even by Canadian standards.

It was close to dark by the time we arrived in Pijijapan and we decided we should stop for the night. There were two *posadas* in the village. The first was clean and the receptionist gave us a price for two rooms with enough beds for the eight of us. After we looked at the rooms Ed told her we would stay and handed over the exact amount of cash she quoted. She counted it out and said we had to pay more than what we were originally informed. We all understood the lower quoted price for the two rooms before we agreed to stay; it's not like we don't understand Spanish anymore. Ed reluctantly gave her the extra but was not pleased. I said, "If you feel like you want to take the money back and look elsewhere I'd be happy to do that." Both of us were put out, so he asked for the money back and told her why. She looked a little surprised but did give Ed the money back and we left. This is not something we usually do, but we don't like being taken advantage of just because of... whatever. Anyway, not this time, it is the principle of the situation. It turned out to be the wrong decision—the only other hotel in town was more than twice the money, and we ended up driving another hour in the dark to Tonala.

We found a place for a price within our budget, arranged to have sandwiches made for supper and agreed on 15 pesos per plate. Each plate had a sandwich sliced in half and some cut-up vegetables on it. When Ed paid, the woman charged 15 pesos per half sandwich and our meal was twice the amount originally agreed upon. We have only been here a day; I hope our impression of Mexico improves.

Doesn't integrity exist here? Don't tell me one thing and expect or do another, an agreement should be an agreement.

December 22, 1999: Oaxaca, Mexico

What a crazy day!!! I am still wound up and not sleeping and I should be exhausted. Ed decided yesterday we would stay at the campground in Tehuantepec and take the afternoon to rest. The van works better in the cooler mornings anyway and we were only four or five hours out of Oaxaca.

At the campground we discovered that our bag of electrical cords, lights and ropes was nowhere to be found. Ed remembered putting it on top of the cooler when packing up the last camp. Tanya, Ben and he figured the morning the window was broken the culprits must have grabbed what was on top and ran. It is not a huge loss but made for an inconvenient night. Since we didn't have light we were in bed earlier than usual. Everyone was so excited about seeing family today that sleep did not come for hours. I consented to reading King Arthur to help settle the kids minds and was concerned the batteries of the flashlight weren't going to outlast the kids.

Without having to urge anyone this morning, they were up before the sun, dressed, packed and had their beds rolled up. Spirits were high and we were ready to move by 7:30 a.m. Ed said we would have no trouble being in Oaxaca by noon. We anticipated checking into the hotel, getting cleaned up and picking up grandparents, aunts, uncles and cousins at the airport.

We stopped at the house of the owners of the campground to ask for directions to the highway for Oaxaca, and the man Ed spoke with said, "It's impossible to get there today." After he and Ed chatted, to everyone's dismay, Ed turned the van off. Earlier this morning, roadblocks were set up on the main highways into the city in a protest of some sort, and nobody was moving through Tehuantepec. The man Ed spoke to went into the house and came back with the owner of the farm and campground. Ed was told there was a possibility of going around but it meant crossing a river without a bridge. If the river is low enough it should be passable. The landowner took Ed to Tehuantepec in his vehicle to see if the situation was hearsay or valid and there were roadblocks.

While inquiring about the roadblocks, Ed met another man with a family who had stayed overnight in a hotel room. He too was checking out the river. Family expected his family for Christmas holidays in Huatulco today. They inspected the river together and found the water a little high but all thought it would be possible. The owner sent his hired man, José, with us to direct us through the riverbed crossing and back roads to the highway.

When we arrived, the other family was not yet at the crossing place, but on the opposite bank, a white Kombi van was stuck and not moving. We stepped out of the van to survey what we were faced with. The river was no more than knee deep and had a solid rocky bottom. Ed felt the only place we may have a problem was at the sandy gravel area after the second small water crossing. I put my running shoes on to protect my feet and suggested the kids to do the same, but Ed didn't put his on so my words held no weight, and the kids stayed in their flip-flops. We waded across the refreshing water in the growing heat of the day. Ed, Ben, José and the man at the house on the edge of the river helped push the Kombi van up onto the river bank. Ben lost a flip-flop in the river bottom; he dug around for it but it disappeared. His third pair of flip-flops in the last six months, and he's not wearing them out. He put his running shoes on.

The guys in the Kombi van were two musicians on their way home from playing in Tapachula until 3 a.m. Their home is a small village a 90-minute drive up the Oaxaca highway. In the area that Ed thought could be a trouble spot, their van had sunk again. Every one of us pushed but it just didn't budge. When we resigned ourselves to thinking it was a hopeless case, a team of six horses arrived from somewhere (??). Between horses and people, the little van moved onto solid ground easily. With the horses, our big van had a good chance of getting through. Ed crossed the main river easily, took a run at the last section and found himself stuck in the soft gravel ahead of where the other van had gotten bogged down. After hooking up the horses to pull and with everyone else pushing the van still didn't budge—in fact started to dig itself into a rut. We put everything we could find under the tires for traction, and attempted it again, but the wheels were really stuck. Eight of us were using all our strength and the horses were puffing. While catching our breath, Dayna suggested, "Why don't we unload the van so it won't be so heavy to push?" A logical idea, from the mouths of babes.

We emptied absolutely everything out of the van and set it aside, lightening the load by several hundred pounds. The little red car of the other family was right behind us waiting their turn at the second section of the big part of the river. By this time, we had caught our breath, and attempted to push the lighter van. Six horses pulling and nine people pushing—slowly it moved. Ben chimed in, "Keep going, keep going!" The rest of us joined in, "Keep going, keep going, keep going!" as if it would keep the van in motion. We pushed with all our strength while the horses pulled and slowly, with more effort than we thought we had, it made it to the dry, solid tire-track lane.

The kids were into fast action reloading the van without being prompted. We were giddy despite the situation. The little red car dug down into the loose gravel too but the guys moved it through easily using the debris we had laid down. Another white car with just one man aboard came up behind us. He was dressed in fine expensive clothing and polished shoes. He got stuck on the first bank and was pushed out. He attempted the crossing again and proceeded to get stuck again. Everyone pushed him out again, and then he got stuck where everyone else got stuck as well. He was pushed out of there too.

The musicians and Ed each gave the man with the horses a generous number of *pesos* for the help. It would have been a long, tough, almost impossible job without him. The track took us through brush. José told us that during wet season, when the river is high, all of what we are travelling through is under water. The track needed to be cleared, brush was taking over and blocking it. It was the first time it had been used since the river had settled to its winter bed. Ben loves any opportunity he has to use a machete, so he and José did the hacking to make the track passable. We encountered another shallow water area with a clay and mud bottom. With a good run at it, the white Kombi van got through easily, as did our van and the little red car. The white car sped through the clay like the others but its back end fish-tailed and it got stuck. The guys pushed the car through and everyone received a mud plastering, while doing so. The driver was still quite impeccably clean and hadn't helped push anyone else out of anywhere.

We travelled through more brush for another short distance until the last river crossing, and at the embankment we were halted. The track out of the riverbed was partly washed away, and a tree stump on the opposite side made it extremely narrow for a vehicle. Our entourage was becoming an amiable group. Everyone was still laughing, joking and generally having a good time while making a plan of attack. We built up the edge of the "roadway" with rocks and anything we could find to add support to the track. If someone should fall from the edge it would be game over. Since there wasn't the same abundance of stones on this side of the river as the other, we searched for anything that could be added and it was slim pickings. The man from the white car stood on a little piece of dry ground and watched everyone else. When we were satisfied that it was the best we could do with what was available he picked up a small stone on the ground in front of him and threw it in amongst what the rest of us had heaped up. The guys from the Kombi van rolled their eyes at each other. They made an attempt but hesitated on the slope and didn't make it up the bank. It took a couple of pushes to get them back through the slippery clay to where they had started from for another run. Ed instructed the driver, "This time don't let up on the gas and use your momentum to keep going." The challenge for the driver was, that if the vehicle was not aimed just right, it would either hit the stump or go over the edge. The second attempt was a breeze for the kombi and the cheering crowd let out a whoop. Now it was Ed's turn, and our big, wide van had no room for error. I couldn't watch—if he missed he would be off the edge, and we would need two teams of oxen to pull us out. He aimed and took a good run. I held my breath and shut my eyes, visualizing success through my fear. When I heard screams and cheers from the kids, my eyes opened to see the back wheel scraping the tree trunk. He did it! What a driver, what a relief! And that was the last crossing for us. The little red car climbed the bank with ease. We cheered again. The white car... well, he hesitated and was stuck on the incline. We managed to push him back to take a second try but he missed and slid off the edge. The guys tried to push him out but he just sank deeper on the passenger side. They were filthy from mud and that finely dressed man tiptoed out of his car through the clay, clean as a whistle to survey the situation. Given that there was not much we could do, and feeling some frustration with this man, the kids and I walked up to the field to explore.

The guys were still trying to do something about the car, and on our return all were extremely frustrated with the situation; no one had strength or energy left. With the car almost on its side, not much more could be done. All were blankly staring at it when four men in a pick up truck arrived from the oncoming direction. If they wanted to pass, they would have to get the car out. The musicians hadn't slept all night, and the other family had two young children who needed attention. Ed said we had done enough and since the events of the morning put us on a tight schedule he told us to get into the van. Our three vehicles left together.

We continued on another one-lane track to a gravel road, then a gravel road to the main highway on the other side of the roadblock. We took José back towards town and honked our good-byes to the others when they headed toward Oaxaca. There was a lot of traffic, despite the roadblocks, and while purchasing gas we were told the roadblock had cleared about forty-five minutes earlier.

We left Tehuantepec at 11 a.m. still with plenty of time to meet the plane in Oaxaca at 7 p.m. After a ten-minute drive up the Oaxaca highway there was a military checkpoint. They asked the regular questions and where we were going. Ed replied, "Oaxaca."

The man asked, "Are you aware the road is blocked?"

Ed's eyes popped open and asked, "Up here too?"

He said, "No, they moved from Tehantepec to El Gramal no more than an hour ago." We sat there in disbelief. Ed asked me what I thought. If we went around we would never be on time and it's a really long drive. We discussed the situation and decided that since it is Christmas, they wouldn't sit there over the entire holiday. The last roadblock lasted only a few hours. Ed decided to bet on this one being a short time too. The kids' spirits were slowly breaking down.

We were stopped in a long line of traffic that went on a good distance further than the point to which we walked up the highway to take a look. We ate our lunch and waited; the morning adventure had enhanced our appetite. It became extremely hot sitting in the sun. The kids asked if we were going to see Grandma and Grandpa tonight. We didn't know. They were looking forward to seeing grandparents and the disappointment for Jake, Whitney and Karina was clearly showing. While we continued to sit, cars and trucks started to roll toward us in the oncoming lane. Several minutes passed and cars were still coming when our line started to move. Smiles and cheers from the kids, excitement again. Ed looked at his watch and said, "We should still have a couple of hours to spare if there aren't any more roadblocks."

The afternoon was incredibly hot. We travelled 12 kilometers before reaching the bridge where the roadblock took control of traffic. The oncoming traffic was still abundant and impatient drivers were passing in both directions on the two lane Oaxaca highway.

By mid-afternoon the van started to chug and choke and Ed pulled it to the side just as it stalled. It always breaks down on uphill climbs when it heats up. The happy spirit of our family was diminished to desperation, and we became downright grumpy with each other. We were stuck in the hot sun and had little water left. The van wouldn't cool down quickly in the heat and direct sun. After a few tries, Ed started it up and it moved, coughing and complaining, a short distance into some shade. The van stalled again before it was entirely under the shade of the trees. Ed said he would wait until three before trying to go any farther. I said four, to let it cool right down, and we would travel when the air was cooler. He and I argued about how long the wait should be, and the kids, who were also upset, argued too. All the good humour of the morning evaporated in the heat and frustrations of the day. Ed gave us all a pep talk. If we let it cool until three we would still have time to get to the hotel and airport (forever the optimist). I began reading aloud to take our minds off the situation and was interrupted several times with questions about Grandma and Grandpa. When Ed decided it was time to move he closed the hood, started the van and it ran as if there wasn't a thing wrong with it. The bulk of the traffic was well ahead and our drive was much safer. (Maybe our angels took us out of a dangerous situation—I need to learn to think that way during tight moments, instead of getting so upset.) The van worked well for an hour then choked and hesitated on another uphill climb—but it kept going.

At our next refueling stop there were two trucks of *Green Angels*—highway helpers. Ed spoke with them about our problem, and the guys agreed it was likely a clogged gas filter. Ed asked if he could have it changed here. We followed the truck to a little out-of-the-way place—literally a hole in a mud brick wall—to purchase the gas filter and then directed to a mechanic who would change it.

The mechanic said if the same thing happened again, the problem probably originates with the fuel pump; they work while cool but will quit when hot.

At 5 p.m. we were on the move again. Ed, still being the optimist, announced, "We can still make it to the airport if we go straight there." This put some enthusiasm back into the kids. I was past expecting to get there on time and worried about Dad and Mom being worried about us, after I'd told them we would be at the airport unless there was a major disaster. I was afraid they were going to think something really awful had happened. Teach me not to say stuff like that. Things have held us back but it's not a major disaster.

Again the van functioned as if there wasn't anything wrong, and we enjoyed the incredible views of mountains, valleys and the sun setting. On another steady, long, uphill climb, we had more difficulties. Hot with the strain of climbing mountains, the engine choked and hesitated. In the darkness of night, Ed pulled into a rest stop and turned the engine off within 60 kilometers of our destination, just one hour before the family was to land in Oaxaca. The mood of our crew was a little hard to describe—defeated and resigned to the fact that we were just not going to meet everybody at the airport. Karina and Jake were almost in tears. Getting to see Grandma and Grandpa shouldn't be so hard. As we stepped out of the van to relieve our bodily needs a police truck pulled up beside the van. Ed explained the situation to the officers and told them the van would go again when it cooled down, then asked if there was much more climbing. There were only a few more uphill kilometers and the rest of the distance to Oaxaca was the same altitude. They moved on.

Evening in the mountains, and the air was downright cold. We had clothes on for 30-degree weather. The van wouldn't take long to cool down. Sitting in the dark and silence, the Whit came out with, "I guess Grandma and Grandpa can't depend on us to pick them up at airports; we always miss them."

She made me laugh, "You're right Whitney, we missed them when they came to Santiago too, didn't we? But we are going to see them, we are going to get there." Trying to be reassuring.

I began reading again, using the flashlight, and then by moonlight when the big white full moon rose over the mountaintop. Ed resumed our trek of tribulations at the exact moment our family was to be touching down at the airport, and the lights of Oaxaca came closer and closer without any more coughing, sputtering or hesitation from the van.

I had written the address of the hotel in the back of my writing book but it was not to be found. We must have torn the page out and mistakenly used it as a score sheet for a game. It's the only thing I could think of. When Mom gave us the hotel name we looked it up to see if it was listed in the *Mexico and Central America Handbook*. What we found then was Regional de Antequera not Real de Antequera and assumed there was a misunderstanding by either Mom or me when putting it down on paper. We assumed it was the hotel. (Never checked to match address??) We were at Regional de Antequera by 8 p.m. Whitney had fallen asleep. Ed and the other five bombarded the reception desk to ask if our people had arrived; if not we were going to head to the airport. Ed and the kids were back within minutes with a not-so-happy look on their faces. There was no reservation under the name of Michlowski, or for a group our size, but the man at reception said he thought there was a Real de Antequera maybe two streets over on the other side of the *zocolo* (Mexican town center square). We didn't have much luck; the one-way streets were busy, narrow and difficult to navigate with the big van. We were lost looking for a place for which we didn't even have an address. Karina had all she could take for one day, began dropping tears, and buried her face in a pillow.

I remembered Mom saying the hotel she booked was within a block of the *zocolo*. Driving being so confusing, Ed parked the van a few blocks away and took Jake and the older kids searching on foot. Whitney slept. Karina had given up, and saying she had a headache, lay on the seat and didn't move.

After 9 p.m. I spotted the girls on the street with Mom and Jenna (my niece). They had found the hotel and our family. I said, "I see Gram." Karina was suddenly better. She had her shoes on before I roused Whitney. They popped their heads in as Whitney slowly wakened and found her smiles. Mom said, "So glad you guys got here, it has been pretty gloomy at the hotel. We were supposed to meet Lee and Clif in Dallas and fly together from there but they didn't show up. We don't know what happened to them." We had some good hugs; it has been a long time.

Dad and Clark (my brother) were waiting in the hotel doorway, all smiles and hugs too. Dad said, "So glad you guys made it; we were worried."

I said, "Well, Dad, you have to give Ed all the credit, Oaxaca was his goal and he just kept going. I didn't think we were going to get here today."

We are in a nice hotel room, In Jake's words as he flopped onto a bed, "This is absolute luxury." Lee called and explained that they only had a photocopy of Eli's birth certificate and the airline wouldn't let him out of the country without proper identification. Clif drove back to San Diego today to find the original, and they'll be arriving tomorrow afternoon. We had lots to talk about over tacos and the kids were running on adrenaline. I still am.

Clark and Jenna had a setback today too. For some reason the flight from Mexico City to Oaxaca was overbooked, and they didn't have confirmed seats. Nobody understood this. All six tickets were purchased and confirmed together, yet two of them were put on standby. Anyway, there were two empty spaces, due to the absence of Lee and Clif. The full moon was playing tricks on us all.

January 13, 2000!!! We are into the New Millennium

I have not written a word since meeting up with family. What a ceaseless paradox we live—time but no time! It has been a busy, fun and a relaxing three weeks getting reacquainted with family. My brother, Clark, hasn't changed at all from Christmas '96 the last time we saw him, but Jenna, his daughter, has certainly grown up. Age six to nine makes a big change in a little person. Lee, Clif and Eli managed to get to Oaxaca easily the next afternoon. It was the first time we've met Eli, and he is now 20 months old. He played shy for a day but soon played with the others.

Ed spent most of the 23rd in the auto repair shop with the van, having the fuel pump changed. It stayed overnight; they couldn't get the timing right and it is still a problem. Will anyone ever figure this thing out?

Monte Alban Ruins was the only place we visited as a group. The recent earthquake has made many structures unsafe, and we were not allowed to enter half of the sites of the ruins that Mom and Lee had visited six years ago. But even so it was an intriguing tour.

Whitney & her cousin Jenna at Monte Alban –Oaxaca, Mexico

Archeologists believe the Zapotec society went through five significant periods. It began to take shape about 650 BC when small groups of Olmec people moved into the fertile valleys. The first period began with excavating and levelling the top of a 1,600-meter mountain after which, stone buildings and temples were constructed. Sophisticated tunnels, as well as water storage and drainage systems, were constructed. The second period saw smaller groups of people from Chiapas and Guatemala merge with the Zapotec, creating vast human resources. The majority of the present-day ruins are what is left of the reconstruction of the third period. When the Zapotec were an influential empire, the city had a population estimated at 35,000, occupying over 65 hectares. The mountain peak is believed to have been the religious center. The plaza aligns perfectly north and south: there is a Palace, the home of the ruling dignitary (four rooms surround a patio), an observatory, ball court, pyramid systems, and several stepped temples. One hundred and seventy tombs were found in the area. The oldest structure on the site is *Los Danzantes,* Building of the Dancers. It houses rectangular stone slabs with glyphs and carvings of human figures illustrating life and death; many of the figures are in contorted positions. There were fabulous views of the valleys from the upper pyramid.

Christmas in Oaxaca was a special time. The 23rd is the day the radish carving and flower arranging festival competition is judged. Huge radishes were carved and shaped into scenes and displays. Most were nativity scenes, but many facets of contemporary life in the state of Oaxaca were represented as well. Hundreds of carvings were set up on tables in the *zocolo*. By the morning of the 24th the show was totally cleared away and the *zocolo* was set up for evening parades. Holy night traditions in the city of Oaxaca are a true celebration. Each church parish creates a float bearing a live nativity scene and puts a procession together from its home church. Bands play, children dress as angels, people sing, extended families walk together and gather in the heart of the city. Processions come from different directions filling the *zocolo* with people in high spirits, along with music and fireworks. People on floats threw candies on the street for children to collect. Many handed out handmade candle lanterns to the crowd of bystanders and giant spiral sparklers were an eye-catcher. Fireworks, sparklers, lanterns, music and dancing filled the centre of the city with light and joy. By midnight, the processions worked their way back to their own parishes, and people returned to their homes and their own meals and celebrations. It was a real festival of light that kept the kids dazzled until they were falling asleep on their feet.

We had a Christmas morning breakfast at the hotel restaurant where Mom gave a little gift bag to each of her grandchildren. It was to be a no-present Christmas, but as always, it was an opportunity for grandparents to dote. In Oaxaca, Christmas day was business as usual; Christmas Eve is the celebration. We walked the city streets and markets, and then had a wonderful Christmas dinner at a second-story restaurant overlooking the Christmas clad *zocolo*—it was magical. Music, food, drink and a celebration of our own, one of the best I remember. We shared Mom's Christmas fruitcake and shortbread with the musicians and waiters. They enjoyed sampling some of our food traditions as much as we enjoyed theirs.

We moved to Puerto Escondido on the 26th to enjoy the beach. Clif, having lived beside the ocean his entire life, is an avid surfer and fisherman. He taught Ben a little surfing, took the kids out snorkeling and arranged to take the guys deep-sea fishing for tuna. So it was at 6 a.m. one morning that Clark, Ed, Ben and Jake followed Clif on an adventure none of them had ever experienced before. Dad was invited but declined; like his visit to Chile, he was there because his grandchildren were there. They caught two bonito and two tuna, gave the two bonito and the 15-kilogram tuna to the captain and came back with the 25-kilogram yellowfin tuna that Ed hauled in. The captain eats the fish that are caught or has the right to sell them. Clif gutted the tuna only after several photos, and it filled our fridges. The 15 of us ate tuna for four days: tuna tacos, sautéed tuna and onions, tuna salad and tuna steaks. The first night alone we must have enjoyed $500 worth of sashimi, which tasted like it did in Japan. What a treat. The guys might have enjoyed the fishing trip more but for the seasickness. Jake apparently spent the morning flat on the floor of the boat and got up only to watch the dolphins or to vomit over the edge. Ben said, "There were so many dolphins they swam in layers

around us and followed the boat. They jumped out of the water together and you could see their whole bodies."

Jake added, "So close, it looked like the boat ran over one. It didn't though, they were too fast, they were so awesome."

That was the only time Jake smiled in the two to three hours after they returned. Ed

The fisherman & their catch. Clif & Eli & Clark with Ed, Jake & Ben
-Puerto Escondido, Mexico

Living Dreams

said, "Just seeing the dolphins was worth going out, and we got fish too." It took a few hours for the healthy colour to return to their blank-looking skin.

The people of Puerto Escondido appear to make a ritual of watching the sunset from the beach. The setting sun never failed to appear as a clear red-orange disc dropping to the horizon, taking less than two minutes to be swallowed by the sea. It was the busiest time of day on the beach. What better opportunity does one have to give thanks for another day? Watching the daily sunsets I couldn't help but feel the days rolling by and questioned if I was using them wisely. All I can do is my best at being conscious about making each day the best it can be.

Jenna was not happy to leave her cousins when she and Clark left to be home for New Year's. Schedules are a fact of life for them. I don't know how I am going to go back to a scheduled life, but it is amazing what a break from the known can do for a person's soul. Our mid-life interlude is coming to an end and I am beginning to believe that every hard-working person should be entitled to a time-out from routine life for a year or two.

We have been living somewhat cut off from the news of the world and had heard little of the fear of computers shutting down when the date changed to 2000. Clif filled us in, and as I listened I couldn't help but think that we have become a society too dependent on things and not on our own personal resources. What if the systems in place really did fail? Our society really would fall apart and it wouldn't matter one breath to the people who live with the earth, the people who at present are considered the "poor" people of the world, self-sufficient and resourceful people relying on nature and themselves. They are the people who would be richer and prepared for survival. For billions of years the sun has risen and set, and it will continue until the sun itself dies, whether the human race is present or not.

Thoughts, thoughts, thoughts, one millennium going, another coming, but that too is just a man-made thing: days, seasons, circles around the sun. From ice age to ice age isn't a human creation, but putting numbers on days, months and years is. I have circled the sun 43 times and if it is destined, look forward to at least that many more. The year 2000 came in with us on the beach of Puerto Escondido, Mexico. There is peace and balance in my life, and on the morning of January 1, 2000, the sun rose as calmly, peacefully, beautifully and consistently as it did the day before.

Our plans were to tour Mexico after everyone had left, but the kids are not interested in driving to see more Mayan ruins. They're all anxious to get home. So, with the van not being in top condition, and after looking at distances, I resigned myself to the fact that other Mayan ruins will have to be visited at another time. Tanya would like to visit others too but said, "It doesn't matter, because one year I'm going to Chichen Itza to see the sunrise on the equinox, whether we go this year or not." At Chichen Itza there is a temple where the rising sun on the morning of the vernal equinox creates a shadow resembling a serpent. It is something she wants to see. These kids are already making future travel plans. When we were talking about them being married and having kids of their own, Jake firmly claimed, "I'm not doing anything like that until I've seen the rest of the world first." I don't know what we are turning these kids into— maybe gypsies. Whitney has been on the move half her life. I wonder if she will be content to live in one place for more than four months. Anyway, we decided to follow our family up the coast to Acapulco to spend a few more days with them before they headed home.

Ben, Dad, Lee, Clif and Eli took the bus to Acapulco, Ed and the rest of us met them at the campground. Mom came with us in the van. She was interested in the sights and kept telling us to look at this or that, and did so enthusiastically all day long. She commented on several women doing their laundry in the river. Dayna rolled her eyes, to which Mom responded, "These guys don't find this interesting? What's wrong with you people?"

Dayna retorted, "It's normal, it's the way people live here—we see it all the time."

"You guys have seen so much it doesn't mean anything anymore," Mom replied.

It's not that it doesn't mean anything to us; after being amongst this lifestyle for the past three years, we know and understand that it is the way of life for the people of this part of the world and it's not so foreign to our senses. Canada really isn't a realistic representation of what the rest of the world is like.

We have camped at Pie de la Questa while in the Acapulco area. There are six groups of people camping here; one has a Mexican license plate and all the rest are from Quebec. Ed says that it is a pretty good indication of who the more adventurous Canadians are. We aren't so unique anymore—we're just more Quebecers in Mexico for the winter. Quebec plates on vehicles appear to outnumber all other foreign plates travelling on the streets, too.

The kids took turns staying with Gram and Grandpa in the hotel overnight. The only sightseeing we did in Acapulco was to take a local bus to see the cliff divers. These people dive 40 meters into a small split in the cliff where the water rolls in; it is death defying. I'm afraid it has given Ben some ideas.

Ed gave the kids another pep talk when it was time for their grandparents to fly back to Canada. "When we say good-bye to Grandpa and Grandma, don't get upset like when they left Santiago, okay? We are going to be home in three months. Sometimes even in Canada we don't see them for that long."

We said good-bye tonight and did all right. Dad was especially happy knowing we would be back in Canada soon. They fly home tomorrow and we are going to look for a place on a beach to spend the Canadian winter before heading home. The constant travelling has been hard work for Ed as much as it is adventure. The couple of months before Christmas were stressful for him. He is entitled to a rest and some real holidays. It is taking a while for him to shake the cough that started in South America and grew worse with the cold he had in Puerto Escondido.

January 17, 2000: Acapulco to Sayulita

Today we are in Sayulita, just north of Puerto Vallarta, and it looks like we have found where we are going to stay for a month or two, although if we had known northern Mexico was going to be so full of non-Mexicans, we would have stayed in Puerto Escondido.

Along the costal highway from Acapulco to north of Barra de Navidad the land was productive with foods. In some places, coconut plantations went on as far as the eye could see. Mango orchards are in full blossom; the fragrance of the flowers fills the air, a delicate yet heady fragrance. Papayas were a common sight as well as that basic food: bananas. There were many coconut palm fields with, I am assuming, cacao plants underneath. We noticed only a few citrus trees. The larger fields of bananas had the whole stem of bananas covered with plastic bags. This is done to protect developing stems from applications of pesticides, and is a common practice in Ecuador, Colombia, Guatemala and Brazil as well.

One tree in particular that I cannot name grows in abundance along the roadside. There are no leaves, just white flowers. At first it looked like a tree covered in white petunias, but these "petunias" have burgundy centres. When they are in fields and on hillsides the white makes them stand out from everything, and they are striking against a brilliant blue sky. Another type of bush or tree has bright yellow, star-shaped flowers that are bigger than the "petunias". This latter tree flowered in Brazil in late July and August, which were the months leading up to spring there. It is blooming here now, in the months leading up to Mexico's spring.

Police checks occur regularly on the highway, but if police are seriously looking for something, they don't look deep enough. Then again, their hearts soften when they see our troop of kids getting out of the van. During one of those police checks Ben noticed one of the supports of the roof box giving away again underneath the last repair work. By the time we arrived at the trailer park in Playa Azul, the support had broken completely. Ed warned us the last time it needed repairs that we would be getting rid of the box when it broke again. The caretaker of the hotel said he could use the wood, so off it came. As a result, the van is more crowded, and it is more of a challenge keeping peace in the closer confinement, but we manage. In the big picture we don't have that much farther to go anyway.

There was a bus from British Colombia and a motorhome from Ontario at the Playa Azul trailer park on our arrival, and as we started setting up, four large motorhomes from Quebec rolled in. Only Canadians were in the Mexican park.

The trailer park in Malaque, five minutes north of Barra de Navidad, wasn't any different. Only two of the 45 spaces in the park were left when we pulled in, and all the visitors were Canadians and Americans. Mexico is a migration destination for people as much as it is for birds and butterflies.

Ed spoke with people from Kitchener in one of the mobile homes and they said finding a house to stay in would be easy. They introduced Ed to a man from Kapuskasing who spends his winters here and owns several houses in the Manzanilla area. He had two that were available to rent immediately and brought us to see them. One was much too small for our family and the other was perfect but a long way from the beach. It would do if we didn't have another choice.

We walked the beach area after leaving the house to see what it was like and where we would be spending time if we rented the house. There was a dead stingray on the beach. Dayna said there was no way she was swimming in that water. It wasn't a clean beach either.

Ed spotted something large in the water and we spent at least an hour watching three whales swim back and forth in the bay from one side to the other; one was much larger than the other two. They swam in unison and we saw a head twice. Most of the time all that was visible was whale backs not with fins but with bumps on them. A tail flipped into the air occasionally and when the whales had been submerged a few minutes, water sprayed from their blowholes. They came so close to shore we could hear them blowing. Tanya said they must be gray whales. She is the one who spent days drawing and colouring whales a few years ago and still remembers many features of each type. They were so huge and yet moved gracefully. A boat full of people hoping to get a closer look followed them; within minutes the creatures were back in the open sea and far out of sight. Anything that is chased usually eludes the one chasing it.

We looked for more houses in Barra de Navidad and found the town to be quaint, tightly built, and to have an amiable character, but we didn't find anything to match our expectations. This is the last of the ocean for us for an indefinite period, and we would like to be close to it for a while. Ed said the people from Kitchener told him Wayne Gretzky and his entourage spent New Year's here, and that there were plenty of fireworks used for the new millennium. They also told him Gretzky is retiring this year. Karina piped in and asked, "Who is Wayne Gretzky?"

Ben exclaimed, "Wayne Gretzky? Karina, what's wrong with you?"

She retorted, "Well then, who is he?"

Ben said, "Only the most famous hockey player in the world and he is Canadian."

She said, "So," and was obviously hurt by Ben's reaction to her not knowing. I hoped to soften the sting and said, "Karina, that just goes to show that we have been away from Canada for a long time. I bet Tanya could name plenty of Brazilian and Chilean soccer players but I'm pretty sure Wayne Gretzky is just about the only hockey player she knows." Tanya confirmed my statement and it consoled her sister. Knowledge comes only from what we are exposed to.

That evening Ed talked with people from Alberta. When he came back he said, "This guy said, 'When you guys go back you're going to find that nothing has changed. Quebec is still talking separation, taxes are still really high, and it takes forever for the government to do anything.'"

He sounded frustrated with the way things are in Canada. But if there is one thing I have learned while visiting other countries, it is that every one of them has its strengths and weaknesses, pros and cons. I don't know whether my saying so is because I am truly Canadian and biased, but Canada is the best country in this world to live in, and if people can't live the life they choose for themselves there, then it is only because of themselves.

The van has been working fairly well since the fuel pump was changed. Occasionally it hesitates while on the road, and it is always slow to move unless it has been warmed up first (it must be getting older).

SAYULITA HOLIDAY

Sunday, January 23, 2000: Sayulita, Mexico

This week has been another example of events throwing us off track but everything working out for the best in the end.

We were at the camping and trailer park in Sayulita before noon Monday morning, but the only space left was in a less than ideal spot for an unreasonable cost. Ed told the owner that we were looking for a place for a month or two, and the owner didn't hesitate to suggest the condominiums next door, explaining that they are summer homes owned by people in Guadalajara, and some of them are rented out during the winter months. He added that real estate agencies in the village would help us look and then offered a monthly rate if we wanted to stay at the campground.

As we walked through the gate of the condos I knew this was the place. The cleaning lady showed us three units available, but we had to make arrangements with the caretaker who wouldn't be back until late afternoon. The unit at the front overlooking the ocean was our first choice but twice the cost of the unit that was five back from the beach. We met Javier, the caretaker, to ask if we could rent the one that suited our needs. We had to wait until 7 p.m. for him to talk with the owner to find out whether it was booked at all over the next two months. We gambled that it would be available and didn't make arrangements for a place to stay the night. On our return, we learned we could have the condo but not until Monday so we needed a place for the week. When Javier realized we still needed accommodations he introduced us to Kathleen. She rents the upstairs bedrooms of her condo, and since she didn't mind us cooking our own food on the upstairs patio, it is where we have been for the week.

Kathleen is American and her husband, Sergio, is Mexican. They both have seasonal work in the northern states and this is their winter home. Their son, Francisco, attends the school across the road as well as keeping up with school in the states.

Monday Ben was not well and didn't eat. For some reason his body rejected any water he drank. Fruit juice was the only thing that would stay down on Tuesday, and on Wednesday, the first thing he said was, "I'm hungry".

Ed retorted, "There goes our budget." Something bothered Ben's digestive system and he is now making up for the days he didn't eat.

On Wednesday morning, the ocean water was clean and clear, but by the afternoon it was fluorescent yellow. It didn't look like water I wanted to set foot in. Kathleen said it gets like that occasionally; the Mexicans call it *mala agua*—bad water, but she says it doesn't take long before it clears again. I told the kids to swim in the pool and it wasn't hard to convince them. Their senses told them to stay out of the ocean water as well, even though some people swam in it.

Tanya kept the kids busy making a Monopoly game. At Finca Ixobel she copied the cards and the board out by hand to make a game for travelling. They made everything, even paper dice. She had Jake and Whitney cutting rectangles and writing out the numbers for money. Screams came from Whitney when a series of 100s were written 001. She just couldn't stand the fact that she had made a mistake and Tanya disapproved. A common error, but with encouragement Tanya had her doing it the right way around. Whitney the wit, discovered if you turn it upside down it said 100 and yelled back at Tanya, quite smugly, that she was writing it so Ben (sitting across from her) could see that it was 100. Tanya put the others to work writing out the rental and mortgage info on the cards and showed Karina how to make the paper cubes for the dice. Tanya constructed the game board. It occupied them for an entire day, and by evening they were playing their game.

Ed called Lisa on both Wednesday and Friday concerning the house. Christiane and Pascal have given notice that they are moving out March 1st. However, when Ed talked with Lisa it was the first of February, which threw a glitch into our two-month condo plans; we are only going to stay a month now. Funny how things work—if we had made arrangements for the condo when we first arrived the two months rent would have been paid.

Early Thursday morning Kathleen was excited when I met her. She asked, "Have you been down to the beach yet this morning? You should see it. The tide has washed up thousands of sardines on the beach and there are so many birds you wouldn't believe it. I've never seen anything like it before". After a lengthy description of what we would find she added, "Did you know there is an eclipse tonight about nine o'clock? It's a lunar total eclipse, I wonder if it has something to do with the fish on the beach. It's going to get very smelly after the sun gets working on them if it doesn't get cleaned up".

It was a curious phenomenon on the beach. There were thousands and thousands of birds. Never in my life have I ever seen so many birds at once: Grey pelicans, brown pelicans, a white gull-like bird with an orange beak, cormorants, another black one with a long black beak and a red beard underneath, another similar-shaped bird but with a longer beak and white markings on their head. Small dead fish littered the beach as the tide receded. There were three kinds: sardines, anchovies and swordfish all between three and six inches long. We watched the birds feed on the live fish in the water. Pelicans skimmed the surface and scooped them out of the water while in flight. The white gulls dove in to fill their bellies, but the other birds flew in circles scooping fish off the surface with a flick of their neck.

The water and sky were full of birds as far as one could see in both directions and several kilometers out from shore as well. The water was the clean clear blue it was when we arrived. As we watched the birds feast that afternoon I wondered if the *mala agua* was the reason for the mass of dead fish on the beach.

The beach smelled of nothing but fish, and the water boiled with them. Black areas in the water just meters from shore turned out to be schools of fish. When the sun caught the waves at the right moment, instead of appearing black with fish they were full of sparkling silver flecks and the ocean appeared carbonated as the fish jumped out of the tossing waves. Little fish were still being washed up live; they either died or managed to catch another wave back into the ocean.

Jake, with his own methods of learning, collected the dead swordfish. (At least that's what we thought they were. There were fewer of them amongst the others.) He played knights, having sword fights and actually ran the dead fish through each other with the "swords". I found it gross, but they were already dead. We walked the length of the beach and discovered that it was no different anywhere else. We spent most of the day watching the birds and fish. By late afternoon clouds rolled in and stayed, which disappointed the kids; they were looking forward to watching the eclipse.

Ed, Tanya, Ben, Dayna and Whitney fell asleep while we read *The Lion Witch and the Wardrobe* while waiting for the eclipse. Karina, Jake and I joined Kathleen. She had been watching from the beginning but clouds blocked the view. We talked about the fish, birds, yellow water and the eclipse all happening at the same time—it seemed so unusual. Javier said he had only ever seen a suicide of fish like that once before about 20 years ago. Jake watched the sky as it cleared and said there were stars but no moon then yelled, "There it is, it's dark red and you can hardly see it." The others wanted to see the eclipse, but only Dayna and Ben managed to pull themselves out of bed. We watched a sliver of white slowly grow into what the kids called a cookie with a bite out of it. Karina and Ben didn't last but Jake and Dayna watched the moon until it was fully restored to how we are accustomed to seeing it.

Sleep didn't come easy for me, yet Ed was sleeping hard. The guys in the condo we were supposed to rent were having a party playing their guitars and bongos. So much was flying through my head and I often lie awake through a full moon. I couldn't help wondering if we were headed home in just a week. We are not prepared for winter and if we end up at home now, the kids will need appropriate clothing. I put some warm clothes on and made a cup of chamomile tea to help calm my senses. The moon had everything lit up and while waiting for my water to boil I noticed my mug was casting no shadow apart from the handle that caused a small rectangle of shade directly underneath. The moon was at the zenith. It never does that in Canada. I turned a plastic cup upside down onto the table. It was wider at the brim than at the base and without a handle, which allowed the entire form of the cup to be illuminated; like the *Hitching Post of the Sun* at Machu Picchu when it casts no shadow. Before I finished my tea the east facing side of the upside down cup darkened and the shadow had begun to grow.

My mind was dwelling on petty human things and was given an opportunity to look at a bigger picture. Anxious negative thoughts just interfere with the positive natural force that makes things work.

Since we are only staying a month now, Ed arranged for us to use the front condo and we move in tomorrow—what a treat. Scrabble and Monopoly have been the time consumers this week and the kids are getting better at the former. Ben's impatience comes through in nonsense but he comes up with some good words too. Jake and Whitney rediscovered the paint box this week; paintings covered the floor and were hanging up everywhere. We sure know how to spread out our things when we have some space.

The condo we will be staying in for the month has three bedrooms. One bedroom is on the ground floor with the kitchen, small eating area and living room. The ground floor outdoor living space has a big table and chairs. The two upstairs bedrooms open out on to the second floor balcony, which gets shaded sun most of the day and I know will be a favourite spot. We are right beside the pool, overlooking the beach and the ocean, and have a little lawn space where the kids can play.

January 25 to February 24, 2000: Sayulita, Mexico

We soon fell into a comfortable daily rhythm of reading and math in the morning after a walk on the beach, midday meals of tacos, afternoons of soaking up sun and playing in the water, and light evening meals followed by cards, Scrabble, Boggle and reading stories aloud.

It is the first time we have spent any length of time in one place where Ed didn't work. He has taken a holiday and enjoyed the down time. The kids found friends on the beach. The campground had several Canadian and American families with children out of school in order to experience a different lifestyle and warm winter weather. Whitney befriended Hannah, and they were back and forth. They swam in the pool, played on the beach, played games of soccer and bicycled at the campground. Eli, Hannah's four-year-old brother, visited as well, but that stopped after he slipped in the pool and ended up face down. Despite the fact the water wasn't over his head, he was unable to get his feet back onto the bottom, and I pulled him out of the water. Whitney, Hannah and I brought Eli back to his mom. Whitney boasted to Beth, "Mom did it again, she pulled another kid out of the water." Beth's mouth dropped open as Eli cried, relieving his fear in the safety of his mother's arms. I explained, "Eli had a scare, he slipped off the step, landed face down in the pool and couldn't seem to get his feet on the bottom. He wasn't face down long, but it frightened him."

Theron, Hannah's dad, came looking for his daughter one afternoon, and we got to know each other's families more. He is an auto mechanic and had neck and shoulder problems. He worked on the van and Ed worked on him. He did a test drive, tuned the engine up and was confident it would get us back to Canada. So we drive it the way it is.

Ben had to have a surfboard and got resourceful in convincing his Dad it would be worthwhile. He worked a deal with John who was selling it, and we didn't see much more of Ben, other than watching him out on the water catching any wave he could. It was easy to recognize him: his sun-bleached blond hair and dark, tanned skin made him stand out from everyone else. I'm sure half the attraction was the girl who waited for a wave beside him. More time was spent straddling the board with feet dangling in the water and just socializing than actually catching waves. He came to shore mostly when his stomach dictated.

Theron and his friends invited Ben on a day trip of sea kayaking and surfing at another beach, and he learned some skills that he had been trying to master through trial and error.

Tanya, Dayna and Karina befriended the teen girls of a family in the condo across from us. They were from southern Ontario on a two-week vacation. Once they got to know each other, they were inseparable.

Jake occasionally played with the boys at the campground but has been content to play alone on the beach for long periods of time; he seems to need that, he just doesn't function well in larger groups yet.

Ed and I often found ourselves alone while the kids were off with the people they had befriended. Having time together without the pressures of living and surviving, we find ourselves content and enjoying each other's company. A dream at Christmas seemed to summarize our relationship through the past few years:

Ed and I were walking together on a gravel road downhill. The road had many shells on it. We both spotted the same one at the same time; Ed picked it up. It was whole and beautiful. I found two more. I almost missed them, they were so covered in dirt, but they cleaned up with some work and were beautiful whole shells.

For Ed, our relationship has always been whole. For me there were so many emotional blocks within myself I couldn't see our relationship for what it was. I am given a second chance.

Ed and I spoke with an interesting retired couple from Vancouver. They have been driving and living nomad style out of their motorhome for the last two years and have travelled most of North America, but the farthest south they have been is Mexico. They were interested to hear about our travels and are contemplating going farther south. The gentleman was curious about the kids and their education and said, "I'm impressed, every time I see your kids at least two of them are reading. I don't think I have ever seen kids read so much." They were obviously watching us. Their morning strolls coincided with our short amount of concentration time and they saw the kids more often than not in the couple of hours during the morning when they were into some bookwork. The girls often read a book for pleasure on the beach in the afternoons as well. I said, "Well, they have time. Reading doesn't happen unless kids have time. If they are too busy doing other things, reading is one of the last things they will do." The couple stayed at the campground almost three weeks and then continued south, saying they thought they might attempt Guatemala.

Ed spent his time exercising, reading some good novels (reading fiction is something he rarely does) and enjoying the beach. He decided we were using the van only for trips to Puerto Vallarta while here in Sayulita, so keeping food in the house meant regularly walking the beach to the village and carrying it home. It was an enjoyable chore we shared. A daily trip to the tortillaria with our cloth

Ed, Lisa & Kids on a walking tour of Puerto Vallarta

to wrap tortillas in gave us warm, fresh corn flour tortillas for tacos. It became a delicious constant food.

We enjoyed Lisa's visit; it was good to catch up on news of family at home. She had our vehicle insurance reinstated and brought both the new ownership and insurance papers to us.

Lisa attempted swimming in the waves with the kids but like me she doesn't like being scraped on the bottom, tossed and turned upside down while waiting for the ocean to spit you back out onto the shore. She used the pool more. The girls in particular spent as much time as they could with her. Evenings of euchre competition and ongoing jokes keep us roaring in laughter much of the time. A day visit to Puerto Vallarta, a day trip and picnic on a different beach, and a day of gift shopping for people at home used up her days with us. Her weeklong visit didn't feel long enough.

Tuesday, February 22, 2000:

Sometimes I am really shown that some higher power listens when I call from within. I have spent many hours on the beach without a pair of sunglasses. I sat on my last pair in the van and was making myself go without for being so careless. Two days ago, I couldn't read on the beach, the sun was just too bright. I gave up, threw my book down, shut my eyes to relax from squinting and claimed, "God, I need a pair of sunglasses." I then walked the shoreline closer to where Ben was surfing to watch him for a while. With nose to the ground and keeping an eye out for new shells along the way I squatted down to grab one from rolling back into the water with a wave and missed. But... there was a pair of sunglasses rolling around in the lapping of the waves. I was somewhat stunned when I picked them up, since I had just claimed I needed a pair of sunglasses. Every once in a while I am given clear proof I am being heard. Gucci, no less, they were perfect. I have a small head, so finding hats and sunglasses to fit is a challenge. I watched Ben without straining my eyes in the sun. I get what I need, and I have more than a pair of sunglasses to be thankful for.

I was up at 5:00 o'clock this morning and the ocean called. I walked to the beach, listened to the waves, and looked out into the darkness before me. The sky was dark but clear. I felt joy and sadness, always two sides to my feelings. The big dipper was before me, the North Star close to the horizon. The north is pulling us home. When returning from the beach, I spotted my kite rising, in the southeast sky. I have not seen it in the last few months. It is still flying and I was reminded it is always there; just at this time of year it flies more of its hours on the light side of the sky.

I have spent many hours on this north facing beach thinking of the future with anticipation, reluctance and often a knot in my stomach over what lies ahead. The next challenge will be living at home again and building on the positive aspects of the life we left behind. I don't know what I am capable of as yet, but I do know my own children will have first dibs on my time. I must be all there, not just physically but mentally and emotionally as well. We are being put back into our community for some reason, and I suppose I will learn what it is sooner or later. I wanted a different life and place than what we had before but whatever this force is, it is stronger than my will. Our travel journey is ending in a few weeks. God's plan is not always my plan, and I have become better at trusting that process.

THE LAST OF OUR WANDERING

Thursday, February 24, 2000: Mazatlan, Mexico

It was a somber, drive to Mazatlan; we didn't like leaving Sayulita. Ed picked out a campsite in Zona Dorada two blocks from the ocean. We are in the middle of the city among several RVs, most belonging to Canadians. Our aim was the beach for the afternoon, but the store with shells from all over the world was more intriguing. It was more a museum than a store. Some of the shells were the size of a beach ball and there were several pieces of coral basketball size. Ed managed to drag us out but not before we'd purchased a few little souvenirs. Despite the cool evening, the kids had a dunk in the pool to refresh themselves. Being in tents in a campground in the middle of the city feels a little weird.

Friday, February 25, 2000: Loreto, Baja Mexico

The ferry left at 5 p.m. to arrive in La Paz this morning. When we boarded, the steward tried to direct us to the overnight berths. He couldn't believe our tickets were for the common room, for the night journey. It was what we had chosen. Tickets were half the price, making them within our budget, and the kids all agreed they would be fine. As it turned out, the common room was barely half full and we had more space than we needed. The sun set shortly after we set sail. The ocean rolled continuously, so a light meal was all we could handle. While I caught up on my journal, Ed and the kids watched a movie in the lounge. A man who spoke English came into the common room with two children, maybe six and eight, giving them a tour of the ship. I didn't take close notice until I heard, "And this is where the poor people stay—can you imagine not having a bed to sleep in?" You know, I really don't consider myself a poor person, especially since I have achieved greater emotional and spiritual wellbeing. I really wonder who the poor people are sometimes. What classifies a person as poor? In that room there were probably 150 people and we were the only non-Latin American people in it. Why did that man classify us as poor? Because we didn't have a bed to sleep in, or because it costs more to pay for a room with a bed and he believed all of us would take one if we had the money to pay for it? I shook my head in disbelief. All kinds of thoughts raced through my head. I was in that room for several hours and I didn't see many poor people. The giggles and laughter that came from the children playing tag was infectious, there was happy chatter and socializing, genuine concern over a hurt child, the sharing of food, a blanket so an angelic toddler could have a cozy, protected space on the floor to sleep. There was a rich content feeling that many people don't recognize even when it is staring them in the face.

Financial freedom may buy whatever you need or want, but my gut feeling says true freedom comes from not needing money to supply what is necessary to live a

---

fulfilled, healthy life. Just as an example: Drug companies are some of the richest corporations in the world, and they control much of how our society is run. Several drugs we pay billions of dollars for every year are available to anyone who knows what plant to use for the ailment that needs healing. Most such drugs are plentiful and easily found in the mountains, deserts, fields, forests, or in water—both fresh and salt. Many even plague city streets and lawns. It is possible to live in more freedom than what our society allows. History has maneuvered us out of our self-sufficiency, and made us dependent on the almighty dollar.

That man struck a discordancy within me. I am caught between the desire to have money to create freedom in my life and the desire to be self-reliant with the ability to live on what the earth provides. Who is the richer human being? What is really more important? It is likely that many of the people in that room don't have extra money or even enough for basic needs but why is it that we classify people by the amount of money and things they have? What was that man teaching those children by the statement he made? If you don't have money or a bed to sleep in you are poor? It was as if he was saying it is awful not to have a bed, or perhaps sowing the beginnings of a guilt complex because they did. Speaking from experience, it is nice to have a bed to sleep in, but it's not like a good night's rest has to come from a bed. One of the most luxurious nights of sleep I had was on a bed of grass in the Valle de Elqui. (Javier in Sayulita had a bed but he slept on the floor; he said his body didn't ache so much in the morning.) The question that man asked those two children is not a question conducive to helping a child be adaptable in a situation when that child did not have a bed. I found myself shaking my head and saying under my breath as he moved the kids through to the outside doors, "Oh dear God, those poor kids." There was an element of control he had that made me feel sorry for them. It is just how we choose to perceive our reality, isn't it?

We crossed the Tropic of Cancer on our ship's journey across the Golfo de California and are no longer in the tropics. Most of us ended up on the floor for the night; the ocean was rough, and being flat was the best remedy.

Going through inspection was a major ordeal. Mazatlan and La Paz are in the same country, and yet we were given the toughest, most thorough search we have ever experienced in our three years of travel. If we were trying to smuggle something, they would have found it. A whole morning was consumed before we were allowed to continue on.

Baja California is that long peninsula, south of San Diego, that always caught my attention on a map, and here we are. My first impression was that it is grey, rocky and barren. But it is desert and has a unique beauty of its own. There are two campgrounds almost side by side here in Loreto, and we chose the quieter one with more space available. A motorhome from British Columbia moved in beside us (almost on top of us), despite all the space that was available. I don't like being cramped when it's unnecessary. The RV's owners, a retired couple, rolled out artificial turf at the side door along with a table and chairs and set up an awning overhead. The man took a look at our setup and said, "You guys camp the old hard way," with an arrogant tone in his voice. It is peculiar how some statements from some people provoke... whatever. I felt as if he was being smug and we weren't living up to his standards. Something about him told me he thought the kids had no business being here. We don't actually have to say words to get a message across, and his body language was loud and clear. Ed spoke with his gentle diplomatic tact, saying, "That is true, but there weren't many places we couldn't get to with our setup." They chatted; I took my turn in the shower. Ed told me afterwards that our neighbour wouldn't believe we had been to Tierra del Fuego and back, and asked why the kids weren't in school... It takes all kinds of people to make a world. Anyway, the couple found their friends at the other campground and the keeper here invited us to watch a movie with him. We did.

February 27, 2000: Parque Natural de Ballinas Gris

(Natural Park of the Gray Whale—beside what is known in English as Scammon's Lagoon)

There are interesting sites along the east coast of Baja Sur—mountainous desert to the west, and rolling highway up, down, around and along the coast of the Gulf of California. Many foreign motorhomes are parked at the water's edge among the small villages. The highway cuts across the saddle of the mountainous desert from Santa Rosalia. The air was hot and dry. Rocky desert and cacti made up the landscape, and we spotted several coyotes; two crossed the road in front of us. Vultures with wings spread, sitting atop cacti were an unusual sight to us but common in Baja California. The wind is always strong, making us wonder if the vultures spread their wings to keep their balance on their perches.

We attempted to arrange a whale watching tour at Guerrero Negro where we learned it was possible to camp in the Parque National de Ballina Gris for free and arrange our own tour there. So we headed for the park, prepared and self-sufficient for a few days, as we were told it didn't have facilities. We easily found the small building on the shore of the lagoon where tours begin. We talked with a man from British Columbia who has been camping here since yesterday. He did a boat tour this morning and is still here watching the whales. He told Ed we wouldn't regret getting out on the water to see the whales, and recommended the morning, when it is calmer. We watched over the lagoon: a tail fin, a nose in the air, splashes and blows of spray. There are several whales out there.

Ed talked with this man for longer than the kid's attention span, and the rest of us walked out onto the landscape. We found white and well-worn shells a long distance from the shore. It was evident that they had not been in water for many years. Tanya, drawing information together, said, "All these shells so far away from the water. It must mean this was ocean before." I was struck with what she said and had a feeling of some success. Whether she was right or not, she was displaying that she is becoming a thinking person, someone capable of drawing conclusions from observations without being primed, prodded or manipulated into it. For me, it was another glimpse of a home-schooling accomplishment.

It was impossible to find any kind of a sheltered camping spot. The only things in abundance here are wind and sand, and it was a challenge keeping the stove lit to make dinner. We set the tents up close together then moved the van in beside them as a windbreak. It helped. We explored the shore, continued to spot whales, and watched a flock of sandpipers undaunted by our presence, in close proximity to our camp. It is a mysterious phenomenon, how the entire flock takes off, circles, and lands together repeatedly, moving as one. It is proof to me of a collective consciousness—will the human race ever become one like that, communicating instinctively and living in true cooperation.

The wind died down after the sun left the sky, allowing the distant sound of coyote yipping to come through. Silence: no other people, no electricity, no wind. Even the water was silent, and my body was given a chance to relax and rest.

Monday, February 28, 2000: Guerrero Negro – San Quintin Baja California

It was cloudy and damp this morning, not really raining, but the air had a fine mist in it. A young American couple, Paula and Michael, arrived here at the same time we did, but the group of us waited close to an hour for the tour operators. When they finally arrived, they complained about the "bad weather." Accustomed to dry air and sunny skies almost every day of the year, a little bit of wet discouraged them. Obviously our tolerances come from what we are used to—they would never last in Canada. Eventually the clouds cracked to let a little sun through, and the guides consented to taking us to see the whales.

We were all outfitted with life jackets and were told to stay seated at all times in the flat bottom boat. Our guide gave us some information about whales as we headed out into the lagoon. They give birth in the winter months of December, January and February here in the warm, shallow lagoons of Mexico. Both male and female reach sexual maturity between five and 11 years of age. Females are larger than males, ranging from 40 to 50 feet long, and can weigh up to 35 tons. The calves are born after 12 months of gestation; at birth they are between 12 and 15 feet long, and weigh one to one-and-a-half tons. They drink 150 to 200 litres

Whale Watching —Guerrero Negro, Baja Mexico

Living Dreams

of milk per day. Migration north starts in April. The males leave first after mating, the females and calves following within weeks; but some linger as late as June. They will travel alone as well as in groups. Mothers aggressively defend their calves from sharks and killer whales on the journey, yet barely 50 percent of them make it to the coast of Alaska where they spend the summer months eating and growing. Gray whales feed on the small animal life of the shallow ocean water: shrimps, crustaceans and worms. They are baleen whales (no teeth), sucking in food and water, then forcing out the water in order to strain out the food. They are coloured in variations of grey and bear patches of barnacles and whale lice. Our guide said the whales are friendly and often curious about the boats on the water.

At first we were not sure we would see many whales, but our guide spotted the spray of a blow and headed toward it. Boats are prohibited from approaching closer than 50 feet, but nothing stops the whales from coming closer than that to the boats. Soon there were several around us. The most common sight was a cow and calf swimming together in unison, neither head nor tail surfacing, just the backs arching up to dive under again. Occasionally a tail flipped above the surface and a few times a huge head came straight out of the water for a look at us. At one point an adult's back arched above the water surface no more than 10 feet away. We were awe-struck. The whales are obviously friendly and don't feel threatened; our boat was barely a quarter of the length of the many whales that surfaced beside us, and could have been demolished easily with just the flip of a tail. The two hours passed quickly, and we were back on shore. Paula asked Whitney what she thought of the whales. Whitney quickly exclaimed with enthusiasm, "They are awesome. The best part was when the big whale stuck his head out of the water and I saw his eye. It was this big," putting all five fingertips of each hand together to make the biggest ball she could.

We collected a small jar of salt at the thousands of commercial salt ponds between the lagoon and main highway. Paula and Michael told us they heard on the news this morning that the company that was trying to obtain permission to build another salt flat in the area was denied the right to do so. The proposal was going to affect a large gray whale birthing area, and the government of Mexico ruled in favor of the whales. The salt flat is already one of the largest in the world, supplying Canada, the U.S. and Japan.

The desert vegetation became more intriguing the farther north we drove—in particular the cacti of which there were several types. The land has a warmer colour to it as opposed to the cool greys of southern Baja. For several kilometers through the park, the boulders are huge, some the size of houses, rounded as if water has been working on them for thousands of years. Between boulders, cacti, coyotes and vultures, the desert landscapes kept us intrigued.

Pebellon Campground at San Quintin is on the beach. Trees were planted in rows to serve as a windbreak and we found the most sheltered spot we could to set up the tents. The wind is as steady and strong as it was at Patagonia, giving no relief. Before us is an incredible white sand beach: wide, flat, littered with giant mussels and clam shells, eight to 10 inches long—sand dollars too. We just wanted to keep walking on it.

It is the middle of the night. I awakened, uncovered and on the move for the tent door, my heart racing as if I had been running. I was dreaming:

The coyotes are around our tents. They want me to come and play with them. I go. I watch my bare feet running on the desert sand, coyotes running with me on both my right and left. I can hear their panting as we are running together. It feels so good to run free, alive and wild with the coyotes.

In the reality of the night, coyotes surround us. Their chorus is in stereo and some are so close I can clearly hear individual voices in the yipping and howling. I am really cold, have put more clothes on, but still can't sleep. I have tried to waken Ed to listen to the coyotes but he is in another world. I just get moans and grumbles.

It is our last night in Latin America; we cross into the States in the morning. I am not sure I want this nomad life to be over. Part of me is so tempted just to go run with the coyotes right now. I don't know how I am going to live life in Canada and not let my free spirit get caged in. I am afraid she will be lost.

Leap Year Day, 2000: San Quintin to San Diego, California

The desert reminded me of the Roadrunner cartoons I watched as a child. Tall cacti, with their big arms, shrubs, sagebrush, rocks and sand soon gave way to agriculture and heavier population, until we were driving on a major four-lane highway and entering city-like suburbs after Ensanada.

While we were stopped in traffic in Tijuana, a young man about 18 to 20 years of age was going from car to car, looking desperate. He spotted us. "Are you guys American?"

Ed replied, "No, Canadian."

"Oh good, somebody who will understand." He started into a long spiel while keeping up to the van on foot. "We went to a bar and got into a fight, it wasn't our fault. The stupid cops put me and my brother in jail last night. They took my car and won't give it back. They let me out this morning, but not my brother. Won't give me my car, stupid people, how do they expect me to get them what they want if I can't have my car? I have to get back to get some money so I can get my brother out. I went to the bus station to see if I can go that way, but the damned bus driver says if I don't pay first I don't get on. Can you spare me some money so I can get a ticket, my brother's sitting in that stinking jail and I gotta get him out? I'll give you my shoes, anything, please help me." His face was bruised. This didn't seem like a put-on. The Mexicans were having no pity on these boys. Ed gave the kid $18 after asking how much the bus fare was. The kid counted out the dollars— "Thank you, thank you" almost kissing Ed through the window. He started to take his shoes off. Ed said, "I don't want your shoes. Just go." The traffic started to move, and we left him behind. He stood and stared, then took off running. We were stunned with the episode we had witnessed. Ben said, "That's pretty stupid, go to a foreign country and get into a fight; you're asking for trouble." Inside I felt thanks—some good sense being displayed here.

We sat in the line-up at the border for more than an hour, eventually finding out it was the American Customs office. We hadn't taken care of the van exit papers. When the agent at the booth saw we were Canadian, all she asked was how long we had been in Mexico and let us through. Ed asked where he could take care of the van papers. She replied, "It should have been done before you came here, but it doesn't make that much difference, just go." We weren't allowed to stop once through (it's not Argentina and Brazil). Ed parked at a mini-mall about a kilometer away and went back into Mexico on foot to have the papers completed.

The rest of us waited in the parking lot and it didn't take long before a comparison in cultures became the topic of discussion. It is so different. The signs are English, the people around speak English, and there is a lack of colour in the storefronts.

We have been in Spanish-speaking countries so long it doesn't feel normal. When Ed returned he said the van had to be at the border—"officials" have to remove the sticker and if it was not done properly, we would have a difficult time entering Mexico again with a vehicle. We really didn't want to face that line-up a second time so continued to Lee and Clif's.

Tuesday, February 29 to Monday, March 6, 2000:

A visit with Lee, Clif, Eli and baby-to-be:

Their house in La Mesa overlooks San Diego, and on clear days the ocean is visible. Eli knew who we were this time. Clif kept coming up with things for us to do during our week, but the kids are toured out. We spent a day visiting Ed's aunt and uncle, another having a picnic at the beach and another wandering the

The last beach we visited of Latin America.

wharf and visiting sea lions sunning themselves. Beyond that, we simply had a good visit.

Clif and Ed went to Tijuana early one morning and it didn't take long to complete the van formalities.

Ed took the van to a mechanic who replaced the rear set of brakes and the two original tires with which we started our journey. Before we left, the cost of the four tires Ed purchased practically made me choke. But they were worth every red cent. No deflation or inflation during altitude changes and not one flat tire. The mechanic couldn't figure out the engine hesitation problem, and said the van would get us back to Canada.

I did some grocery shopping with Lee, having forgotten about the abundance and variety available. The small store we went into was overwhelming, and it is peculiar to hear so much English spoken. I am feeling some culture shock.

Ed's Mom, Dad and some of his family are getting together at Dan's (Ed's brother) for the weekend of the 10th in Toronto, so we decided to crash their party.

March 9, 2000: Toronto, Ontario after "flying" through the States

We thought we would visit the Grand Canyon if the weather was good, but by the time we reached Prescott, Arizona we realized it wouldn't be possible. It was snowing and at the town of William's we were told the road wasn't even open. None of us had clothes for the cold weather, and we tramped through a foot of snow from the parking lot to the motel room. It was a regular snowy night, and it wasn't just I who had trouble warming up. Our bodies are not acclimatized to the cold after being in the tropics for the past year.

We made a snowy, slippery start in the morning, and Ed was thankful he'd had the new tires put on. The van held well in the mountains. Of all the mountains we had driven through in the past three years, we never did have to contend with a snowfall.

When a sign indicated the continental divide in New Mexico, I thought it would be a great opportunity for a geography lesson and started to explain. The kids were way ahead of me. Ben sighed, "Yeah, yeah we know—on that side water goes to the Pacific, on this side water goes to the Atlantic. It's just like the Andes. It's not like water can run uphill Mom." I underestimate their knowledge sometimes. We escaped the snow east of Albuquerque and spent the night in Shamrock, Texas.

Ed asked if anyone minded driving the rest of the way home without stopping for the night. No one did, and it was a 28-hour marathon drive for the two of us. But there were no fights, arguments or complaints, just anxious anticipation.

For some reason the thought of crossing the Canadian border caused some anxiety in Ed. He seemed to think if we told customs how long we had been out of the country and where we had been we would have an extensive delay. I told him we had nothing to hide, were entitled to everything we had with us, and that he had nothing to worry about. Ed and the kids were making up stories. I said, "We can't lie; it would just make a search worse." Ed said, "You're driving through the border, then."

We were in Port Huron by 7 a.m., stopped for gas and cleaned ourselves up in the service station bathroom so that we didn't look like a bunch of bums. I drove, with butterflies in my stomach, more from the excitement of getting our feet back onto Canadian soil than anything, I think. It was a good thing I didn't have to wait long to cross the border. The minutes of waiting for the car in front of us gave just enough time to realize where we had been, what we had accomplished and that we had made it home successfully. I wiped away the tears that started to come, drove up to the customs agent and gave him a cheery, "Good morning". It was returned with, "Good morning. Is everyone travelling in your van a Canadian citizen?"

"Yes, Ed, myself and our six children."

He looked inside, "Where do you live?"

"Wakefield, Quebec, just north of Ottawa."

"How long have you been in the States?" I didn't dare look at Ed but my insides were jumping for joy and I could barely keep a straight face, "Almost two weeks."

"Reason for your visit?"

"My sister lives in San Diego, we visited her and her family."

"Do you have anything to declare?"

"A second-hand surf board" (it was obvious in the back) and Ed interrupted because he knows I volunteer far too much information most of the time. "T-shirts and a couple of sweatshirts," then he gave me a look. I said nothing more.

"Okay, welcome home."

"Thank you."

I drove off holding my breath and too soon the screams and cheers were let go. We didn't lie, we didn't tell him everything, but we didn't lie.

I turned off the highway at the Forest exit. The kids complained, "Mom, where are you going? I thought we were going to Toronto."

"We are, but I'm going someplace else first. My grandpa used to live here and I want to see his house." The farms... wow, the farms. They look so prosperous, cosmopolitan. I wonder if farmers still consider themselves the poor folk of the country. I drove slowly past the house and farm where I had spent so many childhood days. I noticed a few trees gone, but otherwise it still looked like his house. But it isn't a place where I will find comfort again; change happens whether we like it or not.

We were at Dan's by noon, finding some unusually warm weather for the time of year—22 degrees Celsius. Arizona was snowed in, and Toronto has May weather in March.

Ed's parents arrived early in the evening. They weren't expecting us for a couple of weeks and were pleasantly surprised. It took a long time to get through hugs, tears and laughter before any one could say any words. It has been more than three years.

SPRING 2008, WAKEFIELD, QUEBEC

So here we are, 11 years after our dream-vision journey began. We returned to where we started, a closer more functional family, healthy, happy and with expanded minds. The kids settled back into their lives in Canada with ease, and what is interesting to see now is how adventurous their spirits are, how easy-going they have become and adaptable to new things that come their way. Ed takes everything in stride, and decided that since the universe brought us back to Wakefield, this is where we are supposed to be. He purchased the clinic back from Pascal.

For me the culture shock of returning home was overwhelming; a supermarket felt intimidating. Shopping for anything required major decisions, just because of the amount of choice. Our huge house felt small and confining after living in the open for the previous year, and I was extremely frustrated with things that needed to be fixed in it. After four weeks of repairs and making yet another trip to the city for necessary materials, I found myself in tears. I just wanted to be on the road and really going somewhere. As I started to climb the hill on the north end of Highway 5, two crows took off in flight before me. One flew just meters ahead, and the other grazed the windshield yet continued to fly. I was startled out of feeling sorry for myself. They were a pair and each was carrying a mouthful of dry grasses. As the rush of adrenaline in my body subsided, I discovered a deeper meaning to the incident. They were collecting materials to build their spring nest. It is the job of adults to provide a home for their offspring while they are young and dependent and it felt as if I was being told to do what needed to be done. Throughout the initial weeks of our return, without really understanding it, I had mourned the loss of what had made our journey so special: the freedom it gave us, the opportunities we had to learn about the world firsthand and I believe, most of all, the time we had as a family together. During that drive to the city I came to terms with the fact that people grow, and things change; we continue the journey, just in a different form. With that understanding, I felt like the spirit part of me that had stayed in South America rejoined my physical being, helping me to feel whole again here in Canada. Picking up where we left off was best while the kids were still growing up. Wakefield and our house is a good place to live.

Life is the same but different, although maybe the difference is simply in my way of perceiving the reality around me. The big difference is that I have found power in myself, the ability to take time for myself without feeling guilty about it. Since our journey, I have a deeper understanding and acceptance of natural law. My inner peace has grown and a sense of purpose gives way to love, joy and happiness. The challenge of holding onto the spiritual connection, after resuming the lifestyle we left behind, is always a challenge, requiring conscious effort to remain open to the ever-present messages from nature. Being somewhere different from home doesn't have to be the answer. I realized this after being back in Canada for more than a year during a visit from our Brazilian friends Carmen and Roberto. They spent a few days with us after camping in Algonquin Park. In a conversation over dinner one evening Carmen expressed her desire to live in

Canada. One of her reasons was that she found it was so much easier while in Canada to live a spiritual life and be close to the earth, which she said is what she needs more than anything. Those comments opened up a new perspective on my part. Here I am in Canada feeling as if my mind was more open to a spiritual life while I was in South America, feeling as if I might lose that spirituality living here. She sat across the table from me and explained the exact same thing in reverse. After a few days of sorting thoughts, I came to some enlightening conclusions for myself. Mostly as the expression goes, "The grass is always greener on the other side." So why? When Carmen comes to Canada she lives a less cluttered life away from the responsibility that her job and house entails. While visiting them in their home in Salvador, their office was extremely deep in paperwork and files that needed to be dealt with. Even with someone to help in the home, the demands of laundry, cleaning and dishes were always a challenge. We lived without that same cluttered life while in South America and that was what was so liberating. It definitely appears to be the answer. It doesn't matter which continent we are on, it is a conscious choice of lifestyle.

So Ed is serving the community again, and the kids are turning into responsible young adults. We have continued to be a home-based education family and I have continuously worked on putting my journals into book form when time has allowed.

Tanya has educated herself in ways that have interested her. She worked as one of Ed's Chiropractic Assistants since our return and managed the office up until September 2006. As ski racing is one of her favorite pastimes, she obtained her Level II ski coaching certification and coaches during winters for the Vorlage Racing Club in Wakefield. To expand her social life and earn more income, she worked as a server and bartender at the Earle House Restaurant in the village as well. The money she earned has given her the opportunity to travel overland to Alaska and Newfoundland, visit friends in Australia and Mexico on separate occasions, and to travel with girlfriends in Europe for part of a summer. The travel bug has infected her.

She has worked towards her Fashion Design Certificate through Algonquin College and took courses at the University of Ottawa until she was accepted into the Theater Design Program at Concordia University in Montreal. She has been attending school there full-time since September 2006 and has enjoyed the new challenges. We have had some adjusting to do with her living elsewhere, since we had become so dependent on her business skills, computer skills and what she contributed intrinsically to the family. She is still Ed's and my computer coach when the others in the family are stumped.

Ben went to high school for one day after our return and decided he preferred designing his own education. He started working at the Earle House Restaurant as soon as they would let him and he has never looked back. He likes having cash in his pockets. Cars have always been one of his passions, and he owned one before he had a license to drive it. By the time he was 18 he owned four vehicles and had bought and sold several others.

The winter Ben was 17 years old, he and his lifelong friend, Etienne, packed up Ben's van with snowboards and a few living basics and drove across Canada to Whistler, B.C. to work and ride the slopes. One winter was enough for him to decide that he wanted more out of life than that. On his return in the spring, he again worked at the restaurant as a server until doing odd jobs turned into full-time work. He started at the University of Ottawa that September with the ambition of becoming a Chiropractor. It took three semesters for him to figure out that he was going to be broke for seven to eight years and would probably have a huge debt of student loans by the time he was through. The resulting career would depend on his being in a specific location to earn income. He doesn't like being without money, and has been learning business strategies to build passive income with the aim of becoming financially independent. He now says he'll go to school when he doesn't have to worry about where his money comes from. This remains to be seen, but he has always been a person of his word, so I wouldn't put it past him. He has been self-employed in his own odd-job business and has provided work to friends and his brother when he had more than he could manage.

During the fall of 2006, Ben convinced his father and myself to help him purchase the local convenience and movie rental store as an initial investment to the real estate business he plans to create. He is learning through experience and earning a decent income at the same time. He has always enjoyed his freedom and making his own decisions. The lifestyle he has chosen for himself gives him that.

By the time Dayna reached high school age, her home-schooled peers had chosen to attend school. Every teenager needs a social life and she decided to go to school the year she was at a Grade 10 age. I wasn't sure about how she would do academically but her goal was to meet new people, so we enrolled her. She proved to me that when a kid goes to school for her own reasons, she does just fine. She eased into the mainstream system confidently, easily and found a new social circle.

Dayna is an avid skier whose passion is racing. For several years she claimed the regional championship. To help fund her equipment and travel costs, she too worked at the restaurant over the summer tourist season and in the clinic for her father. During ski season, she was noticeably absent from school while travelling to various ski hills throughout Quebec and the northern U.S. to race. For her second year of high school she chose subjects that would allow her to maintain a decent average and still ski. She did advanced math separately over another ski season to obtain the credit she needed to get into college for the business career she intends to pursue. Dayna obtained her Level 1 ski coaching certification and, while attending college worked part-time coaching in Vorlage's Nancy Greene program for ski racers. She has just been accepted into the International Business Management program at McGill University. She has her social life, is doing things she loves to do, and gaining an education. We all should enjoy our lives as such.

When she was 13 years old Karina started babysitting for our friends, Lucie and Gilles, the people who owned and ran the Earle House Restaurant at the time. It didn't take long before she moved to working in the kitchen like her older siblings. She enjoys the financial freedom a job gives her and has financed her own trips to Australia and Mexico with her sister to visit mutual friends.

When she announced that she wanted to follow in Dayna's footsteps in attending school, I had a knot in my stomach. Being a quiet, middle child she so often got lost among the demands of the others. (We have all learned that.) I had spent virtually no time with her as far as bookwork was concerned, apart from helping her get to a level of reading that she could build on herself. My goal was to help her develop her writing skills the year she would be at a grade 10 level. She spent most of her time reading, I didn't even know if she could write a paragraph and make it coherent. She started school a week and a half after classes began, and it took a couple of weeks for her to settle in, but she flourished. After the mid-year exams, she received a form letter of congratulations from the principal for her average being over 85 percent—so much for my concerns. She complains she has less time to read the literature that interests her but it was worth her going to school to see the rise in her self-confidence and certainty. She enjoys the social life of school but recognizes real social problems amongst her peers and is discouraged with how the system demands respect, yet most of the time it is not reciprocal. It is wonderful to see her recognize the downfalls, accept them for what they are without taking them personally and letting them affect her emotionally, and get what she needs from school as a ticket to the future. She continued to follow Dayna's school example and chose to attend the commerce program at college. There is talk of business law but wonders if she can stick out that many years of school. Time will tell.

Jake has had little interest in doing much of anything academically. He was 12 before he was able to sort out letters to a degree that they started to make sense to him. Yet, within two years, he had become a capable, proficient reader. Basic mathematical concepts somehow just became a part of his thinking. But he wouldn't put anything on paper without resistance and usually a confrontation between us. The latter, I admit, only occurred because I was anxious about him not doing bookwork. The one program that each of the kids used more or less daily, was *Saxon Math*. When Jake became bored with being physically active, and he realized his older siblings each had a math text on the go, he said, "Maybe I should do some math." When he was 13, he started putting math concepts on paper at a grade six to seven level and worked at it half-heartedly, with me beside him most of the time. It was in March 2006 that I realized I hadn't helped Jake with math for a few weeks. One day when he was working at the dining room table, I went to sit beside him to help out. I barely got there when he put his hand out policeman style, signaling me to stop and shouted, "I don't need your help!" In the weeks that I hadn't helped him, he had gone through as many lessons as we had done together in the previous four months. So this boy who has taken his time getting over whatever it was that prevented him from settling into some "book learning" is doing just as well as other kids his age and still has a high level of self-confidence and self-esteem.

In August of 2005, Tanya and Ben were figuring out their courses for the fall semester at university. Dayna had decided to work on her advanced math credit, and Karina was tossing around the idea of high school. There was plenty of talk about institutional education. Jake, the boy who came into this world and joined our family the year Ed and I made the decision to home-school his older brother and sister, asked me, "Mom, do I ever have to go to school?" He was obviously feeling some pressure. My reply was simply, "That all depends on what you want to do with your life, Jake. Do you have any idea of how you want to support yourself and earn a living when you are older?"

He was quick to answer. "I just want to have a business of my own."

The kind of business will determine whether the certification of school is necessary or not, but there are many people who run successful businesses without going to university or college. I am sure Jake can learn what is needed through experience if that is the route he wants to take. He lives, loves and knows several sports, I can see him doing something of the sort. Only time will tell and I just need to have the patience to give him that.

Whitney is working through her math program easily, and almost independently, since she has become a more comprehensive reader. Although she is a capable reader, she still enjoys me reading aloud—which still often draws in the entire family. What keeps her from moving at a faster pace is the fact that she has a hard time sitting still. Her body wants and needs to move, and sports are a high priority for her. She too has a passion for skiing and has claimed the regional championship in her age category for two years. Home-based education has given her time to spend on the slopes practicing speed and skills.

Whitney says she might go to school for grade 10. She is a highly sociable person who likes to have interaction with as many people as possible. School is attractive to her from that perspective, although she knows it may interfere with the winter sport she loves so much. It will be her decision.

During the winter of 2006 - 2007, Ben convinced his siblings to work with him and run the local convenience store that had come up for sale. Because each of the kids was willing to put their energy into a business of their own, Ed and I helped them out, purchased the store and created a corporation in which each family member owns shares. Since the store has become ours, it is interesting to watch how these very young business owners have taken charge, discuss at length the changes they want to implement, and then do it. They are loving the responsibility, earning income and contributing to our community. It is a real-life project they are taking to heart. So all those worries, doubts and fears in me about whether the kids were getting an education that would prepare them for life... where does that fit? They are way ahead of me.

Ed and I are enjoying spending time with each other and the children we brought into the world. Some day we may spend part of the year in South America, but until the kids have their own life directions more firmly in place our place is here, being facilitators, helping them find the resources they need to get them where they need and want to go.

Talk around the dinner table often turns to our adventures on the road in South America. Our goal is to return someday to visit the many people we became friends with and the countries we grew to love, but for now our journey is here in Canada—there is never a dull moment. And our dreams... they continue.

Photo by Claude Brazeau

Dayna, Frail
Yon Flower
–Merida,
Venezuela

Our painting & the Artist
–Lago Quilotoa, Ecuador

Equatorial Monument –Quito, Ecuador

Plaza de Armas
–Lima, Peru

Karina & Alpaca
–Huaraz, Peru

Cabillitos and fishnets on the beach.
Huanchaco, Peru

Huaca de la Luna, Moon Temple –Trujillo, Per

Whitney at Rainbow Temple –Trujillo, Peru

A rest on the top of the Sand Dunes –Huacachina, Peru

Oasis –Huacachina, Peru

Piedras de Sumbay –Arequipa, Peru

Colca Canyon
& Snow Capped Mount Mismi

Woman of Colca Canyon.
This style of hat was found only at Colca Canyon.

One of several cathedrals where the sillar is carved in detail.
Arequipa, Peru

The North Side
of Mount Misti and a vicuna
–Arequipa, Peru

Children –Ollantaytambo, Peru

Children of Taquile Island

Taquile Island & the
purchased hats for the kids.

Uros Islands –Lago Titcaca, Peru

Machu Picchu

Tunita & Kids
−Tacna, Peru

Living Dreams

Spring flowers –Mirasol, Chile

The Beach
at Mirasol
–Algarrobo, Chile

The cargo ship Puerto Eden docked
in Puerto Natales with our van
disembarking.

Mom, Dad, Ed & kids
–Torres del Paine
National Park, Chile

Our van and the cuernos –horns. Torres del Paine National Park, Chile

Karina, Jake, Whitney & Dayna. Where they took turns rubbing the Indian's toe. –Punta Arenas, Chile

Rio Cisne & the Carretera Austral

Perito Moreno Glacier, kids and grandparents

Living Dreams

Sheep Ranch
– Patagonia, Argentina

Pelicans –Concon, Chile

Palacio de la Moneda
–Santiago, Chile

Steve, Pamela & Chris with Ed & Kids

Blooming cactus –El Tololo, Chile

Aris & Christina with the kids –Mirasol, Chile

Vinyards –Central Valley, Casablanca, Chile

Countryside hike
–Mendoza, Argentina

Foz do Iguacu, Brazil

Coati – looking for handouts
–Foz do Iguacu, Argentina

Indaia Falls
–Itiquira Campground, Brazil

Toucan –Brasilia Zoo

Collecting fish from the nets – log canoe –Barra Grande, Brazil

Capoiera at the
Mercado Modelo –Salvador, Brazil

Monkey visitor –Aracaju, Brazil

Sugarcane field –Brazil

Ed in his hammock on
the Nielo Correa

Amazon River Sunrise

Whitney with an armful of Sloth
–Cartagena Colombia

Ben's attacker. Scarlet Macaw –Finca
Ixobel, Guatemala

Lago Atitlan, Guatemala

Dad & Mom's family
in Puerto Escondido,
Mexico

Oaxaca Market

After all that road, a holiday
in Mexico agreed with us.

Ben surfing –Sayulita, Mexico

Living Dreams